MEDIEVAL EUROPE

A Short History

Tenth Edition

MEDIEVAL EUROPE

A Short History

Judith M. Bennett

University of North Carolina
Chapel Hill

C. Warren Hollister

Late of the University of California
Santa Barbara

Boston   Burr Ridge, IL   Dubuque, IA   Madison, WI   New York
San Francisco   St. Louis   Bangkok   Bogotá   Caracas   Kuala Lumpur
Lisbon   London   Madrid   Mexico City   Milan   Montreal   New Delhi
Santiago   Seoul   Singapore   Sydney   Taipei   Toronto

Higher Education

MEDIEVAL EUROPE: A SHORT HISTORY

1 2 3 4 5 6 7 8 9 0 DOC/DOC 0 9 8 7 6 5

ISBN   0-07-295515-5

Publisher: *Lyn Uhl*
Senior sponsoring editor: *Monica Eckman*
Freelance developmental editor: *Kristen Mellitt*
Marketing manager: *Katherine Bates*
Lead media producer: *Sean Crowley*
Senior project manager: *Rebecca Komro*
Senior production supervisor: *Carol A. Bielski*
Lead designer: *Gino Cieslik*
Media project manager: *Kathleen Boylan*
Manager, Photo research: *Brian Pecko*
Art manager: *Robin Mouat*
Illustrator: *Patti Isaacs*
Art director: *Jeanne Schreiber*
Cover design: *Gino Cieslik*
Cover image: © *Bodleian Library, University of Oxford, 1999*
Typeface: *10/12 Times Roman*
Compositor: *Interactive Composition Corporation*
Printer: *R.R. Donnelley and Sons Inc.*

Library of Congress Cataloging-in-Publication Data

Bennett, Judith M.
    Medieval Europe : a short history / Judith M. Bennett, C. Warren Hollister.—10th ed.
        p. cm.
    Rev. of: Medieval Europe / C. Warren Hollister, Judith M. Bennett. 9th ed.
    Includes bibliographical references and index.
    ISBN 0-07-295515-5 (alk. paper)
        1. Europe—History—476-1492. 2. Middle Ages—History. 3. Civilization, Medieval. I.
Hollister, C. Warren (Charles Warren), 1930- II. Hollister, C. Warren (Charles Warren),
1930- Medieval Europe. III. Title.
    D118.H624 2006
    940.1—dc22   2004059264

www.mhhe.com

ABOUT THE AUTHORS

Judith M. Bennett teaches medieval history and women's history at the University of North Carolina at Chapel Hill, where she is Martha Nell Hardy Distinguished Professor. Educated at Mount Holyoke College, the University of Toronto, and the Pontifical Institute of Mediaeval Studies, she is the author of numerous books and articles about peasants, women, and families in the Middle Ages. Professor Bennett's research has been supported by the John Simon Guggenheim Memorial Foundation, the National Endowment for the Humanities, the American Council of Learned Societies, the National Humanities Center, the Folger Shakespeare Library, and numerous other agencies. She has held lectureships in Australia and England, as well as in the United States. A Fellow of the Medieval Academy of America and the Royal Historical Society in London, she has held offices in such professional organizations as the Medieval Academy, the North American Conference on British Studies, the Coordinating Council for Women in History, and the Berkshire Conference of Women Historians. Professor Bennett has received several awards for her scholarly books and articles, and she is also an acclaimed teacher at UNC-CH, where she has won a top teaching award and is now a fellow of the Academy of Distinguished Teaching Scholars.

C. Warren Hollister was Professor of History at the University of California, Santa Barbara. He received his BA from Harvard University and his MA and PhD from UCLA. A Fellow of the Medieval Academy of America, the Royal Historical Society (London), the Medieval Academy of Ireland, the Australian National University, the John Simon Guggenheim Foundation, and Merton College, Oxford, he wrote many books that have run through more than thirty editions and have been translated into several languages. His many honors included the E. Harris Harbison National Award for Distinguished Teaching (Princeton University) and the UC Santa Barbara Faculty Teaching Prize.

CONTENTS

PART III

THE LATER MIDDLE AGES: CRISIS AND CREATIVITY, 1300-1500   321-324

ABBREVIATIONS AND CONVENTIONS

Boldfaced words are defined in the glossary at the back of the book. These words are typeset in boldface at first use *only*.

B.C.E.	before the Common Era
C.E.	Common Era
c.	*circa,* used to indicate an approximate date
r.	indicates dates of reign, not dates of life
d.	indicates date of death

BIOGRAPHICAL SKETCHES

MEDIEVAL MYTHS

TIMELINES

MAPS

FIGURES AND COLOR ILLUSTRATIONS

Figures

Color Illustrations

PREFACE

It remains an honor and a challenge to work with *Medieval Europe: A Short History,* a book that for more than three decades was marked by the historical vision and engaging style of C. Warren Hollister. Professor Hollister wrote in the preface to the eighth edition of his fateful realization, while in college, that our world today "is a product of the medieval past." I share his enthusiasm for understanding the medieval roots of our own society, but my own path to medieval history was different and, I must confess, somewhat less intellectual. Professor Hollister read Toynbee's *A Study of History* in college and found his life transformed. I read novels in high school—*any* novel on a medieval topic I could lay my hands on—and found myself hooked.

In the past decade, I have had the pleasure of reliving my first imaginative encounters with the Middle Ages with my grandnephews Bennett and Samuel Kocsis, with whom I have built Lego castles, practiced swordplay, worked out the physics of catapults, played computer games, and read countless books on knights, Robin Hood, and even a medieval peasant or two. They remind me that medieval history is fun as well as important, and I dedicate this book to them. I hope that, should they eventually read it in college, they will not find all the fun gone.

✹ NEW TO THIS EDITION

This tenth edition represents a thorough revision, with every chapter, page, and line subject to review. Some textbooks now seek to encompass Byzantium and Islam fully within the embrace of "medieval." This textbook remains focused on the medieval West, with Byzantium and Islam playing supporting roles to the main story. This approach provides, in my view, a more coherent history that better incorporates women's history, social history, and the history of the Later Middle Ages. In all of these changes, I have been guided, as Professor Hollister was before me, by the late Lynn White's advice to him that a textbook is not "the place to trot out daring new hypotheses" but is instead a place for "canonized orthodoxy."

Users of past editions will note some broad revisions and additions, especially

- *Medieval Myths* is the title of a new series that treats topics—such as King Arthur, Lady Godiva, and the Pied Piper of Hameln—that intrigue students but are seldom mentioned in textbooks. Because this is a new series, I have added these discussions to only half the chapters; if teachers and students like this innovation, I will expand its coverage in the 11th edition. I am grateful to Jenny Stevens, Christine Deaver, and other students in my spring 2004 course for their vigorous and rigorous responses to drafts of these new materials.
- *The Maps* have been reconceptualized, redrawn, and overall improved. I hope that students will be encouraged to refer to these maps not only by references within the text itself but also by the new captions that point out, for each map, a few noteworthy features.
- *Chapter 2* has been reworked and renamed. It now focuses less on Rome and more on barbarian settlement.

- *Coverage of Byzantium and Islam* has been substantively reworked. Part I now boasts a single chapter on Byzantium and Islam to the year 1000, and the later histories of these civilizations have been treated at appropriate places in Parts II and III. I hope readers will agree that this rearrangement has created a more coherent and chronologically sensible treatment. It also better balances the book, with six chapters on the Early Middle Ages, six on the Central Middle Ages, and three on the Later Middle Ages.
- *Citations to all quotations* are now listed at the back so that students intrigued by a quote may easily put their hands on a modern translation.
- *Suggested Primary Sources* have been added at the end of each chapter, for the use of both teachers and students.

✸ SUPPLEMENTS

- The tenth edition is accompanied by a robust **Web site** (www.mhhe.com/bennetthollister10). Paul Halsall of the University of North Florida has designed this rich resource to complement the text. Both an online study guide for students and a starting point for evaluating online sources for medieval history, the site offers mapping exercises, Internet activities, multiple-choice and essay quizzes, timelines enhanced with links to relevant Web sites, links to primary source material, online resource guides, and more. The site also offers resources for instructors, including an online instructor's manual and an image library.
- An **Instructor's Manual/Test Bank** is also available, with materials for both first-time professors and veterans looking for a few new lecture ideas or activities to add to the classroom. For each chapter of the book, instructors will find chapter objectives, a chapter outline, lecture and discussion topics, and music and film references. A full test bank, including essay questions, multiple-choice questions, fill-ins, and map and chronology exercises, is also provided for each chapter.

For information about the price and availability of these supplements, please contact your local McGraw-Hill sales representative. Some restrictions may apply.

✸ ACKNOWLEDGMENTS

I thank with pleasure Blain Roberts, Jennifer Heath, Janelle Werner, and Dana Brinson who, at various points and in various ways, assisted me with research tasks for this revision. I am also grateful for the specific advice offered by Malcolm Barber, Sandy Bardsley, Stanley Chojnacki, Christine Deaver, Robert Frakes, David Ganz, Elizabeth Harper, Daniel Hobbins, Maryanne Kowaleski, Maura Lafferty, Michael McVaugh, Janet Nelson, Richard Pfaff, Colleen Seguin, Miriam Shadis, Jenny Stevens, and William Stoneman. Most of all, I thank Cynthia Herrup, who tolerated this revision with her usual patience and good humor.

McGraw-Hill and I would like to thank the reviewers of this edition for their helpful comments and suggestions: William Bakken, Rochester Community & Technical

College; Robert Berkhofer, Western Michigan University; John J. Contreni, Purdue University–West Lafayette; Randall S. Howarth, Mercyhurst College; Paul Knoll, University of Southern California; Robert Lerner, Northwestern University; Felice Lifshitz, Florida International University; John Ott, Portland State University; Loretta Reed, University of California–Sacramento; Douglas Skopp, SUNY–Plattsburgh.

As to the errors that remain, I can do no better than again to repeat Professor Hollister's words: For all mistakes and stylistic potholes, I cheerfully take the blame. I also welcome your comments and corrections, which I will acknowledge, as he did, with prompt reply and future amendment. And, like Professor Hollister, I take comfort in the words of the twelfth-century historian Henry of Huntington:

> What I have well performed, in grace approve,
> Where I have erred, correct me in your love.

Judith M. Bennett
Durham, NC

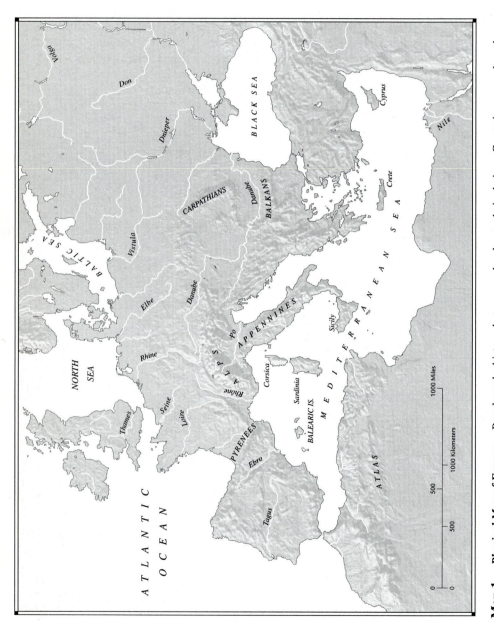

Map 1. *Physical Map of Europe.* People make history, but geography shapes their choices. Great rivers—such as the Rhine and Danube—were liquid highways and boundary markers. Mountain ranges—such as the Alps, Pyrenees, and Balkans—posed formidable obstacles.

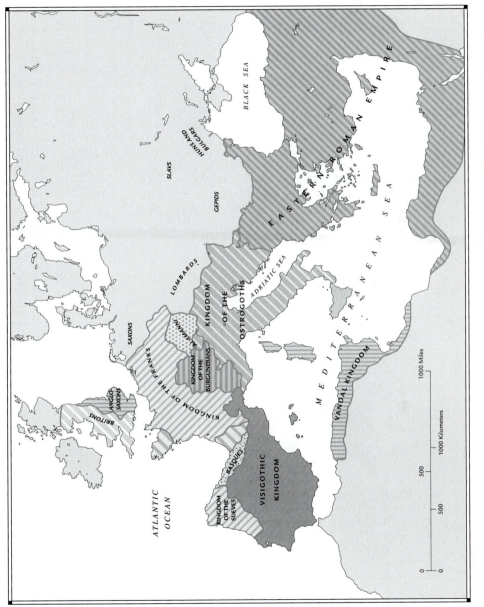

Map 2. *Europe, c. 500.* By 500, "successor states" fractured the old unity of imperial Rome. Some—such as the Vandal kingdom in North Africa—were short-lived. Others—such as the kingdom of the Franks—long endured.

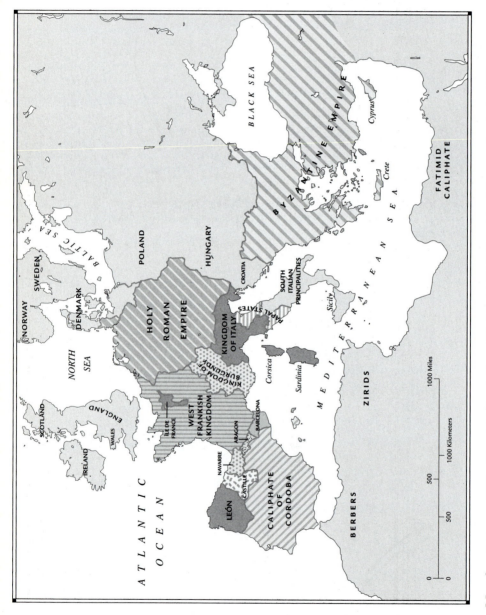
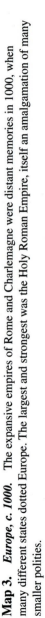

Map 3. *Europe, c. 1000.* The expansive empires of Rome and Charlemagne were distant memories in 1000, when many different states dotted Europe. The largest and strongest was the Holy Roman Empire, itself an amalgamation of many smaller polities.

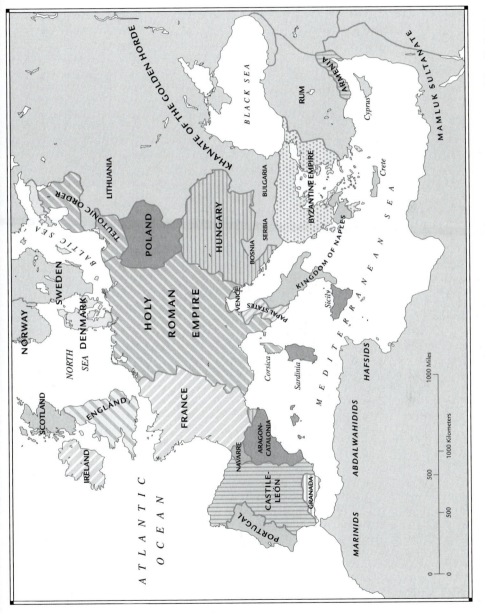

Map 4. *Europe, c. 1300.* By 1300, Christian Europe had expanded its reach. The Christian kingdom of Castile-Leon dominated Iberia, and the Holy Roman Empire had expanded far to the east. The Byzantine Empire was a shadow of its former self.

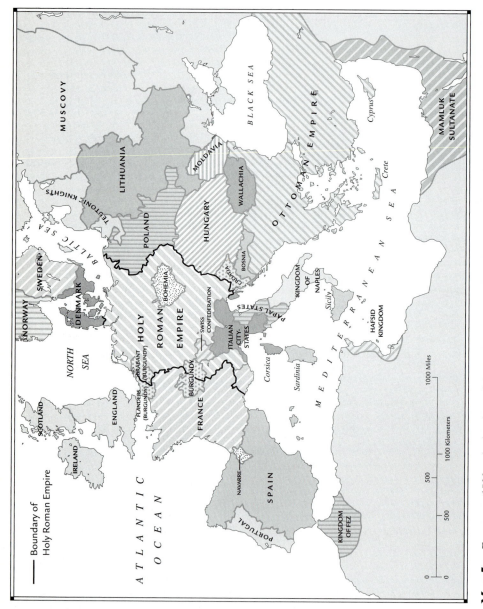
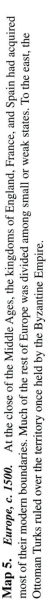

Map 5. *Europe, c. 1500.* At the close of the Middle Ages, the kingdoms of England, France, and Spain had acquired most of their modern boundaries. Much of the rest of Europe was divided among small or weak states. To the east, the Ottoman Turks ruled over the territory once held by the Byzantine Empire.

INTRODUCTION

There is an old-fashioned notion, long discredited yet still popularly accepted, that medieval Europe was a disastrous time. Today, the word "medieval" brings to mind such deplorable things as midnight curfews, repressive governments, tangled graduation requirements, and even, as in a *New York Times* editorial in November 2000, the "medieval voting machines" used in Florida during the Bush–Gore election struggle. The Middle Ages, stretching across a thousand years from the fifth century to the fifteenth, are still viewed by some as a long, stupid detour in the march of human progress—a millennium of poverty, superstition, and gloom that divided the old golden age of the Roman Empire from the new golden age of the Italian Renaissance. During these years, as a famous historian said in 1860, human consciousness "lay dreaming or half awake." Another historian has gleefully described the millennium as wrapped in "a monstrous fog, a heavy, grey, leaden fog." And to many others, the Middle Ages are simply the "Dark Ages," a long mistake wedged between Rome and Renaissance. At length, some time in the fifteenth century, the darkness is supposed to have lifted. Europeans awakened, basked in bright sunlight, and began thinking again. After a long medieval intermission, the Grand March of Human Progress resumed.

This Rip Van Winkle theory was first advanced at the end of the Middle Ages by Renaissance humanists who wanted to return to the triumphs of ancient Rome and Protestant reformers who wanted to return to the earliest traditions of Christianity. For both, the medieval millennium was an obstacle, a sleeping wasteland between past glories and present hopes. Their nasty view of the Middle Ages survives some 500 years later, but for different reasons. Because medieval people are long dead, they cannot protest if we today characterize their customs as primitive, their lifestyles as crude, and their values as horrific. Their silence offers us a safe opposite to ourselves, a bad time against which our own time looks pretty good. Who, after all, would want to live in a time without electricity, running water, or computers? Who, they might respond to us if they could, would want to live in a world plagued by nuclear weapons, global warming, and gargantuan cities?

TIMELINE FOR INTRODUCTION   The Middle Ages, 500–1500

500	1000	1300	1500

Later Roman Empire	Early Middle Ages	Central Middle Ages	Later Middle Ages	Early Modern Europe

In any case, the Middle Ages were neither asleep nor awful, but instead were a time of constant change—so much so that Europe in 600 was vastly different from Europe in 1100 or 1400. Accordingly, this book is divided into three parts, as shown in the accompanying Timeline. The Early Middle Ages (c. 500–1000) span the troubled, formative centuries between the collapse of the Roman Empire in the West and the emergence of Western Europe as a more secure and confident civilization. The Central Middle Ages (c. 1000–1300) embrace a period of growth in population, wealth, cities, education, and territory. These centuries also saw religious reform, intellectual advance, and, alas, persecution of minority groups. The Later Middle Ages (c. 1300–1500) brought both terrible trouble and dynamic change. Between 1300 and 1350 Europe was devastated by both famine and plague, but by 1500, Europe's technological know-how, political structure, and economic organization had given it a decisive edge over all other civilizations on earth. Columbus had begun to explore the Americas; the Portuguese had sailed around Africa to India; and Europeans had developed the cannon, the printing press, the mechanical clock, eyeglasses, distilled liquor, and numerous other ingredients of modern civilization.

In part, this book celebrates this medieval creativity and its effects on our world today. During the "modern" centuries that followed the Middle Ages—that is, from about 1500 to 1945—European fleets, armies, and ideas spread across the globe and transformed it. Even today, non-European countries remain deeply influenced by medieval ideas about education, government, social structure, and social justice. Universities—a medieval invention—dot the globe, and the legislative bodies that govern the United States, Mexico, Canada, Israel, Japan, and the newer democracies of Eastern Europe are, to some extent, descendants of the parliaments and assemblies of the Middle Ages. Even the Communist systems that survive in China, Cuba, and North Korea are based on Western European ideas, some of which can be traced back before the time of Karl Marx to late medieval peasants who attacked their "social betters" with the slogan of a classless society:

> When Adam delved [dug] and Eve span,
> Who was then the gentleman?

In short, anyone who wonders how Western Europe helped to transform the world, for good or ill, into the global civilization that envelops us today must look to the medieval centuries for an important part of the answer. During the Middle Ages, Europe grew from a predominantly rural society, thinly settled and impoverished, into a powerful and distinctive civilization whose history helped to shape the world we now know.

In part, however, this book celebrates difference as well as descent, telling a story of how medieval Europe was not just part-prologue to our own day but also just plain *different*. Many of these differences might look weird and exotic to us today. Why did medieval people imagine that monstrous races—people with no torsos, or one-legged people, or horned people—lived beyond the borders of the known world? What explains medieval flagellants who reacted to plague by whipping themselves into frenzies of religious regret? How could medieval people have found it acceptable for some people to lives as **slaves** and others as semi-free **serfs?**[1] Sometimes these peculiar medieval customs survive today as, for example, in the ways some Hollywood movies depict Martians or other alien beings. Sometimes these customs have parallels in non-European cultures, such as those that accept self-flagellation as a suitable form of religious expression. And sometimes these customs—serfdom is a good example—simply died out, leaving little or no trace in our contemporary world. Even these extinct medieval customs have a place in our story, for they are fascinating examples of the breadth of human experiences, past and present, and they are, of course, integral parts of the medieval world that we seek not merely to observe but also to understand.

SUGGESTED READINGS

David Abulafia et al., *The New Cambridge Medieval History* (from 1995). A 7-volume scholarly series. See also Robert Fossier, ed., *The Cambridge Illustrated History of the Middle Ages* (1986–1997), 3 volumes, translated from earlier French editions.

Judith M. Bennett, *Medieval Women in Modern Perspective* (2000). A pamphlet for teachers. For further bibliography, see also *Feminae: Medieval Women and Gender Index* (www.haverford.edu/library/reference/mschaus/mfi/mfi.html).

Norman F. Cantor, ed., *Encyclopedia of the Middle Ages* (1999). See also H. R. Loyn, *The Middle Ages: A Concise Encyclopedia* (1989). For more extensive coverage, see Joseph Strayer, ed., *Dictionary of the Middle Ages* (1982–1989), 13 volumes. For specific areas, see William W. Kibler et al., eds., *Medieval France: An Encyclopedia* (1995); Phillip Pulsiano et al., eds., *Medieval Scandinavia: An Encyclopedia* (1993); Paul E. Szarmach et al., eds., *Medieval England: An Encyclopedia* (1998); John Jeep, ed., *Medieval Germany: An Encyclopedia* (2000); Michael E. Gerli, ed., *Medieval Iberia: An Encyclopedia* (2003).

Mark R. Cohen, *Under Crescent and Cross: The Jews in the Middle Ages* (1994). A highly readable comparison of Jews in medieval Christendom and medieval Islam. See also Kenneth R. Stow, *Alienated Minority: The Jews of Medieval Latin Europe* (1992), and Norman Roth, ed., *Medieval Jewish Civilization: An Encyclopedia* (2003).

Kevin J. Harty, *The Reel Middle Ages: American, Western and Eastern European, Middle Eastern and Asian Films about Medieval Europe* (1999).

Internet Medieval Sourcebook (www.fordham.edu/halsall/sbook.html). An excellent resource for out-of-copyright primary sources.

Labyrinth: Resources for Medieval Studies (www.georgetown.edu/labyrinth/). This is the best place to start medieval searches on the Web. See also *Online Reference Book for Medieval Studies* (http://the–orb.net).

Carl Lindahl et al., eds., *Medieval Folklore: A Guide to Myths, Legends, Tales, Beliefs, and Customs* (2002). A handy guide to both the mundane and the obscure.

Peter Linehan and Janet L. Nelson, eds., *The Medieval World* (2000). An outstanding collection of articles, some on general topics and others more specific.

Angus Mackay and David Ditchburn, *Atlas of Medieval Europe* (1997). For medieval maps, try *Cartographic Images* (www.henry-davis.com/MAPS/).

---

[1] Words defined in the glossary are indicated, at first use, by boldface.

∞

PART I

THE EARLY MIDDLE AGES
THE BIRTH OF EUROPE, 500-1000

By the end of the fifth century the Roman Empire had disintegrated in the West, and in the 500 years that followed, a new "European" civilization took shape. By the eleventh century that civilization was poised for expansion, growth, and further change. The term "Early Middle Ages" refers here to the period between about 500 and 1000, although such dividing lines are flexible and would have passed unnoticed at the time.

Rather than descending suddenly from the sky onto Europe in 500, we will approach it on foot from out of the Roman past, beginning with the reign of Augustus (r. 31 B.C.E.–14 C.E.), when the old Roman *Republic* gave way to the Roman *Empire*.[1] Looking briefly at the Empire at its height, in the first and second centuries, we will then explore the ways in which Roman civilization was transformed during the third, fourth, and fifth centuries. We will focus on the Christianization of the Roman Empire, for this religious change decisively shaped the future of Europe, both Western and Eastern. We will also trace the collapse of Roman imperial authority in the West, the barbarian settlements and invasions, and the establishment of new kingdoms across vast stretches of Western Europe and North Africa once ruled by Rome. With this running start behind us, we will arrive at 500.

The vast territory once controlled by the Roman Empire was eventually divided into three successor civilizations: Western European, Byzantine, and Islamic. Because the subject of this book is medieval Western Europe, we will keep our eyes on the latter two but not focus on them. Chapter 4 will show how Byzantine and Islamic civilizations came to dominate the eastern and southern reaches of the old Roman Empire. In this

---

[1] Our dating system derives from the calculations of an early medieval monk who reckoned the numbers of years that separated his own time from the birth of Jesus. Years were counted *Anno Domini* ("in the year of our lord"), but the system is flawed, for it counts from a miscalculated year for Jesus' birth. Historians now think Jesus was, in fact, born four to ten years before the year 1 *Anno Domini*. (This embarrassing fact did not slow down celebrations for the beginning of the third millennium, even though it occurred some four to ten years late, by strict reckoning.) In any case, as this system is now accepted as a common dating system for worldwide use by people of many religions, its old abbreviations—B.C. (Before Christ) and A.D. (Anno Domini)—are now conventionally replaced by B.C.E. (Before the Common Era) and C.E. (Common Era). These new abbreviations recognize that this dating system has been accepted, as a matter of convenience not faith, for use throughout the world.

TIMELINE FOR PART I   The Early Middle Ages, 500–1000

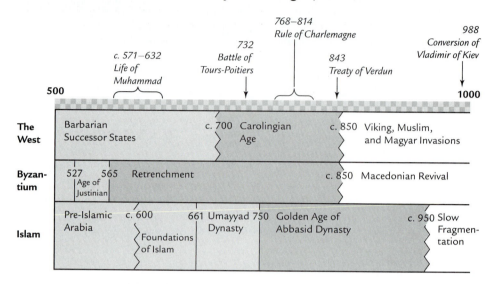

chapter we will consider these civilizations on their own terms, but we will particularly look at the influence of Byzantium and Islam—in terms of culture, religion, and war—on the emerging world of the medieval West. We'll do the same when we return to these "neighbors" of the West in later chapters.

In Western Europe, the sixth and seventh centuries witnessed repeated invasions, accompanied by political and economic turmoil. Illiterate, hard-bitten landholders led their retinues in battle, fighting among themselves, fighting against other barbarians, and eventually fighting also against the armies of an expanding Islamic empire. In the midst of this turmoil, cities became underpopulated and ruinous, while the countryside suffered periodic famines and plagues. Yet Christianity prospered. Many Christian queens, in a process known as **domestic proselytization,** brought their husbands (and kingdoms) into the Christian fold, and intrepid monks and nuns sought still more converts among the Frisians, Saxons, Bavarians, and others. The monasteries that nurtured the pious careers of monks and nuns were places of prayer, but they were also the heartbeat of Christianity. Monasteries provided central hubs for missionary work, agricultural production, and scholarly endeavor—outposts of civilization where the Latin literary heritage of ancient Rome was kept alive through the copying and study of old manuscripts. In Rome itself, the papacy did not exactly prosper after the important foundations laid by Pope Gregory I (r. 590–604), for his successors exercised little authority outside of Rome and its vicinity. But their *claims* to greater authority kept alive the ideal of a single and unified **Church,** governed from Rome.

In the 700s, a new dynasty—the Carolingians—worked closely with monks, nuns, and popes to build an empire that eventually stretched across most of Western **Christendom.** Charlemagne, the greatest of the Carolingians, assumed the title "Roman Emperor" in 800, a title that spoke both to the imaginative power of the Roman legacy and to the real power Charlemagne then wielded. But lacking large cities and an educated bureaucracy, Charlemagne's empire was fragile. It collapsed during the 800s amid a new wave of invaders: Vikings, Muslims, and Magyars. In the course of these invasions, and partly in response to them, strong kingdoms emerged among the Anglo-Saxons in England and among the German states in the old East Francia of Charlemagne's empire. In West Francia, or France, the monarchy long remained feeble, and the burden of defense fell to dukes and counts, who fortified their lands with castles and gradually tightened their control over lesser landholders.

By 1000 the invasions had run their course. The Muslims were in retreat. The Vikings and Magyars had adopted Christianity, becoming participants in Western civilization rather than predators of it. Cities were growing once again in the heartland of Western Europe, and commerce began to flourish. The Church entered a period of reform and spiritual renewal, and literacy slowly spread. In the relative peace that graced the beginning of the second millennium, peasants enjoyed better harvests, townspeople benefited from expanding trade, lords and ladies collected more profits from their lands, and the power of the Church waxed strong. The Early Middle Ages began about 500 with the decay of an old and powerful civilization and ended about 1000 with the maturation of a new one, radically different from ancient Rome yet, in a sense, one of its children.

SUGGESTED READINGS

Lisa Bitel, *Women in Early Medieval Europe, 400–1000* (2002). A survey of the literature now available on this subject. See also Jane Schulenberg, *Forgetful of Their Sex: Female Sanctity and Society, ca. 500–1100* (1998).

Peter Brown, *The Rise of Western Christendom* (2nd edition, 2003). A recent and readable synthesis by an authoritative scholar.

Roger Collins, *Early Medieval Europe, 300–1000* (2nd edition, 1999). Not very readable, but a thorough account of political history.

Robert Fossier, ed., *The Cambridge Illustrated History of the Middle Ages, vol. 1: 350–950* (1989). See also the early volumes of David Abulafia et al., eds., *The New Cambridge Medieval History.*

Judith Herrin, *The Formation of Christendom* (1987). A learned study of the evolution of Christian Europe, East and West, from late antiquity to the Carolingian era.

Rosamond McKitterick, ed., *The Uses of Literacy in Early-Medieval Europe* (1990). Essays by distinguished scholars.

Lawrence Nees, *Early Medieval Art* (2002). A new, richly illustrated overview of art in the first millennium.

Klars Randsborg, *The First Millennium AD in Europe and the Mediterranean: An Archaeological Essay* (1991). Sweeping, provocative, and brief.

CHAPTER 1

ROME BECOMES CHRISTIAN,
C. 31 B.C.E-430 C.E.

❋ INTRODUCTION

The Roman Empire at its height was one of the largest the world had ever known. It encompassed the entire Mediterranean basin and bulged far northward through present-day France and England. During its first two centuries, between the accession of Emperor Augustus (c. 31 B.C.E.) and the death of Emperor Marcus Aurelius (180 C.E.), the Roman Empire extended from the Euphrates River in modern Iraq to the shores of the Atlantic, and from the Sahara Desert of North Africa to the Danube and Rhine rivers of central Europe and the Cheviot Hills of northern Britain (see Map 1.1). Across this vast territory, the power of Rome was firm but not suffocating. The Empire was united by the power of Roman armies, the administration of Roman cities, and the loyalty of local elites who, whatever their mother tongues, adopted Latin as the language of empire. Yet beneath this loose structure lay mind-boggling diversity—a babble of languages, a throng of many races, and a great diversity of religions.

In these first centuries of imperial rule, Christianity was a new and relatively minor player among the many religions of imperial Rome. By the fourth century, however, Christians had won imperial support (see Timeline 1.1), and Christianity, strengthened by numerous converts and nurtured by strong emperors, was a new source of Roman unity. Christianity changed Rome, and Rome returned the favor. Christianity, rooted in the traditions of Judaism and shaped by the teachings of Jesus and his earliest disciples, slowly absorbed many of the intellectual and institutional traditions of the Roman world.

❋ THE ROMAN PEACE (31 B.C.E.-180 C.E.)

Rome's emperors ruled their peoples in relative peace, but not all of them ruled wisely. Several were decidedly dull-witted and a couple were (to put it charitably) demented. Caligula (r. 37–41 C.E.) had his favorite horse wined and dined at imperial banquets and made plans to have the beast raised to the office of Roman consul. (The project

TIMELINE 1.1   The Roman Empire, c. 31 B.C.E.–500 C.E.

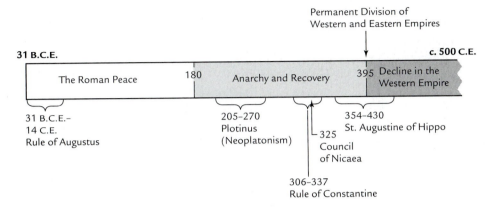

was cut short by Caligula's assassination.) And the less said about Nero (r. 54–68 C.E.), the better. But a number of the early emperors were able and farsighted, and even under the worst of them, imperial government continued to function. An army of some 300,000 to 500,000 men guarded the far-flung imperial frontiers, a superb system of paved roads tied the provinces to Rome, and Roman ships sailed the Mediterranean and Black seas, rarely troubled by pirates or enemy fleets. Scattered across the Empire were cities built in the Roman style with temples, public buildings, baths, schools, theaters, amphitheaters, and triumphal arches. Their ruins are still to be seen all around the Mediterranean and beyond—in Italy, France, Spain, Portugal, England, North Africa, the Balkans, Turkey, and the eastern Mediterranean—bearing witness even now to the tremendous scope of Roman authority and the tasteful uniformity of Roman architecture.

The Empire extended about 3,000 miles from east to west, the approximate length of the United States. According to the best scholarly guesses, its inhabitants numbered more than 50 million (about one-sixth of the U.S. population today), and most lived in the eastern provinces where commerce and civilization had flourished long before Rome. Egypt, Palestine, Mesopotamia, and Greece had all fallen under Roman rule, although Greece—with its distinctive religion, literature, art, and urban-based political institutions—exerted such a dominating *cultural* influence that some Romans doubted who had conquered whom. Most wealthy Romans were bilingual in both Greek and Latin, and they shared a Greco-Roman culture that spanned this enormous territory, a culture found in the cities of Iberia as well as those of Asia Minor and North Africa. But ordinary people, who mostly lived in farms and villages instead of cities, spoke their old languages, followed their local customs, worshiped their traditional deities, and offered obedience and taxes to Rome.

To the east, Rome shared a boundary with the Parthian Empire, which would give way during the third century to a new and aggressive Persian Empire—and new border wars. Elsewhere Rome's expansion from the Mediterranean Basin was halted only by geography—by the Arabian and Sahara deserts, the Caucasus Mountains, the dense forests of central Europe beyond the Rhine and Danube rivers, the barren highlands of Scotland, and the Atlantic Ocean. In short, the Roman frontiers encompassed virtually

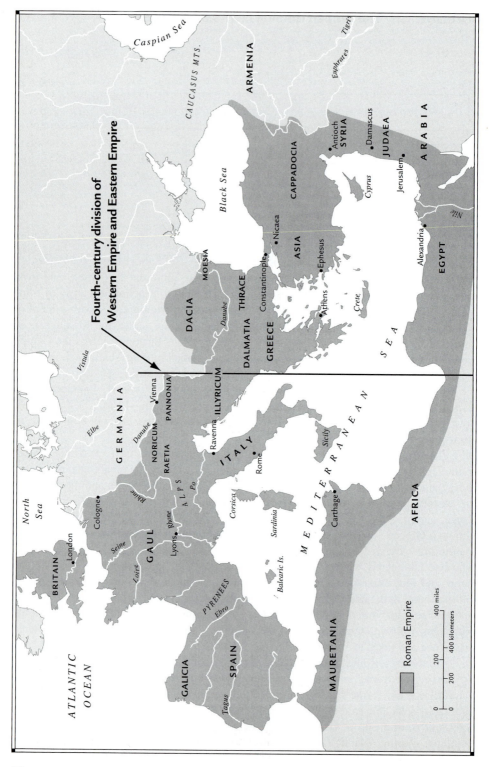

**Fourth-century division of
Western Empire and Eastern Empire**

Caspian Sea

CAUCASUS MTS.

ARMENIA

Tigris

Euphrates

Black Sea

ARABIA

Damascus

SYRIA

Antioch

JUDAEA

CAPPADOCIA

Jerusalem

Cyprus

ASIA

Nicaea

Nile

Ephesus

Alexandria

EGYPT

MOESIA

Constantinople

THRACE

Athens

Crete

DACIA

DALMATIA

Danube

GREECE

S E A

Vistula

ILLYRICUM

Vienna

GERMANIA

PANNONIA

Elbe

NORICUM

M E D I T E R R A N E A N

Danube

RAETIA

Ravenna

ITALY

Sicily

Rhine

A L P S

Po

Rome

North
Sea

Cologne

Corsica

Sardinia

Seine

GAUL

Lyons

Rhône

Carthage

AFRICA

London

BRITAIN

Loire

Balearic Is.

PYRENEES

MAURETANIA

ATLANTIC
OCEAN

Ebro

Roman Empire

GALICIA

SPAIN

400 miles

Tagus

400 kilometers

200

200

0

0

all the lands that could be reached by Roman armies and cultivated profitably by Roman landowners.

Roman institutions and classical culture spread far and wide across the Empire under the canopy of the *Pax Romana,* the "Roman Peace." As distant provinces became progressively Romanized, the meaning of the words "Rome" and "Roman" gradually broadened. By the time of Augustus, these terms embraced not simply a city and its inhabitants but the greater part of the Italian peninsula. Thereafter Roman citizenship was extended to more and more provincials until finally, in 212 C.E., every free inhabitant of the Empire received citizenship. By then the Roman emperors themselves often came from the provinces: the talented second-century emperors Trajan (r. 98–117 C.E.) and Hadrian (r. 117–138 C.E.), for example, were born not in Rome, but in Iberia.[1]

Economic and Social Conditions

Rome was an empire of cities. The city of Rome itself boasted perhaps a million inhabitants, and hundreds of thousands lived in the big eastern cities of Alexandria, Antioch, and later, Constantinople. Yet most Roman cities were much more modest, especially in the western provinces. There, most cities had no more than 5,000 inhabitants, bigger than many colleges today but smaller than most universities. In this case, however, size did not matter, for even small cities played big roles in the Empire's administration. A provincial city essentially governed its surrounding countryside, so that well-off citizens from a small city acted as agents for Rome, administering its edicts, emulating its traditions, and, of course, collecting its taxes. In this way, a small urban elite governed the Empire, spread its culture, and enjoyed its profits. Constituting only 3 percent of the population, this elite controlled perhaps one-third of the Empire's goods and lands.

Wealth was concentrated in Roman cities, but it was mostly not produced there. Although small-scale urban industry flourished, particularly in the East, the cities of the Empire were of only modest importance as commercial and manufacturing centers. Rich citizens supported themselves with rents and produce from landed estates and with the profits of imperial administration, but relatively few lived by trade or industry. This was particularly true in Rome and other western cities, which, like modern Washington, D.C., consumed far more than they produced. In other words, the administration of the Empire relied on cities, but the Empire's economy was rooted in the countryside. As long as fields ripened with grain, flocks multiplied, and olive trees bent low with fruit, landowners prospered and their tenants and slaves had more to eat. This is just what happened during the first two centuries of the Empire. Once the rural economy

◀ **Map 1.1**   *The Roman Empire during the Pax Romana*   This map shows the Roman Empire at its height, c. 180 C.E., when the Mediterranean was entirely encircled by Roman lands. Notice how the Rhine and Danube rivers defined the north-central boundary of Roman authority. Added to this map is a line showing how this empire was later divided—in the fourth century—into western and eastern halves. From this division would eventually emerge medieval Europe (in the west) and the Byzantine Empire (in the East).

---

[1] The terms "Rome" and "Roman" would eventually acquire even broader connotations that extended well beyond the chronological confines of Roman history: in later centuries, a Greek monarch in Constantinople, a Frankish monarch in Aachen, a Saxon monarch in Germany, and a Hapsburg in Vienna would all call themselves "Roman" emperors.

began to falter at the end of the second century, however, cities declined, and with them slowly decayed the administrative structure of the Western Empire.

Roman agriculture varied according to climate, soil, and custom, but the principal crops of the Empire were grain, grapes, and olives—the so-called Mediterranean triad that had dominated agriculture in the Mediterranean basin for countless generations and that, to some extent, still does today. Grain, chiefly wheat and barley, and grape vines were cultivated throughout most of the Empire. From these the Romans produced two of the basic staples of their diet: bread and wine. Olive trees were also grown in abundance, though their vulnerability to cold restricted their cultivation to the frost-free lowlands around the Mediterranean Sea. There, olive oil was much preferred to butter; in more northerly climes, the rich imported olive oil and the poor made do with butter. In the Italian peninsula itself, sheep- and cattle-raising had replaced grain production, and the fertile wheat-growing provinces of Egypt and North Africa supplied bread for the teeming populace of the city of Rome.

By the first and second centuries C.E., agriculture was organized into large estates, not family farms. Small, independent farmers were few and far between, a glorious memory of the Roman past but not part of the Roman present. Instead, wealthy aristocrats owned most of the land, which they often consolidated into large estates tilled by slaves or half-free peasants. Roman slavery was not race-based; almost any person might be enslaved, if captured in war, abandoned by parents, or even sold to pay debts. Most slaves worked in agriculture, but others labored as household servants or in manufacturing. Under Roman law, slaves could not marry or form families.

As the frontiers of Rome jelled and the flow of war captives dwindled, supplies of slaves fell off, too. Landowners responded by leasing farmland to sharecroppers called *coloni,* and over time, these sharecroppers slowly sank into a semi-servile status halfway between slave and free, akin to what would be the status of medieval serfs. Serfdom would emerge as a dominant form of agricultural labor in many regions of medieval Europe, but agricultural slavery also persisted far into the Middle Ages, dying out only around 1000 C.E. (and in some parts of Europe, urban slavery persisted throughout the Middle Ages). But these trends were in the future. During the Roman Peace, the muscles of slaves, poor laborers, and coloni worked the lands on which hinged the leisured lives of the Empire's elite and, indeed, the very survival of the imperial economy.

All in all, the Roman Peace, centered on small administrative cities that themselves relied on the sweat of laborers who worked distant fields, was remarkably fragile for something that prospered for two centuries. It also was not as peaceful as one might suppose. **Barbarians** hammered repeatedly at the imperial frontiers, while, as recent research has made clear, towns and estates deep within the Empire were afflicted by local violence and mayhem to a degree unimagined by earlier historians. Even in the golden age, the Roman provinces were drastically underpoliced and undergoverned.

The Roman Peace was also not a golden age for most people. If we put on the rose-tinted glasses of nineteenth-century historians, the first two centuries C.E. may seem humanity's happiest age, but the lives of slaves, coloni, and the poor should warn us against such happy conclusions. Roman imperial culture was impressive, but it was also narrowly limited, enjoyed only by the Empire's upper crust. Although everyone benefited from the stability of the Roman Peace, most people were impoverished and undernourished. Their misery, which persisted throughout the Roman Peace and beyond, was caused not by economic misfortune but by the privileged needs of the great estates and wealthy households of Rome. Some people prospered during the Roman Peace, but many labored hard for little return.

This disparity was found within households as well as within the Empire. The Roman father was the master of his family and exercised the power of life or death over his newborn children. If he liked their looks, he kept them; if they were weak or physically handicapped, or if the father already had enough children (particularly female children), they were taken from home and abandoned. Some had the good fortune to be rescued by slave traders or adults in need of children; others simply died of exposure. By long tradition, elite Roman women were expected to stay home and obey their fathers and, later, husbands. During the imperial era, many wealthy Roman women acquired control over their own lands, traveled more freely, and attained considerable independence with respect to marriage and divorce. Some upper-class women were even well educated. But these changes affected relatively few. Most Roman women were perpetual minors, subject to either father or husband, and most were, like their fathers and husbands, oppressed slaves, unfortunate sharecroppers, or poor laborers. The labor of ordinary women was far too valuable—to either their owners or their families— to have ever been limited by confinement at home.

Of course, virtually all ancient civilizations were afflicted by mass enslavement, impoverishment, malnutrition, internal violence, the oppression of women, and the abandonment of unwanted infants. In these respects, Roman imperial civilization was probably no worse than others, and in the larger cities, where public baths and other amenities were available (such as free bread in the city of Rome), it was significantly better, even for ordinary people. Life during the Roman Peace could be pleasant enough if one were male, adult, wealthy, and naturally immune to various epidemic diseases. But if this was humanity's happiest time, God help us all!

✳ The Third and Fourth Centuries (180 C.E.-395 C.E.)

Anarchy and Recovery

The prosperity of the Roman Peace was limited to only a wealthy few, but what followed was bad for everyone. During the third century, invading tribes broke through the frontiers again and again, forcing cities to construct protective walls and threatening for a time to tear the Empire to pieces. Imperial survival depended increasingly on military defense, and the Roman legions, well aware of that fact, made and unmade emperors so often that (to exaggerate only slightly) a man might be a general one day, emperor the next, and dead the third. Twenty-odd emperors (depending on how you count) reigned during the calamitous half-century between 235 and 285, and all but one died by murder, in combat, or in captivity. With military troubles and political anarchy came social and economic breakdown. Plagues, famines, and floods were more troubling than before. The cost of living soared 1,000 percent between 256 and 280 C.E., and taxes, needed to pay and feed soldiers, grew apace. Laborers abandoned their fields, harvests fell, towns decayed, and population dropped. The golden age had given way to what one third-century writer described as an age of "iron and rust."

The Empire was saved, though just barely, by imperial reform in the late third and early fourth centuries. With energetic creativity the emperors Diocletian (r. 284–305) and Constantine (r. 306–337) rebuilt the loosely governed Empire of earlier days into an autocracy supported by a huge army and bureaucracy. The regimented government that resulted from their reforms has often been criticized, and with justice. But it enabled the faltering Empire to survive for nearly two more centuries in the West and for more than 1,000 years in the East.

First, by tremendous military effort they threw back barbarian and Persian armies, recovered lost provinces, and restored old frontiers. Second, they just as vigorously (but less successfully) tried to arrest socioeconomic decay, fixing wages and prices at set levels and insisting that people not change occupations, in effect creating a system of hereditary vocations. And third, they reorganized imperial government to compensate for the decay of the cities whose elites had once eagerly administered the Empire. They expanded the civil service and governed on more authoritarian lines. The most out-standing symbol of this new authoritarianism was the emperor himself who assumed godlike proportions. Borrowing from Greek and Persian court ceremonial, Diocletian employed all the known arts of costume, cosmetics, and drama to make himself appear majestic. During the Roman Peace, emperors had striven to work harmoniously with the political institutions of the former Roman Republic, especially the Senate and civic magistracies, and during the third-century anarchy, emperors had fallen victim to the whims of the army. Now, as Figure 1.1 illustrates, there was a new sort of emperor. Exalted in every possible way, this emperor was *dominus et deus,* "lord and god."

Diocletian and Constantine also began to divide the Empire, a process of profound importance for the development of a distinctive culture in what would come to be known as the "Medieval West." The division began as an administrative matter, with a line drawn through the Balkans (where even today, east and west meet in tense confronta-tion) and down through the heart of North Africa (see Map 1.1). To the west of this line lay Rome, the old capital of the Empire, and a society that was more rural, less wealthy, and more vulnerable to invasion. To the east lay Constantinople, a new capital founded by Constantine, and a more urban, secure, and prosperous world. In 395, this adminis-trative division was made permanent, and thereafter Western Empire and Eastern Empire drifted apart while nevertheless sharing a common imperial past.

The New Religious Mood

Amid the crisis of the third century and the recovery of the fourth, Christianity was ini-tially only one of many **mystery religions** in the Empire. For centuries these mystery religions—so-called because they promised mystical union between worshipers and divine beings—had offered release from individual guilt and hope of eternal life. They presented compelling alternatives (or, in most cases, *additions,* as few mystery cults re-quired that members abandon other religions) to traditional Roman veneration of the deities of hearth and household, clan and city. The gods and goddesses of old Rome, like the Greek deities of Mount Olympus whom the Romans adopted early on, had safe-guarded the corporate welfare of social and political groups; the deities of the new mys-tery cults appealed instead to individual worries and hopes. From Egypt came the cult of the goddess Isis; from Persia came the cult of the savior Mithras; and from Palestine came Christianity. As the peace of the second century gave way to the anarchy of the third, the shift from civic god to savior god, from a focus on this world to a longing for the next, gained enormous momentum. With it came a surge of interest in astrology, magic, and other means of connecting everyday life to broader forces, whether natural

Figure 1.1 *Constantine* Constantine and other fourth-century emperors used magnificent statuary to impress their imperial glory and grandeur on the minds of Romans. This colossal marble head is more than eight feet in height, and it was once part of a full-length statue that stood about forty feet tall.

or otherworldly; these had never been absent from ancient culture, but they now dominated popular thinking as never before.

The boisterous deities of Mount Olympus—Jupiter, Juno, Apollo, Mars, Minerva, and the rest—were not abandoned, but they were slowly eclipsed by new pieties. Tormented by economic hardship and insecurity, many urban poor of the third- and fourth-century Empire turned toward mystery cults, and they were joined by wealthy elites for whom the high hopes of classical humanism—the dream of a rational universe, an ideal republic, a good life—were beginning to seem like cruel illusions. The result was a slow but basic shift in religious outlook—a rejection of worldly interests and a concern for life after death—that shaped the intellectual world of the late Empire and the civilizations that would succeed it.

The elegant, worldly culture that elites had developed during the Roman Peace gradually became more mystical, otherworldly, and impressionistic. This trend can be seen in literature and art, but it was especially conspicuous in the leading philosophical movement of the third century, **Neoplatonism** (so named because it was based loosely on the much earlier thought of the Greek philosopher Plato). Neoplatonism received its fullest elaboration in the writings of the third-century philosopher Plotinus (205–270) who taught of one god, a god who was infinite, unknowable, and unapproachable, except through mystical experience. This deity was the ultimate source of everything, spiritual and physical. All existence was imagined as a series of stages radiating outward from this god, this Oneness, like concentric ripples in a pond, each new stage diminishing in excellence with distance from the divine source. Neoplatonists taught that the human soul, trapped at a lesser stage, should seek to return, via **mysticism,** to the perfect oneness of god. As was customary at the time, Neoplatonists did not reject old practices. Regarding the pagan gods and goddesses as crude but useful symbols of the true Neoplatonic god, they gave new life to old Roman cults. In the process, distinctions between the traditional civic veneration of Jupiter, the more recent mystery cults, and the abstractions of Neoplatonism steadily blurred.

✳ CHRISTIANITY

In this intense atmosphere of worldly dissatisfaction and spiritual longing, Christianity slowly won out over its competitors. Some Christian beliefs and practices resembled those of older religions: baptism, eternal salvation, the death and resurrection of a savior-god, the sacramental meal, a human family governed by a divine father—none of these was new. Yet Christianity differed from other mystery religions in two fundamental ways. First, its founder and savior was an actual historical person; compared with the human-god Jesus, such deities as Isis and Mithras might have seemed more distant and less real. Second, the Christian god was not merely the best of many deities but the One God, the God of the Jews, unique in all antiquity in his claims to exclusiveness and omnipotence, and now detached from his association with the Jewish people to become the One God of *all* who would accept Christian baptism.

Jesus lived and died a Jew in the province of Judea, a once autonomous state that was then firmly under Roman control. Most Jews lived in Judea but some lived in Alexandria, Tarsus, Ephesus, and other cities in the eastern Mediterranean. For the people of Judea, subjection to Roman authority was a relatively new and bitter experience; for the Romans, Judea was a difficult province, politically turbulent and also, thanks to Jewish monotheism, religiously peculiar. Jesus was born into this explosive mixture of Jewish and Roman traditions around 4 B.C.E., and when he reached maturity, he began a ministry devoted not to abolishing Jewish laws but to fulfilling them. In the four Gospels, he is pictured as a warm, charismatic leader who miraculously healed the sick, raised the dead, and stilled the winds—miracles that some saw as guarantors of the divine authority with which he claimed to speak. He ministered chiefly to the Jewish poor and outcast, and at first, they accepted his ideas most readily. His sermons stressed love, compassion, and humility; like the earlier Hebrew prophets, he scorned empty formalism in religion and favored a simple life of generosity toward all and devotion to God. He did not object to ritual as such, but only to ritual infected with pride and divorced from feeling. Welcomed by some Jews, he angered others, and to the Roman authorities, he was simply a troublemaker. Brought before the Roman governor Pontius Pilate on the charge of claiming to be king of the Jews, an act of treason against the emperor, Jesus was condemned in 30 C.E. to crucifixion, a common means of executing non-Romans.

According to the Gospels, Jesus' greatest miracle was his resurrection, his return to life on the third day after his death on the cross. He was said to have remained on earth for a short period thereafter, giving solace and instruction to his disciples, and then to have ascended into heaven with the promise that he would return in glory to judge all souls and bring the world to an end. The earliest generations of Christians expected this second coming to occur quickly, but with time, Christians began to organize their communities for survival over the long haul.

From the beginning, most Christians not only accepted the ethical teachings of Jesus but also worshiped him as the Christ—that is, as the incarnation of God. As reported in the Gospels, Jesus had distinguished repeatedly between himself and God ("the Father") but he also stated, "I and the Father are one." Those who followed Jesus interpreted such statements in diverse ways. In the second century some Gnostics (from "gnosis," the revealed "knowledge" that led to salvation) taught that Christ was not truly human but only a divine phantom—that because the physical world was evil, God could not have degraded himself by assuming a flesh-and-blood body. In the third century, **Arians** (named after their leader, Arius) maintained that Christ was not fully divine, not an equal to God the Father.[2] Shortly thereafter, Monophysites (from "monophysis" or "one nature") argued that Christ's divine nature predominated over his humanity. These controversies about the nature of Christ—human or divine or both—drew, to some extent, on long-standing disputes about relations between mind and body, matter and spirit, earth and heaven. These disputes continue to this day. But most Christians slowly became committed to the difficult and sophisticated notion of a Jesus Christ who was both fully human and fully divine (see Figure 1.2 and Color Illustration 2). Most Christians also accepted the notion of a single divinity with three equal aspects: Father, Son, and Holy Spirit. Christ was the Son, or Second Person, in a Holy Trinity that was nevertheless one God. These doctrines produced a great deal of theological controversy but they would eventually produce **orthodoxy,** an agreed-upon theology from which other interpretations were unorthodox or even **heretical.**

The Early Church

The first centuries of Christian belief witnessed a deeply significant process whereby the Judeo-Christian foundations of the new faith were modified and enriched through contact with Greco-Roman culture. Jesus' own apostles were little influenced by Greek thought, and some of them sought to keep their faith strictly within the framework of Judaism. But St. Paul (c. 5 B.C.E.–67 C.E.), an early convert who was both a Jew and a Roman citizen, succeeded in steering Christian communities toward a more encompassing goal. Paul taught that Christians should not be bound by the strict Jewish dietary laws or the requirement of circumcision (which would have severely diminished Christianity's attraction to adult, non-Jewish males). The new faith would be open to all

---

[2] The term "Arian" is not related in any way to "Aryan," a racist classification common in Nazi literature and ideology.

Figure 1.2   *The Good Shepherd*   No contemporary
portraits of Jesus survive, and the earliest ones date from
the fourth century when this statue was made. The "Good
Shepherd" theme of this statue emphasizes the youth,
simplicity, and goodness of Jesus, and it was one of the
most popular images in early Christian art. The nature of
Jesus—whether a human (as emphasized in this image) or
divine (as emphasized in images of Jesus splendidly dressed
or enthroned), or both—was the subject of much debate
among early Christians. See Color Illustration 2 for a
mosaic that emphasizes Jesus' awesome divinity.

people everywhere who would accept Jesus as God and Savior—and open also to the bracing winds of Greco-Roman thought.

Some converts were wealthy enough to provide money and homes for new Christian communities. In Philippi, for example, Paul and Luke stayed with Lydia, a dealer in purple dyes, whose household became the nucleus of the town's Christian community. Lydia's prominent role was not unusual, for women were active in early Christian congregations. Yet although some rich women—and men as well, of course—accepted the Christian faith in its earliest years, Christianity drew converts from a wide swath of Roman society, including artisans, small traders, and even the urban poor. These humble folk might have found it easy to accept a savior who had worked as a carpenter; had consorted with fishermen, ex-prostitutes, and similar riffraff; had been crucified by the imperial authorities; and had promised salvation to all who followed him—free or slave, man or woman. Whether rich, middling, or poor, most early converts lived in cities.

From the first, Christians engaged regularly in a holy meal of bread and wine that came to be called the **Eucharist** (Greek for "thanksgiving"). This ritual was viewed as a **sacrament,** a channel of divine grace through which the recipient was infused with the spirit of Christ. By means of another sacrament, baptism, converts were initiated into the Church, had all sins forgiven, and received God's grace. Because baptism erased all sins, some put it off until they were near death. By the end of the first century, Christians also had written texts that told the stories of their faith. Some of these were lost or rejected by later generations, but four—those ascribed to the authorship of Matthew, Mark, Luke, and John—became the Gospels, the core of the Christian New Testament.

Thus nourished by their rituals, sacraments, and Gospels, Christians were also inspired by holy people or **saints.** In the earliest centuries of Christianity, saints were honored in an informal process of recognition; if people thought you were a saint, you were. Most early saints were distinguished by their exceptional self-denial (celibacy was especially important) or by their martyrdom. Stories celebrating the lives of saintly people added another written tradition—that of **hagiography,** or saints' lives—to the textual treasury of Christianity. In 202, for example, a young woman named Perpetua suffered martyrdom in Carthage. The story of her Christian courage inspired its readers, advanced the victim's status as *Saint* Perpetua, and even today provides an important source for the history of early Christians. By the Central Middle Ages, the saintly free-for-all of early Christianity would be curbed by rules and bureaucracy. Within Roman Catholic tradition today, for example, a special office in the Vatican reviews the lives and miracles of candidates for sainthood and "makes" saints.[3]

At the same time that Christians were developing rituals, texts, and saintly models to guide their faith, they also grew more organized. Most early communities met in homes, but by the fourth and fifth centuries, purpose-built churches grew common (see Figure 1.3). A distinction developed between the **clergy,** who governed the Church and administered the sacraments, and the **laity** whom they served. The clergy, initiated into the Christian priesthood through the ceremony of ordination, were divided into several ranks; particularly, ordinary *priests,* who conducted religious services and

---

[3] Because designation of sainthood is a matter of historical interest (as well as Christian faith), persons recognized by the medieval Church as saints will be so noted in this book, usually just at first reference.

Figure 1.3   *An Early Church*   This shows the nave and apse of Santa Sabina in Rome, begun c. 425 C.E. and built in the style of a Roman basilica. In the fifteenth century, architects inspired by humanist ideals would again emulate the flat roofs and rounded arches of this style (see Figure 15.3).

administered the Eucharist, and ***bishops,*** who supervised priests and led Christian urban communities.[4] The most powerful of the bishops were the *archbishops* (also known as "metropolitans") of the more important cities, who supervised the bishops of their districts. Atop the hierarchy were the bishops of the greatest cities of the Empire: Rome, Alexandria, Antioch, Jerusalem, and later Constantinople. Each of these leaders, known as "patriarchs," governed Christians across a vast swath of the Mediterranean world.

Of the patriarchs, only the bishop of Rome resided in the West. He claimed preeminence over all, based on the tradition that Peter, foremost among Jesus' twelve apostles, had spent his last years in Rome and suffered martyrdom there (c. 65 C.E.). Peter was held to have been the first bishop of Rome—the first **pope**—and later popes regarded themselves as his direct successors. No pope ever convinced the patriarchs of Alexandria, Antioch, Jerusalem, and Constantinople to bow to his authority, and even among Western Christians, it would take many centuries for the bishops of Rome to make good their claim of papal supremacy.

---

[4] The Latin word for bishop is *episcopus,* from which is derived such English words as "episcopal" (having to do with a bishop or bishops) and "Episcopalian" (a member of the Anglican church in the United States).

Christianity and Classical Culture

Early Christianity was especially shaped by Jewish and Greek intellectual traditions. Philo of Alexandria (c. 13 B.C.E.–50 C.E.), who lived in the large Jewish community of Alexandria in Egypt, provided one important inspiration. He used the idea of allegory to reconcile scriptural beliefs with philosophy. To Philo, in other words, the concrete stories of the Jewish Bible had abstract symbolic meaning—so that, for example, the down-to-earth story of Abraham's life spoke abstractly about the soul's journey from sin to salvation. Allegorical interpretation provided one means for Christian theologians to demonstrate that their religion was more than just an appealing myth, that it could hold its own in the highest intellectual circles. For example, they were able to argue that Plato and the Bible agreed on the existence of a single God and the importance of living an ethical life. Christian theologians could also use allegory to interpret the Jewish Bible (or Old Testament) as a text that foretold Christianity—so that, for example, the *wood* Abraham carried as he prepared to sacrifice his son Isaac in response to God's command was a prefiguration of the *cross* on which Jesus died.

Christian thinkers also built on the traditions of Neoplatonism. The otherworldly asceticism of this philosophy made it a good ally for Christians but so too did its notion of a single Oneness from which came all existence. This was easy to associate with the Christian God, and, in the process, Christians incorporated into their theology Neoplatonic ideas about the soul, the role of mysticism, and the material world. To a certain extent, Neoplatonism, like allegory, gave Christian thinkers an acceptable language with which to explain their faith in intellectual terms.

Yet other Christians rejected intellectual attempts to explain their faith. They insisted that God so transcended reason that any attempt to approach God intellectually was useless and, indeed, blasphemous. In the third century, Tertullian (c. 150–225) posed the rhetorical questions:

> What has Athens to do with Jerusalem? What concord is there between the
> Academy and the Church? . . . Let us have done with all attempts to produce a
> bastard Christianity of Stoic, Platonic, and dialectic composition. We desire no
> curious disputation after possessing Christ Jesus, no logical analyses after enjoying
> the Gospel!

Tertullian's rejection of an intellectual approach to Christianity shocked some and appealed to others. Clement of Alexandria (c. 150–215) and his student Origen (c. 185–254) vigorously disagreed. To them, Christians had nothing to fear from philosophy, reason, or even pagan culture, for all these were parts of God's greater plan. They should be used well, not rejected. Yet Tertullian had many followers, and the tension he articulated between reason and faith—between Athens and Jerusalem—would reach its medieval climax in the twelfth century when the logical theology of the philosopher Peter Abelard came into conflict with the loving theology of Bernard of Clairvaux (more about this in Chapter 12).

Christianity and the Empire

From the first, the Christians of the Roman Empire had been a people apart, convinced that they alone possessed the truth and that the truth would one day triumph. They were eager to win new converts and were uncompromising in their rejection of other religions.

In this regard they were distinct from almost all other contemporary faiths, save Judaism, for most people of the ancient world adopted new deities without rejecting old ones. Because Christians were willing to learn from the pagan world but were unwilling to submit to it, they were somewhat worrisome. Their refusal to offer sacrifices to the state gods resulted in imperial persecution, but only intermittently. Violent purges alternated with long periods of official inaction, so that most Christians lived in quiet coexistence with the pagan majority while a few met terrifying—and often unanticipated—deaths. The persecutions could be cruel and sudden, but they were never sufficiently ruthless to exterminate the whole Christian community, and martyrdoms only strengthened the resolve of those who survived. As Tertullian boasted to the pagans who persecuted Christians, "The more you cut us down, the more we multiply. The blood of our Christian martyrs is the seed of our Church." The most severe imperial persecution, and the last, occurred at the beginning of the fourth century under Emperor Diocletian. By then Christianity, although still very much a minority faith, was too firmly entrenched to be destroyed, and the failure of Diocletian's persecution made it evident that the Empire had little choice but to accommodate itself to this new religion.

In 313, the Emperor Constantine undertook a momentous reversal of imperial religious policy when he granted Christians official toleration and protection. Constantine's new approach was partly encouraged by his Christian mother, St. Helena (d. about 330), and partly, it is said, by an extraordinary experience. Before a battle in 312, Constantine dreamt of a cross inscribed with the advice "In this sign, you will conquer." The next day, his soldiers fought under the sign of the cross and won the field. Constantine would not be formally baptized until he lay on his deathbed some three decades later, but soon after the battle of the Milvian Bridge he began not only to tolerate Christianity but also to nurture it. So too did most of his successors. The Christian emperors of the fourth century convened Church **councils** to resolve doctrinal disputes and built great churches that spoke to the awesome power of their God. They replaced the combat of gladiators, which had traditionally provided savage amusement for the urban masses, with the less bloodthirsty sport of chariot racing. They abruptly ended the practice of crucifixion. They prohibited the abandonment of infants, a practice repugnant to Christians, as it had always been to Jews, that was losing much of its social utility in an era of declining population. (They did not, however, eliminate slavery, for it was deemed too essential to the Roman economy.) In grateful return for this imperial patronage, Christian bishops lavished praise on their old enemy and new ally, the emperor. Constantine could no longer claim, as had his imperial predecessors, to be *dominus et deus* (lord and god), but he was lauded as the thirteenth apostle, the master of all churches, the divinely chosen ruler of the Roman people. By offering his imperial support to the Church, Constantine gained for the Empire the support of the Church.

Rich and poor alike now flocked to the Christian faith. **Paganism** would long survive, particularly in the countryside (the word "pagan" derives from the Latin word for peasant, *paganus*), but it slowly withered before the momentum of Christianity. Still a minority faith in 300 C.E., Christianity had become the dominant religion of the Mediterranean world by 400 C.E. No longer persecuted and disreputable, it was now official, respectable, and even supported by imperial subsidies. Of course it lost some of its former spiritual intensity in the process. Bishops and patriarchs now tended to come from wealthy aristocratic families. Women, who had played active roles in the persecuted Church, found their activities more restricted in the institutionalized Church. Doctrinal arguments, once pursued between disagreeing co-religionists, became matters of orthodoxy and heresy. And Christian emperors came to play commanding roles in matters of faith. Constantine was instrumental in the Church council that condemned Arianism at Nicaea in 325, and later in the century Emperor Theodosius I (r. 378–395) added state power to the ban, outlawing the teachings of the Arians and breaking their power. Theodosius outlawed paganism as well, making orthodox Christianity the official religion of the Roman state. The old gods of Rome, deprived of imperial sanction, gradually shuffled off stage, followed, in due course, by the mystery cults associated with Isis, Mithras, and others.

As their religion became more secure, Christians continued to debate its meanings. They argued about the nature of Christ (how could he be both God and human?) and the Trinity (how can three be one?). They also argued about sin (were infants innocent or tainted with original sin?), about priests (was a sacrament administered by a sinful priest valid?), about Mary (was she *theotokos*—the mother of god?), and about many other elements of Christian belief and practice. After long debate, most of these issues were resolved at councils, where bishops and other leaders gathered to settle Christian policy. For example, at the first great council at Nicaea in 325, it was agreed that Christ was fully human and fully divine, a coequal member of the Holy Trinity who had always existed and always would, but who had assumed human form and flesh at a particular moment in time and had walked the earth, taught, suffered, and died as the man Jesus. This agreement satisfied many, but it left others unhappy. The creation of orthodoxy had the positive effect of clarifying Christian doctrine, but it had the negative effect of silencing debate and creating heretics, people whose beliefs were suddenly outside the acceptable mainstream of Christianity.

In the particular case of the decisions of the Council of Nicaea, Arian Christians—who believed that Jesus was not fully divine and was, therefore, a lesser member of the Trinity—continued for centuries to practice and spread their particular version of Christian faith. For many barbarian people, conversion to Christianity was, in fact, conversion to Arian Christianity. Consequently, when in time barbarian kings established successor states on the ruins of the Western Empire, they found themselves divided from their new subjects not only by culture but also by bitter antagonisms between two different Christianities. For centuries, Arian Christians and Catholic Christians—that is, those who remained faithful to the teachings of the Roman pope—would tensely share the lands of the old Western Empire.

Although Arian Christianity eventually disappeared, divergent Christian practices would also slowly culminate in an institutional split that paralleled the divisions of the old Roman Empire. Western Christians usually looked to the pope in Rome for guidance, and because popes claimed authority over *all* Christians, they came to use the term "**catholic**" (or "universal") to describe their faith. Eastern Christians rejected the claims of the Roman pope and looked to the Byzantine emperor and the patriarch of Constantinople for leadership. This division between Catholic Christians and Eastern Orthodox Christians developed over many centuries and around many issues, but the year 1054, when Pope Leo IX (r. 1049–1054) and Patriarch Michael Cerularius (r. 1043–1058) **excommunicated** each other, is usually taken as the date of formal **schism.**[5]

---

[5] The term "Catholic" would take on new meaning when the Western Christians further divided under pressure from "Protestant" reformers in the sixteenth century, but throughout the Middle Ages, it reflected the claim of the bishop of Rome—or pope—to authority over *all* Christians.

In the fourth and fifth centuries, however, divisions between Catholic and Orthodox were in the distant future, and the Christian Church, with all its diverse practices and debates, was closely tied to the imperial traditions of Rome. Before the collapse of the Empire in the West, the Christian Church absorbed and turned to its own purposes many Roman traditions, thereby carrying Roman political organization, administration, and law into the medieval and modern worlds. The pope assumed the old Roman title of *pontifex maximus* (supreme pontiff) and preserved a great deal of the ritual of later imperial courts. The law of the Church—that is, **canon law**—was similarly modeled on Roman civil law. In this organizational sense, the medieval Church has been described as a ghost of the Roman Empire. Yet it was far more than that, for the Church reached its people as Rome never had, giving the impoverished majority a sense of participation and involvement that the Empire had never offered.

Christianity and Judaism

Having started as a Jewish movement, Christianity had quickly developed into an autonomous religion, particularly under the influence of Paul. Judaism itself was also changing in these years, for the failure of two Jewish uprisings in 70 and 135 C.E. devastated Judea. After the revolt of 135, Jews were not even allowed into Jerusalem, except for one day each year. Many left Judea, and those who remained were a minority in their old homeland. By the time of Constantine's edict of toleration for Christianity in 313 C.E., there were Jewish communities not only in the Eastern Empire, as had long been the case, but also in western cities such as Rome, Milan, Cordoba, Marseille, Lyon, and even Cologne along the northern frontier. Thanks to a long tradition of Roman respect for Jewish "ancestral law," Jews were allowed to practice their faith without harassment and even to become citizens of Rome.

In the fourth century, when Christians achieved not only toleration but also imperial sponsorship, Jews continued to be allowed to follow their faith, but somewhat more grudgingly than in the past. When Theodosius banned Arian Christians and pagans, he explicitly extended his tolerant protection to Jews. But most early Christian theologians viewed Judaism in negative or, at best, ambivalent terms. They characterized Judaism as an old religion that had once been useful but was now no longer justified; they saw Judaism as a flawed and even evil faith; they suggested that Judaism could be tolerated only because its "errors" were useful counterexamples to Christians. Jewish theologians had some unkind words for Christianity, too, characterizing Jesus as a magician, rebel, or even the son of a prostitute. But Christians had the power of the state on their side. In these critical centuries, Jewish communities were established throughout the Mediterranean world, but the disinterested acceptance of pagan Rome was slowly replaced by a Christian Empire's more anxious toleration.

The Latin Doctors

Constantine's conversion hastened the process of fusion between Christian faith and Greco-Roman culture. In the generations after him, three Christian scholars— St. Ambrose (c. 339–397), St. Jerome (c. 340–420), and St. Augustine (354–430)— continued the task. Working at a time when the Empire was swiftly becoming Christianized, yet before the intellectual vigor of classical antiquity had diminished, they used their mastery of Greco-Roman philosophy to interpret Christian faith. Since all three were busy administrators, immersed in the political and **ecclesiastical** affairs of their day, their teachings were practical as well as thoughtful. Honored in later years as "Doctors of the Latin Church" (in this case, "doctor" means "teacher," from the Latin *docere* meaning "to teach"), these three men exerted a commanding influence on succeeding generations of Christians.[6]

Ambrose was bishop of Milan, a great city that in the later fourth century replaced Rome as the imperial capital in the West. Ambrose was a superb administrator, a powerful orator, and a vigorous opponent of Arianism. Thoroughly grounded in Greco-Roman literature and philosophy, he salted his sermons and essays with references to Plato, Cicero, Virgil, and other giants of the pagan past. Significantly, he was the first major churchman to assert that in the realm of morality the emperor himself is accountable to the Christian priesthood. When Emperor Theodosius massacred the rebellious inhabitants of Thessalonica, Ambrose barred him from the church of Milan until he had formally and publicly repented. Ambrose's bold stand and the emperor's public submission set a long-remembered precedent for the principle of ecclesiastical supremacy in matters of faith and morality.

Jerome was the most celebrated biblical scholar of his time. A restless, troubled man with a touch of acid in his tongue, he once remarked to an opponent, "You have the will to lie, good sir, but not the skill to lie." Wandering far and wide through the Empire, Jerome lived in Rome for a time, but then founded a monastery in Bethlehem. Jerome's monks devoted themselves to the copying of Latin manuscripts, a task that was to be taken up by countless monastics in later centuries and which, in the long run, resulted in the preservation of important works of Greco-Roman antiquity—by Aristotle, Cicero, Ovid, and others—that would otherwise have perished. Yet Jerome himself was once terrified by a dream in which Jesus banished him from heaven with the words, "You are a Ciceronian, not a Christian." Although torn by doubts about the propriety of a Christian admiring pagan authors, he was much too devoted to the charms of classical literature to do without it. In the end he determined to use Greco-Roman literature in the service of Christian faith.

Jerome's supreme achievement lay in his study and translation of the Christian scriptures. He produced the definitive Latin translation of the Bible from its original Hebrew and Greek. The result of Jerome's efforts was the Latin **Vulgate Bible,** which Catholic Christians used throughout the Middle Ages and beyond, and which has served as the basis of innumerable translations into modern languages. Jerome's translation was an achievement of incalculable significance to Western civilization.

Augustine of Hippo, whose conversion to Christianity is described in the Biographical Sketch on pp. 26–27, was the foremost philosopher of Roman antiquity. As bishop of Hippo (an important city in North Africa), he was deeply involved in the political and religious problems of his age. He wrote voluminously against various pagan and heretical doctrines, and, in the course of these disputes, he examined many of the central problems that have occupied theologians ever since: the nature of the Trinity; the existence

---

[6] Among the many important theologians and leaders of Early Christianity, the Roman Catholic Church today recognizes the sanctity and learning of four Western Doctors (Ambrose, Augustine, Jerome, and Pope Gregory I) and four Eastern Doctors (John Chrysostom, Basil the Great, Gregory of Nazianzus, and Athanasius). The important contributions of Pope Gregory I (r. 590–604) will be discussed in Chapter 3.

BIOGRAPHICAL SKETCH

St. Augustine of Hippo (354–430)

In his *Confessions*—the first major autobiography ever written—Augustine described his long intellectual and moral journey along a twisting path from youthful hedonism to Christian piety. He did so in the form of a prayer, a confession to God, written in the hope that others, lost as he once was, might be led into the spiritual haven of the Christian Church. The *Confessions* is not necessarily a full or even accurate account of Augustine's life, but it is a compelling story that has ever since influenced both the faith of Christians and the writings of autobiographers.

Augustine told of his dissolute youth in the North African region of the Roman Empire. Despite the prayers and admonitions of his Christian mother, St. Monica (333–387; from whence, California's Santa Monica), he rejected her faith. He took a mistress, who bore him a son; he studied philosophy and rhetoric; and he drifted from one popular creed to another: from paganism to **dualism,** skepticism, and Neoplatonism. It was not until the age of thirty-two that he converted to Christianity while he was teaching rhetoric in Milan.

Augustine described his conversion as a painfully gradual process. Out of curiosity he went to hear the preaching of Milan's eloquent and renowned bishop, Ambrose. Delighted by Ambrose's "charming delivery" and "soothing style," Augustine also slowly found himself moved by the *content* of Ambrose's sermons. But he was not yet prepared to abandon his pleasure in wine and women. While in Milan he became engaged to a wealthy heiress not yet of marriageable age. Out of respect for the engagement (and to further his quest for wealth), he parted from his mistress, but he kept his son with him—and eventually took up with yet another mistress. Augustine prayed to God to deliver him from his sexual desires, but he also hoped God's deliverance would be a bit delayed, adding, "Let me wait a little longer."

Yet the tension between Augustine's growing faith and the worldliness of his life slowly became all but unbearable. His great emotional crisis occurred late in the summer of 386, when a friend told him about the ascetic ideals of Christian monasticism and how two young imperial officials, engaged to be married as Augustine was, had abandoned the world and the prospect of marriage to become celibate monks. Profoundly moved, Augustine said to his friend, "What's the matter with us? What does this story mean? These two men have none of our education, yet they rise up and storm the gates of heaven while we, for all our learning, lie here wallowing in this world of flesh and blood."

Augustine reports that he then rushed into his garden "where nobody could interrupt that fierce struggle, in which I was my own opponent, until it reached its conclusion." He tore at his hair and beat his forehead. His past sins seemed to speak to him in tempting whispers: Did he really intend to renounce the joys of sex forever? His conscience countered: "Close your ears to the dirty whispers of your body." Then, as Augustine reported, "a great storm broke within me, bringing with it a deluge of tears." He flung himself beneath a fig tree, wept bitterly and then heard a child's voice repeating over and over again: "Take it and read, take it and read."

In the belief that those words were a divine command, Augustine sought out his copy of Paul's *Epistles,* opened it at random, and read a passage from the letter to the Romans: "No drunken orgies, no promiscuity or licentiousness, and no strife or jealousy. Let your armor be the Lord Jesus Christ, and forget about satisfying your bodies with all their lusts." As Augustine wrote, "I had neither the desire nor the need to read further. When I finished the sentence, as though the light of peace had been poured into my heart, all the shadows of doubt dispersed."

Augustine gave up his wealthy bride-to-be, his licentiousness, and his teaching career. St. Ambrose baptized him in Milan the following Easter, 387, to the overwhelming joy of his mother, who stood at his side.

Augustine subsequently returned to his native North Africa, where he formed a small religious community and headed it for a time. In the 390s he was dragged unwillingly into Church administration, accepting an appointment as bishop of Hippo. There, he produced a great quantity of literary and philosophical works of immeasurable importance to medieval intellectual history, including *Confessions* and, much later, *City of God.*

Augustine was also occupied with the day-to-day cares of his **diocese** and his Christian flock. His contribution to religious thought arose not from the dispassionate working out of an abstract system of theology but rather from his responses to the urgent issues of the moment. One such issue was the survival of the Roman Empire itself. By one of those eerie coincidences of history, within months of Augustine's death in 430, his episcopal city of Hippo would fall to barbarian invaders, the Vandals.

of evil in a world created by a good and all-powerful God; the role of marriage and sexuality in Christian life; the special quality of the Christian priesthood; and the nature of free will and predestination. Out of his diverse writings grew the intellectual foundation for medieval philosophy and theology. Even today, theology students are taught that every good sermon needs a quote from Augustine of Hippo.

Augustine was disturbed, as Jerome had been, by the danger of pagan thought to the Christian soul. But, like Jerome, he concluded that although good Christians ought not to *enjoy* pagan writings, they might properly *employ* such texts for Christian ends. Accordingly, Augustine used the philosophy of Plato and the Neoplatonists as a basis for a new Christian philosophical scheme. Like the Neoplatonists, he believed that the material world was less important than the spiritual world, but it was nevertheless the creation of a loving God who remained actively at work in it. Augustine elaborated on the traditional Christian doctrine, rooted in Judaism, that God had created the first man and woman with the intention that they and all their descendants should attain salvation by living forever in God's loving presence. But rather than creating mere human puppets, God gave humans freedom to choose between good (accepting his love) and evil (rejecting it). As a consequence of wrong choices made by Adam and Eve, humanity fell from its original state of innocence, became incorrigibly self-centered, and thus severed its relationship with God. But God reknit the relationship, Augustine taught, by assuming human form in the person of Jesus—suffering, dying, and rising again. The original sin of Adam and Eve was redeemed by the crucifixion of the sinless God-human, Christ, and the possibility of human salvation was thereby restored.

To Augustine, therefore, the central goal of the Christian life was to attain the salvation that Christ's sacrifice had made possible. Yet Augustine insisted that humans were powerless to achieve this salvation *except through divine grace*. In other words, he saw humans as incapable of finding their own way to heaven and as utterly reliant on the gift of salvation from God. This being so, nobody deserved salvation, in Augustine's view, but some could achieve it because their moral characters were shaped and strengthened by God's grace.

The necessity of divine grace to human salvation is a central theme in Augustine's *City of God.* Here he set forth a comprehensive Christian philosophy of history that was radically new and deeply influential. Rejecting the Greco-Roman notion that history repeats itself in endless cycles, he viewed history as a purposeful process of God's interaction with humanity—beginning with the creation, continuing through Christ's incarnation, and terminating with the end of the world. To Augustine the single determining force in history was human moral character, and the single goal was human salvation. True history, therefore, had less to do with politics, rulers, and states than with the war between good and evil that rages within each state and each soul. Accordingly, Augustine divided humanity into two opposing groups: not Romans and barbarians as pagan writers would have had it, but those who lived in God's grace and those who did not. The former were members of the "City of God," and the latter belonged to the "Earthly City." To Augustine, the two cities were hopelessly intertwined in this life, but their members would be determined at death—by either eternal salvation or damnation. Human history, therefore, had as its purpose the growth and welfare of the City of God.

Augustine's teachings on marriage and sexuality were also influential, both in his own day and ever since. From the earliest days of Christianity, some Christians avoided marriage and embraced chastity. They were inspired by Jesus' words, as reported in Matthew 19:29, "Anyone who has forsaken home, brothers, sisters, father, mother, wife, children, or lands for my name's sake will be repaid a hundred times over and inherit everlasting life." And they also took inspiration from the lives of such holy people as St. Anthony (c. 250–355), who lived as a godly hermit in the Egyptian desert. Anthony and other early celibates—women as well as men—were admired for their disciplined sacrifice, a sort of living martyrdom that became especially important after 313, when imperial toleration eliminated the prospect of martyrdom-by-death. This early Christian asceticism was fully orthodox, and from it would grow Christian monasticism. The desire to withdraw from the world and devote oneself to uninterrupted religious contemplation is not unique to Christianity (it is also found, for example, in Buddhism), but monasticism would become a particularly powerful form of religious expression in medieval Europe.

In Augustine's lifetime, however, monastic communities were just forming, and some Christians took the pious asceticism of Anthony and others to an extreme, arguing that *all* Christians should live celibate lives. Augustine, who himself practiced celibacy, sharply criticized these radicals in *On the Good of Marriage.* He acknowledged that the *ideal* Christian life was a celibate life, especially as exemplified by monks and nuns who devoted themselves to celibacy, prayer, and self-denial. But this ascetic ideal was not, Augustine said, for everyone, and he argued that marriage was a good, honorable alternative for these ordinary Christians. Augustine praised marriage for the children it produced, the conjugal love and sexual fidelity it promoted, and the sacramental grace of God by which it was created. Augustine's defense of marriage would profoundly influence medieval canon law about marriage-making, divorce, and birth control; for example, because canon lawyers accepted Augustine's teaching that the production of children is an essential good of marriage, they opposed birth control. Of course, Augustine's defense also aided the simple survival of Christianity. If ascetic radicals had won the day in the early fifth century, Christians would have produced no children with whom to sustain their faith from generation to generation.

The writings of St. Augustine have shaped Western thought in fundamental ways. His theory of two cities, although often reinterpreted in later generations, influenced political ideas over the next thousand years. His Christian Neoplatonism dominated medieval philosophy until the mid-twelfth century and remains a significant theme in religious thought to this day. His emphasis on divine grace was to be a crucial source of inspiration to the Protestant leaders of the sixteenth century. And his ideas about marriage and sexuality still influence many Christian denominations today.

✳ CONCLUSION

By the time Augustine, Ambrose, and Jerome died, Christian culture was firmly established on classical foundations. At Augustine's death in 430, the Western Empire was tottering, but its classical culture endured within Christianity. The strength of the Greco-Roman tradition within medieval Christianity owes much to the fact that early Christian theologians found it possible, despite Jerome's nightmare, to be both Christians and Ciceronians.

SUGGESTED READINGS

T. D. Barnes, *The New Empire of Diocletian and Constantine* (1982). A persuasive reinterpretation of the late Empire and the consequences of its conversion to Christianity.

Peter Brown, *Augustine of Hippo: A Biography* (2nd edition, 2000). Still the best study.

Kenneth G. Holum, *Theodosian Empresses: Women and Imperial Dominion in Late Antiquity* (1982). For a different perspective on women in this period, see Jo Ann McNamara, *A New Song: Celibate Women in the First Three Christian Centuries* (1983).

Wayne A. Meeks, *The First Urban Christians: The Social World of the Apostle Paul* (2nd edition, 2003). An excellent introduction to early Christianity. See also Ramsay MacMullen, *Christianizing the Roman Empire, A.D. 100–400* (1984), and Robert L. Wilken, *The Christians as the Romans Saw Them* (2nd edition, 2003).

SUGGESTED PRIMARY SOURCES

Bart D. Ehrman, ed., *After the New Testament: A Reader in Early Christianity* (1999). A collection of sources for the first three centuries of Christianity, each with a short introduction.

Ramsay Macmullen and Eugene N. Lane, eds., *Paganism and Christianity, 100–425 C.E.* (1992). A topically organized collection.

Jo-Ann Shelton, ed., *As the Romans Did: A Sourcebook in Roman Social History* (2nd edition, 1998). A wide-ranging collection of fascinating sources.

Carolinne White, ed., *Early Christian Lives* (1998). Translations of seven saints' lives, from St. Anthony to St. Benedict.

CHAPTER 2
━━━━━━━━━━━━━━━

BARBARIAN SETTLEMENT
IN THE WEST, c. 400-500

✴ INTRODUCTION

In the early fifth century, the West was tottering, but it was not without resources. Some of the most important lay in nature itself: reasonably good climate, rich soils, broad rivers, and accessible coastlines. As Map 2.1 shows, the Western European heartland consists of a huge plain of rich soil that fans north from the Pyrenees and the Alps into England and across France and Germany into Scandinavia. Its weather varies greatly but is generally bracing without being intimidating—a happy compromise between the languid, narcotic mildness of southern California and the freezing winters of Maine. Northwestern Europe's dependable year-round rainfall and the fertile soils of its numerous river valleys encouraged agricultural productivity, so much so that a first-century Greek geographer could describe the region as "producing in perfection all the fruits of the earth necessary for life."

The climate was kind to farmers in Western Europe, but so too was the land. Crossing the European heartland are several low, mineral-rich mountain ranges, a broad swath of rich loam for farming, and a remarkable network of broad rivers fed by year-round rains. These rivers connected inland settlements with the sea and with each other, moving people, news, goods, and ideas. Most of Europe's major cities were built on riverbanks—Paris, London, Milan, Cologne, and many others—so that even though they lay far from the sea, their docks received goods from many places and then dispersed them to even more. Europe's long, irregular coastline was a further stimulus to commerce, with not only its huge bays and peninsulas but also its accessible offshore islands such as Sicily, Sardinia, Britain, and Ireland.

Until recently, historians had visualized transalpine Western Europe in late Roman times as a sparsely populated wasteland. But archaeologists have now shattered this traditional picture of Europe as an untamed wilderness—both before Roman occupation and afterward. Their investigations have demonstrated that human settlement throughout Western Europe was far more widespread and more complex than we had previously suspected. As Roman armies marched into Gaul, Iberia, and Britain, they found not wasteland populated by the occasional savage, but instead populous and flourishing agricultural villages. They also encountered hill forts sheltering well-organized communities, farms tilled with the help of highly effective plows, and networks of fields, corrals, and homesteads. Marked by clear boundaries and linked by well-used trackways, these villages, forts, and farms—and the remains they have left for archaeologists today—testify to the complex societies north of the Alps whose people met the Romans, fought them, lived with them, and, in the end, survived them.

Still, the Romans did leave their mark on the landscape of transalpine Europe, reshaping old agricultural patterns to fit new Roman modes of cultivation and introducing to these regions a Greco-Roman model of urban settlement. This latter change was especially important. In their half-millennium of occupation, the Romans built Lyons, Cologne, Vienna, London, and many other cities which, although troubled after the fifth century, usually survived (and many would flourish anew from the eleventh century). These cities are impressive testaments to Roman power, but they were innovations on an already settled landscape. The Romans brought cities to transalpine Europe, but they did not, as we once thought, bring civilization itself.

Before the Roman conquests and long thereafter, most of Western Europe was inhabited by Celts, whom the Romans called Gauls, and by still earlier Bronze Age peoples whom the Celts had subdued when they settled the region in the second millennium B.C.E. "Celt" is a tricky term. Today, it evokes strong ethnic identities associated with Europe's "Celtic Fringe"—from Brittany in France to Wales, Ireland, and western Scotland—where Celtic languages are still spoken. As used for late antiquity, however, "Celt" is a broader and more encompassing term. Then, Celtic-speaking peoples lived throughout transalpine Europe from the Iberian peninsula through Gaul to Britain. In language and culture, Celts were distinct from other language groups, especially Germanic speakers whose homelands lay to the northeast, Slavic-speaking peoples in central Europe, and Latin or Italic speakers from the Italian peninsula. Yet these distinctions were not as neat as they seem. The Celtic language group was large and itself included a great diversity of peoples, tribes, and customs.

The Celts were early recognized for their skills in music, poetry, metalwork, and clothmaking. The Romans were amused at the Celtic custom of wearing pants instead of tunics ("breeches" is a Celtic word). Most Celts were farmers, living in villages surrounded by cultivated fields. Some others were traders, carrying goods across vast stretches of Europe. These traders built fortified towns along their routes, some of which became important provincial cities in Roman times. But it would be misleading to describe these far-flung settlements as a "Celtic Empire" (as some scholars have done), for the Celts were split into hundreds of independent tribes that united only occasionally and grudgingly into larger confederations. They fought hard against the Romans, but in the long run they could not match the military resources of a Mediterranean empire.

Under their Roman conquerors, Celtic villages continued to function much as before. In time, most were incorporated into the great estates of the provincial Roman aristocracy, which had become, through intermarriage, a Gallo-Roman aristocracy. But, although Celtic farmers continued to inhabit their villages and till their fields, their personal status slowly changed, and for the worse. Instead of the free landholders they had once been, many became unfree peasants who were forced to pay rents and dues to the

TIMELINE 2.1   The Waning of the Western Empire, 180 C.E.–700 C.E.

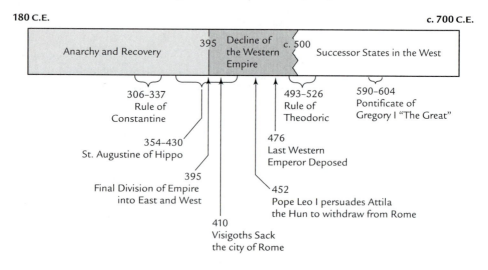

180 C.E.   c. 700 C.E.

Anarchy and Recovery	395 Decline of the Western Empire c. 500 Successor States in the West

306–337
Rule of
Constantine

354–430
St. Augustine of Hippo

395
Final Division of Empire
into East and West

493–526
Rule of
Theodoric

590–604
Pontificate of
Gregory I "The Great"

476
Last Western
Emperor Deposed

452
Pope Leo I persuades Attila
the Hun to withdraw from Rome

410
Visigoths Sack
the city of Rome

Gallo-Roman aristocrats who owned the lands. The sons and daughters of free farmers slowly became serfs and slaves. These men and women still worked the land much as their parents had done, but they were now *compelled* to do so. They also lived in a world of shrinking horizons, a world that was increasingly localized and self-contained. Although a small-scale luxury trade continued to supply aristocratic households, peasants produced most of what they needed, and because their lives were meager, their needs were few.

When barbarians began to move into the West, they were certainly not welcomed by this Gallo–Roman population. Yet they were not an unmitigated disaster. As Celts and Romans had done before them, the barbarians mingled readily with local populations. They brought more expansive ideas of kinship, new forms of military organization, and legal codes that focused more on the concrete challenge of resolving disputes than, as Roman law did, on abstract principles. Amid the political chaos of the late Western Empire (see Timeline 2.1), their kings offered the gift of security, creating from Rome's remains the "successor states" (so-called because they came after—or succeeded—the Western Empire) that both mimicked Roman forms and were so very different from the old empire.

✸ THE BARBARIANS AND THE WESTERN EMPIRE

The last centuries of the Western Empire are a story of Roman accommodation to two old realities that were newly important after 300 C.E.: Christianity and barbarian settlement. We have already seen how, as the once-revered practices of Roman worship became "paganism," new Christian ideas—about such matters as celibacy, the purpose of life, and poverty—challenged classical values. As Map 2.1 shows, barbarian settlement also altered the West. To us today, "barbarian" implies savagery and lack of culture, as exemplified by such fictional characters as Conan the Barbarian. But we must not apply this modern meaning to the past. To the Greeks and the Romans after them, "barbarian" simply meant foreigner (someone whose language sounded—to Greeks or Romans—like gibberish or "ba-ba-ba"). Initially, the Greeks even called the Romans "barbarians."

Map 2.1   *Barbarian Settlement, c. 500*   Some of the peoples shown on this map—such as the Berbers, the Suevi, and the Britons—were old inhabitants of the Western Empire, but by 500 most of the West had been overrun by barbarians who had established "successor states." The Eastern Empire remained relatively untouched by barbarian settlement. For a more expanded view of the Mediterranean world, c. 500, see Map 2 at the front of the book.

In considering barbarian settlement, then, we will examine how outsiders slowly moved into the Western Empire and in the process, both challenged its culture and reinvigorated it.[1]

Barbarian Customs and Institutions

Roman frontiers had always separated those who were under Roman authority from those who were outside it (see Figure 2.1). In the later fourth century, however, life on

---

[1] Sometimes the terms "**Germanic**" and "German" are preferred to "barbarian," but these words were rarely used by Romans to describe the people on their frontiers who eventually settled among them (Tacitus's *Germania* is the outstanding exception). Also, these terms wrongly suggest that all these settlers shared a common Germanic language and were the ancestors of modern Germans. Neither "barbarian" nor "Germanic" are ideal terms, but "barbarian" seems the better of two poor choices.

Figure 2.1   *Roman and Barbarian*   This second-century relief shows a Roman
legionary standing firm against the strong arm and sword of a barbarian warrior. In
contrast to the calm demeanor and well-constructed armor of the legionary, the
barbarian warrior is depicted as wild (notice his flowing hair) and simple (notice
the rustic house in the background).

these frontiers changed, especially on the frontiers created by two great rivers whose
origins lay in the heavy annual snowfalls—and snowmelts—of the Alps: the Rhine,
which flowed to the northwest, and the Danube, which flowed to the southeast.
Outsiders pressed harder against the borders, and Romans were more willing to grant
them entry. Most of the pressure came from central and southeastern Europe, and across
those borders came some people who spoke Germanic languages but also considerable
numbers of Celts, Slavs, and even people from the Middle East. It is therefore hazardous
to make broad generalizations regarding their cultures and institutions, for these varied
widely. Although we tend to think of the barbarian tribes as representing different ethnic
groups within each of which we might find one religion, one language, and one
culture—that is, *one people*—this was not so, at least initially. The tribes were ex-
tremely unstable, taking form around successful war leaders, disintegrating when
military fortunes declined, and then re-forming around new leaders. Eventually a sort of
coherence did take shape as diverse groups coalesced, under growing Roman influence,
into the tribal kingdoms that emerged from the fractured remnants of Roman imperial
governance in the West: those of the Franks, the Vandals, the Angles, the Saxons, the

Ostrogoths, the Visigoths, and others. Once established as kingdoms in the Roman West, these newly formed groups fabricated myths about their allegedly age-old origins in Eastern Europe or Scandinavia. They, in other words, *created* ethnic origins.

Before their first contacts with the Empire, all these peoples were illiterate and therefore "prehistoric," because they left no written records. They preferred to build in wood rather than stone, so they have also left relatively few archaeological remains. Our most reliable evidence comes from Roman commentaries and therefore from a time when barbarians had already been affected by their contacts with Rome. In 98 C.E., the Roman historian Tacitus wrote a short book titled *Germania,* a morality piece written with the intention of criticizing the "degeneracy" of the Romans by comparing them unfavorably with simple, upright barbarians. We can accept his description of tall, blue-eyed people with reddish-blond hair, who lived in agricultural villages and occasionally went on rampages. Less easy to accept is his description of the independence and respect accorded to barbarian women. Because women's agricultural labor freed men for hunting and war, they were certainly valued members of barbarian communities. But barbarian law codes indicate that women were regarded as lifelong minors subject to the guardianship of their fathers or husbands. Tacitus likewise exaggerated when he praised the barbarians for their chastity and virtuous behavior. On the whole their vices seem to have been no less numerous than those of the Romans, but simply cruder. Their standards of personal hygiene are suggested by the later observation of a fifth-century Roman aristocrat: "Happy the nose that cannot smell a barbarian."

Barbarians might have been unpleasant to smell, but they were good for trade and good for soldiering. Trade goods moved regularly across the Rhine and Danube. Romans were not supposed to sell weapons to barbarians, but they traded various luxury goods for which they were paid in good coin, not barter. From the late third century, these borderlands also became prime recruitment areas for the Roman army, and some barbarian groups were even allowed to cross the border, settle in Roman territory, and then defend it against other barbarians. With goods, people, soldiers, and even whole tribes moving back and forth across the frontier, barbarians and Romans came to know each other well. Their interactions were not always happy; Roman armies sometimes undertook campaigns across the border, and barbarians also occasionally ravaged imperial territories. But, like most borders, the Roman frontier saw the daily exchange of people, goods, and customs, as well as the occasional battle. By the 370s, when the major migrations and settlements began, the barbarians were very different from those described by Tacitus some 300 years before. They had absorbed Roman culture to a considerable degree, and many had been converted in the fourth century to Arian Christianity.

We once thought that most barbarians were pastoralists and, therefore, that they moved with their herds across vast stretches of land. New archaeological evidence now suggests that many were settled into farms or villages from which they cultivated the surrounding fields. Their **artisans** produced exceptionally fine metalwork, as shown in Figure 2.2. Like the Romans, the barbarians used iron tools and weapons. Unlike the Romans, they had few cities. Instead, their social and political organization rested on two foundations: kindred and war-band.

Barbarians traced descent through both parents. As a result, only unmarried siblings shared exactly the same kin, and kinship networks were large and amorphous. Barbarians probably often looked to kin, as we do today, for nurturance, love, and

Figure 2.2   *Barbarian Metalwork*   Some barbarians were highly skilled metalworkers, capable of intricate designs that wove together natural images and abstract patterns. This Visigothic royal crown from seventh-century Iberia sets sapphires, pearls, and other precious stones within complex patterns of gold. Designs such as these would long influence Christian art. See, for example, the *Book of Kells* (Color Illustration 3).

companionship, but they also expected their kin to offer a protection that we now expect from police forces and armies. If a person was killed or hurt, kin were bound to avenge the deed. Initially, kin were expected to conduct a feud—declare war, as it were— against the offender's family. Eventually, it became customary to establish a **wergild,** a sum of money that the offender might pay to the relatives of the victim to appease their vengeance. Wergilds varied in size depending on the victim's sex, age, and social status (they were highest for aristocratic adult males and women of childbearing age). They also varied according to injury—large payments for murder and smaller payments for lesser injuries such as cutting off a victim's arm, leg, thumb, or finger, until in time every imaginable injury was covered, down to the little toe. There was no guarantee, however, that the payment would be offered or that the offended kin would accept it. In such cases, blood feuds ensued. Both blood feuds and efforts to forestall feuding through wergild would continue far into the Middle Ages, and both spoke to the importance of kin-as-protectors among the barbarians.

Although ties of kinship were strong, they were rivaled by those of the war-band, or **comitatus**, a group of warriors bound together by their loyalty to a warlord. The comitatus was a kind of military brotherhood based on honor, fidelity, courage, and mutual respect between the leader and his men. In battle the leader was expected to excel in courage and prowess, thereby inspiring his men to fight bravely and loyally. The comitatus was usually a subdivision of a tribe, a group whose members were bound together by their allegiance to a chieftain or king. But sometimes the leader of a comitatus won enough battles and attracted sufficient followers to lead a tribe of his own. The heroic virtues of the comitatus would persist throughout the Early Middle Ages as the characteristic ideology of the European warrior aristocracy.

As the barbarians came under Roman influence, each tribe was bound together by laws as well as military loyalties. The laws developed by the barbarian tribes differed significantly from those of the Roman Empire. Roman law was backed by the power of the Roman state, administered by the work of judges and lawyers, and applicable to all. Barbarian law was based on **custom** and tradition, enforced by general agreement, and applicable only to those within a specific tribe. Each tribe had its own customs and, hence, its own laws, but all barbarian law codes sought primarily to limit violence. Barbarian law, in other words, sought to provide peaceful resolutions to disputes that might otherwise have ended in bloodshed and feud.

For example, wergild schedules—specifying who would be paid what compensation for which offense—offered guilty malefactors and angry victims the possibility of resolving their disputes in peace instead of feud. Wergilds were one way to control violence; divine judgment was another. For people of high rank, divine judgment could be determined by **compurgation,** whereby oaths—by accused and their "oath-helpers"—were sworn as to the veracity of a case. A weak case could be revealed by insufficient oath-helpers or misspoken words. For ordinary people whose oaths carried less weight, innocence or guilt was sometimes determined by a process known as trial by **ordeal.** Supervised by a priest, the accused could be required to grasp a bar of red-hot iron or take a stone from a boiling cauldron. If the accused's hand healed properly, he or she was judged innocent. If not, the verdict was guilty. Similarly, the accused might be tied to a rope and lowered into a pond whose water had been purified by priestly blessing; sinking (acceptance by the blessed water) was proof of innocence and floating proof of guilt.

These legal strategies might sound bizarre today, but at the time, they helped secure peace among people who all too often resolved their disputes with violence. A payment of wergild could stop a blood feud; a solemn oath-taking ceremony might cause guilty people to stumble over words or reveal the wavering doubts of supporters; ordeals offered the judgment of God, a definitive judgment that could reknit a community torn by dispute. To barbarians, our modern reliance on trial by jury would have seemed a less reliable route to either the truth of a case or the making of peace between disputing parties.

Barbarian law codes, then, sought to achieve community consensus—to heal the enmities between families that could lead to divisive violence and bloodshed. Throughout the Middle Ages, the principles behind these law codes vied for authority with the principles of Roman law. Barbarian law emphasized peacekeeping and sought to mend divisions through social consensus and divine intervention. Roman law emphasized broad principles and sought to enforce order through the authority of a powerful state. Roman law survived the fall of the Western Empire in fragmentary form, but it was preserved in the Eastern Empire, and in the twelfth century, its study was revived in the West. From that time, as we shall see in Chapters 10 and 12, Roman law would exert a particularly strong influence on the legal systems of medieval Europe.

The decades just preceding the invasions witnessed the development, under Roman influence, of relatively stable royal dynasties among some barbarian tribes. An unusually gifted warrior and his kindred would gather military followers around him to form a new tribe, rather like the formation of a new criminal gang in the United States today. Then, if the new tribe was successful in war, its leader or leaders might claim royal status and even, in time, descent from some divine ancestor. When a king died, an assembly of the tribe's warriors chose as his successor the ablest member of his family. This might or might not be his eldest son, for the tribal assembly was given considerable latitude in its elective power. The custom of election would persist in many once-barbarian kingdoms far into the Middle Ages. Its chief consequence during the fifth century was to ensure that the tribes were normally led by clever, battle-worthy kings. In leadership, the barbarian tribes had a clear advantage over the Western Empire.

Migration and Settlement

Barbarians had long been a threat to the Empire. They had defeated a Roman army in the first century; they had probed deeply into the Empire in the second century and again in the mid-third. But before the late fourth century, the Romans had always managed to drive the invaders out or absorb them into the Roman political structure. Beginning in the 370s, however, an overtaxed, exhausted Empire was confronted by renewed pressures on its borders.

Lured by the relative wealth, the productive agriculture, and perhaps even the sunny climate of the Mediterranean world, the barbarian peoples saw the Empire as something to appreciate and enjoy, not plunder and destroy. Their yearning for the fair lands that lay on the Roman side of the Rhine and Danube was made suddenly urgent in the later fourth century by the westward thrust of a tribe of Asiatic nomads known as the Huns. These mounted warriors easily conquered one barbarian tribe after another. When they subdued the Goths and made them a subject people, a group of survivors, known subsequently as the Visigoths, sought to preserve their independence by appealing for sanctuary on the Roman side of the Danube. The Eastern Emperor Valens (r. 364–378), an Arian Christian, sympathized with his co-religionists (the Goths were also Arian Christians), and in 376 he took the unprecedented step of permitting the Visigoths and associated peoples to cross peacefully into the Empire.

There was trouble almost immediately. Corrupt imperial officials cheated and abused the Visigoths, who retaliated by going on a rampage. At length, Valens himself took the field against them, but he lost both his army and his life at the battle of Adrianople in 378, a military debacle of the first order. Valens' successor, Theodosius I (r. 378–395), pacified the Visigoths, permitting them to settle peacefully in the Balkans and providing them with food and revenue in return for their loyalty and military backing. This story of Visigothic incorporation into the Empire contains elements that would be repeated many times in the next century: a barbarian group under pressure on their

MEDIEVAL MYTHS

King Arthur

Probably no medieval legends are as rich and long-lived as those that tell of King Arthur, Queen Guinevere, the Knights of the Round Table, the valiant knight Lancelot, the good-humored wizard Merlin, and, of course, the castle of Camelot. And probably few debates today are as heated as between those who insist that Arthur was a real historical person and those who claim he was a fictional character only. To some, Arthur is a genuine Celtic hero, a petty king in the western part of Britain who organized fierce resistance against Saxon invaders. He is most often placed at the head of the local forces who won an important victory over the Saxons at Mount Badon in 516. Stories about Arthur's victory seem to have been popular in early medieval folktales, especially in Wales, Cornwall, Brittany, and other regions where Celtic traditions remained strong even after barbarian settlement. In this historical guise, Arthur grew into a symbol of Celtic identity, with his brave stand against the Saxons inspiring even today those who espouse Welsh or Cornish nationalism. Yet if this rugged warlord ever existed, he must have been a far cry from the gentle, chivalric Arthur of the written tales that proliferated around his name in the Central Middle Ages. In the early 1100s, the historian Geoffrey of Monmouth first elaborated on the Arthurian legends in his *History of the Kings of Britain;* later in that century, the writer Chrétien de Troyes created five Arthurian romances to entertain his aristocratic audiences; and the rest is history, if only literary history. To get a taste of what twelfth-century people believed about this sixth-century hero, you can read the section on "Arthur of Britain" in any translation of Monmouth's *History* (you'll find it on pages 212–261 of Lewis Thorpe's edition), or you can read the *Arthurian Romances* translated by William B. Kibler (1991). Then, you might find it fun to look at "Arthuriana" some 800 years later, in T. H. White's classic *Once and Future King* (1958) or Marion Zimmer Bradley's *Mists of Avalon* (1982). A warlord Arthur of west Britain might have led a successful uprising against barbarian settlers around 500, but the fictional King Arthur of Camelot has led a much longer and more interesting life.

eastern or northern flanks; Roman authorities agreeing to allow their immigration; some subsequent conflict; and eventual accommodation and settlement.

When Theodosius died in 395, imperial authority was split between his two young sons. Arcadius (r. 395–408), barely eighteen, became emperor in the East, and Honorius (r. 395–423), a child of eleven, assumed authority in the West. As it happened, the two halves of the Empire were never again rejoined under a single ruler. Not long after Theodosius's death, a skillful new Visigothic leader named Alaric led his people on a second pillaging campaign. In 406 the Western Empire, desperate to block Alaric's advance, recalled most of its troops from the Rhine frontier, with the disastrous result that in late December the Vandals and other barbarians crossed the frozen, ill-guarded Rhine into Gaul. Shortly thereafter, the Roman legions abandoned distant Britain, and the island was gradually overrun by Angles, Saxons, and other barbarian war-bands.

In 408 Emperor Honorius, by then an adult in his mid-twenties, engineered the murder of his ablest general, a man of barbarian ancestry named Stilicho. Honorius might have been right to suspect Stilicho's devotion to the imperial cause, but without Stilicho, the Italian peninsula was virtually defenseless. Honorius and his court barricaded themselves behind the impregnable marshes of Ravenna, leaving the city of Rome to the mercies of Alaric and his Visigoths. In 410 the Visigoths entered the old imperial capital unopposed and plundered it for three days.

The sack of Rome had a devastating impact on imperial morale. "My tongue sticks to the roof of my mouth," wrote St. Jerome on hearing of the catastrophe, "and sobs choke my speech." But in historical perspective, the event was merely a single milestone in the disintegration of the Western Empire. Alaric died in 410, shortly after the sack, and the Visigoths moved northward into southern Gaul and then Iberia where they established a Visigothic kingdom that endured until the Muslim conquest of the eighth century.

Meanwhile other barbarian tribes, most of them newly formed, were carving out kingdoms of their own. The Vandals moved through Gaul, Iberia, and across the Straits of Gibraltar into Africa in the 420s and 430s. In 430, the year of Augustine's death, they captured his episcopal city of Hippo. They established a North African kingdom centered on the ancient city of Carthage, and they then took to the sea as buccaneers, devastating Mediterranean shipping and sacking coastal cities, including Rome itself in 455.[2] The Vandal conquest of North Africa cost Rome much of its grain supply, while Vandal piracy so shattered the peace of the Mediterranean that it crippled the already fragile commercial networks of the Western Empire.

Midway through the fifth century the Huns themselves moved against the West, led by Attila (r. 433–453), the "Scourge of God" (see Figure 2.3). Attila's atrocities, although reported in hair-raising detail by contemporary Roman observers, were probably no worse than those of Roman generals. By about 440, Attila and his horsemen had made themselves virtually supreme over the barbarian tribes of central Europe and had frightened the Eastern Empire into paying an annual tribute. They had also established a capital, not far from modern Budapest. Then, in 450 the Eastern Empire discontinued its payments of tribute, and Attila, rather than seeking revenge on Constantinople itself, turned to the more vulnerable West.

Attila suffered defeat at the hands of a Roman-Visigothic army in 451. But he returned the following year, sacking and pillaging cities as he moved steadily toward the city of Rome. There, he found a city defended not by its emperor, who had fled, but by its pope. On the outskirts of Rome, Attila was confronted by Pope Leo I (r. 440–461) heading a delegation of Roman senators. According to one account, Pope Leo, an "old man of harmless simplicity, venerable in his gray hair and majestic clothing," was suddenly and miraculously joined by St. Peter and St. Paul, swords in their hands and clad in bishops' robes. Their appearance at this critical moment was especially noteworthy because both saints had been dead for nearly 400 years. Perhaps moved by Leo I's appeals but more likely concerned that his men were dying from heat and plague, Attila withdrew once again from the Western Empire. He would never return. Within two years, he was dead, and the Huns were absorbed into the settled populations of Europe.[3]

---

[2] Historians have had few good things to say about the Vandals, but of course they are no longer here to defend their reputation. We are indebted to them for providing our language with such colorful words as "vandal," "vandalize," and "vandalism."

[3] Attila and his troops only briefly troubled Europe, but their terrifying memory has long endured. For centuries, the Byzantines would name as "Huns" any who troubled their borders, and even in the world wars of the twentieth century, Germans were vilified by their enemies as "Huns."

Figure 2.3   *Attila in Hollywood*   This still photograph from the 1954 movie, *The Sign of the Pagan,* depicts Attila as a *noble* savage. Yet to the Goths and Romans who actually encountered Attila and his men, they seemed more savage than noble. Jack Palance, the actor who portrayed Attila in this film, went on to star in many westerns.

In its final years the Western Empire, whose jurisdiction now scarcely extended beyond the Italian peninsula, fell under the control of hard-bitten military adventurers of barbarian birth. Emperors continued to reign for a time, but their barbarian generals were the power behind the throne. In 476 the barbarian general Odovacar, who saw no point in perpetuating the charade, deposed the last Western emperor, a boy named Romulus Augustulus, "little Augustus" (r. 474–476). Odovacar sent the imperial insignia to Constantinople, claiming he did not seek to be emperor himself but merely to rule as an agent of the Eastern Empire. But the emperor in the East, Zeno (r. 474–491) had his own troubles, and Odovacar was really on his own. Not for long. About a decade later, Zeno asked a group known as Ostrogoths, now free of Hunnish control and led by an astute king named Theodoric, to invade the Italian peninsula. When a rough peace was established after several hard-fought years, Theodoric invited Odovacar to a banquet, murdered him, and established his own rule. If Odovacar (r. 476–493) was a figure of transition between Western Empire and Middle Ages, Theodoric (r. 493–526) was the first medieval king.

Theodoric

Ruling the Italian peninsula for more than three decades, Theodoric became the dominant power in a Western Europe now cut adrift from the Eastern Empire. Although apparently illiterate, he respected Roman culture and administrative expertise. Under his governance, Arian Ostrogoths and Catholic Romans worked together to repair aqueducts, erect new buildings, and bring a degree of prosperity to the long-troubled Italian peninsula. Ostrogoths provided military security, elite Romans ran the civil government, and ordinary people paid taxes much as before but to a new ruler. The improved political and economic climate gave rise to an intellectual revival that, in turn, facilitated the transmission of Greco-Roman culture into the Middle Ages.

At a time when knowledge of Greek was dying out in the West, the philosopher Boethius (c. 480–524), a high official in Theodoric's court, produced a series of works that laid the groundwork for what would evolve into a new, *medieval* intellectual tradition. First, he set out to make Latin translations of the Greek writings of Plato (c. 429–347 B.C.E.) and Aristotle (384–322 B.C.E.). For reasons that will soon become apparent, he managed to translate only a few of Aristotle's texts on elementary logic before he died, but his translations and commentaries on them became fundamental texts for the next 500 years. Second, Boethius laid the basis for the medieval curriculum of the **quadrivium** (or the meeting of the "four paths" of arithmetic, geometry, astronomy, and music) and the **trivium** (a junction of the "three paths" of grammar, rhetoric, and logic), and for each of these seven liberal arts, he provided basic Latin texts that would guide students for centuries to come. Third, Boethius wrote his own masterpiece, *The Consolation of Philosophy,* in which he argued that spiritual development is more important than worldly successes or fortunes. Because he wrote this in prison, awaiting execution after being implicated in a plot to overthrow Theodoric, Boethius spoke from personal experience about the importance of spiritual growth over material glories. Although he was a Christian, he drew his ideas primarily from Plato and the Stoics. *The Consolation of Philosophy* remained immensely popular throughout the Middle Ages and is long overdue for a modern revival, more likely on the beaches of southern California than in the cubicles of Wall Street.

Cassiodorus (c. 490–583), the man who took over the high office vacated by the executed Boethius, was another scholar of considerable distinction and lasting importance. He had more political savvy or perhaps just more luck than Boethius, for he managed to outlive Theodoric. Cassiodorus undertook his most important work after he "retired" to his family lands in the southern Italian peninsula in the 550s. There, he founded a monastery where he began two projects for which every modern student can be thankful. First, he assembled a sort of reading list, *On Divine and Human Readings,* that guided would-be scholars through the great works of Christian and pagan antiquity. In a sense, this book resolved the struggle that had terrorized the dreams of Jerome more than a century before: for Cassiodorus and all who followed his advice, being a Ciceronian and a Christian was a natural combination, not an abomination. Second, he encouraged the monks in his monastery to copy texts as a holy duty. He set standards for scribal copying, wrote a spelling guide for his scribes, and even served as a sort of cheerleader for those bored by hours of endless copying. With great enthusiasm, he praised scribes who, as he put it, "preach to the people with only the hand . . . and fight against the illicit temptations of the devil with pen and ink." In this regard, too, Cassiodorus built on foundations laid by Jerome; both ensured that future generations of monks and nuns would copy and therefore preserve the literary works of both pagan and Christian antiquity.

Clovis

While Theodoric was establishing his control over Ostrogothic Italy, another barbarian king, Clovis (r. 482–511), was creating a Frankish kingdom in the former Roman province of Gaul. Although much less Romanized then Theodoric, Clovis possessed a keen instinct for political survival. He adopted the straightforward policy of murdering all possible rivals (a tactic not unknown to either Roman emperors or Theodoric). A few generations later, Bishop Gregory of Tours (c. 538–594) quoted Clovis as saying, "Oh woe, for I travel among strangers and have none of my kinfolk to help me!" But Bishop Gregory added, "He did not refer to their deaths out of grief, but craftily, to see if he could bring to light some new relative to kill."

It will perhaps seem odd that a bishop like Gregory would approve wholeheartedly of Clovis's bloody rule. Yet Clovis, a ruthless monarch who lacked even the family loyalty of a mobster, is pictured in Gregory's *History of the Franks* as one who "walked before God with an upright heart and did what was pleasing in his sight." The explanation is that, thanks in part to the influence of his wife, Clotilda (described in the Biographical Sketch on pp. 44–45), Clovis converted to Catholic Christianity. At a time when most barbarian kings were either pagans or Arian Christians, Clovis became a defender of Bishop Gregory's Catholic Christianity. Other barbarian rulers ignored Catholic churches or even handed them over to the Arian Christians; Clovis nurtured them. So, although Clovis himself regarded Christianity as a kind of magic to help him win battles (much as Constantine had done), the Church promoted him as a hero of Catholic orthodoxy.

Another reason for Clovis's good press was that he maintained relatively warm relations with the old landholding aristocracy, an elite to which Bishop Gregory belonged by birth. Because of the depopulated condition of the countryside, there were lands enough for all—Frank and Gallo-Roman alike. So the great landowning families of Roman times were for the most part left in peace to enjoy their fields, their bishoprics, and their parties, and to serve as high officials in the Frankish regime. From their point of view, Clovis's victory was not so much a conquest as a coup d'état.

In succeeding generations, Frankish and Gallo-Roman landowners, already joined by a common Catholic Christianity, fused through intermarriage into a single aristocratic order. As centuries passed, the royal name "Clovis" was softened to "Louis," the "Franks" became the "French," and the alliance between the Frankish monarchy and the Church developed into one of the most enduring elements of European politics.

✵ THE DECLINE OF THE WESTERN EMPIRE

In the fourth century, the West experienced not only barbarian settlement but also a slow withdrawal of imperial power toward the East. In the year 330, Emperor Constantine founded a new imperial capital in the East, locating it on the western edge of the Bosphorus, a strategic waterway that connects the Mediterranean with the Black Sea. The city was built on a grand scale and adorned with monuments pillaged from throughout

BIOGRAPHICAL SKETCH

Clotilda, Queen of the Franks (470–548)

Clotilda's life wove together old worlds and new, for she was born when the last Roman emperor ruled in the West, was married as a young woman to the Frankish king Clovis, and was recognized as a Christian saint after her death.

Clotilda's mother, from the old Roman aristocracy of Gaul, was a Catholic Christian, but her father represented a rougher sort. He was son of the king of Burgundy, a Romanized barbarian, and like most Burgundians, he was an Arian Christian. Clotilda was raised in her mother's faith. When she was in her teens, her uncle Gundobad murdered her parents, exiled her sister (who became a nun), and kept Clotilda in his home, perhaps because her intelligence and beauty promised a good marriage.

If her uncle had hoped to marry her to an ally, he was to be outfoxed. Clotilda secretly began to arrange her own marriage. It was no love story. When Clovis, king of the Franks, heard about the unmarried niece of the powerful Gundobad, he sent an envoy to offer marriage. The envoy disguised himself as a pilgrim and secretly presented Clotilda with a ring and other gifts. Clotilda hid these and sent a message back to Clovis. She appreciated his proposal, but she asked him to keep it secret. And, although she expressed concern about Clovis's paganism, she added, "Whatever my Lord God orders, I will do."

A year later, Clovis made his move. He asked Gundobad to send Clotilda to him so that their marriage could be finalized. Gundobad, still in the dark about the proposal, reacted with fury. But when he found Clovis's gifts stashed away in a corner of his treasury, he considered these to be evidence of an irrevocable betrothal and angrily allowed the marriage to go forward. Clotilda probably first met Clovis just before they were married in Soissons in 493, when she was no more than 20 years old. All told, this was a hardheaded match. Made more through negotiation than courtship, it was a common arrangement for the aristocracy of the day.

Brought up in a court of Arian Christians but faithful to Catholic Christianity, Clotilda now found herself married to a pagan. She is said to have started converting Clovis on their wedding night, with a well-timed lecture on Christianity. (With somewhat less charitable intent, she also harangued him about the importance of avenging her parents' murders.) When their first son was baptized as a Catholic Christian and soon thereafter died, Clovis blamed his wife's faith, but Clotilda was soon pregnant with another heir. That son, too, was baptized, and he lived, a fortunate turn for the future of Catholic Christianity among the Franks. Clotilda continued to press her husband to convert, and after three years of marriage, Clovis finally gave in.

He chose a strategic moment. Losing a disastrous battle against the Alemanni, he raised his eyes to heaven and invoked the god of his wife, shouting "Jesus Christ, you who Clotilda maintains is the son of the Living God . . . if you will give me victory over my enemies, then I will be baptized in your name." In the next instant, the Alemanni turned and fled. Clovis accepted baptism, along with 3,000 of his men. He thereby achieved domestic peace (no more late-night lectures from his wife) and also ensured that the Franks—first among the barbarian tribes—accepted Catholic Christianity. At Clotilda's further urging, Clovis became a firm ally of Catholic Christianity, destroying pagan shrines, building churches, and funding a variety of religious projects.

This story of female persuasion and Catholic triumph comes from later Frankish histories that weave together fact and fiction. Historians today would tell the tale differently. Clovis's battlefield conversion recalls Constantine at the Milvian Bridge too neatly to be credible, and it now seems that Clovis might have been an Arian Christian, not a pagan, be-fore Clotilda persuaded him to accept Catholic Christianity. In any case, Clovis had good political reasons to accept his wife's faith, for his Franks had to coexist with a Gallo–Roman population faithful to Catholic Christianity. And because his choice of Catholic Christianity distinguished the Franks from all other barbarian tribes, Clovis positioned his dynasty as champions against the Arian Christianity embraced by the Burgundians, the Visigoths, and others. Yet, although Frankish histories might have emphasized Clotilda's pious work over Clovis's political savvy, both seem to have worked together to the same end: the conversion of the Franks to what eventually became orthodox Christianity in the West.

Like many aristocrats of her day, Clotilda lived between barbarian and Roman cultures and among many different faiths. Like many aristocratic women, Clotilda forged active links between these diverse traditions, and her work as a domestic proselytizer was not unusual. Both the Lombards and Visigoths eventually abandoned Arian Christianity thanks to pious Catholic queens married to Arian husbands. The later conversions of Bohemia, Poland, and Russia would also come about, in part, by the marriages of Christian women to pagan kings. But Clotilda would have likely taken most pleasure in the efforts of her great-granddaughter Bertha, Christian wife of the pagan King Ethelbert of Kent. When Queen Bertha welcomed Christian missionaries to Kent in 579, she nurtured a fledgling faith that would eventually take hold throughout Britain, as it had almost a century earlier among the Franks.

the Roman Empire. It was a second Rome, with its own senate, its own imposing palaces and public buildings, and its own poor kept alive with free bread and diverted by chariot races in an enormous hippodrome (the oval course of which can still be traced). Situated on the site of a Greek town called Byzantium, this new city was named Constantinople ("Constantine's City"). Now renamed Istanbul, it is the largest city of Turkey, and with a population in excess of nine million it is today, as it was in the Middle Ages, one of the largest cities in the world.

Constantine's founding of a new capital in the East continued a process that had begun a half-century earlier when Diocletian had first divided the empire into two administrative units, Western and Eastern. Thereafter, the Roman imperial office had been split from time to time between a Western emperor and an Eastern emperor, and in 395 the split became permanent. This political split reflected a linguistic division of long standing, for although the Latin of the early Romans had spread across the Western provinces, Greek remained the major language of the East. This split also reflected social and economic differences in which the Eastern Empire—Greece, Egypt, and the eastern Mediterranean provinces—had an advantage. The East had been civilized far longer than the western lands of North Africa and Europe, far longer than Rome itself; it contained the bulk of the population; its agriculture relied less than the West on vast plantations whose wealthy owners were able to resist imperial taxation and even, to a degree, imperial authority; and its cities were larger, more numerous, and more commercially active than the newer cities of the West. The East also enjoyed a favorable balance of trade with the West. In exchange for Eastern silks, spices, jewels, and grain, the West had relatively few goods to offer, apart from slaves, warhorses, and a diminishing supply of gold coins. Thus, with the coming of large-scale barbarian migrations in the fifth century, the Eastern Empire managed to survive while the more brittle political superstructure of the Western provinces slowly disintegrated.

The "decline and fall" of the Western Empire has fascinated historians across the centuries, for it involves the collapse of one of the world's most impressive empires. Many reasons have been proposed—no less than 210 different causes according to a recent survey. They include such factors as unfavorable climatic changes, overreliance on slavery, the otherworldliness of Christianity, sexual orgies, bad ecological habits, even lead poisoning. None of these make much sense. Classical civilization began and ended with slavery. The Eastern Empire was more thoroughly Christianized than the West, yet it survived for another thousand years. The most spectacular Roman orgies occurred during the glories of the Pax Romana, not in the waning centuries of the Western Empire. One otherwise respectable historian even proposed the bizarre idea that the fall of Rome was a result of male homosexuality, a practice that is much more easily documented in the fifth century B.C.E. than the fifth century C.E. and might, therefore, more plausibly be associated with the rise than the demise of classical civilization.

Other explanations are more convincing. No single cause can explain the long and tortuous decline of imperial power in the West, but among many possible factors, political, military, and socioeconomic troubles were especially acute. At a time when strong leadership especially mattered, the fifth-century Western emperors were less competent than their Eastern colleagues. For example, Valentinian III (r. 425–455) came to the throne as a child, left most decision making to his mother Galla Placidia (c. 388–450), and soon after her death in 450 promptly murdered his best general and got himself murdered in return. During his long and inglorious reign, Rome lost North Africa to the Vandals and failed to hold most of Gaul against the Franks and Burgundians. The first-century Empire was sufficiently entrenched to endure the rule of Nero and Caligula; the far weaker Western Empire of the fifth century was hard put to survive similar imperial incompetence.

This was particularly true because the Western Empire faced the growing challenges posed by barbarian migrations—and sometimes invasions. These accelerated in the late fourth century when various tribes found themselves attacked by the westward movement of the Huns. Pushed by the Huns across the Danube and Rhine rivers, Goths, Vandals, and other barbarians disrupted and sometimes terrorized the Western provinces. In the long run, these barbarian tribes settled in the Western provinces, preserved Roman culture, and revitalized their regions, but in the short run, their migrations were grudgingly endured and their raids were unwelcome.

Political and military troubles were exacerbated by socioeconomic woes. During the Pax Romana, agricultural productivity, supplemented by a constant influx of plundered goods and slaves, had ensured prosperity. But in the third century, when farm production was hard hit by the ravages of soldiers (both barbarian and Roman), and territorial expansion had ceased, the West responded poorly. Basic farming techniques changed very little. The Roman plow was adequate but rudimentary, and windmills were unknown. There were some water mills, but nowhere near as many as in, say, eleventh-century England. Continuing to rely on slaves and coloni, Roman landowners had little interest in labor-saving devices or agricultural innovation. They viewed large-scale industry and commerce with similar disdain. Accustomed to drawing their wealth from plantations, their status from public office, and their pleasure from the company of fellow aristocrats, Roman landowners faced rural poverty, agricultural decline, population stagnation, runaway inflation, and high taxes. Their response was self-interested and defensive. They withdrew from civic affairs, abandoned their town houses, retired to their country estates, fortified their villas, and assembled private armies to ward off marauders and imperial tax collectors alike. This reaction was to have long-term consequences: in many parts of Western Europe, aristocrats would avoid cities and prefer the countryside for the next thousand years.

As the cities of the West declined, more than the economy was crippled. After all, cities had been essential to the administrative structure of the Western Empire, and they had also nurtured the civic culture of Greco-Roman antiquity. Simply put, the culture of Athens, Alexandria, and Rome could not flourish in fields and pastures. Romans had once been deeply influenced by Greek culture; now a Greco-Roman culture was influenced by new developments: rural living, Christianity, localism, and of course, barbarian settlement. All through the fifth century barbarians—Goths, Franks, Alemanni, and others—settled peaceably within the Western Empire. Sometimes they also attacked Roman armies and raided Roman territories, but they were more often settlers than pillagers. Indeed, barbarians became *defenders* of the Western Empire: they abounded in the army, their tribes were sometimes hired to defend the frontiers, and their generals held high positions in the administration of the Western Empire.

The riddle of Rome's decline and fall will probably never be completely solved, and even the question itself is misleading for imperial Rome did not literally fall. First, it survived in the Eastern Empire. From this perspective, the changes of the fourth and fifth centuries seem merely a strategic withdrawal of imperial interest from the less productive West to the wealthier provinces of the eastern Mediterranean. Second, it survived, albeit in attenuated form, even in the West. From this perspective, the deposition of the last Western emperor in 476 C.E. seems much less momentous than the survival, for many centuries to come, of Roman institutions and traditions within the new kingdoms that succeeded the Western Empire.

The Roman Legacy

Greco-Roman culture never died in the West. It exerted a profound influence, as we have seen, on Augustine and other early Christian theologians and, through them, on the theologians, philosophers, and writers of the Middle Ages. It was the basis of repeated cultural revivals, great and small, down through the centuries—in the era of Charlemagne, in the Central Middle Ages, in the Italian Renaissance, and in the neoclassical movements of the eighteenth and nineteenth centuries. Roman law profoundly shaped the canon law of the medieval Church and even today influences jurisprudence in many European countries. The Latin tongue remained the language of educated Europeans for well over a thousand years, while evolving among ordinary people into the Romance languages of modern Europe: Italian, French, Spanish, Catalan, Portuguese, Romanian, and others. And the dream of creating a new Rome has inspired empire-builders from Charlemagne to Napoleon.

Even though much fragmented, Roman administrative structures also survived in the West, after a fashion. In most of the barbarian successor states, kings relied on the advice of Roman bureaucrats and fiscal experts. Similarly, the organizational units of the

Church—dioceses and provinces presided over by bishops and archbishops—were patterned on Roman administrative units that had borne identical names. In fact, Church and imperial administration blended together in other ways too. The bishops of the late Empire became increasingly involved in imperial governance, participating in civic functions and monitoring the activities of Roman officials. With the demise of imperial authority in the West, these bishops sometimes assumed political control of their dioceses, seeing to the maintenance of the food supply and supervising the repair of fortifications. They became *political* leaders as well as religious leaders. Since most bishops came from office-holding families of the old Roman aristocracy, such duties came easily to them.

In these ways and many more, the legacy of classical antiquity was passed to the medieval West. Europeans for centuries to come would be nourished by Greco-Roman culture and haunted by the memory of Rome.

✵ CONCLUSION

As the sixth century dawned, the Western Empire was only a memory, albeit a potent one. In its place were successor states that vaguely prefigured the nations of modern Western Europe. Theodoric headed a relatively tolerant Arian-Ostrogothic regime in the Italian peninsula. The Catholic Clovis was completing the Frankish conquest of Gaul. The Arian Vandals lorded over a restive Catholic population in North Africa, seizing wheat plantations and introducing former Roman aristocrats to the joys of field work. The Arian Visigoths were being driven out of southern Gaul by the Franks, but they would hold onto Iberia for two more centuries. And the Angles and Saxons were in the process of establishing a group of small, non-Christian kingdoms in Britain that would one day coalesce into "Angle-land," or England. Western Europe had, in a sense, returned to a localism it had known long before Rome and would know long after. Conquest and annexation would at times impose unity on some areas—during, for example, the times of Charlemagne, Napoleon, and Hitler. But only recently has the localism of Western Europe been complemented by peaceable consolidation—that is, in the late twentieth-century treaties that have created the European Union.

Still, a new and different unity promised, in the year 500, to offer common cause to the peoples of Western Europe. At the same time as barbarian kings fractured the political unity of the West, the Roman **papacy** consolidated its position as an independent power of "catholic" authority. We have seen how Pope Leo I assumed the task of protecting the city of Rome from the Huns, thereby winning for himself the moral leadership of the Italian peninsula. Leo and his successors declared that the bishop of Rome—the pope—constituted the highest authority in the Church, and following the example of St. Ambrose's disciplining of the Emperor Theodosius (see Chapter 1), they also insisted on the supremacy of Church (and its pope) over state in spiritual and ethical matters. In proclaiming these doctrines of papal authority over all Christians and ecclesiastical independence from state control, fifth-century popes wisely distanced themselves from faltering Western emperors. They also thereby began building a free-standing institution of considerable moral and political authority. The mighty papacy of the Central Middle Ages was yet far off, but it was partly created by the boldly independent stance of Pope Leo I. The Western Empire was crumbling, but eternal Rome claimed a new sort of allegiance from the peoples of the West.

Suggested Readings

Averil Cameron, *The Later Roman Empire, A.D. 284–430* (1993) and *The Mediterranean World in Late Antiquity, AD 395–600* (1993). Two works of original scholarly synthesis. See also A. H. M. Jones, *The Later Roman Empire, 284–602: A Social, Economic, and Administrative Survey* (1986).

Donald Kagan, ed., *The End of the Roman Empire: Decline or Transformation?* (3rd edition, 1992). A short anthology of modern scholarly debates.

Malcolm Todd, *The Early Germans* (1992). A readable archaeological and historical study. See also Walter Goffart, *Barbarians and Romans, A.D. 418–584: The Techniques of Accommodation* (1980). For individual groups, see especially Peter Heather, *Goths and Romans, A.D. 332–489* (1991), and E. A. Thompson, *The Huns* (1996).

Raymond Van Dam, *Leadership and Community in Late-Antique Gaul* (1985). An original reinterpretation of receding imperial administration, the regional aristocracy, and the evolution of Christian communities.

Suzanne Fonay Wemple, *Women in Frankish Society: Marriage and the Cloister, 500 to 900* (1981). Argues that the status of elite Frankish women declined over these centuries.

Suggested Primary Source

Alexander Callander Murray, ed., *From Roman to Merovingian Gaul: A Reader* (2000). An eclectic collection accompanied by helpful editorial commentary.

CHAPTER 3

EARLY WESTERN CHRISTENDOM, c. 500-700

✸ INTRODUCTION

In the sixth and seventh centuries, Roman authority in the West was no more. Political unity under Rome had given way to political localism under barbarian kings and aristocrats. The Church provided an alternative sort of unity, but the umbrella of Christendom—of a dominion unified by Christian faith and obedience—was then little more than nice rhetoric and dim promise. Divisions between Arian and Roman Christians still rocked some parts of the West, and in other parts, pagans were either uninterested in Christianity or had never even heard of it. The city of Rome itself lay in the West, but by 500, Western Europe had become a poor partner of a relocated Roman Empire that flourished far to the East.

Historians have often viewed the sixth and seventh centuries in the West as a dull time, a dark age, a tedious stop on an otherwise fine journey. As a result, these centuries are sometimes taught, as some critics recently put it, "as a corpse to be dragged quickly offstage so that the next great act of the drama of the Middle Ages should begin." Let us not be so hasty. These first centuries of the Middle Ages were hard times indeed, yet they were not without important developments in society, politics, religion, and thought (see Timeline 3.1).

✸ EARLY MEDIEVAL SOCIETY

There is reason to believe that some Western European farmlands were abandoned altogether in the fifth and sixth centuries—and resettled only much later. Aerial photographs of the southern French countryside disclose fields of a typically medieval pattern, radiating outward from a central village. But often these radiating fields appear superimposed on earlier Roman patterns—square or rectangular fields, systematically laid out. This suggests that the Roman fields had reverted to wilderness and that people long after had resettled the land. Aerial photographs do not permit precise dating, but the silent

TIMELINE 3.1   Western Christendom, 500–800

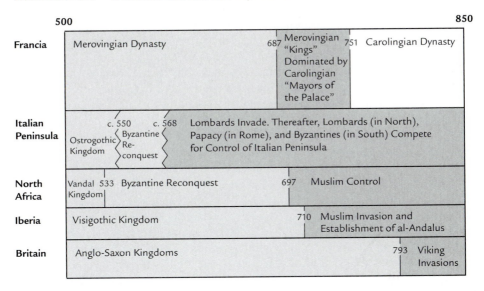

catastrophe they record may well have resulted from violence following the collapse of imperial authority in the West, aggravated by a great plague cycle that commenced in the 540s. Certainly, this is what happened in the cities. Archaeological investigations have disclosed a process of urban collapse during the 600s and early 700s; in many places north of the Alps, cities simply disappeared.

Barbarian settlement also transformed the ethnic character of Western Europe. Ethnicity had long been a hodgepodge in the West, so that by 500, as we have seen, varieties of Celtic groups had merged with various levels of Roman society to create the world we call Gallo-Roman, only then to merge again with the various cultures of barbarian settlers. What this meant in terms of ethnicity has exercised historians ever since. Some argue that ethnicity emerged as a political tool—that, in other words, the Franks became Franks because they had kings who forced that identity on them. Others find ethnicity in more ordinary things, such as shared dress, burial customs, and language. In these arguments, perspective matters a great deal. Is ethnicity something that is imposed by leaders or even outsiders? Or it is something that individuals or groups can claim as their own? Since these questions still worry us today, it is scarcely a surprise that we cannot fully resolve them for early medieval society. Still, it is clear that new groups of Europeans were emerging from the various cultures of Celts, Romans, and barbarians, and that many of them were identified by the names of old barbarian tribes: Franks, Burgundians, Visigoths, Lombards, Bavarians, Saxons, and the like.

Among the landed classes, these new ethnicities were accompanied by new militarism. As the pleasures of gentle living and sophisticated leisure gave way before the heroic virtues of the barbarian comitatus and its warlord, the civility of Roman villa life was replaced by a warrior ideology. From this blending of Roman and barbarian elites into a single social order grew the aristocracy of medieval Europe: rich, haughty, ready to command, and ready, also, to kill. They entertained themselves much as they lived, with epic songs of the brave deeds of warriors faced with fearsome enemies. Of these, the greatest is *Beowulf,* an Anglo-Saxon tale of Danish origin that was tempered by Christian sentiments by the time it was committed to parchment sometime between the eighth and tenth centuries. It begins by telling of young Beowulf's fiercely fought victories over the monster Grendel and then Grendel's vengeful mother; it ends by describing how these feats were followed, some fifty years later, by a final battle in which Beowulf, then an aging king, slew an angry dragon but received a mortal blow in return.

Polygyny was standard practice among these elites in the sixth and seventh centuries, as were various different sorts of union: *formal marriage* required the father's transfer of authority over his daughter to her new husband and the exchange of properties; *informal marriage* involved the transfer of neither authority nor property; and *concubinage* was so informal that the children of such unions were illegitimate. Only wealthy men found it possible to maintain many wives or concubines, and the Church opposed such arrangements. Nevertheless, polygyny continued well into the eighth century. It created intricately complex family entanglements, nasty struggles over inheritance among half-brothers, and extraordinary opportunities for some elite women. A few women were able to rise, through the flexibility offered by Frankish marriage, from humble status to queenship; others were critical allies for sons who had to fight half-brothers; still others, as widows, exercised considerable powers over extensive lands. And a few chose to avoid the hurly-burly of polygynous marriage altogether (or perhaps their parents chose this for them) and found refuge in monasticism.

✳ EARLY MEDIEVAL POLITICS

The Roman system of administration survived after a fashion in the West, particularly in Ostrogothic Italy and Visigothic Iberia, less so in the kingdom of the Franks, and scarcely at all in Britain. But long before the imperial collapse of the fifth century, Roman government in the West had been disintegrating. All through the late imperial era, government and economic life had grown steadily more localized, and as resistance to imperial taxes grew, great landowners had begun to keep private armies on their own fortified estates. The barbarian kings of the sixth and seventh centuries were by no means incompetent to manage a Roman provincial government. Themselves the products of many generations of Roman influence, they could always rely on the help of administrators from the Gallo-Roman population, eager to survive and prosper in the new regime. But when the barbarian kings established themselves in the former Western provinces (see Map 3.1), the administrative machinery they inherited was in bad repair. The unfavorable trade balance with the East persisted, gold coins remained scarce, violence disrupted the countryside, and powerful aristocrats were no more willing to pay taxes to barbarian kings than to Roman emperors.

Localism and Kingship

In this atmosphere of widespread suffering, violence, and dispossession, local power was the most effective power, but this meant different things in town and country. In the countryside, aristocratic families governed the areas around their estates. If you had been a peasant in the sixth century, you would have looked no further than your local

Map 3.1   *Europe, c. 600* In 600, the Byzantine Empire had briefly extended its authority over parts of the West (more about this in the next chapter), but most of Western Europe was divided among barbarian kingdoms. Some, such as the Visigothic kingdom, were large and unified, but others, such as the many kingdoms of the Anglo-Saxons and Merovingians, were much more modest.

lord or **lady**—the rich landowner who might have lived in a fine house within easy reach of your fields—to demand taxes from you, provide some protection, and offer a rough sort of justice. In the cities, bishops stepped into the breach. The economy of many towns had collapsed, but some survived because they became the sites of the bishops' **cathedrals** and the headquarters of episcopal government over surrounding districts. If you had been an artisan in the sixth century, you would have relied on your city's bishop for religious guidance, but you would also have expected him to demand taxes from you and provide protection and justice in return.

Bishops even took on economic importance when, in some towns, the profits made from pilgrims began to replace the profits of trade. The cathedral at Tours, for example, possessed the body of St. Martin (bishop of Tours from 372 to 397), who was said to heal many who touched his tomb. Holy men such as Martin were revered in their lifetimes as vessels for the transmission to ordinary folk of God's power, wisdom, and love, and their saintly bodies were thought to retain this function after death. Christians from far and wide would travel to cathedral churches to venerate holy **relics**—the bodies or clothing of deceased saints—which were regarded as agents of spiritual power and physical healing. Buttressed by possession of relics, proceeds from pilgrimages, profits from estates in the countryside, and the absence of other competing authorities, the bishops of early medieval Europe were, in effect, the rulers of their cities.

Localism did not mean the collapse of kingship, but it did mean that kings often *claimed* more authority than they actually had and that, to exercise any authority, they had to cultivate the support of local aristocrats and bishops. Personal loyalty was essential to early medieval kingship; in essence, a king's friends and trusted warriors were the agents of his government.

The sixth century witnessed a virtual earthquake among some of the states that succeeded Rome. In 500 Theodoric's Ostrogothic kingdom provided some security and peace in the Italian peninsula; a century later it had been destroyed by invasions both north and south. By 600 the decimated—and much impoverished—Italian peninsula was divided between the Byzantines in Ravenna and the south, the papacy around Rome, and the Lombards in the north. The Lombards were the last major barbarian confederation to enter Western Europe; their state would eventually be conquered by Charlemagne (r. 768–814), but their legacy survives in the Italian province of Lombardy, as well as in Lombard Street in London (so named because merchants from Lombardy traded in London in later centuries). North Africa was as shaken as the Italian peninsula by the sixth century. In 500 the Vandals ruled North Africa; a century later North Africa had become Byzantine rather than Vandal.

In Britain at the beginning of the century, various barbarian tribes—collectively identified by modern historians as "Anglo-Saxons"—were slowly expanding their settlements. By the end of the century, Anglo-Saxons occupied much of the island. Their advance drove some of the indigenous Gallo-Roman inhabitants (also known more simply as "Britons") into the western hills of Cornwall, Wales, and southern Scotland, but the Anglo-Saxons mostly mingled with the population—intermarrying and settling alongside them so that, with time, the two cultures became one. Britain became a confusing patchwork of small, independent kingdoms. Most were pagan, and in 600, the process of Christian conversion was just underway.

Merovingian Gaul

Gaul underwent political changes in the sixth century, but not seismic upheavals. As we saw in Chapter 2, Clovis and his Franks were conquering Gaul in 500, and by 600 the region was thoroughly dominated by his successors, known as the Merovingian dynasty (after Clovis's legendary ancestor, Merovech). But there was little unity or peace. Following long custom, the Merovingian kings treated their sons equally in inheritance, dividing the kingdom among them all. This might sound like a fair practice of kindly fathers, but it often resulted in bitter sorts of brotherhood. After a father's death, sons would often fight each other until one of them emerged as sole king or they agreed to be content with their own bits of inheritance. This sad story was repeated, generation after generation, and it contributed to a proliferation of petty kings. In sixth-century northern Europe (taking into account not only Merovingian territories but also Britain and other regions), there were, at any one time, about 200 kings. Even kingship was localized.

The Merovingians have suffered from bad press, thanks partly to the fondness of Gregory of Tours, their major chronicler, for tales about bloody atrocities, and thanks partly to the desire of the Carolingians, the dynasty that succeeded in the eighth century, to malign their predecessors. Some of the bad press is justified. The Merovingians were never able to rid themselves of the habit of murdering rivals, usually fellow kin. And with the passage of generations, the Merovingian kings became less and less effective as their power and estates slipped into the hands of aristocrats. They were kings in a society where local power mattered more than royal power.

But on occasion an able Merovingian king ruled effectively over a united Frankish kingdom or a significant portion thereof. The most celebrated of the later Merovingians, Dagobert I (r. 629–638), received part of the kingdom in 622 from his father Clothar II, who himself had united Francia by seizing power from his aunt, Queen Brunhilde (whom he tortured to death). Dagobert acquired the remainder of Francia on Clothar's death in 629 and thereafter ruled strongly over all the Franks until his own death in 638. He was a generous and savvy benefactor of the Church; for example, by granting permission to his favorite **abbey** of St. Denis to hold an annual fair, he managed at one blow to please God and stimulate commerce. He was also a strong administrator; he issued Latin charters that employed Roman legal formulas and had Latin law codes drawn up for the barbarian tribes under his sway. Despite interfamilial squabbles and localism, the Merovingians managed to endure in Francia for two and a half centuries—much longer than any other barbarian dynasty—until giving way in 751 to the Carolingians (who will be turning up in Chapter 5).

Visigothic Iberia

Visigothic Iberia also saw no political earthquakes in the sixth century. The Arian kings of the Iberian peninsula were more successful than the Merovingians in retaining vestiges of the old Roman administration, particularly systems of tax assessment and collection. During the early generations of their rule, they lacked the Merovingians' crucial advantage of a shared faith with their Hispano-Roman Catholic and Jewish subjects. This problem was solved when the Visigothic king Reccared (r. 586–601) converted from Arianism to Catholicism in 587. As was usual with the conversion of kings, he brought with him most of the Visigothic aristocracy and most of the Arian clergy as well. This mass conversion—a virtual holy stampede—opened the way for the integration of the Roman and Visigothic landholding classes into one aristocracy. Two years later, Reccared authorized the holding of a great church council at his capital of Toledo in 589, where Arianism was officially extinguished and the two churches fused. Figure 3.1 shows one of the churches built in the wake of this Christian consolidation.

Christian harmony was accompanied, however, by Christian-Jewish disharmony. In 613, the Visigothic and Catholic king Sisebut (r. 612–620) ordered the Jews of his realm to accept Christian baptism, and for almost a century thereafter—until the Arab conquest of the peninsula in 711—Visigothic kings periodically attempted to convert

Figure 3.1   *Visigothic Church*   This mid-seventh-century church of St. John the Baptist in Baños de Cerato, Spain, is a highly original reinterpretation of the classical style. Many early churches were built on the sites of old pagan temples or shrines.

Jews by force. This policy was designed, it seems, to promote homogeneity within a kingdom where Visigoths governed native Hispano-Romans and Jews. If so, even success brought failure, for converted Jews seem to have been regarded as a distinct group of Christians—Jewish in culture, if not religion. It also failed on a more basic level, for forced conversions were never imposed on all the Jews of the realm. Christian clergy were generally ambivalent supporters of the policy, questioning the "hazy zeal" of Sisebut and preferring the opinion of Pope Gregory I (r. 590–604) that Jews should be turned toward Christianity by words, not violence. The aristocracy also sometimes protected Jews from forced baptisms, as a way of flouting royal authority.

On other fronts, the Visigothic kings enjoyed more success when in the 620s they reconquered the Mediterranean shore from the Byzantines (whose attention was focused just then on the Persians). But, like the Merovingians, the Visigothic kings allowed their power and wealth to pass little by little to the landed aristocracy. The regime would finally fall before conquering Muslims in the early 700s.

✳ THE EARLY MEDIEVAL CHURCH

Monasticism

As we saw in Chapter 1, St. Augustine and other early Christians unhesitatingly regarded chaste asceticism as the most perfect form of Christian life. Those who could not be chaste should marry, but chastity was best. Encouraged by popes and supported by kings, monasteries—communities of chaste monks and nuns—grew into potent forces in the early medieval West.

When St. Anthony (c. 250–355) retired to the Egyptian desert to live the ascetic life of a godly hermit in the third century, he sought solitude but ended up creating one of the first communities of Christian ascetics. As word of his sanctity spread, other would-be ascetics gathered around him, and Anthony responded by organizing them into a community of hermits who lived together but had little communication with one another—rather like apartment dwellers in an American city. Similar hermit communities soon arose throughout Egypt and elsewhere. Hermit saints abounded in the fourth and fifth centuries. One of them, a Syrian holy man named Simeon the Stylite (c. 390–459), achieved the necessary isolation by living atop a sixty-foot pillar for thirty years, evoking widespread admiration and imitation. Despite their relative isolation, Simeon the Stylite and other hermit saints were of fundamental importance in their communities. To the people who admired and supported them, these holy men and women were transmitters of divine favor and protection, as well as sources of holy wisdom, practical advice, and even profits from pilgrims. They stood, in a sense, between God and ordinary folk.

Some critics objected to these practices as too extreme, too chaotic, and too antisocial, and they began to develop forms of monasticism that were more moderate and more communal. This new movement began in the East, where Pachomius (c. 287–346) and Basil the Great (c. 330–379) guided more down-to-earth communities of monks (and sometimes nuns, too). Rather than a hermit's life, these new communities prized companionship and joint striving toward holy life. Their members lived in closer proximity to each other, they met together more often, and they shared with each other a common spiritual journey. This sort of cooperative monasticism was to prove especially popular in the West. In 404 John Cassian (c. 360–435), who had served as a monk in both Bethlehem and Egypt, returned to the West and began to encourage communal monasticism. Cassian wrote influential Latin treatises on the monastic life and founded two monasteries in Marseilles on the Mediterranean coast of Gaul, one monastery for women and the other for men.

To the northwest, in Ireland, still another strain of Christian monasticism was emerging. The Irish had been introduced to Christianity in the fifth century by St. Patrick (c. 389–461) and other missionaries; by 600 they had developed an astonishingly creative and distinctive Christian culture. Having never been incorporated into the Roman Empire, the Irish had no cities on which to build an ecclesiastical structure of bishops and dioceses, as was common elsewhere in the Christian West. Therefore, Irish monasteries assumed many of the functions that were elsewhere performed by bishops. In Ireland, in other words, heads of great autonomous monasteries took on the administrative functions of bishops. (There *were* bishops in the Irish Church, but their duties were spiritual and sacramental only, and in some places, they even lived in monasteries.) Irish monasticism was unusual in another respect: Irish monks (but not nuns, so far as we know) enthusiastically embraced pilgrimage-as-mission. Because this required a pilgrim not only to leave home but also to take on the hard work of converting pagans or establishing new monastic communities, Irish pilgrimage was a form of self-denial—a penitential exile, as it has been called. Thanks to it, St. Columba (521–597) and his companions founded the great monastery of Iona off the Scottish west coast, and St. Columban (c. 540–615) founded Luxeuil in France and Bobbio in the northern

Italian peninsula. Others did the same, but few were as hardheartedly determined as St. Columban, who stepped over his mother's grieving body as he left his home. And few traveled as far as St. Brendan (died c. 577) is said to have done, in a ship blown so off course that he may have been the first European to reach the Americas (in his case, the coast of Canada). In organization, Irish monasticism was initially closer to Anthony than John Cassian; within a monastic compound, each monk or nun kept a separate cell or hut.

Early medieval monasteries were not always single sex. In Ireland, Britain, Gaul, and Iberia, some monasteries included both women and men, and in most of these, an abbess ruled over both sexes. For example, the community founded by St. Bridget (c. 460–528) at Kildare housed both nuns and monks. Now known as **double monasteries,** these dual-sex houses caused no scandal. Writing of the community at Armagh, one seventh-century scholar noted matter-of-factly that "both sexes are seen to live together in religion from the coming of the faith to the present day almost inseparably."

Early medieval monasteries were also closely linked to the powerful local families that supported them. Often, this meant that the abbot or abbess was a descendant of the donor and that the monastery offered hospitality and other favors to the donor's family. Like double monasteries, this practice of **family monasteries** was readily accepted early on but would come under harsh scrutiny in later centuries.

St. Benedict and His Rule

Although monasticism was well established in the West long before the time of St. Benedict of Nursia (c. 480–550), he is often called the "father of Western monasticism." His great contribution was to synthesize the ideas of Pachomius, Basil, Cassian, and others into a written *Rule of St. Benedict* that remains deeply influential to this day.

Like many other Christian leaders of his time, Benedict was a Roman of good family. Born in the central mountains of the Italian peninsula, he was sent to Rome for his education. But he fled the city before completing his studies and took up a hermit's life in a cave near the ruins of Nero's country palace. In time, word of his saintliness circulated, and disciples gathered around him. As it turned out, Benedict was more than a simple ascetic; he was a man of keen psychological insight, a superb organizer who learned from the varied experiences of his youth how the monastic life might best be lived. His tremendously influential *Rule* prescribed a monasticism marked by moderate asceticism, gentle discipline, and flexible orderliness.

Benedict founded a number of monasteries, but he built his greatest at Monte Cassino atop a mountain midway between Rome and Naples. His sister, St. Scholastica (d. 543), established herself in a nearby hermitage and visited him once a year to talk of spiritual matters. Scholastica was to become the patron saint of Benedictine monasteries for women, and Benedict's abbey at Monte Cassino remained for many centuries one of the chief centers of religious life in Western Europe.

The *Rule of St. Benedict* provided for a busy, regulated life, simple but not ruthlessly austere. Although designed for communities of men, it was readily adapted to nunneries. Benedictine monks and nuns were decently clothed, adequately fed, and seldom left to their own devices. Theirs was a life dedicated to God and the attainment of personal sanctity through prayer and service, yet it was also a life that could be led by any dedicated Christian. In other words, Benedict welcomed into his monasteries not only would-be saints but also ordinary people who sought, within the limits of their abilities, to lead pious lives. Benedictine communities were even open to children, many of whom were dedicated to religious life (without being asked) by their parents or guardians and were then educated in their monastery's school. This practice was known as **oblation** and the children as oblates.[1]

The monastic day was filled with carefully prescribed activities: communal prayer, devotional reading, and work—field work, household work, or manuscript copying, according to need and ability. Benedictine communities included priests to conduct the sacraments, but it was by no means necessary that all monks be consecrated as priests, and most were not. Monks and nuns alike were pledged to the fundamental obligations of poverty, chastity, and obedience. By relinquishing all personal possessions, living a celibate life, and obeying the abbot or abbess, Benedictines sought to resist the three great worldly temptations of money, sex, and ambition. The heads of Benedictine houses were elected for life, and they exercised unquestioned authority, governing as parents ("abba" means "father" in Aramaic) over their monastic families. They were strictly responsible to God and were instructed to govern justly in accordance with the *Rule*. But they were also to be caring and patient rulers, wary of overdriving their charges or giving them just cause for what Benedict called "murmuring."

Contributions of Benedictine Monks and Nuns

Within two or three centuries of Benedict's death, his *Rule* had spread throughout Western Christendom. The result was not a vast hierarchical organization but rather a host of individual, autonomous monasteries sharing a general way of life. In this sense, early monasteries were similar to modern colleges and universities, where each institution is independent of all others (except in state systems with multiple campuses), but all share a common purpose. No formal hierarchy links the University of Chicago to either Northwestern University or Lake Forest College, but on all three campuses, students work toward degrees in roughly similar ways. So it was with early monasteries: they were administratively separate, but linked in objective.

Benedict had visualized his monasteries as spiritual sanctuaries into which pious Christians might withdraw from the world. But Benedictine monks and nuns were soon thrust into the nexus of early medieval politics, thanks to the vast estates their abbeys accumulated, the ties that linked many monks and nuns to powerful aristocratic families, and the need in **secular** society for the skills that could be acquired only in monastic schools. As a result, Benedictine monks and nuns had an enormous impact on the world they renounced. They controlled the main repositories of learning, producing most of the scholars of the age and preserving many texts that would otherwise have been forever lost. They were eager vessels of missionary activity, spearheading the penetration of Christianity into the forests of modern-day Germany and later into Scandinavia, Poland, and Hungary. They produced scribes to record the business of lay courts, advisers to princes, and candidates for high ecclesiastical offices. And as recipients of

---

[1] Child oblation was usually opposed by the Church, but it was nevertheless common in these centuries. Although the thought of parents choosing a religious career for a child might seem cruel, it worked well in practice; not surprisingly, most children reared in monasteries grew up comfortable with the challenges of monastic life.

numerous gifts of land from pious donors, they held and managed large estates, some of which were models of intelligent agricultural organization and technological innovation. For although each Benedictine monk or nun was pledged to *personal* poverty, a Benedictine abbey might acquire immense *corporate* wealth. Some Benedictine abbeys became great landholders, responsible for political and legal administration and military recruitment over the large areas under their control. In short, Benedictine monasticism became a major civilizing influence in the early Christian West. But in theory always, and in practice sometimes, these monasteries remained dedicated to one primary purpose: prayer, meditation, and service to God.

Pope Gregory the Great (r. 590–604)

In its earliest years, the monastic vision of St. Benedict and his *Rule* was very nearly destroyed. A generation after Benedict's death, Monte Cassino was pillaged by the Lombards (c. 577), and its monks were scattered. Some took refuge in Rome, where they came into contact with the pious, well-born monk and future pope, Gregory the Great. Though not himself a Benedictine monk, Gregory was deeply impressed by their accounts of Benedict's holiness and his *Rule*. Gregory wrote a biography of the saint that achieved tremendous popularity and drew widespread support to Benedictine monasticism.

As a theologian, Gregory's work was highly influential in subsequent centuries, particularly because he helped to popularize the thought of St. Augustine of Hippo. His real genius lay, however, in his keen understanding of human nature and his ability as an administrator and organizer. His *Pastoral Care,* a treatise on the duties and obligations of a bishop, is a masterpiece of practical wisdom and common sense. It answered a great need of the times and became one of the most widely read books in the Middle Ages. Also, his commentary on the Book of Job was instrumental in passing along the techniques of allegorical interpretation that had been developed, as we saw in Chapter 1, by Philo of Alexandria in the first century C.E.

Gregory loved the monastic life and ascended the papal throne with genuine regret. On hearing of his election he went into hiding and had to be dragged into the basilica of St. Peter's to be consecrated. But once resigned to his new responsibilities, Gregory bent every energy to the extension of papal authority. He believed fervently that the pope, as successor of St. Peter, was the rightful ruler of the Church. He reorganized the financial structure of the papal estates and used the increased revenues for charitable works to ameliorate the wretched poverty of his times. His integrity, wisdom, and administrative ability won him an almost regal position in Rome and its region, at a time of crisis when Lombards and Byzantines were struggling for control of the peninsula.

The Conversion of the Anglo-Saxons

Gregory also had the wisdom to dispatch a group of monks to convert the pagan Anglo-Saxons. The mission was led by a monk named Augustine (d. 604), who is now known as St. Augustine of Canterbury so as not to confuse him with the great theologian of an earlier day, St. Augustine of Hippo (354–430). In 597, when Augustine and his followers began their momentous work in Kent, Britain was divided into a number of independent kingdoms, of which Kent was momentarily the most powerful. Augustine was assured a friendly reception by the fact that Queen Bertha (died c. 612), wife of King Ethelbert of Kent (r. 560–616) was a Frankish Christian. Great-granddaughter of Queen Clotilda, who had converted Clovis in 496, Bertha was as skilled at domestic proselytization as her progenitor. She so thoroughly prepared the way for Augustine that within a few months of his arrival, King Ethelbert and thousands of his subjects were baptized. The chief town of the realm, Canterbury, became the headquarters of the new Church, and Augustine himself became Canterbury's first archbishop. Under his influence Ethelbert issued the first written laws in the Anglo-Saxon language.

During the decades that followed, the fortunes of Christianity in Britain rose and fell with the varying fortunes of the Anglo-Saxon kingdoms. Kent declined after Ethelbert's death, and by the mid-600s political power shifted to the northernmost of the Anglo-Saxon states, Northumbria. This remote outpost became the scene of a deeply significant encounter between the two great creative forces of the age: Irish Christianity moving southward from monasteries Irish monks had established in Scotland and Roman Christianity moving northward from Kent.

Although the two movements shared a common faith, they had different cultural backgrounds, different notions of monastic life and ecclesiastical organization, and different systems for calculating the date of Easter. This last might sound unimportant, but it caused considerable awkwardness; for example, the Northumbrian king Oswy (d. 670), who followed Irish practice, found himself celebrating Easter while his wife, Eanfled (died c. 704), who followed the Roman tradition, was still observing the penitential season of Lent. The Roman date for Easter won official recognition at a **synod** convened in 664 at the monastery of Whitby, which was guided by the renowned Abbess Hilda (see Biographical Sketch on pp. 62–63). Five years later, in 669, the papacy sent the scholarly Theodore of Tarsus (c. 602–690) to assume the archbishopric of Canterbury and reorganize the Anglo-Saxon Church into a system of bishops and dioceses. As a consequence of the Whitby synod and Archbishop Theodore's tireless efforts, the Anglo-Saxon kingdoms, only a century out of paganism, became one of Europe's most vigorous Christian societies.

Popular Christianity

Because a bishop's authority usually stretched no farther than his city and its immediate environs, the Church had less religious sway over the countryside than towns. Only gradually were rural **parishes** organized to meet the needs of the peasantry. In the meantime, some peasants were fortunate if they saw a priest once a year. Monasteries, with their walled precincts and broad fields, provided some religious services for ordinary people, but they were usually independent of episcopal control and sometimes wary of pastoral duties. In the British Isles and perhaps elsewhere, however, it seems that "minster churches" housed clerical communities active in pastoral case ("mynster" is Old English for "monastery"). By overseeing lesser churches, a minster church supervised pastoral care over a wide area. In this case, as in others, the distinctions of the Central Middle Ages between **regular clergy,** who followed **monastic rules,** and **secular clergy,** responsible for pastoral care, were not so distinct in the first centuries of the

Hilda, Abbess of Whitby (614–680)

A lmost everything we know about Hilda of Whitby comes from a short biography in Bede's *Ecclesiastical History*. Writing some fifty years after Hilda's death, Bede included events that are suspiciously like those found in other saints' lives: a mother who dreamed of the brilliant future of the child in her womb; a life crisis at the age of thirty-three (the age at which Jesus was thought to have died); and a joyful death, followed by heavenly ascension. These we may discount as better hagiography than history, but Bede's other information is more historically reliable.

Bede tells us that Hilda was nobly born into a collateral branch of the Northumbrian royal family. She was raised a pagan, but when she was thirteen, she converted to Christianity on the same day that her great-uncle, King Edwin (d. 632), accepted baptism. Of her next twenty years, Bede is silent. Because he never praises her virginity, Hilda might have married and then been widowed; because he never mentions her husband, she might have married a pagan or endured an otherwise unsuitable union. In any case, Hilda turned in a new direction at midlife when she decided to join her sister at the monastery of Chelles, near Paris. At the last minute she was persuaded to pursue her monastic vocation in England, and she founded two monasteries before settling down at a third which she established at Whitby, a cold and windy harbor on the Yorkshire coast. To one side of her monastery lay rocky cliffs; on the other, the North Sea.

At Whitby, Hilda governed a community of both nuns and monks to whom, in the words of Bede, she "taught the observance of righteousness, mercy, purity, and other virtues, but especially of peace and charity." Her wisdom was so renowned that bishops, kings, and ordinary people traveled to Whitby to speak with her, and, as Bede tells it, even people who never met her were inspired by "the story of her industry and goodness." Of all Hilda's accomplishments, three especially stand out. First, she made Whitby into a "nursery of bishops," from which came no fewer than five men who were raised to episcopal power. Second, she hosted the Synod of Whitby at which long-standing disputes between Irish and Roman forms of Christianity were finally resolved in 664. Third, she encouraged the development of Old English poetry. When a cowherd named Caedmon began to compose religious verses in his native tongue, he was brought before Hilda. She determined that his skills were heaven-sent, admitted him to her monastery, and arranged for his religious instruction. Thereafter Caedmon, like a cow chewing its cud (in Bede's memorable phrasing), turned the lessons of his teachers into poetry. His verses were sung and praised throughout England.

This is what Bede tells us, but we would like to know much more. Hilda was born a pagan but became a great Christian leader. What was the story behind the depth of her new faith? Hilda was converted to Roman Christianity, but she stood on the Irish side at Whitby. When and why did she come to prefer the traditions of Irish Christianity? Hilda wielded great power in an age when men dominated church and state. Did she transcend the limitations placed on women by her extraordinary virtue, by her privileged birth, or just by force of personality? And although Hilda supervised the early training of Wilfrid, Bishop of York (r. 669–678), she grew bitterly opposed to his policies. What went wrong in their relationship? Like the years between Hilda's conversion and her turn toward religious life, we can speculate on these matters, but we cannot be sure. If Bede has not told us, we simply do not know.

Hilda's monastery was destroyed by Vikings in 867. Only one manuscript survives from its flourishing scriptorium and only one letter written by its many nuns and monks. Nothing survives of the monastery itself. The ruins that today stand off Whitby harbor are of a male monastery founded in 1078. The fate of the manuscripts and buildings of Hilda's monastery are like her own place in history. Hilda presided over a powerful and pious monastic community but, in the end, her fame would lie in the hands of one man who added a few paragraphs about her to his book. Such is the nature of historical memory and the fragility of fame.

Middle Ages. Peasants benefited from this overlap of functions because it likely mattered little to them whether a cleric from the local minster or a parish priest assigned by the bishop provided their religious care.

Still, all in all, churchmen and churchwomen were better known among the peasantry as wealthy landowners than as fountains of justice and divine grace. This is no wonder, because bishops, abbots, and abbesses were the brothers and sisters of kings, queens, and nobles. Hilda, seventh-century abbess of the great monastery at Whitby, was born into a noble Northumbrian family and related to East Anglian royalty; Gregory, bishop of Tours in the sixth century, hailed from the Gallo-Roman aristocracy; and Pope Gregory I had been born into a wealthy Roman family. Their high birth was the norm among men and women who built careers in the Church. Through most of the Middle Ages, aristocratic children had only two options—either the Church or lay life. In both, they could expect to be supported by landed estates whose fields were tilled by enslaved, semi-servile, and rent-paying peasants.

Old pagan customs lingered for centuries among ordinary people, blending into Christianity in interesting ways. Pagan holidays were assimilated into the Christian calendar (for example, the winter solstice became the occasion for the celebration of Christmas, joining birth of sun and Son); pagan sites became Christian shrines and churches; and old customs and prayers took on new Christian meaning. Here, for example, is a charm to be used against elves, invoked in Anglo-Saxon England long after its conversion, in which Christian and pre-Christian remedies are strangely mixed:

> Make a salve [of various herbs, including] wormwood, bishopswort, garlic, and
> fennel. Put the herbs into a cup, place them under the altar, sing nine masses over
> them, then boil them in butter and sheep's grease. . . .

This spell might not have troubled Pope Gregory I, who advised his missionaries to move gently in converting the Anglo-Saxons so that the converts would feel comfortable in their new faith. A practical man, he knew that it would be impossible "to cut everything at once from their stubborn minds," and that, therefore, old pagan temples could be converted into Christian churches and old festivals into new Christian feasts. As long as there was no pagan belief, he taught, little harm was done in accompanying Christian prayers with meaningless old customs. Gregory's advice was well taken, and even today, a holiday such as Halloween (the eve of the Christian feast of All Saints) brings together traditions that were first blended in Gregory's time.

✳ INTELLECTUAL LIFE

As the culture of old Rome faded, new intellectual traditions began to develop in Western Europe. Bishops took the lead in many places, but monks and nuns also played important roles.

To some historians, this culture seems derivative, credulous, and unimpressive. Gregory of Tours (c. 538–594), whose *History of the Franks* is our best source for the reigns of Clovis and his successors, wrote in ungrammatical Latin, was guilty of blatant political bias, and tended to dwell on improbable miracles and bloodcurdling atrocities. Similarly, Pope Gregory wrote with practical wisdom and psychological insight, but he could not approach the philosophical depth and scholarly sophistication of Augustine of Hippo and other fourth-century theologians. And, although Isidore, Bishop of Seville (560–636), pulled his wide knowledge together in the *Etymologies,* an encyclopedia studied for many centuries thereafter, he lacked critical powers, including in his work every scrap of information he could find, whether likely or unlikely, profound or super-ficial. He also collected more than he created, lifting freely from the works of other scholars in a massive cut-and-paste effort. In fairness to Isidore, it should be said that his borrowings were weakened by the credulity of the ancient Roman writers on whom he depended. Nevertheless, he betrayed a certain lack of sophistication. On the subject of monsters, he wrote:

> The Cynocephali are so called because they have dogs' heads and their very barking betrays them as beasts rather than men. These are born in India. The Cyclopses, too, hail from India, and they are so named because they have a single eye in the middle of their forehead. . . . The Blemmyes, born in Libya, are believed to be headless trunks, having mouth and eyes in the breast; others are born without necks, with eyes in the shoulders. . . . They say the Panotii in Scythia have ears so huge that they cover the whole body with them. . . . The race of Sciopodes is said to live in Ethiopia. They have one leg apiece, and are of a marvelous swiftness, and . . . in summertime they lie on the ground on their backs and are shaded by the greatness of their feet.

Finally, with a touch of much-needed skepticism, Isidore concluded:

> Other fabulous monstrosities of the human race are said to exist, but they do not; they are imaginary.

It is well to remember, however, that scholars such as Gregory of Tours, Pope Gregory I, and Isidore of Seville were making the best of difficult circumstances. They were often well aware of their limitations. Gregory of Tours apologized to his readers for his poor Latin, and Pope Gregory wrote movingly about the decline of Roman culture "wasted away with afflictions grievous and many." Moreover, if we look elsewhere, we find genuine intellectual vigor in these centuries.

In Ireland, after all, monks (and perhaps nuns, but our evidence is thin)—using a Latin language that they had never encountered before, thanks to Ireland's distance from the imperial power of Rome—were capable of writing in perfect Latin. They excelled in the rigor of their scholarship, the depth of their sanctity, the austerity of their lives, and the scope of their missionary work. Irish monastic schools were the best in Western Europe at the time. The Irish boasted the only schools where Greek was studied along-side Latin; they adapted the Roman alphabet to the Irish language, thereby preserving in written form the oral traditions of the Irish past; and they developed a rich artistic tradition that culminated in fabulous illuminated manuscripts of which the Book of Kells (see Color Illustration 3) is just one example. These manuscripts were the wonder of their age and still excite admiration in our own. The triumphs of Irish monasticism did not enliven Ireland alone, for Irish missionaries sought to revitalize monastic life beyond their own shores by establishing communities in Britain, Francia, and as far afield as the northern Italian peninsula.

Benedictine monasteries were also important centers of learning, and their schools produced most of Europe's readers and writers during the Early Middle Ages. Because many included a **scriptorium** where manuscripts were copied as well as studied, monasteries also served as cultural bridges, where the writings of Latin antiquity were transcribed and preserved. Scribal work could be demanding and exhausting, as we learn from occasional postscripts tacked onto the ends of medieval manuscripts: "Now I've copied it all out," wrote one weary scribe, "for Christ's sake, give me a pot of wine."

These two monastic traditions—Irish and Benedictine—encountered each other most directly along the remote, cold, and windy coast of seventh-century Northumbria, producing a cultural awakening known as the "Northumbrian Renaissance." The luster of Northumbrian culture in the late 600s and early 700s can be seen in many ways: bold illuminated manuscripts that use a curvilinear style both Celtic and barbarian in inspiration; a new script; a vigorous **vernacular** epic poetry; an impressive architecture; and the achievements of the greatest scholar of the age, St. Bede the Venerable (c. 673–735).

Bede, who unlike most other major scholars of the 500s and 600s had no family ties to the old Roman aristocracy, entered the monastery at Jarrow (see reconstruction in Figure 3.2) as a child and remained there until his death. The greatest of his many works, the *Ecclesiastical History of England,* displays a critical sense far superior to that of his contemporaries, and it established him as the foremost Western intellect since Augustine of Hippo. Reflecting a remarkable cultural breadth and a penetrating mind, the *Ecclesiastical History* is our chief source for early English history. It is also the first major historical work to employ the modern chronological framework based on the Christian era: A.D., *Anno Domini,* the "year of the Lord," now still used but designated as C.E., Common Era.

By Bede's death in 735, Northumbrian culture was beginning to fade. But its tradition of learning would be taken to the Continent during the eighth century by a group of Anglo-Saxon missionaries. In the 740s the Anglo-Saxon monk St. Boniface (c. 675–754) reformed the Church of Francia, infusing it with Benedictine idealism, systematizing its organization, and binding it more closely to the papacy. Boniface and other Anglo-Saxon missionaries also founded new Benedictine monasteries east of the Rhine from which they undertook the long and difficult task of Christianizing the Bavarians, Thuringians, and other Germanic-speaking tribes, just as Pope Gregory's monks had Christianized Kent little more than 100 years before. By the later 700s the cultural center of Western Christendom had shifted southward again—this time, from Anglo-Saxon England to the rising empire of the Frankish leader, Charlemagne. Scholars from as far afield as Iberia and Lombardy would enliven Charlemagne's court, but the greatest of them all was the Northumbrian monk Alcuin (c. 732–804), a student of one of Bede's own pupils.

Figure 3.2   *Reconstruction of the Monastery at Jarrow*   Jarrow was the home of the
Venerable Bede. The religious buildings are at the back (the main church on the left and a
chapel to the right); the other buildings were for sleeping, eating, meeting, studying, and
housing guests. The river provided a critical means of transport and communication, but it also
made it easy for the Vikings to attack. Bede died in 735, and his beloved monastery was
pillaged by Vikings in 794.

✸ CONCLUSION

Perhaps the most important distinction between West and East to emerge during the
sixth and seventh centuries was the independence with which the Western Church was
able to develop. Church and state often worked hand in hand in the Christian West,
but religion and secular politics were never merged to the degree that they were in
Constantinople and, indeed, in most ancient civilizations. This separation between cultural leadership, which was ecclesiastical and monastic, and political leadership, which
was in the hands of early medieval kings and aristocracies, creatively fueled the dynamism of Western culture. The tension of their interplay—sometimes cooperation,
sometimes conflict, sometimes indifference—profoundly shaped the development of
early medieval civilization. Now, let us turn to another creative tension and profound
influence on medieval Europe: its Byzantine and Islamic neighbors.

SUGGESTED READINGS

Lisa Bitel, *Land of Women: Tales of Sex and Gender from Early Ireland* (1996). Bitel's analysis
     is both interesting and accessible.
James Campbell, ed., *The Anglo-Saxons* (1982). An aptly illustrated survey. See also Henry
     Mayr-Harting, *The Coming of Christianity to Anglo-Saxon England* (3rd edition, 1991).

For other histories of specific groups or regions, see Neil Christie, *The Lombards* (1995); Roger Collins, *Early Medieval Spain: Unity in Diversity (400–1000)* (2nd edition, 1995); Peter Heather, *The Goths* (1996); Edward James, *The Franks* (1988); Chris Wickham, *Early Medieval Italy: Central Power and Local Society 400–1000* (1981).

Richard Fletcher, *The Barbarian Conversion: From Paganism to Christianity* (1997). A persuasive history of the meaning of conversion from the fourth to the fourteenth centuries.

Patrick J. Geary, *Before France and Germany* (1988). An excellent and highly readable book that concisely reviews recent historical and archaeological interpretations.

R. A. Markus, *Gregory the Great and his World* (1997).

Jeffrey Richards, *The Popes and the Papacy in the Early Middle Ages, 476–752* (1979). A welcome effort to revisit the early medieval papacy on its own terms.

Pauline Stafford, *Queens, Concubines and Dowagers: The King's Wife in the Early Middle Ages* (1983). Traces the lives of "royal bedfellows" from marriage negotiation through widowhood.

SUGGESTED PRIMARY SOURCES

Paul Fouracre and Richard A. Gerberdling, eds., *Late Merovingian France: History and Hagiography 640–720* (1996). Translations of eight narrative accounts of the age.

J. N. Hillgarth, ed., *Christianity and Paganism 350–750* (revised edition, 1986). Organized by topics, this collection follows on the coverage provided in Ramsay Macmullen and Eugene N. Lane, eds., *Paganism and Christianity, 100–425 c.e.* (1992).

Jo Ann McNamara and John E. Halberg, eds., *Sainted Women of the Dark Ages* (1992). Translations of the lives of seventeen saints from the fifth through seventh centuries. See also Thomas F. X. Noble and Thomas Head, eds., *Soldiers of Christ: Saints and Saints' Lives from Late Antiquity and the Early Middle Ages* (1995).

CHAPTER 4

NEIGHBORS: BYZANTIUM AND ISLAM, c. 500-1000

✴ INTRODUCTION

The Eastern and Western halves of the old Roman Empire followed different trajectories from the fifth century, but they remained in close contact. They were soon joined by a third power in the Mediterranean, Islam, so that by 700, the lands of the old Roman Empire had fallen under three influences. To the west lay political disintegration, a promise of religious unity, and an emerging social synthesis of Celtic, Roman, and barbarian traditions. Out of this was growing the medieval West, the focus of our story. To the east lay the most direct successor of Rome: an Eastern Roman Empire that continued to wield authority, for a while at least, over the Balkans, Asia Minor, the Middle East, and Egypt. Out of this inheritance, the Byzantine Empire was taking shape. And to the south, a new power had emerged in the middle of the seventh century, a power born of a new religion, Islam, and an old part of the world, Arabia. By 700, a Muslim dynasty was claiming as its own all of the southern Mediterranean, and for several centuries thereafter, a unified Islam was by far the greatest of the three civilizations that encircled the Mediterranean Sea.

Historians sometimes talk of these three civilizations as the "three heirs" of Rome or even as "three siblings." But "neighbors" might better capture the relationship, for the proximity of these civilizations to each other was as important as any shared Roman inheritance. Indeed, medieval Europeans seldom dwelled on the cultural inheritances they shared with Byzantines and Muslims, and many might have been bemused or even outraged by the sibling analogy. But they knew that to their east lay the Byzantines, a people who were sometimes allies, sometimes enemies, and always perplexing. And they knew that Muslims, a pressing presence to their south, threatened the very existence of their fragile "Christendom." For medieval Europeans, these neighbors were, for better or worse, never far away (see the Timeline for Part I).

❊ From Eastern to Byzantine Empire

At the same time that the Western Empire fractured into a variety of successor states, the Eastern emperors, with their capital at Constantinople, retained control of an immense, crescent-shaped empire that stretched across the eastern Mediterranean, from the Balkans through Asia Minor, Syria, and Palestine to Egypt. As we have already seen, the East boasted civilizations that were far older and more deeply rooted than those in the West; it had larger cities and more of them; and its prosperous peasants enjoyed freedoms that were only dim memories for the coloni of the Western Empire.

In the fifth century, the political, military, and socioeconomic troubles of the Western Empire were matched by advantages in the Eastern Empire. To begin with, the Eastern Empire was better governed. While the Western Empire was collapsing, able Eastern emperors carefully husbanded their resources, fattened their treasuries, and strengthened the fortifications of Constantinople. The East also enjoyed important military strengths. During the cataclysmic fifth century in the West, when barbarian kings were establishing new states in former Roman provinces, Asia Minor (that is, Anatolia, or modern-day Turkey) was the bulwark of the Eastern Empire. Protected from invaders by the Black Sea and the walls of invulnerable Constantinople, Asia Minor was a vast reservoir for both soldiers and the tax revenues that paid them. Finally, with more cities, more industry, more commerce, and more free peasants than the West, the Eastern Empire prospered. This prosperity was further enhanced by the central location of Constantinople, whose wharves and ports controlled virtually all commerce between the Black Sea and the Mediterranean. During the fifth century, gold coins steadily flowed out of Western coffers to enrich the merchants, farmers, emperors, and soldiers of the East.

Understandably, then, the East proved far more resilient than the West, and, indeed, it generally prospered for another half-millennium (see Timeline 4.1). It changed in size, expanding in the 500s so that it controlled—briefly—almost all the Mediterranean coastline, west as well as east; it then lost many of those territories so that by 800 it had **sovereignty** over only Asia Minor and parts of the eastern Balkans; it then grew again until about the mid-eleventh century (see Map 4.1). Whether expanding or shrinking, the empire endured, safely protected by the massive landward and seaward walls of Constantinople. The Eastern Empire also changed in character, losing many of its ties to Latin culture by 700 and becoming more of a Greek state. Long after the decline of the Western Empire, the emperors who governed from Constantinople continued to call themselves "Roman" and to claim that they governed the "Roman Empire," but they usually looked East across the Bosporus, not west toward Rome. Modern historians have applied a distinction these Eastern emperors denied, labeling their jurisdiction as a "Byzantine Empire," after the old town of Byzantium.

Byzantine Government

Byzantium took its religion from Christianity and its culture from Greece, but its governmental structures were largely Roman. Indeed, Byzantine laws and bureaucracies were direct offspring of the later Roman political system: Byzantine autocracy had its roots in the glorification of such late Roman emperors as Diocletian and Constantine; the close involvement of emperors in the Byzantine Church harked back to the policies of Constantine (r. 306–337) and Theodosius I (r. 378–395); and Byzantine taxation continued the heavy exactions of late Roman times.

TIMELINE 4.1   The Eastern Empire and Byzantium to 1000

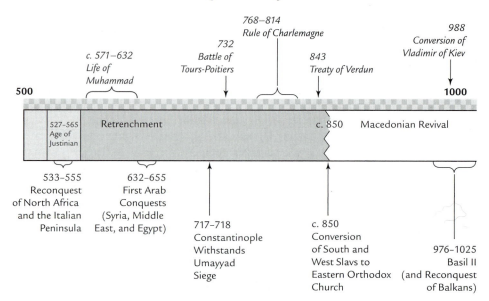

In addition to these institutional inheritances from Rome, Byzantium inherited a political mind-set from the late Roman Empire that emphasized defense and self-preservation. Byzantine history includes some daring emperors and some expansionary eras, but the prevailing political trend was defense, not conquest. To the Byzantines, their state was the ark of civilization—the political embodiment of Christian faith—in an ocean of barbarism, and as such it had to be preserved at all costs. The appropriate virtues in such a state were entrenchment not expansion, caution not daring.

This defensive, conservative approach shaped both the Byzantine bureaucracy and the Byzantine army. The bureaucracy, huge and precedent-bound, abhorred change and seldom took risks. It resisted the policies of Byzantium's more vigorous and imaginative emperors, but it also provided cohesion during the reigns of fools. The army, small and highly trained, also clung to a policy of few risks. Its generals practiced their art with cunning and caution, well aware that the preservation of the Empire might depend on the survival of their troops.

Although Byzantium took both political structures and outlook from Rome, it also elaborated on them in new ways. The "big government" of the Byzantine Empire—elaborate imperial ceremonies, huge bureaucracies, heavy-handed state regulation—eventually exceeded anything the late Roman Empire had seen. And the complex, sometimes devious schemes of Byzantine rulers went so far beyond the cautious mind-set of late Roman politics that even today the word "Byzantine" is a synonym for inflexible or complicated political strategies.

Byzantine Christianity

Christianity had first taken strong hold in the Eastern Empire, and it remained a dominant force in Byzantium. The patriarch of Constantinople eventually came to head an Eastern Orthodox Church that defined both doctrine and authority in different ways

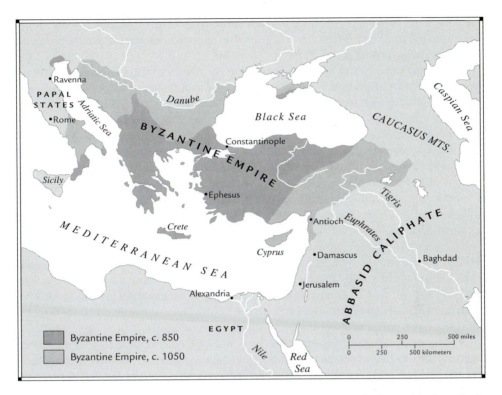

Map 4.1 *Byzantine Retrenchment and Expansion, c. 850–1050*   The Byzantines lost all of the southern part of their empire to Islamic conquest. Thereafter, they wielded authority over just Greece, the Balkans, Asia Minor, and the extreme south of the Italian peninsula. The different hatchings of this map show how Byzantine authority over these regions was reduced by the 800s and then slowly expanded until c. 1050.

from the Catholic Church headed by the Pope in Rome.[1] For Byzantines, Christian faith was a compelling identity that defined their very existence. When they fought against Avars, Slavs, and Bulgarians on their northern borders in the sixth century and against Arabs to their south and east from the seventh century, they saw themselves as defending Christianity against heathen hordes. As we shall see in Chapter 9, Byzantine dealings with Western crusaders after 1095 would be similarly tinged by religious antipathy, although, in this case, between disagreeing Christians.

The Byzantine emperors drew invaluable strength from the loyalty of their Christian subjects. To Byzantines, their emperor was much more than an ordinary secular sovereign. He was God's vice-regent, and his voice was, in theory, a decisive one in all matters affecting Christian governance, practice, and doctrine. He was the protector of the Holy Church; his armies fought not only for the Empire but for God; his warriors

---

[1] In this instance, capitalization really matters. "Orthodoxy" specifically signifies the Eastern Orthodox Church (which embraces self-governing branches in Greece, Russia, Serbia, and elsewhere), and "orthodoxy" has a more general meaning of a "correct opinion" as judged by a designated religious authority. As a result, an orthodox opinion according to the Catholic Church might not be accepted by Orthodox Christians; papal infallibility, accepted by Catholic Christians and rejected by Orthodox Christians, is a good example.

were not mere soldiers but crusaders. In Byzantium, Christianity became a potent stimulus to patriotism, and Byzantine emperors thus enjoyed popular support to a degree unknown in the days of pagan Rome.

But the emperor's dominating position in Byzantine Christianity was a source of weakness as well. Because religious controversy was a matter of direct imperial concern, heresy became a threat to the state. This was especially true in conflicts over the nature of Christ, old disputes that took on new meaning in the fifth-century Eastern Empire. Was Christ a human being? Was he God alone? If he was both God and human, how did these merge into one person? Two main positions developed. On one side stood those who argued that Christ was both perfect God and perfect human, with these two natures united in one person. This was the orthodox position defined at the Council of Chalcedon in 451 and accepted by both the pope in Rome and the patriarch of Constantinople. On the other side stood those who insisted on a single nature for Christ, a single nature in which divinity tended to supersede humanity. Known as "Monophysites," they particularly predominated in the cities of North Africa and the Middle East, areas with religious traditions that had long regarded the divine as irrevocably separate from earthly things. To Monophysites, it made sense that God had walked the earth and suffered crucifixion, but it was illogical to believe that God had become as fully human as divine. Their position was clear, strong, and supported by many bishops in Egypt, Syria, and Palestine, and even some emperors.

The quarrel raged long and bitterly. Emperors, convinced that doctrinal unity was essential to the preservation of their state, followed first one policy, then another. Sometimes they persecuted the Monophysites, sometimes they favored them, and sometimes they worked out compromise doctrines that were intended to satisfy both sides but in fact satisfied neither. Controversy dragged on until the seventh century, when the Monophysite provinces were swallowed by conquering Islamic armies. Indeed, this swallowing was made easier by the disaffection of Monophysite Christians who resented imperial persecution and welcomed the more tolerant attitudes of their new Arab rulers. Thereafter, at the Ecumenical Council of Constantinople in 680, the orthodox position first articulated at Chalcedon won its definitive victory within what then remained of the Byzantine Empire.

In the eighth century, a new doctrinal conflict arose, this time over the use of **icons** (that is, holy statues and pictures). This conflict not only divided Christians within Byzantium but also exacerbated tensions between East and West. Icons had gradually come to assume an important role in Christian worship, particularly in Byzantine monasteries that often possessed impressive painted images and thereby profited from pilgrims who came to see them. Icons were useful: they taught the illiterate about Christian faith, and, as *symbols* of the holy persons they represented, they could inspire intense religious devotion. But there was a tendency among some people to worship the icons themselves, and this was unacceptable. A series of reform emperors in Constantinople, beginning with Leo the Isaurian (r. 717–741), decided to ban icons altogether and to promote iconoclasm (literally, icon-smashing). If there were no holy images, iconoclasts thought, there would be no risk of improper worship. Because this new policy undermined monasteries, which had hitherto controlled huge estates free from imperial taxation, it had a political as well as a religious basis. In any case, the iconoclastic decrees offended a great many Byzantines, image-worshippers and thoughtful traditionalists alike.

Iconoclasm ultimately failed even in Byzantium, but as long as the controversy raged, it aroused intense enmity between Rome and Constantinople. In the West, the decrees of iconoclastic emperors found little support. The papacy opposed iconoclasm as heretical, and as we shall see in Chapter 5, this issue was so important that it helped turn Rome away from Byzantine alliances and toward the Frankish rulers to their north. Other East-West arguments also raged—especially about differences of liturgical practice, the nature of the Trinity, and the pope's claim to be sole head of a single Church. These disagreements slowly led the two Churches down separate paths, and in 1054, pope and patriarch formally excommunicated each other. This event—just one moment in a long series of misunderstandings and controversies—marks the traditional date of a schism between Catholic Christians (guided by the pope in Rome) and Eastern Orthodox Christians (guided by the patriarch in Constantinople). Even today, these two ancient branches of Christianity have not fully healed this almost 1,000-year-old schism.

Byzantine Culture

Shaped by Roman government and Christian religion, the Byzantine Empire drew on Greece for most of its cultural traditions. The Greek culture that Byzantium inherited was by no means the culture of classical Athens, with its superbly proportioned architecture, its advances into uncharted regions of speculative thought, and its controlled, tensely muscular sculpture. That tradition had undergone successive modifications in the ages that followed and, above all, during the late Roman Empire. The mood of otherworldliness that permeated imperial culture in the third and fourth centuries had especially transformed the classical legacy. There had always been a potent spiritual-mystical element in Greco-Roman culture, coexisting with traditional interests in the earthly and concrete. In the late Empire, this mystical element had grown stronger. More and more of the better minds had turned away from worldly concerns to study theology, interpret the scriptures, and seek the path to individual salvation. St. Augustine, for example, had believed that studying the physical sciences was simply a waste of time. Artists had followed suit, growing less interested in portraying beauty and more interested in portraying sanctity. The new Christian art of the later Roman Empire had depicted slender, heavily robed figures with solemn faces and deep, deep eyes that seemed windows into their very souls. Techniques of perspective, which artists of the classical era had once developed to a fine degree, mattered less to the artists of this new age (as they would later matter less to modern artists). De-emphasizing physical realism, the artists of the late Empire had embellished their works with rich, glittering colors that conveyed a sense of heavenly radiance and religious solemnity.

Such was the artistic tradition Byzantium inherited. It conformed so perfectly to the Byzantine spirit that the artists of the Byzantine Empire were able to produce enduring masterpieces without ever departing far from its basic aesthetic canons. Majestic churches in the Byzantine style were graced with interiors that shone with glistening mosaics of Christ, the Virgin, saints, and various rulers, set off against backgrounds of shining gold. Hagia Sophia in Constantinople is the classic example; Figure 4.1 shows its majestic interior, and Color Illustration 2 shows how its rich mosaics emphasized Christ's divinity. Yet the continuing political influence of Byzantium in parts of the Italian peninsula also left its artistic mark on such churches as San Vitale in Ravenna. The mosaics there (see Color Illustration 2 and Figure 4.2) illustrate

Figure 4.1   *Interior of Hagia Sophia, Constantinople*   Notice how the windows that encircle the dome make it appear to float on air. Once a church and later a mosque, this magnificent building is now a museum.

how Byzantine art evoked imperial majesty and as well Christ's divinity. In these churches and others was an art vastly different from that of Greek antiquity, with different techniques and different goals, yet every bit as successful as the art of classical Athens.

In this new, visionary environment, Byzantine civilization developed unique expressions, but it remained Greek nonetheless. Most Byzantines spoke Greek as their primary language, and despite their deep commitment to the Christian faith, they never forgot their ancient Greek heritage. Indeed, their increasing dissociation from a Latin past is what most marks the slow transition from an Eastern Roman Empire to a Byzantine one. Even though the Byzantines never ceased to regard themselves as Romans and their state as the Roman Empire, Greek became the language of their imperial court. The Byzantine Church, guided by the emperor and the patriarch of Constantinople, gave no allegiance and little thought to the Roman pope. Byzantine scholars ignored their Latin to the point where they could no more be expected to read a Latin literary text than could a modern professor of business, journalism, or American history.

Latin literature fell by the wayside, but in Constantinople and other Byzantine cities, scholars long studied the poems, plays, speeches, and philosophic treatises of the ancient Greeks. Byzantine students, untrained in Latin, honed their skills with Homer, Demosthenes, and Plato. Students in the medieval West, untrained in Greek, read Virgil, Ovid, and Boethius. Study of the Bible was common to both traditions, but it was a Greek Bible in the East and Jerome's Latin Vulgate in the West. Divided by politics and religion, East and West also drifted apart in culture.

Figure 4.2   *The Emperor Justinian*   This mosaic from San Vitale in Ravenna shows Justinian, patron of the church, surrounded by his courtiers. Color Illustration 1 offers a close-up from the matching mosaic of Theodora and her courtiers. The frontal poses and large eyes are characteristic of Byzantine imperial art, and these features would be imitated in Ottonian art (see Figure 6.2).

✳ THE BYZANTINE CENTURIES

For its first half-millennium, the Byzantine Empire drew on the governmental traditions it had inherited from the later Roman Empire, on its Eastern Orthodox understanding of Christianity, and on the Greek culture of late antiquity. It saw great emperors and foolish ones, religious hatreds and Christian unity, many wars and occasional peace. Viewed from a distance—that is, from our perch in the medieval West—it also broadly went through two periods of greatness, with a great trough of decline in the middle.

The Age of Justinian, 527–565

The first creative surge of Byzantine civilization occurred during the reign of Justinian (r. 527–565). In many respects Justinian stands as the last of the Roman emperors. He and his court still conversed in the Latin tongue; he was driven by the vision of reviving the old Roman Empire by recovering its lost Western provinces; and it was under his direction that the vast heritage of Roman law was assembled into a single, coherent body of jurisprudence. Yet Justinian was as much a Byzantine as a Roman—and he would surely have perceived no distinction between them. His reign witnessed a golden age of Byzantine art and the full development of an imperial autocracy that would endure over the centuries that followed.

The achievements of Justinian's reign were products not only of his own determination and ambition but also of the wise and cautious rule of his predecessors, who endured the worst of the barbarian invasions, nurtured the financial resources of the Byzantine Empire, and gradually accumulated a sizable surplus in the treasury. Justinian was also fortunate that the successor states of the West, which he would determine to conquer, were losing some of their early vigor. Theodoric, king of the Ostrogoths (r. 493–526), died a year before Justinian ascended the Byzantine throne, and the Vandal kingdom of North Africa had grown disorganized and corrupt.

Lucky in his predecessors and his timing, Justinian was also aided immeasurably by his wife and co-ruler, Empress Theodora, a woman no less ambitious than he and even more resolute (see Biographical Sketch). Together, she and Justinian brought new energy and boldness to an old, conservative regime. The achievements of the Justinian Age are usually ascribed to Justinian himself, but since he consulted Theodora on all matters of policy, it is often impossible to distinguish her ideas from his. In any event, without Theodora's iron will in the face of riotous mobs who burned Constantinople in 532 and sought to depose her husband, Justinian's reign would have been a short and undistinguished one. But they survived, and their audacious policies shaped Byzantium—and the West too—in three particular ways.

First, after the riots of 532, Justinian and Theodora devoted immense funds to rebuilding Constantinople on an unprecedented scale. The most notable product of this construction program was the church of Hagia Sophia ("Holy Wisdom"), one of Byzantium's foremost works of art: its interior shone with gold, silver, ivory, and dazzling mosaics, and its vast dome seemed almost to float on air (as shown in Figure 4.1). The total effect was such as to stun even Justinian; he is said to have exclaimed on its completion, "Glory to God who has thought me worthy to finish this work. Solomon, I have outdone you!"[2]

Second, at Justinian's bidding, a talented group of lawyers set about to codify the untidy mass of legal precedents, juridical opinions, and imperial edicts that then constituted Roman law. They arranged these materials in a systematic collection known in later centuries as the *Corpus Juris Civilis,* the "body of civil law." Justinian's *Corpus Juris Civilis* became the keystone of future Byzantine jurisprudence, and it also served as the vehicle in which Roman law returned to Western Europe in the late eleventh century. At that time, as we shall see in Chapters 10 and 12, the *Corpus Juris Civilis* presented a challenging alternative to centuries-old legal practices that had grown from the barbarian law codes, and from this alternative would develop more systematic legal systems in the European states. But the importance of the *Corpus Juris Civilis* extended even beyond this. Roman law had formerly contained strong elements of popular sovereignty, but in Justinian's hands it acquired some of the autocratic flavor of the Byzantine state. Thus, in the late medieval and early modern West, the *Corpus Juris Civilis* tended to support the rise of royal absolutism, acting as a counterpoise to notions of limited monarchy that especially drew on barbarian legal traditions. Many monarchs in late

---

[2] Unlike the temple of Solomon, Hagia Sophia still stands, although it is now a museum.

BIOGRAPHICAL SKETCH

Empress Theodora (500–548)

Born the daughter of a bear trainer, Theodora died an empress in whose presence everyone—save her husband—had to show their reverence by throwing themselves face down on the floor. In between, Theodora worked as an actress and prostitute, bore at least one illegitimate child, and participated in one of the most remarkable marriages in history. Most of the details of her life come to us filtered through the unfriendly eyes of the historian Procopius (c. 500–562), who reserved an entire chapter of his *Secret History* for what he called "The Crimes of Theodora." Yet, if we dig beneath his nasty rumors and innuendo, we find an extraordinary woman who lived an extraordinary life.

Although raised in poverty, Theodora had three advantages—beauty, brains, and ambition. With her two sisters, she was sent as a young girl into the hippodrome of Constantinople, where citizens were entertained by chariot races, wild animal shows, acrobatic feats, theater, and even political rivalries. Like modern football teams, racing squads in the hippodrome were supported by their own factions, and the principal two factions—the Greens and the Blues—enjoyed such fanatical support that they developed into quasi-political parties.

The hippodrome mingled pornography and prostitution with more legitimate entertainment, and this licentious atmosphere was the unmaking of many young girls and boys. But Theodora prospered, especially, if Procopius is to be believed, by putting her sexual skills to good use. On her way up, she offered herself as a prostitute to paying clients and became the mistress of at least one powerful man. Eventually, she achieved enough prominence to meet Justinian, then the heir apparent to the imperial throne. The attraction between them was immediate, deep, and long-lasting. When they married, she was only 20 years old and he was about 35. For more than two decades, their dynamic partnership reshaped the Eastern Empire and redrew its boundaries.

Theodora exercised behind-the-throne power, but her influence over Justinian was strong. It can be especially seen in his legislation on women's issues, in his religious policies, and in their charities, which included a home for reformed prostitutes. Her moment of greatest glory came early in Justinian's reign during the Nika riots of January 532. Angered by a series of political missteps and demoralized by cold damp weather, the Blues and Greens put aside their rivalries and formed a coalition against Justinian. They rampaged through the streets of the city, shouting "Nika," or "Victory." (Yes, this is the same word from which the modern shoe company takes its name.) For several days and nights, the city literally burned. When neither troops nor political concessions quelled the disturbances, Justinian tried to speak from the imperial box in the hippodrome. His words were drowned out by the cries of the angry mob.

In a panic, Justinian made preparations to flee the city, but Theodora stopped him in his tracks. First, she scolded him by noting that she, a woman, was now forced to be more daring than men. Then, she firmly stated her position: death with imperial dignity was preferable to safety in exile. As she put it, *she* fully intended to be buried in a purple shroud (purple cloth was reserved for members of the imperial family). Her words—and her apparent unwillingness to join Justinian in his flight—turned the tide. Justinian stayed in Constantinople, the rioters were suppressed, and Constantinople was rebuilt.

Theodora and Justinian did not always agree. Justinian embraced the orthodox view that Christ combined human and divine natures in one person, whereas Theodora ardently

Continued

BIOGRAPHICAL SKETCH

Empress Theodora (500–548)   *Continued*

supported the Monophysite emphasis on the divinity of Jesus. Justinian relied heavily on the advice of his friend John the Cappadocian (c. 500–550); Theodora constantly worked to undermine John's influence. But their disagreements seemed only to strengthen their marriage. After Theodora died of cancer in 548, the wind went out of Justinian's sails. He never remarried; "by the name of Theodora" became his most solemn oath; and even many years later, he would halt a huge victory parade to pause, while all of Constantinople waited, for a moment of prayer and reflection before Theodora's tomb.

medieval and early modern Europe found much to admire in Justinian's precept that the emperor's decree should be unquestioned law.

Third, Justinian, keenly sensitive to the Roman imperial tradition, could not rest until he made an all-out attempt to recover the lost provinces of the West and reestablish imperial authority in the city of Rome. His armies, small but led by brilliant generals, conquered the strife-torn Vandal kingdom of North Africa with ease in 533–534 and also succeeded in wresting a long strip of the Iberian coast from the Visigoths. For twenty years his troops struggled against the Ostrogoths in the Italian peninsula, crushing them at length in 555 but only after enormous effort and expense. The Italian campaigns, known as the Gothic Wars, ravaged the peninsula and left Rome itself in ruins. The Visigothic sack of 410 was a mere puff of smoke compared with the havoc wrought by Justinian's armies. Yet for a time, Justinian succeeded in bringing almost all the Mediterranean coastline under the domination of his "Roman" authority. For a few glorious years, the Mediterranean was again a Roman sea.

The final years of Justinian's reign were less happy. Theodora died in 548, leaving Justinian demoralized and irresolute. The Gothic Wars so drained the treasury that the Byzantine Empire ended up bankrupt. The so-called Perpetual Peace that Justinian had arranged with Persia (at the cost to him of some 11,000 pounds of gold) ended in 540 with renewed war—and a series of Byzantine losses—in Syria. A devastating outbreak of plague swept across Byzantium and Western Europe in 541–543, taking a fearful toll of human lives and crippling the Byzantine economy. Worst of all, Justinian found it difficult to hold onto his newly reunited Empire. With his military attention focused westward, Justinian could not prevent a great flood of Slavs and Bulgars from moving into the Balkans. In 561, the Avars, warlike nomads from the Asian steppes, settled on the Danube shore and proceeded to subjugate the Slavs and Bulgars. Byzantium now found itself living in the shadow of a hostile Avar state and an expanding Persian empire, forces far more threatening than Vandal North Africa or Ostrogothic Italy.

Retrenchment, c. 570–850

Justinian's western conquests did not long endure. In 568, just three years after Justinian's death, a barbarian tribe known as the Lombards (Langobards, or "Long

Beards") burst into the Italian peninsula, further devastating that tormented land and carving out an extensive northern kingdom centered on the Po Valley and known ever since as Lombardy. Byzantium retained much of the southern Italian peninsula and clung to Ravenna and other cities along the Adriatic coast, but its hold on the Italian peninsula was appreciably loosened. Shortly afterward, the Visigoths reconquered Byzantine territories in southern Iberia, and eventually, in the 690s, Byzantine North Africa—the former Vandal state—fell to the Muslims. Then, in 751 the Lombards seized Ravenna, reducing still further the Byzantine presence in the Italian peninsula. Thereafter, all the Byzantines could claim of the old Western Empire was a small foothold along the southern Italian coast.

Justinian's successors had no choice but to abandon his ambitious dream of a reunified Empire. Facing hostile peoples to the immediate north and east, they were forced to turn their backs on more distant and less worrisome threats in the West. The Persian Empire pressed dangerously against Byzantium's eastern frontier, and the Avars with their Bulgar and Slavic subjects won control over most of the Balkans. By the early 600s, Persian armies occupied Syria, Palestine, and Egypt, and in 626, Constantinople itself just barely survived a furious combined siege of Persians and Avars.

In the midst of these crises, a great emperor came forward to defend Byzantium's borders. In the 620s, the Emperor Heraclius (r. 610–641) succeeded in reestablishing imperial control over the Balkans and so crushed the Persian army that he reclaimed all the lands that had once been lost. He even recovered from the Persians what was alleged to be the True Cross on which Jesus had been crucified—the holiest of all Christian relics. Had time stopped at that moment, Heraclius would have been the great hero of Byzantine history.

But no sooner had Heraclius defeated the Persians when Arab armies, united and inspired by Islam, raced across the Middle East, wresting Syria, Palestine, and Egypt from the Byzantines. These forces dealt a devastating blow to Byzantium in the seventh and eighth centuries, even putting Constantinople itself in peril. Muslims besieged the city on several occasions, most determinedly in 717–718, at which time the dogged defense of the Byzantines may have prevented not only their Empire but also much of eastern and central Europe from being absorbed into Islam and the Umayyad Empire. The shield provided by Constantinople's walls even aided the Christian kingdoms of the West in their struggles against Islamic armies. Yet, although Constantinople withstood the powerful northward thrust of Islam, the Byzantine Empire was much reduced. By 800, the Byzantines retained only Constantinople, Asia Minor, and an unsteady overlordship in parts of the Balkans and the Italian peninsula.

In short, Byzantium survived, but just barely. As it shrank in size, it also changed in character. In the course of the seventh and eighth centuries, in Asia Minor and the Balkans alike, the cities of the Byzantine Empire declined and disappeared. With their security and trade threatened by the constant movement of armies, many cities were either abandoned or converted into fortified villages. Even in Athens, the populace withdrew to the fortified acropolis—literally, the "hill town." Other major urban centers—such as Damascus, Alexandria, Antioch, and Carthage—fell to the Arabs and were lost to Byzantium. By 800, the Byzantine Empire was far smaller and poorer, yet more homogeneous, more unified in religion and culture, and more tightly centered on Constantinople, the one great city remaining in what otherwise was now a largely agrarian civilization.

The Macedonian Revival, c. 850–1050

Yet the highpoint of Byzantine civilization was yet to come. In the middle of the ninth century, a peasant boy transformed himself from stable-hand to emperor (murdering his predecessor on the way), and as Basil I (r. 867–886), he created a dynasty that would expand once more the territories of Byzantium and in the process, would revitalize imperial cities, support a rich literary and artistic revival, and convert many Slavs to Eastern Orthodox Christianity. Basil's dynasty was misnamed "Macedonian" because Basil had been imprisoned as a child in an area north of the Danube that was itself misnamed Macedonia because so many of the prisoners held there were Macedonians. One mistake led to another, and the label has stuck.[3] Basil himself was Armenian, with not a drop of Macedonian blood.

The Macedonian emperors reconquered northern Syria for a time and expanded their northeastern frontiers in Asia Minor. But their most significant military accomplishment, in the long run, was the establishment of firm Byzantine rule over the Balkan Slavs and Bulgars (see Map 4.1). The most celebrated ruler of the dynasty, Basil II, "the Bulgar-Slayer" (r. 976–1025), campaigned year after year in the Balkans, demolishing a Bulgarian army in 1014 and eventually crushing all resistance to Byzantine imperial authority.

Perhaps the greatest story of the Macedonian revival, however, is a story of conversion. In the middle years of the ninth century, Byzantine missionaries—especially St. Cyril (c. 826–869) and his brother St. Methodius (c. 815–884), "the Apostles to the Slavs"—evangelized tirelessly among the western and southern Slavs, spearheading the conversion of large portions of the Balkans to Eastern Orthodox Christianity. (Other Balkan and East European peoples—Hungarians and Poles, for example—converted to Catholic Christianity, which was being introduced just then by missionaries from the West.) In the later ninth century, the first Slavonic alphabet was developed by Byzantine missionaries—reputedly by Cyril and Methodius themselves—for the purpose of creating a Slavic vernacular Bible and liturgy. Thus the Slavonic written language and Slavonic Christianity came into being side by side.

The conversion of the Russian states came next. When Kiev (now the capital of Ukraine) formed the nucleus of the new state of Kievan Rus in the tenth century, the Macedonian emperors in Constantinople were careful to develop warm diplomatic relations—not only in the interest of trade and peace, but also to promote Eastern Orthodox Christianity. The latter proved easy to accomplish. One chronicle reports that Vladimir I (r. 980–1015) sought out a monotheistic faith that might help to unify the tribes under his command. He rejected Islam because, among other things, it prohibited the drinking of alcohol. He rejected Judaism because he could not understand how a chosen people could not have a country of their own. He rejected Catholic Christianity because its churches seemed drab and uninspiring. And then, when his emissaries to Constantinople reported that as they entered Hagia Sophia they "knew not whether we were in heaven or on earth," Vladimir knew he had found the religion for his young state. His conversion was accomplished by marriage, but, in this case, the Christian wife

---

[3] Even today "Macedonia" is a disputed term. In describing a *geographical* area, the term covers the south-central Balkans, including territories in Greece, Bulgaria, and the Republic of Macedonia. In describing a *political* unit, the term designates both the Republic of Macedonia (an independent state along Greece's northwestern border) and a province of Macedonia within Greece.

was an unwilling agent of "domestic proselytization." When Basil the Bulgar-Slayer proposed to marry his own sister Anna to Prince Vladimir of Kiev, she retorted that she would rather die than go through with the marriage. But she eventually had to give in, and as part of the deal, Vladimir agreed to adopt Christianity. His people quickly did the same. Neither Vladimir I nor his successors ever submitted politically to the Byzantine emperors, but the Russian princes and their people became spiritual subjects of the Eastern Orthodox Church. For his part, Basil got 6,000 soldiers to help him against the Bulgars.

Ultimately, the evangelism of the Macedonian age brought much of the Balkans and Eastern Europe into the Eastern Orthodox Church and hence into the sphere of Byzantine influence. The enduring effects of this process are exemplified by the alphabet used to this day in portions of the Balkan peninsula and throughout Russia and Ukraine; it is known as the "Cyrillic alphabet," after St. Cyril.

Byzantine civilization contributed much to the medieval West: Roman law, Greek texts, Christian alliance (and sometimes, misunderstanding), and maritime trade that stimulated the economic awakening of such Western commercial centers such as Venice, Genoa, and Pisa. For medieval Europe, Byzantium was a military bastion, a cultural treasure chest, and a fairly reliable ally. But it was on the Slavic peoples of Eastern Europe that Byzantine culture would leave its deepest imprint. There, Eastern Orthodox Christianity remains a powerful force to this day, and memories of Byzantium—good and bad—still linger.

✸ The Ascent of Islam

The remarkable story of Islamic expansion has roots in a compelling religion that was born in seventh-century Arabia and then spread outward with remarkable speed. It carried to the Mediterranean not only a new faith but also a distinctive Arabic culture. In the first hundred years of its existence, the faith of Islam shattered Christianity's hold over the Mediterranean basin, and soldiers of Islam annexed the Persian Empire, expanded far into southern Asia, seized Byzantium's richest provinces, and conquered Visigothic Iberia. Islamic armies claimed as their own significant parts of the old Roman Empire, east as well as west, but they also conquered places that Roman soldiers had seen but never vanquished. Today, the influence of Islam is, like modern Christianity, worldwide. Its areas of strongest influence extend from North Africa and parts of the Balkans, through the Middle East, southwest Asia and Pakistan, to Indonesia and the Philippines.

The Islamic conquest of Iberia was especially important for the medieval West, as it brought Islam to its very doorstep. When the Muslim general Tariq crossed from Africa to Iberia in 711, he began a process that would soon establish an Islamic state of al-Andalus in a land over which Visigothic kings had once ruled.[4] For three centuries, al-Andalus, an Islamic state, flourished in Europe's southwestern peninsula. In the eleventh century, al-Andalus broke into smaller principalities, each thereafter vulnerable to annexation by Christian warriors engaged in a process they termed "reconquest."

---

[4] Tariq also gave his name to the massive rock in the straits between Europe and Africa: Gibraltar, or Gib al-Tariq, Mount Tariq.

TIMELINE 4.2   Islam to 1000

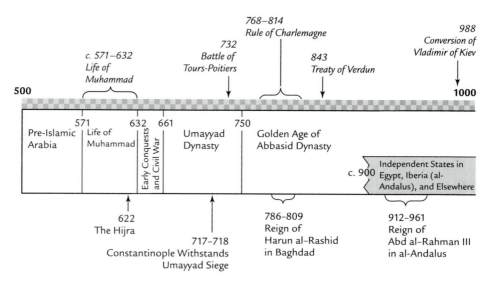

But it was not until the very end of the fifteenth century that Granada, the last Islamic state in Iberia, fell to Christian armies.

Like Byzantium, Islam has a rich history separate from that of medieval Europe (see Timeline 4.2), a history that merits our attention here for its influences over the medieval West. In some ways, Islamic contacts with the West paralleled those of Byzantium: war and diplomacy, religious competition, trade, and preservation of ancient manuscripts. But Islam brought much more than these to medieval Europe and, indeed, to Byzantium. Along with the power of Islamic faith and the might of its soldiers came new technologies, new crops, new products, and new ideas. This inheritance is heard today in the Arabic roots of such common English words as tariff, check, sugar, bazaar, arsenal, orange, apricot, artichoke, zero, and algebra. It would so critically shape medieval society from the eleventh century that it is possible to describe Islam as *the* force in the "awakening" of Europe with "the prince, a speaker of Arabic, bestowing the kiss of delivery from centuries of deep sleep." We will not go so far, but there is no doubt that medieval Europe was deeply challenged and enriched by its Islamic neighbors.

Arabia and Muhammad (c. 571–632)

Arabia was not a new force in the Mediterranean. Many empire-builders of the ancient Near East had come originally from the Arabian peninsula: the Amorites, the Chaldeans, the Canaanites, even the Hebrews. Situated at a critical juncture between Europe and Asia, Arabia had long been crossed by trade routes and cities, and, in the time just before Muhammad's birth, some Arabian tribes in the north of the peninsula had allied themselves with Rome or Persia.

In Muhammad's time, most Arabs were nomadic Bedouins, but others lived in cities, where they supported themselves by industry or trade. Although these cities challenged some old ways, both city-dwellers and nomads were polytheistic and revered tribal deities. The greatest trade route then ran between the Mediterranean and southern Arabia, and the greatest city along this route, Mecca, was a bustling commercial center that sent its own caravans northward and southward and grew wealthy from their profits. It was in Mecca, around the year 571, that the prophet Muhammad was born.

A member of a lesser branch of one of Mecca's leading clans, Muhammad grew up in the very center of Arabian life and culture. To his north lay the Mediterranean, a world of enduring Roman influence in the East and wavering recovery from Rome's decline in the West. In 571, Emperor Justinian had been dead for six years; the man who would eventually become Pope Gregory I was just about to turn 30; and St. Columban had not yet traversed his mother's body on his way out of Ireland.

As a young man, Muhammad managed the camel caravans of a wealthy widow named Khadija (see Biographical Sketch on p. 84). Through his travels and perhaps also his contacts with Jewish and Christian communities in Mecca itself, he encountered at least three of the most prominent religions of his day: Judaism, Christianity, and Zoroastrianism (a highly sophisticated dualist faith from Persia that emphasizes a cosmic battle between good and evil). A respected man with a powerful personality, Muhammad eventually married Khadija. She offered him unwavering support when he underwent, in his late thirties, a prophetic experience.

Muhammad's revelations first began when he was on spiritual retreat in the countryside, and they continued thereafter. In these visions, the angel Gabriel recited to Muhammad the words of a single, almighty God, known in Arabic as Allah. These recitations were, Muhammad taught, the ultimate revelation of divine truth, completing earlier revelations received by such prophets as Moses and Jesus. *Islam*, an Arabic word that means "submission" or "surrender," described Muhammad's new faith, for he taught his followers to submit to the will of God. They came to be known as *Muslims*, or "those who surrender."

When Muhammad began to preach about his revelations, he found little support in Mecca, apart from his wife, his relatives, and a few humble converts. The ruling merchants of Mecca ignored or rejected his teachings, partly because of its egalitarian bent and partly because they feared the new religion would discredit the chief Meccan temple, the *Kaaba,* a profitable center of pilgrimage. History would prove this latter concern to be a staggering miscalculation, but in the meantime, their hostility forced Muhammad and his supporters to flee Mecca in 622 and settle in the town of Medina, 280 miles northward on the caravan route.

The flight to Medina, known as the *Hijra,* was such a momentous turning point in the development of Islam that it marks the beginning of the Muslim calendar. At Medina, Muhammad achieved a fusion of religion and politics that became basic to his new faith, for, as Muhammad won the inhabitants of Medina to Islam, he also assumed political leadership of the city. This made sense for at least two reasons. First, since his teachings defined not only religious belief but also the nature of a just society, religion and government were indistinguishable. Second, because submission to God required submission to his messenger, Muhammad was logically both a religious and a political leader. By thus merging religious and civil authority, Muhammad built a sacred state in Medina. He also provided a model of religious governance that would be copied by many great Islamic states in later years.

Biographical Sketch

Khadija (555–619) and Aisha (614–678)

Muhammad married at least a dozen women, but two of them played especially important roles in the early development of Islam.

Khadija, Muhammad's first wife, was a well-off and well-connected widow who had employed Muhammad to manage her caravan between Mecca and Syria. When she was 40 and he was 25, she proposed marriage. He accepted, and she remained his only wife until her death some 25 years later. Her unwavering support—financial, social, and emotional—was critical in Muhammad's development as a religious leader. When he came home dazed from his first revelation, she wrapped him in a blanket, assured him that he was not mad, and arranged for others to hear his story. Khadija was Muhammad's first convert, and when few others stood by him, she stood firm. Her death in 619 so seriously weakened Muhammad's position in Mecca that within a few years he was forced into exile in Medina.

Aisha (c. 614–678), usually remembered as Muhammad's favorite wife, was born into a family already faithful to Islam. About ten years old when she married Muhammad, she lived with his other wives in an environment that increasingly stressed that they were "not like any other women." As "Mothers of the Believers," they were enjoined to be especially pious, to "stay in your houses," and to be approached by others only from "behind a curtain." As was appropriate for Aisha's age, her marriage was not consummated for several years; just a few years thereafter, when she was 18, Muhammad died. Aisha lived as a widow for another four decades, and she actively participated in the civil wars of 655–661. At the Battle of the Camel, she even took to the field, urging on troops by placing her own life in jeopardy.

Historians have long debated how we might best understand the lives of Khadija, Aisha, and other women in early Islam. To some, Khadija, the widow who boldly proposed marriage, exemplifies how powerful Arab women had been before Islam, and Aisha, married young, secluded, and veiled, shows how Islam lowered the status of her sex. Others take the opposite view, arguing that Khadija grew up in a male-dominated society, whereas Aisha was protected by the new laws of Islam (which, for example, limited polygyny to four wives and then, only if a husband could treat all four equally). And still others say "comme si, comme ça," stressing that there is strong evidence of gender asymmetry in Arabia, both before and after the teachings of Muhammad. Similar debates enliven the histories of other religions, as, for example, in discussions about early Christianity or the Protestant Reformation. Although debates of this sort will likely never reach any grand resolution, they greatly advance research—in this case, into gender issues as reflected in Islamic law, in early chronicles, and in the first biographies of Islam.

In the meantime, Khadija, Aisha, and Fatima—the only child of Muhammad who had children—stand at the very beginning of Islamic history. They do not stand alone. More than 1,200 women are recorded as knowing Muhammad and working for his cause. They are among those privileged to be remembered as "Companions of the Prophet."

Under Muhammad's guidance, Medina made war on Mecca, raiding its caravans and blockading its trade until, in 630, Mecca was incorporated into Islam. During the two remaining years of his life, Muhammad, by then an almost legendary figure in Arabia, received the voluntary submission of many tribes in the peninsula. By the time of his death in 632, he had united Arabs as never before into a coherent political-religious group, well organized, well armed, and inspired by a powerful new monotheistic religion.

Islam

Islam, the cement with which Muhammad unified Arabia, was a faith extensively supported by written texts. Muslims were relatively tolerant toward Jews and Christians, whom Muhammad and his followers recognized as "peoples of the book" (see Color Illustration 4). But Muslims also had a book of their own, the *Quran*, which superseded its Jewish and Christian predecessors and was believed to contain the pure essence of divine revelation. The Quran contains Muhammad's revelations, the bedrock of the Islamic faith. Muslims regard it as the word of God, recited to Muhammad by the angel Gabriel from an original in heaven. Accordingly, its divine authority extends not only to its precepts but also to its every letter (of which there are 323,621). In strictest terms, even translation is not allowed, for it is best read in its original Arabic. As a result, as Islam spread, the Arabic language spread with it.

The supreme authority not only in religion but also in law, science, and the humanities, the Quran became the standard text in Muslim schools for every imaginable subject. It was also the text from which non-Arab Muslims learned their Arabic. But it was soon joined by *hadiths,* stories about the activities and sayings of Muhammad. These narratives circulated orally for several generations, but they were eventually gathered into several collections known collectively as the *Hadith.* The Hadith lacks the divine authority of the Quran—Muhammad, after all, taught he was a prophet, not divine himself—but it usefully supplemented the teachings of the Quran.

Muhammad offered his followers a straightforward faith that assured eternal salvation to those who led upright, sober lives and followed the five *pillars of Islam:* the simple declaration of faith that "There is no God but God, and Muhammad is his messenger"; prayers five times a day; fasting during the daylight hours of the month of Ramadan; charity toward the needy; and pilgrimage to Mecca, if possible. Followers were also asked to work devoutly toward the welfare and expansion of the sacred community, a responsibility that came to involve *greater jihad* (the internal struggle to become a better Muslim) and *lesser jihad* (the external struggle against the disbelief of others). Lesser jihad sometimes resulted in what Westerners called "holy wars," but these also drew on customs of tribal raiding in pre-Islamic Arabia.

Following Muhammad's example in Medina, public law in Islamic lands had religious sanction, and the fusion of religion and politics remained fundamental to Islam. In practice, religious authority often rested with Muslim scholars and the traditions they collectively articulated. But in theory, there was no division between secular and religious authority, and Muhammad's political successors, the caliphs (Arabic for "successors") were to guard both the faith and the faithful. The tension between church and state that troubled and enlivened medieval Europe was thus muted in the Muslim world, as it also was in Byzantium.

✹ THE ISLAMIC EMPIRE

The Early Conquests: 632–655

Immediately after Muhammad's death in 632, the military prowess of the Arab tribes, long honed by inter-tribal conflicts and now harnessed by the teachings of the Prophet, became abundantly evident to the Mediterranean world (see Map 4.2). Their spectacular conquests resulted in part from the youthful vigor of Islam and in part from the

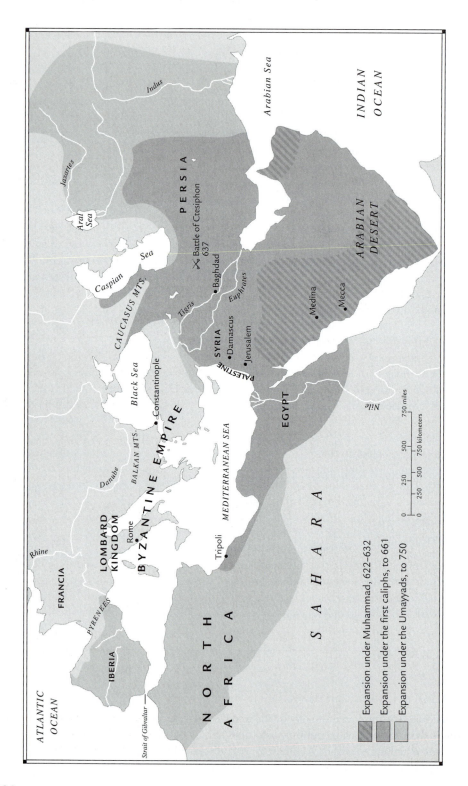

ATLANTIC
OCEAN

FRANCIA

Rhine

PYRENEES

IBERIA

Strait of Gibraltar

N O R T H
A F R I C A

S A H A R A

Tripoli

Rome

LOMBARD
KINGDOM

B Y Z A N T I N E   E M P I R E

MEDITERRANEAN SEA

Danube

BALKAN MTS.

Black Sea

Constantinople

Caspian
Sea

CAUCASUS MTS.

Aral
Sea

Jaxartes

Indus

P E R S I A

Battle of Ctesiphon
637

Baghdad

Tigris

Euphrates

SYRIA

•Damascus
•Jerusalem

PALESTINE

EGYPT

Nile

Medina

Mecca

A R A B I A N
D E S E R T

Arabian Sea

INDIAN
OCEAN

0   250   500   750 miles

0   250   500   750 kilometers

Expansion under Muhammad, 622–632

Expansion under the first caliphs, to 661

Expansion under the Umayyads, to 750

weakness of its enemies. When Arab armies appeared on their borders, the Persian and Byzantine Empires had just concluded a long, desperate conflict that left both powers exhausted. Furthermore, the Byzantine government had so mistreated the Monophysite Christians of Syria and Egypt that they seem to have welcomed new, more tolerant governors.

As Arabs entered these tired, embittered lands, their conquests were driven by momentum, not master planning. Most of the early campaigns began as plundering expeditions aimed at the wealth of Byzantium and Persia, but with each victory the pace grew. Striking into Syria (an area much larger than the modern-day state of the same name), the Arabs annihilated a huge army in 636, captured Damascus and Jerusalem, and by 640 had detached the region more or less permanently from Byzantine control. In 637 they inflicted an overwhelming defeat on the army of the Persian Empire and entered the capital of Ctesiphon, gazing in wonder at the opulence of that great city. Within another decade, they had subdued all Persia. Eventually most Persians would accept the new faith, abandoning Zoroaster for Muhammad, while nevertheless retaining much of their native culture and language. In later years, Muslim armies penetrated deeply into the Indian subcontinent and laid the religious foundations of such modern Muslim states as Pakistan and Bangladesh.

Meanwhile, other Arab armies were pushing westward toward Egypt. In the 640s, they captured Alexandria, the great metropolis that had for centuries been a center of Hellenistic science, and, later, Jewish and Christian theology. With Egypt and Syria in their hands, Arabs then took to the sea, where they proved to be extraordinary sailors. They captured the island of Cyprus and raided ancient Rhodes; then, in 655, they destroyed the Byzantine navy in a sea battle so devastating that the emperor escaped only by trading clothes with one of his men.

Civil War: 655–661

In that same year, expansion ceased momentarily when a dynastic struggle transfixed Islam. The succession to the religious and political authority of the caliphate was contested between the Umayyads, a leading family in the old Meccan commercial elite, and Ali (d. 661), the cousin and son-in-law of Muhammad himself. Ali's followers insisted that the leader of the Islamic community must be a direct descendant of the Prophet. As it happened, Muhammad had only one surviving child who had issue, a daughter Fatima (d. 633), who had married Ali. His Umayyad opponents included a widow of Muhammad named Aisha (see biographical sketch), who in 656 rode a camel into battle to rally troops against Ali's forces. The battle has henceforth been known as "The Battle of the Camel."

By 661, Ali had lost considerable support, and he was assassinated. This cleared the way for the establishment of the Umayyad dynasty. The Umayyad caliphs moved the Islamic capital to Damascus and ruled there for nearly a century. But the legitimist

◄**Map 4.2**   *The Islamic Empire, c. 750*   In little more than 100 years, Islam embraced most of Spain, all of North Africa, all of Arabia, and much of the Near East. By 750, where Visigoths, Vandals, Byzantines, and Persians had once ruled, the Umayyad caliphate reigned supreme from its capital in Damascus.

faction that had once supported Ali persisted as a dedicated minority, throwing its support behind various descendants of Ali and Fatima. In time, this movement evolved into a distinctive form of Islam known as Shi'ism, which held that the true caliphs—the descendants of Muhammad through Fatima and Ali—were sinless, infallible, and possessed of a body of secret knowledge hidden in the Quran. In these beliefs, Shi'i Muslims were distinct from the majority of Muslims, the Sunnis, who based their faith firmly on the Quran and the practices of the Prophet. In their opposition to the Sunni majority, Shi'is occasionally mounted civil uprisings. In the tenth century, they gained control of Egypt and established a Fatimid dynasty of caliphs in Cairo. In various forms, Shi'i Islam survives to this day. It is, for example, the doctrine of most Muslims in Iran.

The Umayyad Dynasty: 661–750

Umayyad victory over Ali in 661 left the old Arabian aristocracy in firm control, with a new capital in Damascus. They next aimed at Constantinople, but the Byzantine capital repulsed a series of powerful attacks between 670 and 680. Constantinople's defense was aided by a secret weapon known as "Greek fire," a liquid containing quicklime that ignited on contact with water and could be extinguished only by vinegar or sand. In 717–718 a combined Arab fleet and army launched a new assault, but it also failed; thereafter, the Umayyads abandoned their effort to take the city. Byzantium survived as an Orthodox Christian city for another seven centuries, effectively barring Muslim inroads into southeastern Europe until the Later Middle Ages.

In the meantime, Muslim armies were enjoying spectacular success in North Africa. They took the old Vandal kingdom, by then ruled from distant Byzantium. And in 711 they crossed the Strait of Gibraltar into Iberia and crushed the Visigothic kingdom at a blow, bringing its Jewish and Christian populations under their dominion, driving its Christian aristocracy into mountain hideaways in the Pyrenees, and eventually creating the Muslim state of al-Andalus. They next threatened the kingdom of the Merovingian Franks, but their advance northward came to an abrupt halt in 732. Exactly a century after the Prophet's death, an Arab raiding party was turned back on a battlefield between Tours and Poitiers by a Christian army led by the Frankish leader Charles Martel (r. 714–741). The Arabs whom Charles Martel defeated had intended to loot the shrine of St. Martin of Tours, and their army was small and makeshift in comparison with the great force that had besieged Constantinople in 717–718. But taken together, the defeats at Tours-Poitiers and Constantinople brought an end to the Arab advance into the old Roman Empire. By 750, Muslims held more than half of the territory once governed by Rome, but their expansion was over.

Converts and *Dhimmi*

Although their conquests were driven partly by religious zeal, Muslims did not seek converts to their new faith. In fact, the earliest generations regarded Islam as a religion for Arabs only, and people of other monotheistic faiths—especially Christians and Jews—were allowed to practice their religions unmolested. Yet in Syria, Egypt, and North Africa—areas that boasted some of the earliest and best-organized Christian churches—many people converted within a few generations of the conquest. The same happened in al-Andalus. Some people might have converted to Islam for such practical reasons as to avoid the special taxes due from non-Muslims or to position themselves better in their new societies. But other converts accepted in heartfelt devotion the straightforward teachings and obligations of Islam.

Others, however, chose not to convert, and they continued in their old faiths. These non-Muslims—or *dhimmis*—acquired distinct status in most Muslim states. As long as they accepted the rule of Islam, paid special taxes, and did not attempt to proselytize among Muslims, their religious communities were tolerated. In many places, dhimmis even constituted the majority of the population. This was the case in al-Andalus, where Christians—known as *Mozarabs* because they adopted the dress, diet, and language of their Arab conquerors—predominated through the eleventh century. Jews also flourished in al-Andalus, where their numbers increased about threefold between 700 and 1000. In al-Andalus, Muslims ruled, but Christians and Jews lived in fairly peaceful concord with their rulers (and with each other, too).

The Golden Age of the Abbasids: 750–c. 950

In 750, eighteen years after the battle of Tours, the Umayyads were overthrown. Their successors, the Abbasids (750–1258), were also of Arabian descent, but they were more interested in Asia than Arabia. They relied on Persian aristocrats in their government, and they even moved the capital of the caliphate from Damascus to Baghdad on the Tigris River, in the old Persian Empire. This move marked an eastward shift in Islam's political interests, a shift that relieved some of the pressure against both Constantinople and Francia. In 751 an Islamic army won a major victory over the Chinese at the battle of Talas in central Asia, and in later years Islam expanded deep into India and onward to the large offshore islands of Indonesia.

The rise of the Abbasids marks the end of the Arabian aristocracy's monopoly on political power within Islam. The new government at Baghdad was run by a medley of peoples. Arabic language united these people, but Arabs now shared power with Persians, Syrians, and others. As befitted their eastward turn, the Abbasid government drew heavily from the administrative traditions of Persia and, to a lesser degree, Byzantium. A sophisticated, complex bureaucracy worked from the capital at Baghdad, keeping in touch with the provinces through a multitude of tax gatherers, judges, couriers, and spies. Court ceremonies followed suit, emphasizing the awesome power of the caliphs in ways reminiscent of other Eastern empires. Persian and Byzantine customs also began to affect gender roles, as the Abbasids adopted a variety of customs—such as the seclusion of women in private quarters, and the covering of women behind veils and draperies—which had not hitherto been a general part of Islamic practice. Literature also reflected a merging of Arabic and Persian traditions (see Figure 4.3).

The status of peasants and unskilled laborers in the Abbasid caliphate was kept low by the competition of multitudes of slaves, many of them from sub-Saharan Africa. Although no more sensitive to social justice than other governments of its day, the Abbasids did make more land available for ordinary people by draining swamps and installing extensive irrigation works. They also sometimes allowed individuals of very humble origin to rise high in their service. As one disgruntled songwriter groaned, "Sons of concubines have become so numerous amongst us; Lead me, O God, lead me to a land where I shall see no bastards."

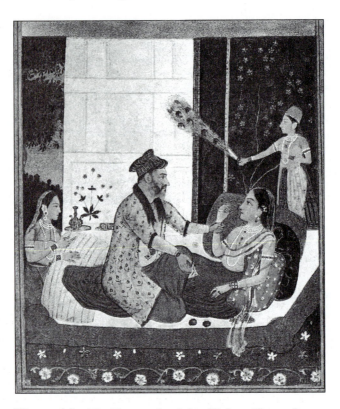

Figure 4.3   *The Thousand and One Nights*   These tales
were written down during the Abbasid caliphate, and they
combine the oral traditions of Arabia and Persia. This
illustration shows Scheherazade entertaining her royal husband
with her nightly tale.

Baghdad, under the early Abbasid caliphs, became one of the world's great cities.
It was the center of a commercial network that spread across Europe, Africa, and Asia.
Silks, spices, and fragrant woods flowed into its wharves from India, China, and
Indonesia; furs, honey, and slaves were imported from Scandinavia; and gold, slaves,
and ivory from sub-Saharan Africa. Baghdad was also the hub of a far-flung banking
system with branches in other cities across the Islamic world. A check could be written
in Baghdad and cashed in Morocco, 4,000 miles to the west. The Abbasid imperial
palace, occupying fully a third of the city, contained innumerable apartments and public
rooms, and a remarkable reception room known as the "hall of the tree," which
contained an artificial tree of gold and silver on whose branches mechanical birds
chirped and sang. (The Byzantine imperial throne room in Constantinople boasted a
similar contrivance.)

The culture of Baghdad reached its height under the Abbasid caliph Harun al-
Rashid (r. 786–809), whose opulence and power became legendary. Harun was accustomed to receiving tribute from the Byzantine Empire itself. When on one occasion the

tribute was discontinued, he sent the following peremptory note to the Emperor Nicephorus (r. 802–811) at Constantinople:

> In the name of Allah, the merciful, the compassionate.
> From Harun, the commander of the faithful,
> To Nicephorus, the dog of a Roman.
> In truth I have read your letter, O son of an infidel mother.
> As for the answer, it shall be for your eyes to see, not for your ears to hear.
> Goodbye.

What Nicephorus eventually saw was a Muslim army, and he soon resumed the customary tribute.

The era of Harun al-Rashid was notable, too, for its vigorous intellectual life. Scholars studied, synthesized, and surpassed the learned traditions of Greece, Rome, Persia, and India. In Baghdad, Harun's son and successor founded the House of Wisdom, a great intellectual institute that was at once a library, an institute of advanced study, and a center of translation. There, scholars of many faiths—Muslim, Christian, Jewish, and even pagan—pushed learning in new and exciting directions. At a time when Charlemagne was struggling to civilize his rustic, illiterate Franks, Harun reigned over a glittering Baghdad.

During these centuries, a mystical movement known as *Sufism* became immensely powerful within Islam. For centuries Sufi mystics, although never tightly coordinated, converted millions of people to Islam in Africa, India, Indonesia, central Asia, and China. And it was often they, rather than the religious scholars and lawyers of Sunni orthodoxy, who brought hope to the Muslim populace in times of trouble. Drawing from the Neoplatonic notion that only the divine is real, the Sufis sought mystical union with God, and they, therefore, stressed God's love over the Sunni emphasis on God's authority. Some Sunni scholars were influenced by Sufi mysticism, but many fought vigorously against it. By the tenth century, Sufism was the most powerful religious force among the people of Islam.[5]

Fragmentation after c. 950

Within a few generations of its founding in 750, the loosened structure of the Abbasid Empire began to unravel in the face of dynastic wars, religious conflicts, economic woes, and persistent localism. Even in the palmy days of Harun al-Rashid, the extreme western provinces—al-Andalus, Morocco, and Tunisia—were ruled by independent local dynasties. By the later ninth century the trend toward disintegration gained momentum as Egypt, Syria, and eastern Persia (Iran) severed ties with the government in Baghdad. As province after province broke free, the centralized power of the Abbasids became more notional than real.

Of these former provinces that developed into independent states, the most important for the medieval West would be the caliphates of Egypt and al-Andalus. Established in the tenth century, the Fatimid dynasty (r. 909–1171) drew its strength from Shi'i Islam, and as their name suggests, the Fatimids traced descent from Muhammad's

---

[5] The division between Sunni and Shi'i Muslims is strong and mutually exclusive, but the influence of Sufism transcends it—that is, Sufis can also be adherents of either Sunni Islam or Shi'i Islam.

daughter, Fatima. From their capital in Cairo, the Fatimids at times controlled not only Egypt but also most of North Africa, Sicily, and even Damascus. In Iberia, the first decades after Muslim conquest were chaotic, but in the 750s Abd al-Rahman (r. 756–788), a prince of the just-deposed Umayyad dynasty, established firm authority. He formally broke all ties with the Abbasid caliphate a few years later, and in 929, his descendants took the title "caliph" (as the Fatimids had also done just a few years earlier). Where there had once been a single caliph who oversaw the whole Muslim community, there were now several. Al-Andalus was an exceptionally diverse society, with many sorts of Muslim immigrants (especially Berbers from North Africa, Yemenis, and Syrians), a large indigenous Christian population, an indigenous Jewish minority, and even Slavs, who were brought as slaves in the tenth century to form the core of a new army. Al-Andalus particularly flourished during the long and competent reign of Abd al-Rahman III (r. 912–961), when his state was the most powerful in Western Europe and his capital of Cordoba its intellectual center (see Figure 4.4). Shortly after the year 1000, however, al-Andalus began to disintegrate into small princedoms, and the caliphate was formally abolished in 1031. In the centuries that followed, as we will see in Chapter 9, its Muslim principalities would be slowly swallowed by Christian conquerors.

Figure 4.4   *The Mosque at Cordoba*   Built in the tenth century, this stunning building rivals that of Hagia Sophia (see Figure 4.1).

MEDIEVAL MYTHS

The Flat Earth

Just about everyone has heard that medieval people thought the earth was flat, and that when Columbus sailed across the Atlantic in 1492, many predicted he and his crew would literally fall off the edge of the world. Not so. Ancient scientists had established the roundness of the earth and even estimated its circumference. Arabic astronomers went even further. Ahmad al-Farghani (who lived c. 850) estimated the diameter of the earth to be about 6,500 miles, and he levelheadedly pointed out that earth's roundness could be seen every time a ship's mast slowly disappeared in the distance. In the medieval West, natural philosophers—so-called because they studied nature—accepted these calculations and arguments. The Bible presented a bit of a challenge because some passages suggest that the earth is not round (see, for example, Psalm 104). But as early as the fourth century, St. Augustine was observing that the biblical evidence on this point was not definitive, especially because the earth's shape was not critical to salvation, and that, in any case, it certainly seemed reasonable to conclude that the earth was round. The Venerable Bede (673–735) described the earth as a globe; so too did Roger Bacon (1220–1292) and Thomas Aquinas (1225–1274), and by the last centuries of the Middle Ages, some natural philosophers were even postulating that the spherical earth rotated on an axis. Their ideas were not just abstract science; medieval monarchs held orbs—globes with crosses inscribed or added at the top—to show their authority over a Christian world (for an example, see Figure 6.2). So, why can you still read, even in some history books, that medieval people thought the earth was flat? Washington Irving is part of the problem, for he popularized the "flat earth myth" in the nineteenth century. And our prideful tendency to think of the Middle Ages—or any past time—as a relatively ignorant age compared to our own, more enlightened, time is another part. To find out more, look at this short, fascinating study by Jeffrey Burton Russell, *Inventing the Flat Earth: Columbus and Modern Historians* (1991).

As for the Abbasids themselves, they had become mere figureheads by 945, even in the city of Baghdad itself; they retained the title of caliph, but others ruled what was left of the Abbasid state under the title of *amir.* The future lay with the Seljuk Turks, a nomadic tribe that had converted to Islam in the 900s and whose chief in 1055 conquered Baghdad, assumed the title of *sultan,* and began to exercise effective power over the heartland of the old Abbasid Empire.

✳ ISLAMIC CULTURE

Although the Muslim world was only briefly united either politically or religiously, Islam provided a common culture and faith that united a great diversity of peoples in Europe, Africa, and Asia—Goths, Berbers, Egyptians, Syrians, Persians, Arabs, Turks, and many others. In the end, Europeans would often apply the term "Arab" to every Muslim from Iberia to Iraq, regardless of ethnicity, and Arabic was, as Latin had been before it, a language that spanned continents.

Muslim scholars proved remarkably adept at drawing from the legacies of the civilizations they conquered, while creating from them a new cultural synthesis that was uniquely their own. All across the Islamic world, from Cordoba to Baghdad and farther still to the east, scholars and artists borrowed, but never without digesting. Architects molded Greco-Roman forms into a graceful and distinctive new style. Philosophers elaborated on the writings of Plato and Aristotle, even in the face of hostility from orthodox Islamic theologians. Physicians built on the ancient medical doctrines of Galen and his Greek predecessors, describing new symptoms and identifying new curative drugs. Astronomers tightened the geocentric system of Ptolemy, prepared accurate tables of planetary motions, and gave the stars Arabic names that are used to this day—names such as Altair, Deneb, Alberio, Aldebaran, and (regrettably) Zubenelgenubi and Zubeneschamali. Mathematicians learned geometry and trigonometry from the Greeks, developed algebra from the Hindus, and appropriated from them the so-called Arabic numerals—the set of nine number symbols plus the zero—which would ultimately revolutionize European mathematics. Writers excelled in both poetry and prose, of which perhaps the best examples are the quatrains of the *Rubaiyat* written by Omar Khayyam (c. 1048–1123). And cities flourished as centers of simply brilliant cultural achievement. During the tenth century, for example, Cordoba, the capital of al-Andalus, had no rival in Western Europe in terms of population, wealth, or municipal organization. It was the wonder of the age—with its mansions, mosques, aqueducts, and baths, its bustling markets and shops, its efficient police force and sanitation service, its street lights, and its splendid sprawling palace flashing with brightly colored tiles and surrounded by minarets and sparkling fountains.

Legend has it that the Frankish monk Gerbert of Aurillac (c. 945–1003) traveled to Cordoba in the tenth century as part of his effort to learn mathematics and astronomy from Muslim scholars. He was the first of what would become a long stream of Christian scholars eager to benefit from Islamic learning. To them, Cordoba and other Muslim cities seemed to be, as one tenth-century nun put it, an "ornament bright" of learning. Although the monastic schools from which these Europeans came belie the notion of a deeply asleep Europe kissed awake by an Arabian prince, there is no doubt that the intellectual development of medieval Europe was profoundly stimulated by the richness of Islamic libraries and the wisdom of their scholars. When Gerbert returned to France, he seemed to his contemporaries to be armed with fearsome and almost supernatural knowledge. No wonder so many followed in his footsteps. They would bring back to Europe not only ancient texts preserved in Islamic libraries but also the works of Islamic scholars. The medical writings of Ibn Sina (980–1037), known to Europeans as Avicenna, became the most authoritative texts on the healing arts in medieval Europe, and the rationalist philosophy of Ibn Rushd (1126–1198), known as Averroes in Europe, laid the foundation for a school of intellectual thought in thirteenth-century Paris. But we are getting ahead of ourselves; we will return to this story of intellectual exchange in Chapter 12.

✸ CONCLUSION

By the mid-700s, Islam, Byzantium, and Western Christendom had divided the old Roman Empire among themselves, and despite later skirmishes, wars, and even exchanges of territories, the equilibrium of the eighth century would remain in balance for centuries to come. As we shall see in later chapters, the Crusades were an exception to this generalization, but ultimately only a minor one; the Christian reconquest of Iberia and the victory of the Seljuks over the Byzantines in Asia Minor were more important exceptions. But it would not be until the fourteenth century, when the Ottomans swept into the Balkans, that the balance of the three powers was upset altogether. In the interim, the three civilizations that succeeded Rome would tend to expand not at one another's expense but away from each other—Byzantium into the Balkans and Russia; Islam into south Asia; the medieval West into modern-day Germany, Scandinavia, Hungary, and Poland.

In the early centuries of this tense equilibrium among neighbors, there is no question that the successor states of the old Western Empire were bounded on east and south by more powerful and sophisticated civilizations. Like many neighbors, Westerners, Byzantines, and Muslims sometimes cooperated (especially in trade) and sometimes argued (especially over matters of religion). But Westerners were the weakest of the three, a neighbor who inspired more disdain than respect. To one tenth-century Arab geographer, this is how Europeans seemed:

> . . . their bodies are large, their natures gross, their manners harsh, their understanding dull, and their tongues heavy. Their color is so excessively white that they look blue . . . their hair is lank and reddish because of the damp mists. The farther they live to the north, the more they are stupid, gross and brutish.

Suggested Readings

Dionisius A. Agius and Richard Hitchcock, eds., *The Arab Influence in Medieval Europe* (1994). A collection of highly useful essays on trade, technology, literature, and culture.

Michael Angold, *Byzantium: The Bridge from Antiquity to the Middle Ages* (2001). A new summary by a distinguished scholar.

Guglielmo Cavallo, ed., *The Byzantines* (1997). Up-to-date essays on various aspects of Byzantine history.

Norman Daniel, *The Arabs and Medieval Europe* (2nd edition, 1979). A very useful survey. For a short, readable survey, try Richard Fletcher, *The Cross and the Crescent: Christianity and Islam from Muhammad to the Reformation* (2003).

Richard Fletcher, *Moorish Spain* (1992). A highly readable account running to the early seventeenth century. See also Bernard F. Reilly, *The Medieval Spains* (1993), and Roger Collins, *The Arab Conquest of Spain, 710–797* (2nd edition, 1994).

Lynda Garland, *Byzantine Empresses: Women and Power in Byzantium, A.D. 527–1204* (1999). Offers thorough studies of individual empresses. See also the texts in Alice-Mary Talbot, ed., *Holy Women of Byzantium: The Saints' Lives in English Translation* (1996).

Albert H. Hourani, *A History of the Arab Peoples* (rev. ed., 2002). Includes an outstanding account of medieval Islam. See also Hugh Kennedy, *The Prophet and the Age of the Caliphates* (2nd edition, 2003).

Nikki R. Keddie and Beth Baron, eds., *Women in Middle Eastern History* (1991). A useful collection of diverse interpretations, fully half related to medieval subjects.

John Meyendorff, *Byzantine Theology: Historical Trends and Doctrinal Themes* (2nd ed., 1979). A clear and concise survey of a complex subject.

Warren Treadgold, *A History of the Byzantine State and Society* (1997). See also Speros Vryonis, *Byzantium and Europe* (1967) for a short, well-illustrated interpretive survey.

SUGGESTED PRIMARY SOURCES

Olivia Remie Constable, ed., *Medieval Iberia: Readings from Christian, Muslim, and Jewish Sources* (1997). An eclectic and useful collection, with substantial sections on Muslim conquest and settlement.

Bernard Lewis, ed., *Islam, from the Prophet Muhammad to the Capture of Constantinople*, 2 vols. (1974). See also William H. McNeill and Marilyn Robinson. Waldman, eds., *The Islamic World* (1973).

Michael Anthony Sells, *Approaching the Qur'an: The Early Revelations* (1999). Provides explanations, translations, and recitations (on a CD) of 35 passages from the Quran.

CHAPTER 5

CAROLINGIAN EUROPE, c. 700-850

✸ INTRODUCTION

In the year 700, the Byzantine emperor controlled a large area that fanned out to the south of Constantinople, reaching as far west as Sardinia, passing east through the southern Balkans, then stretching over Asia Minor. Byzantium was a smaller and less prosperous empire than it had been 100 years earlier, but it still claimed impressive political and cultural power. In the year 700, the Umayyad dynasty was basking in the capture of Carthage two years earlier, and its soldiers were moving so quickly across the western reaches of North Africa that they would soon press into Iberia itself. The political and cultural power of Islam in 700 was not as impressive as it would be 100 years later, but it doubtless seemed impressive enough to the Berbers of North Africa.

The powers of Byzantium and Arabia in 700 dwarfed Francia and other successor states in the West. Constantinople and Damascus were great cities—centers of far-flung commerce, homes of superb libraries, and capitals of emperors who wielded as much centralized power as was possible in an age of poor communication and localized government. The Franks were an agrarian people who had no cities worth the name; they boasted just a few monastic libraries of any note (and these few were thanks more to the learning of Irish and Anglo-Saxon exiles than the efforts of Frankish monks or nuns); and their territory, divided into various Merovingian realms, had no effective center of government.

Yet in the course of the 700s, Francia would unite much of the West into a single dominion, which historians today call the Carolingian Empire. This was a vast constellation of territories welded together by the Frankish king Charlemagne (r. 768–814), who built brilliantly on the accomplishments of his wily father and hardnosed grandfather.[1] Yet Charlemagne did more than merely conquer, for in his realm the various cultural ingredients of the past—Gallo-Roman, Christian, and barbarian—began to merge together into

---

[1] Although the Carolingians are so-named from *Carolus* (Latin for "Charles"), they take their name not from the greatest of their dynasty, Charles the Great (or Charlemagne), but instead from his grandfather Charles Martel (r. 714–741).

TIMELINE 5.1   Carolingian Europe, c. 680–850

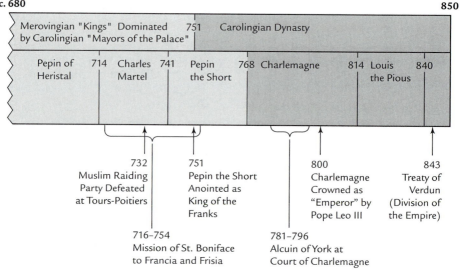

a new synthesis. The person of Charlemagne himself was witness to this fusion. He wore Frankish trousers but took the title of Roman emperor; he understood Latin and Greek but could not write himself; and although he prayed with devout fervor, he also discarded wives at will and allowed his daughters to consort openly with their lovers. This mingling of Gallo-Roman, Christian, and barbarian traditions slowly created a new *European* culture. In 800, Francia was still a modest power in comparison to the Byzantine and Islamic empires, but it had come a long way in just 100 years (see Timeline 5.1).

In Charlemagne's lifetime, "Europe" and "Christendom" were very much on the mind. Scholars wrote about *Europa* and called Charlemagne's empire a *Regnum Europae,* or "realm of Europe." Today, many historians agree, characterizing Charlemagne's accomplishments as creating the "First Europe." Some geographers might reasonably protest that Europe was always *there*—a continent clearly noted on maps and changed little in recent millennia by earthquakes, volcanoes, and erosion. Perhaps so, but the *idea* of Europe was relatively new in the 700s. The word was an inheritance from the Greeks and Romans, whose mythology included the story of how Europa, the beautiful daughter of the king of Tyre (roughly, modern-day Lebanon), was pursued westward and raped by Zeus. Yet it was not until the Early Middle Ages that a clear idea of Europe, as distinct from Asia to the east and Africa to the south, began to emerge.

Although we today usually define Europe as a geographical continent, Charlemagne and his contemporaries would have defined it as a religious entity—as a "Christendom," literally a realm of Christians. In his *Etymologies,* Isidore of Seville (560–636) popularized the idea that the sons of Noah had divided the world among them—Japheth getting Europe (land of Christians), Shem getting Asia (land of Semites), and Ham getting Africa (land of servants). This linkage of geographical continents with religious and racial identities would long endure, for even in the nineteenth century, American slaveholders justified their abuse of Africans by reference to the Bible's stipulation that Ham would be servant unto his brethren. But the differences between Europe and Christendom are as important as their affinities. By the geographical standard, Iberia was fully a part of Europe; by the religious standard, Iberia would lose its place in Western Christendom with the Arab conquests that began in 711. By the one, Jews were as European as their Christian neighbors in the Middle Ages; by the other, they were aliens with only a marginal place in a Christian world.

Whether Europe or Christendom (or better, *Western* Christendom, because the Byzantine Empire constituted, of course, another realm of Christians), the Carolingian Empire differed profoundly from the Western Roman Empire of old. It was predominantly agrarian in economic organization, and its culture was centered on monasteries, cathedrals, and aristocratic courts instead of urban marketplaces. Moreover, although Charlemagne extended his authority into the Italian peninsula, the center of his activities and interests remained northern Francia. In a word, his empire did not, as Rome had done, face the Mediterranean; its axis lay to the north, along the Rhineland.

✳ The Early Carolingians

Francia in 700

Simply put, life in Francia in 700 was difficult, very difficult. It had been slightly colder and rainier for centuries, and although the climate would shortly improve, no one in 700 would have bet on it. The land was sparsely populated, with each village an isolated dot in a landscape dominated by vast forests and crossed only by rough roads (except where old Roman roads remained in use). Extended families were still important; kin still avenged wrongs through feud or wergild; marriage was hard to differentiate from concubinage; and the most basic unit of social organization was the familial **household.** Harvests were poor, yielding a return of two bushels for every bushel sown. Because every household had to save some grain to use as seed the following year, this meant that each harvest was more or less just a matter of running in place. Even running in place was hard for a peasantry who worked with crude tools and owed substantial dues to their landowners. Some were slaves, working full-time on their owners' estates; others were serfs who worked part-time for an estate and part-time on lands allotted to their households; a few were still **free peasants**—that is, they held land on their own account, owing no dues or services to the aristocracy. A peasant woman, for example, might have been a slave, obliged every day to weave cloth in a workshop; she might have been a serf who labored twice a week in her landowner's fields and the rest of her time in fields held by her own household; or she might have been free, cultivating a bit of land that owed no rent to anyone—and got no protection from anyone either.

This landscape of isolated villages, hard-working peasants, and poor communication was dominated by landowners: kings and queens, aristocrats, monasteries, and bishops. The "well-born" relied on networks of extended kin, as did the peasantry, but their networks were larger and more complex, thanks to polygyny (which only they could afford) and informal marriages. They sought to enrich themselves through family lands, plunder, and gifts. Among aristocrats, the giving of gifts was a means of impressing rivals and gaining prestige; it was also the motivation for the followers of a lord or lady to serve faithfully. At the highest level, in the relationships between the kings and their followers, royal gifts from the plunder of conquests bound the upper aristocracy to their monarchs.

Conquest and war defined the aristocratic world. War expressed the personal loyalty that bound one aristocrat to another. War allowed men to display their masculine prowess on battlefields. War provided opportunities for women to advance family interests through encouragement, planning, and estate management, and it also produced, thanks to high male mortality, an extraordinarily large number of widows and heiresses. War was also an important source of profit to aristocratic households, generating new lands, rich loot, and fine gifts received in return for exemplary services. Well armed and well born, aristocrats dominated their localities, providing the daily reality of military might translated into practical power.

During the 600s, aristocratic families in Francia grew more powerful at the expense of the Merovingians, the royal family to whom they theoretically owed allegiance. Merovingian kings and queens, like other early medieval monarchs, were obliged to give away royal lands, generation after generation, in order to attract loyal followers. By 700, they were relatively impoverished, and their aristocracies were relatively enriched. The Merovingians were also divided among themselves. After generations of civil strife among the widows, sons, and brothers of deceased Merovingian kings, Francia had split into several separate districts, the most important of which were Neustria (Paris and northwestern France), Austrasia (the heavily Germanized northeast, including the Rhineland), and Burgundy in the southeast (see Map 5.1 later in this chapter).

As the power of the Merovingians waned, the power of another family—eventually known to historians as the Carolingians—increased. The Carolingians built a power base in their native Austrasia by gathering around them, in the tradition of the old barbarian comitatus, considerable numbers of trained warriors. These men placed themselves under the protection of the Carolingians, pledging loyalty and accepting food, shelter, and support. Wise marriages also were a critical strategy, for wives brought land and alliances into the dynasty. And the rise of the Carolingians was further enhanced by their claim of saintly ancestry in both Gertrude of Nivelles (died in the 650s) and Arnulf, bishop of Metz (c. 582–641). When the Carolingians became "mayors of the palace" (the chief administrative officer) for the Austrasian royal household, they expanded their power still more by making the post hereditary. As the Merovingians became increasingly land-poor, bereft of aristocratic followers, and powerless, the Carolingians became the real rulers of Austrasia.

In 687 Pepin of Heristal (r. 680–714) led his Austrasian army to a decisive victory over the Neustrians at the battle of Tertry, and the Carolingians thenceforth controlled both districts. With Neustria in their grip, they were able to dominate Burgundy as well. Francia was again united, albeit under a Merovingian figurehead behind whom loomed the powerful presence of a Carolingian mayor of the palace. The servant had become his master's master.

Charles Martel (r. 714–741)

Pepin of Heristal's son Charles Martel, "the Hammer," was a skillful and ruthless military chieftain. When Muslim armies attacked Francia in the early 730s, his leadership provided a united response. His greatest victory came in 732 when he turned back an Arab force at the battle of Tours-Poitiers, but he won many other battles over Muslims and Christians alike, consolidating his power over the Franks and extending the boundaries of the Frankish state. Charles Martel rewarded his military followers with estates in conquered lands and with other properties confiscated from the Frankish church. Although the Church complained loudly, there was little it could do to oppose the hero of Tours-Poitiers and master of the Franks.

The Carolingians followed the same practice of divided succession among male heirs that had weakened the Merovingians. But, as it happened, over several generations the Carolingian rulers had only one long-surviving heir. Unity was maintained not by policy but by luck. When Charles Martel died in 741, his lands and authority were divided between his two sons, Carloman and Pepin the Short. Carloman ruled only six years, retiring in 747 to the monastery of Monte Cassino (voluntarily, so it appears) and leaving the field to his brother, Pepin.

Pepin the Short (r. 741–768) and the Franco-Papal Alliance

Carloman's piety left his brother with undisputed power over Francia, but Pepin the Short faced another problem: he was king in fact but not in name. The Merovingians were mere puppet-kings, but replacing their prestigious dynasty was a tricky business. Pepin found the solution in alliance with the papacy. Pepin sent messengers to Rome with a far-from-theoretical query, asking whether it was right that a powerless figurehead should continue to be called "king." Pope Zacharius I (r. 741–52) answered that Pepin should henceforth be king of the Franks and should be anointed into his royal office by a papal representative. The anointing ceremony was duly performed at Soissons in 751, and it buttressed the new dynasty with the strongest of spiritual sanctions: Carolingians henceforth ruled not by force alone but also by God's favor. The last of the Merovingians were shorn of their long hair (a symbol of their royalty) and packed off to a monastery. A few years later, a new pope, Stephen II (r. 752–757), traveled northward to Francia where he personally anointed and crowned Pepin at the royal monastery of St. Denis, thereby conferring every spiritual sanction at his disposal on the upstart Carolingian monarchy.

Zacharius I and Stephen II supported Pepin the Short for a good practical reason: they needed a strong ally in their struggle to secure their position within the Italian peninsula. In return for offering spiritual support to Pepin the Short, they sought his military aid. For many years the papacy had been trying to establish its own autonomous state in the center of the Italian peninsula. In pursuing this goal, popes had often turned to Byzantium for protection against the Lombards who, although Christian, remained an ominous threat to papal independence. But by the time Pepin the Short was seeking legitimacy for his rule, two developments encouraged the papacy to turn away from Byzantium and toward the Franks.

First, the Byzantine emperors had recently embraced iconoclasm, a practice opposed by the Roman popes. As we saw in Chapter 4, this controversy centered on the role of icons—that is, statues and pictures of Christ and the saints. Some thought these were useful spurs to contemplation; others considered them idols that were improperly worshipped. When the Byzantine emperors began to ban all icons, their decrees troubled Western popes who considered iconoclasm heretical and contrary to Christian traditions. As long as the iconoclast controversy raged, popes were apprehensive about depending on the troops of heretical emperors for their defense.

Second, even without the iconoclast controversy, it was increasingly doubtful that Byzantium could supply the military power that the papacy needed. The Byzantines faced serious threats closer to home, especially the Avars in the Balkans and the Arabs in the Middle East, but they also lacked the might to stand up to the powerful Lombards. By 750 the Lombards were on the march once again, threatening not only Byzantine holdings but also papal territories. In 751 the Lombards captured Ravenna, which had long served as the Byzantines' capital in the West and had hitherto been considered impregnable. With the fall of Ravenna, the pope's position became more precarious than ever.

So when Stephen II crowned Pepin at the Abbey of St. Denis, he also asked for Pepin's military support against the Lombards. Pepin obliged, leading his army into the Italian peninsula, defeating the Lombards, and giving some of the lands he conquered to the papacy. The pope got relief from the ominous pressure of the Lombards, but he also got something more long-standing: the "Donation of Pepin," a formal recognition by Pepin of a territory in the center of the Italian peninsula governed by the pope. From this would slowly grow the Papal States, a region ruled by the pope. The Papal States would remain important in Italian politics until the late nineteenth century, and even today the Vatican, a vestigial remain of a once greater papal territory, is an autonomous polity within Italy, as all stamp collectors know. In return for giving spiritual sanction to the practical power won by the Carolingians, the papacy was rescued from the Lombards and established as a secular power in the center of the Italian peninsula.

At about the same time, popes began to make an even broader claim to secular power. In the 740s, the papal chancery produced a document called the "Donation of Constantine" by which that first Christian emperor allegedly sent the pope the imperial crown and ceded to him governance over Rome, the Italian peninsula, and all the West. The pope was said to have returned the crown but kept the power of governance. Hence, popes could regard the Carolingians as subordinates—stewards who exercised political authority by delegation from the papacy. The "Donation of Constantine" is perhaps the most famous forged document in history. The ingenious clerk who produced it would probably have protested that his forgery did not rewrite history but merely manufactured evidence for an event that had actually occurred (and for which the documentation had unfortunately disappeared). Others would have vigorously disagreed, for the forgery buttressed an exceptionally broad claim to papal monarchy over all of Western Christendom. This claim would be met throughout the Middle Ages with skepticism and opposition, but it was more successful in some times than others. The document itself would not be definitively proven as forged until the fifteenth century.

Pepin the Short, like all successful kings of the Early Middle Ages, was an able war leader who followed in the militaristic tradition of his father, Charles Martel. In addition to defeating the Lombards in the Italian peninsula, he drove the Muslims from Aquitaine and maintained peace within Francia. He died in 768, leaving Francia larger, more powerful, and better organized then he had found it. But perhaps his most significant contribution was his alliance with papal Rome, which would affect medieval kingship for many generations to come.

St. Boniface (c. 675–754) and Missions from the Anglo-Saxons

While Charles Martel and Pepin the Short were solidifying the Carolingian dynasty, another sort of consolidation was happening outside the borders of Francia: the expansion of Western Christendom through missionary activity. Anglo-Saxon monasteries, enriched by the dual traditions of Ireland and Rome, were then the most vibrant in the

West, and they produced monks—and sometimes nuns—who became the evangelists of the seventh and eighth centuries. They brought with them not only Christianity but also organizational discipline and devotion to the papacy.

The key figure in this effort was an Anglo-Saxon Benedictine monk, St. Boniface. Reared in the monasteries of southern Britain, Boniface left his native Wessex in 716 to evangelize among the Frisians. From then until his death in 754, he devoted himself above all to Christianizing the pagans of Frisia, Thuringia, Hesse, and Bavaria. Well over six feet tall (a giant of a man by contemporary standards), he became famous among pagans for chopping down one of their sacred oak trees. He won converts, founded Benedictine monasteries in the wilderness, and erected the organizational framework of a disciplined church in lands east of the Rhine. He suffered moments of discouragement, as when he wrote to an Anglo-Saxon abbot, "Take pity upon an old man worn out by the storms of the German sea." Yet the monasteries Boniface established—particularly the great house of Fulda in Hesse—were to become centers of learning and evangelism. Throughout his career he was a devoted representative of the Anglo-Saxon church, the Benedictine Rule, and the papacy. As he promised in a letter to the pope, "I will show in all things a perfect loyalty to you and to the welfare of your Church."

Boniface enjoyed the support of Charles Martel and his sons, Carloman and Pepin the Short. But Charles Martel, willing enough to support Boniface's mission among the Frisians and other pagans, did not want Boniface interfering with his own Frankish church and perhaps raising awkward questions about his seizing of Church lands. After Charles Martel's death in 741, Boniface was able to turn his energy to Francia itself. Well before Boniface's arrival, a monastic reform movement was flourishing in Francia, but the Frankish church as a whole stood in urgent need of reform. Many areas had no priests at all; the beliefs of some peasants veered close to paganism at times; and priests themselves were even reported to have hedged their bets by sacrificing animals to pagan deities. With encouragement from Carloman and Pepin the Short, Boniface called a series of synods to reform the Frankish church. Working closely with the papacy, he remodeled Frankish ecclesiastical organization on the more disciplined pattern of Anglo-Saxon bishoprics and papal Rome. He reformed Frankish monasteries along the lines of the Benedictine Rule, saw to the establishment of **monastic schools,** encouraged the appointment of dedicated bishops and abbots, and worked toward the development of an adequate system of local parishes and parish churches. Thus, Boniface laid the groundwork for both a new church east of the Rhine (in modern-day Germany) and a reformed church in Francia. In doing so, he also served as a chief architect of the Carolingian cultural revival. And since the bishops, abbots, and abbesses of his reformed Frankish church were valuable servants of the Carolingians, Boniface can also be partly credited with the administrative innovations of Carolingian government.

Boniface ended his career much as it had begun. In 754, he returned to Frisia, the site of his first mission almost four decades before and a source of continuing concern. Before the year was out, he died a martyr.

Manorialism

The early eighth century was, then, an age of political consolidation under the early Carolingians and religious consolidation under Boniface. A third consolidation of an entirely different sort also took full shape during these years: the emergence of the rural institution we now call **manorialism.** The origins of manorialism are shrouded in mist and haunted by controversy, but its main features emerged in eighth-century Francia, as a manorial grid began to be imposed on a landscape of village, forest, and wasteland. Sometimes the borders of manors coincided with the boundaries of villages, but sometimes not. In essence, manorialism linked the landed elite to the peasantry in a web of social obligations. The land of the manor belonged to one owner—a lord or lady, bishop, or monastery; the labor that worked the land belonged to the peasantry—some slaves, some serfs, some free. Most manors consisted of a **demesne** (that is, the lands whose produce went directly into manorial barns) and tenements that were rented out to peasants. Ideally, each tenement consisted of a *manse,* enough land to support one household (the exact acreage of the manse varied by region). Slaves were housed and fed by the manor, and they owed all their labor to it. Serfs worked their own tenements and paid part of their rent by laboring on the demesne as well. Free peasants usually owed no labor services, but paid for their tenements in cash or goods. Interestingly, women and men were not equally distributed among these three groups; more women lived as slaves who worked full-time for the manor, and more men lived as serfs on manses. Whether this reflected manorial policies, the effects of a particular sexual division of labor, or even female infanticide is unclear.

Looming over all these workers—women and men; young and old; slaves, serfs, and free—was the authority of the owner of the manor, a person or institution who not only profited from their labor but also governed their lives. Most manors had jurisdictional powers attached, so that the owner of the manor was able to issue regulations, judge disputes, punish crimes, and otherwise wield public authority. The lord or lady of the manor was also expected to protect the tenants, a promise with considerable appeal in a violent age.

With the development of the economic and jurisdictional powers of manors, the centrifugal tendencies of early medieval Europe reached their fullest expression. For many peasants, "government" was in effect their manor, for it was within this local context that their lives were protected and regulated. For many aristocrats, their power as manorial lords or ladies brought wealth, authority, foot soldiers, and sometimes control over whole regions. And for a king like Charlemagne, the manor would become a building block in plans to centralize a decentralized world. He eventually tried, for example, to require that every four manses provide a foot soldier for his army.

✵ CHARLEMAGNE (R. 768-814)

Charles Martel and Pepin the Short were remarkably successful men, but they were bested by their grandson and son, Charlemagne, a talented military commander, a statesman of rare ability, an ally of the Church, and a friend of learning (see Figure 5.1).

Charlemagne towered over his contemporaries both figuratively and literally. He was 6' 3½" tall, thick-necked, and potbellied (a good feature in a society that knew more starvation than plenty). Thanks to his able biographer, Einhard (c. 770–840), whose *Life of Charlemagne* was written within a decade or so after the emperor's death, Charlemagne has come down to posterity as a three-dimensional figure. Einhard, who was small in stature, wrote enthusiastically of his oversized hero. Although he lifted whole passages from Suetonius's biography of the emperor Augustus, there is much in

Figure 5.1 *Charlemagne*   This later depiction of Charlemagne is
from the treasury of the Cathedral of Metz, now held at the Louvre
Museum, Paris.

Einhard's *Life* that represents his own appraisal of Charlemagne's deeds and character.
Reared at St. Boniface's monastery of Fulda, Einhard served for many years in
Charlemagne's court and thereby gained an intimate knowledge of the emperor.
Einhard's warm admiration of Charlemagne emerges clearly from the biography, yet the
author was able to see Charlemagne's faults as well as his virtues:

> He was moderate when it came to food and drink, but he was even more moderate
> in the case of drink, since he hated drunkenness in anybody, especially himself or
> his men. But he was not able to abstain from food and often complained that fasts
> injured his health . . . So restrained was he in the use of wine and all sorts of drink
> that he rarely allowed himself more than three cups in the course of a meal.

Because Carolingian wine cups were closer in measure to modern pints than cups,
Charlemagne's moderation in matters of drink was relative.

Charlemagne could be warm and talkative, but he could also be hard and cruel, and his subjects came to regard him with both admiration and fear. The most fascinating passages in Einhard's biography, however, bear on the emperor's way of life and personal idiosyncrasies that reveal him as a human being rather than as a shadowy hero of legend:

> He thought that his children, both daughters and sons, should begin their education with the liberal arts, which he himself had studied. Then, he saw to it that when the boys reached the right age they were trained to ride in the Frankish fashion, to fight, and to hunt. But he ordered his daughters to learn how to work with wool, how to spin and weave it, so that they would not grow dull from inactivity and instead might learn to value work.

Einhard portrayed the emperor as a fluent master of Latin, a student of Greek, an effective speaker, a devotee of the liberal arts, and in particular a student of astronomy who learned to calculate the motions of the heavenly bodies. But he also noted that Charlemagne, despite long hours of practice, never mastered the skill of writing, for he had begun his education too late in life to train his hands to form letters.

Charlemagne possessed a strong piety that prompted him to build churches, collect relics, and promote a Christian cultural revival in Francia. In keeping with the views of his papal ally, he issued laws forbidding the practice of polygyny. In time, his insistence on monogamy simplified inheritance patterns drastically, creating an important legal distinction between legitimate children (who could inherit) and illegitimate children (who often could not). But his laws in support of Church policy on marriage did not prevent Charlemagne himself from divorcing unwanted wives and filling his court with concubines. In one four-year period, he divorced twice and married twice! Even his daughters, whom he never permitted to marry, consorted openly in his court with their lovers and presented him with grandchildren born of unsanctified unions. As Einhard tells us, Charlemagne's response was to "pretend there was nothing wrong at all."

The Expansion of the Empire

Above all else Charlemagne was a warrior-king, and he took to the battlefield each year as a matter of course. When his **magnates** and their retainers assembled around him each spring (war was a good weather activity), the question was not whether to go to war but whom to fight. It was only gradually, however, that Charlemagne developed a coherent scheme of conquest built on the goal of unifying and expanding the Christian West. At the behest of the papacy, he followed his father's footsteps into the Italian peninsula. There he conquered the Lombards completely in 774, incorporated them into his growing state, and assumed for himself the Lombard crown. Thenceforth he titled himself "King of the Franks and the Lombards."

In 778 Charlemagne launched a campaign against al-Andalus that met with little success, although he did manage subsequently to establish a border district south of the Pyrenees Mountains known as the "Spanish March" (march, as in "frontier"). In later generations part of Charlemagne's Spanish March evolved into the county of Barcelona, which still remains more receptive to the influence of French institutions and customs than any other district in modern-day Spain. Some 300 years later, Charlemagne's brief sojourn in al-Andalus would take on epic—and fictional—proportions in the *Song of*

Roland, a tale of a devastating attack on the rearguard of Charlemagne's army as it was withdrawing across the Pyrenees into Francia. The *Song of Roland* describes Charlemagne as a godlike conqueror, 200 years old, and it transforms the Christian Basques who attacked Charlemagne in 778 into Muslims, making the battle a heroic struggle between the rival faiths. But as a stirring tale of brave men, true friends, and loyal warriors, it reflects the aristocratic spirit of Charlemagne's time, as well as the late eleventh century when it was written down.

Charlemagne devoted much of his energy to the expansion of his eastern frontier. In 787 he conquered and absorbed Bavaria, organizing its easternmost district into a forward defensive barrier against the Slavs. This East March, or *Ostmark,* became the nucleus of a new state which would later develop into Austria. In the 790s Charlemagne pushed still farther to the southeast, destroying the rich Avar state, which had long tormented Eastern Europe, plundering some victims and demanding tribute from others. Charlemagne had the good fortune to seize a substantial portion of Avar treasure; it is reported that fifteen four-ox wagons were required to transport the hoard of gold, silver, and precious garments back to Francia. The loot of the Avars contributed significantly to the resources of Charlemagne's treasury and broadened the scope of his subsequent building program and patronage.

Charlemagne directed his most prolonged military effort against the pagan Saxons to his northeast. With the twin goals of protecting the Frankish Rhineland and bringing new souls into the Church, he campaigned for some thirty-two years, conquering the Saxons repeatedly and baptizing them by force, only to have them rebel when his armies withdrew. In a fit of savage exasperation in 782, he ordered the execution of more than 4,000 Saxons in a single day. At length Saxony submitted to the remorseless pressure of Charlemagne's soldiers—and the missionaries who followed in their wake. By 804 Frankish control of Saxony was well established, and in subsequent decades Christianity seeped gradually into Saxon society. By the middle of the tenth century, Saxons would boast the most powerful Christian state in Europe.

The Imperial Coronation of 800

By incorporating extensive lands east of the Rhine into his realm, Charlemagne succeeded where the generals of ancient Rome had failed. No longer a mere Frankish king, Charlemagne, by 800, was master of the West. A few small Christian states remained outside his jurisdiction—most notably, the principalities of the southern Italian peninsula and the Anglo-Saxon kingdoms—but Charlemagne's political sway extended throughout Western Christendom (see Map 5.1). On Christmas Day, 800, his immense accomplishment was formally recognized when Pope Leo III (r. 795–816) placed the imperial crown on his head and acclaimed him "Emperor of the Romans."

This dramatic act had several meanings. First, from the standpoint of legal theory, it insulted the Empress Irene (r. 797–802) in Constantinople, for it implied that the imperial throne on which she sat was empty. Leo III argued that because Irene, as a woman, was ineligible to rule over men, Charlemagne was just filling a vacancy.[2] Second, from

---

[2] Charlemagne had recognized the Empress Irene's authority just two years before. When she queried his Christmas Day coronation, he replied with an offer of marriage that would have legally united the Byzantine and Frankish empires. This idea so appalled Irene's supporters that she was forced to retire to a monastery.

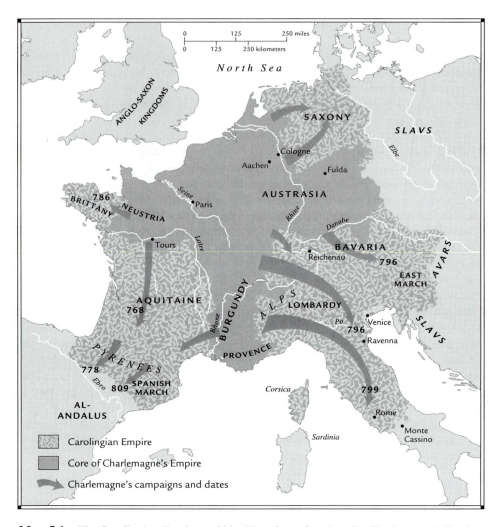

Map 5.1 *The Carolingian Empire, c. 800*   Historians often describe Charlemagne's Empire as "the first Europe," and this map shows why. Charlemagne's power did not extend very far into Spain nor did it reach into the British Isles. But it encompassed much of modern-day Italy, Austria, and Germany and all of modern-day France, Belgium, the Netherlands, Luxembourg, and Switzerland.

the standpoint of practical effect, it reconstituted the Western Roman Empire after a 324-year intermission: Charlemagne's empire now stood in its place. Third, from the standpoint of diplomatic history, it was the ultimate consummation of the Franco-papal alliance begun in 751 with Pepin the Short's pointed question to Zacharius I.

    According to Einhard, Pope Leo III took Charlemagne by surprise on that Christmas Day and bestowed on him a dignity so unwanted that "he would not have set foot in the church the day that it was conferred, although it was a great feast day, if he could have foreseen the pope's design." Many modern historians tend to be more

Figure 5.2   *Charlemagne's Church at Aachen*   This is
an impressive building, but it is modest compared to similar
buildings in Constantinople (see Figure 4.1) and Cordoba
(see Figure 4.4).

skeptical, arguing that Charlemagne was too firmly in control of events to permit a coronation he did not want. Moreover, it seems clear that Charlemagne's imperial coronation
of 800, like the papal anointing of Pepin the Short in 751, represented a blend of
Carolingian and papal interests.

As to Charlemagne's interests, he had long been attempting to attain a status comparable to that of the rulers of Byzantium. To this end, for example, he modified the traditional practice of traveling constantly with his court, consuming the surplus food of
one estate and moving on to the next. In 794 he established a permanent capital at
Aachen, where he sought to create a Constantinople of his own. Aachen was called
"New Rome," and an impressive palace-church was built in the Byzantine style—almost
literally a poor man's Hagia Sophia (see Figure 5.2). Even though Charlemagne's

church at Aachen was a far cry from Justinian's masterpiece, it was a marvel for its time and place. It was the product of a major effort on Charlemagne's part, an effort not only to create a beautiful church but also to ape the Byzantines. The coronation of 800 may well have been an expression of this same imitative policy.

As to the papacy's interests, Leo III may have regarded the coronation as an opportunity to regain some of the initiative lost to the all-powerful Charlemagne. To be sure, Leo III's action on Christmas Day "promoted" Charlemagne from a king to an emperor, but Charlemagne's empire would thenceforth bear the stamp "Made in Rome." Later popes would insist that what Leo III gave they could also take away—that is, if the papacy could make emperors, it also could depose them. The Donation of Constantine worked to buttress this claim: if the West belonged to the pope, then only the pope could rule or designate other rulers.

Charlemagne, of course, had a different perspective on this matter, and although he respected the papacy, he was unwilling to cast himself in a subordinate role. After 800, he always retained the title "King of the Franks and the Lombards" alongside his new imperial title. And when the time came to crown his son as emperor, Charlemagne excluded the pope from the ceremony and did the honors himself. These maneuvers between Charlemagne and Leo III were the prologue to a long, bitter struggle over the correct relationship between empire and papacy, a struggle that would reach a crescendo in the eleventh, twelfth, and thirteenth centuries.

For the present, however, Charlemagne's power was unrivaled, and Leo III and other popes were much too weak to resist him. Indeed, the papacy was nearly smothered in Charlemagne's affectionate embrace, for Charlemagne exerted by far the greater influence over the Carolingian church. Papal anointing gave him, as it had his father, a sacred, almost priestly quality. Driven by a sense of responsibility for systematizing Church discipline and by the need to incorporate educated churchmen into the structure of Carolingian government, he used his immense authority to govern not only the body politic but also the Church. At the Synod of Frankfurt in 794, he even legislated on Christian doctrine. Charlemagne saw the Church as an essential buttress of the Carolingian state, and he regulated it accordingly.

The Empire

Charlemagne made great advances, but his realm remained economically underdeveloped. Towns were small and scattered, with minimal industry or trade. A few centers of craft production, especially pottery and glass, did develop, and there was some trade in iron, salt, and wines for ordinary people and in luxury goods for the rich. Because roads were miserably bad, most trade moved along rivers, especially the Rhine. Charlemagne tried to encourage economic growth: he maintained a silver coinage of good quality (though many ordinary transactions continued to be based on barter); he concluded a reciprocal agreement with an Anglo-Saxon king guaranteeing the safety of merchants; he encouraged the construction of roads, bridges, and lighthouses; he even contemplated building a canal to link the Rhine and Danube rivers.

Charlemagne might also have tried to jump-start the Frankish economy by encouraging the further settlement of Jews within Francia. Contemporary evidence is frustratingly thin on this point, but later generations of Jews preserved a folk memory that Charlemagne had welcomed them into the Rhineland and elsewhere. If Charlemagne did, indeed, encourage Jewish immigration, he likely especially encouraged the immigration of Jewish *merchants*. Later, when Charlemagne's son Louis the Pious (r. 814–840) issued charters of protection to Jewish communities, he explicitly included provisions related to **tolls,** trading, and mercantile law. Jews were engaged in many occupations, including medicine, agriculture, and crafts, but in the predominantly rural world of Carolingian Francia, Jews were particularly valued for the mercantile expertise they brought with them as they moved north from bustling cities along the Mediterranean coast to the small towns of West and East Francia.

Charlemagne responded with similar vigor to challenges in government. Yet despite considerable innovation on his part, his empire remained administratively undergoverned. Charlemagne issued laws and regulations known as **capitularies** that were to be observed throughout his realm, and he also sent out envoys known as **missi dominici** to see that his capitularies were being obeyed and his revenues collected. But these innovations did not end his reliance on the loyalty of local aristocrats. Like his predecessors, Charlemagne depended on local officers who held land in return for their services: dukes, lords of the marches (margraves), and, most commonly, counts of the nearly 300 counties of his Empire. These men were oath-bound to obey their king and emperor. But oaths were frail threads, and counts acted on their own when loyalty no longer suited their interests. Because many were drawn, of necessity, from aristocratic Frankish families, they boasted land and followers of their own. Because, in place of the salaries that Charlemagne could not afford to pay, they were granted use of royal lands (from which they could not easily be dislodged), office-holding expanded their local power. And because of vast distances and poor communications, they had to be entrusted with broad powers over royal tribunals, taxation systems, and military recruitment in their counties. Enriched by family and royal lands and empowered with extensive authority, many counts were the de facto rulers of their territories.

Even under the overarching authority of Charlemagne, the Empire was afflicted by widespread local and regional violence: blood feuds between aristocratic families, private warfare over disputed lands, plundering raids, and highway robberies. The imperial government was much too weak to contend effectively with well-entrenched regional aristocratic elites, especially if they were not too blatantly conspicuous in pursuing their self-interests. Charlemagne's missi dominici, usually one churchman and one layman sent into each area, were only moderately effective at keeping track of his regional administrators, and they would become less so under later monarchs who lacked Charlemagne's power to punish and reward. Counts and other local officials obeyed royal commands and capitularies not out of patriotic allegiance to the Carolingian state but because of loyalty to Charlemagne himself—a loyalty based on the bonds of common interest that linked a warrior king and his aristocracy.

✺ INTELLECTUAL REVIVAL

Charlemagne and Alcuin

As part of his effort to raise the intellectual standards of his realm, Charlemagne assembled scholars at Aachen from all over Europe. From eastern Francia came the emperor's biographer, Einhard. From Monte Cassino came the poet-historian Paul the Deacon (c. 720–799), who compiled a book of sermons so that busy priests could know what to

BIOGRAPHICAL SKETCH

Walafrid Strabo (c. 808–849)

B orn in about 808, Walafrid was dedicated by his parents to lifelong service as a monk. Accordingly, when he was eight years old, he entered the Benedictine monastery of Reichenau, an important center of Carolingian learning set on an island in Lake Constance. An enthusiastic pupil in the monastic school, he quickly learned Latin and then mastered the Bible, the writings of the Latin Doctors, and the principles of the liberal arts. He especially excelled at poetry, and by the age of fifteen, he was sending his verses to bishops, always with characteristic Benedictine humility. He addressed one verse "as a mouse to a giant" and identified himself thus: "It's the boy with the squinty eye, Father, who writes these words to you."

As was expected of him, Walafrid took monastic vows on coming of age. He did so happily, because he had by then developed a deep religious faith and a devotion to Benedictine monasticism. One of his friends was not so lucky. Gottschalk, born of a Saxon count who offered his son to a monastery, grew up so unhappy with monastic life that he eventually asked for release from his vows. This provoked anguished debate. Could a vow made before God be broken? Could a child be forced into religious life? Gottschalk was eventually released from his monastic obligation, but only with great scandal and bad feeling. Walafrid, a kind and loving man, stood by Gottschalk in all his troubles, later writing him, "Be unto me a friend, as I in all loyalty shall be a friend to you."

Walafrid flourished in the monastic culture that seemed so stifling to Gottschalk. At the age of eighteen, he was sent to study under Rabanus Maurus, abbot of the great monastery of Fulda, which Boniface had founded a century before. Walafrid was fascinated by Rabanus Maurus's project of compiling Biblical commentaries, and he enthusiastically joined in. The two became lifelong friends.

Walafrid remained at Fulda for only three years, for at the age of twenty-one, he was summoned to the imperial court at Aachen. There he tutored the son of Louis the Pious by his second wife, the Empress Judith (c. 800–843): Charles, who, being only five years old, had not yet won his nickname, "the Bald." Walafrid remained at court for nine years (829–838), tutoring, studying, writing, and reveling in the intellectual world created by the Empress Judith whom he called "Lover of peace, Seeker of light." Again, he would prove himself a true friend, standing by the Empress and her young son when Louis's sons from his first marriage rose up against their father and briefly deposed him (from 832 to 835). Throughout these upheavals Walafrid remained faithful to his duties as tutor, with the result that Charles the Bald turned out to be the best educated of the Carolingian monarchs.

In 838, Walafrid, then about thirty, was rewarded by being made abbot of Reichenau, the abbey he had entered as a child. But with the death of Louis the Pious in 840, the civil war between his sons intensified, and Walafrid suffered exile for two years. He was restored to his abbey in 842 and spent there some of his happiest years, studying, writing letters and poetry, and gardening. Although he regretted the division of the Empire between Lothar, Louis the German, and Charles the Bald (accomplished by the Treaty of Verdun in 843), he enjoyed the trust of all three royal brothers. In 848, at about the age of forty, Walafrid traveled to the court of his former pupil Charles the Bald, now king of the West Franks, to represent Louis the German, now king of the East Franks, on a diplomatic mission. There, he died in a boating accident while crossing the Loire. His body was carried back to Reichenau and buried on his beloved island. His former teacher and grieving friend, Rabanus Maurus, wrote his epitaph.

Walafrid Strabo balanced perfectly the many tensions of his world. Given as a child oblate to Reichenau, he might have suffered from his parents' choice, but he instead flourished on what he called his "happy isle." Delighted with monastic life, he nevertheless served his emperor through long and fruitful years at the imperial court. Fascinated with the preservation efforts that were so characteristic of Carolingian scholarship, he not only compiled and conserved but also created some of the best poetry of his age. And born at the height of Charlemagne's powers, he lived to see both peace and scholarship decline—to see that, as he put it, "enthusiasm for study is slipping back from high tide to low tide." Throughout all these challenges and changes, he retained a refreshing optimism and love for others, and indeed, above all else, he was simply a good friend. In some unforgettable lines, he wrote of his affection for one fellow cleric:

In love's dear service and with heart's devotion true
To Luitgar, Strabo sends this little note . . .
As mother loves her only boy, as sun to earth,
As dew to grass, and stream to thirsty fish,
As air to birds that sing, as flowing brooks to meadows,
So dear thy face, my little one, to me.

preach on which holy day. From Iberia came Theodulf (c. 768–821), later bishop of Orléans and abbot of Fleury, a poet of considerable talent. And from York in England came the greatest of all, Alcuin (732–804). Like Boniface before him, Alcuin brought from Britain ideas and skills that directly stimulated the intellectual development of Carolingian Francia. These scholars and others worked, under Charlemagne's energetic guidance, to build a revitalized Christian society.

They began at the most basic level, by providing basic education for as many children—girls as well as boys—as possible. Alcuin introduced Boethius's notion of seven liberal arts, divided into those related to effective communication (the trivium) and those related to study of the natural world (the quadrivium). Because Francia had no professional teachers, either lay or clerical, the only hope for educational reform lay with the Church, the only institution where literacy—then defined as the ability to read Latin—was at all common. So Charlemagne ordered the cathedrals and monasteries of his realm to operate schools. His capitulary of 789 commands, "Let schools be established in which children may learn to read," and then further stipulates that these schools should have accurate copies of the psalms, calendars, grammars, and other useful books. It went without saying that Latin was the language of literacy in these schools, for although children grew up speaking languages from which would eventually grow French, German, and Italian, they learned in school to read and write in Latin. These schools provided training for external students who would not pursue Church careers, as well as priests, monks, and nuns.

Many Carolingian monasteries and cathedrals fell short of the modest standards ordered by Charlemagne, but most did vastly improve the quantity and quality of the schooling they offered. It was above all in monastic schools that learning flourished—in monasteries such as Fulda, Tours, and Reichenau. The students they trained pursued careers as teachers or administrators. The schools of Reichenau and Fulda, for example, produced Walafrid Strabo, a writer of saints' lives, a poet, a diplomat for Francia, and tutor to a future king (see Biographical Sketch on pp. 112–113). The book of advice that the noblewoman Dhuoda (fl. c. 810–850) wrote for her sixteen-year-old son William provides another example. Although she was an aristocratic wife and he was a young man destined for a career at court, both valued their Latin literacy for the Christian faith it nurtured. As Dhuoda succinctly put it, "God is learned about through books." More than likely, Dhuoda learned her Latin at a monastic school and then passed the skill along to her son, as his first teacher. Only a tiny fraction of Charlemagne's subjects acquired literacy, but they used their knowledge well.

In addition to improving basic education, Alcuin and other scholars sought to preserve and build on the great works of the Classical-Christian cultural tradition. To this end, they produced accurate copies of important past texts; Alcuin himself, for example, prepared a precise new edition of the Latin Vulgate Bible, a text that had been much corrupted—thanks to the inevitable errors of copyists—since the days of Jerome. In his capacity as chief scholar in Charlemagne's court school, Alcuin sought as much to preserve and honor past scholars as to create new scholarship. "There is nothing better for us," he once wrote, "than to follow the teachings of the Apostles and the Gospels. We must follow these precepts instead of inventing new ones or propounding new doctrine or vainly seeking to increase our own fame by the discovery of newfangled ideas." This might seem a limited aim today, but we should be grateful to Alcuin and his colleagues: more than 90 percent of the Roman poems, epics, essays, and other writings that we can still read today have survived in their earliest form in manuscripts copied during Carolingian times.

Carolingian scholars also developed a clearer form of handwriting, a form so clear that it is the basis of the font you are reading right now (see Figure 5.3). This "Caroline

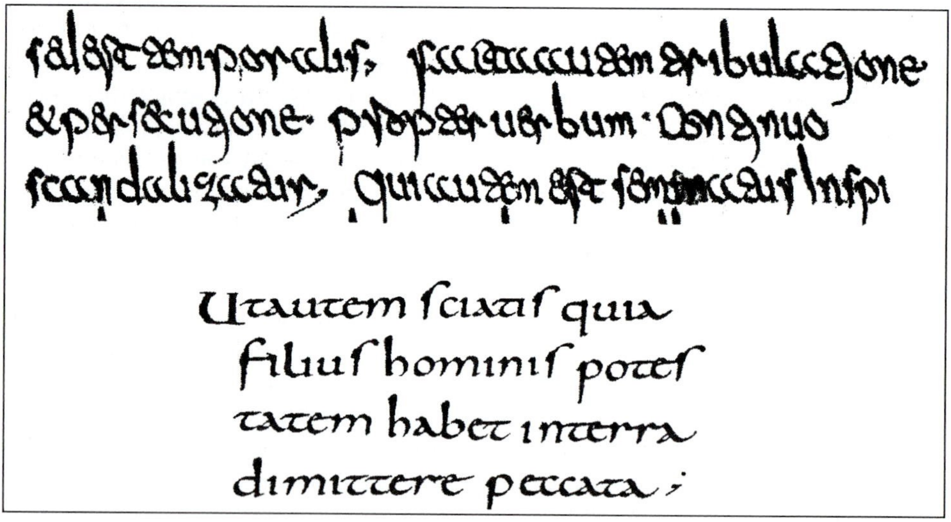

Figure 5.3   *Caroline Script*   The top three lines show a typical Merovingian manuscript, with cramped and hard-to-read lettering. The first three words are "sed est temporalis," and if you can make them out, you should consider a career in Medieval Studies. The bottom four lines are typical of the clarity introduced at the nunnery of Chelles and elsewhere. This second text begins, "Ut autem sciatis quia filius hominis . . ." Aside from the distinctive letter "s," this Caroline script is very close to modern typefaces.

script," as it came to be called, derived in part from earlier Irish scripts and in part from Frankish monasteries, particularly, it seems, female monasteries, such as the famous convent of Chelles whose manuscripts clearly show the change. Caroline script involved several improvements that aided reading: more punctuation, spaces between words (a positive innovation on the old practice of runningwordstogether), clear separation of each letter from those beside it; and the use of both capital and lowercase letters. As a result, books and documents were much more legible, and more students could learn to read more easily. Because Carolingian monks and nuns copied manuscripts on an unprecedented scale, this new script quickly spread.

Alcuin and Charlemagne also sought to continue Boniface's reform of the Frankish church. They turned some of their attention to pastoral care. In their view, the clergy were the "soldiers of the Church" who had to lead "the people of God to the pasture of eternal life." To help priests in this task, they regularized the liturgy, provided ready-made sermons for harried priests, urged both men and women to avoid hard work on Sundays, created handbooks for clergy, and distributed copies of the revised Vulgate. Monastic reform was another important part of the agenda, and to that end, an accurate copy of the Benedictine Rule was obtained from Monte Cassino and urged on all monastic houses. These efforts were not everywhere successful, but they helped improve pastoral care and standardize monastic life.

Intellectual Trends after Charlemagne

Although these achievements were accomplished more through royal than papal initiative, the intellectual revival continued as Charlemagne's empire began to crumble after his death. In the monasteries and cathedrals of ninth- and tenth-century Europe, documents continued to be copied, schools continued to operate, and commentaries and summaries of ancient texts continued to appear. These achievements were impressive: by one estimate, 50,000 books were produced by monks and nuns, working in scriptoria, during the ninth century. Three other trends were especially notable.

First, in keeping with the Carolingian intellectual program of preserving past traditions, these later scholars devoted themselves to preparing encyclopedic accounts of existing knowledge. For example, Rabanus Maurus (c. 780–856), abbot of Fulda, produced a learned collection, on the pattern of Isidore of Seville's *Etymologies,* of all information available to him on all possible subjects.[3]

Second, monastic reform continued but took on a deeper spiritual element under the impetus of a reform movement begun in Aquitaine under the leadership of St. Benedict of Aniane (c. 750–821), not to be confused with St. Benedict of Nursia (c. 480–c. 550). Charlemagne's son Louis the Pious gave Benedict of Aniane the right to tighten the discipline of any monastery he visited, to the chagrin of numerous abbots and abbesses anxious to protect their prerogatives. And in 817, he promulgated for all the monasteries of the Empire a significantly expanded version of the Benedictine *Rule,*

---

[3] Rabanus Maurus, also known as Raban Maur, Hraban Maur, Hrabanus Maurus, and even "Robin Moore" (as one professor once playfully called him), is an example of how modern historians differently render the Latin names found in medieval documents. Similarly, the Carolingian forename Pepin is sometimes styled Pippin. All (save Robin Moore) are correct, and as a result, students of medieval history have to be flexible when encountering one person identified in different ways by different scholars.

based on the strict monastic regulations of Benedict of Aniane. These measures shifted monastic reform toward a deeper concern for the Christ-centered lives of monks and nuns. The elaborated Benedictine *Rule* of 817 lost its status as imperial law in 840, with the death of Louis the Pious, but it remained an inspiration to monastic reform movements in the centuries that followed.

Third, Neoplatonic ideas again became important in Christian philosophy, thanks largely to John Scottus Eriugena (c. 810–877), the most innovative scholar of his day. John Scottus was an Irishman (the Scots in his day were inhabitants of Ireland as well as Scotland). He served for years in the court of Charlemagne's grandson, Charles the Bald (r. 840–877), and he was a wit as well as a philosopher, if we can believe the legend of a conversation between John and his king. The two of them were sitting across the dinner table from each other when Charles the Bald, intending to needle his court scholar, asked him whether there was anything that separated a Scot and a drunkard. "Just a table," was John's reply.

John Scottus was trained in Greek as well as Latin, and he translated into Latin an important Greek philosophical treatise, *On the Celestial Hierarchy,* written by an anonymous late-fifth-century Christian Neoplatonist known as "the Pseudo-Dionysius." This author has perhaps the most confused identity in history. He was thought to be Dionysius the Areopagite, a first-century Athenian philosopher described in the *Acts of the Apostles* as being converted to Christianity by St. Paul. But he was also linked—as if the same person—to St. Denis, missionary to the Gauls and first bishop of Paris, in whose honor the great royal monastery of St. Denis was built ("Denis" is the French equivalent of "Dionysius"). Both attributions were wrong, but they gave the Pseudo-Dionysius—and his idea that the Christian God was the same as the unknowable and indescribable Neoplatonic god—the commanding credentials of an early Christian author, a Pauline convert, and a martyred missionary who brought Christianity to Gaul. Because this God could be approached only by means of a mystical experience, Neoplatonism became an important source of inspiration to later Christian mystics, as it also was to Sufi mystics in Islam. Stimulated by the work of the Pseudo-Dionysius, John Scottus wrote a highly original Neoplatonic treatise of his own, *On the Divisions of Nature.* In its blurred distinction between God and nature, the treatise tended toward pantheism. It was controversial in its own time and would be even more so in later centuries.

❈ Conclusion

The Carolingian Empire would prove to be ephemeral. Rising out of a chaotic past, it disintegrated in the turbulent era that followed. The Carolingians had achieved their early successes not only through strong leadership but also because of the sizable landed resources that they controlled and the loyal, well-armed aristocrats whom these resources could attract. Making effective use of armored horsemen, Carolingian armies were better organized and better disciplined than those of most neighboring powers. And once Carolingian expansion was under way, it fed on its own momentum. Conquests brought plunder and new lands with which the Carolingians could enrich themselves and reward their supporters. Indeed, it became Carolingian policy to install loyal Franks as counts and dukes of conquered provinces. Accordingly, the interests of the Frankish landholding aristocracy became ever more closely tied to the political and military fortunes of their king. As long as the Carolingians could bring in profits from military campaigns, they commanded the enthusiastic obedience of disciplined followers.

In short, Carolingian expansion was like a snowball, growing as it rolled, rolling as it grew. A Frankish lord would gladly obey Charlemagne if it meant a cut of the Avar treasure or a lordship in Saxony. But after the final submission of Saxony in 804, the flow of lands and plunder dried up, and aristocratic loyalty diminished accordingly. Disaffection and rebellion clouded the final decade of Charlemagne's life and brought political chaos to the reign of his son and heir, Louis the Pious. Once the snowball stopped rolling, it began to melt.

The family politics of the Carolingians also eventually worked against them. Because the Carolingians continued the traditional Frankish practice of dividing a father's inheritance among his sons, each generation of males faced either division (as happened at Verdun in 843 when Charlemagne's three grandsons divided his empire) or bitter enmity. Carolingians were remarkably effective at eliminating male claimants to the throne, usually through murder or monastic life. This was so common that Charlemagne had to order his sons explicitly not "to kill, blind, or mutilate their nephews, or force them to be tonsured against their will." He might have known what he was talking about; the sons of his own brother Carloman had disappeared without a trace in 771.

Marriage was another Carolingian policy that produced mixed results. Carolingian males wisely used marriage to enrich their patrimony and enhance their political connections. Pepin of Heristal's marriage to the heiress Plectrude (c. 670–720) brought him rich lands between the Meuse and Moselle rivers; Pepin the Short's marriage to Bertrada (726–783) yielded a similarly rich inheritance; Charlemagne's own numerous alliances (he had at least eleven wives and concubines) helped to consolidate his hold over conquered areas or to strengthen alliances. Yet these men seldom allowed would-be husbands to benefit at their expense, for Carolingian daughters were rarely allowed to marry (many entered monasteries). These policies of marriage, murder, mutilation, and forced monastic vocation helped to consolidate the power of early Carolingian kings, but by the late ninth century, their line of royal descent was dangerously thin.

Moreover, it is important to remember that the centralized authority of Charlemagne was never more than a thin veneer laid over a heavy foundation of regional interest and localism. Under the umbrella Charlemagne created by the force of conquest and the unsteady loyalty of his warriors were many peoples separated from one another by custom, culture, language, and religion. These differences endured. Within a few decades of Charlemagne's death, when two of his grandsons swore an oath at Strasbourg (allying themselves, in good Carolingian fashion, against a third grandson), they chose to take their oaths in different languages. Charles the Bald took his oath in the German vernacular so that Louis's East Frankish army could understand him; for the same reason, Louis the German (r. 840–876) swore his loyalty to the king of the West Franks in the ancestral tongue of modern French. Different cultures do not necessarily make for weak states (as the twentieth-century history of the United States well illustrates), but the Carolingians were never able to balance the diversity of their empire with common, unifying concerns.

Even though Charlemagne's "Roman Empire" was short-lived, he did a great deal with very little. Charlemagne was a fearsome conqueror, but he also knew what he wanted to do with his conquests: he sought to bring pagans into Christianity and to improve the worship of those who were already Christian. His vision of a Christian state—a Christendom—would inspire later rulers. When later generations emulated him, they named their dominion a *Holy* Roman Empire. The Carolingian idea of Europe as a Christian empire was to dominate political theory—and political practice, too—for the rest of the Middle Ages.

SUGGESTED READINGS

Roger Collins, *Charlemagne* (1998). A traditional approach that is up-to-date on research.
Eleanor Shipley Duckett, *Carolingian Portraits: A Study in the Ninth Century* (1962). Walafrid Strabo's biographical portrait has been adapted from this lively collection.
Richard Hodges and David Whitehouse, *Mohammed, Charlemagne, and the Origins of Europe: Archaeology and the Pirenne Thesis* (1983). Uses archaeology to reexamine the Carolingian economy. See also Georges Duby, *The Early Growth of the European Economy: Warriors and Peasants from the Seventh to the Twelfth Century* (1974).
Janet L. Nelson, *The Frankish World* (1996). A collection of essays by a leading authority. See also her *Politics and Ritual in Early Medieval Europe* (1986).
Thomas F. X. Noble, *The Republic of St. Peter: The Birth of the Papal State 680–825* (1984). A lucid study.
Timothy Reuter, *Germany in the Early Middle Ages, 800–1056* (1991). An excellent account with an interesting reinterpretation of Charlemagne.
Richard E. Sullivan, ed., *The Gentle Voices of Teachers: Aspects of Learning in the Carolingian Age* (1995). See also Rosamond McKitterick, ed., *Carolingian Culture: Emulation and Innovation* (1994).
Pierre Riché, *The Carolingians: A Family Who Forged Europe* (1993). A lively study, translated from French. See also his *Daily Life in the World of Charlemagne* (1978), and Rosamond McKitterick, *The Frankish Kingdoms under the Carolingians, 751–987* (1983).

SUGGESTED PRIMARY SOURCES

Paul Edward Dutton, ed., *Carolingian Civilization: A Reader* (1993). A wide-ranging collection of sources, each carefully introduced. See also his *Charlemagne's Courtier: The Complete Einhard* (1998).
Carol Neel, trans., *Handbook for William: A Carolingian Woman's Counsel for Her Son* (1991). A translation of Dhuoda's *Liber Manualis*.

COLOR ILLUSTRATION 1

The Empress Theodora   This mosaic from San Vitale in Ravenna is thought to be a true likeness of the empress. Her large eyes (windows into the soul) are typical of Byzantine art, as is the rich mosaic itself.

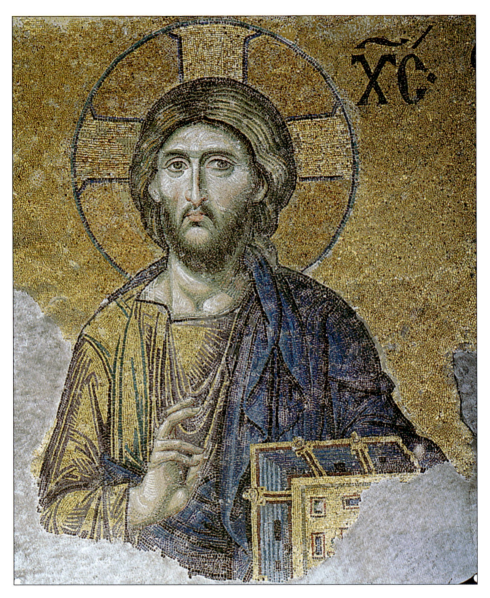

COLOR ILLUSTRATION 2
Jesus, a Mosaic from Hagia Sophia   Contrast this awe-inspiring mosaic of Jesus with the good shepherd image shown in Chapter 1 (Figure 1.2). This image emphasizes the divinity of Christ; the good shepherd emphasizes Jesus' humanity.

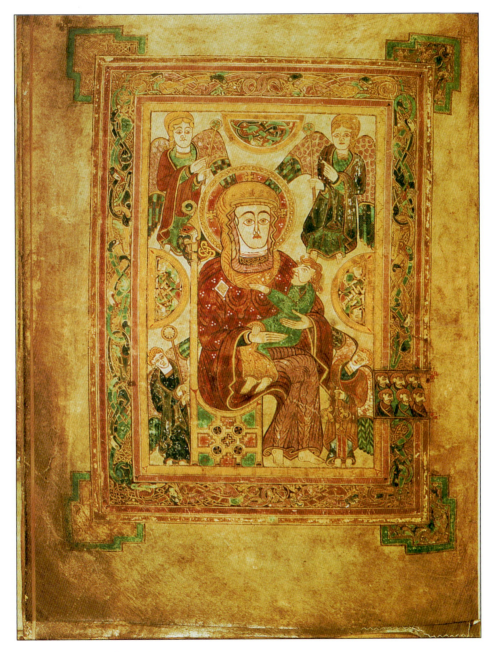

COLOR ILLUSTRATION 3
The Book of Kells Produced around the year 800, the Book of Kells so fuses Irish and Anglo-Saxon styles that we are not certain whether it was produced in Ireland, Scotland, or Northumbria. Notice how the intricate border around this image of Virgin and Child echoes the detailed metalwork characteristic of barbarian art (see Figure 2.2).

COLOR ILLUSTRATION 4

Jesus and Muhammad   Islam taught that Jesus was a respected prophet but that his teachings were superseded by those of Muhammad. This illustration, from a history book written by Rashid al-Din, illustrates this concept. It shows Jesus (on the donkey) with Muhammad (on the camel).

COLOR ILLUSTRATION 5

The Three Orders   This illustration shows the three orders: those who pray, those who fight, and those who work. Notice how the cleric and knight dominate the picture, with the peasant squeezed into the picture and excluded from their animated conversation. Notice, too, how all three orders are depicted as male. Some theorists included women in the three orders, but others did not.

COLOR ILLUSTRATION 6
Knights, Ladies, and Tournaments As this rich picture made c. 1300 shows, knights honed their battle skills at tournaments, but they also sought to impress the ladies who watched them.

COLOR ILLUSTRATION 7
The Gero Cross (c. 970) Carved of oak and then painted, this is the first in-the-round depiction of the Crucifixion. It shows Christ dead, but evokes his suffering through his sagged head and posture. This emphasis on Christ's redemptive suffering was a strong theme in Christian spirituality during the Central Middle Ages, and by the late twelfth century, artists evoked it even more strongly by depicting a suffering Christ—that is, before death and in great pain.

COLOR ILLUSTRATION 8

Eucharistic Piety and Christian Fear of Jews   Among the many false rumors that circulated among medieval Christians were stories of host desecration—that is, that Jews wantonly harmed the consecrated Host that was so central to the eucharistic piety of medieval Christians. Here, the Host is in the middle of the table, and two Jewish men are stabbing it with knives, causing blood to flow across the white tablecloth. Drawn about 1400, this graphic scene was part of a vicious slander that provoked Christian attacks on Jews in many parts of central and late medieval Europe.

COLOR ILLUSTRATION 9

The Confrontation at Canossa   This illustration shows Emperor Henry IV (on bent knee in the center), asking Countess Matilda of Tuscany (to the right) to intercede on his behalf with Pope Gregory VII. It was at Matilda's castle at Canossa that the fateful encounter between Henry and Gregory occurred. The Countess was a firm supporter of the papacy in its effort to eliminate lay investiture.

COLOR ILLUSTRATION 10
The Crusader Castle at Crac des Chevaliers Held by the Hospitalers, this formidable castle—
placed so as to dominate its countryside—withstood many assaults.

COLOR ILLUSTRATION 11
Abelard and Heloise This illustration,
from a fourteenth-century manuscript of
the *Romance of the Rose,* shows Abelard
and Heloise after the end of their love
affair and marriage, when they were both
in monastic orders. In the letters they
then exchanged, they sometimes
discussed their past love, but they more
often discussed matters of monastic life
and discipline.

COLOR ILLUSTRATION 12

A Mystical Vision   This illustration of a mystical revelation of St. Birgitta of Sweden shows how a mystic could bypass clerical authority (note the clerics kneeling in awe before St. Birgitta) and communicate directly with God (note the book being passed between Christ and St. Birgitta). Indeed, since St. Birgitta is handing material received through her mystical revelation to the kneeling clerics, *she* instructs *them*. Through mysticism some medieval women acquired considerable religious authority, despite their exclusion from universities and most Church positions.

COLOR ILLUSTRATION 13

Giotto, **Lamentation**   With his emphasis on realism, detail, and perspective, Giotto was one of the first artists to reject the more stylized techniques of Byzantine and Gothic art.

CHAPTER 6

DIVISION, INVASION, AND REORGANIZATION, c. 800-1000

✳ INTRODUCTION

Charlemagne's empire, great as it was, never rivaled those of Byzantium and Islam. Between 800 and 1000, his empire disintegrated while those of his neighbors flourished. In Byzantium, these were glorious centuries marked by the conquests of Basil the Bulgar-Slayer, the conversion of the Slavs by the sainted brothers Cyril and Methodius, and the extension of Byzantine influence over Russia. In Baghdad, the Abbasids continued to rule over an extensive empire, a glittering court, and an awesome intellectual and artistic culture. To be sure, the once-unified empire of the Abbasids was broken into several caliphates in the 900s, but even these independent Islamic states were large and well run by Western standards.

The West was not so lucky. The built-in weaknesses of Charlemagne's empire were evident by the time the aged emperor died in 814, but to these weaknesses were soon added the devastating effects of internal division and external invasion. By 843, Charlemagne's empire had been divided among his grandsons, and divisions among later heirs only further fragmented the fragile political unity of the Carolingian world. At the same time, Western Europe was hammered by attacks from three directions: Magyars from the east, Muslims from the south, and Vikings from the north. Charlemagne's dream of a united Christian Europe would survive, but, as Timeline 6.1 shows, from the disintegration of his empire and the power of these invaders would emerge distinctive new political arrangements: a centralized kingdom in England, autonomous duchies and counties in West Francia, a **Holy Roman Empire** in East Francia, and powerful cities in the Italian peninsula.

✳ DIVISION: THE LATER CAROLINGIANS

Like the good Frank that he was, Charlemagne made arrangements to divide his Empire among his several sons, but, as it happened, only one legitimate son, Louis the Pious

TIMELINE 6.1   Division and Invasion, 800–1000

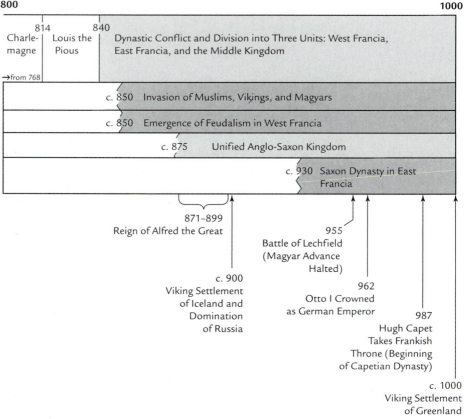

800   1000

814	840	
Charle-magne	Louis the Pious	Dynastic Conflict and Division into Three Units: West Francia, East Francia, and the Middle Kingdom

→from 768

c. 850   Invasion of Muslims, Vikings, and Magyars

c. 850   Emergence of Feudalism in West Francia

c. 875   Unified Anglo-Saxon Kingdom

c. 930   Saxon Dynasty in East Francia

871–899
Reign of Alfred the Great

955
Battle of Lechfield
(Magyar Advance
Halted)

c. 900
Viking Settlement
of Iceland and
Domination
of Russia

962
Otto I Crowned
as German Emperor

987
Hugh Capet
Takes Frankish
Throne (Beginning
of Capetian Dynasty)

c. 1000
Viking Settlement
of Greenland

(r. 814–840), survived him. So, by accident not plan, Charlemagne's empire passed intact to a single heir.

Louis the Pious (r. 814–840) was well named. He ran Charlemagne's concubines out of the imperial court; he gave his wholehearted support to the monastic reforms of Benedict of Aniane; and far more than his hardheaded father, Louis committed himself to the dream of a unified Christian Empire—a City of God brought down to earth. But Louis lacked the resources necessary to maintain cohesion throughout the wide dominions won by his father Charlemagne (r. 768–814), his grandfather Pepin the Short (r. 741–768), and his great-grandfather Charles Martel (r. 714–741). He was neither as politically astute as they nor as militarily successful. Moreover, as wars of conquest gave way to wars of defense, he had fewer gifts of land and treasure with which to reward his aristocratic followers. With the flow of royal largesse drying up, great landholders—many of them made great by past royal generosity—began to desert the monarchy and look to their own interests.

But one of Louis's greatest threats came closer to home: unhappy sons. Early in his reign, he made preparations to pass his imperial authority to his eldest son, giving modest kingdoms to the other two. These younger sons were unhappy about their brother's greater inheritance, and their unhappiness was later exacerbated by the birth of a fourth son, for whom provision also had to be made. Eventually, the sons of Louis the Pious rebelled openly against him and plunged the Empire into civil war. Louis was even captured and briefly deposed.

The animosities among Louis's sons ran deep, but their disputes also tapped into long-standing cultural and linguistic divisions among the people of the Empire. In Strasbourg in 842, when one son took his oath in the ancestral language of modern German and the other in the language that would evolve into modern French, their accommodation to the different native tongues of their soldiers was a practical matter. Today, the Strasbourg oaths seem symbolic as well as practical, for they illustrate the cultural divisions that the political unity of the Empire never obliterated. When the civil wars were finally resolved the following year, the Treaty of Verdun (843) had to reconcile not only competing brothers but also competing regions.

As Map 6.1 shows, this pivotal treaty divided the Carolingian Empire into three new states (one of the four brothers had died, leaving only three claimants). The borders created by the Treaty of Verdun looked to both the past and the future, respecting the distinctive regions of the old Carolingian Empire while also drawing the rough outlines from which would eventually emerge the modern states of France and Germany.

Lothar (r. 823–855), the eldest brother, kept the prestigious imperial title but retained practical authority over only a third of the old empire—a "Middle Kingdom" that embraced Rome as well as Aachen, stretching in a long swath from the center of the Italian peninsula to the North Sea. This kingdom quickly dissolved after Lothar's death in 855, but the middleness of his inheritance would long shape European history. Its shadow can be seen in Burgundian influence in the Netherlands in the fifteenth century, in territorial conflicts between France and Germany in the nineteenth and twentieth centuries, and in the easy mingling of French and German speech in towns like Strasbourg even today. Lothar's two brothers took inheritances that proved more enduring. Louis the German (r. 840–876) took East Francia, the nucleus of modern Germany, and Charles the Bald (r. 840–877) took West Francia, from which would evolve modern France.

At first, however, it looked like none of the three new states would endure, for all coped poorly with the military crises of the later ninth century. By 843, Muslim pirates and Vikings raiders were already wreaking fearsome damage along the Mediterranean and Atlantic coasts, and Magyar horsemen would soon similarly ravage eastern parts of the old Carolingian Empire. Charlemagne's descendants proved incapable of defending their land and people against these attacks. Plagued by internal weakness and external threat, the leadership of the Carolingians simply crumbled in the later ninth and tenth centuries.

✳ INVASION: MUSLIMS, MAGYARS, AND VIKINGS

The invasions of the ninth and tenth centuries might have seemed terrifyingly new to their victims, but invasions were a fact of life in early medieval Europe. Muslim pirates in the ninth and tenth centuries were but a distant echo of the disciplined Umayyad armies that had seized Iberia from the Visigoths in the early eighth century. The Magyars who began to trouble the eastern borders of Europe in the late ninth century came in the footsteps of Attila the Hun (r. 433–453), who had also once moved west from the Asiatic steppes. And Viking raiders came, as had Franks, Saxons, and other

Map 6.1 *The Partition of the Carolingian Empire, 843*   When Charlemagne's grandsons divided the empire among themselves, Charles the Bald took West Francia, from which would eventually emerge the medieval realm of France. Louis the German took East Francia, from which arose in the tenth century the Holy Roman Empire. And Lothar, the eldest brother, took the imperial title and an impossible-to-govern swath of territory known as the Middle Kingdom.

barbarians before them, from north central Europe. Indeed, what was odd about the history of invasions of Europe between 300 and 1000 was Europe's relative freedom from incursion between 750 and 850—that is, between, the Muslim conquest of Iberia in the early 700s and the intensifying raids of Muslims, Vikings, and Magyars in the later 800s. This century of relative peace was a great buttress to Carolingian empire building, and the return of peace after 1000 would be a similar blessing for those who lived during the Central Middle Ages.

But this longer perspective would have offered little comfort in the later eighth and ninth centuries when, as Map 6.2 shows, Western Christendom was attacked on all

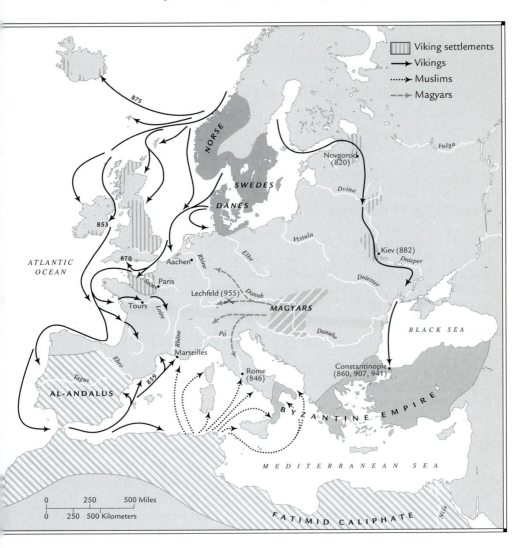

Map 6.2   *The Viking, Magyar, and Muslim Invasions, c. 800–1000*   In the ninth century, Europeans faced threats on all sides. To the east, they faced Magyars who raided deep into the Holy Roman Empire and down the Italian peninsula. To the south, they feared Muslim raiders who harried the French and Italian coasts and all islands in between. And to the north and west, they dreaded the sight of Viking ships. The Danes and Norse settled in some places and ravaged elsewhere, whereas the Swedes swept through central Europe, following the Dnieper to the Black Sea and Constantinople.

fronts. In the southern parts of Charlemagne's old empire, people prayed for divine protection against the Muslims: "Eternal Trinity, deliver thy Christian people from the oppression of the pagans." To the north they prayed, "From the savage nation of the Northmen, which lays waste our realms, deliver us, O God." And in the northern Italian peninsula: "Against the arrows of the Magyars be thou our protector." Like the barbarians who had both troubled Rome and revitalized it in the fourth and fifth centuries, the invaders of the ninth and tenth centuries would eventually bring good as well as harm to the European West. But at first contact, Muslim pirates, Viking raiders, and Magyar horsemen caused suffering and terror.

Muslim Pirates and Magyar Horsemen

As we have already seen, in the seventh and early eighth centuries, Arab armies sought to settle in Europe, and after overrunning Visigothic Iberia, they established the flourishing state of al-Andalus. Charlemagne had created a Spanish March (or borderland) between his empire and al-Andalus, and the two states thereafter coexisted in a tense equilibrium, with some trade, some skirmishes, and much religious misunderstanding. When Muslim pirates began to threaten the Mediterranean coast in the ninth century, they came, unlike their predecessors, as raiders rather than settlers. From bases in North Africa, Iberia, and Sicily, Muslim pirates preyed on shipping, plundered coastal cities, and sailed up rivers to raid inland settlements. They also established lairs on the southern coast of West Francia (today's French Riviera), from which they ravaged the countryside, even kidnapping pilgrims crossing the Alpine passes. Charlemagne had never possessed much of a navy, and his successors found themselves helpless to defend their coasts. In 846 Muslims even raided Rome itself, desecrating its churches and stealing its treasures.

For the people of Western Christendom, the terror of Muslim marauders fostered further intolerance of Islamic culture and religion. Referring insultingly to Muslims as Saracens ("heathen nomads") or **infidels** ("people without faith"), Christians endured their raids almost until the year 1000. As late as 982 a German king was severely defeated by a Muslim army in the southern Italian peninsula. But by then southern Europe, bristling with fortifications and organized around tough local warlords, had learned to defend itself and was even beginning to challenge Muslim domination of the western Mediterranean.

The Magyars, descendants of fierce nomadic horsemen from the Asiatic steppes, harassed East Francia, the northern Italian peninsula, and eastern and central portions of West Francia in the first half of the tenth century. After settling in the shelter of the Carpathian mountains in the 890s, the Magyars sent out raiding parties that plundered defenseless settlements, avoided fortified towns, and outmaneuvered any army sent against them. In time, however, the Magyars became more sedentary and took up farming. In 955 King Otto the Great (r. 936–973) crushed a large Magyar army at the battle of Lechfeld and brought their incursions to an end. Within another half-century, the Magyars had established a kingdom of their own and adopted Christianity. By the end of the first millennium, the Hungarians (a name derived from one Magyar group) were becoming part of Western Christendom.

Viking Raiders

The Vikings (or Northmen) of Scandinavia were the most fearsome invaders of all. Their Scandinavian homeland was a patchwork of petty states, populated by landowning aristocrats, free farmers, and slaves. As elsewhere, women were subordinated to men, and there were instances of Viking lords having several wives (as had Frankish aristocrats until Charlemagne's reforms). The Scandinavian economy was based on grain growing, fishing, and stock-raising, but land was so limited that property squabbles and private wars were common. Although only a few small towns dotted the landscape,

Figure 6.1   *Viking Ship*   Excavated in Norway, this ship was used c. 800 to bury two women, along with their clothes and household implements. Beautifully carved and of elegant shape, it was a practical machine of trade and war. Propelled by oars and sail, ships of this sort had great speed on the open sea, but they could also navigate rivers and be easily pulled ashore.

Scandinavian merchant-seafarers were well known in the ports of Europe for the many goods they brought across great distances. In this world, fame and reputation were all-important. According to a tenth-century Viking maxim, "Cattle die, kinsfolk die, we ourselves must die. But one thing I know will never die: the dead man's reputation." In many cases, a Viking's reputation or distinguishing characteristic was expressed in nick-names. Among the more intriguing names (a few of them half-legendary) were Harold Bluetooth, Swen Forkbeard, Eric Bloodax, Ivar the Boneless, Gorm the Old, Magnus Bare-Legs, and Eystein Fart.

By the year 800, several factors were sending this restless energy abroad. First, population had so increased that landless sons began to seek their fortunes elsewhere. Second, as a few kings began to assert their authority, some malcontents were driven to seek new opportunities abroad. And third, these landless sons and malcontents traveled on eminently seaworthy ships, propelled by sail as well as oars and carrying crews of forty to a hundred warriors at speeds up to ten knots (see Figure 6.1). Capable of voy-ages on the open sea, these vessels nevertheless rode so high in the water that they could also navigate rivers easily and be pulled ashore onto beaches. These ships had long been used for traveling, fishing, fighting, trading, and even burial; by 800, they also became important weapons of raiding. Viking warriors struck the ports of northern Europe, and they sailed up rivers, plundering towns and monasteries and taking large numbers of captives, whom they sold as slaves in the markets of al-Andalus, the Russian states, and the Mediterranean. Sometimes they left their boats, stealing horses and riding across the countryside to spread their devastation still further.

Vikings particularly delighted in attacking monasteries, defenseless places rich in gold and silver plate, fine vestments, and books. Their attacks were so violent, brutal, and terrifying that some nuns are said to have resorted to "heroics of virginity" to discourage Viking rapists. One chronicler reports that after Ebba, the abbess of Coldingham (d. 874), learned that Vikings were approaching her abbey, she used a razor to cut off her nose and upper lip. All her nuns did the same. When Vikings arrived the next day, they were so horrified by the sight of these mutilated and bloody women that they left—but not before burning the monastery and all the nuns within it. The nuns perished, but they died, as their self-mutilation had intended, as virgins. Let us hope that few took such extreme action, but from such measures—or stories about them—might have come the expression "cut off your nose to spite your face."

Viking raids were often preceded by such extraordinarily good intelligence gathering that their success was almost guaranteed in advance. Vikings always seemed to know when a realm had an inept king, or if a town was weakened by political factionalism, or whether a monastery was rich with treasure. Strong trade networks helped Vikings know where and when to attack. Raiding, in turn, promoted more trade, as Vikings would sell in one place what they had plundered in another. So, for example, they sold some English gospel books back to their victims, one of which today bears this inscription: "I Ealdorman Alfred and Waerburh my wife obtained these books from the heathen army with our pure money, that is with pure gold, and we did this for love of God and for the benefit of our souls and because we do not wish these holy books to remain longer in heathen possession."[1] Vikings were canny traders as well as cruel raiders.

The Vikings shared so much that distinctions among them were by no means sharp. But as a general rule, during the great age of Viking expansion in the ninth and tenth centuries, the Danes focused their attention on West Francia and the Anglo-Saxon kingdoms; the Norwegians raided and settled in Scotland, Ireland, and the North Atlantic; and the Swedes turned toward the east, concentrating on the Baltic shores, the Russian states, and the Byzantine Empire. Nevertheless, too much can be made of these general divisions, and it is proper to regard Viking raids, explorations, and commercial enterprises as a single great international movement. In this movement, men raided but both men and women settled. In places as far afield as Reykjavik and Kiev, Viking women joined their men in founding new colonies and consolidating new conquests. All told, the impact of the Vikings on Europe was new, terrifying, and lasting.

Vikings in England and the Continent

To mariners such as the Vikings, the English Channel was a boulevard instead of a barrier, and their raiding parties attacked British and continental shores indiscriminately.

---

[1] An ealdorman was a great lord, the Anglo-Saxon equivalent of a West Frankish count.

The Anglo-Saxon kingdoms were the first to suffer. In 793, the Northumbrian monastery of Lindisfarne was annihilated, and other nearby abbeys soon met a similar fate. In 842 the Danes plundered London, and they soon thereafter established permanent winter bases, which freed them from returning to Scandinavia after each raiding season. By the later 800s, they had turned from piracy to large-scale occupation and permanent settlement. One after another, the Anglo-Saxon kingdoms were overrun until, in the 870s, only the southern kingdom of Wessex remained free of Danish control. On the continent, Viking raiders established permanent bases at the mouths of large rivers and sailed up them to plunder monasteries and sack towns. Antwerp was ravaged in 837, Rouen in 841, Hamburg and Paris in 845, and Charlemagne's old capital at Aachen in 881.

The Vikings easily overcame most opposition they encountered. They were sometimes turned away with bribes, but seldom by armed resistance. Slowly, however, a few kings managed to protect their lands. King Alfred the Great of Wessex (r. 871–899) won a great battle in 878 that saved his kingdom from Danish conquest, and he thereafter began to roll back the Danish presence in England. King Arnulf of East Francia (r. 887–899) won a decisive victory in 891 that lessened Viking pressure on this region (this gave him only brief respite, however, for Magyar raids soon began on his eastern borders). King Charles the Simple of West Francia (r. 898–922) created in 911 a relatively friendly Viking buffer state in the north by concluding a treaty with a Norse chieftain named Rolf. Rolf's band had established a settlement at the mouth of the River Seine, and Charles, less simple than his name would imply, reasoned that if he could make Rolf his ally, the Seine settlement might prove an effective barrier against further raids. Rolf married Charles the Simple's daughter, became a Christian, and recognized Charles as his lord. Expanding gradually under Rolf and his successors, this land of the Northmen—that is, Normandy—would produce in the eleventh century some of Europe's best warriors, crusaders, administrators, and monks.

Vikings in the North Atlantic and the Russian States

The North Atlantic was as enticing to the Vikings as the English Channel. They quickly took the Scottish isles and most of the Scottish west coast, and by the mid-800s, they controlled the greater part of Ireland and had turned Dublin into an important Viking town. Between 875 and 930, they settled remote and desolate Iceland, from which grew not only a distinctive Norse culture but still further exploration and settlement. In Iceland the magnificent oral traditions of the Vikings were preserved in sagas that enlivened dark Icelandic winters with stories of brave warriors and strong women. From Iceland, sailors settled in the late 900s on the coast of Greenland (which would be ruled by the King of Norway until 1944), and they later established temporary settlements on the northern coast of North America itself (Newfoundland), anticipating Columbus by half a millennium.

To the east, Swedish Vikings overran what is today Finland and penetrated southward along rivers to trade with Constantinople and Baghdad. The Swedes attacked Constantinople in 860, 907, and 941, never taking the city but wresting valuable trading privileges from the Byzantines. Impressed by the big and bellicose Swedes, Byzantine emperors even incorporated them into the imperial guard.

In the Russian states, a Swedish dynasty established itself at Novgorod in the later ninth century, ruling over the indigenous Slavic population. In the tenth century, a

prince of Novgorod captured the city of Kiev, which became capital of the powerful, well-organized state of Kievan Rus (and is today capital of Ukraine).[2] Deeply influenced by the culture of its subjects, the dynasty at Kiev eventually became more Slavic than Scandinavian. Around the turn of the millennium, as we have seen, Prince Vladimir of Kiev (r. 980–1015) chose Eastern Orthodox Christianity for his new state, preferring its lustrous pageantry to sober Islam, stateless Judaism, and drab Catholic Christianity. By submitting himself and his subjects to the spiritual authority of the patriarch of Constantinople, Vladimir opened his fledgling state to the influence of Byzantine culture.

Twilight of the Viking Age

The young monarchies that began to develop in Denmark, Norway, and Sweden in the 700s had initially driven some Viking adventurers to seek their fortunes elsewhere, but they ultimately pacified Scandinavia itself. As kings grew stronger, they encouraged peaceable settlement of disputes, discouraged roaming warrior bands, and promoted a more humdrum life. Their efforts were enhanced by Christianity which, by the year 1000, was winning converts all across the Scandinavian world. In Iceland, in the Russian states, even in the kingdoms of Scandinavia itself, the Vikings slowly adopted the religion of the monks and nuns whom they had once terrorized. The Viking threat would continue for a while, but in a changed form. Although England continued to face attacks from the North far into the eleventh century, these invaders were no longer pirate bands; instead, they were armies led by Scandinavian kings. As the new millennium dawned, Scandinavians, like Hungarians, were becoming members of Western Christendom.

✵ Reorganization: New Polities

The invasions of the ninth and tenth centuries brought significant changes to the political and social organization of Western Europe. In West Francia, as unwieldy royal armies failed to cope with the Viking raids, royal authority waned and aristocratic power waxed strong. Elsewhere the invasions had the effect of augmenting royal power. The monarchy of East Francia, after a period of relative weakness, underwent a spectacular recovery in the tenth century, while in England the hammer blows of the Danes had the ultimate result of unifying the several Anglo-Saxon states into a single kingdom. In short, Europeans submitted to whatever leadership could provide an effective defense— whether kings, territorial princes, or, as in the northern Italian peninsula, bishops.

England: Unification

In the later eighth century, on the eve of the Viking invasions, southern Britain was politically fragmented, as it had been ever since the Anglo-Saxon conquests. But it was less fragmented than before, for several smaller kingdoms had gradually passed under the control of four larger ones: Northumbria in the north, Mercia in the Midlands, East Anglia in the southeast, and Wessex in the south. The Danish attacks of the ninth century destroyed the power of Wessex's rivals, clearing the field for the Wessex monarchy to

[2] Today, "prince" often refers to a male member of a royal family (e.g., Princes William and Harry, grandsons of Queen Elizabeth II of Great Britain). In earlier centuries, however, "prince" meant a chief ruler of a region (from the Latin *princeps*). Hence, Machiavelli's *The Prince* (1532) was a guide for rulers, not a guide for sons of rulers, and Elizabeth I of England (r. 1558–1603) called herself a "prince," without any sense that this was a peculiar term for either a monarch or a woman. It is this second, more general sense of "prince" that is used here and throughout this book.

MEDIEVAL MYTHS

Pope Joan

A few years ago, I picked up a novel so good that it kept me wide-awake through a long transatlantic flight. It told a dramatic tale of a young medieval girl whose thirst for learning led her to dress as a boy, become a monk, and eventually even be elected pope. I enjoyed every fictional minute until, at the end of the book, the novelist tried to make her tale into history, claiming that her heroine was a *real* pope of the ninth century. This myth of a medieval Pope Joan has a long history, but not one that goes back as far as the 800s. The story was first concocted some 400 years later, around 1250. Although my twentieth-century novel depicted Pope Joan as a sympathetic, strong-minded woman, even a sort of feminist heroine, the thirteenth-century story made Pope Joan into a figure of horror and even abomination. A weak woman, the medieval "she-Pope" could not even keep her vow of celibacy; worse yet, she got pregnant; worst of all, she gave birth in the midst of a papal procession through the streets of Rome. In the hands of medieval authors, in other words, Pope Joan exemplified the moral and physical weaknesses that were then often attributed to women. The story was so horrible to contemplate, it was said that later popes took de-tours to avoid the site of this one-and-only papal childbirth and that a new papal throne was introduced with a hollow seat that allowed the male genitals of each new pope to be checked. By 1300, the tale of Pope Joan was widely believed, and after 1500, it took on new life as a form of anti-Catholic propaganda. But Pope Joan was never more than a story, one that horrified medieval people, delighted Protestant polemicists, and entertains us mod-erns. If you'd like to be so entertained, read Donna Woolfolk Cross's *Pope Joan* (1997), but then please also read Alain Boureau's *The Myth of Pope Joan* (1993), a scholarly demoli-tion of the story's historical basis. Pope Joan is fun to imagine, but her existence is purely imaginary.

undertake further consolidation. But if the Danes were doing the Wessex monarchy a favor, neither side was aware of it during the troubled years of the later ninth century. At the time it appeared that the Danes might conquer Wessex itself.

King Alfred the Great (r. 871–899)

At the moment of worst crisis a remarkable leader, Alfred the Great, rose to the Wessex throne. Like other Anglo-Saxon kings, Alfred sometimes bribed Vikings to steer clear of his kingdom and sometimes met them in pitched battle. In the winter of 877–878, when the Danes mounted a surprise attack, Alfred had to take refuge, with a handful of com-panions, in a remote swamp on the Isle of Athelney (if you drive today from Bristol to Exeter, you'll pass near the place). Athelney was Alfred's Valley Forge. In the following spring, he rallied his forces and smashed a Danish army at the battle of Edington. This victory turned the tide of the war; the Danish leader accepted Christianity, withdrew from Wessex, and agreed to a permanent peace.

But other Danes refused to honor the peace, and in fighting them, Alfred extended his authority to the north and east. By 886 he had captured London—even then Britain's chief city—and shortly thereafter a new peace treaty gave him most of southern and southwestern Britain. To extend his influence still further, he married his daughter Ethelfled (c. 869–918) to the Mercian king and thereby sealed an alliance with that

Map 6.3   *England under Alfred the Great (d. 899)*   In several hard-fought victories over the Danes, King Alfred secured London and all the south coast for Wessex. He then allied with Mercia by marrying his daughter to the Mercian king. Much of the east of Britain—the Danelaw—remained under Danish control, but the Danes agreed by treaty that they would not attack Alfred's realm.

Anglo-Saxon kingdom to his north. The rest of England—the "Danelaw"—remained under Danish control, but virtually all of non-Danish England was now united under a single king (see Map 6.3).

Like all successful leaders of the age, Alfred was an able warrior, but he was also an imaginative leader who looked to the future. As Alfred himself described his efforts, he was someone who wandered through a great forest collecting timber with which others could build. Among other innovations, Alfred issued a far-reaching law code, systematized military recruitment, assembled a navy, and built defensive strongholds throughout his lands. Many of these forts (or burgs) eventually developed commercial as well as strategic importance because their walls provided security for artisans to work and merchants to trade. Like Charlemagne, Alfred had his biographer, and from the stories of Asser's *Life of Alfred* would grow still more legends until Alfred, like Charlemagne, became a sort of folk hero. In English villages and towns today (including Athelney), you can still encounter heroic statues of Alfred, most of them erected during the nineteenth century when Victorians were fascinated by their medieval heritage.

Alfred was also a scholar and patron of learning. But the great days of Bede (673–735), Boniface (c. 675–754), and Alcuin (735–804) were far in the past, for Viking pillaging of English monasteries had so undermined education that Latin—the key to Classical-Christian culture—was little known. Alfred responded with an intellectual salvage operation that focused on encouraging literacy (among laity as well as clergy) and the translation of Latin works into Anglo-Saxon. Alfred gathered talented scholars around him, and he participated himself in the work, helping to translate such books as Boethius's *Consolation of Philosophy,* Pope Gregory the Great's *Pastoral Care,* and Bede's *Ecclesiastical History.* In his preface to *Pastoral Care,* he wrote nostalgically of the days "before everything was ravaged and burned, when England's churches overflowed with treasures and books." Alfred also likely ordered the keeping of the *Anglo-Saxon Chronicle,* a remarkable record of events and documents that stretches back to 450 (and even earlier, as it includes comments on Jesus' birth) and would continue until 1154.

Alfred's work of reconquest was carried on by his able successors in the first half of the tenth century. His two children—Edward, king of Wessex (r. 899–924) and Ethelfled, lady of the Mercians (r. 900–918)—worked in close harmony to defend their realms against the Vikings, and in the process, they helped to consolidate what Alfred had begun: the creation of an English kingdom out of the many realms of the Anglo-Saxons. In the 950s even the Danelaw came under the control of Wessex; Danish settlers remained in northern and eastern England (where they would leave their mark in, among other things, villages and towns whose names today end in -by or -thorpe), but they were under Wessex rule. By the 990s almost all of Britain south of the Firth of Forth was in the hands of Alfred's successors, and the kings of Wessex had become the kings of England. Out of the agony of invasions the English monarchy had been born.

The Renewal of the Danish Attacks: Ethelred and Canute

For a generation after the Wessex kings conquered the Danelaw, England enjoyed relative peace and prosperity. English fleets patrolled the shores; towns grew up around some of the fortresses Alfred had built; new kings were selected from among Alfred's descendants at the Witan, an assembly of great officers, landowners, and churchmen; and St. Dunstan (c. 909–988), Abbot of Glastonbury and later Archbishop of Canterbury, engineered a monastic revival throughout the realm. But the Danish inhabitants of northern and eastern England remained only half committed to the new English monarchy, and with the succession of a child-king, Ethelred "the Unready" (r. 978–1016), the Danish invasions resumed—this time, in a campaign of conquest directed by the Danish monarchy.[3]

---

[3] "Unready" is the traditional but incorrect translation of Ethelred's nickname. "Ethelred the Unred" is closer to the original, but this makes sense only to those familiar with the Anglo-Saxon language. It was a kind of joke: since the name "Ethelred" meant "noble counsel," "Ethelred the Unred" meant "noble counsel the uncounseled" or something of the sort. It was perhaps more amusing in the tenth century than it is today. Ethelred the Ill-Advised is probably the best English translation.

Ethelred's response was plagued by incompetence, treason, and panic, and he soon had to agree to a desperate measure: the paying of an annual tribute to the Danes, known thereafter as *danegeld,* which was raised by a tax on all English lands. The danegeld is a testament to the efficiency of Anglo-Saxon government (which had to collect it), and long after the Danes had left England, it would remain a lucrative source of income for the English monarchy. But in Ethelred's time it was a costly embarrassment.

When Ethelred died in 1016, he was soon succeeded as ruler of the English by Canute of Denmark (r. in England, 1017–1035). Canute ruled long and well. He conquered Norway as well as England, and joining these two lands to his kingdom of Denmark, he became the master of a huge North Sea empire held together by the wealth of England. A product of the new civilizing forces at work in eleventh-century Scandinavia, Canute was no footloose Viking. He issued law codes, practiced Christianity, and kept the peace. Devoting much of his time to England, he cast himself as a king in the old Wessex tradition, respecting the ancient customs of the land and giving generously to monasteries. "Merry sang the monks of Ely," we are told, "as Canute the king rowed by."

But Canute's Danish-Norwegian-English empire failed to survive his death in 1035, and his own complicated marital history was partly to blame. When Canute seized the English throne, he promptly married Emma (c. 985–1052), daughter of the Duke of Normandy and widow of King Ethelred. Having been married to Ethelred in 1002 to seal a Norman-English alliance against Danish attackers, Emma found herself married in 1017 to one of those attackers. Her second marriage legitimated both Canute's claim to the English throne and his conversion to Christianity, but it was a bit awkward since he had already contracted a union with Aelfgifu of Northampton, by whom he had two sons. Canute never repudiated Aelfgifu, but only Emma was made a consecrated queen. Emma chose to regard Aelfgifu's children as illegitimate, but Canute's two unions and the sons born of them created an uncertain succession after his death. Emma's own marital history complicated matters still further. She had two sons by Ethelred and one by Canute—each could claim the throne as son of an English king. In the uncertainty that followed Canute's death, two of his sons—one by Aelfgifu and one by Emma—briefly held the throne, and then the realm fell peacefully to one of Emma's sons by Ethelred, Edward the Confessor (r. 1042–1066), who had grown up among his mother's kin in Normandy. Edward disliked his mother and exiled her from court, but in an age of multiple royal marriages and self-interested royal motherhood, he owed his crown, in large part, to her.[4]

Edward ruled England in relative peace, but his own marriage was childless, and this created another disputed succession that set the stage for the invasion of William the Conqueror, duke of Normandy in 1066. When William won the English crown in the Battle of Hastings, he inherited a prosperous kingdom with well-established political and legal traditions—a kingdom still divided by differences in custom but with a deep-seated respect for royal authority. With the timber that Alfred collected, his successors had built a sturdy edifice.

---

[4] Mindful of her place in history, Emma commissioned a fascinating history of her life and times, *Encomium Emmae Reginae,* available in a translation by Alistair Campbell (1949, reprinted with a new introduction by Simon Keynes in 1998).

West Francia: Fragmentation

In England the invasions promoted the growth of royal power. In West Francia—the territory from which modern France would evolve—the invasions encouraged a breakdown of royal authority, with local aristocrats assuming powers once reserved for kings. Faced with Viking plunderers who descended unannounced, wreaked enormous damage, and then disappeared into the mists, the Carolingian kings of West Francia failed to defend their realm. Distances were too great, communications too primitive, and the royal army too unwieldy. Into this power vacuum stepped dukes, counts, and local nobles—warriors who were better able than distant kings to protect their regions from the Viking threat.

As the monarchy became a far-off and irrelevant institution, dukes and counts changed from men empowered by royal office into territorial princes tied only loosely to their king. Powers they had once held by grant of the king—custody of royal lands, tribunals, tax revenues, and military conscription—ripened into hereditary possessions that they held by virtue of their fathers or mothers. Lands and powers that they had once administered for the king they now administered for themselves. The heartland of Charlemagne's Empire was transformed into a mosaic of hundreds of largely independent duchies and counties.

The Carolingian kings of West Francia grew so powerless that in 987 the crown passed permanently to a new dynasty, the Capetians (named after its founder, Hugh Capet). In the twelfth and thirteenth centuries, the Capetians would produce some of France's most celebrated kings, but at its beginning, the new dynasty was nearly as feeble as its predecessor. Hugh Capet's power base was the royal domain around Paris known as the Ile de France. As Map 6.4 illustrates, it was no greater in size and wealth than any of a number of French principalities of the period. In theory the Capetian monarch was king of the French, but in reality he was merely one prince among many.

Over the course of the tenth and eleventh centuries, some French aristocratic families combined groups of counties, through marriage and conquest, into larger territorial blocs and grew especially powerful. This process gradually reversed the political disintegration that had begun at Verdun in 843, but it led to great dukes, not great kings. In the eleventh century, the dukes of Aquitaine and Normandy and the counts of Flanders, Anjou, Blois, Champagne, and Burgundy were in most practical respects the equals of the king of France. They based their power on the control of lands, tribunals, taxes, and public services that had formerly pertained to the Carolingian monarchy. Their governance was more effective than that of the Carolingians had ever been. They had the advantage of ruling compact territorial units, which they governed fairly efficiently. Some continued to administer their dominions through regional landholders who were bound to them by oaths of loyalty, but others were wealthy enough to employ salaried officials who could be transferred or removed at will. They also encouraged a commercial revival and then benefited from the higher tax revenues it generated.

Of course, all was not peaceful and prosperous. Private warfare was almost incessant, thanks not only to Muslim, Magyar, and Viking threats, but also to territorial wars between rival princes. The situation was so bad that the Church tried, around the year 1000, to impose a Peace of God (which proscribed attacks on clergy and the poor) and a Truce of God (which forbade violence during important Christian holidays). These

Map 6.4   *France, c. 1000*   In 1000, the Capetians *claimed* authority over all of this territory, but most counts and dukes ruled with little thought about their royal overlords in the Ile de France. The territory directly controlled by the Capetians (that is, their "royal domain") was small and remote. For the Counts of Toulouse and many other great lords, it was easy to ignore Capetian claims.

peace movements curbed violence a bit, but not much. Still, with their increased wealth, efficient bureaucracies, and loyal armies, the princely regimes of early France were able to govern with an effectiveness that was more reminiscent of Rome than Aachen. In the meantime, the royal authority of the Capetian kings remained more theoretical than real, and France was a land of duchies and counties, not a true kingdom.

Feudalism

Feudalism grew out of the political disintegration of West Francia in the ninth and tenth centuries, but it would eventually become a building block of political centralization. "Feudalism" must be reckoned among the most abused and confusing terms in the historical lexicon. To begin with, feudalism is a modern word; a medieval person would probably have talked about *vassalage*. To make matters worse, historians disagree about the meaning and usefulness of the term. Some historians argue that we should stop talking about feudalism altogether, for, in their view, it describes a system that exists more in the minds of historians today than it ever did during the Middle Ages. Other historians, following a practice that dates back to Karl Marx, use feudalism to describe the *economy* of the Middle Ages; to a scholar trained in this tradition, feudalism is a stage in economic development, located between slavery and capitalism, in which serfs on their manors were forced to labor on behalf of a warrior class. (You might encounter this definition of feudalism in economics and sociology classes.) Many other historians use feudalism to describe the *political* and *social* structures whereby the landowning elite governed ordinary people, but not the economic structures that supported the elite, which are treated separately as manorialism. It is this last definition we will use here. *Manorialism* (which, as we saw in the last chapter, encompasses the economic arrangements whereby the landowning elite was supported by the peasantry) and *feudalism* (the political and social arrangements whereby the landowning elite governed) were related but separate medieval practices.

The political and social customs of feudalism developed in France in response to the terror of invasions and the ineffectuality of the later Carolingians. It was rooted, first of all, in a relationship between mounted warriors—a lord and his **vassal.** Like so many medieval practices, this relationship drew on Roman and barbarian customs. Romans had fostered relations of patronage, whereby one man would be a patron to many clients; Franks and other barbarians had joined men under one warlord in a comitatus. By the early eighth century, a technological advance—the use of the stirrup—gave renewed importance to these past methods of creating bonds between men. The stirrup made it possible for a soldier to fight with confidence on a horse, and it had two direct effects: first, it led to a strategic reliance on cavalry instead of infantry, and second, it created a new class of full-time fighters. Before the stirrup, all freemen had been both peasants and warriors; after the stirrup, horse-borne soldiers needed so much equipment and training that fighting became a career. These professional soldiers (or **knights**) needed to be supported—fed and housed, of course, but also equipped with horses, weapons, and protective armor and trained in their use. Vassalage answered that need. Wealthy men who needed soldiers (lords) promised to support and protect the men under their command (vassals).

This lord-vassal relationship quickly began to have a basis in land. Many knights and nobles of northern France came to hold estates in return for service—usually military service—rendered to a greater lord. An estate held on these *conditional* terms (if no service was rendered, the estate could be reclaimed) was often called a **fief** (rhyming with "beef"). Because this tie between landholding and military service grew so important, the term feudalism derives from *feudum,* the Latin term for fief. Typically, the holder of a fief became the vassal of his lord, rendering him loyalty and service in a solemn ceremony of homage. The granting of estates to armed supporters was a convenient way for a lord to maintain a retinue of warriors in an age when money was scarce and land abundant.

Charlemagne had given estates to his dukes and counts in return for their service to him. And he had relied on oaths of personal loyalty to bind together the political structures of his empire. So this first aspect of feudalism was not new in the later 800s. But two other aspects were: the weakness of centralized government and the wielding of public power by private persons. Both of these characteristics arose in the uncertainties of the late ninth century, when local government became the only effective government. Charlemagne's heirs (and the Capetians after them) still continued to *claim* authority over all their territories, but their claims were empty. Centralized government collapsed, and when Vikings or other marauders threatened, local lords took over the responsibilities of government. These lords sometimes supported their regional dukes or counts and sometimes did not; they seldom paid attention to the royal heirs of Charlemagne. Together with dukes and counts, these local lords constituted a single class of landowning and vassal-commanding **nobles,** and it was these nobles—minor as well as great— who began to do what Charlemagne's government had once done: they sent out troops to resist attackers; they hanged thieves and murderers; they minted new coins; they issued orders and laws that they expected to be obeyed. In the absence of central government, local landowners took public power into their own hands.

By 900, in some regions of France, a series of feudal regimes had emerged. Local nobles commanded armies that offered resistance against Vikings and protection against the armies of other nobles. They paid little attention to their putative kings, the later Carolingians. And they held, by right of sheer armed force, the power to govern. This was government by armed thugs, but it was also effective government. If you had lived in a small town along a wide river in western France, you would have been more than grateful to your local lord and his vassals when the Vikings came ashore.

Among the warrior aristocracy of post-Carolingian France, vassalage touched both great and small. A powerful count or duke was often, in theory at least, a vassal of his king, and lesser nobles might, in turn, hold estates as vassals of counts or dukes, while granting even smaller fiefs to vassals of their own. Thus, a single person might be both the vassal of a greater lord and the lord of lesser vassals. But all knights were not noble. Nobles were, like all knights, trained in techniques of mounted combat, but in addition to their knightly prowess, they were empowered by good birth, extensive landholding, or both. The knights who fought under these nobles were similarly trained but not as socially advantaged; they stood midway in status between the nobility and the peasantry. They were knights but not titled lords. Nobles and knights shared a common military vocation, were similarly equipped with arms, armor, and warhorses, and of course were exempt from agricultural labor. But whereas nobles possessed large estates, many knights had little or no land, and whereas nobles led armies into battle, mere knights followed and obeyed. There was always some movement between these groups, especially in the earliest years of feudalism, but the distinction was a lasting one. For more on noble life in the early centuries of feudalism, see the Biographical Sketch of Hugh, Earl of Chester (c. 1048–1101) on pp. 138–139.

By the tenth century another military innovation of surpassing importance was becoming an essential part of the feudal landscape: castles. The earliest castles bore little resemblance to the great turreted fortresses of the later Middle Ages; many were nothing more than small, square towers, usually of wood, planted on hilltops or artificial mounds and encircled by wooden stockades. But when effectively garrisoned, castles were powerful instruments of defense and territorial control. Many castles were built by nobles; others were built (or seized) by ambitious warriors of less exalted status. Eventually known as *castellans,* these men assembled knightly retinues of their own, subjected surrounding lands to their control, and ascended in time into the older nobility. The coming of castles changed the character of the aristocracy by giving great families, old and new, a specifically located center of power. Soon many of them began identifying themselves by the name of their chief castle, their *family seat.* Nobles previously known simply by their first names—Geoffrey or Roger—became Geoffrey de Mandeville and Roger de Beaumont, hereditary lords of the castles of Mandeville and Beaumont.

Castles fostered a new sense of family identity within the nobility. So too did the tendency for fiefs to become hereditary. Fairly quickly, the heirs of vassals came to expect to inherit fiefs as well as the service obligations attached to them. Both castles and heritable fiefs encouraged male **primogeniture** (inheritance by the first-born son), and as fiefs, castles, and lordship passed from father to eldest son, the meaning of "family" slowly changed. Where once "family" had signified an amorphous group of relatives in which one brother might be as important as another and all kin mattered, regardless of whether traced through mother or father, nobles and their vassals increasingly began to focus on one segment of that family, the *male lineage.* To the warrior class of medieval Europe, lineage (a line that stretched back through many generations, usually from father to son) slowly grew more important than kinship (a web that embraced in-laws, cousins, aunts and uncles, and more distant kin).

In early feudal society, daughters and wives were both active participants and awkward appendages. Because men were busied by military matters, they left many other responsibilities—provisioning households, managing estates, and overseeing accounts—to women. And because so many men died in battle, they left many women as bereaved but enriched widows or heiresses. Yet, in a world that most valued military prowess and loyalty, women were somewhat peripheral. They did many things, but what they did was not particularly valued. Moreover, female heiresses were downright worrisome. How was a daughter to provide the military services due from the fief of her deceased father? The answer—that her husband could provide those services on her behalf—led lords to control closely the marriages of their vassals' daughters. If they did not, they faced the risk of being saddled with undesirable vassals. Among the landowning elite, marriage had long been a way to seal alliances and advance Christianity; now it also became a tie between lords and their vassals.

As an ad hoc response to hard times, feudalism was a lot messier than the term implies. There were no hard-and-fast rules, and everywhere, feudal relationships coexisted with entirely different arrangements: estates that were held without any obligation of service; landless knights who slept and ate in noble households (a common practice); political power based on public authority rather than on personal lordship; and loyalties based on kinship, friendship, or wages rather than on a fief. Even when relationships were "feudal," they were not necessarily systematic. As feudalism spread beyond

Biographical Sketch

Hugh, Earl of Chester (c. 1048–1101)

Hugh, Earl of Chester, pursued a life broadly typical of his age and class, but because he was born smack in the middle of the eleventh century, his life looked in two directions—back to the traditions of the early medieval nobility that we have examined in this chapter and forward toward the feudal class as it would develop under the strong kings of the Central Middle Ages.

Hugh was born in Normandy, of Viking descent: his great-grandfather was Ansfrid the Dane. But by Hugh's time, the Viking settlers of Normandy had changed into a French-speaking aristocracy hardly distinguishable from the aristocracies of neighboring French provinces. Hugh's father was a wealthy viscount (an important regional lord) of William, duke of Normandy. Hugh inherited his father's estates and office, and along with this lucrative legacy came his obligations as a vassal to William. These obligations probably called Hugh, as a teenager, to the forces that accompanied William in his conquest of England in 1066. There, Hugh made his fortune, for the new king showered wealth on his young vassal, granting him estates scattered across some twenty counties and raising him to the prestigious office of earl (roughly, the English equivalent of a duke). It was Hugh's responsibility as Earl of Chester to consolidate Norman power on the Welsh frontier and to expand Norman authority in the northern regions that were as yet unconquered. To assist Hugh in meeting these responsibilities, King William gave him all the lands of Cheshire, except those belonging to the Church, and granted him virtually kingly authority there. Hugh was empowered to summon all the Cheshire knights on his own authority, to collect his own taxes, and to appoint his own sheriff and lesser county officials. The new Earl of Chester ruled his own land, even though he ruled it on William's behalf.

Like other nobles of his time, Hugh physically embodied power. He was a large, generous man, given to excesses that impressed his followers and intimidated his enemies. His nickname—Hugh the Fat—might not stimulate admiration today, but in the eleventh century, it evoked his wealth, generosity, and fine feasts. Still, not everyone was impressed, and this is how an unsympathetic monk described the earl:

> He was a great lover of the world . . . always in the forefront of battle, lavish to the point of prodigality, a lover of games and luxuries, actors, horses, dogs, and similar vanities. He was always surrounded by a huge following, noisy with swarms of boys of both high and low birth. Many honorable men, clerics and knights, were also in his entourage, and he cheerfully shared his riches with them. . . . His hunting was a daily devastation of his lands, for he thought more highly of hawkers and hunters than of peasants or monks. . . . He was given over to carnal lusts and sired a multitude of bastards by his concubines.

Hugh was, in short, a typical noble: brave in battle, generous at home, and always surrounded by the accoutrements—people as well as things—of his power.

Hugh's disregard for others and sexual license suggest he was not a paragon of Christian virtue. So, too, do his savage campaigns against the Welsh, whom he slaughtered in large numbers. But Hugh was a good friend of the Church. He founded and endowed two large abbeys, one with his wife, Ermentrude, the daughter of a French count and countess. He cultivated a close friendship with Anselm, abbot of Bec and then archbishop of Canterbury (r. 1093–1109), one of the holiest saints of the Middle Ages. And when he fell gravely ill, he, like other noble patrons facing death, took vows as a monk at one of the monastic communities he had founded. His timing could hardly have been better; having lived a worldly life for half a century, he submitted to monastic discipline for only four days before he died.

Hugh was of Viking descent, but very much a member of the French aristocracy. He was well born, but he made his fortune as a loyal warrior and administrator. He wielded unquestioned power in his earldom but looked to a king as the source of that power. He had a faithful wife but did not bother to be faithful to her. He flouted basic Christian rules but loved the Church. These might seem contradictions, but they were not contradictions to Hugh and his ilk. To the nobility of the tenth and eleventh centuries, Hugh's life was an admirable combination of good birth, physical prowess, feudal loyalty, and firm faith.

France and developed over the course of the Middle Ages, it would adapt to new circumstances and grow even more varied, thereby multiplying the historical challenge of describing exactly what "feudalism" was. In its initial form, however, around the year 900 in the region that would become France, feudalism was a brutal, rugged, and hard sort of government. But it was a creative response to challenging times, and most important of all, it worked. Viking marauders were discouraged, thieves were punished, and coins were available for trade.

The German States: Fragmentation and Unification

The invasions gave birth to unified monarchy in England while undermining it in France. In East Francia, the response was different still: first, the emergence of a few very large and powerful semi-independent duchies, and then a resurgence of royal power.

Although the German states of East Francia were subject to Viking attacks, the greater threat came from mounted Magyar warriors in the southeast. When the later Carolingian kings of East Francia proved unable to cope with the lightning raids of the Magyars, their royal authority descended, as it did also in West Francia, to great regional aristocrats: the dukes, who had formerly administered these regions as agents of the monarchy. During the turbulent years of the ninth century, the tribal duchies (so-called because they were based on earlier tribal divisions) of East Francia became virtually autonomous. Their dukes took direct control of royal lands and powers, and they dominated the bishoprics and monasteries within their districts.

In the early tenth century, East Francia was dominated by five duchies: Saxony, Swabia, Bavaria, Franconia, and Lorraine. The first three had been incorporated only recently into the Carolingian state, whereas the western duchies of Franconia and Lorraine were much more strongly Frankish in outlook. The five dukes of these tribal units might well have become the masters of their domains, but they were unable to curb the Magyars, and they eventually fell under the control of a reinvigorated German monarchy. By 919, the Carolingian line had withered away, and Henry the Fowler (r. 919–936), Duke of Saxony, had seized the crown. Thus began a dynasty of illustrious German kings, men whose power rested in a northern region that had only recently been brought under Carolingian authority and into the Christian faith. Their power also rested on election by the other great dukes, for Henry the Fowler and his successors ruled not only by virtue of raw power and good birth but also by the assent of the men who ruled the separate regions of East Francia.

The Saxon Kings

Henry the Fowler concentrated on building up his base in Saxony and could not vigorously exercise his authority over the other great dukes of East Francia. The full assertion of German monarchy awaited the reign of his son, the ablest of the Saxon kings, Otto I, "the Great" (r. 936–973).

Otto the Great directed his considerable talents toward three goals and achieved them all: (1) the defense of the German states against the Magyar invasions, (2) the recovery of royal lands and powers that the dukes had seized, and (3) the extension of royal control into the crumbling Middle Kingdom that the Treaty of Verdun had assigned to Emperor Lothar in 843. By Otto's time, this Middle Kingdom was a political shambles; parts had been absorbed into neighboring French and German states but the southern districts—in Burgundy and the Italian peninsula—retained a chaotic independence. The dukes of Swabia and Bavaria both had notions of seizing these still-independent territories. To forestall the development of an unmanageable rival power to his south, Otto led his armies into the Italian peninsula in 951 and assumed the title "King of Italy."

Thereafter, events developed rapidly. First, Otto strengthened his power at home by decisively defeating a rebel insurgency. Then in 955 he won a critical victory over a large Magyar army at Lechfeld, bringing their raids to an end at last. Otto's triumph at Lechfeld served as a vivid demonstration of his royal power, and it vindicated his royal claim that he, not the dukes, was the true defender of the German states. The eastern borderlands were secure and open to the gradual penetration of German-Christian culture; the tribal duchies were overshadowed; and the monarchy was supreme. Otto the Great towered over his contemporaries as the greatest monarch since Charlemagne.

Not long after his victory over the Magyars, Otto had to turn his attention again to the Italian peninsula, where a Lombard magnate had seized control and was harassing the pope. In response to a papal appeal (one that dovetailed neatly with Otto's imperial ambitions), Otto crushed his Lombard rival, and in 962 the pope hailed Otto as "Roman Emperor" and placed the imperial crown on his head. It is this event, rather than the coronation of Charlemagne in 800, that marks the true genesis of the medieval Holy Roman Empire, even though the term itself would not be actually employed until the twelfth century. See Map 6.5 for the extent of the Empire and the five tribal duchies that controlled election to the imperial throne.

A later cynic would observe that the Holy Roman Empire was neither holy nor Roman nor an empire, but the idea of a revived empire linked to both Rome and the Christian Church would be a driving force in the history of the German states. Although the imperial claim was a broad one, Otto and his successors exercised only loose authority in the Italian peninsula and no jurisdiction over France or the remainder of Western Christendom. The Holy Roman Empire had its roots deep in German soil, and most of its rulers subordinated imperial interests to those of the German monarchy. From its advent in 962 to its long-delayed demise in the early nineteenth century, the Holy Roman Empire remained fundamentally a German phenomenon.

As had been the case in 800, Otto's imperial coronation was coolly received in the Byzantine court, whose emperors not surprisingly considered themselves to be the true

Map 6.5 *The Holy Roman Empire, 962*   When Otto I was crowned emperor in 962, he controlled not only the traditional five tribal duchies of East Francia but also a variety of border states (or "marches") and several associated states, such as the Kingdom of Burgundy. Before he died, he expanded his territory still more, pushing so far into the Italian peninsula that his authority extended to Rome and beyond.

heirs of Rome. Otto patched up the situation by marrying his son, the future Otto II (r. 973–983) to the Byzantine princess Theophano (956–991). She brought Byzantine territories in the Italian peninsula as her dowry (this was a largely empty gift, since Byzantine control there was weak, but it furthered Ottonian claims in the Italian peninsula); she stimulated the cultural growth that is now associated with the Ottonian court; and as advisor to her husband and regent for her son Otto III (r. 983–1002), she directed the Saxon dynasty at the end of the tenth century toward securing its interests in the Italian peninsula and along the eastern frontier. See Figure 6.2 for a portrait of Otto III that evokes the imperial style of Byzantium.

Figure 6.2   *The Emperor Otto III, from the* **Gospel Book of Otto** *(c. 1000)*   Otto III was
the son of the Byzantine princess Theophano, and her influence over his court can be seen in this
portrait, which borrows freely from Byzantine imperial art (compare to Figure 4.2). Otto holds
the orb and scepter, symbols of imperial power. The orb demonstrates that, contrary to modern
myths about Columbus and a flat earth, medieval geographers knew that the world was round.

For more than a century after Otto I's imperial coronation, his power and that of
his successors was so overwhelming that feudal relationships had little importance in
the German states. The great magnates became vassals of Otto, but they normally had
no vassals of their own. Instead of relying on nobles and knights as agents of his government, Otto and his successors relied on the Church, especially bishops, abbots, and
abbesses. As Otto extended his authority over the other tribal duchies, he made the
clergy of these regions into loyal supporters of the emperor. They were well born and

well educated; they were likely to be less self-interested than were lay nobles (who had legitimate children whose interests and inheritances had to be protected); they often owed their appointments to Otto's influence; and they held estates from Otto for which they had to render military service. They were, in short, ideal royal officials: loyal, competent, and devoted to the success of the emperor.

A hundred years later, the imperial-episcopal alliance begun by Otto would lead to an epic struggle between emperors and popes over who controlled the appointment—and loyalty—of the bishops, abbots, and abbesses of the German states (as we shall see in Chapter 8). But at its inception, Otto's claim to appoint *his* churchmen and rule *his* church made good sense. Like Charlemagne, he had been sanctified by holy anointing, thereby rendering him the natural leader of the church. Like Charlemagne, he sought not only to control the church but also to improve it. Yes, he controlled appointments to most major Church offices (including, in some cases, the papacy), but he reorganized bishoprics, established new ones, defended monasteries and bishoprics against armies of hostile Danes and Slavs, and encouraged German clergy and laity to move eastward into the lands of the Slavs, thereby extending German (and Christian) influence to the borders of modern-day Poland.

Perhaps most importantly, Otto's involvement in Church matters merely exercised on a grand scale what many nobles exercised in their local areas. At this time, many monasteries and churches were treated as **family churches,** the personal property of the families that had built them and endowed them. As founder and supporter of many ecclesiastical institutions in the German states, Otto claimed what others also claimed—that lay founders and lay supporters should have a controlling interest over ecclesiastical institutions. Indeed, such claims still live, albeit in new forms, in modern universities, where big donors to athletic programs sometimes acquire not only good seats and excellent parking but also influence over broader university policies.

Ottonian Culture

Otto, like Charlemagne, used the Christian Church in both pious and practical ways, and he also, like Charlemagne, encouraged learning. This intellectual revival reached its culmination under Otto's two successors, Otto II and Otto III, both deeply influenced by the learning and culture that Theophano brought with her from Constantinople. The Ottonian revival produced a series of able administrators and scholars, many of them associated with the royal court. Richly endowed monasteries, particularly female monasteries, became centers of learning and literary production. The Abbey of Gandersheim was one such royal foundation, headed by a series of royal and noble daughters. Among others, it produced the writer Hroswitha (c. 935–1003), renowned for her legends, poems, and histories but especially for six comedies that she modeled on classical forms. Her plays were meant to inspire as well as amuse, and they were directed at the virginal nuns who were her primary audience. One of her best, *Dulcitius,* tells of three Christian virgins who successfully resist the ludicrous advances of a Roman governor. At one point, the governor becomes so deluded that he starts kissing pots and pans, in the belief that these are the women he seeks. Hroswitha's nuns doubtless laughed at such antics, but they were also probably inspired by the resistance of her heroines and their enduring virginity. Hroswitha was the first playwright of the European Middle Ages and the best Latinist of her time.

The greatest scientific thinker of the Ottonian era was also raised in the monastic tradition, the monk Gerbert of Aurillac (c. 945–1003). An enthusiastic traveler, he was the first scholar from Western Christendom to study in al-Andalus. There, he gained expertise unknown in the West, and others would soon follow in his footsteps, seeking new insights from the libraries and scholars of Islam. Gerbert developed such an encyclopedic knowledge of classical literature, logic, science, and mathematics that he was even rumored to be a wizard in league with the devil, a rumor quashed by his elevation to the papacy as Pope Sylvester II (r. 999–1003). Gerbert was an advance agent of the intellectual awakening that would grip Europe in the twelfth century, stimulated, as his own thought had been, by contact with Islamic teachers and libraries.

In 1024 the Saxon dynasty died out, and a new Salian dynasty (1024–1125) came to power. Working hand in glove with the German church, the Salian emperors improved royal administration and ultimately came to exercise even greater authority than Otto I. In the mid-eleventh century the strongest of the Salian emperors, Henry III (1039–1056), held sway over the German states and appointed popes almost as freely as he selected his own bishops. In 1050, at a time when the French monarchy still dozed, Emperor Henry III dominated central Europe and held the papacy in his palm.

The Italian Peninsula: Autonomous Cities

When Charlemagne conquered Lombardy in 774, he gained control of a kingdom very different from that of Carolingian Francia. For one thing, urban life had retained far more vitality in the Italian peninsula. For another, the Lombard kings exercised strong authority only over the northern part of this peninsula, a rich, fertile region dominated by Milan and irrigated by the River Po. They enjoyed only loose control over the dukes of Friuli to the northeast (near Venice) and Spoleto to the south, and their rule was nonexistent below Rome. There a swarm of small powers waged incessant war on one another: independent duchies, coastal towns, Muslim military settlements, and Byzantine enclaves left from Justinian's conquests.

Charlemagne never asserted his authority south of Rome, and his successors did not long exercise power in the north either. After the quick disintegration of Lothar's Middle Kingdom, control of the northern Italian peninsula became by the late 800s an object of a brutal struggle among various ambitious families, including the dukes of Spoleto and Friuli. There was an almost complete break with the Carolingian past. And as dynastic struggle distracted and weakened the aristocracy, the cities that they governed grew more and more independent.

When Magyars and Muslims began to trouble this region in the ninth century, it was the cities, under the leadership of their bishops, that became the chief centers of resistance. Bishops effectively governed their cities during this time of crisis, and they just as effectively organized urban defenses (sometimes by creating feudal relationships with knights who held land from them and served in their armies). As a result of their de facto governance, bishops were slowly able to extract extensive concessions from local counts and dukes—especially the right to collect tolls and taxes, and eventually also the right to administer justice. By the early 900s, bishops and their cities had won full exemptions from the local aristocracy. Counts and dukes governed the countryside, but bishops governed the cities.

At the urging of a group of Lombard bishops, Otto the Great intervened in the mid-900s, ending the dynastic squabbles of the aristocracy, destroying many enclaves of Muslim pirates, and incorporating the northern part of the Italian peninsula into his empire (see Map 6.6). Otto's conquest brought peace to the north, and it also enhanced

Map 6.6   *Italy, c. 1000*   At the end of the first millennium, "Italy" was a patchwork of states. Almost all of northern Italy fell under the loose umbrella of a Kingdom of Italy, which was itself part of the Holy Roman Empire, but many cities were governed day-to-day by their bishops. Central Italy contained several small states, including the area around Rome, which was controlled by the bishop of Rome—that is, the pope. The far south of the peninsula was under loose Byzantine rule, and Sicily was a Muslim emirate.

the power of bishops and their cities. First, because Otto and his successors usually ruled from a distance, they relied on bishops to maintain stability at home. Second, by providing a settled environment, Otto encouraged urban growth and commercial revival. By the late 900s, the northern ports of Genoa and Pisa were developing a vigorous, widespread Mediterranean trade and a growing merchant class, and in the course of the next century, they would seize the offensive from the Muslims, expelling them from the important

Mediterranean islands of Sardinia and Corsica and launching raids against Muslim ports in Iberia and North Africa. Other Italian coastal cities, beyond the lands ruled by the German emperor, were taking to the sea as well: Amalfi, Salerno, and Naples in the south and, above all, the republic of Venice on the northern shore of the Adriatic Sea.

Long a Byzantine dependency, Venice had achieved virtual independence by the ninth century, even though it continued to send fleets to assist Byzantium in its wars. By carefully cultivating its relations with both Constantinople and Islamic North Africa, Venice developed into the foremost commercial center in Western Christendom. Enriched by the exporting of salt from their lagoons and glass from their furnaces, and by the profits of commerce linking Western Christendom, Islam, and Byzantium, Venetians were able to live by trade alone. In a Europe that was still overwhelmingly agrarian, the Venetians astonished visitors with their ability to grow no crops at all and to rely exclusively on *purchased* food and drink.

In this respect Venice was unique, but other Italian ports—Genoa, Pisa, and Amalfi—also competed in the lucrative Mediterranean trade. In turn, their bustling commercial life stimulated the growth of inland cities such as Milan, Bologna, and Florence. Milan's population in the year 1000, although probably no more than 20,000, made it the largest city in Lombardy and one of the most populous in Western Christendom. With the closing of the age of invasions, the Italian peninsula had thus achieved the reversal of two trends: its cities were growing once more, and its well-armed fleets were at last challenging Byzantine and Muslim domination of Mediterranean commerce.

In later generations, the townspeople of the northern Italian peninsula would rise up against their bishops and claim as their own the privileges bishops had once won from dukes and counts. They would then subject the surrounding countryside to the authority of their cities. These processes would be aided by the economic revival of the eleventh century and the political vacuum then created by struggles between popes and emperors. But even in the tenth century, forces were hard at work that would one day transform much of the Italian peninsula into a land of self-governing city-states.

❋ CONCLUSION

In the year 1000, Western Christendom was still a poor neighbor of Byzantium and Islam, and it had even seemingly slipped from the days of its brief unification under Charlemagne's strong hand. But it was growing stronger, thanks in part to the foundations Charlemagne had laid. By 1000, Charlemagne's empire had been replaced by strong kingship in England, feudal lords in France, a new empire built on tribal duchies in the German states, and powerful cities in the northern Italian peninsula. Yet, although Charlemagne's empire had crumbled, his legacy endured. Charlemagne's imperial crown was a powerful memory at Otto I's coronation in 962; his close work with Alcuin (732–804) and Pope Leo III (r. 795–816) provided a model for later collaboration between church and state; his enthusiasm for evangelical work helped inspire the incorporation of Vikings, Magyars, and Slavs into Western Christendom; his reliance on personal loyalty and local administrators left its mark on medieval government; and his enthusiasm for learning would prove a later inspiration to both Alfred the Great and Otto I.

In the first decades of the new millennium, strength built on strength. Both England and the Holy Roman Empire proved to be comparatively stable, well-organized kingdoms. The French monarchy was still weak, but French principalities such as Champagne, Flanders, Normandy, and Anjou were well along the road to political coherence. Centralization proved similarly elusive in the Italian peninsula, but there cities provided strong government and growing prosperity. Yet, most important of all, the invasions were over. By 1000, the Vikings, Muslims, and Magyars had been stopped, subdued, or settled, and Europeans would not see their like again. From that time to the present, Europe has had the unique opportunity of developing on its own, sheltered from the alien attacks that have so disrupted other civilizations over the past thousand years. Europe was, in short, on the verge of a creative explosion.

SUGGESTED READINGS

Richard Abels, *Alfred the Great: War, Kingship, and Culture in Anglo-Saxon England* (1998). See also Alfred P. Smyth, *King Alfred the Great* (1995). For primary sources, see Simon Keynes and Michael Lapidge, eds. and trans., *Alfred the Great* (1983).

Geoffrey Barraclough, *The Crucible of Europe* (1976). A clearly written political analysis of Western European politics from about 800 to 1050. For national histories, see items cited in earlier bibliographies and also Jean Dunbabin, *France in the Making, 843–1180* (2nd edition, 2000); Timothy Reuter, *Germany in the Early Middle Ages, 800–1056* (1991); Karl J. Leyser, *Rule and Conflict in an Early Medieval Society: Ottonian Saxony* (1979); Giovanni Tabacco, *The Struggle for Power in Medieval Italy* (1989).

Thomas Head and Richard Landes, eds., *The Peace of God: Social Violence and Religious Response in France Around the Year 1000* (1992). Perceptive essays by an international pantheon of scholars.

Susan Reynolds, *Fiefs and Vassals: The Medieval Evidence Reinterpreted* (1994). A recent interpretation. See also J. P. Poly and Eric Bournazel, *The Feudal Transformation, 900–1200,* trans. C. Higgitt (1991). See Lester K. Little and Barbara H. Rosenwein, *Debating the Middle Ages: Issues and Readings* (1998) for a useful selection of readings on feudalism.

Janet L. Nelson, *Charles the Bald* (1992). A deeply learned and brief study emphasizing the politics, economy, and institutions of ninth-century West Francia.

Timothy Reuter, ed., *The Medieval Nobility* (1979). Excellent essays on the French and German nobility to the twelfth century.

Peter Sawyer, *Kings and Vikings: Scandinavia and Europe A.D. 700–1100* (1982). A succinct survey and reinterpretation of the Viking age. See also his edited *Oxford Illustrated History of the Vikings* (1997).

SUGGESTED PRIMARY SOURCES

Carl I. Hammer, *A Large-Scale Slave Society of the Early Middle Ages: Slaves and Their Families in Early Medieval Bavaria* (2002). Includes translated documents about slaves and serfs in the eighth and ninth centuries.

David Herlihy, ed., *The History of Feudalism* (1970). A still useful survey, built around primary sources.

R. I. Page, *Chronicles of the Vikings: Records, Memorials and Myths* (1995). Presents sources within a seamless commentary.

PART II

THE CENTRAL MIDDLE AGES

REFORM, REVIVAL, AND EXPANSION, 1000-1300

Historians disagree about how Europeans greeted the year 1000. Certainly, apocalyptic ideas were common in medieval Europe, and among at least some groups, the approach of the 1000th anniversary of Jesus' birth suggested that the world's end was near. As one monk concisely put it, "Satan will soon be unleashed because the thousand years have been completed." Yet many medieval people let the year 1000 pass without much notice. The dating system of *Anno Domini* was so new that many ordinary people were probably entirely unaware of the anniversary; they used systems that counted from well-known recent dates, so that instead of speaking of "the year 1000," they spoke, for example, of "the seventeenth year of the reign of Otto III." Other people used the new dating system but predicted apocalypses for other years (1033, the 1000th anniversary of Jesus' crucifixion, was a favorite). For its part, the Church steadfastly opposed any such predictions, arguing that it was not for humans to determine God's timing. Still, the millennium was an especially important year to *some* medieval people, and when a meteor streaked across the sky in September, they considered it a "sure sign of some mysterious and terrible event."

Although the millennium provides a particularly convenient date for students to remember, it is not because of anniversaries and apocalypses that the period conventionally known as the Central or High Middle Ages is dated here as beginning around the year 1000. As we have already seen, many new possibilities were coalescing in Europe at this time: effective governance provided by nobles, bishops, and in some cases, kings; a waning threat of invasion; and commercial revival, especially in Italy. To these must be added other factors we will soon examine: agricultural innovations that more than doubled the food available in Europe; a slow expansion of education and literacy; and a Church revitalized by monastic reform and papal leadership. Because none of these changes happened overnight and some took many generations, the year 1000 is a reasonable date but a highly negotiable one. Some historians would prefer to begin the Central Middle Ages as early as 950; others would push for a later date such as 1050 or 1100. All would agree that the process was gradual, commencing in the tenth century, gathering momentum in the eleventh, and achieving full speed in the twelfth (see the accompanying timeline).

TIMELINE FOR PART II   The Central Middle Ages, 1000–1300

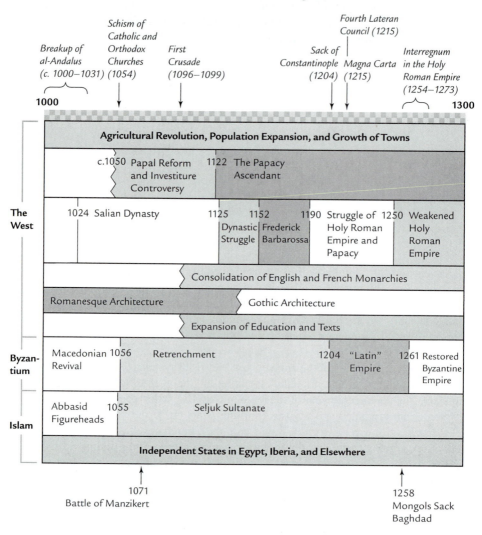

All would also agree that the balance among the three civilizations that bordered the Mediterranean—Byzantium, Islam, and Western Europe—began to shift at this time. While the fortunes of the West improved, those of Byzantium and Islam declined. Part of this teeter-totter effect was produced by the West's good fortunes, for Western knights in the centuries that followed the year 1000 slowly "reconquered" large parts of al-Andalus, temporarily established kingdoms in the Middle East, and even plundered Constantinople. But Western knights were not the sole cause of the troubles that beset Byzantium and Islam.

Byzantium in the Central Middle Ages

In the year 1000, Byzantium was powerful and secure. Basil II the Bulgar-Slayer (r. 976–1025), the most successful ruler of the successful Macedonian dynasty, was campaigning relentlessly in the Balkans, where he would soon bring the Bulgars under the control of his government and the faith of his Eastern Orthodox Church. A few years before, he had married his reluctant sister Anna to the soon-to-be-baptized Vladimir I (r. 980–1015) and thereby brought Kievan Rus under Byzantine influence. But these glories did not last long. When Basil died without issue, the Macedonian dynasty soon ended (in 1056). Even more troubling was the threat posed by the migration into the Middle East of a new Asian power, the Seljuk Turks, a pastoral, horseback-riding people who were moving steadily westward. Recently converted to Sunni Islam, the Seljuks (who took their name from an early chief) first made themselves de facto rulers of the Abbasid Empire; they allowed the Abbasid caliphs to live in powerless splendor in Baghdad, but Seljuk sultans were the real power behind the throne. Then, in 1065 they wrested Armenia from Byzantium, and when an imperial army attempted to drive them from Asia Minor, they annihilated the Byzantines at the Battle of Manzikert in 1071.

Manzikert was a turning point in Byzantine history. Even though the Seljuks did not adequately follow up their triumph, the disaster broke Byzantium's age-long hold on Asia Minor. Without Asia Minor, Byzantium was a very small empire indeed—and much impoverished too. Worse yet, as the Empire began to shrink on its eastern borders, it faced further losses to its west. In the same fateful year of 1071, the Byzantines also lost—to the Normans—their vital port of Bari in the southern Italian peninsula. With the loss of Bari, Byzantium's presence in the West was effectively ended.

Shortly thereafter, Emperor Alexius Comnenus (r. 1078–1118) sought outside help in his struggle against the Seljuks. He turned to the West, which, after centuries of being viewed by Byzantines as an impoverished and insignificant neighbor, now seemed a powerful ally. Alexius Comnenus begged assistance from Pope Urban II (r. 1088–1099), then the leading figure of Western Christendom. Urban II responded by urging Western knights to go on crusade—in aid of Byzantium, yes, but really in aid of the Holy Land. The century of Manzikert ended with the First Crusade (1096–1099) and its capture of Jerusalem, a Christian triumph accomplished not by Byzantine warriors but by Western crusaders.

For the Byzantines, the crusades were a nightmare, quite the opposite of the help that Alexius Comnenus had sought. The fervor and disorder of the earliest crusades alarmed the Byzantines, but it was the Fourth Crusade (1202–1204) that devastated their capital and empire. In 1204, the soldiers of the Fourth Crusade, frustrated by their failed attempt to intervene in Byzantine imperial politics, pillaged Constantinople for three long days and nights, massacring people, seizing valuables, and setting fires. They then established a new "Latin" Empire, whose rulers exercised little authority beyond ravaged Constantinople and its hinterland. The Byzantines set up various courts-in-exile, and eventually, in 1261, Michael VIII Palaeologus (r. 1259–1282) restored the Byzantine Empire to its home in Constantinople. But the restored Empire was a mere shadow of its former self. Its wealth had been looted, and its provinces had grown into independent states. For Byzantium, the three centuries between 1000 and 1300 brought much more woe than glory.

Islamic States in the Central Middle Ages

By the year 1000, the Abbasid heirs who ruled in Baghdad had long been figureheads. They lived in incredible luxury but left the business of ruling to others. In 1055, the leader of the Seljuk Turks conquered Baghdad and assumed the new title of *sultan*. He and his heirs retained effective power over the heartland of the old Abbasid Empire through most of the Central Middle Ages. Other Seljuks ruled in Rum (derived from "Rome"), the part of Anatolia that had been wrested from Byzantine control. By the mid-thirteenth century, the Seljuks faced a new threat from the Mongols, another pastoral people who were moving, as the Seljuks had done several hundred years earlier, westward from the Asian steppes. In 1258, the Mongols took Baghdad, massacred its inhabitants (allegedly 800,000 people), and murdered the last Abbasid figurehead (either by wrapping him in a carpet and kicking him to death, or locking him in a tower with his treasure to starve). The Seljuks shortly thereafter regained control, but only for a few more decades; as we will see in Part III, they were permanently deposed by the Ottoman Turks in the early fourteenth century.

The autonomous Islamic states of Egypt and al-Andalus faced similar challenges during the Central Middle Ages. At the start of the new millennium, the Fatimid dynasty (r. 909–1171) was firmly ensconced in Cairo, ruling a state that extended, at times, from Sicily in the west to Damascus in the east. The waxing and waning of Fatimid borders was one factor in the launching of the First Crusade. When the Fatimids lost Jerusalem to the Seljuks, Christian pilgrims were not as welcome as they had once been, and thus, when Pope Urban II responded to Alexius Comnenus's request for help against the Seljuks, he was thinking more of Jerusalem than Constantinople. In any case, the Fatimids were eventually replaced by a dynasty of Kurdish descent, the Ayyubids (1169–1260), and the founder of this dynasty, Salah al-din Yusuf or Saladin (1137–1193), would become famous in the West when his recapture of Jerusalem in 1187 prompted the Second Crusade. In 1250 the Mamluks, former warrior-slaves, took control of Egypt (r. 1250–1517). They oversaw a cultural revival in Egypt, and they also expanded into Palestine where, in 1291, they captured what was then the last crusader stronghold.

The year 1000 was glorious in al-Andalus. There, al-Mansur (r. 976–1002) was overseeing a time of great prosperity, impressive building, and awesome scholarship. His glittering cities of Cordoba, Valencia, and Seville were peaceably populated by Jews and Christians as well as Muslims. And his armies were fearsome. Christian princes fell easily before him as he burned Barcelona, sacked Leon, and even took Santiago de Compostela. In the south, he so extended his influence over the Berbers of North Africa that, from 997, his governors managed northern Morocco from a new capital at Fez. But al-Mansur's awe-inspiring caliphate disintegrated after his death. Formally abolished in 1031, it was replaced by many small, Muslim principalities. These small Muslim states were much less of a threat to the Christian principalities that still survived in the north of the peninsula, and before the century was out, Christian princes began to "reconquer" them. The first major city, Toledo, came into Christian hands in 1085. In response to Christian advances, Muslim princes sought help from the Berbers of North Africa, with the result that, for most of the eleventh and twelfth centuries, what remained of Muslim Spain was dominated in succession by two groups of fundamentalist and reform-minded Muslims from North Africa: first, the Almoravids (until 1148) and then the Almohads (until 1223). Neither the Almoravids nor the Almohads were much loved by the native Muslims of Spain; rather like Western crusaders in Byzantium, they came to help co-religionists but overstayed their welcome. In the meantime, Christian armies continued to push southward until, by the middle of the thirteenth century, only Granada in the southern tip of Iberia remained of the once great al-Andalus.

The West in the Central Middle Ages

While its Byzantine and Islamic neighbors stumbled, the medieval West came of age. Europe's population grew steadily in the Central Middle Ages, so that it accommodated roughly twice as many people in 1300 as in 1000. At the same time, living standards improved because agricultural innovation and land clearances provided more than enough resources for this growing number of people. In 1300, most Europeans lived in better houses, ate better food (especially protein-rich peas and beans, as well as more cheese, eggs, fish, and meat), and wore better clothing than in 1000. Also, many more of them lived in cities and towns. Although agriculture dominated all preindustrial economies (including the Middle Ages), by 1300, cities had become a critical part of European life. Milan rose in population from about 20,000 to something like 100,000, and Venice, Florence, and Genoa reached comparable size. Urban populations north of the Alps tended to be smaller, but by 1300, cities of 25,000 to 50,000 were not uncommon, and Paris was approaching 200,000. The roots of these changes in agrarian and commercial life lay primarily within Europe itself. As the historian Robert S. Lopez has noted of this period, "For the first time in history an underdeveloped society succeeded in developing itself, mostly by its own efforts."

The Central Middle Ages also witnessed the centralization of governing authority, both within secular states (especially England and France) and within the Church (as ideas of papal monarchy began to have real effect). Simply put, kings were more powerful and so too were popes. In addition, Christian theology was more clearly articulated; cathedrals were built and staffed; universities trained men (but men only) for service to Church and state; and a new style of architecture graced the European landscape. Moreover, in a series of small shifts that added up to a momentous change, Europe evolved during these centuries from a preliterate to a literate society. Whereas much had been left to memory and oral tradition in the Early Middle Ages, much was committed to parchment in the Central Middle Ages. By the fourteenth century, even illiterate peasants understood the power of the written word. When they rose up in revolt, they sought to burn documents that they believed recorded loathsome customs, and, in some cases, they sought out other documents in which were noted, they thought, ancient traditions of their freedom. Most people still could not read in 1300 and many more men had acquired the skill than women, but Europeans had nevertheless come to depend on written records—deeds, letters, government surveys—to define their rights, property, and status.

This explosion of documentary evidence speaks to a profound change in European society, but it also makes history a richer business. Historians interested in popes of the Early Middle Ages have precious few documents on which to base their research; even as late as 1100, only about 35 papal letters survive for each year. But historians interested in later popes can use an archive increased a hundredfold; by 1300, about 3,600 papal letters survive per annum. Financial records, too, were becoming more widespread and systematic. Annual accounts of royal revenues began to be committed to writing in England around 1110, in France around 1190. All across Europe, skills such as reading, writing, and mathematical calculation were becoming vital to the functioning of secular and ecclesiastical governments, urban businesses, and even agricultural enterprises.

Those who possessed these skills—scribes, clerks, lawyers, and accountants—moved into positions of considerable power, as did Europe's first large cadre of professional intellectuals—professors, scholars, and teachers. Because clever social nobodies could now wield influence in royal and ecclesiastical administrations, social mobility increased, and so too did social complexity. Most sons and daughters continued to follow in their parents' footsteps, but some found opportunities to break from old patterns. Cathedral schools and, later, universities began to eclipse the modest aims of the monastic schools so encouraged by Charlemagne; monastic reforms and new religious orders expanded the options of those who sought to devote their lives to Christian piety, and to restless serfs and poor freeholders, towns and cities beckoned.

The social vitality of these centuries offered mobility and opportunity, but it also gave rise to increased social anxiety. Some medieval people found it disconcerting—or even traumatic—to face a life of social change and uncertain prospect. From such social anxieties might have grown the xenophobia and persecutions that are as much a part of the Central Middle Ages as its great cathedrals and new universities. From it, too, sprang an eleventh-century ideal of Christian community, an ideal that sought to put everyone in a proper place with a proper role. Constructed by clerics and much popularized thereafter, this "tripartite" ideal saw Christendom as divided into *three orders:* "those who pray" (*oratores*) whose prayers benefited all; those who fight (*bellatores*) whose military prowess protected all; and "those who work" (*laboratores*) whose sweated labor supported all (see Color Illustration 5). This ideal was most definitely not egalitarian (a peasant's work was less valued than a monk's prayers), but it did emphasize *mutual* aid and obligation within a hierarchical society. It was also never more than an ideal, for it poorly accommodated many medieval social groups: (a) women were sometimes included within each of the three orders, but some medieval commentators considered women a "fourth order"; (b) townspeople, who were relatively few in number in the eleventh century but more numerous thereafter, fit with difficulty into the category of "those who work"; and (c) Jews, a significant minority in some parts of the medieval West, had no place at all in this Christian schema. Yet, although the tripartite schema was bad sociology, it was powerful ideology, and it gave new force to teachings that sought to control social flux. By its logic, each person was born into a particular social place with particular social obligations.

From the social vitality of the Central Middle Ages also grew a greater self-awareness, shown not only in more attempts to collect and preserve personal letters but also in the first autobiographies to appear since St. Augustine (354–430) wrote his *Confessions.* The era also saw new, rational attitudes toward the cosmos. Early medieval people had viewed the world as a theater of miracles in which a storm or fire was a divine punishment for sin and a military victory was a sure mark of God's approval. But in the view of Peter Abelard (1079–1142), one of the greatest philosophers of the Central Middle Ages, and many others who followed him, God's creation was a natural order that could function by its own rules, without constant divine tinkering. Miracles were possible, of course, but they were rare. This rationalism flourished not only in the arcane discussions of philosophers but also in the everyday life of the time. For example, people slowly grew skeptical about judicial ordeals which appealed to God for a "miracle on demand" to determine guilt or innocence. In 1215, a papal council prohibited priests from participating in ordeals, and thereafter the judgment of God gave way to the testimony of witnesses or the deliberation of juries.

These deeply significant shifts in attitude toward self and the world, and the vast economic and social changes that accompanied them, make the three centuries of the Central Middle Ages very distinct from the half-millennium before the year 1000. They would also prove critical for the development of European civilization in the years after 1300. Behind the fifteenth-century invention of printing lay the central medieval shift from a preliterate to a literate society. Behind Columbus's fateful voyage in 1492 lay the "reconquest" of Iberia, begun in the eleventh century and completed in the very year he set sail. Behind the seventeenth-century scientific revolution lay the central medieval idea of a universe functioning by natural rules and open to rational inspection. Behind the nineteenth-century industrial revolution lay the commercial revolution of the twelfth and thirteenth centuries. In examining the Central Middle Ages, then, we will see both the maturing of medieval civilization and the earliest hints of modernity.

Part I of this book was organized more or less chronologically. Because we had to cover some 700 years (taking into account Chapter 1's prologue on the last centuries of the Roman Empire), it made sense to move steadily through the changing circumstances of Europe—from late antiquity to barbarian settlement, to Carolingian revival, to the crises and adjustments of the ninth and tenth centuries. Part II shifts to a topical organization, made possible by the compactness of the "mere" 300 years before us. We will explore the Central Middle Ages from a variety of historical perspectives: economic and social change, the deepening and broadening of religious life, territorial expansion, the struggle between papacy and Empire, the evolution of England and France into coherent states, and concurrent developments in literature, art, and thought.

SUGGESTED READINGS

Robert Bartlett, *The Making of Europe: Conquest, Colonization and Cultural Change, 950–1350* (1993). A path-breaking analysis of territorial expansion and the evolution of medieval civilization.

Marcia L. Colish, *Medieval Foundations of the Western Intellectual Tradition, 400–1400* (1997). An extraordinarily skilled synthesis.

Philippe Contamine, *War in the Middle Ages* (1984). A political, institutional, and intellectual history that covers especially the period 900–1500.

Robert Fossier, ed., *The Cambridge Illustrated History of the Middle Ages, vol. 2: 950–1250,* trans. Janet Sondheimer (1989). See also volumes 4 and 5 of David Abulafia et al., eds., *The New Cambridge Medieval History.* For textbooks, see especially: Christopher Brooke, *Europe in the Central Middle Ages, 962–1154* (3rd edition, 2000); John H. Mundy, *Europe in the High Middle Ages, 1150–1309* (3rd edition, 2000); and Malcolm Barber, *The Two Cities: Medieval Europe, 1050–1320* (1992).

Jacques Le Goff, ed., *Medieval Callings* (1990). Translated from a French edition of 1987, this collection considers medieval people in various walks of life.

Penny Schine Gold, *The Lady and the Virgin: Image, Attitude, and Experience in Twelfth-Century France* (1985). An interesting synthesis of literary, artistic, and historical evidence.

R. I. Moore, *The Formation of a Persecuting Society: Power and Deviance in Western Europe, 950–1250* (1987). A somber reappraisal of the Central Middle Ages. See also his new *The First European Revolution, ca. 970–1215* (2000).

Alexander Murray, *Reason and Society in the Middle Ages* (1978). Argues for a shift in mental outlook that brought into power men skilled at reasoning and accounting.

Susan Reynolds, *Kingdoms and Communities in Western Europe, 900–1300* (2nd edition, 1997). A perceptive work stressing the horizontal bonds of lay society.

CHAPTER 7

❦

ECONOMIC TAKEOFF AND SOCIAL CHANGE, c. 1000-1300

✳ INTRODUCTION

Along with fewer invaders, stronger kings, and expanding literacy, the Central Middle Ages also saw better weather, especially for those who lived to the north. Between roughly 800 and 1300, Europe was less rainy and cold by several degrees than it had been previously or is now. The summer growing season was longer, and vineyards flourished some 300 miles farther north than they do today. Marshes and bogs receded, and seafarers on the North Atlantic faced less ice and milder storms.

Historians are not sure what caused this improvement, but we are sure about the results: better weather was one of several factors that encouraged the growth of the European economy between 1000 and 1300 (see Timeline 7.1). During these centuries, peasants dramatically increased their yield per acre, and they began to use weekly or monthly markets to sell their surplus food and to purchase tools, cloth, and other goods that they no longer had to produce themselves. Townspeople and towns proliferated with the expansion of trade and industry. And nobles and knights experienced a dramatic transformation in taste and style, moving from grim, square towers filled with rough and dirty warriors into elaborate, well-furnished castles that echoed with the songs of troubadours. Behind this story of more prosperous villages, more bustling towns, and more opulent castles was an economic transformation that laid critical foundations for the religious, political, and cultural achievements of the Central Middle Ages.

✳ AGRICULTURAL REVOLUTION

Throughout the Middle Ages (and for several centuries thereafter), most Europeans lived in the countryside, and the products of their labor—grain, vegetables, meat, eggs, wool, and the like—were the lifeblood of the European economy. The countryside was a varied place: rich fertile soils and much rain in England, northern France, and the German states; lighter soils and much drier climate in the Italian and Iberian peninsulas; and

156

TIMELINE 7.1   Economic and Social Change, 1000–1300

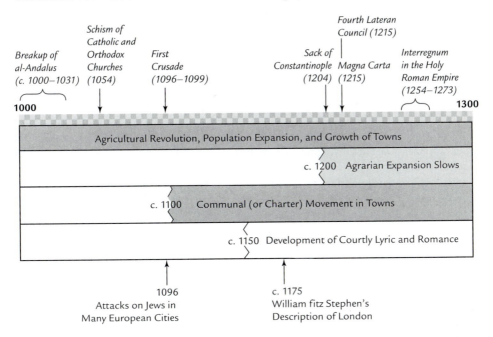

within each region, some flatlands that were easy to plow and some mountains more suited to the raising of sheep or cattle than crops. In southern Europe, along the Mediterranean basin, people cultivated grapes and olives, drinking wine as a basic beverage and relying on olive oil. In northern parts that looked more to the Atlantic, Baltic, or North Sea than to the Mediterranean, grain cultivation and dairying prevailed, and people there drank beer as their basic beverage and used butter instead of oil. These distinctions had existed in antiquity, and they would endure throughout the Middle Ages—and, indeed, to the present day. But in all the regions of Europe, whenever peasants began to produce more goods more efficiently, the economy grew. This is what happened in the tenth and eleventh centuries, when the landscape of Europe, particularly northern Europe, was transformed by small changes that accumulated into big effects.

First, more land—much more land—was brought under cultivation, as people drained swamps, cleared forests, and built dikes to reclaim land from the sea. Some expansion was local, with villagers adding an acre or two to their fields by felling trees or turning wetlands into arable. Other expansion resulted from outright colonization encouraged by nobles who would "plant" a village on uncultivated land and offer inducements to settlers. Whether modest additions of a few acres or expansive new villages, these operations vastly increased Europe's cultivated land.

Second, some peasants not only cultivated more land but also cultivated it more intensely. Here, rotation of cropped and **fallow** land was key. Because fertilizers were scarce in medieval Europe (so scarce that court cases were fought over rights to manure), the best way to keep land productive was to let it lie fallow (that is, uncultivated). Early systems of rotation worked on a two-field basis: peasants would cultivate one field and let the other lie fallow. Beginning as early as the eighth century, a better **three-field**

system of rotation slowly took hold. Three fields were moved through a three-year cycle—spring planting for fall harvesting, fall planting for early summer harvesting, and fallow. This simple change kept two-thirds of the cultivated land in use at any one time, a huge improvement on using one-half of the land in any given year. Not all villages were able to adopt the three-field system; some had soils that could not sustain the extra cultivation, and some had summers too hot for spring planting. But other villages were even able to improve on it, creating four or five fields subject to still more complex rotations.

Third, productivity was improved still more by gradual improvements in agrarian technology. Devices such as tandem harnesses, redesigned horse collars (the old collar had choked horses as they pulled!), and horseshoes increased the power of horses and oxen. The use of axles on wagons also helped, as too did the greater use of metal tools. But the crucial improvement was a new sort of plow. The old Roman or "scratch" plow worked well in the light and dry soils of southern Europe, but it was ineffective on the heavier soils of the north. The new heavy, wheeled plow was (a) heavy enough to cut through rich soil, (b) wheeled and hence maneuverable, and (c) tipped with a metal cutting blade that withstood hard use. This plow was driven by teams of well-harnessed oxen or horses. Another improvement was the expanding use of water mills and, later, windmills. By substituting the power of wind or water for the power of human muscle, these mills freed women—to whom hand-milling, one of the dreariest and most exhausting of farm tasks, had traditionally fallen—for other work. Windmills were also important in draining wetlands, and both sorts of mills eventually developed industrial applications as well (such as driving the hammers that were used to finish cloth).

The results of this agricultural revolution are easy to trace. More food encouraged population growth, fostered an improved standard of living, and encouraged specialization of production and the trade that flowed from it. But to my mind, the results of these broad changes are best remembered by three specific trends. First, crop yields doubled. In Charlemagne's time, a peasant family could hope to harvest two bushels for every bushel sown; by the twelfth century, a yield of four bushels was more normal. A 1:4 yield would be stunningly bad by modern standards, but it was a miracle of sorts for medieval peasants.

Second, famine eased. Between 1000 and 1300, some villages and regions sometimes suffered from food shortages, but there were no widespread famines.[1] Instead, people ate more protein-rich and iron-rich foods than before: peas and beans (products of the three-field rotation), cheese and eggs, fish and meat. Pork was beginning to appear more often on peasant tables, and the rabbit, introduced from Iberia, had hopped to France by late Carolingian times and to England by the twelfth century. Over the course of the Central Middle Ages, Europeans became some of the world's most enthusiastic meat eaters.

Third, this improved diet appears to have changed the relative life expectancies of women and men. In ancient and early medieval times, men usually outlived women, but during the Central Middle Ages, women began to outlive men. Why? The improved, iron-rich diet of the Central Middle Ages dramatically reduced female anemia and, hence, female mortality. Everyone lived longer, but the benefits of the new diet on women (who required iron in greater amounts than men) were particularly

---

[1] As we shall see in Chapter 14, the troubles of the *Later* Middle Ages began with the first widespread famine in centuries—the Great Famine of 1315–1322.

striking—and enduring. In the United States today, the average life expectancy for women is more than 79 years, whereas men can only hope to live to the age of 74. This differential had its European roots in the agricultural revolution of the Central Middle Ages.

✳ VILLAGE, MANOR, AND PARISH

Agricultural innovation was a piecemeal business. Sometimes monasteries developed new techniques that they passed on to peasants, and sometimes a lord or lady encouraged land clearances or new methods of cultivation. But most of the improvements came from the people who worked the land, with peasants trying new tools and methods, keeping those that worked and rejecting others. Expanding productivity was therefore rooted in the rural communities in which most medieval people passed their lives. In northern Europe, in particular, these communities were built around three critical institutions: the village, a community of peasants; the manor which joined landowner and tenants; and the parish of priest and his parishioners (see Figure 7.1).

Of course, most peasants were simultaneously villagers, manorial tenants, and parishioners. Each of these institutions had different functions: mostly social and agricultural for villages, mostly legal and economic for manors, and mostly religious for parishes. They often had different constituencies as well, because sometimes their boundaries coincided but often they did not. Some manors covered two or more villages and so too did some parishes; in these cases, people from several villages shared a manorial court or parish church. But sometimes a manor or parish covered only part of a village, so that people in the same village owed rents to different manors or **tithes** to different parish churches. This messiness reflects the distinct origins and functions of each institution. For a peasant, the village regulated the agrarian routine, the manor defined the claims and powers exercised by the elite, and the parish was the source of Christian consolation and obligation.

Given all this variation, it is as difficult to discuss the "typical" medieval farm as to discuss the typical American business today. That said, let us try, focusing particularly on the more fertile and heavily populated regions of northwestern Europe.

The Village

In the European countryside today, you can still see the traces of medieval villages: houses set close together, surrounded by great fields and gathered about a village green, common well, or fish pond. These "nucleated villages"—the term is meant to evoke a nucleus of houses encircled by fields—began to dominate the landscape of northern Europe around the turn of the millennium. They were not new in the ninth through twelfth centuries, but they were becoming more common, slowly replacing the more scattered and less permanent settlements in which many early medieval peasants had passed their lives. Sometimes a cluster of farms began to attract more settlers, sometimes a lord or lady sought to colonize a new district with a planned settlement, and sometimes a church or castle became an "anchor" for a village that grew in its shadow. In regions where the soil was poor or the terrain mountainous, peasant families continued to live in separate farms or hamlets, but across the fertile lowlands of northern France, England, and the German states, village life became the norm.

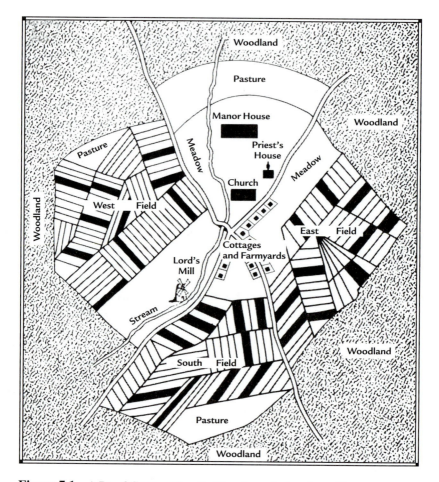

Figure 7.1 *A Rural Community*   In this schematic drawing, village, manor, and parish share the same boundaries. The dark strips in each field indicate how the holdings of one family—in this case, a fairly well-off family—were dispersed through the fields of the village. The extensive woodland shown here would have slowly shrunk over the Central Middle Ages, as peasants brought more land into arable or pastoral use.

The arable lands that surrounded such northern villages were known as **open fields,** because they were normally divided into unfenced **strips** that were separated only by rocks or other low markers. Each strip was about 220 yards long (that is, about twice the length of a football field) and comparatively narrow (perhaps only a few dozen yards wide). Typically, a family possessed several strips, scattered throughout the fields, on which grew the grain that they ate, sold, or used to pay rent. In plowing, seeding, weeding, and harvesting these strips, the members of a family worked for the family's own benefit, but their work was, in every instance, guided by extensive cooperation with other tenants. Because plows and oxen were expensive, families often shared them. Because all strips in an open field had to grow the same crop, families had to agree on which field would be sown in the fall, which sown in the spring, and which left fallow. This cooperative process was partly guided by custom, but new problems were worked out in village meetings or by agreement between family heads. When peasants argued about strip boundaries or plowing rights, they were under strong practical pressure to resolve their conflicts without violence and without the intervention of manorial officers. The shape, contour, and method of cultivation of the open fields varied from place to place, depending on the topography of the region and the fertility of the soil.[2]

The open fields were fundamental to the rural economy of northern Europe, but there was much more to villages than a cluster of peasants' cottages and encircling fields. Peasants ordinarily had farmyards next to their cottages where they raised vegetables, fruit trees, and fowl. They also grazed their animals on village pastures and cut hay for winter feeding from nearby meadows.[3] In addition to oxen and horses, both kept for their pulling power, most peasants also raised sheep and cattle for their cheese, milk, skins, and wool. Certain districts, particularly in Flanders and northern England, took up sheep-raising on a scale so large as almost to exclude the growing of grain.

Villages also had woodland from which fuel and building materials were gathered and in which pigs fed. A stream or pond supplied water, fish, and perhaps a water mill for grinding grain. Some villages also had a common oven or winepress. Almost all boasted a few artisans and tradespeople who combined field work with other labor. Some worked as the wheelwrights, blacksmiths, and carpenters who maintained buildings and tools in good repair; others worked as butchers, bakers, and brewers who provided food and drink for sale. Many of these by-industries were men's work, but brewing was the particular province of women. In some villages of medieval England, the generic term "brewer" was replaced by "brewster" (-*ster* was a female ending in Middle English) because all people in the trade were female. Many villages also accommodated another sort of worker: men, women, and children who had little or no land and survived by hiring their unskilled labor to others.[4]

With fields, woods, streams, mills, artisans, victualers, and wage-laborers, villages were complex economic machines, driven by many resources. But they were seldom economically self-sufficient, and this was especially true by the twelfth century when the commercial revival was well underway. It was then common for peasants to take their food surpluses to local markets or towns, and with the cash they obtained, to buy items they could not produce themselves (such as salt) or chose not to produce (such as cloth or pottery). As towns and trade grew, the village economy was integrated more and more into regional trade networks, and some enterprising peasants even acquired considerable wealth from selling grain or wool.

---

[2] Because it was hard to turn a team of oxen or horses, these long strips grew from the use of the heavy, wheeled plow. Peasants would plow straight ahead until the team of oxen or horses needed to rest; after a breather, they would turn the plow and make a second, long furrow parallel to the first. In southern Europe, rectangular fields, created by cross-plowing with the scratch plow, remained common.

[3] Peasants also fed animals on the stubble of harvested fields, thereby nourishing both animals and fields (since the animals dropped manure as they fed).

[4] Women got about two-thirds to one-half the wages paid to men. Clever bailiffs exploited this differential for, as one writer advised in the late thirteenth century, it was wise to hire a woman for certain tasks because she will "work for much less money than a man would take." These lower wages for women were common in towns and cities too.

The Manor

Compared to the village, the manor—whose lord or lady profited from the labor of peasants and exercised authority over them—was a more artificial unit. As we saw in Chapter 5, manorialism had taken shape in some parts of West Francia by the eighth century, and, in the centuries thereafter, a grid of manors was overlaid on the agrarian landscape of northern Europe. The process was slow and incomplete. In the eleventh century, manorialism was scarcely evident at all in Scandinavia, the Italian peninsula, some northern German states, and southern France, but it was common in northern France and soon thereafter took firm hold in England and elsewhere. The owner of a manor might be a king or queen, a great nobleman or noblewoman, a bishop or monastery, or even a mere knight or lady. For any of these privileged people or institutions, a manor was an efficient way to get support from the land without actually working the land. A monk or nun would have explained manorialism in terms of mutual obligation and the tripartite ideal of medieval society: it was through manorialism that "those who work" supported "those who pray" and "those who fight."

On most manors in the Central Middle Ages, peasants were either free or enserfed. Freemen and freewomen owed rents, paid in cash or goods, but little more. Serfs also paid rent in cash or kind, but they also usually had to labor for a certain number of days each week—often three—on whatever tasks the manor required (see Figure 7.2). Serfs were also bound to the land, forbidden to leave the manors into which they had been born. By the eleventh century, serfdom had expanded considerably, as both former slaves and formerly free peasants joined its ranks. For slaves, serfdom was an improvement, as it often also was for slaveowners who, by changing slaves into serfs, escaped obligations of housing and feeding. For free peasants, serfdom had a certain appeal during troubled times, when protection from Vikings and other armed marauders might be gotten in return for submission to manorialism. Faced with loss of life or loss of freedom, serfdom could then seem the better alternative.

Figure 7.2 *Labor-Rent*   This bailiff is supervising serfs harvesting grain from the manorial demesne. Labor-rent was among the most hated obligations of serfdom.

The owner of a manor profited from it in several ways. First came the produce harvested from the demesne lands that were cultivated directly for the owner's use. The demesne often covered one-fourth to one-third of the acreage, but its strips were scattered, like the strips of peasant tenants, among the open fields. The demesne was cultivated by slaves (if they remained), by wage-laborers, and especially by serfs. Second, manors generated profit through the rents paid by tenants—in cash, goods (sometimes a percentage of the harvest or a stipulated number of eggs, hens, or other commodities), and labor. Free tenants paid rent only in cash or goods; serfs were burdened with labor-rent as well. Third, manors charged various fees for the use of pastures, woodlands, mills, winepresses, and ovens. These fees were so onerous that some peasants tried to pasture animals elsewhere or use handmills; if caught, they were forced to use and pay for manorial facilities. Some fees applied to all of a manor's tenants, but others—such as charges levied when land was inherited or when a young woman married—were directed particularly at serfs. Fourth, profit also accrued from the jurisdictional rights associated with a manor. At manor courts, disputes were settled, misdeeds punished, and obligations enforced—and almost every such transaction resulted in a fee or fine paid to the manor. Manorial justice, like all justice in the Middle Ages, was a money-making enterprise.

Some lords or ladies possessed only one manor, and if so, they usually resided there in a castle or manor house. But many possessed more than one manor, and this was especially true of institutions, such as monasteries, that relied on multiple manors for support. In such cases, a manorial agent known as a **bailiff** or **steward** supervised the manorial court, oversaw the farming of the demesne, and collected the dues and rents of the tenants.

Whether laboring in the shadow of a manor house or under the sharp eye of a manorial officer, medieval peasants worked in a regime designed to extract profit from them in a variety of ingenious ways. But peasants were not limitlessly exploited, for custom stipulated that no manorial lord or lady could demand more from tenants than had been demanded in the past. Some ignored this restraint and abused their serfs pitilessly. But some were forced, by custom, to retract new policies and be content with old ways. All told, serfdom was hardly enviable, but it was better than the slavery of ancient times. Serfs were not chattel slaves: they could not normally be sold away from their lands or families, and after paying their manorial dues, they were entitled to the remaining produce of their fields.

The Parish

Parishes—that is, the area served by local churches and their priests—were also evolving in most parts of Europe by the ninth and tenth centuries. Some were founded by bishops eager to extend pastoral care to rural communities; others evolved out of churches built by monasteries for the same purposes; and many others were originally family churches, built by a local noble whose descendants then claimed the right to appoint its priest and manage its affairs.

During the Central Middle Ages, the parochial system came under the firmer control of bishops who took responsibility for appointing priests and overseeing their work. Because there were no seminaries in medieval Europe, parish priests usually knew the rudiments of reading and writing but were not well educated. Priests were primarily supported by *glebe* lands (that is, land assigned for their use), by *tithes* (parishioners had to pay one-tenth of all they produced to support the church), and by *oblations* (fees that parishioners paid for such services as marriage or burial). Until the reforms of the eleventh century (about which more in the next chapter), priests were not required to be celibate, and many lived with wives and children, much like other peasants. But even married priests were special people, endowed with the sacramental powers of Catholic Christianity. When they celebrated mass before their parishioners, sanctified a marriage, or buried the dead, they brought the power of God and the Church to ordinary people.

Built in stone, if possible, parish churches were among the largest and sturdiest buildings in the countryside (their only rivals in their regard were castles and monasteries). Many were decorated inside with religious paintings and statues that offered an elementary form of religious instruction for an illiterate congregation. Because few churches had pews, worshipers stood or squatted during services—women on one side, men on the other. Although sacred in design and function, parish churches were also community centers. Meetings were held in their naves, grain stored in their driest corners, and markets held in their churchyards. On festival days the church and churchyard were used for dancing and drinking, much to the impotent dismay of bishops. In short, parish churches, like the priests who labored within them, were simultaneously part of their rural surroundings and distinguished, by their sacred functions, from them.

The same was true of the feast days of the Christian calendar: Christmas, Easter, and many lesser holy days (hence "holidays"). These were pious occasions, but they also provided joyous relief from an otherwise grinding routine. Christmas was preceded by several weeks of fasting, but it ended with twelve days of feasting and play. A month later, the feast of Candlemas (February 2) was celebrated by a candlelight procession, often followed by pancakes. Since this feast commemorated the purification of the Virgin six weeks after the birth of Jesus, it was especially important to medieval mothers (who underwent a similar rite after each childbirth), but everyone enjoyed the relief it provided at a dark and dreary time of year. (Groundhog Day, with its ritual of trying to predict the early or late coming of spring, does much the same in the modern United States.) Easter was anticipated by 40 days of springtime austerity (Lent), but it was followed by several days of good food and games. At midsummer, the feast of St. John the Baptist brought bonfires and dancing. At these times and many others throughout the year, holy days provided opportunities for dancing, drinking, and informal sports—wrestling, archery, cockfights, and even a rough form of soccer.

✳ RURAL SOCIETY

The life of a medieval peasant is almost beyond our imagining, tied to the cycle of the seasons and vulnerable to the whims of nature: droughts, floods, epidemics among humans and animals, crop diseases, the summer's heat, and the winter's chill. Today we are insulated from nature by a screen of modern technological wonders: central heating, refrigeration, air conditioning, a secure food supply, plumbing, deodorants, modern medicine, and many more. We enjoy the protection of police and fire departments; we defy distance and terrain with our highways and jets. All these things and others we take for granted, but they are all products of the recent past, undreamed of in the Middle Ages.

From the viewpoint of a modern middle-class American, medieval peasants lived in unspeakable filth and poverty. A typical house in the Central Middle Ages, although much improved on earlier houses, consisted of a thatched roof resting on a timber framework, with the spaces between the framing filled with webbed branches covered with mud and straw. The houses of wealthier peasants sometimes had two rooms, furnished with benches, a table, and perhaps a chest. But most peasants lived in one-room cottages virtually bare of furniture.

People slept on straw that crawled with vermin. The smells of sweat and manure were always present, and therefore largely unnoticed. Flies buzzed everywhere. Cottages sheltered not only people but also domestic livestock: chickens, dogs, geese, and occasionally even cattle. In winter these animals provided added heat, and for the same reason, many people usually shared the same straw bedding. Windows, if any, were small and few (and of course had no glass). The floor was usually of earth; it froze in the wintertime and oozed with the coming of a thaw. Arthritis and rheumatism were common, along with countless other diseases whose cures lay far in the future. A simple fire served for cooking and heating, but because there were no chimneys, the smoke filled the room before escaping through holes or cracks in the ceiling. Candles were luxury items, and peasants had to make do with smoky, evil-smelling torches made of rushes soaked in fat. There was always the danger that a stray spark might set the roof afire. Most people spent as much time as possible out-of-doors, preferring to sit on benches set against the outside walls of cottages.

The peasant "family" was really a "household," for many houses accommodated servants and lodgers, in addition to a nuclear family of husband, wife, and children.[5] Yet some households were small—two brothers who lived together, a widow and her children, even just one person living alone. And some were large, with three generations—grandparents, parents, and children—sharing a single roof.

Work was apportioned according to gender, age, and ability. Men did most of the field work, such as plowing, seeding, and weeding. Women assisted in the fields as needed (especially at harvest), but they also worked in the farmyards around their cottages and in nearby woods and pastures. They cleaned and prepared meals, milked cows, fed livestock, tended vegetable gardens, fetched water, made cheese and butter, turned wool to yarn and yarn into cloth, brewed ale, and collected nuts or fallen wood from the forest. Infants and toddlers did not work, nor did the very old or infirm. But as soon as children were sufficiently mobile and strong, sons assisted their fathers in the fields and daughters worked with their mothers in cottages, yards, and woodlands. Even the elderly and ill helped out as best they could, watching children, spinning wool into yarn, or weeding garden plots. In the winter, when the fields were often frozen, everyone stayed around the cottage, repairing tools, mending clothes, spinning, perhaps even grinding grain in a handmill. In the evening, dinner offered a pot of vegetable broth, coarse black bread, ale, and possibly an egg. Then it was early to bed, to rest for the toils of the following day.

Even this somber picture is a bit idealized. Often one or more members of a household would be immobilized by illness (for which there were few effective medicines) or tormented by injuries, wounds, aches, and pains (no aspirin, just ale). Because

---

[5] Today, only wealthy people employ live-in servants, but in the Middle Ages even modest households kept a servant or two. Medieval servants were not maids or butlers; they were simply hired hands who did whatever needed doing—in field, forest, yard, or home. For a household with too many children, sending a child out to service eased expenses; for a household with too few workers, taking in a young servant was a good solution. In most cases, service was a short-term occupation, employing young people in the years between childhood and marriage.

fertility was limited only by malnutrition and some relatively ineffective forms of birth control and abortion, wives endured many pregnancies. Childbirth was a mortal danger to mother and newborn alike, and infant mortality was very high. Children received a lot of special attention and care from their parents, but they lived in a world of many dangers: open hearths in the houses, ditches filled with water outside, and infections and diseases all around. Well over a third of children died during their first year and another third died before the age of ten. In other words, a woman might live through six childbirths but see only two children reach adulthood. Childhood itself was brief, for children worked as soon as they were able, and by the age of twelve or so, some had already left home to work as servants for others or to seek a living elsewhere.

Flood or drought occasionally worried peasants, but warfare was the biggest threat. Feudal armies did not hesitate to pillage or burn villages or even turn them into battlegrounds. From a French poem of c. 1200 comes this chilling tale:

> They start to march. The scouts and the incendiaries lead. After them come the foragers who are to gather the spoils and load them into the great baggage train. The tumult begins. The peasants, having just come out to the fields, turn back uttering loud cries. The shepherds gather their flocks and drive them toward the neighboring woods in the hope of saving them. The incendiaries set the villages afire and foragers visit and plunder them. The distracted inhabitants are burned to death or led away with tied hands to be held for ransom. Everywhere alarm bells ring. Fear spreads from one side to another and becomes general. Everywhere one sees helmets shining, pennons floating, and horsemen covering the plain. Here money is seized; there cattle, donkeys, and flocks are taken. The smoke spreads; the flames rise; the terrified peasants and shepherds flee in all directions.

Some villages never saw such disasters, but none lived in confident security. And some suffered plundering of a different kind: forced requisition of grain, animals, and other supplies to support a "friendly" force. Whenever faced with ravaged fields or barns emptied by confiscation, helpless peasants had no choice but to rebuild, replant, and pray for survival through a cold, hungry winter.

Hollywood movies have given us images of perfectly happy peasants like those in *Camelot* or horribly oppressed ones like those in *Braveheart*. The truth is somewhere in between. Medieval peasants did not live back-to-nature lives (close to nature, living in rhythm with the seasons, free of urban anxieties, and the like), but their lives were not unremittingly awful either. Some peasants held more land than others, and if so, they lived in relatively well-built houses, ate relatively better diets, and even raised relatively healthier children. By the thirteenth century, most villages included largeholders (who might have about 30 acres of land), middling tenants (with about 15 acres), and smallholders (5 acres or less).

Even serfdom was not always terrible. Because the rents paid by serfs were set by custom whereas rents on free lands could go up without restraint, serfs often paid more favorable rents than did free tenants, especially when land became more scarce (and valuable) in the thirteenth century. Moreover, because manorial rules sometimes prohibited serfs from dividing an inheritance among all children, whereas free tenants regularly did so, serf holdings eventually ended up larger than many free holdings. By 1300, a serf who held a thirty-acre tenancy and paid a rent set by custom was, in many practical respects, better off than a free tenant who had to pay the market rent on a small tenancy of just five acres.

Good Times and Bad

Generally speaking, peasants did well in the expanding opportunities of the eleventh and twelfth centuries, but less well thereafter. The agricultural innovations that clustered around the year 1000 created good circumstances for almost everyone: production was increasing; so too was population (and hence, the labor supply); and there was more than enough land for all. Peasants were in such demand that enterprising landowners who sought to turn woods and marshes into arable had to compete to attract tenants. Others had to compete simply to keep their serfs from running away. Sometimes rents were lowered; sometimes peasants were elevated from servile status to freedom; sometimes demesne fields were leased out to peasants and serfs allowed to pay a cash rent in lieu of their traditional work on the demesne. Some landowners even allowed rural **communes** to develop—that is, communities of peasants whose lord or lady had granted them a **charter** of self-governance that effectively freed them from the daily exactions of manorialism.

Even in the booming twelfth century, however, the reduction of demesne farming and the freeing of serfs occurred slowly and unevenly. By the thirteenth century, these trends were beginning to reverse themselves. Population growth then began to outstrip available arable, raising land values and devaluing peasant labor. As land became more scarce than workers, manors throughout northern Europe began farming their demesnes more intensively than before, often employing landless peasants at low wages or strictly enforcing the labor services of their remaining serfs. At the same time, legal changes began to harden distinctions of status, making it much more difficult for serfs to gain their freedom, and much easier for the free to sink into serfdom. It became firm law in some districts, for example, that a free peasant forfeited freedom by marrying a serf. In other districts, land grew so scarce that some freemen and freewomen submitted to serfdom simply to get a few acres to farm. Moreover, quite apart from the matter of legal status, peasants of the thirteenth century, lacking the leverage they had enjoyed in earlier times of abundant land and labor shortage, were subjected to intense manorial exploitation. They were burdened with higher rents and taxes, higher fines at manorial courts, and higher charges for the use of manorial mills, winepresses, and ovens. Tenants who complained or refused to pay might have had custom on their side, but they faced the prospect of losing their tenancies, which could then be given to any one of the growing number of landless laborers roaming the land.

✴ THE COMMERCIAL REVOLUTION

Before agricultural expansion stalled in the thirteenth century, however, it stimulated an impressive expansion of trade and industry. From richer harvests grew more people, more specialization, more demand, and more trade. Even during the troubled years following the breakdown of Charlemagne's empire, trade had continued, especially along Europe's great rivers—the Rhine, Seine, Po, Loire, Danube, and Thames. Indeed, it was the growing wealth of these river valleys that had attracted Viking, Magyar, and Muslim raiders. When not raiding, Vikings themselves participated in this commerce, bringing furs, amber, walrus tusks, and other Baltic products to European towns and fairs, as well as trading with Islamic and Byzantine merchants. Jewish merchants, who were able to draw on long-standing ties among Jewish communities throughout the Mediterranean

MEDIEVAL MYTHS

Lady Godiva

It is not clear how Lady Godiva became associated with fancy chocolates, but she has been known for hundreds of years as the woman who rode naked through the streets of the medieval English town of Coventry. Her tale was first told by chroniclers in the thirteenth century. Godiva pleaded with her husband Leofric, lord of the town of Coventry, to lower the high taxes he charged its citizens; he replied that he would not consider her request unless she rode through the town naked; she immediately "loosed her hair and let down her tresses which veiled her whole body and . . . rode naked through the town center"; and Leofric responded by granting Coventry a charter that guaranteed freedom from taxes. The story has been much loved and much elaborated on. A Peeping Tom was added to the drama in the seventeenth century; Godiva processions were an annual event in eighteenth-century Coventry; statues and paintings of Godiva's ride proliferated in the nineteenth century; and in the mid-twentieth century, Dr. Seuss wrote about a family of *seven* Lady Godivas. There's a bit of hard fact to the story. A woman named Godifu was a powerful landowner in the mid-eleventh century, and she was married to Leofric, earl of Mercia. But other facts tell against the tale. Godifu held Coventry in her own right, so she did not need her husband's permission to lower its tolls. Instead of enjoying the freedom provided by the eleventh-century charter of this tale, Coventry did not achieve self-governance until the mid-fourteenth century. Perhaps most importantly, although we have many contemporary documents that tell us about the activities of Leofric and Godiva, our first mention of a naked ride occurs some 150 years after Godifu's death. All told, the ride of Godiva is a powerful story, but unlikely history. Still, the story has historical uses, for it shows how medieval people preferred to believe that women exercised power, if at all, through indirect means: in the tale, Godiva does not solve the problem herself but instead convinces her husband to solve the problem. The most revered female intercessor in the Middle Ages was the Blessed Virgin Mary, about whom we'll learn more in the next chapter. To find out more about Godiva, look at David Donoghue's *Lady Godiva: A Literary History of the Legend* (2003).

region and beyond, also helped to link ninth- and tenth-century Europe with the wealthier civilizations of Islam and Byzantium. Vikings had exceptional ships that aided their trade; Jews had exceptionally far-flung contacts. But Europe's trade did not rely on Vikings and Jews alone, for throughout Europe, enterprising young men and women responded to new opportunities by buying goods in one place, transporting them to another, and then selling them at a profit. This was how Godric of Finchale, described in the Biographical Sketch on pp. 173–174, made his fortune.

As the invasions diminished in the late tenth century, Europe's commerce surged. French dukes, English kings, and German emperors alike encouraged weekly markets that served villages in their immediate vicinity and annual fairs that attracted an international array of merchants and goods. The greatest of these were the fairs of Champagne, encouraged from the early twelfth century by the Counts of Champagne, which attracted merchants from throughout Europe, not only from nearby French and Flemish towns but also from English, Iberian, Italian, and German cities. Many rulers also sought to systematize the minting of silver coins, thereby enhancing their power, enriching their treasuries, and providing a more reliable medium of exchange. The commerce of Italian towns flourished under the Ottos and their successors, and when Otto the Great opened a rich silver mine in Rammelsberg in the 970s, a new wave of precious metal flowed across Europe.

Towns and Commerce

Cities had been critical to imperial government in Rome, and from some Roman cities evolved the cathedral towns of the Early Middle Ages, with their episcopal courts, grand churches, and sacred legends of patron saints. When commerce revived in the tenth and eleventh centuries (see Map 7.1), these old towns were invigorated and new ones emerged. Some were "planted" by enterprising nobles who sought to encourage trade and tax it, some developed outside the walls of monasteries, and some flourished around a castle or fortification. These fortifications, or *burgs,* eventually gave their name to urban institutions, for by the twelfth century a "borough" was a town or city, inhabited by **burghers** or **burgesses**.[6] Even today, the association lingers in such places as Edinburgh, Hamburg, and (for a U.S. example) Pittsburgh. The medieval city remained faithful to its saints and religious establishments while expanding its commercial districts and developing its political and legal institutions. Church, commerce, and urban government coexisted within city walls, but it was commerce that transformed Europe's cities into economic centers that, for the first time, earned their own way from the activities of their merchants and artisans.

The earliest and largest commercial towns were those of the northern Italian peninsula, where, as we have seen, Venetian merchants established early contacts with the profitable markets of Constantinople, Alexandria, and North Africa. Other Italian ports—Genoa, Pisa, and Naples—soon followed. After Muslims were virtually driven from the seas in the tenth century, Italian merchants dominated the Mediterranean, bringing goods from Islamic and Byzantine ports to Italian cities and carrying them overland across the Alps into France and the German states. This far-flung trade even brought vigorous new life to inland towns such as Milan and Florence. In the Central Middle Ages, urban life in the Italian peninsula so prospered that several cities reached populations of about 100,000.

After 1095, the crusades initially disrupted Mediterranean trade, but they proved a long-term economic stimulus, especially for Pisa, Genoa, and Venice, whose merchants helped the crusaders and profited from their wars. Eventually many Arab cities established separate enclaves for Italian merchants, and these grew into bustling, busy places. In Tunis in 1289, more than 300 Europeans brought business to the city in a mere seven-month period. They carried furs, slaves, metal, timber, silver, and cloth; they returned home with dyes, spices, silks, cotton, and gold. The breadth of this trade has silent testimony today in coins of Arab origin dug up by archaeologists as far north as England, Poland, and Scandinavia. It was a trade that produced know-how as well as profits. From Arabs, Christians learned about the cultivation of such crops as oranges, sugar, and rice, about better techniques of irrigation, about papermaking and the compass, and about a new lateen sail that allowed ships to tack upwind.

Far to the north, the cities of Flanders also grew wealthy from commerce, trading throughout northern France and the British Isles, the Rhineland, and the shores of the

---

[6] From the same root comes the world "bourgeoisie," a word used to describe the *modern* middle class.

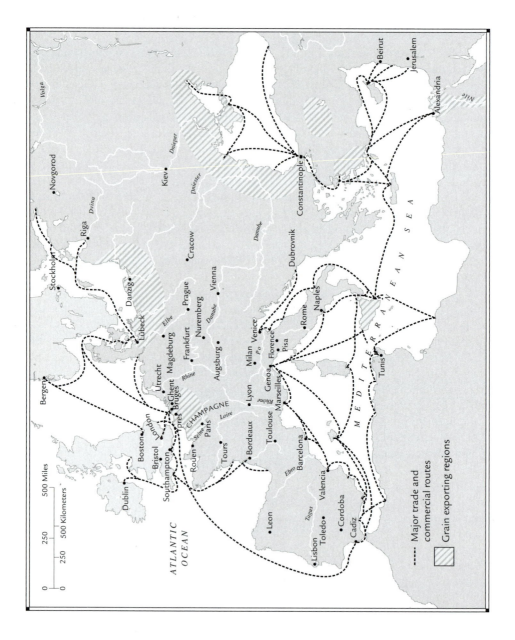

Novgorod

Volga
Dnieper
Dniester
Divina
Danube
Rhine
Elbe
Loire
Seine
Rhône
Ebro
Tagus
Po
Nile

Stockholm
Riga
Kiev
Cracow
Danzig
Lübeck
Bergen
Magdeburg
Frankfurt
Prague
Vienna
Nuremberg
Augsburg
Utrecht
Ghent
Bruges
Ypres
London
Boston
Bristol
Southampton
Dublin
Rouen
Paris
Tours
CHAMPAGNE
Lyon
Bordeaux
Toulouse
Milan
Venice
Florence
Pisa
Genoa
Marseilles
Rome
Naples
Dubrovnik
Constantinople
Barcelona
Valencia
Leon
Lisbon
Toledo
Cordoba
Cadiz
Tunis
Beirut
Jerusalem
Alexandria

ATLANTIC
OCEAN

MEDITERRANEAN SEA

500 Miles
250
0

500 Kilometers
250
0

- - - - Major trade and
commercial routes

Grain exporting regions

Baltic Sea. Manufacturing also enriched Flemish cities. Flanders had long been a great sheep-raising district, and its cities and towns—Bruges, Ypres, and Ghent—soon became centers of woolen textile production. In time, international demand for Flemish cloth grew so great that Flemish merchants had to import wool from England to supplement the once sufficient output of Flemish flocks. By then Flanders was the industrial center of northern Europe, with a textile industry that was the supreme manufacturing enterprise of its age.

Early commerce focused on specific sorts of goods: luxury items such as silk and spices, human cargo for the slave trade, and good quality cloth. As the economy expanded, local areas were able to specialize in whatever goods they produced most efficiently. By selling these goods to distant markets, they could then import the necessities of life. Thus, the Paris basin exported grain, Scandinavia exported timber, Poland exported salt, the northern German states exported salt and fish, England exported wool, Flanders exported cloth, and Burgundy exported wine. A thirteenth-century visitor to a Burgundian monastery reported that the monks devoted all their farmland to vineyards; because their wine sold for such a good price in Paris, they were able to specialize in this one product and use the profits to buy their food, clothing, and other necessary supplies.

In the attenuated commerce of the Early Middle Ages, essential goods had moved across long distances through the few cities that could accommodate such trade; in the Central Middle Ages, a much wider array of goods moved through a much wider assortment of local, regional, and international networks. *Market villages* handled the trade of peasants, offering them weekly opportunities to sell such produce as eggs or grain and to buy such commodities as cloth or pottery (see Figure 7.3 for an illustration of an urban market). *Regional towns* were pumps for these small markets, sending goods to them and receiving other goods in return. For example, a peasant woman in the English village of Brigstock might have sold some wool at the Thursday market of Corby (some eight miles away from her village); this wool might then find its way to the regional town of Lincoln (about sixty miles from Brigstock), and thence across the Channel to Flemish weavers. With the profit made from her wool, this countrywoman could have purchased at Corby cloth made in Bruges, salted herring from the Netherlands, or maybe just a plowshare hammered out by a local blacksmith. She never traveled to Lincoln, but through Lincoln—via Corby—went goods she made and goods she needed to purchase. And from Lincoln some goods from Brigstock went to the top stage of this marketing hierarchy—to the *cities* of the Central Middle Ages, centers of international trade, banking, and industry. England boasted only one genuine city: London, with a population of about 40,000 at the end of the twelfth century, and double that only a century later.

Many trading networks were informal, such as the axis that ran through the Rhine and Rhône valleys, linking the fortunes of Flemish and Italian towns. Other connections were more formal and predictable. For example, the annual fairs of Champagne

◀ **Map 7.1**   *Medieval Trade*   This map shows the *sea routes* that linked medieval cities not only with each other but also with North Africa and the Middle East. Merchants from these cities also moved goods along the *inland rivers* you can see on this map and on *overland routes* (which were too numerous to show without rendering this map illegible). Many of these inland routes led to the fairs of Champagne, located in the region east of Paris. Of the many commodities that were traded within this vast nexus, the most important—grain—has been used to illustrate how far goods and merchants traveled.

Figure 7.3   *Urban Markets* At the center of most towns was a
marketplace where traders displayed goods from tables, benches, or
stalls. In this picture, a woman is selling poultry to a cleric. The
shaved crown of the customer's head—known as a *tonsure*—was a
sign of his clerical status.

eventually provided a rotation of six fairs per year at which European merchants met to
trade. For another example, merchants from various towns sometimes formed leagues to
ensure safer transport and better trading privileges. The greatest of these, the Hanseatic
League, focused on the Baltic trade. It took shape in the mid-twelfth century, had more
than 150 member or allied cities by 1500, and lasted well into the seventeenth century.

Whether in small markets or big cities and whether through individual merchants
or leagues, commerce lubricated the high medieval economy with an ever-increasing
flow of money. It was money that built the great cathedrals, supported the crusades,

BIOGRAPHICAL SKETCH

Godric of Finchale (c. 1069–1170)

The life of St. Godric of Finchale provides a unique example of the rags-to-riches careers of many merchants and traders in the expanding economic climate of the eleventh and twelfth centuries. But we know of Godric's rise to fortune only because he later rejected his worldly wealth to become a hermit-saint whose austere life of prayer and self-sacrifice came to be known and admired throughout Western Europe. For that reason, he was the subject of no less than three pious biographies.

Godric was born shortly after the Norman Conquest of England in a small town in Norfolk. He was of Anglo-Saxon parentage, the firstborn son of Ailward and Aedwin. At about the age of sixteen, Godric left to seek his fortune. For four years, he worked as a wandering peddler, scavenging for lost or castoff goods and then selling them. By then, he had enough money to afford a pilgrimage to Rome, which he probably undertook not only for reasons of piety but also out of curiosity and a longing for adventure. After this first of his many pilgrimages, Godric became a seafaring merchant, plying his wares between England, Flanders, Denmark, and Scotland. Soon he was able to buy a half-share in one merchant ship and a quarter-share in another. He became an accomplished sea captain, steering his own ships from port to port and sometimes saving them from shipwreck by his uncanny skill at weather forecasting (or so it was later said). In these years, Godric was far from the saint he would later become, committing sins of lust and dishonesty which he would later bitterly repent.

In 1101 Godric sailed to the Holy Land on what was said to have been a pilgrimage to Jerusalem, and he doubtless set out on the voyage with a pious intent. Nevertheless, he probably did some trading and perhaps even plundering along the way. Crusade chroniclers describe how an English pirate named Godric rescued King Baldwin I of Jerusalem in 1102 after a major defeat at the hands of a Muslim army. Then in his early thirties, Godric was described by a friend as short, agile, and strong, with a broad forehead, sparkling gray eyes, and bushy eyebrows that almost met. He had an oval face, a long nose, a thick beard, and black hair that in later years would turn pure white.

On his return to England, Godric was torn between resuming his worldly life and devoting himself to God. He served for a time as business manager for a rich nobleman but soon gave it up to go on more pilgrimages—to Rome, to the shrine of St. Gilles in southern France, and then to Rome again. Finally, in his mid-thirties, Godric abandoned his mercantile career for good. He disposed of all his wealth and became a hermit, moving from place to place in the forests of northern England. Eventually, after returning from one last penitential pilgrimage to Jerusalem, he settled down at a lonely, beautiful site on the River Wear, just north of Durham, called Finchale (pronounced, regrettably, "Finkle").

There Godric lived as a pious hermit for well over sixty years, and his reputation for sanctity spread across England and Europe. He was personally visited by some of the great abbots and bishops of northern England. He was so venerated as a prophet that some of the most celebrated leaders in Western Christendom, prelates such as Archbishop Thomas Becket (c. 1118–1170) and Pope Alexander III (r. 1159–1181) sought his prayers and his counsel. He was admired as a poet who set his pious verses to music (and who produced what is today the earliest surviving Middle English verse). He was also revered for his love of animals and was said even to bring rabbits and field mice into his cottage to enjoy the warmth of his fire during the frosts of winter.

Continued

BIOGRAPHICAL SKETCH

Godric of Finchale (c. 1069–1170)   *Continued*

Godric lived to be at least one hundred years old. During his final illness he was nursed by the monks of Durham Cathedral, and after his death, the monks built a priory on the site of his hermitage at Finchale, the ruins of which remain to this day in an unspoiled vale alongside the River Wear. His life was recorded for its remarkable piety, and we can still admire his sanctity today. But what makes him unique, from a historian's point of view, is the information contained in his life story about his youthful years as a merchant and seafarer. Godric regretted the sins of these years, but they provide us today with an unparalleled portrait of a self-made entrepreneur in the early phases of the medieval commercial revolution.

financed the charities of Christian princes, and gave substance to the magnificent religious culture of the thirteenth century—money and, of course, ardent faith. Princes could now collect their taxes in silver coins rather than in goods, govern through salaried officials, and wage war with hired troops. Aristocrats could pamper themselves with imported luxury goods. Enterprising peasants could accumulate wealth to build better houses or buy more land. And burghers, the chief beneficiaries of the new economy, could honor their civic saints by building vast, richly decorated churches. Often, too, they honored themselves by building elaborate town halls, and even more so by building impressive stone houses where they dwelt in conspicuous elegance.

✳ URBAN SOCIETY

Town dwellers were drawn primarily from the wealthier peasantry, but they also included vagabonds, runaway serfs, ambitious younger offspring of the lesser nobility, and, in general, the surplus of a mushrooming population. In the eleventh century, when towns were just getting established, immigration was essential; thereafter, towns (always unhealthy places with high mortality) continued to rely on newcomers to keep up their numbers. Women were especially important immigrants to towns, so much so that they often outnumbered townsmen by the thirteenth century. Women might have been drawn to towns by specific work that catered to female skills (such as the spinning so essential to textile production), but they also might have been pushed to towns by limited opportunities in the countryside (caused, for example, by inheritance practices that favored sons over daughters). In any case, if you had walked down the streets of a central medieval town, you would have encountered as many country-born folk as native urbanites and at least as many women as men.

Logically enough, towns were initially subject to the authority of the noble, bishop, or monastery within whose territory they lay. Thus, a local landowner could levy tolls and taxes on townspeople and could also administer justice within town walls. At an early date, however, the wealthiest inhabitants of towns—that is, the merchants—began to band together to oppose these exactions. They agitated for privileges essential to the pursuit of business: freedom from servile dues; freedom of movement; freedom from inordinate tolls at every bridge or castle; freedom to hold town property without any feudal or manorial services; and freedom of legal self-management. By the twelfth century, local landowners were granting their towns written guarantees of many or all of these privileges, contained in "charters of freedoms" or more simply, **urban charters.** Some nobles were forced to issue such charters in response to urban riots and revolts; others did so voluntarily, recognizing the economic advantages of prosperous commercial centers within their territories; and still others chartered new towns on their own initiative, laying out streets on a grid plan, building protective walls, *and* attracting traders by offering a generous charter of freedoms.

Agitation for urban self-government was so widespread that historians describe a **communal movement** in twelfth-century Europe. In effect, each urban charter created a semi-autonomous political and legal entity, called a **commune** in many parts of Europe, that had its own local government, its own court, its own tax-collecting agencies, and its own customs. The earliest urban charters varied greatly from one another, but soon charters were patterned after certain well-known models. The privileges enjoyed by the burghers of Newcastle-on-Tyne under King Henry I of England (r. 1100–1135) and the charter granted by King Louis VI of France (r. 1108–1137) to the community of Lorris became prototypes for charters elsewhere. The citizens of a commune paid enormous sums to receive such a charter, and they afterward also paid their lord or lady on a yearly basis to renew the charter or keep it effective. But—and this is all-important—they did so collectively, through their urban governments. Townspeople enforced their own laws in their own courts, arranged their own methods of tax collection, and paid their fee to their local landowner in one lump sum. In short, they had won the invaluable privilege of handling their own affairs. Wise nobles had little objection to gathering the golden egg—the annual sum paid for these chartered freedoms—without any administrative effort.

Urban charters grew out of collective effort and were sustained by collective responsibility, but medieval towns were not bastions of democracy or equality. Inequality sprang from many factors, but socioeconomic status, gender, and religion were especially important. Prosperous merchants had the most to gain from charters, as it was they who controlled town governments, ruling over more humble men and all women. In many towns, merchant oligarchies ruled, generation after generation, and they looked out for themselves over everyone else. A grain merchant and a shoemaker shared the same town walls, but their economic interests often strongly diverged. The merchant, for example, might encourage high prices for grain and the profits it would bring him; the shoemaker would pray for cheap grain and affordable bread. For merchants in medieval towns, political privilege worked hand-in-hand with economic privilege.

Women worked in a wide variety of craft and merchant enterprises, even sometimes collecting taxes, lending and exchanging money, illuminating and copying books, and working as druggists or barbers. But women predominated in almost none of these occupations, except for the least lucrative and most unpleasant, such as preparing the dead for burial or spinning wool into yarn. Widows sometimes managed businesses, but in this capacity, they were substitutes for their dead husbands rather than independent businesswomen (for example, if they remarried, they sometimes lost their businesses). Wives worked as helpers to their husbands or took up occupations that complemented those of their husbands (for example, wives of butchers sometimes worked as sausage-makers).

Daughters were much less likely than sons to be apprenticed in skilled trades, and most young women worked alongside their parents until they married or found employment as live-in servants.

As we have seen, Jews had played a vital part in the early phases of medieval urban growth. Jewish communities in Iberia, having survived the forced conversions of the Visigoths, thrived under Islamic toleration. In Italian cities, Jewish communities had similarly deep and strong roots. From the ninth century on, more and more Jews settled in northern Europe. The Carolingians had encouraged Jewish settlement in their Empire, and after the Norman Conquest of 1066, Jews were also welcomed in England. Because Christian rules made it difficult for Jews to own and till land, they usually had to make their livings within an urban milieu. Because it was essential for Jews, as a dispersed people, to maintain contact with other Jewish communities, they were well positioned as merchants—knowledgeable about distant lands, skilled in multiple languages, and armed with trustworthy contacts in many cities. And because Jews were not bound by Christian rules against loaning money at interest (credit cards had no place in the moral universe of the medieval Church), some were available to take on that essential economic function.[7] Yet only a small, highly visible minority of medieval Jews worked as merchants or moneylenders, and most Jews—butchers, bakers, tailors, teachers, and the like—worked much as did other townspeople.

Nevertheless, Jews were always a distinctive element within medieval towns. In part, this distinction was constitutional, for Jewish communities often held charters of their own from local nobles or kings, charters that ensured protection and sometimes even offered exemption from municipal jurisdiction. In such cases, Jews constituted, in a sense, a separate corporation within the corporation of the town in which they lived. In part, however, the distinctive place of Jews in medieval towns grew from Christian attitudes toward Jews which, as we saw in Chapter 1, had long mingled acceptance with anxiety. Jews were unable to participate in civic politics; they could not join most trade or craft **guilds;** and they were often segregated from Christians by residence in a district called the "Jewry," *Jüdengasse,* or *rue des Juifs,* or by specially prescribed clothing. These restrictions intensified over the course of the Central Middle Ages.

When a maelstrom of hatred was unleashed on Jewish communities from the late eleventh century, Christian townspeople led the way. In 1096, in attacks prompted in part by the fervor of the First Crusade, Christians murdered all the Jews of Mainz, Worms, and Cologne. These assaults continued in other towns, and they were soon buttressed by **ritual murder** stories, of which the first arose in the English city of Norwich in 1144. There, a false rumor that Jews had murdered a young Christian boy in a mock crucifixion spread through the town. The boy was made a saint, his tomb became a site of pilgrimage, and the Jews of Norwich narrowly escaped with their lives. This ludicrous accusation mingled misplaced Christian fury about the Crucifixion with

---

[7] Moneylending was and is a much vilified occupation, but it was essential to the growth of the medieval economy. An up-and-coming merchant like Godric of Finchale (see biographical sketch) simply had to be able to borrow money to expand his trade. In this way, he could have cash to continue trading, even when his money was tied up in a shipping venture, or he could get cash to take advantage of a good price on goods that he otherwise would not have been able to buy and then sell at a profit. In any case, although Jews were often maligned for moneylending, only a few Jews supported their families in this way and it was never exclusively a Jewish occupation. Some Christians developed ingenious ways to practice **usury** while hiding it (folding profit into inflated rates of exchange between two currencies was one favorite method). And some Christians simply ignored Church teachings; particularly famous in this regard were moneylenders from Lombardy and the French city of Cahors.

anxieties about present dangers, and it would be repeated again and again, with often deadly results, in the towns and cities of medieval and early modern Europe.[8] We shall consider the origins and effects of Christian persecution of medieval Jews more fully in Chapter 9; for now, it suffices to note their distinctly urban character.

Guilds and Households

Compared to assaults prompted by crusading fervor or false stories of ritual murders, the exclusion of Jewish townspeople from guilds was a minor matter. But guilds were vital to most medieval towns. Some of the first guilds were formed by merchants who organized to wrest urban charters from the aristocracy, and these merchant guilds long retained the political functions from which they had sprung. In other words, to participate in town government, it was often necessary to belong to the single merchant guild of the town or one of several powerful merchant guilds. But other guilds soon began to form, especially guilds of artisans. Although these guilds had many functions—social interaction, charitable activities, and religious observances—their economic functions were all-important.

To limit competition and ensure good quality, craft guilds, or rather, the **masters** of these craft guilds, established strict admission requirements and stringent rules on prices, wages, standards of quality, and operating procedures. Masters ran their trade, and they supervised two other sorts of workers. Young men learned their trade as **apprentices** in the shops of master craftsmen. After a specified period, sometimes as long as seven years, apprenticeship ended, and with good luck and rich parents, it might be possible to open a shop. But young artisans normally had to work for some years as day-laborers improving their skills and saving money; they were known as **journeymen** (after *journée,* the French word for "day"). Many never managed to become masters and open their own shops, and this would become more common as the economy cooled in the thirteenth century. Thereafter, many artisans had to spend their whole lives as wage earners.

These formal stages of artisanal work—apprenticeship, day work, and status as a master—were part of the lives of many men but few women. Occasionally a young woman was apprenticed in a male trade, but her eventual destiny was to marry a master in the trade, not become a guild **mistress** herself. Although a few female trades (such as embroidery or silk spinning) formed guilds of mistresses, journeywomen, and female apprentices, these female guilds were governed entirely or in part by men, and, in any case, they were so rare that they existed in only a handful of medieval towns.

For most merchants and artisans, the shop or workshop was also the home. In other words, the same place in which goods were produced and sold directly to the public was also the place of eating, sleeping, and family living. This urban "family" was, like peasant families, really a "household," for in addition to people related by blood or marriage, it often included apprentices, servants, and lodgers. The blurring of business life and domestic life in medieval shops and workshops sometimes worked to women's advantage. A master's wife and daughters could learn his skills just as his apprentices did, by observing, practicing, and working. Of course, the training of apprentices was

---

[8] As we'll see in Chapter 8, the story of Jesus' crucifixion became especially central to Christian piety in the Central and Later Middle Ages. As Christians dwelt with mournful sorrow on Jesus' redemptive suffering on the cross, they often also dwelt with vengeful hatred on what they erroneously saw as Jewish culpability for that death.

formally recognized, whereas a daughter, skilled from working at her father's side, had no such formal seal of approval. Still, the mingling of domestic space and home space solved, for medieval townswomen, one of the problems that now plagues modern mothers: child care was easily accommodated to work rhythms because the cradle was within easy reach of the workbench.

As in the countryside, urban children began to work at young ages—as soon as they could run errands, execute easy tasks at the workbench, or assist in shops. This was good training as well as drudgery, for children learned critical skills working alongside their fathers and mothers. By their early teens, many lived as apprentices or servants in households elsewhere in the town; others worked at home or as day-laborers. Once grown, children often continued in their parents' occupations. It was not unusual for sons to be apprenticed in their fathers' crafts, and the marriages of many daughters were similarly arranged. In this way, familial ties were strengthened by ties of trade and craft.

Life in Twelfth-Century London

We can gain some impression of life in a medieval city by looking at London as it existed toward the end of the twelfth century. With a population of about 40,000, London was by far the largest city in the British Isles and one of the leading commercial centers of northwestern Europe. Many of England's bishops, abbots, and barons maintained townhouses there, and the king himself conducted much of his business at a palace (completed in 1099 and standing to this day) in the western suburb of Westminster. Londoners of the later twelfth century were served by 139 churches, whose pealing bells marked the hours of every day.

London's streets, narrow and mostly unpaved, were crowded with people, dogs, horses, and pigs. (Half a century earlier, a crown prince of France was killed when his horse tripped over a pig in the streets of Paris.) The streets were lined with houses and shops, most of them built of wood and thatched with straw. Fire was an ever-present danger. Yet from the perspective of its twelfth-century inhabitants, London was a great, progressive metropolis. The old wooden bridge across the River Thames was being replaced by a new London Bridge made entirely of stone.[9] City sanitation workers cleared the streets of garbage. There was a sewer system of sorts, the only one in England: it consisted of open drains down the centers of streets. There was even a public lavatory established in the early twelfth century.

By today's standards, the city was a small, filthy, odoriferous firetrap. But twelfth-century Londoners were proud of it. One of them, William fitz Stephen, writing around 1175, described it in these glowing words:

> London is happy in the healthiness of its air, in its observance of Christian practice;
> in the strength of its fortifications, in its natural setting; in the honor of its citizens,
> and in the modest behavior of its matrons. It is cheerful in its sports and the fruitful
> mother of noble men.

All medieval cities were fortified, and London more strongly than most, with the Tower of London to the east, strong castles in the west, and a massive wall with towers

---

[9] This is not the London Bridge that is now a major tourist attraction in Arizona. Purchased by an entrepreneur and reassembled in the Arizona desert in 1971, this "London Bridge" was built less than 200 years ago (in 1831).

and gates placed at regular intervals. Within these walls came goods from far places: furs from the Russian states, gold from Arabia, spices from the Middle East, precious stones from Egypt, silk from China, and, of course, wine from France. More humble commodities were also produced and sold, including the medieval equivalent of fast food—ale sold in the streets by brewsters, wine sold directly from the ships that carried it from France, pies and cakes sold by hucksters, and cook-shops down by the river where, as William fitz Stephen described it, "you may find food according to the season, dishes of meat, roast, fried, and boiled; large and small fish; coarser meats for the poor and more delicate for the rich, such as venison and big and small birds."

William fitz Stephen also described the leisure pleasures of Londoners: miracle plays, carnivals, and athletic contests (a virtual medieval Olympics: "archery, running, jumping, wrestling, slinging the stone, hurling the javelin beyond a mark, and fighting with sword and buckler"). And in winter, he said that young people played on the frozen Thames:

> Some, gaining speed in their run, with feet set well apart, slide sideways over a
> vast expanse of ice. Others make seats out of a large lump of ice, and while one
> sits thereon, others with linked hands run before and drag him along behind them.
> So swift is their sliding motion that sometimes their feet slip, and they all fall on
> their faces. Others, more skilled at winter sports, put on their feet the shinbones of
> animals, binding them firmly around their ankles, and, holding poles shod with
> iron in their hands, which they strike from time to time against the ice, they are
> propelled as swiftly as a bird in flight. . . .

Of women, William fitz Stephen made only the most cryptic of remarks: "The matrons of this city are very Sabines." In Roman legend, the Sabine women, victims of a plot whereby they were seized, raped, and made pregnant by Roman men (who lacked any women to marry), heroically made peace between their de facto Roman husbands and their angry Sabine fathers. Presumably, fitz Stephen meant the allusion to be the highest of compliments, probably signifying the fierce loyalty of London women to both their husbands and their fathers.

As a proud Londoner, William fitz Stephen emphasized London's strengths and downplayed its weaknesses. He wrote of the healthiness of London's air, and yet we know that London had a smog problem even in the twelfth century. Not all shared his chamber-of-commerce enthusiasm. We are told that one twelfth-century Jewish merchant from France gave this warning to a friend about to leave for England:

> When you reach England, if you come to London, pass through it quickly. . . .
> Whatever evil or malicious thing that can be found in any part of the world, you
> will find in that one city. Steer clear of the crowds of pimps; don't mingle with the
> throngs in eating houses; avoid dice and gambling, the theater, and the tavern. You
> will meet with more braggarts there than in all of France. . . . If you don't want to
> dwell with evildoers, don't live in London.

The same merchant provided equally bad reports about other English towns. In Exeter both men and beasts ate the same food. Bath, lying amidst "exceedingly heavy air and sulphurous fumes, is at the gates of hell." At Bristol, "there is nobody who is not or has not been a soap maker." Ely "stinks perpetually from the surrounding fens." And York is "full of Scots—filthy and treacherous creatures, scarcely human."

�֎ THE LANDHOLDING ARISTOCRACY

As agriculture expanded and towns grew, aristocratic life in northern Europe was also transformed. For one thing, money began to erode the lord-vassal relationship, replacing personal services with cash payments. Nobles and kings, first in England and later on the Continent, began to depend less on the services that vassals personally performed and increasingly on mercenary troops and paid officials. From the twelfth century, English kings began to require their aristocratic vassals to pay a tax called *scutage* ("shield money") in lieu of service in royal armies, and in time this practice spread to France and elsewhere.

Moreover, money and commerce brought new luxuries into aristocratic households: pepper, ginger, and cinnamon for baronial kitchens; finer and more colorful clothing, jewelry, fur coats for cold winters; and for the castle, carpets, wall hangings, and more elaborate furniture. The cost of these amenities drove many aristocrats into debt, but in a culture where overspending was a virtue—the mark of a generous spirit—debt was preferable to frugality.

Professional Warriors

The medieval aristocracy was, above all, a military class, its men trained from early youth in mounted combat and its women reared to encourage male valor. As we saw in the last chapter, the feudal aristocracy was originally two-tiered, divided between nobles (the great landholders) and knights (their followers). During the Central Middle Ages, the social boundary between nobles and knights grew less clear. On the one hand, noblemen—impressed by the heroic virtues of such fictional knights as Tristan and Lancelot and influenced by the idea of "Christian knighthood"—grew more content to think of themselves as "knights" who just happened to be wealthy and powerful. On the other hand, ordinary knights began to acquire more extensive lands, along with privileges and jurisdictional rights formerly limited to the old nobility. By the thirteenth century, knights and noblemen, along with their wives, sisters, and daughters, were blending into a single aristocratic order. The two groups continued to vary greatly in wealth and power, but they shared a common code of behavior known as "chivalry" (from *cheval,* the French word for "horse").

For all the romantic images that today surround the medieval knight, he was, in essence, an armed thug. Mounted on a charger and clad in helmet and chain mail, he was the medieval equivalent of the modern tank (see Figure 7.4). Fighting was what he had been trained for; it was the chief justification for his existence; and it was how he grew wealthy (through plundered goods, ransoms, and gifts from grateful nobles). Knights claimed that they protected Church and society, and they sometimes did. But knights were violent men, primarily interested in defending and extending their own estates. Indeed, to some, nothing was more fun than battle. As one twelfth-century French nobleman put it,

> I tell you, eating or drinking or sleeping hasn't such pleasure for me as the moment
> I hear both sides shouting *Get 'em,* and I hear riderless horses crashing through the
> shadows, and I hear men shouting *Help! Help!,* and I see men—great and small—
> falling in the grassy ditches, and I see the dead with splintered lances, decked with
> pennons, through their sides.

This French knight probably led a very happy (and violent) life, for warfare was everywhere to be had in the Central Middle Ages. Monarchs and princes slowly managed to

Figure 7.4   *Human Tank*   This knight, from a twelfth-century manuscript, is ready for war. He has a firm seat, thanks to his saddle, stirrups, and reins. He is well armored and well armed. And his horse, specially bred and trained, is well shod and protected with padding.

discourage private wars between local barons, but progress was slow and problems persisted into the thirteenth century and beyond.

War was devastating for the villages and towns that lay in the paths of armies, but not very dangerous for knights themselves. Most medieval warfare consisted of castle sieges and the harrying of an enemy's lands and peasants. Great battles were rare, and even when they occurred, the knight was so well protected by his armor that captivity was more common than death. Indeed, opponents preferred to capture rather than kill, for a captive was obliged to pay a large ransom for his release.

✺ FEUDAL SOCIETY

In peacetime, tournaments took the place of battles (see Color Illustration 6). The Church legislated against tournaments, fruitlessly but with good reason, for they often involved day-long mock battles among as many as a hundred knights, in the course of which participants might be killed or maimed. Aristocratic men relished these "melees" as opportunities to demonstrate their skills and collect ransoms from those they captured. So too did the ladies who watched from the sidelines, encouraging their favorites and placing bets on the outcome. Peddlers, ale-sellers, pie-bakers, prostitutes, and pickpockets also liked tournaments for the business they provided. All told, tournaments were not unlike big-league football today—a sport of controlled violence, masses of spectators, lots of money to be made on the side, even a sort of cheerleading with the tokens and other favors that ladies would bestow on their preferred knights. Unlike football players, however, knights had a practical application for their athletic prowess: in tournaments, they trained for war.

Knights loved to fight in mock or real battles, but they had more mundane duties too, and all grew in importance from the eleventh century. They had to preside at manorial courts; they had to attend on their lords or ladies and give them counsel; they had to manage their estates (or get their wives to do this for them). For recreation, lords and ladies went hunting or hawking in their private forests or parks. In addition to the sheer enjoyment of it, hunting rid the forests of dangerous beasts—wolves and wild boars—and provided tasty venison for the baronial table. But enjoyment was an important part of hunting, so much so that peasants were forbidden to trap or kill the deer and other animals that provided their "social betters" with good sport. In bad weather, chess, a game of war, was a favored amusement. Others were drinking, eating, and listening to minstrels and storytellers.

Over the course of the Central Middle Ages, aristocratic life underwent a much needed refinement. Most early medieval castles were nothing more than square wooden towers, set atop hills or artificial mounds, enclosed with moats or stockades (or both), and surrounded by barracks, storehouses, stables, workshops, kitchen gardens, manure heaps, and perhaps a chapel. The tower, or "keep," was apt to be stuffy, leaky, gloomy, and badly heated. Because it was built for defense, not comfort, its windows were narrow slits for outgoing arrows, and its few rooms accommodated not only the lord, lady, and their family but also servants, retainers, and guests. It was a world of enforced togetherness in which only the wealthiest of aristocrats enjoyed the luxury of a private bedchamber.

By the thirteenth century, however, nobles were living in much more commodious dwellings, usually built of stone and mortar. When chimneys began to replace central fires in the twelfth century, it became possible to heat individual rooms, and this encouraged new notions of privacy, including private bedrooms and separate servants' quarters. Privacy remained relatively rare, for great nobles now commanded larger retinues than before. But the sweaty, swashbuckling life of the nobility in 1000 had evolved by 1300 into a new, courtly lifestyle of good manners, troubadour songs, and gentle behavior. The old warrior elite was becoming "high society," increasingly conscious of itself as a separate class. Distinguished from lesser folk by its good breeding and good taste, the aristocracy became more exclusive and rigidly defined than in its earlier, less stylish days.

Yet feudal society remained a warrior's world that accommodated aristocratic women only awkwardly. Alert readers will have already noted that food, drink, and sleep—but not relationships with women—were the favorite leisure activities of the twelfth-century knight quoted earlier in this chapter. By his time, however, some of his contemporaries were finding some pleasure in women, singing troubadour lyrics that celebrated love between the sexes. **Courtly love,** as it has come to be called, was more a literary ideal than real practice, and it idealized women to an absurd extent, placing them on pedestals from which they are only now descending. But it did signal an alternative male attitude toward women, one that competed with older views of women as evil temptresses, as vessels for guilt-free knightly rape, or as inferiors rightly punished by boorish, wife-beating husbands.

Although women were not expected to fight in battle, some did, either because of necessity or choice, and they were more often praised for their man-like courage than condemned for unfeminine behavior. In about 1100, Lady Isabel of Conches was admiringly described as generous, daring, and high-spirited: "In war she rode armed as a knight among the knights." Although inheritance customs favored men, women did hold fiefs—either as heiresses or as widows who claimed one-third of their husbands' estates. And although women were not expected to rule over men, some wielded such authority long and well. Blanche of Castile (1188–1252), mother of King Louis IX of France (r. 1226–1270), ruled on his behalf, first during his minority and later when he was off crusading. A person of uncommon intelligence and resolution, Blanche of Castile should, as one modern French historian has observed, "To all intents and purposes . . . be counted among the kings of France." Other women were not so lucky. Anxiety about female rulers provoked resistance in England to the rule of Matilda (c. 1102–1167), daughter of King Henry I (r. 1100–1135) in the mid-twelfth century, as well as the roughly contemporaneous troubles of Queen Melisende of Jerusalem (c. 1102–1161), whose inherited right to rule was challenged by both her husband and son.

Aristocratic women sometimes fought in battles, sometimes held fiefs, and sometimes ruled over men, but most of all, they were expected to marry and produce children. Although the central medieval Church insisted that both bride and groom had to consent for a marriage to be valid, feudal alliances usually involved lord or lady, parents, and friends more than the principals themselves. Indeed, heiresses and widows could be compelled to marry men chosen by their lords or ladies, a practice that became an important element of royal revenue. In the financial accounts of King Henry I of England (1100–1135) are such items as these:

- Robert de Venuiz renders account to the king for sixteen shillings eightpence for the daughter of Herbert the Chamberlain with her dowry.
- The sheriff of Hampshire renders account to the king for a thousand silver marks for the office and daughter of the late Robert Maledoctus.

One great female landowner, the thrice-widowed Lucy, countess of Chester, paid handsomely just for the privilege of not having to marry again for five years.

As male lineage grew more important to the feudal elite, so too did the production of legitimate children. Eleanor of Aquitaine (c. 1122–1204) was rich, well married, and powerful, but she found time to bear no less than eleven children. She was not unusual among aristocratic women, most of whom married at young ages (Eleanor first married at age 15), ate relatively good diets, and fulfilled their obligation to secure the next generation by bearing exceptionally large numbers of children. As the legitimacy of male lineage grew more valued, an age-old double standard gained new force: a baron might sire bastards across the countryside under his control, but he expected his wife's children to be his own. Like children of more humble birth, many aristocratic children died in infancy or youth. And because noble children (especially boys) were sent away at early ages to train in other noble households, they spent relatively few years under the direct tutelage of their parents. But despite large families, high child mortality, and distance, parents seem to have loved their children well. In part, this love was practical, for aristocratic lineages were made powerful by loyal children who married well or pursued successful careers in the Church. In part, however, this love was simple human feeling. Even in the Early Middle Ages, Gregory of Tours had written of a plague that killed many children: "And so we lost our little ones, who were so dear to us and sweet, whom we had cherished in our bosoms and dandled in our arms, whom we had fed and nurtured with such loving care. As I write, I wipe away my tears."[10]

✳ Conclusion

For peasants, townspeople, and aristocrats, the Central Middle Ages brought many new opportunities—better food, better housing, better clothing, and simply a world of more choices. These improvements rested on foundations that were humble but secure for several centuries. From the tenth through twelfth centuries, Europe's land was more fertile than before, cultivated more intensely in terms of both techniques and sheer acreage. From this more productive agriculture grew an economy that supported more people, more trade, and a wealthier elite. Until the thirteenth century, when population growth finally began to outstrip the productivity of land, medieval people enjoyed a world of expanding possibility and opportunity.

Suggested Readings

Guy Bois, *The Transformation of the Year One Thousand: The Village of Lournand from Antiquity to Feudalism* (1992). Translated from the French, this study argues for a rapid transformation of the European economy and society.

Constance Brittain Bouchard, *Strong of Body, Brave and Noble: Chivalry and Society in Medieval France* (1998). An outstanding new study. See also Theodore Evergates, ed., *Aristocratic Women in Medieval France* (1999); C. Stephen Jaeger, *The Origins of Courtliness: Civilizing Trends and the Formation of Courtly Ideals* (1985); and Richard W. Kaeuper, *Chivalry and Violence in Medieval Europe* (1999).

Mark R. Cohen, *Under Crescent and Cross: The Jews in the Middle Ages* (1994). A prize-winning study of medieval Jews and Jewish communities in both Christian and Islamic societies. See also Kenneth R. Stow, *Alienated Minority: The Jews of Medieval Latin Europe* (1992).

Hans-Werner Goetz, *Life in the Middle Ages: From the Seventh to the Thirteenth Century* (1993). A very readable study of medieval life, from peasants to nobles.

David Nicholas, *The Growth of the Medieval City: from Late Antiquity to the Early Fourteenth Century* (1997). See also Edward Miller and John Hatcher, *Medieval England: Towns, Commerce and Crafts, 1086–1348* (1995).

N. J. G. Pounds, *An Economic History of Medieval Europe* (2nd edition, 1991). Still an excellent account, written for students.

Werner Rösener, *Peasants in the Middle Ages* (1992). An excellent account, translated from German. See also Leopold Genicot, *Rural Communities in the Medieval World* (1990); Edward Miller and John Hatcher, *Medieval England: Rural Society and Economic Change, 1086–1348* (1978); and Robert Fossier, *Peasant Life in the Medieval West* (1988).

---

[10] Affection for children was not confined to the feudal elite. Peasant and urban parents have left less written evidence of their deep feelings for children, but their affection was sometimes clear in their actions (as, for example, in reports of parents who dashed into burning houses to save their children). Parental pleasure in children was sweetly evoked in popular verse, as in this song in which the bereaved Virgin Mary envies mothers whose children are still alive: "Your children you dance upon your knee/With laughing, kissing, and merry cheer. Behold my child; behold now me/for now lies dead my dear son dear."

Suggested Primary Sources

Georges Duby, *Rural Economy and Country Life in the Medieval West* (1968). Translated from French, this is an excellent introduction to the medieval rural life; it also contains more than 200 pages of primary sources.

Maryanne Kowaleski, ed., *Medieval Towns and Town Life: A Reader* (2005). A new collection that treats social as well as economic history.

Robert S. Lopez and Irving W. Raymond, *Medieval Trade in the Mediterranean World: Illustrative Documents* (2001). A classic, now available with an updated bibliography.

CHAPTER 8

꩜

NEW PATHS TO GOD,
c. 1000-1250

✸ INTRODUCTION

The social transformation of the Central Middle Ages, resulting in part from economic and demographic expansion and the rise of cities, produced fundamental changes in other areas as well. Europeans began to push beyond their boundaries, conquering some regions and mounting crusades against others; scholars traversed new intellectual horizons; artists and writers added new dimensions to Western culture; administrators pushed forward the science of government. Underlying all these changes was the subject of this chapter: the new ways in which Christians began to express and organize their faith. The Central Middle Ages witnessed an intensification of lay piety, a growth of heresy, the development of new forms of monasticism, and the rise of a vigorous papacy dedicated to reform and the creation of a Christian world order.

Medieval Christianity followed many paths. It could be devoutly conventional, it could be anti-clerical, and it could be openly heretical. Yet its basic institutional expression was the Catholic Church, based on the authority of the papacy in Rome and claiming a universality that, although it had little purchase in Constantinople, had considerable meaning in Cologne, Paris, and London. To medieval Christians, this was "the Church" pure and simple. This Church gave medieval Christians, most of whom traveled little beyond their immediate region, a consciousness of belonging to an international commonwealth: a Christendom that, although fragmented politically, was united by a common faith, by the expanding power of the papacy, and by a shared enthusiasm for Christian militancy. Before nationalism had any meaning in Europe, internationalism—in the form of the universal or Catholic Church—was a powerful ideal.

Yet the Catholic Church did not claim the hearts of all Europeans during the Central Middle Ages, and during these critical centuries, Jews were also seeking new paths to God. Medieval Jews had no central authority to compare to the pope in Rome, and their communities were small and scattered. But Jewish rabbis built a great authoritative tradition, based primarily in the schools that were as essential to their communities as synagogues. Rabbinical *responsa*—that is, decisions issued in response to questions or disputes—guided ordinary life, as did the Talmud, commentaries on religious and moral law. The Central Middle Ages saw a revival of Talmudic scholarship that was characterized by relative theological flexibility and openness to new ideas.

In response to the perceived legalism of Talmudists, some Jews turned toward pietism, a movement that stressed inner religious life. One of the greatest Jewish pietists, Bahya ibn Pakuda (1059–1111) distinguished between the "duties of the limbs" (ritual and ceremony) and the "duties of the heart" (inner piety). As his name suggests, ibn Pakuda lived in Muslim Iberia, but pietism flourished within many medieval Jewish communities in the Rhineland and elsewhere. Still other Jews were inspired by neither Talmudists nor pietists, but by mystics. This blossoming of Jewish mysticism, particularly centered on writings known as the Cabala, was viewed with suspicion by many mainstream Jews. Cabalists espoused many unorthodox ideas; for example, some distinguished so thoroughly between the masculine and feminine sides of God that monotheism seemed to wither away. It enjoyed some popularity among medieval Jews, but always remained marginal.

Jewish thinkers also grappled with a question that vexed Christian thinkers: the proper relationship between faith and reason. Moses Maimonides (1135–1204), born in Iberia but settled in Egypt, struggled with this problem in his wonderfully titled *Guide for the Perplexed.* His objective was to synthesize the writings of Aristotle—who represented, to Maimonides, the apogee of human reasoning—with his own religious traditions. Arguing that there was no inherent conflict between faith and reason, he sought to recast his Jewish faith within an Aristotelian framework. His ideas would later influence such Christian theologians as Albertus Magnus (c. 1200–1280) and Thomas Aquinas (c. 1225–1274). They regarded him with such awe that he was to them simply "the Rabbi," just as Aristotle was simply "the Philosopher."

In the Middle Ages, Judaism developed as a law-bound faith, as a faith of inner piety, as a mystical faith, and as a faith that grappled with profound questions about the ability of human reason to comprehend the mysteries of God. In these and other developments, neither Jews nor Christians moved in isolation. Christian ideas about chastity seem to have influenced some Jewish mystics in the Central Middle Ages, just as Jewish biblical commentaries stimulated the thinking of some Christian scholars. But Christians were the dominant and dominating majority, and it is on their religion that we shall focus in this chapter.

✸ THE EVOLUTION OF PIETY

To say that central medieval Europe was dominated by the institutional Church, although true to a point, is dangerously misleading. The Church was by no means monolithic, nor were its members always obedient to papal commands, or even aware of them. Like all human institutions, the Church functioned imperfectly and often fell short of its ideals. Despite its theoretically centralized command structure (pope → archbishops → bishops → priests), lines of communication were slow and clogged. It might take half a year for an archbishop of Canterbury to journey to Rome, consult with the pope, and return to England. Any bishop who ignored or deliberately "misunderstood" a papal order was difficult to dislodge.

The Church was also not free from corruption among its own personnel, a result of the inevitable fallibility of human beings. Some historians have delighted in cataloging instances of larcenous bishops, licentious priests, and gluttonous nuns. But cases such as these were clearly exceptional. The great shortcoming of the central medieval Church was not gross corruption but rather a creeping complacency that sometimes resulted in a shallow, mechanical attitude toward the Christian religious life and an obsession with ecclesiastical property. The medieval Church had more than its share of saints, but among its clergy the profundity of faith was often lost in the day-to-day affairs of the pastoral office, the management of large estates, disputes over land, and ecclesiastical status-seeking. Anyone familiar with modern politicians and university administrators will appreciate the problem.

Yet not all clergy were inclined to ignore papal commands or to be more careerist than holy. Spearheading a new Christian spirituality in Europe, some clerics replaced the awe and mystery characteristic of earlier Christianity with a new emotionalism and dynamism. We can perhaps best see this shift today in ecclesiastical architecture, which moved in the twelfth-century from the earthbound **Romanesque** style to the tense, upward-reaching **Gothic** style (more on this in Chapter 12). It also profoundly affected devotional practice, as the divine Christ sitting in judgment gave way to the tragic figure of the human Christ suffering on the cross for the sins of humanity (see Color Illustration 7 for the very first sculpted-in-the-round Crucifixion). This image of Christ's redemptive suffering was to exercise a profound hold on the consciousness of medieval Christians, for whom the contemplation of Christ's wounds, pain, and suffering grew central to understanding the gift of salvation. This shift toward a more emotive Christianity also contributed to the emergence of the Virgin Mary as a central figure of religious veneration (see Biographical Sketch on p. 190). During the Central Middle Ages, the Virgin was especially revered as a compassionate intercessor for hopeless sinners, a task at which she was reputed to be so successful that, as one legend told it, the devil complained to God that the tender-hearted Queen of Heaven was cheating hell of its most promising candidates. Christianity became, as never before, a religion of love, hope, and compassion. The God of Justice became the merciful, suffering God of Love (see Figure 8.1).

Ordinary people also embraced this new theology of a loving God, assisted by a suffering Son and a forgiving Virgin Mary, but a considerable gulf sometimes separated the religious practices of popes and theologians from those of common townspeople and peasants. The supernatural ideas of ordinary people in any society, including our own, inevitably include a variety of notions that are not embraced by theologians (witness, in our own society, the proliferation of psychic advisers, available for instant consultation by anyone with both telephone and credit card). The Middle Ages were no exception. The God of theologians in the Central Middle Ages was a God of love and reason. But in the popular mind, God was also sometimes a kind of divine magician who could shield his favorites from the horrors of hunger, pain, disease, and premature death. To many people, the best way to approach such a God was through acts that, although heartfelt, were more mechanical than mystical. By possessing a relic or going on pilgrimage or repeating short prayers at a roadside shrine, people often hoped to win God's favor and aid.

The most cherished relics of all were those associated with Christ and the Virgin Mary. Because both were believed to have ascended bodily into heaven, relics of the bodily sort were out of reach, but there remained pieces of their clothing, fragments of the True Cross, vials of Christ's blood and the Virgin's milk, Christ's baby teeth, his umbilical cord, and the foreskin removed at his circumcision. Reading Abbey, founded in southern England in the 1120s, had acquired hundreds of relics by the end of that

Figure 8.1   *Michelangelo's* **Pieta**   Completed at the very end of the fifteenth century, this sculpture illustrates two important aspects of Christian piety in the Central and Later Middle Ages: contemplation of Jesus's suffering and veneration of the Virgin Mary.

century, including twenty-nine relics of Christ, six of the Virgin Mary, nineteen of the Old Testament patriarchs and prophets, and fourteen of the apostles. As a result of its avid collecting, Reading became a prosperous pilgrimage center, yet it was merely one of many. Chartres had the Virgin Mary's tunic; Canterbury had the body of St. Thomas Becket (c. 1118–1170); Santiago de Compostela in northwestern Iberia had the bones of St. James the Apostle (except for one of his arms, which was at Reading); Paris acquired Christ's crown of thorns after it had been taken from Constantinople following the Fourth Crusade (1201–1204). Indeed, scarcely a town or rural district in all Western Christendom did not possess some relic or protective image. This passion for relics prompted an economic expansion of its own, as traders carried relics to willing customers. Unfortunately, there was often more cheating than truth in this trade. By the

BIOGRAPHICAL SKETCH

The Blessed Virgin Mary

The woman who is believed by Christians to be the mother of Jesus was not, of course, born in the Central Middle Ages. But her veneration is very much a product of the time.

Mary is mentioned less than two dozen times in the New Testament and not always in the most positive contexts. For example, Matthew 12:46–50 reports that when Jesus was told that his mother and brothers wished to speak with him, he gestured toward the people he was then addressing and said, "Who is my mother? Who are my brothers? Here are my mother and my brothers. For whoever does the will of the heavenly father is my brother, sister, and mother." Other biblical references are more promising. Luke 1:26–38 tells the story of the Annunciation, when the angel Gabriel is said to have hailed Mary as the future mother of God.

Among early Christians, the Virgin Mary's purity quickly became a matter of intense interest. As early as the second century, some were arguing that Mary was a *perpetual* virgin, a view eventually confirmed as doctrine in 649. (Biblical references to the "brothers and sisters" of Jesus were understood as metaphors or as references to adopted siblings.) Early Christians also focused on Mary's maternal role, and she was proclaimed in 431 as *Theotokos,* mother of God. In this role, Mary literally embodied the humanity of Jesus: it was through his mother that Jesus gained the humanity that was central to his sacrifice and the salvation that it brought to others.

The comparison with Eve was irresistible and common: the evil done by one woman was undone by another. This analogy grew so strong that one Middle English song even celebrated Eve's sin in the Garden of Eden because it brought forth the need for Mary:

> Had not the apple been taken,
> The apple been taken,
> Then never had our Lady
> Been heaven's queen.
> Blessed be the time
> That the apple was taken!

It was in the eleventh and twelfth centuries that Marian devotion intensified in the West (see Figure 12.6). In part, this devotion grew from crusaders, pilgrims, and merchants who observed the prominent role of the Virgin in Eastern Orthodox Christianity. In part, it spread with the preaching of St. Bernard of Clairvaux, who once claimed that nothing gave him more pleasure than to preach a sermon on the glories of the Virgin Mother. His Cistercian monks were dedicated to the Virgin: they put her image on their seal, they wore white in memory of her purity, they sang in her honor at daily services, and they often built *lady chapels* dedicated to her. And in part, Marian devotion simply grew from popular sentiment. It was in these years that the prayer, *Ave Maria* (or "Hail Mary"), began to take shape, as well as the cycle of prayers that would eventually form the rosary. Lilies and roses were associated with her; so too was Saturday; so too were many parish churches and shrines named in her honor, as well as newborn girls. And the Virgin as "Notre Dame" (Our Lady) was a product of the twelfth century. The great cathedrals of Paris and Chartres were among those that took this new name.

From all of these sources developed two new emphases in Marian devotion. First, Mary was revered as *Mater Dolorosa,* the sorrowing mother (for an example, see

Michelangelo's *Pietà,* Figure 8.1). In this role, Mary complemented medieval piety, for her pain echoed and emphasized the redemptive suffering of her son. Second, Mary was revered as *Mediatrix,* as an intercessor between ordinary Christians and their God. The *Salve Regina,* even today the best loved of Catholic hymns, was composed around 1100, and it entreats Mary on behalf of sinners:

> To thee we cry, banished children of Eve.
> To thee do we sigh, groaning and weeping
> In this vale of tears.

Along with these new devotions came new debates. Was Mary so pure that she was born free of original sin—that is, immaculately conceived in the womb of her mother Anne? St. Augustine (354–430) had argued against this idea in the fifth century, and later theologians such as St. Thomas Aquinas agreed. But popular sentiment ran the other way during the Central Middle Ages, and although not confirmed by the modern Catholic Church until 1854, the doctrine of the Immaculate Conception was widely accepted by medieval Christians. The same was true of the tradition that Mary fell asleep and rose into heaven, rather than suffering ordinary human death and decay. A belief widely accepted in the Middle Ages, the Assumption was confirmed as Catholic dogma in 1950.

As a mother who was also a virgin, the Blessed Virgin Mary presented an impossible role model to ordinary women, but her veneration must have comforted those who sought lives of virginal purity as well as those who bore children. Interestingly enough, medieval men, especially monks, seem to have been particularly attracted to her veneration (one monk sweetly described himself and his fellows as "curled up against her breast"). Nuns certainly revered the Virgin, but their devotional practices often centered elsewhere, particularly on the infant Jesus or on Jesus as bridegroom. Nevertheless, for all Christians in the Central Middle Ages, the Blessed Virgin Mary inspired awe for her purity, comfort for her motherly love, pity for her sorrows, and, perhaps most of all, hope that merciful Mary would successfully intercede on their behalf.

early sixteenth century there would be, as Desiderius Erasmus (c. 1466–1536) then sarcastically put it, enough relics of the True Cross in Europe to fill a ship.

People looked to God for aid and to the Virgin Mary as an intercessor for such aid, but they also looked to individual saints, each of whom had specialties that appealed to specific worshipers. There was an appropriate saint for almost every known disease: plague sufferers prayed to St. Roch, St. Romane specialized in mental illnesses, St. Clare in afflictions of the eye, and St. Agatha in sore breasts. (These attributions were linked to saints' lives. For example, St. Agatha's martyrdom had included chopping off her breasts, which were then miraculously restored.) Saints were also associated with occupations: potters offered special devotions to St. Gore, painters to St. Luke, horse doctors to St. Loy, and dentists to St. Apolline. In southern France, a cult developed around a greyhound who was said to have been mistakenly killed while defending his master's infant child; peasants began bringing their sick children to the grave of the blessed dog in hope of miraculous healing.[1]

---

[1] For more on this story, see Jean Claude Schmitt, *The Holy Greyhound: Guinefort, Healer of Children since the Thirteenth Century* (1983).

No theologian would have welcomed the idea of a sainted greyhound, and, indeed, the proliferation of human saints in this era was such that the Church established procedures to determine which holy men and women would be formally honored by sainthood. Yet many of the practices associated with popular piety received encouragement from clergy, who shared in the general devotion to relics and who also rejoiced in the flood of pilgrims that relics attracted to their cathedrals and monasteries. The cult of relics was even justified up to a point by the theological doctrine of the Communion of Saints—that is, a caring fellowship of all Christians, whether in this world or the next. Nevertheless, some theologians and Church leaders were disturbed by popular practices, especially those that seemed to carry a residue from long-ago days of pagan magic. But their doubts were drowned out by the clamor of popular demand.

At the same time as relics, pilgrimages, and charms proliferated in ways that the Church could not control, other aspects of Christian practice were more firmly regulated by the Church, especially the sacraments through which religion was brought home to ordinary Europeans. Long part of Christian practice, the sacraments were fully articulated at the Fourth Lateran Council in 1215. They guided Christians through every stage of life. Births were sanctified by the sacrament of *baptism,* in which infants were cleansed of the taint of original sin and initiated into the Christian fellowship. At puberty Christians received the sacrament of *confirmation,* which reaffirmed their membership in the Church and gave them the additional grace to cope with the problems of adulthood. Christian couples were united in the sacrament of *matrimony.* And if a man chose the calling of the Christian ministry, he was spiritually transformed into a priest and "married" to the Church by the sacrament of *holy orders.* As death approached, the sacrament of *extreme unction* prepared the soul for its journey into the next world. Throughout their lives, Christians could receive forgiveness from the damning consequences of mortal sin by repenting their transgressions and receiving the comforting sacrament of *penance.* They could also partake of the central sacrament of the Church—the *Eucharist*—receiving the body of Christ into their own bodies.[2] Thus, the Church through its seven sacraments brought God's grace to all its members, great and humble, at every critical juncture of their lives. The sacramental system, which assumed final form only in the Central Middle Ages, was a source of comfort and reassurance: it made communion with God not merely the elusive goal of a few mystics but the periodic experience of all believers. And, of course, it established the Church as the essential intermediary between God and humanity, making it ever more important that the staff of the Church—that is, the priests who administered sacraments—distinguish themselves from the laypeople they served, by both autonomy of office and style of life.

Orthodoxy and Heresy

In the hot-house religious climate of the Central Middle Ages, the line between orthodoxy and heresy was often painfully thin. Sometimes the difference hinged on important theological points, such as the question of whether priests were special people endowed with sacramental powers that ordinary laypeople lacked. Sometimes the line was drawn

[2] During the Middle Ages, theologians articulated the concept of transubstantiation: that the Eucharistic sacrament transforms the substance of the bread and wine into the body and blood of Christ. This doctrine was confirmed at the Fourth Lateran Council in 1215; it would be rejected by many Protestant faiths in the sixteenth century and later.

TIMELINE 8.1   Christian Heresies, 1000–1300

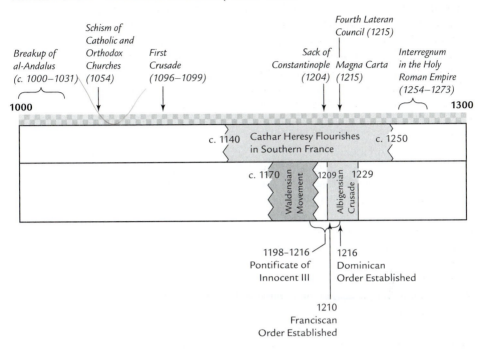

over matters of ecclesiastical discipline and obedience, such as concerns raised about holy women who, however pious they might have been, were not subject to the authority of local bishops or other clergy. Sometimes people stumbled unknowingly into heresy and quickly reconciled with the Church, whereas sometimes people—spurred by heartfelt piety or dissatisfaction with the workaday Church, or both—turned self-consciously toward forms of Christian expression that the Church deemed heretical.

The heresies of the Central Middle Ages flourished particularly in the expanding towns of southern Europe. The eleventh-century urban revolution had caught the Church somewhat unprepared to minister effectively to the new, vigorous, and widely literate burgher class. Too often, townspeople viewed their bishops more as political oppressors and enemies of burghal independence than as spiritual directors. Too often, they felt that the Church failed to understand their problems. Too often, they grew suspicious of ecclesiastical wealth and power. Although most townspeople remained loyal to the Church, a minority, particularly in southern France and the northern Italian peninsula, turned to new alternatives that crossed the line.

Of all the groups that troubled the Church, the **Cathars** of southern France were the most troublesome of all (see Timeline 8.1). Also known as **Albigensians** (after the town of Albi where they were particularly strong), the Cathars fused two traditions: (1) protest against ecclesiastical wealth and power, and (2) a dualistic theology that derived, in part, from Persian Zoroastrianism. The Cathars recognized two gods: a god of good who reigned over the universe of the spirit and a god of evil who ruled the material world. Christ, whom they regarded as a purely spiritual being with a phantom body, was the god of good; the Old Testament God, creator of the material universe, was their god of evil. Their morality stressed a rigorous rejection of all material things—of physical appetites, wealth, worldly vanities, and sexual intercourse—in the hope of one day escaping from the prison of the body and ascending to the realm of pure spirit. In reality this severe ethic was practiced only by a small elite of spiritual men and women known as *perfecti* ("perfect ones"); the rank and file normally ate well, made love, and participated only vicariously in the rejection of the material world (usually, by criticizing the affluence of the Church). Indeed, their opponents accused them of gross licentiousness. Although such accusations were exaggerated, it does seem likely that some Provençal nobles were attracted to the new teaching by the opportunity of living well while appropriating Church lands in good conscience.

By the dawn of the thirteenth century, Catharism was expanding so swiftly that it posed a dangerous threat to the unity of Western Christendom and the authority of the Church. In some parts of southern France, Cathar bishops, monasteries, and perfecti constituted an institutionalized Church, commanding the support of noble and poor alike. Catholic Christians regarded the Cathars as a horrible infection spreading through the body of Western Christendom. As we shall see in the next chapter, the fight to eradicate Cathar beliefs created both a crusade within Europe (1209–1229) and the establishment of inquisitorial procedures. By the middle of the thirteenth century, a few Cathars persisted in some isolated parts of the south, but the Cathar Church was no more.

Catharism drew heavily on popular **anti-clericalism**—that is, popular resentment of the influence, wealth, and sacramental power of the clergy. For other sects, this rejection of the special privileges of the clergy was even more central, and this was especially true of the Waldensian sect, founded by a merchant of Lyons known to history as Peter Waldo. Around 1173, Waldo gave all his possessions to the poor and took up a life of apostolic poverty. He and his followers sought the Church's permission to preach in towns. The Church refused, for it worried about preaching by untrained laypeople (especially, untrained lay*women*), and it preferred to leave religious instruction in the hands of ordained males. But Peter Waldo continued to preach, and so too did the men and women who followed him. These acts of defiance, along with Waldo's growing doubts about the special spiritual status of priests, earned the Waldensians the condemnation of the Church.[3] Similar groups, some that remained orthodox and some that were deemed heretical, arose in the communes of Lombardy and were known as *Humiliati*. These groups proved worrisome to the local ecclesiastical hierarchies, but generally they escaped downright condemnation, unless they themselves took the step of denying the authority of the Church. By the opening of the thirteenth century, anti-clerical sects were spreading across the northern Italian peninsula and southern France, and even into Iberia and the German states.

✸ CHANGES IN MONASTIC LIFE

The men and women who made their careers within the Church were as affected by these changes as were ordinary people, and they responded with institutional change as well as spiritual redirection. In the Central Middle Ages, institutional change within the church was driven first by monastic reform and then by papal reform.

---

[3] The town of Valdese, North Carolina, claims to have been founded in the late nineteenth century by members of a church descended from these Waldensian origins.

Complacency is a recurring threat for all religions, and it was an especially strong force in Christian monasticism during the Middle Ages. Again and again, the idealism of a monastic reform movement was eroded until, at length, new reform movements arose in protest against the growing worldliness of old ones. Indeed, the sixth-century Benedictine movement was itself a protest against the excesses and inadequacies of earlier monasticism. Although St. Benedict (c. 480–550) had stressed withdrawing from the world and devoting full effort to communion with God, his followers eventually became so deeply (and productively) involved in teaching, evangelism, and ecclesiastical reform that by the tenth and eleventh centuries the whole Benedictine movement was itself immersed in worldly affairs. Benedictine monasteries controlled extensive lands, operated Europe's best schools, supplied contingents of knights to feudal armies, and worked closely with secular princes in affairs of state. Moreover, the very process of creating each new generation of monks or nuns was fraught with problems. Many early medieval monasteries accepted novices only from the aristocracy and required a substantial entrance gift (usually a landed estate) from the novice's family. And many of these novices had little choice in their religious vocation, for they were oblates, designated for monastic careers at the time of their birth. Some developed into devoted servants of God; others simply went through the motions. This was not what St. Benedict had envisioned for his monks and nuns in the early sixth century.

At the beginning of the tenth century, the Cluniac movement, which was itself Benedictine in spirit and rule, arose in protest against this worldliness and complacency. The movement was named after its home: the Burgundian abbey of Cluny founded in 910 by the duke of Aquitaine. Its founder tried to ensure that Cluny was free of aristocratic and episcopal control and subject only to the pope, whose authority was then feeble and remote. The new monastery was blessed with a series of able and long-lived abbots. Following the modification of the original Benedictine *Rule* that St. Benedict of Aniane (c. 750–821) had introduced, Cluniac monks devoted themselves to an elaborate sequence of daily prayers and liturgical services and a strict, godly life. Richly endowed, holy, and seemingly incorruptible, Cluny was widely admired. Gradually other monasteries attached themselves to Cluny until it became the nucleus of a large group of reform monasteries extending across Europe, each a **priory** subject to the abbey (and abbot) of Cluny. By thus binding different monastic houses together, Cluny created, in a sense, the first **monastic order**—the first forging of formal links between monasteries that had hitherto shared only a general acceptance of the Benedictine *Rule*. In the mid-eleventh century the monastery of Cluny was both powerful and wealthy, the recipient of countless gifts from the landed nobility from near and far, and its new abbey church, completed in the early twelfth century, was the most splendid building in Western Christendom. It was a favored place for bereaved Christians to arrange for the saying of masses or other prayers for the dead.

During the twelfth century, however, Cluniac monks began to show traces of the very complacency against which their predecessors had originally rebelled. Prosperous, respected, and secure, Cluny was too content with its majestic abbey and priories, its elaborate liturgical program, and its bounteous fields to give its wholehearted support to the radical transformation of society for which many Christian reformers were then struggling.

Moreover, the Cluniac reform was threatened from another direction: the slow erosion of the traditional educational preeminence of monasteries. As we shall see in

TIMELINE 8.2   Monasticism, 1000–1300

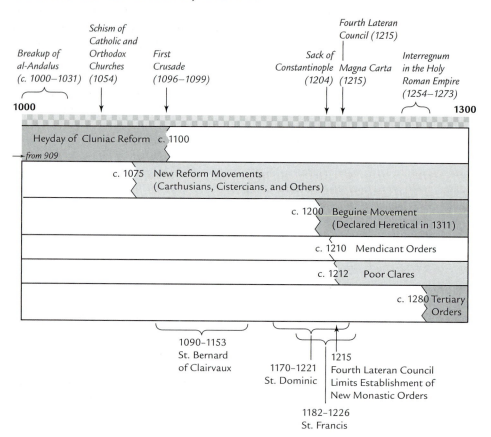

Chapter 10, by the early twelfth century the monastic monopoly on education was being gradually eroded by **cathedral schools,** and by the early thirteenth century, the new universities of Europe's expanding cities added to the challenge. These urban schools produced well-trained scholars who in time rivaled monks and nuns as scribes and advisers to princes. With the steady advance of urbanization, some traditional monastic contributions to medieval society were no longer as urgently needed as before. This gave new force to the spiritual quest at the heart of the monastic life.

New Monastic Movements: Carthusians, Cistercians, and Others

As the monks of the Cluniac order fell into complacency, a wide variety of new religious movements emerged (see Timeline 8.2). Founded by ardent reformers, they were staffed by men and women who had chosen their religious vocations for themselves, as adults. The possibility of personal career choice resulted in part from a heightened sense of self. But this self-consciousness was not the lonely sort of individualism we know today; instead it was a new freedom to choose among a number of different kinds of communal life—a discovery of self through community, whether towns, guilds, peasant communes, or new monastic foundations. The personal choice and serious

self-examination of its members gave these new monastic movements a spiritual intensity absent from both traditional Benedictine monasticism and the Cluniac reform
thereof. Indeed the idea of entering religious life out of free, adult choice was so well at-
tuned to the new world of the twelfth century that many older monasteries, including
Cluny itself, ceased to admit child oblates.

Perhaps the most demanding of the new orders, the Carthusians emerged in eastern France in the late eleventh century and spread across Western Christendom in the
twelfth. Isolated from the outside world, the Carthusians lived in small groups, wor-
shiping together in communal chapels but otherwise living as hermits in individual cells.
This austere order has survived to the present day, and, unlike most monastic movements, its discipline has seldom waned. Yet even in the spiritually charged atmosphere
of the twelfth century it was a small movement, offering a way of life for only those capable of heroic holiness. Too ascetic for the average Christian, the Carthusian order was
much admired but seldom joined.

The greatest monastic force of the twelfth century, the Cistercians, managed for
a time to be both austere and popular. The motherhouse of the movement, Cîteaux,
was established by a small group of Benedictine dissenters led by Robert, one-time
abbot of St. Michel de Tonnerre, who, in about 1075, grew dissatisfied with the luxurious lifestyle of his monks and led a band of disciples to the wilderness site of
Molesme. There, they founded a new abbey, building huts of tree limbs. Today, the site
of this abbey is a luxury-class hotel with sumptuous bedrooms and a superb Michelin
two-star restaurant, one of the best in France. Robert of Molesme (c. 1029–1111)
would have been appalled, for to him even these rustic beginnings were insufficiently
challenging, and in 1098 he led his disciples onward to the wilderness site of Cîteaux.
This new abbey became the motherhouse of what in time became a great Europe-wide
congregation of Cistercian houses. The Cistercian reform grew slowly at first, then acquired impressive momentum. In 1115 Cîteaux had four monasteries attached to it; by
the end of the century it had 500. Cistercian houses were bound together not by the
authority of a central abbot, as at Cluny, but by an annual council of all Cistercian
abbots meeting at Cîteaux. Without such centralized control it is unlikely that the individual houses could have clung for long to the strict ascetic ideals Robert and his
followers espoused.

In contrast to the elaborate Cluniac monasteries of the time, Cistercian abbeys
were stark and undecorated. Cistercian life was stark as well—less severe than that of
the Carthusians but far more so than that of the Cluniacs. Their houses were poorly
heated, even in chilly north European winters; their diet was limited to black bread,
water, and a few stewed vegetables; they were forbidden to speak except when it was absolutely essential. Like other new monastic movements, the Cistercians admitted no
children. The minimum age for entry was fifteen, and new recruits underwent a year-
long *novitiate* (trial period) before taking lifetime vows, so that they would be certain of
their religious vocation. The year-long novitiate had been prescribed in St. Benedict's
Rule but had hitherto been largely ignored.

The Cistercians also admitted to their communities lay brothers and sisters,
known as *conversi*, many of peasant origin. Some conversi were imported from afar to
till newly cleared lands; others were recruited from the local peasantry who had long
been cultivating fields that pious donors now gave to the Cistercians. The conversi
were bound by vows of chastity and obedience but were permitted to follow a less

demanding form of the Cistercian spiritual life. Some wealthy women and men attached themselves to Cistercian monasteries in this fashion, but most conversi were laborers and working people. Their admission into Cistercian monasteries constituted a compassionate outreach to the illiterate peasantry and, at the same time, a solution to the labor shortage on Cistercian lands. Occasionally Cistercians joined the conversi in their field labor, but not often. The importance of the labor provided by conversi is also indicated by the fact that, although Cistercian monks accepted only lay brothers, nuns accepted conversi of both sexes, in part because lay brothers were such useful agents in business dealings with the outside world.

The key figure in the incredible twelfth-century expansion of the Cistercian movement was St. Bernard of Clairvaux (1090–1153), an incisive, charismatic leader. Bernard joined the community of Cîteaux in 1112 as a young man; three years later he became the founder and abbot of Clairvaux, one of Cîteaux's earliest new foundations. Bernard was the most admired Christian of his age—a mystic, an eloquent religious orator, an exceptionally gifted and prolific writer, and a crucial figure in the meteoric spread of Cistercian practice. His moral influence was so immense that he became Europe's leading arbiter of political and ecclesiastical disputes, inducing the king of France and the German emperor to participate in the Second Crusade (1147–1148) and successfully backing one candidate in a hotly disputed papal election. On one occasion he even dared to rebuke the pope himself: "Remember, first of all, that the Holy Roman Church, over which you hold sway, is the mother of churches, not their sovereign mistress—that you yourself are not the lord of bishops, but one among them."

Bernard also took a firm stand against one of the major intellectual trends of his day: the attempt to reconcile Catholic faith with human reason, led by the brilliant philosopher Peter Abelard (1079–1142). We shall explore this controversy more fully in Chapter 12, but, in brief, against Abelard's rationalism, Bernard advocated pure faith and simple love. He was not opposed to reasoned argument and logical thought, but he was certain that these were not the best ways to approach God. Instead, Bernard stressed personal mysticism, devotion to the Virgin Mary, and God's love. As such, he spoke powerfully to the contemporary turn toward a more personal and loving Christianity. In the long run, Bernard failed to convince many theologians and philosophers, most of whom preferred the Christian rationalism which Abelard's ideas so powerfully represented. In the short run, however, he did succeed in making life miserable for Abelard, even securing official condemnation of certain of Abelard's teachings.

Above and beyond his obvious talents for diplomacy and persuasion, Bernard won the devotion of twelfth-century Europe through his reputation for sanctity. He was widely regarded as a saint in his own lifetime, and stories of his miracles circulated far and wide. Pilgrims flocked to Clairvaux to be healed by his touch. This aspect of Bernard's reputation made his skillful preaching and diplomacy even more effective than it would otherwise have been. For here was a holy man, a miracle worker, who engaged in severe fasts, overworked himself to an extraordinary degree, wore coarse clothing, and devoted himself single-mindedly to the service of God.

When confronting an enemy, Bernard could be absolutely terrifying. On one occasion, for example, he commanded Duke William X of Aquitaine (r. 1127–1137) to reinstate certain bishops whom the duke had driven from their cities. When, after much persuasion, the duke remained obstinate, St. Bernard celebrated a High Mass for him.

Holding the consecrated **Host** in his hands, Bernard advanced from the altar toward the duke and said,

> We have besought you, and you have spurned us. The united multitude of the servants of God, meeting you elsewhere, have entreated you, and you have scorned them. Behold! Here comes to you the Virgin's Son, the Head and Lord of the Church which you persecute! Your Judge is here, at whose name every knee shall bow. . . . Your Judge is here, into whose hands your soul is to pass! Will you spurn him also? Will you scorn him as you have scorned his servants?

The duke threw himself on the ground and submitted to Bernard's demands.

Bernard's career demonstrates the essential paradox of the Cistercian movement. For although the Cistercians strove to dissociate themselves from the world, Bernard was drawn into the vortex of secular affairs. Indeed, as the twelfth century progressed, the entire Cistercian movement became increasingly involved in the world outside. The Cistercians had begun as great colonizers and settlers of wilderness lands, but as the expansion of European settlement continued apace, the world caught up with their once-isolated monasteries. The Cistercians also discovered, as would Puritans and Quakers in later centuries, that their twin virtues of austere living and hard work resulted in an accumulation of wealth and, eventually, a corrosion of their spiritual simplicity. They consolidated their estates and managed them with considerable skill, introducing improvements in the breeding of horses, cattle, and sheep. The English Cistercians even became the greatest wool producers of the realm, and throughout Europe, their estates were rich, powerful, and often in the vanguard of agricultural innovation. Economic success brought ever-increasing wealth to the order. Cistercian abbey churches became more elaborate, and the austerity of Cistercian life was progressively relaxed.[4]

For the Cistercians, then, withdrawal from the world had proven to be elusive and temporary. Other monastic orders began to move in a different direction, engaging with the world and working toward its regeneration. The Augustinian **canons,** for example, submitted to the rigor of a rule, yet carried on normal ecclesiastical duties in the world, serving in parish churches, hospitals, and cathedrals. Their fusion of monastic discipline and worldly activity would culminate in the twelfth-century **military orders**—the Knights Templar, Hospitalers, Teutonic Knights, and similar groups—whose knight-monks helped to expand the political frontiers of Western Christendom (as we shall see in the next chapter). These and other efforts to direct the spiritual vigor of monastic life toward the regeneration of Christian society typify the visions of the new, emotionally charged Christian piety of twelfth-century Europe.

Women and the New Monastic Orders

Whether oriented toward withdrawal from the world or involvement in it, most of these new monastic orders incorporated women, but with some difficulty. The Cluniac reform, with its stress on ordained monks saying masses for the dead, initially created only one female house under its umbrella, a monastery at Marcigny that was established to provide for the wives of men who entered the Cluniac order.[5] Cistercian reformers

---

[4] The modern day Trappists, founded in the seventeenth century, have returned to the strict observance of the early Cistercians.

[5] The monks of Cluny so distrusted nuns that they made the Virgin Mary the permanent abbess of Marcigny and the abbot of Cluny her earthly stand-in. In effect, the nuns of Marcigny were ruled by an abbot, not an abbess.

included a few women from the start, but, as the Cistercian order grew into a European-wide congregation, female houses were accommodated only grudgingly and slowly. In the thirteenth century, for example, Cistercian abbesses were not included in the annual council of abbots; they met separately, in a meeting at which the decisions of the abbots' council were announced to them. Some new orders began with better promise, fully accommodating women as well as men, but then ended up expelling its nuns. This is how one abbot justified such an expulsion:

> Recognizing that the wickedness of women is greater than all the other wickedness of the world, and that there is no anger like that of women, and that the poison of asps and dragons is more curable and less dangerous to men than the familiarity of women, we have unanimously decreed for the safety of our souls no less than that of our bodies and goods, that we will on no account receive any more sisters... but will avoid them like poisonous animals.

The abbot's explanation opens with classic misogynous ideas about women as especially evil and dangerous, ideas we can today dismiss along with notions that dragons actually existed. But he ends by noting that nuns threatened the goods as well as the bodies of his monks. In other words, these new orders sought to be free of nuns not only because of concerns about male chastity but also because nuns could be expensive. Why? Because nuns usually were more closely cloistered than men, their economic opportunities were more limited. Because nuns often had to employ priests to perform the sacraments, their spiritual maintenance was more costly. And because nuns inspired less generosity from lay donors, the endowments of their monasteries were smaller. The economic differences could be striking. In Normandy in the mid-thirteenth century, the average net worth of a female monastery was about £60, as compared to almost £400 for a male monastery.

When faced with reforming monks who were unenthusiastic about their holy sisters, women often responded with initiatives of their own. Some followed charismatic preachers in such numbers that arrangements simply had to be made for them. From such pressures came several new sorts of double monasteries—congregations primarily of nuns that included some monks to provide religious services: the Gilbertines founded by Gilbert of Sempringham (c. 1085–1189) and the abbey of Fontevrault founded by Robert of Arbrissel (c. 1047–1117). The Premonstratensians, founded by Norbert of Xanten (c. 1080–1134), also initially included many nuns. Other women made more informal arrangements, of which by far the most important was the **beguine** movement that flourished in the towns of the thirteenth-century German states and the Low Countries. Like nuns, beguines lived in communities of religious women, but unlike nuns, their vows were temporary, and they could leave if they wished. Some worked outside the beguinage during the day, and most importantly, their grassroots communities were less closely regulated by the Church.

Renowned for their piety, beguines produced some women of extraordinary sanctity. In what must have been one of the most unusual wedding nights in history, one beguine, Marie of Oignies (1176–1207), convinced her husband that they should not only live chastely but also devote themselves to the care of lepers. Another beguine, Mechthild of Magdeburg (1207–1282), expressed her mystical experiences in poetry and prose of great immediacy. Her *Flowing Light of Divinity* seems to have inspired an outpouring of mysticism in the monastery of Helfta, where she ended her days, and it is still awe-inspiring reading today. Yet, despite their piety, beguines were regarded with suspicion by Church authorities, accused sometimes of sexual misbehavior and sometimes of such religious irregularities as preaching by women or unsupervised study of the Bible. Their movement was finally condemned by papal decree in 1311. In later centuries, it was revived, but the beguinages you can visit today in Bruges and other northern cities reflect more the culture of the nineteenth century than that of the Middle Ages.

The Papacy and Its Church

Through most of the Central Middle Ages, a vibrant papacy was at the center of the trends we have just traced: the spiritual regeneration of Christian society, the fight against heresy, and new forms of monastic life. Yet, at the very beginning of this era, around the year 1000, the papacy was desperately weak. A great chasm then divided any grand theories about the papal leadership from the chaotic realities of the contemporary Church.

Since late Roman times, theories of papal government had envisaged a sanctified Christian commonwealth in which nobles and kings accepted the spiritual direction of priests and bishops who, in turn, recognized the leadership of the pope. Popes claimed to be the successors and representatives of St. Peter (died c. 65), who was thought to have been the first bishop of Rome—the first pope. Just as St. Peter was the chief of Christ's apostles, the papacy argued, so too the pope was the monarch of the apostolic Church. And as eternal salvation was more important than earthly prosperity—as the soul was more important than the body—so priestly power overshadowed that of nobles, kings, and emperors. The properly ordered society, the truly Christian society, was one dominated by the Church, which, in turn, was led by the pope. In the intellectual climate of the Central Middle Ages this view provided a persuasive justification for the idea of papal monarchy, and it won the support of many thoughtful people.

The reality of early eleventh-century society was far different. Almost everywhere the Church was under the control of aristocrats. Manorial lords and ladies appointed the priests who managed their parish churches; dukes and kings selected their bishops, abbots, and abbesses. Moreover, these laypeople not only controlled appointments to ecclesiastical offices but also expected churchmen and churchwomen to work on their behalf: to help in administration (as was particularly the case in the Ottonian Empire), to provide warriors from Church estates for feudal armies, and to serve as their advisers and as clerks for their administrations. The Church was a vital part of early medieval society, but in the years after 1000, it was almost always subordinate to "those who fight."

Lay influence was not always bad. Charlemagne (r. 768–814) had guided his Frankish church toward reform; so too did the duke who founded the abbey of Cluny in 910; so too would Emperor Henry III (r. 1039–1056) who moved the papacy toward reform in the mid-eleventh century. But lay influence too often proved inadequate or even corrupting. Many aristocrats grew accustomed to selling bishoprics and abbacies to unworthy, self-seeking candidates, who then turned out to be horrible moral leaders and just as horrible administrators (since they had to recoup the purchase price by exploiting their tenants and subordinates). To many lay princes, this sale of Church offices was merely an ecclesiastical version of what happened when a fief changed hands—the new holder had to pay a sort of inheritance tax. To some career-oriented clergy, it was a good and workable system. Archbishop Manasses of Reims (r. 1070–1077), who had paid handsomely for his office and then enriched himself from it, is supposed to have said, "The archbishopric of Reims would be a fine thing if it didn't mean having to sing Mass." But to reformers who began to protest in the eleventh century, this commerce in ecclesiastical appointments was shamefully corrupt, and they labeled it **simony,** after Simon the Magician, a New Testament figure who had tried (unsuccessfully) to purchase the Holy Spirit.

The papacy itself was not immune from lay influence, for it had fallen into the greedy hands of the Roman nobility and become a prize tossed among several leading aristocratic families. In 1032 the prize fell to a young aristocrat who took the name of Benedict IX (r. 1032–1048). He had no talent for piety, and his immoral behavior was scandalous even by contemporary standards. To make matters even worse, he grew bored with his papal office and sold it to a would-be pope, but then changed his mind and tried to reclaim it. By 1046, three different men claimed to be the true pope.

Ecclesiastical Reform

When reform came, its general purpose was clear: to improve the moral character of the clergy and to limit lay influence over Church matters. About the first, there was little disagreement but much protest, for the issue of "moral character" hinged particularly on sexual practices. In theory, all clergy had long been enjoined to celibacy, but in practice, most priests married and only those who held high office (for example, bishops) could not live openly with wives. For eleventh-century reformers, the marriage of priests was a moral problem of high importance, so much so that some claimed that married priests could not properly administer the Church's sacraments (a heretical position). But priestly marriage was a practical problem as well as a moral one, because a married priest might use Church lands to provide for his wife and children, and if such lands passed as inheritance, they became family property, not Church property. For their part, many priests were horrified at the notion that they should put aside their wives, who not only offered them sexual and emotional comfort but also, in many cases, were simply essential for the effective running of priestly households. Priests loudly complained that they could not live like angels, and some even claimed that it was evil-minded *lay*people who wanted to force celibacy upon them. In 1072, the archbishop of Rouen was even stoned when he attempted to discipline his married clergy. He escaped with his life, but just barely.

About the second reform item—limiting lay influence—there was even more disagreement. A moderate group sought to eliminate simony, enforce clerical celibacy, and improve the moral caliber of churchmen, but without challenging the Church's traditional collaboration with kings and princes, a collaboration that had been strengthened by countless gifts of lands and privileges to the Church. A more radical group sought to demolish the tradition of lay control and to rebuild society as a Christendom governed by a papal monarchy. They sought to establish an ideal Christian commonwealth in which laypeople no longer appointed clergy, and in which kings deferred to bishops and bishops deferred to the pope, rather than the other way around. The moderate reformers endeavored to heal society; the radicals were determined to transform it into an international spiritual monarchy centered on the pope.

Although the ensuing struggle is often figured as a "conflict between Church and state," this is misleading. Many bishops, abbots, and abbesses opposed the reform agenda, whether moderate or radical, because it subordinated them to papal power. After all, they were accustomed to working partnerships with regional princes, to whom they were often connected by bonds of kinship, interest, and gratitude. They had no desire to become the pawns of some overmighty pope. As one German archbishop exclaimed, "The man is a menace! He wants to boss bishops about at his pleasure, as though they were his bailiffs." Conversely, many nobles were great supporters of Church reform, at least in its moderate form. One of eleventh-century Europe's more active reformers was the Holy Roman Emperor Henry III (r. 1039–1056), who used his imperial authority to intervene decisively in the politics of papal Rome. Shocked by the antics of Pope Benedict IX and the three-way tug-of-war for the papal throne, Henry III marched into the Italian peninsula in 1046. He deposed Benedict and his two rivals and appointed the first of a series of German-born reform popes.

The Gregorian Reform

The ablest of Henry's appointees, Pope Leo IX (r. 1049–1054) opened his **pontificate** in dramatic fashion when, at a synod held a few months after taking office, he condemned the bishop of Sutri for simony—and the bishop promptly fell dead. More encouraged than deterred by this event, Leo IX waged a vigorous campaign against Church corruption, holding yearly synods at Rome, sending papal **legates**—that is, papal ambassadors given broad discretionary powers—far and wide to enforce his orders, and traveling constantly to preside personally over local synods and depose guilty clergy. Leo IX struggled on all the fronts that had become central to ecclesiastical reform: enforcement of canon law, cleansing the Church of simony, elimination of clerical marriage, and assertion of the supreme authority of the pope. This last agenda item aggravated relations with the Eastern Orthodox Church, which had never acknowledged the special authority of the bishop of Rome, and in 1054 Leo IX excommunicated the patriarch of Constantinople, precipitating a split between the two Christian churches that has still not fully healed.

But despite the breadth and vigor of Leo IX's reforms, some felt that he was not going far enough. The real evil, in the view of these radical reformers, was the power of laypeople over the Church. To them Henry III's seizure of the papal office in 1046, however well intentioned, was the supreme example of that evil. Henry III might have appointed Leo IX and supported most of his reform initiatives, but his authority in Church matters was—to them—anathema. Many of these ardent reformers, who would dominate papal reform for the next several decades, came from monastic backgrounds, and they sought to bring to papal government the pure piety of the monastic revival that was then surging through eleventh-century Europe.

One such reformer was St. Peter Damian (1007–1072), a leader of a movement of hermits before Leo IX brought him to Rome and made him a **cardinal.**[6] Peter Damian was a forceful preacher and writer dedicated to the eradication of sin—some of which he described so graphically that a sixteenth-century editor felt constrained to tone down his language. Damian served the reform papacy tirelessly, traveling far and wide to enforce prohibitions against simony, to eradicate clerical marriage, and to reform the

---

[6] Originally, cardinals were churchmen—often bishops but sometimes just priests or even **deacons**—who stood in for the pope when he had to be elsewhere. Most were from the area immediately around Rome. Leo IX expanded the office by appointing outsiders like Peter Damian, and soon thereafter, cardinals were designated as the sole electors of each new pope. They retain this function today.

clergy. Yet he drew back from what seemed to him the irresponsible efforts of his more radical associates to challenge and transform the lay-dominated social order.

Among these more radical associates, two especially stand out. Humbert of Silva Candida (c. 1000–1061) and Hildebrand (1020–1085) had, like Peter Damian, left monastic lives to join the **papal curia,** but they disagreed with Damian on the issue of lay involvement in Church affairs. Humbert of Silva Candida used his subtle, well-trained intellect to support papal reform in its most radical aspects. He was uncompromising on the issue of papal supremacy, personally placing on the high altar of Hagia Sophia the document that excommunicated the patriarch of Constantinople in 1054. He was similarly firm in his attack on lay control of Church offices, producing a bitter, closely reasoned attack, *Three Books against the Simoniacs,* in which he extended the meaning of simony to include not merely the buying or selling of ecclesiastical offices but any instance of lay interference in clerical appointments. In Humbert's view the Church ought to be utterly free of lay influence and utterly supreme in European society.

Hildebrand lacked Humbert's intellectual depth but he gave vigorous practical force to his friend's ideas. He became the most controversial figure of his age. Contemporaries described Hildebrand as a small, ugly, pot-bellied man, but they also recognized that he was a spellbinding leader, an effective mover of events, and a man who simply burned with religious fervor. Some even thought he had the power to read minds—and he may well have believed so himself. Consumed by the ideal of a godly society dominated by the Church and a Church dominated by the papacy, Hildebrand served with prodigious vigor and determination under Pope Leo IX and his successors. At length he became pope himself, taking the name Gregory VII (r. 1073–1085). His pontificate was to be one of the most violent and unforgettable of the Middle Ages. He would die in exile, reviled by some as a "holy Satan" and "false monk," but when he died, Church reform—now called the Gregorian (or sometimes Hildebrandian) Reform in his honor—had become a fixed reality in Europe.

First, the Gregorian Reform regularized the selection of popes and firmly removed the process from imperial influence—or any other lay involvement, for that matter. At the death of Henry III's last papal appointee in 1057, reformers began electing popes on their own. (They were encouraged in this move by the untimely death of Henry III the year before, leaving behind a six-year-old heir and a weak regency government.) In 1059, under the influence of Humbert and Hildebrand, they issued a daring declaration of independence known as the "Papal Election Decree," which stated that thenceforth the pope would be chosen by cardinals. The emperor and the Roman laity would merely give formal approval to what the cardinals decided. In the years that followed, this revolutionary proclamation was challenged by both the Holy Roman Empire and the Roman aristocracy, but in the end the reformers won out. The papacy had broken free of lay control; cardinals elected the pope, and the pope appointed the cardinals. The decree of 1059 thus created at the apex of the ecclesiastical hierarchy a reform oligarchy of the most exclusive sort.

Second, priestly celibacy was firmly established as the *rule* of the Church. In 1000, priests' wives were common and respected members of their communities; by 1125, no priest could formally marry within the Catholic Church. Abstinence from marriage was, of course, easier to enforce than abstinence from cohabitation. In many cases, a priest's wife simply became his concubine (a significant demotion in social status!), and in other cases, priests lived alone but frequented brothels or other venues for sexual pleasure. But real change had occurred. What had been *encouraged* in the past was now *required*. Under the vigorous leadership of Gregory VII, priests were firmly ordered to live chastely, with no wives and children to distract them from parochial duties or to claim Church property as their own. Many individual priests failed to live up to the new standard, but the new standard was firm.

Third, the papacy slowly gained control over the entire hierarchy of ecclesiastical offices. The early death of Henry III in 1056 provided a golden opportunity for radical reformers who sought to annihilate lay control over the Church and to subordinate bishops and archbishops to the pope. Milan was the first site of struggle. On one side stood the supporters of old ways: the emperor, the local nobility, and the bishops of Lombardy. On the other side stood the reform papacy, backed by merchants and artisans, derisively called **patarenes** ("rag-pickers") by their enemies but newly powerful in the expanding commercial economy of the city. The reformers in Rome had no sympathy for the archbishop of Milan who was, in effect, an imperial agent and who, by condoning simony and marriage among his clergy, symbolized the traditional Church at its worst. In 1059 Peter Damian journeyed to Milan where he humbled the archbishop and the higher clergy, forcing them to confess their sins publicly and making them promise to change their ways. Thus, the Milanese church, despite its friendship with the Empire and its tradition of independence, was made to submit to the power of the papacy. The same would happen again in 1072 when the young emperor Henry IV (r. 1056–1106) attempted to name his own man as archbishop of Milan. After the pope excommunicated Henry's counselors, he was forced to back down. This was the first stage of what was to become an epic struggle over **lay investiture.**

Gregory VII, Henry IV, and Lay Investiture

The struggle over lay control of ecclesiastical appointments broke out in earnest in 1075 when Hildebrand, newly installed as Pope Gregory VII, issued a proclamation banning lay investiture. Traditionally, a newly chosen bishop was "invested" into office by receiving two items from the layperson who controlled the appointment: a ring that signified marriage to the Church and a pastoral staff symbolic of the duty to be a good shepherd. Gregory attacked this custom of lay investiture as a crucial symbol of inappropriate lay authority over clergy. His attack was a challenge to the established social order and a threat to the authority of every ruler in Western Christendom—none more than the Holy Roman emperor, whose administration was particularly dependent on the support of German and Lombard bishops.

By 1075, Henry IV was showing promise of becoming as strong a ruler as his father. He had been forced to back down in Milan a few years earlier, but he was not inclined to do so again. When Gregory VII suspended a group of imperially appointed German bishops, Henry IV responded with a vehement letter of defiance. Backed by his bishops, he asserted that as a divinely appointed sovereign, he was authorized to lead the German Church without papal interference, and he challenged Gregory's very right to the papal throne. The letter was insultingly addressed to Gregory under his previous name, "Hildebrand, not pope but false monk." It concluded with the dramatic words, "I, Henry, king by grace of God, with all my bishops, say to you: 'Come down, come down, and be damned throughout the ages.'"

Henry's letter was a defense of the traditional social order of divinely ordained kings, sanctified by the ceremony of holy consecration and anointment that accompanied their coronations, ruling as vicars of God over their lay subjects and their semi-autonomous bishops. Gregory's view of society was vastly different: he denied the sacred qualities of kings and emperors, he suggested that most of them were murderous thugs destined for hell, and he repudiated their claim to question his status or his decrees. Emperors had no power to appoint bishops, much less depose popes. But the pope, as the ultimate authority in Western Christendom, had the power to depose not only bishops but kings and emperors as well. Accordingly, Gregory responded to Henry IV's letter with a devastating counterpunch: he excommunicated and deposed Henry IV. It was for the pope to judge whether or not the king was fit to rule, and Gregory had issued his judgment.

Radical though it was, the deposition was effective. Under the relatively placid surface of centralized authority in the Holy Roman Empire, aristocratic opposition had long been gathering force. Relatively subdued during the reign of Henry III, local and regional princes had asserted themselves during the long regency following his death, and Henry IV, on reaching maturity, was on much less secure ground than his father had been. In 1075 he succeeded in stifling a long, bitter rebellion in Saxony and seemed to be on his way toward reasserting his father's imperial power. Then, the controversy with Rome exploded. Gregory VII's excommunication and deposition—awesome spiritual sanctions to the minds of eleventh-century Christians—unleashed in the German states all the latent hostility that the centralizing policies of the Salian dynasty had long evoked. Many Germans, clergy and aristocrats alike, refused to serve an excommunicated sovereign. The German nobility even took the revolutionary step of threatening to elect a new emperor in Henry's place, thereby challenging the ingrained tradition of hereditary selection.

Desperate to keep his throne, Henry crossed the Alps to seek the pope's forgiveness. In January 1077, at the castle of Canossa in the north of the Italian peninsula, the two men met in what was perhaps medieval history's most dramatic encounter: Henry IV, humble and barefoot in the snow, clothed in rough, penitential garments, and Gregory VII, torn between his priestly duty to forgive a repentant sinner and his conviction that Henry's change of heart was a mere political subterfuge. Finally Gregory lifted Henry's excommunication, and the king, swearing to amend his ways, returned to the German states to rebuild his authority (see Color Illustration 9).

The struggle between Henry IV and Gregory VII did not end at Canossa. Henry would later invade and appoint an alternative pope. Gregory VII would excommunicate Henry again, but die in forced exile in Salerno. And their disagreement over lay investiture would fester for several generations, until heated positions had been cooled by the passage of time. In 1122, the differences were reconciled in the Concordat of Worms by which the emperor (then Henry V, r. 1106–1125) agreed to give up lay investiture, while the pope (Calixtus II, r. 1119–1124) conceded to the emperor the important privilege of bestowing on a new bishop the symbols of *territorial* and *administrative* jurisdiction (as distinct from the ring and staff, both symbols of *spiritual* authority, which the pope bestowed). This agreement was similar to those already reached in France (1104) and England (1107), where the struggle had been less bitter. Bishops and other ecclesiastical officers were thenceforth to be elected according to the principles of canon law, but the emperor had the right to be present at such elections and to make the final decision in the event of a dispute. These reservations enabled the emperor to retain a considerable degree of de facto authority over the appointment of high-ranking German clergy. The exercise of lay control over an acceptable Church election is illustrated by the command of King Henry II of England (r. 1154–1189) to the monks at Winchester Abbey when they needed to elect a new abbot: "I order you to hold a free election, but nevertheless I forbid you to elect anyone except Richard, my clerk."

The Reformed Papacy

Gregory VII died in exile, bitterly reflecting with his last breath, "I have loved justice and hated iniquity: therefore I die in exile." Yet his vision of papal monarchy long outlived him. The papacy soon fell into the expert hands of Urban II (r. 1088–1099), a monk who had served Gregory VII as one of his most faithful and effective cardinals. Ideologically, Urban was firmly part of Gregory's radical tradition, and he added further fuel to the papal fire when, in 1095, he called the First Crusade (1096–1099), thereby wedding the papal reform movement to the fervor of Christian militancy. Urban was, however, much more practical and diplomatic than Gregory. He began to rebuild the papal administration, which had disintegrated during Gregory's final years, into a smoothly functioning bureaucracy suited to the needs of a centralized papal government in regular communication with the bishops of Western Christendom. Papal correspondence increased, financial management improved, and the papal tribunal became steadily more active and effective. In the long run, the powerful papal monarchy of the Central Middle Ages might have owed more to the administrative reforms of Urban II than to the excommunications of Gregory VII.

At a time when the Church—its pope, its bishops, its monasteries, and its parishes—possessed perhaps a third of the land in Europe, the full realization of Gregory VII's vision of papal monarchy would have crippled secular power, destroyed episcopal autonomy, and revolutionized the European political order. This was, in fact, just what Gregory and other radical reformers wanted, for only in this way, they believed, could a justly ordered Christian commonwealth be achieved. Although they did not achieve their goal, they did lay the foundations for a vigorous papal monarchy that was a powerful and effective force in later centuries. By the year 1200, Innocent III (r. 1198–1216) was not just a pope; he was far and away the most powerful ruler in Europe, exercising rigorous control over his Church and wielding extraordinary authority over the princes of Europe. The popes of the Central Middle Ages spearheaded the crusades, sought to eliminate heresy, defined theological positions with great clarity, encouraged the development of canon law, responded to developments in monastic life and ordinary piety—and continued to vie with dukes and kings for ultimate power within Europe. We shall return to all of these themes in later chapters. But they all are rooted in a papacy that controlled its Church in 1200 in ways that would have been almost inconceivable in 1000.

✳ THE MENDICANT ORDERS

It is, therefore, not at all surprising that the papacy played a central role in the development, in the early 1200s, of the Franciscan and Dominican orders. With their devotion to poverty, preaching, and charity, these orders responded to powerful trends in popular piety. They also provided new weapons in the fight against heresy. Franciscans and

Dominicans fought heretics directly, but they also eventually drained urban heresy of much of its allure by demonstrating to townspeople that Christian orthodoxy could be both relevant and compelling. Franciscans and Dominicans also introduced a new sort of religious life to Western Christendom. Like monks, these **friars** took vows of poverty, chastity, and obedience, but they rejected the life of the cloister in favor of working directly in the world and they also rejected the corporate wealth of monasticism by pledging themselves to both personal and corporate poverty. They were proudly known as **mendicants,** or "beggars."

The Dominicans

St. Dominic (1170–1221), a well-educated Spaniard, conceived the idea of an order of men trained as theologians and preachers who could win over heretics through argument, oratory, and the example of their own dedication to poverty and the simple life. At the urging of Pope Innocent III, Dominic traveled to southern France to preach against the Cathars. His eloquence and simplicity won him considerable renown, a few converts, and some volunteers who joined in his work. From this small cadre eventually grew a new religious order known as the Order of Friars Preachers. Achieving permanent shape between its formal establishment in 1216 and Dominic's death in 1221, the order attracted people who could not be satisfied with the enclosed, tradition-bound life of monasticism but were challenged by the austerity of the Dominican life, the disciplined vitality of the order, and the goal of working toward the moral regeneration of society.

In ordering the Dominican way of life, Dominic drew freely on the earlier ordinances of the Augustinian canons, in part because he had been an Augustinian canon in his youth and in part because the Fourth Lateran Council of 1215 had just decreed that any new monastic movements had to be based on older monastic rules. But Dominic essentially crafted a new direction for his followers. The order was to be headed by a minister-general, elected for life, and a legislative body that met annually. The friars themselves belonged not to a particular house but to the order at large. Their life included such rigors as midnight services, total abstinence from meat, frequent fasts, and prolonged periods of mandatory silence. And the entire order was strictly bound by a rule of poverty: it had no possessions except churches and priories, and it was to subsist through charitable gifts alone. Dominic had learned to emphasize institutional as well as individual poverty from his contemporary, St. Francis (c. 1182–1226), but their emphasis was different. For Dominic, the poverty of his preachers was a way to attract converts and save heretics. For Francis, as we shall see, poverty was good in and of itself.

The Dominican order expanded at a phenomenal rate during the course of the thirteenth century. Dominican friars carried their evangelical activities across Europe and beyond, into the Holy Land, central Asia, Tibet, and China. The Dominicans were, above all, preachers, and their particular mission was to preach among heretics and non-Christians. Yet their contact with Christian heretics led them to be inquisitors as well as preachers—if they could not persuade, they sometimes sought to root out. Dominicans took pride in their nickname *Domini canes,* "hounds of God," which suggested their role as watchdogs of the Catholic faith. To European heretics and Jews, the nickname came to have a more ominous connotation.

Dominicans also became intellectual leaders. Dominic himself had insisted that his followers acquire a broad education before undertaking their mission of preaching, and he also expected that each Dominican priory would maintain a school of theology. Within a few decades after his death, his order included some of the foremost intellects of the age. Dominicans dominated the faculties of many of the new universities of Europe; they became the leading proponents of Aristotelian philosophy; and they included in their numbers such notable scholars as Albertus Magnus (c. 1200–1280) and Thomas Aquinas (c. 1225–1274). In deference to the great truth that scholar-teachers cannot be expected to beg or do odd jobs, the rule of corporate poverty was slowly softened until, in the fifteenth century, it was dropped altogether.

The Franciscans

Dominic's contemporary, St. Francis, is perhaps the most widely admired figure of the Middle Ages (see Figure 8.2). A product of the medieval urban revolution, he was the son of a wealthy merchant of Assisi in the central Italian peninsula. As a youth he was generous, high-spirited, and popular, and in time he became the leader of a boisterous group of teenagers. As one writer aptly expressed it, he "seems altogether to have been rather a festive figure."

In his early twenties St. Francis underwent a profound religious conversion that occurred in several steps. It began on the occasion of a banquet that he gave for some of his friends. Afterward Francis and his companions went into the town with torches, singing in the streets. Francis was crowned with garlands as king of the revelers, but after a time he disappeared and was found in a religious trance. Thereafter, he devoted himself to solitude, prayer, and service to the poor. He went as a pilgrim to Rome, where he is reported to have exchanged clothes with a beggar and spent the day begging. Returning to Assisi, he encountered an impoverished leper, and notwithstanding his fear of leprosy, he gave the poor man all the money he was carrying and kissed his hand. Thenceforth he devoted himself to the service of lepers and hospitals.

To the consternation of his father, who sold fine clothing, Francis began to go about Assisi dressed in rags and giving to the poor. His former companions pelted him with mud, and his father, fearing that Francis's almsgiving would consume the family fortune, disinherited him. Francis left home singing a French song and spent the next three years of his life in the environs of Assisi, living in abject poverty. He ministered to lepers and social outcasts and continued to embarrass his family by his unconventional behavior. Then, even though still a layman, he began to preach to the poor.

Lay preaching was not approved by the Church, but Francis soon sought papal approval for his work and for those disciples who were now gathering around him. When he arrived in Rome in 1210, his timing was excellent. Pope Innocent III had recently given his blessing to similar movements—first, an orthodox group of Humiliati in 1201, and then, a group known as the "Poor Catholics," founded by a one-time Waldensian in 1208. He doubtless saw in the Franciscan mission an orthodox counterpoise to the Waldensians, Cathars, and other heretical groups that had been winning masses of converts from the Church by the example of their poverty and simplicity. For here was a man whose loyalty to Catholicism was beyond question and whose own artless simplicity might bring erring souls back into the Church. And it may well be that Francis's glowing spirituality appealed to the sanctity of Innocent himself, for the pope, even though a great man of affairs, was deeply pious. However this may be,

Figure 8.2   *St. Francis*   Although much restored, this fresco is the earliest known depiction of St. Francis, ascribed to the Italian painter Cimabue (c. 1240–1302).

thirteenth-century Europe deserves some credit for embracing a movement that in many other ages would have been persecuted or ridiculed. Our own society, to its shame, would probably place St. Francis in a mental hospital. But the medieval West took Francis to its heart and made him a saint. In the process, however, the hard edges of his religious austerity were blunted by those who followed him.

Francis and his followers began by constructing a makeshift headquarters near Assisi, basically little more than rough huts built with branches and twigs. This central location mattered little, for they were always on the move, wandering in pairs over the countryside, dressed in peasants' clothing, preaching, serving, and living in self-conscious imitation of Christ. During the next decade the movement expanded at a spectacular rate, and by Francis's death in 1226, Franciscan missions were active in France, England, the German states, Hungary, Iberia, North Africa, Turkey, and the Holy Land, and his friars numbered in the thousands. The captivating personality of Francis himself was a crucial factor in his order's popularity, but it also owed much to the fact that his ideals harmonized with the religious aspirations of the age. Urban heresy lost some of its allure as cheerful, devoted Franciscans began to pour into Europe's cities, preaching in the crowded streets and setting a living example of Christian sanctity.

The Franciscan ideal was based above all on the imitation of Christ. Fundamental to this ideal was the notion of poverty, both individual and corporate. The Franciscans subsisted by working in return for their food and other necessities. Humility was also an essential element; Francis gave his followers the modest name, *Friars Minor* ("little brothers"). And also characteristic of the Franciscan life was joyous acceptance of the world as God's handiwork. The Cathars had rejected the material world as evil, as had Neoplatonists before them, but Francis, known as "God's own troubadour" to his contemporaries, saw beauty and holiness in nature. In his "Song of Brother Sun" he expressed poetically his holy commitment to the physical universe:

> Praise be to you, my Lord, for all your creatures,
> Above all Brother Sun
> Who brings us the day, and lends us his light;
> Beautiful is he, radiant with great splendor,
> And speaks to us of you, O most high.
> Praise to you, my Lord, for Sister Moon and for the stars;
> In heaven you have set them, clear and precious and fair.
> Praise to you, my Lord, for Brother Wind,
> For air and clouds, for calm and all weather
> By which you support life in all your creatures. . . .

Yet the early Franciscan life was too good to last—for all but St. Francis and a few others. The order quickly grew too large to retain its original disorganized simplicity. By 1220, thousands of men had become Friars Minor, and they were joined by a new phenomenon: lay men and women in **tertiary orders,** who dedicated themselves to the Franciscan way while continuing their careers in the world. Francis's little band of brothers had evolved into a holy multitude.

Francis himself was no administrator, and as his order grew, he withdrew from the practical challenges that necessarily arose. In 1220, when a rule for the order was formally established, he resigned his leadership of the movement with the words, "Lord, I return to you this family that you have confided to me. Now, as you know, most sweet Jesus, I have no longer strength or ability to keep on caring for them." At his death in 1226 he was universally mourned, and the order that he had founded had become the most powerful and attractive religious movement of its age. It is not clear, however, what Francis would have thought of a Franciscan order which was, by then, rent with dissension. Most Franciscans were willing to amend Francis's strict rules in the interest of practicality—for example, to accept gifts of houses or land so that their communities could continue on a more orderly financial basis. Yet a few others insisted on the strict imitation of Francis's life and struggled against any modification. Known in later years as *Spiritual Franciscans,* they sought to preserve the apostolic poverty and artless idealism of Francis himself. Their goals were admirable, but their numbers few.

As mainstream Franciscans began to modify Francis's ideal of absolute poverty, they also began to downplay his disparagement of formal learning as irrelevant to salvation. Devoting themselves to scholarship, they eventually took their places alongside the Dominicans in thirteenth- and fourteenth-century universities. Franciscan scholars such as Roger Bacon (c. 1214–1294) played a role in the revival of scientific investigation, and the minister-general of the Franciscan order in the later thirteenth century, St. Bonaventure (1221–1274), was one of the most illustrious theologians of the age. Necessary though they might have been, these compromises diminished the radical idealism that Francis had instilled in his order. In the progress from huts of twigs to halls of ivy, something precious was left behind. Franciscans continued to serve society, but by the end of the thirteenth century they had ceased to inspire it.

Women and the Mendicant Orders

The reforms of St. Dominic and St. Francis were particularly difficult to adapt to the religious needs of women. The specialty of those who followed St. Dominic was preaching, an activity explicitly forbidden to women by the medieval Church. Dominic himself founded three monasteries for women, and by the beginning of the fourteenth century more than 140 Dominican nunneries graced Europe. But unlike their male counterparts, Dominican nuns led cloistered lives and were permitted no active ministry. All told, their religious life was not very different from that of nuns in older Benedictine houses. The specialty of those who followed St. Francis was apostolic poverty, a way of life entirely unsuited for women (who, among other things, would have been vulnerable to rape and accusations of prostitution). Francis himself resisted incorporating women into his order, reportedly saying "God has taken our wives from us, and now Satan has given us sisters." But he was a good friend to St. Clare of Assisi (1194–1253), and she founded a female order that sought to complement the absolute poverty of male Franciscans with the absolute claustration of women (see Figure 8.3). Women who entered her order, the Poor Clares, did not preach or beg as Francis had done, but they were literally dead to the world, enclosed perpetually behind walls. Dominic and Francis inspired women as well as men, but the imitation of Christ was difficult to reconcile with then acceptable roles for women. In both cases, the cloister beckoned more than the world.

✳ CONCLUSION

Catholic Christianity was a powerful unifying influence in Europe during the Central Middle Ages. The papacy never completely succeeded in breaking the control of kings and nobles over local clergy, but by the twelfth century it was coming to exercise a very real authority over the bishops and other clergy of Europe. A parish system had spread across the European countryside to bring the sacraments and at least some Christian instruction to the peasantry. An intense spirituality that looked more to God's love than his anger inspired both ordinary lay piety and monastic reform. And even the vitality of Christian heresy speaks to the importance of spirituality in the towns and villages of

Figure 8.3   *Poor Clares in Their Chapel*   The Poor Clares, unable to undertake the life of preaching, poverty, and wandering embraced by the early Franciscans, opted instead for a life of strict enclosure within monastic walls.

Europe. Reform movements ebbed and flowed, but there was no lack of new ideas to tackle problems, both old and new.

There was, however, a price to pay for all this religious enthusiasm and fervor. As Christians became increasingly devoted to their faith, they tended to become less tolerant toward those who deviated from their beliefs. Thus, the Central Middle Ages witnessed an intensification of hostility toward "others"—a group that included Jews, heretics, Muslims, and even lepers, prostitutes, and men who engaged in homosexual acts (female same-sex relations were apparently deemed too trivial to cause much worry). The growth of spiritual self-awareness was thus accompanied by the emergence of what one historian has called "a persecuting society," many aspects of which endure to this day. This is one of the subjects to which we shall turn in the next chapter.

Suggested Readings

Constance Hoffman Berman, *The Cistercian Evolution: The Invention of a Religious Order in Twelfth-Century Europe* (2000). A major revisionist history of the first century of Cistercian reform.

Uta-Renate Blumenthal, *The Investiture Controversy: Church and Monarch from the Ninth to the Twelfth Century* (1988). The best account of the investiture controversy in English.

Rosalind and Christopher Brooke, *Popular Religion in the Middle Ages* (1985). For primary sources, see John Shinners, ed., *Medieval Popular Religion, 1000–1500: A Reader* (1997). See also Kathleen Ashley and Pamela Sheingorn, *Writing Faith: Text, Sign and*

History in the Miracles of Sainte Foy (1999); Jean-Claude Schmidt, *Ghosts in the Middle Ages* (1998); and Benedicta Ward, *Miracles and the Medieval Mind* (1982).

Caroline Walker Bynum, *Jesus as Mother: Studies in the Spirituality of the High Middle Ages* (1982). Perceptive essays on Christian spirituality. See also Giles Constable, *The Reformation of the Twelfth Century* (1996).

H. E. J. Cowdrey, *Pope Gregory VII, 1073–1085* (1998). The definitive biography.

Malcolm Lambert, *Medieval Heresy: Popular Movements from the Gregorian Reform to the Reformation* (3rd edition, 2002). See also Jeffrey B. Russell, *Dissent and Order in the Middle Ages: The Search for Legitimate Authority* (1992).

C. H. Lawrence, *Medieval Monasticism* (3rd edition, 2001). See also the texts in Douglas J. McMillan and Kathryn Smith Fladenmuller, eds., *Regular Life: Monastic, Canonical, and Mendicant Rules* (1997).

Lester K. Little, *Religious Poverty and the Profit Economy* (1978). A skillful and highly original study of the relationship between the mendicants and the merchant class. See also C. H. Lawrence, *The Friars: The Impact of the Early Mendicant Movement on Western Society* (1994).

Joseph H. Lynch, *The Medieval Church: A Brief History* (1992). An excellent survey. See also Gerd Tellenbach, *The Church in Western Europe from the Tenth to the Early Twelfth Century* (1993). For the papacy per se, see the bibliography for Chapter 10.

Jo Ann Kay McNamara, *Sisters in Arms: Catholic Nuns Through Two Millennia* (1996). Includes extensive coverage of female monasticism in the Central Middle Ages. See also Penelope Johnson, *Equal in Monastic Profession: Religious Women in Medieval France* (1991), and Bruce L. Venarde, *Women's Monasticism and Medieval Society: Nunneries in France and England, 890–1215* (1997).

SUGGESTED PRIMARY SOURCES

Thomas Head, ed., *Medieval Hagiography: An Anthology* (2000). A wide-ranging collection of newly translated texts—from Athanasius of Alexandria to Joan of Arc. See also Mary-Ann Stouck, ed., *Medieval Saints: A Reader* (1999). Organized by topic, not by saint, this collection also spans the entire medieval millennium.

John Shinners, ed., *Medieval Popular Religion, 1000–1500* (1997). An outstanding collection.

Diana, Webb, *Pilgrims and Pilgrimage in the Medieval West* (1999). The thematic sections of this collection are preceded by concise, accessible essays.

CHAPTER 9

CONQUESTS, CRUSADES, AND PERSECUTIONS,
c. 1100-1300

✳ INTRODUCTION

As we have now seen, the Central Middle Ages saw considerable change, much of it impressive and good. Peasants drew ever more harvest from their fields, and population surged. Trade expanded, and towns sprang up to accommodate new goods and merchants. The nobility consolidated their military power with better administrations and created a chivalric culture that mingled violent values with Christian virtues. The Church revived under a reformed papacy and a variety of new religious orders. These same centuries also saw the "Europeanization of Europe," to borrow historian Robert Bartlett's memorable phrase. In other words, the "First Europe"—Charlemagne's old imperial heartland of France, the German states west of the Elbe, the northern Italian peninsula—spread its values and culture through an ever larger and ever more homogeneous Western Christendom.

Part of this process involved external conquest and colonization. Western Christendom roughly doubled in area during the Central Middle Ages. Some newly absorbed areas—such as Hungary, land of the Magyars, and the Iberian peninsula, home of the Muslim state of al-Andalus—were simultaneously Christianized and Europeanized. The absorption of these regions into Western Christendom is most vividly symbolized by the ever-growing popularity of the Virgin Mary as the namesake for female children. In Christian Iberia, a girl christened Maria bore a name that proclaimed both her faith and her European-ness.

Another part of this process involved internal cultural homogenization. Hints of pressure for uniformity can be found as early as the Council of Whitby in 664, when Irish Christianity had been brought—some would say "forced"—into conformity with Catholic customs. This trend continued through the Central Middle Ages, with results that are perhaps best symbolized in the naming of male infants. In 1000, boys were usually given names that reflected local customs and local saints—Malcolm in Scotland, Raymond in southern France, Herman in the Baltic. By 1300, parents still sometimes favored these local names, but they more often chose from a few European-wide

TIMELINE 9.1   Conquests, Crusades, and Persecutions, 1000–1300

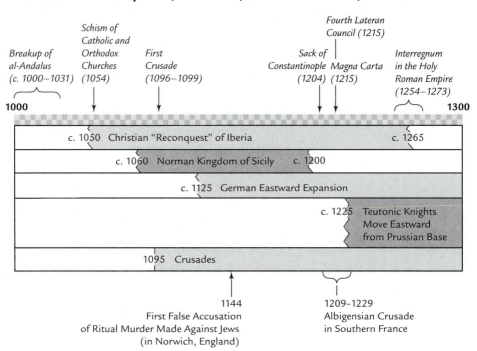

1144
First False Accusation
of Ritual Murder Made Against Jews
(in Norwich, England)

1209–1229
Albigensian Crusade
in Southern France

favorites. Whether born in Scotland, southern France, or the Baltic, a male infant in the early fourteenth century was likely to be given one of a small number of *European* names. Among the most popular were John, William, Thomas, and Henry.[1]

This Europeanization of Europe fueled cultural understanding, but, as Timeline 9.1 sets out, it also gave rise to brutal conquest and terrifying persecution. At the same time as some people were absorbed more fully into European culture and society, others were expelled from it. Jews provide the classic example, for, as we shall see, they often faced forced conversion, death, or expulsion during these centuries. Yet many other people suffered, too. Behind the diverse stories of conquests, crusades, and persecutions that we shall examine in this chapter lay many causes and motivations, but all drew, in part, on a growing Christian militancy. For many medieval people, Christianity—that is *Catholic* Christianity—defined the limits of what was civilized, acceptable, and hospitable. Anything that lay outside that boundary was assumed to be savage, intolerable, and hostile.

✸ CONQUESTS AND TERRITORIAL EXPANSION

Europe's transformation during the Central Middle Ages was marked, as we saw in Chapter 7, by the conquest of a great *internal* frontier: the clearing of forests, the draining of swamps, and the reclamation of land from the sea. This internal colonization was

---

[1] The form of these names varied, of course, in different vernaculars. For example, in Italian, they are Giovanni, Guglielmo, Tommaso, and Enrico.

complemented by an *external* expansion along the periphery of Western Christendom that brought parts of the Muslim, Byzantine, and Slavic worlds within the ballooning boundaries of European civilization.

European expansion was not new in the eleventh century. Charlemagne (r. 768–814) had introduced Frankish government and Christianity into many of the German states, and he had established a Christian bridgehead around Barcelona in Iberia. The tenth-century conversion of Bohemia and Poland pushed the limits of Western Christendom still farther to the east and north. The Bohemians converted in the early tenth century, when they were seeking help against the Magyar onslaught and were therefore open to German (and especially Bavarian) influence.[2] The conversion of Poland was facilitated by yet another case of domestic proselytization; the marriage in 964 of Dobrava (died c. 985), Christian daughter of Boleslas I of Bohemia, to the Polish prince Mieszko (ruled c. 962–992); he was baptized two years later. By the turn of the millennium, the waning of the Magyar and Viking threats and the accompanying conversion of both Hungary and Scandinavia to Christianity had pushed out still more the boundaries of Western Christendom. Then, in the eleventh, twelfth, and thirteenth centuries, multitudes of aristocratic younger sons (made landless by the growing popularity of inheritance by primogeniture) began to seek wealth and military glory on Western Christendom's frontiers. They were joined by peasants (made more numerous by the population boom) who provided a labor force for newly conquered lands. And they were encouraged by a Church (made stronger by papal and monastic reform) that taught that a young warrior who carved out new estates for himself on the frontier was also storing up treasures in heaven by promoting Catholic Christianity among Muslims in Iberia, Sicily, and Syria and among the Slavs of Eastern Europe. Land, gold, and eternal salvation—these were the alluring rewards of the medieval frontier.

Iberia

So it was that knightly adventurers from all over Western Christendom, particularly France, began to flock southwestward during the eleventh century to aid in what they saw as a "reconquest" of the Iberian peninsula from Islam. Al-Andalus had flourished throughout the tenth century, particularly during the long reign of Abd al-Rahman III (r. 912–961) and the long regency of Ibn Abi Amir (r. 976–1002), who took the name al-Mansur, "The Victorious." But this long century of territorial security, internal peace, and economic prosperity was followed, after al-Mansur's death in 1002, by the slow disintegration of the caliphate into small, warring principalities. Christian princes in the north of the peninsula also ruled small territories, regularly fought among themselves, and were seldom capable of united action. But they were slowly able to respond to the opportunity provided by the break-up of al-Andalus, conquering their Muslim rivals one by one, or as was often the case, merely extorting tribute from them (see Map 9.1).

The Christian kingdom of Castile first took the lead, capturing the great Muslim city of Toledo in 1085. In later years Toledo would become an intellectual entrepôt, a crucial contact point between Islamic and Christian cultures, with local Jewish intellectuals

---

[2] Unfortunately, the Good King Wenceslas of Christmas carol fame was neither a king nor particularly good. He was a Christian prince of Bohemia murdered by his Christian brother in 929. In later years, his murder was transfigured into a mythic martyrdom, but with no basis in historical fact.

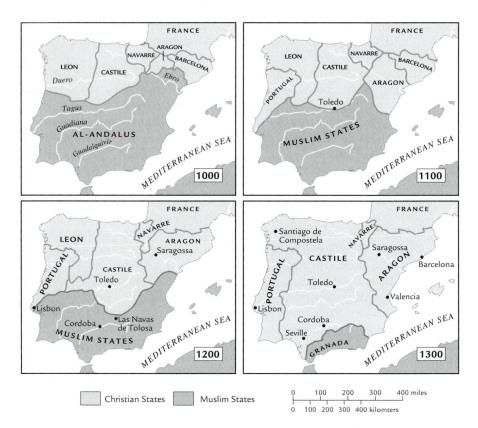

Map 9.1 *The "Reconquest" of Iberia, c. 1000–1300*   The first of these maps shows how the Muslim caliphate of al-Andalus controlled most of the Iberian peninsula in the year 1000. The next three maps show how, in the centuries that followed the disintegration of al-Andalus in 1031, Christian states slowly extended their power southward. As the expansion of Castile and Aragon shows, the princes of some Christian states extended their territories at the expense not only of Muslim princes to their south but also of their Christian neighbors.

often serving as intermediaries. From Toledo in the twelfth century would flow Arab scientific and philosophical works, newly translated into Latin and eagerly sought by Western scholars.

For decades after the capture of Toledo, Christian armies made only slow progress. In the far west, Portugal was established as a new Christian kingdom. In the center of the peninsula, Castile continued to annex areas to the immediate south of Toledo. And in the northeast, the Christian kingdom of Aragon slowly grew more powerful, capturing Muslim Saragossa in 1118 and uniting with the prosperous Christian county of Barcelona (the "Spanish March" of Charlemagne's time) in 1137. But further progress was slowed by both stiffened Muslim resistance and internecine warfare.

By the late eleventh century, Spanish Muslims were receiving help from their co-religionists in North Africa, help that more or less annexed what remained of Muslim Spain into a Berber empire. That empire grew, in part, from two waves of religious fundamentalism. The *Almoravids,* who insisted on a literalist approach to the Quran, dominated North Africa from the mid-eleventh to the mid-twelfth century. When their greatest leader, Yusuf ibn Tashufin, received an appeal for aid from Muslims in Seville, he first helped them and then subdued them; by 1090, he controlled much of Muslim Spain, as would his successors until 1148. They were then replaced by another Berber power, the equally fundamentalist *Almohads* who contended that a too-literal reading of the Quran (like that embraced by the Almoravids) encouraged the heresy of polytheism. Spanish Muslims initially welcomed Berbers for both their military support against Christians and their inspiring religious reforms. But they eventually tired of their Berber overlords, offering them half-hearted support or even outright resistance.

While Muslims exhausted themselves with internecine struggles, so too did Christians. The Christian states of northern Iberia constantly fought against each other, and some also intervened in the affairs of southern France. As a result, the early "reconquest" was little more than a series of wars among princes, with each prince primarily seeking to secure or expand the territory of his realm. These wars usually pitted Christian prince against Muslim prince, but not always. Indeed, it was not uncommon for Christians to ally with Muslims against other Christians. Land and conquest mattered more than faith.

The slow pace of conquest quickened after 1212, when Pope Innocent III (r. 1198–1216) proclaimed an all-out crusade against Iberian Muslims. The king of Castile, backed by a huge army of knights from throughout Europe, advanced from Toledo and won a decisive victory over the Muslims at the battle of Las Navas de Tolosa. Thereafter, Muslim power was permanently crippled. Cordoba itself—once the opulent capital of al-Andalus, the center of the civilization that had attracted the intrepid Gerbert of Aurillac (945–1003)—fell to Castile in 1236. With its largely agrarian economy and its great sheep-raising ranches, Castile now dominated the center of the Iberian peninsula. To the west, the Portuguese, pushing steadily southward against Muslims settled along the Atlantic coast, expanded their kingdom to its present dimensions by 1250. During these same years the kings of Aragon advanced southwestward across the rich coastal district of Valencia (1238) and overran Majorca, Minorca, and the other Balearic islands.

By 1264 Muslim power was confined to the small southern kingdom of Granada, which would remain a Muslim enclave until its fall in 1492. Yet from the mid-thirteenth century, Christians controlled nearly all of the Iberian peninsula, now reorganized into three major kingdoms: Castile, Aragon, and Portugal. In a political sense, the "reconquest" was virtually done.

Christian militancy fueled the rapid advances of Christian princes in the thirteenth century, and these princes sought to promote their faith by importing Christian peasants for massive resettlement. But they did not initially force conversion on their new Muslim and Jewish subjects. In theory, no Muslims should have been left in the lands conquered by Christian princes. Both religions concurred on this point; by Islamic teaching, they were obliged to emigrate to Muslim states, and by Church decree, they were to be expelled. But most Muslims stayed, and in some areas, such as Valencia with more than 250,000 Muslim subjects, they predominated. A certain rough separation was maintained, with Muslim villages distinct from Christian villages and Muslim districts carved out in Christian towns. And certain restrictions were imposed, with Muslims often forbidden, for example, from buying or selling land to Christians. But a workable coexistence was established, and Muslims in the new Christian principalities can even be said to have prospered through much of the thirteenth and fourteenth centuries. Still the Muslim community was, as one historian has graphically put it "decapitated intellectually as well as politically" by Christian conquest.

Jews were far less numerous than Muslims, perhaps no more than 50,000 in the entire peninsula. Most lived in small communities of a thousand or so, especially in cities. Toledo, with about 2,000 Jews, boasted the largest single community. Like Muslims, Jews were considered a "people apart," subject to the special attention and taxation of Christian princes. Initially, Jews were well treated by conquering Christians, but the fourteenth century was disastrous for them. They were forced to listen politely as Dominican preachers maligned their faith, they were required to wear distinctive badges, and they had to pay tithes to the Church. Then, they faced mob violence: an attack on the Jewish community of Navarre in 1328, another in Gerona in 1331, a massacre (led by royal troops) in Toledo in 1355, and either death or forced conversion for the Jews of Seville in 1391. Throughout the peninsula, many Jews were killed, some converted, and many emigrated. By the end of the century, the Jewish population of Iberia had been cut almost in half.

Sicily and the Southern Italian Peninsula

The warrior-aristocracy of Normandy was probably the most militant force in eleventh-century Europe. Viking in ancestry, French in tongue, and Christian in faith, Normans plied their arms across the length and breadth of Europe: in the Christian conquest of Iberia, on the crusades to the Middle East, on the battlefields of England and France, and in the southern Italian peninsula and Sicily.

Population pressure, greed, adventure, and even the pressures of political centralization within Normandy drove its young warriors far and wide on distant enterprises. This is the impression they made on one Italian chronicler:

> The Normans are a cunning and revengeful people; eloquence and deceit seem to be their hereditary qualities. They can stoop to flatter, but unless curbed by the restraint of law they indulge in the licentiousness of nature and passion and, in their eager search for wealth and power, despise whatever they possess and seek whatever they desire. They delight in arms and horses, the luxury of dress, and the exercise of hawking and hunting, but on pressing occasions they can endure with incredible patience the inclemency of every climate and the toil and privation of a military life.

The key figures in the Norman conquest of the southern Italian peninsula were sons of a minor baron of northwest Normandy named Tancred de Hauteville (d. 1041). Tancred had twelve sons, and eight of them headed off to the Italian peninsula in the 1030s and 1040s, poor in goods but rich in ambition. Even before the first of them arrived, other Norman adventurers had already been drifting south to serve as hired soldiers for the Byzantine coastal cities, the Lombard principalities, and the independent seaport republics that were struggling for power in the military-political snake pit of the eleventh-century south. Before long, they were building principalities of their own.

Robert Guiscard (1025–1085) and Sichelgaita (c. 1040–1090)

In 1047 the most formidable of Tancred de Hauteville's sons, Robert Guiscard ("the Cunning"), arrived in the southern Italian peninsula. A tall, blond man, with a terrifying voice and eyes that sparked with fire, he was, as the Byzantine princess and historian Anna Comnena put it, "ready to submit to nobody in all the world." Robert Guiscard began his Italian career as a bandit leader, plundering villages and robbing travelers in the south of the peninsula. Encouraged by his success, he turned to conquest, and winning victory after victory, he emerged by the mid-1050s as the leader of all Normans in the region. He then secured his position with a strategic marriage in 1058 to the Lombard princess Sichelgaita (pronounced more or less as spelled: "sickle-gate-a"). This marriage eventually brought Salerno under Giscard's influence, but it also created a formidable husband-and-wife partnership. Also tall and powerfully built, Sichelgaita was as bellicose as her husband and just as awesome. Anna Comnena tells us that "When dressed in full armor, the woman was a fearsome sight."[3] Strengthened by both conquest and marriage, Guiscard won papal acknowledgment of his power the following year. At the Treaty of Melfi (1059), the pope gave Guiscard the title of duke and received in return his homage as a papal vassal.

From the Treaty of Melfi onward, the Normans were partners of the popes, and their conquests were holy wars. For its part, the papacy, which was then asserting its claims against the overmighty interests of German emperors in the north of the Italian peninsula, came more and more to depend on the military support of Duke Robert. In 1060, with papal blessings, Guiscard invaded the populous Muslim island of Sicily, driven more by Norman greed than Christian zeal. The island was prosperous and well defended, and its conquest consumed more than thirty years. Once the invasion was well under way, however, Guiscard turned the campaign over to his younger brother Roger and launched an attack against Byzantine holdings in the southern Italian peninsula. In 1071 he captured Bari, Byzantium's chief Italian seaport. Then, returning to Sicily, he combined forces with his brother Roger to seize the great Muslim metropolis of Palermo in 1072. Palermo had been one of the leading urban centers of the Islamic world, and its bustling harbor was the key to the central Mediterranean. With Palermo, Bari, and all of the southern Italian peninsula under his control, Guiscard was in position to dominate Mediterranean commerce.

His ambitions were limitless. In 1080, again with papal backing, he attacked the Byzantine Empire, hungering for Constantinople itself. As Anna Comnena describes the crucial battle of Durazzo, the Normans were first put to flight by the Byzantines. But Sichelgaita galloped majestically after her husband's retreating army, her long hair streaming out beneath her helmet and her spear raised above her head. In a deafening voice, she shouted, "How far will you flee? Stand and acquit yourselves like men!" Reinvigorated by this challenge to their masculinity, the Normans ceased their flight, returned to battle, and won the victory.[4]

In 1084, in the midst of his Byzantine campaign, Guiscard was called back to the Italian peninsula by his political ally Pope Gregory VII (r. 1073–1085), whose conflicts with Emperor Henry IV (r. 1056–1106) had left him besieged within a fortress in Rome.

---

[3] Anna Comnena (1083–c. 1155) was the daughter of the Byzantine Emperor Alexius Comnenus. Well educated and well liked by the populace, she tried to place her husband on the Byzantine throne after her father's death. Her brother foiled her plans and placed her in a monastery. There, she wrote the *Alexiad,* a history of her father's reign and an essential source for, among other things, the history of Sicily and the First Crusade.

[4] For more on Sichelgaita's career, see Patricia Skinner, "'Halt! Be Men!': Sikelgaita of Salerno, Gender and the Norman Conquest of Italy," *Gender and History* 12:3 (2000), pp. 622–641.

When Guiscard and Sichelgaita returned to rescue Gregory VII, the news of their advance sufficed to send Henry IV fleeing northward. But their rescue turned into a riot. The Normans entered Rome peacefully, restored the pope, and then plundered the city. These Norman soldiers—Christians and allies of the papacy—caused greater devastation than ever had the Visigoths and Vandals in the fifth century. They even sold some of Rome's leading citizens into slavery.

In 1085 Robert Guiscard died, with Sichelgaita at his side, in the midst of still another campaign against Byzantium. His rags-to-riches career displays in full measure the limitless opportunities and ruthlessness of the age. His epitaph displays his (justified) arrogance:

> Here lies Guiscard, the terror of the world,
> Who out of Rome the Roman Emperor hurled . . .

The Norman Kingdom of Sicily

Guiscard was a bandit and warrior, but he established in Sicily and the southern Italian peninsula one of the most sophisticated states in medieval Europe. Norman control of the region was given formal recognition in 1130 when a pope sanctioned the coronation of Guiscard's nephew, Roger the Great (r. 1130–1154), as King of Sicily. With his capital at the Sicilian metropolis of Palermo, Roger surveyed a Kingdom of Sicily that included most of the southern Italian peninsula as well as Sicily proper. His government effectively blended the lord-vassal structure of Norman feudalism with the administrative sophistication of Italian Byzantines and Sicilian Muslims. Its culture just as effectively blended Norman, Byzantine, and Muslim traditions. The result can be seen in the stunning Capella Palatina ("Palace Chapel") built in the twelfth century inside the Norman palace at Palermo (see Figure 9.1). The design of high nave and lower side aisles probably derives from other churches of Western Christendom; the interior glitters with mosaics in the Byzantine style; and the decor of the vaulted ceiling suggests a Muslim paradise, inhabited by jinns instead of Christian angels. The overall effect of the church, despite its diverse cultural ingredients, is one of unity—echoing the achievement of the Norman kingdom of Sicily in unifying peoples of many tongues and many pasts into a single, cohesive realm.

Roger the Great ruled strongly but tolerantly over the assorted peoples of his realm—Normans, Byzantines, Muslims, Jews, Latins, and Lombards—with their variety of faiths, customs, and languages. Palermo, with its superb harbor and magnificent palace, its impressive public buildings and luxurious villas, was at once a great commercial center and a crucial point of cultural exchange. Known as the city of the three-fold tongue, Palermo drew its administrators and scholars from Latin, Byzantine, and Muslim traditions alike. Perhaps the greatest of these was the Muslim scholar al-Idrisi (1100–1166), who created a comprehensive study of geography, which he dedicated to Roger the Great (the treatise has been known ever since as "The Book of Roger"). Like Toledo and Constantinople, Palermo became a significant site for the translation of texts from Arabic and Greek into Latin. Sicilian translators provided European scholars with a steady stream of texts drawn from both Greek and Islamic sources, and these translations, together with others passing into Europe from Toledo and Constantinople, would serve as essential foundations for the intellectual achievements of Western Christendom in the thirteenth century.

Figure 9.1   *Capella Palatina*   The relatively small palace church of Roger the Great in Palermo combines Byzantine, Latin, and Islamic artistic traditions. It is one of the gems of twelfth-century architecture.

German Eastward Expansion

While Christian princes were moving south through the Iberian peninsula and Norman warriors were claiming Sicily and the southern Italian peninsula, Germans were pushing to the east, across the Elbe and down the Danube. Eastward expansion differed, however, from expansion in the Iberian and Italian peninsulas in that it was not a planned product of wealthy aristocrats, nor was it sealed with papal approval. Instead, it was more of a grassroots affair, led by local nobles and consolidated by peasant settlers. This was a gradual but steady movement that succeeded, between about 1125 and 1350,

Map 9.2   *German Expansion to the East*   This map shows how German-speaking people moved east in the Central Middle Ages, across the Elbe River and down the Danube, into lands once held by the Slavs. Between 1100 and 1300, these settlements roughly doubled the area of German influence. This map also shows a later development: that is, the control that the German military order of the Teutonic knights exercised over the north Baltic by the late fourteenth century.

in pushing the eastern boundary of German settlement far to the north and east. This boundary moved at the expense of the resident Slavic population, which sometimes adopted the customs of its German conquerors and sometimes was displaced by them. Some German lords merely absorbed conquered Slavic villages into their regime, but others consolidated military gains by building villages populated by German peasants. Through both settlement and assimilation, then, these new areas were in large part Christianized, Germanized, and, of course, Europeanized (see Map 9.2).

In this region, as well as regions to the south, Catholic Christianity competed with Orthodox Christianity. Sometimes the two Churches cooperated, as they had done when the brothers St. Cyril (c. 826–869) and St. Methodius (c. 815–884) went as missionaries to the Slavs in the ninth century. But sometimes they argued vigorously, as happened in the case of the Bulgarians (whose first Christian king cleverly courted both the Roman pope and the patriarch of Constantinople). In the end, Poles, Bohemians, Hungarians, and Croats looked westward, accepting the authority of the pope in Rome. Russians, Serbs, and Bulgarians looked to the east and the patriarch of Constantinople. These choices created a profound and fractured divide through eastern Europe, one that can still fuel hostilities, as, for example, in the states of the former Yugoslavia. It can also still fuel uncertain historical categories. In many history departments today, Russian history is categorized sometimes as part of European history and sometimes not. In such cases, the Carolingian assumption that "Europe" was equivalent to "Western Christendom" has continued into the present.

✳ CRUSADES

In the Central Middle Ages, then, a "Europe besieged" gave way to an "expanding Europe." We have traced the main frontiers and conflicts, but there were others, too. In 1171, for example, Henry II of England (r. 1154–1189), armed with papal authority, invaded Ireland, thereby beginning the long, tortured, and as yet unfinished history of Anglo-Irish conflict. These conquests expanded what it meant to be "European," for as Europe pushed out its frontiers, it also opened itself to new possibilities—to Jewish and Muslim cultures in Christian Iberia, to Muslim and Byzantine traditions in Norman Sicily, and to Eastern Orthodox Christianity in the Balkans and eastern Europe. Yet Europeans, although open to the new influences brought by these conquests, were also propelled by Christian militancy. They brought their own culture—and political power—with them. Nothing better illustrates the possibilities and dangers of this Christian militancy than the Crusades.

The crusading movement grew out of developments in both east and west. In the east, the balance of power between the Byzantine empire and various Muslim caliphates (particularly the Abbasids in Persia and the Fatimids in Egypt and Palestine) was upset by the eleventh-century arrival of a new power: the Seljuk Turks who had swept into Persia from central Asia, converted to the Islamic faith, and turned the Abbasid caliphs of Baghdad into their pawns. In 1071 the Seljuks inflicted a nearly fatal wound on the Byzantine Empire when they smashed a Byzantine army at the battle of Manzikert and occupied Asia Minor. That same year, they took Jerusalem from the Fatimids.

In the West, as we have seen, a new power was emerging that would have a special interest in these events: the papacy, reinvigorated and reformed by the Gregorian movement. When stories began to filter into the West of Seljuk atrocities against Christian

MEDIEVAL MYTHS

Right of the First Night

In the movie *Braveheart,* William Wallace (played by Mel Gibson) is a law-abiding Scot until the English impose an abominable new practice on Scotland: the right of an overlord to sleep with a bride on her wedding night. When this primitive custom threatens Wallace's own bride, he rises in rebellion, heroically fights the English, and eventually dies a fearless death. Variously called *jus primae noctis* (right of the first night) and *droit de seigneur* (right of the lord), this custom makes for great drama, but it never actually existed. The false tale of its existence began after the close of the Middle Ages, when the author of a sixteenth-century book concocted a story about how, some five centuries earlier, a saintly king and queen had convinced their nobility to give up this barbarous custom. The idea that medieval people endured such a horror caught on quickly, and within a few generations, it was widely believed to have been practiced, especially in such "barbaric" places as Scotland, Ireland, and Wales. No contemporary evidence for the practice has ever been found, and Alain Boureau's recent study *The Lord's First Night* (1995) has firmly established it as fabrication, not fact. Medieval lords enjoyed many powers, but these did not include the "legal rape" of their female serfs. There is no doubt that medieval lords sometimes fathered bastards from their female servants and tenants. For example, perhaps as many as five bastards of Philip de Somerville lived on his manor of Alrewas in fourteenth-century England. But there is also no doubt that this raw, lordly power was never backed up by formal law or accepted custom. Lords could intimidate, cajole, threaten, and take; they could not command sexual intercourse with their bondwomen as a matter of right. This medieval myth, then, is a modern myth *about* the Middle Ages. So too is the related story that medieval knights, about to head off on crusade, clasped "chastity belts" on their wives. Medieval people never constructed chastity belts or practiced any right of the first night, but modern people have often believed they did.

pilgrims to Jerusalem (the Fatimids had allowed Christians to visit the city in relative peace), the papacy grew concerned. And when the desperate Byzantine emperor, Alexius Comnenus (r. 1081–1118), swallowed his pride and appealed to the West for help, he wrote not to the Holy Roman Emperor or any other secular monarch but to Pope Urban II (r. 1088–1099). Europe, under the leadership of Urban II, was ready to respond.

The crusades fused three characteristic medieval impulses: piety, pugnacity, and greed. All three were essential. Without Christian idealism, the crusades would have been inconceivable, yet the dream of liberating Jerusalem from "the infidel" and reopening it to Christian pilgrims was reinforced mightily by the lure of new lands and vast wealth. The crusaders were provided a superb opportunity to employ their knightly skills in God's service—and to make their fortunes in the bargain.

A crusade presented many advantages to the Church, and when he received the appeal of Alexius Comnenus, Urban II, a masterful reform-minded pope, was quick to grasp the opportunity. First, a crusade enabled the papacy to put itself at the forefront of an immensely popular movement and grasp the moral leadership of Europe. Second, it promised a partial solution to the problem of private warfare. When Urban II proclaimed the crusade, he also proclaimed a peace throughout Western Christendom, forbidding all warfare between Christian and Christian. In this way, he extended the peace movements—both the Peace of God (which prohibited attacks on noncombatants) and the Truce of God (which outlawed warfare on holy days)—by which churchmen, with the backing of the peasantry and some nobles, had been *attempting* to curb the violence of the aristocracy within Western Europe for more than a century. The crusade, strangely enough, was the climax of these earlier peace movements. Although Urban's peace was not everywhere honored, it did have the effect of protecting, to some degree, the estates of crusaders from the greedy designs of their stay-at-home enemies.

Third, crusading also contributed to peace within Western Christendom by redirecting the ferocity of aristocratic warriors outward toward Muslims. Knights who had previously been condemned by the Church for their random violence and cruelty were now lauded as soldiers of Christ fighting against the heathen. Thus Christian knighthood became a holy vocation; instead of begging the Church's forgiveness and doing acts of penance for their military violence, knights were invited to achieve salvation *through* the exercise of their martial skills. Indeed, the Church pictured crusading as an act of Christian love—toward persecuted fellow Christians in the East, certainly, but also toward Christ himself, who had suffered, in the Church's view, from the loss of his rightful lordship over the Holy Land and its "pollution" by nonbelievers. Just as a good vassal must help his lord recover a stolen lordship, so too must the Christian knight endeavor to restore Jerusalem to his God.

The Popular Crusade and the First Crusade

Accordingly, in 1095, Pope Urban II summoned Christian warriors to take up the cross and reconquer the Holy Land. He delivered a spellbinding address to the Frankish aristocracy at Clermont in central France, calling on them to emulate the brave deeds of their ancestors, to avenge Seljuk atrocities (which he described in bloodcurdling detail), to win the biblical land of milk and honey for Western Christendom, and to drive "the infidel" from Jerusalem. Finally, he promised those who undertook crusading the highest of spiritual rewards: "Set out on this journey and you will obtain the remission of your sins and be sure of the incorruptible glory of the Kingdom of Heaven."

With shouts of "God wills it!" French warriors poured into crusading armies. So too did ordinary people—peasants, townspeople, women, children, even the infirm and the aged. It was their "Popular Crusade" that first reached Constantinople in 1096. Led by the spellbinding preaching of Peter the Hermit (c. 1050–1115), this "army" was poor, ill-equipped, disorganized, lacking in military discipline, and driven by simply extraordinary religious faith. Many died even before reaching Constantinople; most of the rest died shortly thereafter when Alexius Comnenus, horrified by their ragtag army, shipped them across the Bosphorus where they were quickly cut down by Seljuk troops; a few (including Peter) survived to join the more professional force that arrived the following year.

That force, composed primarily of knights from central and southern France, Normandy, and Norman Sicily, was better prepared, more disciplined, and armed for war. It made its way across the Balkans and assembled at Constantinople. Altogether the warriors of the First Crusade numbered 25,000 to 30,000, a relatively modest figure by modern standards but immense in the eyes of contemporaries. Emperor Alexius, already disconcerted by the Popular Crusade, was also disturbed by the magnitude of the aristocratic response to his request for military support. As he put it, he found that he had a new barbarian invasion on his hands. Cautious and apprehensive, he demanded and obtained from the crusaders a promise that they would do homage to him for all the lands they might conquer.

From the beginning, Western crusaders and their Byzantine allies differed in both temperament and objective. The Byzantines wanted only to recapture the provinces of Asia Minor lost at Manzikert and related defeats; Western crusaders were determined on nothing less than the conquest of the Holy Land. Alexius promised military aid, but it was never forthcoming, and not long after the crusaders left Constantinople, they broke with the Byzantines altogether. Hurling themselves southeastward across Asia Minor into Syria, they encountered and defeated Muslim forces, captured Antioch after a long and complex siege, and in the summer of 1099 took Jerusalem itself.

The crusaders celebrated their capture of Jerusalem by plundering the city and pitilessly slaughtering its Muslim and Jewish inhabitants. A Christian eyewitness described the sack of Jerusalem in these words:

> If you had been there, your feet would have been stained up to the ankles with the
> blood of the slain. What more shall I tell? Not one of them was allowed to live.
> They did not spare the women and children.

With the capture of Jerusalem after only three years of campaigning, the goal of the First Crusade had been achieved. No future crusade was to enjoy such success, and during the two centuries that followed, the original conquests were gradually lost. For the moment, however, Europe rejoiced at the triumph of its crusaders. Most of them returned to their homes and received heroes' welcomes. But several thousand stayed to enjoy the fruits of their conquests. A long strip of territory along the eastern Mediterranean shore had been wrested from the Seljuks and was now divided among the crusader knights. These warriors consolidated their conquests by erecting elaborate castles, whose ruins survive to this day, sometimes as tourist attractions and sometimes still as sites of military operations (see Color Illustration 10).

As Map 9.3 shows, the conquered lands were organized into four **crusader states**: the county of Edessa, the principality of Antioch (ruled by a son of Robert Guiscard), the county of Tripoli, and the kingdom of Jerusalem. This last was the most important, and the king of Jerusalem was theoretically the overlord of the other three states. In fact, however, he had difficulty enforcing his authority outside his own kingdom and sometimes even within it. Thus, the crusader states were tormented from the beginning by rivalries and dissension. Despite their earlier promises, neither the king of Jerusalem nor his counts offered any homage to the emperor in Constantinople.

The Second and Third Crusades

Gradually over the years, Muslim armies began to recover their lands. For many chroniclers and commentators, the cause was obvious: both the soldiers of crusading armies and those who had settled in the crusader states had succumbed to wickedness and debauchery. As one churchman lamented in a letter written home from the Holy Land, "I weep and am sorely grieved to report that our army has given itself over to disgraceful pursuits and indulges in idleness and lust instead of the practice of virtue. The Lord is not present in the camp; there is no one who does good." Whatever the reasons, when Edessa fell before a Muslim army in 1144, the disaster gave rise to a renewal of crusading fervor in Europe.

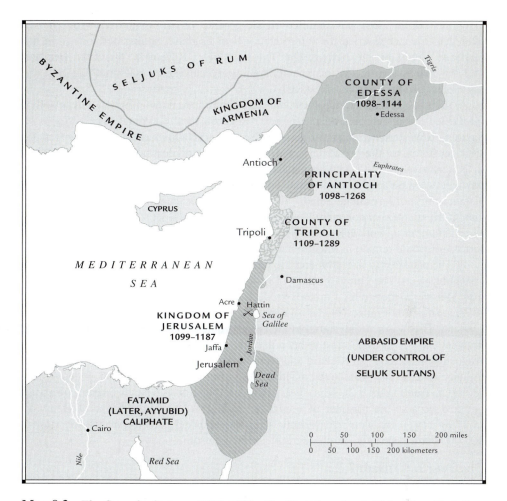

Map 9.3 *The Crusader States, c. 1100–1300*   The First Crusade established four "Latin" states in the Middle East that were ruled by crusaders from Western Europe and their descendants. As this map shows, these four states formed a small sliver of Catholic-controlled territory that faced the Mediterranean on one side and various Muslim states on most other sides. These fragile crusader states eventually crumbled, but for much of the twelfth and thirteenth centuries, they were outposts of Western culture in the East.

The Second Crusade (1147–1148) was inspired by the powerful preaching of Bernard of Clairvaux (1090–1153) and led by a king of France and a Holy Roman Emperor. It began with high hopes but ended in defeat. The crusaders returned home shamefaced and empty-handed, prompting Bernard to describe the campaign as "an abyss so deep that I must call him blessed who is not scandalized by it." Among other things, the Second Crusade helped to end the marriage of Eleanor of Aquitaine (c. 1122–1204) and King Louis VII of France (r. 1137–1180). Married young and always ill-matched, they went their separate ways on the crusade—Louis careening from one defeat to the next and Eleanor reveling in the sophisticated court culture of the crusader states. Within a few years of their return, the marriage (which had produced two daughters but no sons) was annulled on the grounds of consanguinity. A few months after that, Eleanor married the future Henry II of England; among her sons from this marriage would be the hero of the Third Crusade, Richard I "the Lion-Hearted" (r. 1189–1199), featured in this chapter's Biographical Sketch (see pp. 232–233), and his hapless brother John (r. 1199–1216).

In the 1170s and 1180s, a new, unified Islamic state grew in Egypt, galvanized by the skilled leadership of a warrior-prince named Salah al-din Yusuf (1137–1193)—or Saladin, to Western ears. Chivalrous as well as able, Saladin negotiated a truce with the crusader states, but the rise of his new principality nevertheless posed an ominous threat to their survival. In 1187, a hotheaded Christian baron broke the truce and forced a show-down between Saladin's army and the combined forces of the crusaders at Hattin, some distance north of Jerusalem. Saladin surrounded the crusader army and virtually annihi-lated it. He then easily conquered large portions of the crusader states and next occupied Jerusalem after a two-week siege. Save for one brief interval in the thirteenth century, Jerusalem would remain in Muslim hands for the remainder of the Middle Ages.

The catastrophe at Hattin and the fall of Jerusalem resulted in still another major crusading effort. The Third Crusade (1189–1193) was led by three of medieval Europe's most illustrious monarchs: Emperor Frederick Barbarossa (r. 1152–1190), King Philip II "Augustus" of France (r. 1180–1223), and King Richard I "the Lion-Hearted" of England. This was a strong start, but the crusade quickly faltered. Frederick Barbarossa drowned on the way, and most of his army trudged back to their German homes. Philip Augustus quarreled with Richard and went home. Richard, although he enjoyed much military success and won back considerable portions of the Holy Land, failed to take Jerusalem (see Figure 9.2). Worse yet, Richard fell into hostile hands on his return jour-ney and became the prisoner of Frederick Barbarossa's son, the Emperor Henry VI (r. 1190–1197). He won release only after England had paid the staggering sum of 100,000 pounds sterling—quite literally a king's ransom.

The Fourth Crusade

Within a decade, Europe was ready for still another attempt on Jerusalem. The Fourth Crusade (1201–1204) had as its instigator the most powerful of medieval popes,

Figure 9.2 *Richard the Lion-Hearted and Saladin*   This drawing from the fourteenth-century Luttrell Psalter depicts a legendary event: a joust between Richard the Lion-Hearted (on the left) and Saladin (on the right).

Innocent III. Like the First Crusade, it was led not by kings but by great territorial princes—most notably, Baldwin IX, count of Flanders (r. in Flanders 1194–1206). It was the oddest of the crusades. It never reached the Holy Land at all; it wreaked horrific damage on Constantinople; and yet in its own way, it was spectacularly successful.

The crusaders resolved to avoid the perils of overland travel by crossing to the Holy Land in Venetian ships. Unfortunately, they overestimated their numbers and, as a result, contracted with the Venetians for many more ships than were necessary (and at far too great a cost). Venice nevertheless agreed to take what money the crusaders had and to transport them to the Holy Land *if* they would do a small errand on the way: re-capture for Venice the Adriatic port of Zara, which the king of Hungary had seized some years before. Innocent III was infuriated by this bargain, since it pitched the crusaders against a Christian king who was not only a good Catholic but a papal vassal as well. When he heard that the crusaders had attacked Zara, Innocent excommunicated them and washed his hands of the whole enterprise.

Nevertheless, the crusaders went doggedly on. After capturing Zara in 1202, the crusaders were again diverted, this time by a dispute in Constantinople over the imperial succession. The crusaders slowly grew frustrated by their inability to navigate the complex waters of Byzantine politics, and they turned from allies into conquerors. They resolved to take Constantinople for themselves, to elect a new Byzantine emperor from their own ranks, and to divide the Byzantine empire among them.

Accordingly, in 1204 the crusaders besieged Constantinople, took it by storm, and subjected it to three long-remembered days of pillage and massacre. The impregnable Byzantine capital had fallen at last to enemy conquerors; the crusaders had succeeded where barbarians, Persians, Bulgars, Avars, and Muslims had failed. Count Baldwin be-came emperor, and he and his successors ruled in Constantinople for over half a century. The crusaders under his command, although permanently diverted from the Holy Land by the wealth of Constantinople, could claim to have accomplished a great deal. After all, the Eastern Orthodox and Catholic Churches had been reunited by their efforts, and what Pope Leo I (r. 440–461) had claimed long ago—that the pope in Rome should govern *all* Christians, east as well as west—was finally achieved. The patriarch in Constantinople was no longer the pope's rival, but instead his subordinate. Innocent III, who had absolved the crusaders from excommunication after the fall of Zara and had excommunicated them anew for attacking Constantinople, readmitted them once again to communion when he realized the "great blessings" that had befallen Western Christendom by their seizure of the "schismatic" city.

Baldwin stayed in Constantinople, but most of the crusaders returned to Europe with plunder from the Byzantine metropolis: precious gems, money, and gold. The greatest prize of all was the immense store of holy relics that they brought home from the Byzantine capital: bones, heads, and arms of saints, Jesus' crown of thorns, St. Thomas the Apostle's doubting finger, and many similar treasures. Although much was lost in the conflagration of Constantinople, its conquest also offered Western Christendom a third access point to the intellectual legacies of Greek and Byzantine civilization. Like the conquests of Iberia and Sicily but to a more limited extent, the conquest of Constantinople and its libraries—those that were not destroyed—opened new intellectual worlds to the scholars of Europe.

Although successful from its own perspective, the Fourth Crusade was simply a disaster for Byzantium. A nucleus of the old Byzantine state held out in Asia Minor,

BIOGRAPHICAL SKETCH

Richard the Lion-Hearted (1157–1199)

Only a few people have been memorialized with statues in front of the Houses of Parliament in London, and one of these was king of England from 1189–1199: Richard I, the Lion-Hearted. In a sentimental sculpture of Victorian design, Richard is shown astride a horse, crowned, and raising his sword high above his head. The sculpture is inspiring artistry, but somewhat peculiar history, for Richard spent almost no time at all in England. He was born in England (in 1157) and king of it for the last decade of his life, but his heart lay elsewhere—in France and the Holy Land. There he established himself as the foremost soldier of his day, as Coeur de Lion, Lion-Heart.

The second son of Henry II of England and Eleanor of Aquitaine, Richard was expected to inherit only the Duchy of Aquitaine. Thus, he was raised there and much favored by his mother. His parents' marriage was, to put it mildly, tumultuous, and Richard took his mother's side. He first joined his mother and brothers in a revolt when he was just sixteen; it ended with his mother imprisoned, his brothers subdued, and Richard prostrate at his father's feet, begging for forgiveness. He got it, but he got his revenge too. Some fifteen years later, he joined with Philip Augustus of France in a second revolt against his father. He won victory after victory. No matter that his father was mortally ill: a conference was held, humiliating concessions were secured, and within two days, Henry II was dead. Richard, heir to England since the death of his elder brother some six years before, was now king.

He immediately went to England to be crowned and to arrange the realm's governance: four months sufficed. Then, he went on crusade, on what history now calls the Third Crusade. On the way, he harried Sicily and conquered Cyprus. He extracted himself from one marriage promise (to the sister of his fellow crusader Philip Augustus) and contracted another (to the daughter of the king of Navarre). And he got seasick a lot, for he was a notoriously bad sailor. When once again on dry land, he put his genius for war to good work. He took the stronghold of Acre. He met and defeated Saladin at the battle of Arsuf. He took Jaffa, a critical supply point. And then he headed for Jerusalem.

Richard got within a few miles of the city, but he had to turn back when word reached him that Philip Augustus, once his friend and now his enemy, was conniving with his brother John to seize his lands. On his way back home, Richard ran into even harder luck: he was captured and held for ransom by Emperor Henry VI (r. 1190–1197). After languishing in prison more than a year and writing some self-pitying songs while there, he was finally set free. He traveled briefly to England to stabilize his position there (it took all of two months), and then he returned to France where he spent the next five years fighting— and winning—various territorial wars.

One evening, at the age of 42, Richard rode out without armor to inspect the works of his latest siege. When he spied a lone crossbow-man on the ramparts of the besieged castle, a soldier brave enough to show his face but ill-equipped enough to have to use a frying-pan as a shield, Richard applauded his bravery in one minute and found himself shot in the shoulder in the next. The wound became infected, and he died within a few days.

There is no doubt that Richard inspired the loyalty, love, and admiration of his contemporaries. He shared the same hardships that he asked his soldiers to share; he was fearless in battle; and his troops would, as one contemporary put it, wade through blood as far as the Pillars of Hercules [that is, Gibraltar] for his sake. Or, as another bragged, "I say with pride that my lord is the finest knight on earth." Even his enemies admired him. As one

Muslim chronicler conceded, "Richard's courage, shrewdness, energy, and patience made him the most remarkable ruler of his times."

Yet Richard the Lion-Hearted has also been the subject of much myth-making: that he met with Robin Hood and amiably supported his grievances; that he jousted with Saladin (as in Figure 9.2); that he killed a lion by reaching through its mouth to rip out its heart. And he has been the subject of just as much historical debate. Was he a good warrior but an awful king? Was he a married man but homosexual in his preferences? Was he courageous in battle but foolhardy about his own safety? These debates will long continue, for the sources are contradictory and obscure.

Of one thing we can be certain. Richard spent no more than six months of his reign in England, and he levied extraordinary taxes on the English in order to finance his crusade and, later, his ransom. His statue before Parliament celebrates his military prowess, but for the English of Richard's day he was possibly most remembered for the unprecedented ways in which he managed to get money—and then more money—out of them. To one of them, he seemed less a great warrior and more "like a robber permanently on the prowl, always probing, always searching for the weak spot where there is something for him to steal." Before the English Parliament, then, stands not only a great warrior but also an ingenious and relentless collector of taxes.

nursing its grievances and gathering its strength, until in 1261 Baldwin's dynasty was overthrown and, after a fifty-seven-year hiatus, Greek emperors reigned once again in Constantinople. The irksome power of the Roman pope was shrugged off, and the patriarch of Constantinople resumed his traditional role as head of the autonomous Eastern Orthodox Church. To his successors, few things would be as distasteful as the thought of another union with the Catholic Christians who had so violently and so briefly imposed their authority on the East: 'Better the sultan's turban than the cardinal's hat' became their watchword. All told, however, the sack of Constantinople in 1204 delivered a blow from which Byzantine society—and the political authority of its emperors—never entirely recovered.

Hostility between the two heirs of Rome—old Western Empire and old Eastern Empire—was nothing new in 1204. The Catholic and Eastern Orthodox Churches had long argued about their relative authority, an argument symbolized, as we have seen, by the mutual excommunications of pope and patriarch in 1054. And almost from the moment the first crusader entered Constantinople in 1096, Alexius Comnenus seemed to regret his request for Western aid; his lukewarm enthusiasm for the crusaders and the crusader states was shared by all his successors. Yet the Sack of Constantinople in 1204 created a virtually insurmountable wall of hatred. Western Christians had ravaged Constantinople, killing innumerable people and virtually killing a society, too. As they wantonly destroyed churches, icons, buildings, and statues, crusaders destroyed some of the greatest artifacts of a great culture. Even today in Istanbul (the former Constantinople), local guides still mutter about "those accursed crusaders."

Later Crusades

During the thirteenth century, a variety of other crusades—mostly notable for their failures—launched fervent Western Christians toward the Holy Land. In 1212 a visionary, ill-organized enterprise known as the "Children's Crusade" ended in tragedy. Thousands of boys and girls flocked into the ports of southern Europe, gripped by religious fervor and convinced (wrongly) that the Mediterranean would dry up so that they could walk to the Holy Land. Some returned home; some were sold into slavery; some died. In 1217–1221, the Fifth Crusade (the Children's Crusade, as a movement more than a military campaign, does not count in the reckoning of crusades) was directed at a new target: Egypt, the real center of Muslim power in the eastern Mediterranean. When the crusaders captured the key Egyptian port of Damietta in 1219, they soon found themselves caught between a Muslim army and the flooding Nile. Theirs was another joyless homecoming.

A decade later, the brilliant Emperor Frederick II (r. 1215–1250) led a largely peaceful expedition that in 1229 obtained possession of Jerusalem by treaty. This crusade—too bloodless to be counted in the reckoning—marked an important shift in crusading from papal to royal initiative. Indeed, Frederick II was under a papal decree of excommunication when he sailed to the Holy Land. Royal initiative lay behind the next two crusades as well, the Sixth and Seventh Crusades led by the saint-king of France, Louis IX (r. 1226–1270). Both failed, and the latter cost St. Louis his life. Crusades continued to be organized and mounted in subsequent generations, but in 1291 the fall of Acre—the last Christian bridgehead on the Syrian coast—brought an end to the crusader states in the Holy Land.

Military Orders

Several religious orders of Christian warriors grew out of the crusading ideal. Bound by monastic rules and dedicated to advancing the crusading cause in every possible way, these crusading orders combined the two great medieval institutions of monasticism and knighthood. One such order was the Knights Templar, an international brotherhood that acquired great wealth through pious gifts and intelligent estate management and gradually became involved in far-flung banking activities. Another was known as the Hospitalers, an order that drew chiefly on French knights for its membership. A third order, the Teutonic Knights, drew entrants mainly from the German states. With the waning of crusades in the thirteenth century, the Teutonic Knights transferred their activities from the Holy Land to northeast Europe, where they advanced German and Christian interests against the Slavs. They penetrated, for a time, as far northward as Lithuania, Latvia, and Estonia and even into the Russian states (see Map 9.2). Similar military orders arose on other frontiers of Western Christendom. The Knights of Santiago de Compostela, for example, were dedicated to fighting Muslims in Iberia.

Combining Christian life with military prowess, men in these orders were widely admired in their time for fighting "against spiritual weakness with the virtues of the heart and against physical enemies with the strength of your bodies." But they were not invulnerable to criticism. Because they were largely free of royal or episcopal supervision, they posed a threat to both, and after crusading enthusiasms waned, they remained powerful but less admired.

The Crusades in Perspective

By the time Acre fell in 1291, the crusading ideal had crippled the Byzantine Empire, which had good reason to regret Alexius Comnenus's request for help in 1095. In a curious twist, crusaders had strengthened Muslim power in the Middle East, for

Muslims had responded to Christian threat by reorganization, not retreat. For Western Christendom, the crusades expanded the boundaries of "Europe," at least briefly, to the crusader states of the Middle East. The crusades also enhanced the growing power of popes who, as monarchs of Western Christendom, caught the militant imagination of European Christians and united them in a single vast effort. Merchants benefited, too, for crusaders extended Christian maritime dominion into the eastern Mediterranean and the Black Sea, firmly establishing Western commercial interests in these areas. And, perhaps most of all, the crusades brought many more Europeans than before into close contact with Muslims and Byzantines. It is no mere coincidence that Arabic was first studied in Europe in the twelfth century or that, at the same time, European libraries began to fill up with books that had been long lost to Western scholars, but were now "found" in Muslim and Byzantine libraries and translated into Latin.

✷ Persecutions

The greed, violence, and religious militancy at the heart of the crusading movement also fostered the growth of a persecuting mentality within Europe. Heretics faced new threats; so too did Jews, other minorities, and eventually, even some militant Christians.

Crusades and Inquisition within Europe

During the thirteenth century, popes called for crusades not only against Muslims in the Holy Land and Iberia but also against Europeans, including at one point the Holy Roman Emperor. Of these internal holy wars, the most devastating was the Albigensian Crusade launched against the Cathar heresy in the early thirteenth century.

As we saw in the last chapter, Cathars were thick on the ground in southern France in the early thirteenth century. They had, in effect, their own institutionalized Church, with priests, bishops, liturgy, theology, and even monasteries. Pope Innocent III, recognizing the gravity of the situation, tried with every means in his power to eradicate the heresy. He removed incompetent and corrupt clerics, he urged the nobility to help suppress the Cathars, and he encouraged the revitalization of orthodoxy through the preaching of such men as St. Dominic (1170–1221). When none of these measures succeeded, Innocent III summoned a crusade against the Cathars.

The Albigensian Crusade (1209–1229) was a savage affair that crushed Catharism only after two decades of relentless bloodshed. The French monarchy intervened in its final stages and brought it to a successful conclusion, thereby extending royal authority to the shores of the Mediterranean. Southern France recovered quickly from the ravages of northern knights, but north-south antagonisms long endured. The task of searching out hard-core heretics and keeping the region free of heresy gave rise to inquisitorial practices that exemplify the medieval Church at its most repressive.

Although heretical ideas and heretics were nothing new in the history of Christianity, it was not until after the Albigensian Crusade that the papacy deemed it necessary to establish firmer methods of combating heresy. Bishops had long been expected to inquire into heresy within their dioceses; in the 1230s, Pope Gregory IX (r. 1227–1241) began to augment episcopal inquiries with men he appointed as **inquisitors.** Most were Dominican or Franciscan friars, and they were well educated, deeply religious, and responsible to the pope himself. They were also endowed with sweeping powers. As they traveled through southern Europe looking for heretics, they employed torture, secret testimony, conviction on slight evidence, denial of legal council to the accused, and other practices that far exceeded the carefully defined limits of medieval canon law. To the inquisitors and those who supported them, this excess was absolutely necessary; they exercised a kind of martial law, required by the urgency of the war against heresy.

Inquisitors aroused strong regional opposition, less on humanitarian grounds than because they usurped the traditional rights of bishops and lay lords. Most inquisitors endeavored to act fairly, and the great majority of heretics were imprisoned or given lesser penances (such as wearing crosses over their clothing). Some were condemned to death, but even these were handed over to lay authorities for execution so that no inquisitors themselves took human life. In time, Dominicans, members of an order that St. Dominic had founded to preach to heretics, became the leading inquisitors of heretics.

Inquisitorial procedures cannot be justified, but, like all historical developments, they can be explained. To orthodox Christians in the medieval West, heresy was a hateful thing, a betrayal of Christ, a source of eternal damnation, and a plague that could spread its infection to others. Inquisitors fought against what they perceived as a near and present danger. They would be neither the first nor the last instance of people unable to respond calmly to the presence of beliefs or practices different from their own.

Jews and Other European Minorities

As we saw in Chapter 1, the institutionalization of Christianity in the Late Roman Empire had been accompanied by some deterioration in the status of Jews. By the Early Middle Ages, Jewish communities were sometimes under threat and sometimes secure. In seventh-century Iberia, Jews had to contend with a royal policy of forced conversion; yet in Carolingian Francia, they were welcomed and protected by royal charters. By the eleventh century, many towns boasted Jewish families that, while distinct from the Christian majority, nevertheless coexisted with them in relative harmony.

Then, in the twelfth century and after, this uneasy cooperation was replaced by violent persecution. We have already briefly glimpsed the persecutions to which Jews were subject from the twelfth century on: attacks during the First Crusade, the ritual murder accusations that began in Norwich in 1144 and spread rapidly thereafter, and the plight of Jews in the Christian kingdoms of Iberia in the fourteenth century. These were part of a much larger trend, for from the twelfth century Christians often required Jews to wear special badges or hats, to practice only certain occupations, and to live only in specified localities. Christians also began to attack and even murder Jews.

Historians disagree about the causes for this momentous change, but two factors seem especially important. First, Christian self-awareness and devotion to the suffering Christ played a role. Color Illustration 7 shows the first fully sculpted depiction of Christ on the cross. Completed in the late tenth century, it marks a new Christian emphasis on the redemptive suffering of Christ, an emphasis that grew ever stronger through the Central and Later Middle Ages. Popular sentiment, ignoring the sound reasoning of theologians that Christ had *voluntarily* died for the sins of all, held that he was *murdered* by the Jews. And some Christians, aroused by the pious practice of contemplating the painful story of Christ's suffering at the crucifixion, arrived at the grotesque conclusion that this "murder" should be avenged. In this sense, a shift in Christian practice toward a focus on the redemptive suffering of Christ prompted a rise in Christian prejudice.

Second, the crusades heightened anti-Jewish sentiment. At the outset of the First Crusade, it occurred to some crusaders that their mission to subdue "infidels" abroad might be prefaced by slaughtering the Jewish minority in Western Christendom itself. According to one Christian writer, the maddened crusaders "rose in a spirit of cruelty against the Jewish people scattered throughout these cities and slaughtered them without mercy." Jewish communities in central Europe were especially hard hit. Massacres of Jews did not begin with the crusades, but they became more frequent thereafter. As in Norwich in 1144, most were prompted by absurd rumors that Jews had murdered Christian children or had desecrated the Eucharist (see Color Illustration 8). Pope Gregory X (r. 1271–1276) ordered in 1272 that Jews arrested on such slanderous pretexts be freed, but such orders were usually ignored.

As Gregory's decree suggests, the papacy, although never a friend of Jews, did endeavor to protect them from the violence of popular prejudice. Kings and emperors sometimes did the same, but they demanded much in return for their protection: they forced Jews to lend them money, milked them through arbitrary taxes, seized the property of Jews who had died without heirs, and charged enormous sums for the right to travel freely, enjoy a fair trial, and bequeath property. In the end, even these monarchs abandoned their Jewish subjects, expelling them from one kingdom after another (this was especially easy to do by the thirteenth century, when Italian bankers provided alternative sources of commercial and royal credit). Jews were expelled from Jerusalem in 1099, England in 1290, and France in 1306 (with repeated decrees thereafter); various self-governing German cities in the 1420s; and Spain, Portugal, and Lithuania in the 1490s.

Christian theologians also contributed to this incessant beat of anti-Jewish sentiment. Early Christians had tolerated but often denigrated Judaism, and their ambivalent views survived in medieval theology. Some medieval theologians argued that Jews were worthy witnesses to the faith of the Old Testament. Many others were less tolerant, and they began to teach that Jews of their own time overemphasized the Talmud at the expense of the Bible, thereby committing a heretical lapse from their original faith. According to this twisted logic, Jews could even be punished for blasphemy if they refused to convert to Christianity.

To some historians, these medieval attacks on Jews mark the beginning of a sad history that culminated in the horrors of the concentration camps of Nazi Germany. To other historians, these attacks seem rooted in the special circumstances of Western Christendom in the Central and Later Middle Ages and are not related much—or at all—to modern instances of anti-Semitism. Both arguments have some validity, for the past belongs both to its own time and to the future it creates. In any case, attacks on Jews—although particularly vicious and intense—were part of a larger persecuting trend in medieval Europe. From the twelfth century not only Jews and heretics but also prostitutes, lepers, and men who participated in homosexual acts caused much more anxiety among their neighbors than ever before. Interestingly enough, rumors about all these groups repeated the same themes, again and again: these minorities were supposedly a source of pollution to good Christians; they were portrayed as sexually unregulated; and they were thought to worship the devil. And even more interesting, fears about these groups blended together, as this description of a group of heretics shows:

> About the first watch of the night . . . each family sits waiting in silence in each of
> their synagogues; and there descends by a rope which hangs in their midst a black
> cat of wondrous size. On sight of it they put out the lights and . . . hum with their

closed teeth, and draw near to the place where they saw their master [that is, the black cat], feeling after him and when they have found him they kiss him. The hotter the feelings the lower their aim: some go for his feet, but most for his tail and genitalia. Then as though this disgusting contact has unleashed their appetites, each lays hold of a nearby man or woman and enjoys him or her as much as possible.

This description of Christian heretics includes references to Jewish synagogues, to devil worship (the black cat was a classic stand-in for the devil), sexual orgy (including homosexual acts), and even the first-ever mention of what would develop into a common accusation: the "obscene kiss." This merging of prejudices was not a mere matter of imagination and rhetoric, for attacks on one group sometimes quickly spread to others. In 1321, for example, a French rumor that lepers were plotting to poison wells led to attacks on Jews as well as lepers. From this combination of anxieties came not only persecutions that afflicted many medieval Europeans, but also another trend that would reach a fearsome fruition after 1500: witch-hunting.

The Templars

In the early fourteenth century, charges of this sort were marshaled against a new victim: the Knights Templar. Born of Christian militancy, the Knights Templar were destroyed, in part, by its effects, for they fell victim, as did heretics, Jews, and other minorities, to trumped-up charges of religious and sexual irregularities. In one of the most sordid episodes of medieval history, the Knights Templar were attacked by Philip IV of France (r. 1285–1314). He accused them of blasphemous and homosexual acts; he tortured them to secure confessions; he forced the pope to agree to the order's suppression; and, in March 1314, he burned their leaders—all of whom had retracted their forced confessions—at the stake. Some of the Templar's properties ended up in Philip's hands; others were transferred to the Hospitalers, who have survived to this day in the charitable organization known as the Knights of Malta.

✳ CONCLUSION

The Europe that welcomed the year 1300 was very different from the Europe that had ushered in a new millennium three centuries earlier. By 1300, Europe's internal frontiers of forest and swamp had been transformed into field or pasture, and Europe's external frontiers had been pushed far to the south and east. Europeans had walked in and dominated such wealthy metropolises as Palermo, Toledo, Antioch, Cordoba, and Constantinople. Thanks to these crusades and conquests, Europe was tied as never before to the trade, culture, and intellectual traditions of Islam and Byzantium. In this sense, Europe was opening up, reaching out to the possibilities of a broader world. This process, once started, had a momentum of its own that would lead in many directions—to Marco Polo's travels to China in 1271, to Portuguese explorations of West Africa in the fifteenth century, and to Columbus's fateful voyage in 1492. Yet at the same time that medieval culture opened itself to new influences, it also, in another sense, closed down; Europeans seeking a homogeneity within their borders that would prove highly dangerous and ever elusive. In 1300, the abundance of girls named Maria and boys named John spoke not only to the greater unity of European culture but also perhaps to its growing intolerance of diversity within.

SUGGESTED READINGS

David Abulafia, *The Western Mediterranean Kingdoms 1200–1500: The Struggle for Dominion* (1997). For the centuries it covers, this is the place to start for the history of Spain, Sicily, and the southern Italian peninsula. See also Bernard F. Reilly, *The Medieval Spains* (1993), and Donald Matthew, *The Norman Kingdom of Sicily* (1992).

Robert Bartlett, *The Making of Europe: Conquest, Colonization and Cultural Change, 950–1350* (1993). An essential new analysis; see pages 269–291 for the "Europeanization of Europe." See also J. R. S. Phillips, *The Medieval Expansion of Europe* (2nd edition, 1998).

Robert Chazan, *In the Year 1096: The First Crusade and the Jews* (1996). Brief and readable. See also Miri Rubin, *Gentile Tales: The Narrative Assault on Late Medieval Jews* (1999).

Eric Christiansen, *The Northern Crusades: The Baltic and the Catholic Frontier, 1100–1525* (2nd edition, 1997). The best study of the German advances and reversals to the northeast.

David Douglas, *The Norman Achievement* (1969) and *The Norman Fate* (1976). Expert, readable studies of Norman activities through Europe, 1050–1154.

R. I. Moore, *The Formation of a Persecuting Society* (1987). A pathbreaking study of the rise of persecutions in medieval Europe. See also Jeffrey Richards, *Sex, Dissidence and Damnation: Minority Groups in the Middle Ages* (1991).

Joseph F. O'Callaghan, *Reconquest and Crusade in Medieval Spain* (2003). A new study that conceptualizes the Spanish "reconquest" as part of crusading history.

Edward Peters, *Inquisition* (1989). A fascinating study that traces both the medieval history of inquisition and modern myths about it. See also his *Heresy and Authority in Medieval Europe: Documents in Translation* (1980).

Jonathan Riley-Smith, ed., *The Oxford Illustrated History of the Crusades* (1995). A valuable and splendidly illustrated introduction. See also his *The Crusades: A Short History* (1987), and Jean Richard, *The Crusades, c. 1071–c. 1291* (1999). For religious motivations, see Benjamin Z. Kedar, *Crusade and Mission: European Approaches toward the Muslims* (1984). On specific crusades, see John France, *Victory in the East: A Military History of the First Crusade* (1994), and John Godfrey, *1204, The Unholy Crusade* (1980), on the Fourth Crusade.

John V. Tolan, *Saracens: Islam in the Medieval European Imagination* (2002). Traces how the medieval West first developed derogatory images of Islam.

SUGGESTED PRIMARY SOURCES

S. J. Allen and Emilie Amt, *The Crusades: A Reader* (2003). See also Carole Hillenbrand, *The Crusades: Islamic Perspectives* (2000).

Simon Barton and Richard Fletcher, eds., *The World of El Cid: Chronicles of the Spanish Reconquest* (2000). Four chronicles, each separately introduced and carefully annotated.

Michael Goodich, ed., *Other Middle Ages: Witnesses at the Margins of Medieval Society* (1998). Primary sources on Jews, heretics, "sexual nonconformists," "victims of the devil," and others.

Edward Peters, *Heresy and Authority in Medieval Europe: Documents in Translation* (1980).

CHAPTER 10

WORLDS IN COLLISION
PAPACY AND HOLY ROMAN EMPIRE,
c. 1125-1300

✳ INTRODUCTION

In Germany today, the expression "to make a journey to Canossa" has one clear meaning: surrender. Yet, as we saw in Chapter 8, when Emperor Henry IV (r. 1056–1106)—standing barefoot and penitent in the snow outside the castle at Canossa in 1077—sought the forgiveness of Pope Gregory VII (r. 1073–1085), this was only a strategic move, just one foray in a long and drawn-out controversy over lay investiture. Gregory VII eventually proffered his forgiveness to the shivering emperor at Canossa (see, again, Color Illustration 9), but the two quickly fell out again, and it would take another two generations before their quarrel was resolved by compromise at the Concordat of Worms in 1122. Moreover, their disagreement over lay investiture, although very important, was only one of many issues that pitted the interests of the German emperor against the interests of the Papal **See** in the Central Middle Ages. As we shall see in this chapter, these disputes profoundly shaped both Empire and papacy.

Although Henry IV did not "surrender" at Canossa, the dispute that was so dramatized by his penitence there would, in the long run, have tragic consequences for his Empire. On the eve of Canossa, the German king (or "Holy Roman Emperor," although the term was not regularly used until the twelfth century) was the strongest monarch in Western Christendom. His power extended not only throughout the German states but also into the northern and central Italian peninsula, and it stretched over ecclesiastical affairs as well as matters of secular governance. Some 200 years later, in 1300, the German states were fragmented into largely independent principalities, the northern Italian peninsula was fragmented into city-states, and although there was a Holy Roman Emperor in name, he wielded little practical imperial power.

The trajectory was different for the Papal See. When Gregory VII sat, warm and comfortable, in the castle at Canossa, he was the head of a newly invigorated papacy. He and other reformers had great plans for the growth of papal authority, but in 1077, that authority was more hoped for than realized. Over the next two centuries, many—but not all—of their dreams would come to fruition. No medieval pope ever governed

Western Europe as fully as radical reformers hoped—as a Christendom under the pope's unquestioned *secular* as well as religious authority. But medieval popes did gain better control over ecclesiastical structures, did exercise considerable moral authority throughout the West, and did consolidate their base of secular authority, the Papal States, in the heart of the Italian peninsula.

In a broad sense, then, the equivalence of "to make a journey to Canossa" and "surrender" is not so far off the mark. Henry IV rebounded after Canossa, but the drama of that day—his cold atonement and Gregory VII's warm superiority—presaged the future of Empire and papacy during the Central Middle Ages. While the power of emperors waned, the power of popes waxed strong—at least, for a while.

✳ Papacy and Empire at the End of the Investiture Controversy, c. 1125

In 1122, the investiture controversy finally ended with the Concordat of Worms. The pope agreed that the emperor could be involved, in limited ways, in the selection of bishops and other ecclesiastical officers. Henceforth, the emperor could preside over ecclesiastical elections, he could designate winners in disputed cases, and he could hand to the newly elected officer any symbols of his *secular* power (usually a scepter). But in gaining these concessions, the emperor made concessions of his own. He agreed to the general principle that Church law governed the selection of Church officers, and he also agreed not to confer on a new bishop the symbols of his *religious* power (specifically the episcopal ring and staff). Thus ended in compromise an argument that had begun nearly fifty years before. During that half-century, a lot changed for both German emperors and Roman popes, as Timeline 10.1 shows.

Political Theory

To begin with, the investiture controversy itself stimulated a lot of discussion about the relative roles of church and state—or, to put it another way, a lot of political theory. Was the emperor, as an anointed king, divinely empowered to govern over his realm in matters religious as well as temporal? This had been the vision of Charlemagne (r. 768–814), who sought to rule Christendom with fearsome military prowess and firm Christian piety. It was an ideal that launched many good changes within the Church: the efforts of Charlemagne and Alcuin (c. 732–804) to improve monastic life and pastoral care in the eighth and ninth centuries; the origins in the early 900s of the Cluniac monastic reform (initiated by a pious duke); and even the eleventh-century papal reform, whose first proponents had been elevated to the papacy by none other than the Emperor Henry III (r. 1039–1056). By 1122, however, this *imperialist* position had run its course, and for the rest of the Middle Ages, no king or emperor could credibly claim to govern clergy as well as laity—to be, in effect, God's vicar on earth.

For many others, a *papalist* position then presented the most compelling alternative. Although this position was based in earlier arguments and documents (especially the Donation of Constantine, forged in the eighth century but considered genuine during the Central Middle Ages), it grew more popular in the hands of Humbert of Silva Candida (c. 1000–1061) and other radical reformers in the eleventh century. They argued that the pope was properly the head not only of his Church but also of Christendom. The

TIMELINE 10.1   Papacy and Empire during the Investiture Controversy, 1075–1125

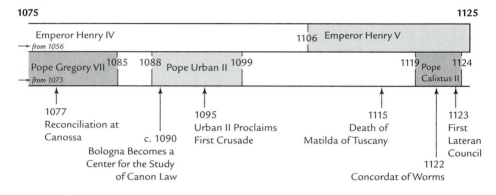

pope was, in other words, a temporal ruler as well as a religious one: he was God's vicar in *all* matters. This argument did not eliminate kings, dukes, nobles, and other secular leaders, but it placed them below the pope and accountable to him. Gregory VII put it very straightforwardly in his "Two Swords Theory": (a) God placed both the spiritual and temporal swords in the pope's hands, (b) the pope might delegate his secular authority by passing the temporal sword to a king or other ruler, but (c) the pope could always reclaim the temporal sword and the authority that came with it. This position was much discussed in the late eleventh and twelfth centuries, and it would reach its fullest potential during the pontificate of Innocent III (r. 1198–1216).

Despite the strong popularity of the papalist position, a third perspective—the *clericalist* argument—continued to find some support. This held that the Church as an institution was properly separate from the political institutions—kingdoms, dukedoms, and the like—of the West. Church and state coexisted, each doing important work specific to its own task and respecting the work of the other. Popes and other clerics guided the Christian faithful; monarchs and other rulers provided peace and stability; and both groups worked together in a fruitful partnership. Yet (and this was an important proviso) in matters that touched religion or morality, the Church was superior, and it could, if necessary, intervene in secular matters to reprimand or otherwise discipline an immoral ruler. The Church was the conscience of the state, but otherwise the two worked independently. This theory, like the other two, had firm roots in Carolingian Europe. Like the other two, it sought not to eliminate either Church or state, but to find the best working balance between the two. Although the clericalist position had little appeal during the surge of papal power that occurred in the late eleventh and twelfth centuries, it never entirely died out.

Papal Authority

The fifty years of the investiture controversy saw steadily increasing papal authority, so that when the controversy ended in 1122, popes were stronger than ever before. Some of this new authority extended beyond the Church itself to Europe in general. As we saw in Chapter 9, when the Byzantine Emperor Alexius Comnenus (r. 1078–1118) sought help from the West in his struggle against the Seljuks, it was to Pope Urban II (r. 1088–1099) that he turned, and when Urban II responded by preaching the First Crusade, he un-leashed people and resources far beyond those he directly controlled. The early cru-sades, all instigated by popes, testify to the expansive moral and religious authority of the reformed papacy.

Yet, a lot of the pope's increased authority was internal to the Church—and no less important for that. By 1122, popes had gained much closer control over the vast structure of the Church, from archbishops and bishops down to lowly priests. The Gregorian reform had insisted on priestly celibacy: married priests were fewer and more embattled with each passing year. The Gregorian reform had insisted that the Church should control clerical appointments: the pope now sat as the acknowledged head of an ecclesiastical hierarchy that stretched across Europe. The Gregorian reform had sought to have the presence of the pope felt by all Christians: papal legates now regularly car-ried the pope's authority with them as they traveled throughout the West. The power of the pope over the officers of the Church was made especially manifest the year after the Concordat of Worms. In 1123, at the First Lateran Council in Rome, Pope Calixtus II (r. 1119–1124) presided over the first Church-wide assembly in centuries. Over the next few centuries, there would be a total of five Lateran Councils (1123, 1139, 1179, 1215, 1517), two councils in Lyons (1245, 1274), and one at Vienne on the Rhône (1311–1312). All were summoned by popes, and all strengthened papal authority. Among other edicts, the First Lateran Council formally forbade the marriage of priests, giving firm injunction to the piecemeal prohibitions of the past.

By 1123, papal power over its Church was also manifest in a critically important development: the systematization of canon law (that is, ecclesiastical law). For a ruler of the Central Middle Ages, law was a means to power, a way to draw authority, income, and respect toward oneself. This was true of secular monarchs, as we shall see in the next chapter; it was also true of popes. During the investiture controversy and subse-quent church-state struggles, popes looked to canon lawyers to support their claims with cogent arguments and documented precedents. Popes also recognized that ecclesiastical courts, staffed by canon lawyers and backed by canon law, were an effective way to ex-tend papal authority over both clergy and laity.

In the late eleventh century, canon law was a messy collection of rules, or *canons,* that drew on the Bible, the writings of early Christian theologians, the edicts of Church councils, and the decrees of popes. The first attempts to produce comprehensive canon-ical collections date from the Early Middle Ages, but it was not until an eleventh-century revival at Bologna that serious scholarly standards were applied to the task. This revival was stimulated, in part, by the study of Roman law and especially the *Corpus Juris Civilis* of the Emperor Justinian (r. 527–565). Although this massive compilation had remained important in the Byzantine Empire, it was all but unknown in the West until it "reappeared" at Bologna in the last quarter of the eleventh century. Its study then stimulated the development of both Roman law (see Chapter 12) and canon law.

The essential goal of canon lawyers was to systematize their sources, explaining what was unclear and reconciling what seemed contradictory. Out of an immense vari-ety of edicts and opinions, they worked to impose order, to assemble their diverse sources—their canons—into a single coherent work. They sought, in short, to accom-plish for Church law the task that Justinian had performed for Roman law in the sixth century: to create their own compendium of *ecclesiastical* law. This task first took shape as a scholarly discipline in eleventh-century Bologna and later spread to other major centers of learning. In Bologna canon lawyers developed a method built on commentary; scholars known as *glossators* studied existing canons and wrote commentaries (or **glosses**) that clarified difficult points and reconciled apparent contradictions. The definitive collection was completed around 1140 by the great Bolognese canon lawyer Gratian. Its original title, *The Concordance of Discordant Canons,* encapsulates Gratian's objective of creating a harmonious system out of what had previously been a hodgepodge of often contradictory opinions. But Gratian's great work has usually been known to posterity by a simpler, if less illuminating, title: the *Decretum.*

Gratian took the immense body of canons at his disposal and framed them in a logical, topically organized scheme. Using methods that were just beginning to be employed by philosophers, he (*a*) raised questions in logical sequence, (*b*) quoted the relevant canons, and (*c*) endeavored to resolve contradictions in the canons. The result was an ordered body of general legal principles validated by excerpts from various authorities: the Bible, early theologians such as St. Augustine of Hippo (354–430), popes, and councils. The *Decretum* became the authoritative text in ecclesiastical tribunals and the basis of all future study in canon law. Together with later supplements that dealt with canons issued after 1140, it was eventually given the title *Corpus Juris Canonici,* the ecclesiastical equivalent of Justinian's great compilation of the sixth century. The *Corpus Juris Canonici* reflects not only the genius of Gratian and other canon lawyers but also the administrative and jurisdictional authority of the papacy. Popes solidified their authority, in part, through canon law.

In the early twelfth century, popes also extended their territorial claims, particularly in relation to the disputed gift of Matilda of Tuscany (1046–1115). Born to power, Matilda had twice married well, so that by the time she was in her 30s, she was Countess of Tuscany, holding vast lands on both sides of the Alps. For almost fifty years, she was a fierce opponent of imperial claims and a fierce supporter of the papacy. Indeed, it was at her castle at Canossa that Henry IV humbly sought the forgiveness of Gregory VII in 1077. She arranged and long intended for her lands, which extended across nearly one-fourth of the Italian peninsula, to pass at her death into the hands of the papacy. Toward the end of her long life, however, she reconciled to the Emperor Henry V (r. 1106–1125) and made him her heir. But because she never revoked her earlier gift to the papacy, her death a few years later began a long struggle between papacy and Empire for her rich inheritance. When the Papal States took their full shape in the twelfth century, they drew, in part, on this Mathildine inheritance, as well as on the long-established authority of the pope over territories in the immediate vicinity of Rome and the long-advanced claims of the pope to govern the Italian peninsula (as supported especially by the Donation of Constantine).

Imperial Authority

When Pope Calixtus II sent his envoys to Worms in 1122, then, he represented a papacy whose position had been much strengthened since the days of Canossa. When Emperor Henry V met those envoys, he was not nearly as powerful as his father had been in 1077. At Canossa, Henry IV had dealt expediently with a situation that threatened to explode out of control. Because his prompt submission forced Gregory VII to lift his excommunication, Henry IV was able to rally political support and reassert his authority over the princes of the German states. Within a few years, he was even able to renew his struggle with Gregory VII, leading his army to Rome and only withdrawing, as we saw in Chapter 9, when Robert Guiscard (1025–1085) and Sichelgaita (c. 1040–1090) came to Gregory's aid. Even so, Henry IV had the last laugh. After Guiscard's boisterous Normans sacked Rome, Gregory was so disliked within the city that he was obliged, for his own protection, to accompany his Norman "rescuers" when they withdrew to the south. In 1085 Gregory died at Salerno, consumed by bitterness and a sense of failure.

Pope Urban II and his successors continued, however, to harass Henry IV, stirring up rebellions in the German states and eroding the power of his imperial government. By the time Henry IV died in 1106, his own son and heir, the future Henry V, was in rebellion against him. Henry V enjoyed a happier reign, but only because he ruled with a lighter hand. Forsaking his father's struggle to recover the fullness of imperial power as it had existed in the mid-eleventh century, he sat on an ever weakening throne. On the one hand, he could no longer rely on bishops, abbots, and abbesses, for they looked increasingly to the pope rather than the emperor. On the other hand, his authority over the great princes of the German states, not strong to begin with, grew ever weaker as these men consolidated their territories and asserted their independence.

Henry V tried to compensate as his father had done, by relying on **ministerials** (lowborn knights who worked as royal servants) and by cultivating good relations with towns (especially through the generous granting of **urban charters**). But neither of these strategies could stem the tide. During the chaotic half-century between Canossa and Worms, a newly empowered aristocracy emerged in the German states. Ambitious landowners rose to great power, built castles, extended their estates, and usurped royal rights. They compelled lesser landholders to become their vassals and, in some instances, forced free peasants to become their serfs. Henry IV had not been able to curb this trend, and his son Henry V was just as helpless.

When Henry V died without an heir three years after the Concordat of Worms, imperial authority suffered another blow. From that moment on, the imperial crown was weakened not only by overmighty aristocrats and a resplendent papacy but also by the reassertion of the custom of *electing* the German king. Kings had been elected in East Francia after the death of the last Carolingian in 911, but the practice had become a formality under the Saxon (919–1024) and Salian (1024–1125) dynasties, both of which had successfully imposed the principle of direct hereditary succession. Although the old custom of election had been resurrected to harass Henry IV at the time of Canossa, he had successfully quashed it. After 1125, however, genuine election again became common practice. The choice always fell to a man of royal blood but not necessarily to the most direct heir. In the decades after 1125, an intense rivalry developed between two great families whose sons could claim the crown: the Welfs of Saxony and the Hohenstaufens of Swabia. Through it all, the German princes grew stronger at the expense of their weakened monarchy.

At the same time as the power of Henry V was withering away in the face of papal reform and territorial princes, his imperial authority over Lombardy was also eroding. The fierce struggle that had transfixed Milan in the mid-eleventh century—with the local nobility and bishop supporting the emperor on one side, and papal reformers and upstart patarenes ("rag-pickers") supporting the pope on the other—was thereafter repeated throughout Lombardy. In this communal movement, Lombard burghers sought to establish urban communes free of the wide jurisdictional powers exercised by their pro-imperial bishops. Allied with proponents of papal reform, they rebelled against the control of nobles, bishops, and emperor alike, and established quasi-independent city-states. By 1125, Milan and other cities in Lombardy were free communes, over which the Holy Roman Emperor exercised only nominal authority.

Between Canossa and Worms, then, in both the German states and the Italian peninsula, imperial power receded before the whirlwind of local particularism, fanned by the investiture controversy, the rise of independent towns, and the old principle of elective monarchy. The decline of the Holy Roman Empire had begun.

✸ The Battle for the Italian Peninsula (1125–1250)

The Expansion of Education: Better Lawyers and Better Bureaucrats

Developments in education might seem a curious topic for a chapter on political conflicts between popes and emperors, and it is certainly true that some aspects of educational development—for example, the composition of systematic treatises on theology and philosophy or the writing down of literary works that had long been transmitted by oral tradition—had little political relevance. We shall delay examination of these intellectual and literary issues until Chapter 12. But in other respects, the vast expansion in education and increase in the use of the written word in the Central Middle Ages had direct importance for the power wielded by kings, emperors, and popes.

Simply put, during these centuries, there was an enormous proliferation of government documents (written commands, property deeds, financial accounts, and judicial transcripts) and records of the transactions of individuals (wills, business records, and property transfers). Power came to be *justified* less by personal loyalty and more by political theories or hard documentation (such as that provided by canon lawyers to buttress the power of the papacy). And power came to be *exercised* less by physical force and more through parchment, by documents that verified claims, listed taxes, or issued royal decrees. Thus, law, which had long been based on local and long-remembered custom, came to rely more on coherent, written systems of secular and ecclesiastical jurisprudence. All told, this shift "from memory to written record," to borrow the words of historian Michael Clanchy, resulted in basic changes in administrative and social organization, encouraging a much more logical and systematic approach to every aspect of human experience.

These changes also provided more opportunities for ambitious young men. With knowledge beginning to offer as good a route to power as military prowess, the ability to reason, read, and compute provided a direct avenue into the governmental institutions of Church and state. Accordingly, schools sprang up everywhere, and skilled teachers found themselves in great demand. When the abbot Guibert of Nogent (1053–1125) looked back to the days of his youth, he remembered a time when "scarcely any teachers could be found in the towns and very few in the cities, and those who by good luck could be found didn't know much." By the time he wrote, those days were long past, for by 1100 Europe abounded with students and teachers.

The greatest of the new schools were established in cities. The commercial revolution that fueled the growth of towns slowly brought about the eclipse of the old monastic schools, which had done so much to preserve and enrich culture during the times of Charlemagne and Otto the Great (r. 936–973). Monastic schools were

Map 10.1   *Some Medieval Universities*   No European region can claim to be the "birthplace" of university education. In 1200, the first universities were spread across the European landscape—from Oxford in England to Salerno in southern Italy, with Paris, Montpellier, and Bologna in between. In the centuries that followed, universities were rapidly founded elsewhere, so that by the fifteenth century, almost every region of Europe had its own university.

superseded north of the Alps by schools in urban churches, often cathedrals, and in Lombardy by semi-secular municipal schools. Both cathedral schools and municipal schools had long existed, but only in the eleventh and twelfth centuries did they rise to prominence. Many now became centers of higher learning of a sort that Europe had not known for centuries. Their enrollments increased and their faculties grew until, in the later twelfth century and after, some of them evolved into universities (see Map 10.1).

From the outset, universities served only a limited sector of the medieval population. First, they were for men only; not until the nineteenth and twentieth centuries did

European—and North American—universities admit women. In the meantime, monastic schools continued to offer some training for a few women, but as education expanded beyond the capacities of monasteries in the twelfth century, it expanded for only one sex. Second, these new educational institutions were for clerics only, at least during the Central Middle Ages. Almost all students and teachers at cathedral schools and universities were in Church orders, usually sub-deacons, deacons, priests, or friars.[1] And third, they were for the wealthy only. Many students lived on small budgets and in humble lodgings, and they doubtless considered themselves "poor." But most were the sons of well-off landowners, merchants, and artisans; these were the families that had both the money and incentive to send their sons to school. For peasants and laborers, education was out of reach; for the higher nobility, whose sons were born to fight and to rule, education of this caliber was simply superfluous.

In the Middle Ages, "university" was a vague term denoting nothing more than a group of persons gathered for any purpose. For example, the word was commonly applied to the merchant and craft guilds found in towns. Fundamentally, then, the medieval university was neither a campus nor a complex of buildings, but a privileged corporation of teachers, or sometimes of students. It differed from lesser schools in that students traveled great distances to receive instruction from scholars expert in medicine, philosophy, or law. Students followed a basic program of instruction in the trivium and quadrivium, the seven "liberal arts" for which Boethius (480–524) had provided the foundational texts in the sixth century: grammar, rhetoric, logic, astronomy, geometry, arithmetic, and music. On the successful completion of the liberal arts curriculum, a student could apply for a license to teach, but he could also continue his studies by specializing in medicine, philosophy (which was synonymous with theology), or law. The advanced instruction that universities offered in one or more of these "higher" disciplines—medicine, philosophy, and law—was one of their defining characteristics.

In the thirteenth century, universities especially flourished at Paris, Bologna, Naples, Montpellier, Oxford, and Cambridge. With classes normally held in rented rooms, the university was a highly mobile institution. On more than one occasion when a university was dissatisfied with local conditions, it won important concessions from the townspeople simply by threatening to move. If students moved, they took with them the money with which they paid rent, bought food, and drank wine. The universities at Paris, Oxford, and elsewhere in the north were dominated by corporations of instructors, a system not unlike most modern American universities in which the faculty determine curricula, degrees, and instructors. The university at Bologna was governed by a corporation of students, a pattern followed by other southern universities. The Bologna student corporation managed to reduce exorbitant local prices of food and lodgings by threatening to move en masse to another town, and it also established strict rules of conduct for the instructors. Professors, for example, were placed under the obligation to begin and end their classes on time and to cover the announced topic. Because Bologna specialized in legal studies, its pupils were older professional students for the most part—students who had completed their liberal arts curriculum and were determined to secure sufficient training for successful careers in law.

---

[1] Deacons were just below priests in the clerical hierarchy, celibate and able to perform some but not all of the sacraments. Sub-deacons were also celibate, but had more limited religious functions.

Figure 10.1   *A University Lecture*   This fourteenth-century illustration shows an instructor commenting on a text, while his students pay varying degrees of attention. Peter Lombard's *Sentences* was the standard text for theology lectures; Gratian's *Decretum* was the main text for the study of canon law.

Notwithstanding the enormous differences between medieval and modern university life, the modern university is a direct outgrowth of its high medieval predecessor. We owe to the medieval university such customs as the formal teaching license, the practice—unknown to antiquity—of group instruction (see Figure 10.1), the awarding of academic degrees, the notion of a liberal arts curriculum, and the tradition of dressing in priestly garb (caps and gowns) for commencements.

Just as we today can appreciate the medieval university, so too did medieval princes and popes. For them, universities produced bureaucrats and lawyers who were more efficient, better trained, and also, since so many owed their social rise to merit not birth, more loyal. In 1158, for example, Frederick Barbarossa (r. 1152–1190), acknowledging that educated men were a benefit to the Holy Roman Empire, extended his protection to all students, who were thereby free to travel and study as they wanted.[2] By thus fostering education, he ensured a steady supply of skilled clerks to manage his affairs in efficient and profitable ways. For both Frederick Barbarossa and Innocent III, in short, the expansion of education facilitated the expansion of their political reach.

---

[2] Because other monarchs also recognized this freedom of students to travel, the international flavor of medieval education became another contributing factor in the Europeanization of Europe.

TIMELINE 10.2   The Battle for the Italian Peninsula, 1125–1250

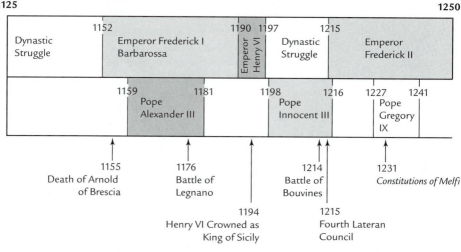

Emperor Frederick Barbarossa (r. 1152–1190) and a Reconstructed Empire

After Henry V died without an heir in 1125, the first two men elected to the German monarchy were chosen largely because they were weak. The territorial princes of the German states wanted emperors who neither established new dynasties nor asserted imperial claims. Lothar III (r. 1125–1138) was old, unrelated to the Salian dynasty, and without any sons. Conrad III (r. 1138–1152) succeeded Lothar, partly because he represented the opposition side, which now got its turn to rule, and partly because he was neither wealthy nor powerful. Their reigns are an interlude between the Salian dynasty which ended with Henry V's death in 1125 and the Hohenstaufen dynasty which began in 1152 with the election of Frederick I, Barbarossa ("Red-Beard"), duke of Swabia (see Timetable 10.2). Frederick took as his mission the reconstruction of the Holy Roman Empire.

Recognizing that the sturdy imperial structure of Henry III was beyond recovery, Frederick Barbarossa strove to harness regional forces to his imperial wagon. To that end, he pursued a policy of limited feudalization. First, he deliberately encouraged his great territorial princes to expand their power at the expense of lesser landowners; by backing the greater nobility against lesser ones, he sought to limit the decentralization of power within his Empire. Second, he forced these greater princes to recognize his own overlordship; in other words, at the same time as he supported their regional power, he sought to secure his imperial authority over them. In the long run, Barbarossa's policy did not work, for the personal loyalty of princes to their emperor was too unreliable, but in the short term, he greatly enhanced the real power behind his throne.

Barbarossa also recognized that his effective lordship over the great princes of the German states required two assets: educated bureaucrats and money. To improve his bureaucracy, he supported education. To increase his revenues, he began extending the territories under his direct authority so that he could boast an extensive royal demesne to compete with the sizable territories of his chief vassals. Frederick accordingly enlarged his Swabian holdings by bringing many new monasteries and towns under imperial jurisdiction.

With the same fiscal objective in mind, Barbarossa also reasserted imperial authority over the wealthy cities of Lombardy. With Lombardy under his control and its revenues pouring into the imperial treasury, he knew that no German prince would challenge him. But this Lombard policy was costly. First, the intensely independent Lombard cities opposed his claims. Second, the papacy, which had long resisted the growth of imperial power in Lombardy, was just as hostile. And third, when Barbarossa became too deeply embroiled in Italian politics, he made himself vulnerable to rebellion within the German states—and especially rebellion fomented by the rival Welf family, which was then headed by the ambitious Duke Henry the Lion of Saxony (1129–1195).

The papacy of the mid-twelfth century was having problems of its own. Pope Hadrian IV (r. 1154–1159), who began as Frederick Barbarossa's ally and ended as one of his most bitter foes, was faced at the beginning of his pontificate with rebellion within Rome itself. A man of humble origins whose name was originally Nicholas Breakspear, Hadrian IV was the only Englishman ever to occupy the papal throne. He had the misfortune to face an exceptionally turbulent Rome, for the ideals of the communal movement had reached the city, turning much of the populace against the pope. In Milan and other northern cities, revolutionaries had once allied with the papacy to break the power of imperial bishops over their cities; now, revolutionaries in Rome turned against their own bishop, the pope. In the 1140s the city was torn by a rebellion whose leaders dreamed of driving out the pope and reestablishing the ancient Roman Republic.

Arnold of Brescia (1100–1155), a gifted scholar and spiritual revolutionary who sought to strip the Church of its wealth and political authority, led the rebellion. In the 1140s, his movement was suppressed by the troops of papal ally King Roger the Great of Sicily (r. 1130–1154), but it blossomed anew when Hadrian IV took the papal throne. Hadrian responded to Arnold and his followers by placing Rome itself under **interdict** (that is, he ordered the suspension of religious services throughout the Holy City). By curtailing Rome's lucrative pilgrimage business, the interdict took the wind out of the rebellion, and Hadrian's supporters drove Arnold of Brescia from the city. Hadrian and Barbarossa then joined forces to hunt him down, and once he fell into their hands he was hanged, burned, and thrown into the Tiber. Thus Arnold was emphatically eliminated, and his relics were put out of the reach of future admirers.[3]

The growing hostility between the papacy and the Roman citizenry was an ominous indication that papal leadership of urban reform was at an end. Popes had once made common cause with the explosive ambitions of newly wealthy merchants and artisans, as Gregory VII had done with the patarenes of Milan. By the mid-twelfth century, however, Hadrian IV and his successors were on the other side: opposing the political ambitions of independent-minded citizens and striving also to suppress urban spiritual movements, which too often struck anti-clerical themes.

Hadrian IV could not have beaten Arnold of Brescia without Frederick Barbarossa's help, but the two quickly quarreled. At Frederick's imperial coronation in 1155, Hadrian insisted that Frederick follow a humiliating point of protocol—assisting the pope onto his mule and then leading both pope and mule through the streets of Rome. At first Frederick refused to demean his imperial status in such a manner, but

---

[3] Arnold of Brescia died a painful death, but his criticisms of ecclesiastical wealth and power were an early example of what would become a recurrent theme in central medieval Christianity. Both anti-clerical heresies, such as the Waldensians and the Cathars, and orthodox movements, such as the Franciscans and Poor Clares, sought spiritual regeneration through rejecting the riches and powers of the institutional Church.

when it appeared that there would otherwise be no coronation at all, he grudgingly submitted. This small conflict symbolized far greater ones, for Hadrian and his successors proved to be implacable opponents of Frederick's drive to win control of the cities of Lombardy. The two became firm enemies.

The struggle over Lombardy reached its height during the pontificate of Hadrian's successor, Alexander III (r. 1159–1181). Shrewd and learned, Alexander was Frederick Barbarossa's most formidable opponent. He was also a new sort of pope. Whereas many popes before him came from monasteries, he and many of his successors were trained in canon law and active in papal politics before their elevation to the papal throne. This shift reflected the growing size of the papal curia and the importance within it of canon lawyers, trained at Bologna and elsewhere in the careful logic and order of Gratian's *Decretum*. It was also facilitated by a new argument put forth by canon lawyers that bishops, once thought to be "married" to their bishoprics and unable to move, could, in fact, take up the papal throne. In any case, Alexander III was one of the first among twelfth- and thirteenth-century popes to take his early training in canon law and then work within the papal curia. He was also one of the ablest.

Determined to prevent Frederick Barbarossa from dominating Lombardy, Alexander briefly returned to the old alliance of papacy and urban communes, making common cause with the towns of Lombardy. These towns had long fought against each other, but they now combined forces against the Empire in a new military confederation known as the *Lombard League.* Alexander III backed them. When Barbarossa threw his support behind a rival claimant to the papal throne, Alexander excommunicated him. What followed was a prolonged struggle between Barbarossa, on one side, and Alexander and the Lombard League, on the other. In 1162, Frederick besieged and then burned the great city of Milan, both intimidating and infuriating the Lombards. In 1176 they got their revenge, winning a decisive victory at the battle of Legnano. In the wake of this defeat, Barbarossa was forced to grant de facto independence to the cities of Lombardy; they promised in return to acknowledge a vague imperial overlordship. As to the papacy, Barbarossa tearfully embraced Alexander and promised to be a dutiful son. For the moment, all was at peace.

But Barbarossa did not abandon his designs on the Italian peninsula; he merely shifted his theater of operations to two different sites. First, he began to press imperial claims in Tuscany, the rich province at the center of the Mathildine inheritance that the papacy claimed as its own. Second, he arranged a marriage between his son, the future Henry VI (r. 1190–1197), and Constance of Sicily (1154–1198), who stood first in line to inherit that Norman kingdom. The marriage would ultimately bring the Kingdom of Sicily (that is, both Sicily itself and the southern Italian peninsula) into the imperial fold, placing the papacy in the chilling embrace of the Holy Roman Empire, now to the south of Rome as well as the north (see Map 10.2). In 1180 Barbarossa tightened

Map 10.2 *The Holy Roman Empire and the Italian Peninsula in the Central Middle* ▶
Ages   By the twelfth century, medieval popes controlled a large swath of territory at the center of the Italian peninsula. But they had trouble extending their power to either north or south. To the north, popes competed with Holy Roman emperors for influence over the city-states of Lombardy and Tuscany. To the south lay the Norman Kingdom of Sicily, under papal control until it fell into Hohenstaufen hands in 1194. For the next half-century, the Papal States were uncomfortably sandwiched between imperial interests.

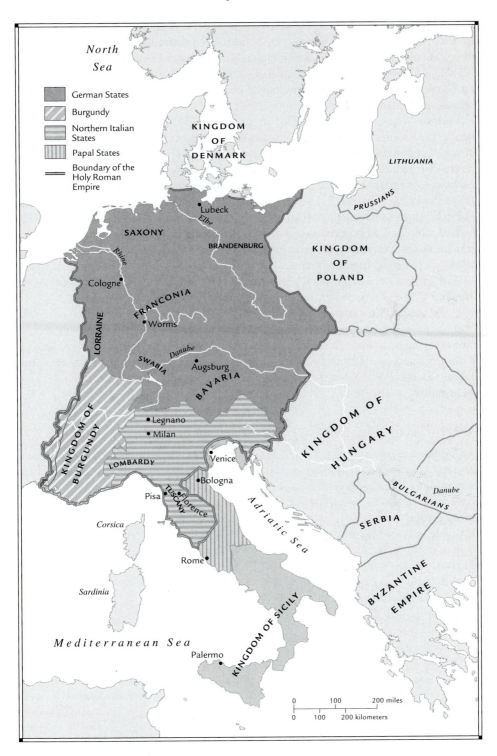

North Sea

German States

Burgundy

Northern Italian States

Papal States

— Boundary of the Holy Roman Empire

KINGDOM OF DENMARK

LITHUANIA

PRUSSIANS

Lubeck

Elbe

SAXONY

BRANDENBURG

KINGDOM OF POLAND

Rhine

Cologne

FRANCONIA

LORRAINE

Worms

Danube

SWABIA

Augsburg

BAVARIA

KINGDOM OF BURGUNDY

Legnano

Milan

LOMBARDY

Venice

KINGDOM OF HUNGARY

Bologna

Pisa

TUSCANY

Florence

Adriatic Sea

Danube

BULGARIANS

SERBIA

Corsica

Rome

BYZANTINE EMPIRE

Sardinia

Mediterranean Sea

Palermo

KINGDOM OF SICILY

0   100   200 miles

0   100   200 kilometers

his hold on the German states by crushing the most formidable of his vassals, Henry the Lion, the Welf duke of Saxony. In the next year, Alexander III died, and until his own death nine years later, the far-sighted and determined Frederick Barbarossa was at the height of his power. In an accident with disastrous consequences for the future of the Empire, he drowned while leading his army toward the Holy Land on the Third Crusade in 1190.[4]

Barbarossa had taken pains to circumvent the custom of elective monarchy by forcing the election of his eldest son as ruler over the German states. Hence, in 1190 Henry VI succeeded his father without difficulty, and in 1194 he made good the claim of his wife Constance to Sicily and the southern Italian peninsula. He was crowned king of Sicily on Christmas Day 1194, and on the next day Constance gave birth to their son, the future Frederick II (r. 1215–1250). The papacy—along with the lands in the central Italian peninsula over which it claimed dominion—was now encircled by a Holy Roman Empire whose reach had never been so extensive. This vast empire was both a great triumph and a future danger, for in a time when regional rebellion always threatened, particularly among imperial vassals in the German states, the frontiers of the Holy Roman Empire were perhaps too broad. In the meantime, however, the revenues of the kingdom of Sicily fattened the imperial purse, and Henry VI held his ground.

Then, in 1197, Henry VI died of malaria in his early thirties, leaving as heir his three-year-old son, Frederick II. The challenges the Empire faced in 1197—vast borders, antagonistic papacy, restless vassals—would have taxed the ablest of leaders, yet at this moment the imperial leadership fell into the hands of a child. Frederick Barbarossa had brilliantly rebuilt the Holy Roman Empire, but the papacy now had its opportunity.

Pope Innocent III (r. 1198–1216) and the Papacy Ascendant

During the twelfth century the papacy developed into a huge, complex administrative institution. Taxes flowed into its treasury from all of Western Christendom; bishops traveled vast distances to make their spiritual submission to the Roman pontiff; and the papal curia served as a court of final appeal for an immense network of ecclesiastical courts across Western Christendom. In brief, papal authority over the Western Church had increased immeasurably since the days of Gregory VII. As the dream of papal monarchy came nearer realization, the traditional theory of papal supremacy over Christian society was further magnified by canon lawyers. These subtle and skilled scholars were beginning to dominate the papal curia and some, like Alexander III, even occupied the papal throne itself.

Innocent III, featured in the Biographical Sketch on pp. 256–257 and pictured in Figure 10.2, was the most powerful of all the lawyer-popes, and he began his pontificate in the year following Henry VI's death. Innocent had the wisdom to support the Franciscans, the ruthlessness to fight Cathars, the enthusiasm to launch the Fourth Crusade (1201–1204), and the administrative savvy to establish firm control over the Papal States. He also dominated the Church more completely than any of his predecessors had done. In

---

[4] Frederick Barbarossa has long remained a favorite of German folklore, the hero of stories about a sleeping king who will return to unify his country. In one version, the timing of his return was related to the length of his beard: once the beard grew long enough, it was said, Frederick Barbarossa would arise to fight again.

Figure 10.2   *Innocent III*   This fresco from the
monastery of Sacro Speco in Italy shows Innocent III with
the monastery's foundation charter. One of only two
contemporary portraits of Innocent III, it might be more
idealized than realistic (the other portrait shows Innocent
with a moustache). Innocent's regal appearance is enhanced
by the admiring gaze of the monk in the lower left corner.

1215 he summoned the Fourth Lateran Council and guided it through a remarkable quantity of significant ecclesiastical legislation: clerical dress was strictly regulated, a mora-
torium was declared on new religious orders, Jews were required to wear special badges,
clerics were forbidden to participate in the barbarian legal procedure of the ordeal, fees
for the administration of sacraments were forbidden, bishops were ordered to maintain
schools and to preach sermons at their services, and all Catholics were bound to receive
the sacraments of penance and the Eucharist at least once a year. The efficient organization of the Fourth Lateran Council and the degree to which Innocent dominated it are
illustrated by the fact that the churchmen in attendance—more than 1,200 bishops, abbots,
and priests—produced their important new legislation in meetings that lasted a total of
only three weeks.[5] By contrast, the Council of Basel met off and on for eighteen years
(1431–1449) and accomplished a lot less.

     Inspired by papalist theory, Innocent forced his will on the leading monarchs of
Europe, playing off one ruler against another with consummate skill. He managed to
make England, Hungary, Portugal, and Aragon into papal fiefs whose rulers recognized
him as their overlord. In England, the struggle began when King John (r. 1199–1216)
and Innocent disagreed over the appointment of an archbishop of Canterbury; Innocent
then laid John's kingdom under interdict, threatened to depose John himself, and backed

---

[5] Abbesses attended some early councils of the Church, but by the Central Middle Ages, churchwomen were excluded from
these assemblies.

BIOGRAPHICAL SKETCH
Pope Innocent III (1160–1216)

A forceful leader at a propitious moment, Innocent III led the papacy to the height of its temporal and spiritual powers. No pope before or after him had so much sway over the princes of Europe. No pope before or after so influenced the development of Christian worship and spirituality. His were great deeds indeed, yet he has not been honored with the title "the Great." Why is Innocent III not also known as "Innocent the Great"? Perhaps because, for all the good he did, Innocent III was born to power and delighted in its exercise.

Born in 1160, the boy who would become Innocent III was named Lothar by his parents. His father Trasimund was count of Segni, a region to the southeast of Rome; his mother Clarissa hailed from the powerful Scotti family of Rome that had long counted popes among its members. From an early age Lothar was destined for a career in the Church. Perhaps this was his fate as a younger son; perhaps he had an aptitude for study and piety; perhaps his family needed someone to advance its interests within the Church; perhaps all these. We do not know the reasons, but we do know the results. Lothar received his earliest education in Rome and then studied in both Paris and Bologna.

In the late twelfth century, every ambitious young man longed to study in Paris and Bologna. Paris was the intellectual center of Europe, particularly in the study of theology. There Peter Lombard (c. 1095–1160) had produced his *Book of Sentences,* a book that did for theology what Gratian's *Decretum* did for canon law: it set out conflicting opinions and used logic to reconcile their differences. Lombard's *Sentences* soon became the basic textbook for theology students, and this was what Lothar studied in Paris. Decades later, when Innocent III guided the Fourth Lateran Council in its decisions about heresy, transubstantiation, pastoral care, and the like, he put into practice what he had learned in Paris as a young man. He also rewarded his teachers and fellow students, several of whom became archbishops after Lothar became Innocent III.

Lothar left Paris a trained theologian who had made the acquaintance of some of the best minds in Europe. He went next to Bologna, a place as central to the study of canon law as Paris was to theology. There, he studied under Huguccio of Pisa (d. 1210), a scholar renowned for his commentary on Gratian's *Decretum.* Lothar spent only a year or two in Bologna, but when he became pope some ten years later, he showered Huguccio with honors, and he surrounded himself with canon lawyers. His time in Bologna taught Lothar to appreciate the powerful reach of the law.

In 1189, Lothar returned to Rome and the embrace of his powerful family. Soon his kinsman Pope Celestine III (r. 1191–1198) made him a cardinal deacon, a position from which he took an active role within the papal curia. He also took up writing, none of it distinguished, but some of it very popular. His treatise *On Contempt for the World* was widely copied and read—the medieval equivalent of a best-seller.

When Celestine III died at the age of 93, Lothar, well traveled, well connected, well educated, and even well written, was in an excellent position to succeed him. But he had two marks against him. He was not the dead pope's preferred successor, and at the age of 37, he was considered too young, especially because some feared that, should Lothar live as long as Celestine III, one man would hold the papacy for 50 years or more. Still, Lothar won on the second vote, and according to tradition, God's pleasure was immediately shown when three white doves flew into the assembly and the whitest settled on Lothar's shoulder. As soon as possible, Lothar was ordained a priest, and on the very next day he became bishop of Rome and pope, taking the name Innocent III.

The white dove was a nice touch, but there was no hiding the fact that Lothar's rise to the papal throne had been facilitated by birth, privilege, and planning. It is a far cry from the story of the accession of another medieval pope, Gregory I (r. 590–604), who *is* titled "the Great." Gregory had also been Roman-born, wealthy, and well educated, but he had forsaken his privilege to become a monk. Indeed, according to legend, Gregory was so humble and so uninterested in papal power that he tried to escape his selection as pope by hiding in a cart leaving Rome. Gregory's accession was a story of humility and reluctant acceptance of a duty; Innocent's accession was a story of preparation and, indeed, excellent career planning.

In 1198, when Lothar became Innocent III, he was brilliantly prepared to lead a Church that needed a brilliant leader. His birth, education, and connections helped to make him the great pope he became: a strong administrator, a major player in the political affairs of Europe, a theological innovator, a hammer of heretics, a preacher of crusades, and, to sum it all up, a man who could credibly claim (as, indeed, he did) that he was "placed between God and humans, lower than God but higher than humans." Yet these same assets, so critical to Innocent's success, have also made him seem too careerist for a holy man, despite his many charitable projects and pious deeds. In his own life and its remembrance in history, then, Innocent III embodies the central challenge of the medieval Church: to be both "in" the world and "above" it. That historians of the papacy have judged him too worldly to be "Great" might say more about our unrealistic expectations for religious leaders than about Innocent III's own accomplishments.

a French invasion of England. Finally, John submitted, installing Innocent's man as archbishop of Canterbury *and* consenting to papal lordship over England. In other places, Innocent III was unable to claim feudal overlordship, but he made his power felt. In France, for example, Innocent imposed proper marital behavior on an unwilling King Philip II Augustus (r. 1180–1223) who had married a Danish princess named Ingeborg (1175–1237) but cast her aside after their wedding night. He had then married again, against all precepts of canon law and theology. After laying France under interdict and excommunicating Philip, Innocent obtained his submission (but only after the death of Philip's second wife).

These papal triumphs in England and France were important, but throughout Innocent's pontificate one political issue took precedence over all others—that of the German imperial succession. This was a marvelously complex problem that taxed even Innocent's diplomatic skill. Involved were the questions of whether the kingdom of Sicily would remain in imperial hands, whether the imperial throne would pass to the Welfs or the Hohenstaufens, and whether an accommodation could be achieved between the traditionally hostile forces of papacy and Empire. The problem of the imperial succession also touched the interests of the French and English monarchies: the Welf claimant could count on the support of his kinsman King John of England, whereas the Hohenstaufens enjoyed the friendship of the French king, Philip Augustus.

The direct Hohenstaufen heir in 1197 was the three-year-old Frederick, son of the late Henry VI. But since a child could hardly be expected to fight for the throne, the Hohenstaufen claim was taken up by Frederick's uncle, Philip of Swabia (1178–1208) against the Welf claimant, Otto of Brunswick (c. 1175–1218). The young Frederick remained in Sicily while Philip of Swabia and Otto of Brunswick battled for the imperial throne. Innocent recognized the German princes' right to elect their own monarch, but, as it happened, Philip and Otto had both been elected, each by a different group of princes. In the case of a disputed election such as this, Innocent claimed the right to intervene by virtue of the traditional papal privilege of crowning the emperor. He delayed his decision considerably, and in the meantime civil war raged in the German states.

At length Innocent III settled on Otto of Brunswick, from whom he had extracted promises to support papal interests in the German states. Because Otto, as a Welf, had no dynastic claim on the Hohenstaufen kingdom of Sicily, his coronation also promised to ease the Holy Roman Empire's threatening embrace—from both north and south—of the Papal States. But when Otto was crowned emperor in 1209 (a feat achieved, in part, by the death of Philip of Swabia the year before), he repudiated his promises to Innocent, asserted his mastery over the German church, and even launched an invasion of the kingdom of Sicily. Innocent responded by deposing Otto, excommunicating him, and throwing his support behind the young-but-growing Frederick. But before backing Frederick for the imperial title, Innocent wrung several promises from him: to abdicate as king of Sicily and sever the Sicilian kingdom from the Empire, to lead a Crusade, to follow the spiritual direction of the papacy, and in general to confirm the pledges that Otto of Brunswick had made and then broken.

Innocent's decision revived the Hohenstaufen cause in the German states and renewed the civil war. The pope employed all his diplomatic skill to win German nobles to Frederick's cause. He was supported in these maneuverings by Philip Augustus of France, now on friendly terms with the papacy, traditionally sympathetic to the Hohenstaufens, and hostile to the English and their Welf allies. Then, in 1214 at the battle of Bouvines, the complex currents of these international politics reached their climax and their resolution: Otto's army was routed by the troops of Philip Augustus.

Bouvines changed the political face of Europe. Philip Augustus emerged as Europe's foremost monarch, Otto's imperial dreams were dashed, Frederick II (r. 1215–1250) became emperor in fact as well as in theory, and Innocent III had his choice, at last, on the imperial throne. But the German states were in chaos. Imperial involvement in the affairs of the Sicilian kingdom and long years of dynastic strife, during which the German princes usurped royal privileges and lands on a vast scale, had taken their toll. By the time Frederick II acquired the throne, the imperial authority that his grandfather Frederick Barbarossa had carefully and cleverly built was almost beyond recovery.

For Innocent III, these were triumphant years: he launched crusades, humbled kings, presided over Church councils, and everywhere made his will felt. Yet even for Innocent III, papal power was fragile and limited. It was restrained in many ways—by the growing power of the Western monarchies, by the fragility of royal promises of good behavior, and by long-standing difficulties in enforcing papal decrees throughout the length and breadth of Western Christendom. Innocent's Fourth Lateran Council, for example, had decreed that all Christians must go to confession at least once a year, yet the implementation of this and other provisions of the council varied from region to region. The Council's decrees were rigorously enforced in England, which had recently passed under papal lordship, and in Poland, where bishops were strongly papal in their sympathies. But a study of late medieval Flanders has disclosed that a good many Flemings never confessed to a priest at all, much less confessed once a year. Even in international diplomacy, where Innocent achieved such conspicuous triumphs, he also faced crushing disappointments; he had been able, for example, to extract promises from Otto of Brunswick, but he had not successfully forced their fulfillment.

Emperor Frederick II (r. 1215–1250)

In the years after Innocent III's death in 1216, Frederick II made it clear that he would ignore his promises to the pope as completely as Otto of Brunswick had done earlier. Refusing to relinquish his kingdom of Sicily, he sought instead to bring all the Italian peninsula within his Empire. This policy won him the implacable hatred of Innocent III's successors and prompted some churchmen to view him quite literally as the incarnate Antichrist.

Frederick was a talented, many-sided man, a flamboyant product of an intensely creative culture. Having been raised in Sicily, Frederick II had considerable first-hand knowledge of Islam and Islamic culture. He grew up to be a brilliant, anti-clerical skeptic whose dazzling career earned him the name *Stupor Mundi,* the "Wonder of the World." He was a writer of considerable skill and an amateur scientist, curious about the world around him, but in some matters deeply superstitious. After much delay he kept his promise to lead a crusade, but instead of fighting Muslims, he negotiated with them, and with such success that Jerusalem itself came into his hands for a time. The amicable spirit of Frederick's crusade appalled many churchmen, and its success infuriated them.

As king of Sicily, Frederick II was one of the great organizers of his age. In 1231, he convened a great council that established a uniform legal code, the *Constitutions of Melfi,* that greatly enhanced his royal power. He also tightened and broadened the centralized administration of his Norman-Sicilian predecessors; encouraged agriculture, industry, and commerce; abolished internal tariffs and tolls; and founded a great university in Naples. The German states, however, he left largely to their princes. He always preferred his cosmopolitan and warm Sicilian homeland to the forests and snowy winters of the German north. Like Frederick Barbarossa, he tried to expand the royal demesne in the German states and to enforce the feudal obligations of his great German vassals. But he did so halfheartedly. The German states were important to Frederick chiefly as a source of money and soldiers with which to pursue his dream of bringing all of the Italian peninsula under his command.

As it happened, this policy proved disastrous to the Holy Roman Empire as a whole. On the Italian side, Frederick's aggressions provoked the fierce opposition of a revived Lombard League, and worse yet, he impoverished his beloved Sicily with taxes to support his wars. On the German side, he gave up important royal prerogatives in an effort to win the support of German princes for his persistent but inconclusive Italian campaigns. And in both the Italian peninsula and the German states, the papacy remained his implacable foe. Astute lawyer-popes such as Gregory IX (r. 1227–1241) and Innocent IV (r. 1243–1254) devoted all their diplomatic talents and spiritual sanctions to blocking Frederick's enterprises, building alliances to oppose him, and hurling anathemas against him.

The denouement began in 1245 when Innocent IV presided over a Church council at Lyons that condemned and excommunicated the emperor. Frederick was deposed, a rival emperor was elected in his place, and a crusade was called to rid the Empire of its ungodly tyrant. Revolts now broke out throughout Frederick's dominions. Many royal lands in the German states slipped out of his grasp, and even the kingdom of Sicily seethed with rebellion. Against this unhappy background, Frederick II died in 1250. In a very real sense, the hopes of the medieval Empire died with him.

✱ PAPACY AND EMPIRE IN DECLINE (1250-1300)

The German States after 1250

Frederick II's son succeeded him as emperor but died in 1254 after a brief and inglorious reign. For the next nineteen years, the German states suffered a crippling interregnum (1254–1273) during which no recognized emperor held the throne (see Timeline 10.3). Castles sprouted like mushrooms from the German soil as princes and nobles, lacking a royal referee, undertook to defend and advance their own interests. Finally, in 1273, a vastly weakened Holy Roman Empire reemerged with papal blessing under Rudolph of Habsburg (r. 1273–1291), the first emperor of a family that was destined to play a crucial role in modern European history.

Rudolph attempted to rebuild the shattered royal demesne and shore up the foundations of imperial rule, but it was too late. His strategy—to extend and strengthen the crown lands to the point where royal resources were overwhelmingly superior to those of any rival magnate—was a good one. This was the policy on which the medieval French monarchy had risen to a position of dominance in France, and it was also the policy that Frederick Barbarossa had pursued so promisingly in the twelfth-century German states. But it aroused the unremitting opposition of the German princes of the thirteenth century, who had no desire to see their own rights and territories eaten away by royal expansion. Instead, they had been extending their own principalities at the expense of the crown.

The civil strife prompted by Innocent III's indecision over the imperial throne, the Italian involvements of Frederick II, and the interregnum of 1254–1273 had given the German princes their opportunity, and by 1273 crown lands were diminished and disorganized. Rudolph could not turn back the tide. The German states were now drifting toward a loose confederation of independent principalities and weak, elective monarchy. This constitutional structure—strong princes and weak emperors—would characterize the Holy Roman Empire for the next 600 years.

The Italian Peninsula after 1250

The Italian peninsula also emerged from the struggles of the Central Middle Ages as a cluster of regional principalities. The Papal States, straddling the center of the peninsula, were torn with unrest and disaffection, and some popes even had trouble maintaining authority over Rome itself. North of the Papal States, Tuscany and Lombardy became a mosaic of independent and competitive city-states: Florence, Siena, Venice, Milan, and many others. Their rivalries and wars would eventually form the political backdrop of the Italian Renaissance.

Political struggles in and between these city-states would long be couched in terms that echoed the epic struggle of emperors and popes for control over the Italian peninsula in the Central Middle Ages. From the thirteenth century, two factional names dominated Italian politics. On one side stood the *Guelphs*—that is, those who originally

TIMELINE 10.3   Papacy and Empire in Decline, 1250–1300

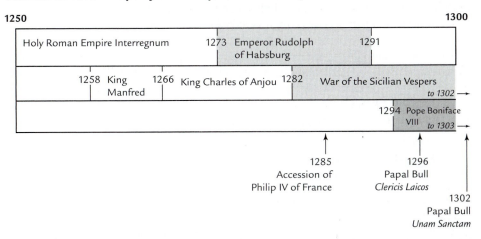

supported Welf imperial ambitions, and through the Welfs, the policies of the papacy. On the other side stood the *Ghibellines,* who supported the imperial ambitions of Frederick Barbarossa, Henry VI, and Frederick II (the name derived from the Waibling lordship of the Hohenstaufen). Conflicts between Guelph and Ghibelline factions disrupted the internal politics of many late medieval city-states and also motivated conflicts between them. But they soon lost their connection to the controversy between papacy and Empire; as early as 1355, a jurist noted that the names Guelph and Ghibelline had no connection "either to the church or to the Empire, but only to those factions which exist in a city or in a province." Yet in their continued use through centuries, these terms bore witness to the traumatic disruption visited on the Italian states by the epic struggle of popes and emperors in the twelfth and thirteenth centuries.

The kingdom of Sicily, established by the Normans and cherished by the Hohenstaufens, passed shortly after Frederick II's death to his illegitimate son, Manfred (r. 1258–1266). The papacy, determined to rid the Italian peninsula of Hohenstaufen rule, bent all its energies toward securing Manfred's downfall. In an effort to harness the power of France to this project, it offered the Sicilian crown to Charles of Anjou (1227–1285), a younger brother of King Louis IX of France (r. 1226–1270). Charles—dour, cruel, and ambitious—defeated and killed Manfred in 1266 and established a new French dynasty on the throne of the kingdom.

But the inhabitants of the realm, particularly those on the island of Sicily, preferred Hohenstaufen rule, resented Charles of Anjou, and looked on his French soldiers as an army of occupation. When, on Easter Monday 1282, a French soldier insulted a young Sicilian wife on her way to evening services (vespers) in Palermo, he was struck down, and on all sides rose the cry, "Death to the French!" The incident resulted in a general massacre of Frenchmen, which spread swiftly throughout the island. When the French retaliated, the Sicilians offered the crown to Peter III of Aragon (r. in Aragon, 1276–1285), Manfred's son-in-law. He claimed the Hohenstaufen inheritance and led an army to Sicily.

There ensued a long, bloody, indecisive struggle known by the romantic name, the *War of the Sicilian Vespers.* For twenty years, Charles of Anjou and his successors, backed by the French monarchy and the papacy, fought against the Sicilians and Aragonese. In the end, the southern Italian peninsula remained under Charles of Anjou's heirs, who ruled it from Naples, whereas the island of Sicily passed under the control of the kings of Aragon. But the dispute between France and Aragon over the former kingdom of Sicily, both the island and the southern Italian peninsula, persisted for generations and became a major irritant in the politics of modern Europe. For the kingdom of Sicily itself, the dispute was devastating. Once one of the wealthiest and best administered states in Europe, it became impoverished and divided, a victim of the ruthless struggle between papacy and Empire.

The Papacy after 1250

Judging from the disintegration of the Holy Roman Empire after the death of Frederick II, one might conclude that the papacy had won an overwhelming victory. But as popes such as Innocent III, Gregory IX, and Innocent IV became absorbed in power politics, the papacy slowly lost its hold on the hearts of Christians. By the second half of the thirteenth century, popes often seemed less like pastoral leaders and more like worldly monarchs.

Ironically, the fiscal and political cast of the late thirteenth-century papacy was a direct consequence of its earlier dream of becoming the spiritual dynamo of a reformed Western Christendom. Many of the ambitions of eleventh-century reformers such as Peter Damian (1007–1072), Humbert of Silva Candida, and Gregory VII did, in fact, come to pass: the papacy became a moral and political leader in twelfth- and thirteenth-century Europe, and popes used that authority to do great good. Under the guidance of central medieval popes, the Church sponsored the rise of universities, the establishment of schools and hospitals in vast numbers, and the founding of hostels for the poor and refuges for orphans. Under papal direction, canon law and Church doctrine were refined, and theological systems emerged that explored in rational terms the mysteries of Christian faith. With papal diplomacy and armies, the Church also played a critical role in inhibiting the rise of royal absolutism; popes had self-interested reasons for opposing emperors such as Henry IV and Frederick Barbarossa, but their opposition provided a critical counterweight to imperial pretensions. All told and notwithstanding historical myths to the contrary, the papacy did far more to stimulate European rationalism than to shackle it, to limit autocracy than to encourage it, to affirm human dignity than to diminish it.

But the power to do all this good came at a cost. An ascendant papacy needed money to finance its operations, a bureaucracy to handle its complex business, and armies to protect its interests. It also needed popes who were effective administrators as well as pious priests. Most thirteenth-century popes, despite their piety, good intentions, and continuing concern for ecclesiastical reform, were lawyers and diplomats rather than charismatic spiritual leaders. The papacy was still a mighty force in the world, but it failed to satisfy the spiritual hunger of many devoted Christians. Indeed, some people were coming to doubt that papal government was the true spiritual center of the apostolic Church and the true citadel of Christ's kingdom on earth. To them, papal tax collectors, papal bureaucrats, and papal use of spiritual sanctions (such as excommunication and interdict) to achieve political ends were worrisome and even noxious developments. The papacy, in other words, had become a great political power and a big business, and like many large, unwieldy institutions, it began to acquire an unsavory reputation for greed. As one contemporary complained, the supreme pontiff was supposed to lead Christ's flock, not to fleece it.

This spiritual malaise at the heart of the papacy was a serious matter, for ultimately, papal authority was based on spiritual prestige. As spiritual prestige waned, so too did worldly preeminence. The popes of the twelfth and early thirteenth centuries had humbled the Holy Roman Empire, but their successors in the late thirteenth century and afterward would be themselves humbled by the rising power of centralized monarchies in northern Europe. By then, the kings of England and France, whose rise we will trace in the next chapter, were chafing under the presence within their realms of a semi-independent, highly privileged, transnational Church. They wanted to bring these ecclesiastical "states within states" under royal control. Popes understandably disagreed. By 1300 their conflict was coming to a head, not over lay investiture (an old dispute that had run its course) but instead over a new issue—royal taxation of the Church. After 1294, when England and France were locked in a costly war with each other, both monarchies adopted the novel policy of systematically taxing the clergy of their realms. Pope Boniface VIII (r. 1294–1303) retaliated in 1296 by issuing the **papal bull** *Clericis Laicos,* which expressly forbade this practice. Once again, monarchy and papacy were at loggerheads.

Boniface VIII was another lawyer-pope—proud, aged, and inflexible—whose visions of papal power transcended even those of Innocent III. He made it known that the pope, as God's deputy on earth, exercised a power that was "not human but rather divine." But Boniface was unable to bend his stupendous concepts of papal authority to the realities of European politics. And in King Philip IV "the Fair" of France (r. 1285–1314), Boniface encountered a dangerous antagonist. Ignoring *Clericis Laicos,* Philip continued to tax his clergy. He also set his agents to work spreading scandalous rumors about Boniface's morals, and he squeezed Boniface's treasury by cutting off all papal revenues from the French realm. Boniface was briefly cowed, but in 1302, encouraged by a vast influx of pilgrims to Rome in the Jubilee Year of 1300, he issued the bull *Unam Sanctam,* which asserted the doctrine of papal monarchy in uncompromising terms: "We declare, announce, affirm and define that, for every human creature, to be subject to the Roman pontiff is absolutely necessary for salvation."

Philip the Fair responded by summoning the **Estates General**—a kingdom-wide assembly—at which he accused Boniface of every imaginable crime from murder to black magic to homosexual acts to keeping a demon as a pet. A small French military force in 1303 took Boniface prisoner at his palace at Anagni, intending to take him to France for trial. The French plan failed—local townspeople freed Boniface a couple of days later—but Anagni stands as the antithesis of Canossa, symbolizing the humiliation of the medieval papacy. The proud old pope died shortly after his release, outraged and chagrined that armed Frenchmen had dared to lay hands on his sacred person. Contemporaries found it significant that his burial was cut short by a furious thunderstorm.

Within a few years, the circumstances of the papacy went from bad to worse. In 1305 the cardinals elected Clement V (r. 1305–1314), a native of Gascony, who pursued a policy of cautious accommodation to the French throne. Clement submitted on the question of clerical taxation and publicly burned *Unam Sanctam,* even saying that Philip the Fair had shown "praiseworthy zeal" in his accusations against Pope Boniface. Clement never traveled to Rome, abandoning its faction-ridden streets for a new papal capital at Avignon on the Rhône river, a city that belonged to the papacy but was tucked within the warm embrace of French lands and the strong influence of the French crown. As we shall see in Chapter 13, during its almost 70 years in Avignon, the bureaucracy of the papacy prospered and its spiritual prestige dwindled.

Although it is easy to criticize Boniface VIII's inflexibility and Clement V's eagerness to please, the waning of papal authority in the years around 1300 did not result primarily from personal shortcomings. It stemmed from an ever-widening gulf between papal government and the spiritual thirst of ordinary Christians, combined with the enduring hostility of secular princes—whether Holy Roman emperors or French kings—for the international claims of a pope who sought to wield authority over all of Western Christendom. At times, the central medieval papacy certainly behaved in ways that today seem corrupt, but this corruption was only an ancillary plot within a larger story. Between 1050 and 1300 men of high purpose sat on the papal throne. Not satisfied merely to chide the society of their day by innocuous moralizing from the sidelines, they plunged into the world and struggled to sanctify it. Tragically, and perhaps inevitably, they soiled their hands.

✸ CONCLUSION

For both popes and emperors, centralized power—power held in a single hand and emanating out from there—was a strong, elusive, and perhaps dangerous dream. The papal ideal of a centralized ecclesiastical structure constantly ran up against the untidy realities of episcopal autonomy, noncompliance with papal commands, and disputes between archbishops, bishops, abbots, and abbesses. By 1300, the papacy was well administered and reasonably centralized, but it inspired little fear in the likes of Philip the Fair and much anti-clericalism among ordinary Christians. The imperial ambitions of Henry IV, Frederick Barbarossa, and other Holy Roman Emperors also encountered the untidy practicalities of powers that were easy to claim and hard to administer. These emperors governed with great authority, but they faced many petty rebellions, some defeats, and occasional humiliations. By 1300, the Holy Roman Empire was not centralized but instead disintegrated—into princely territories north of the Alps, independent city-states to their south, and shattered battlegrounds in the former kingdom of Sicily.

SUGGESTED READINGS

David Abulafia, *Frederick II: A Medieval Emperor* (1988). The best of several accounts of Frederick II. See also his *The Western Mediterranean Kingdoms 1200–1500: The Struggle for Dominion* (1997).

Benjamin Arnold, *Medieval Germany 500–1300: A Political Interpretation* (1997). Emphasizes the regionalism of the medieval German states. See also his *Princes and Territories in Medieval Germany* (1991).

James A. Brundage, *Medieval Canon Law* (1995). A clear introduction to a complex subject.

M. T. Clanchy, *From Memory to Written Record: England, 1066–1307* (2nd edition, 1992). Studies the emergence of a literate mentality in central medieval England.

Horst Fuhrmann, *Germany in the High Middle Ages, c. 1050–1200,* trans. Timothy Reuter (1986). See also Alfred Haverkamp, *Medieval Germany, 1056–1273,* trans. Helga Braun and Richard Mortimer (2nd edition, 1992). These two works replace all earlier surveys of the medieval German states.

Hilde de Ridder-Symoens, ed., *Universities in the Middle Ages* (1992). Essays on both
intellectual and institutional matters by leading scholars. See also bibliography for
Chapter 12.

Jane Sayers, *Innocent III* (1994). Brief and judicious.

Bernard Schimmelpfennig, *The Papacy,* trans. James Sievert (1992). A brief and readable
account of the medieval papacy. See also Colin Morris, *The Papal Monarchy: The
Western Church from 1050 to 1250* (1989), and I. S. Robinson, *The Papacy, 1073–1198:
Continuity and Innovation* (1990). For other books on Church history, see especially the
bibliography for Chapter 8.

SUGGESTED PRIMARY SOURCES

Lynn Thorndike, *University Records and Life in the Middle Ages* (1944). A classic collection
that is still unsurpassed.

Brian Tierney, *The Crisis of Church and State, 1050–1300* (1964). Classic texts, organized
chronologically.

CHAPTER 11

※

STATES IN THE MAKING

ENGLAND AND FRANCE, c. 1050-1300

✳ INTRODUCTION

In the eleventh, twelfth, and thirteenth centuries, while the Holy Roman Empire and papacy were engaged in a drawn-out struggle from which neither would emerge fully victorious, England and France evolved into centralized states. Strong monarchy came sooner to England than to France, yet, in a curious twist that makes good historical sense, by the early fourteenth century the English had gone further than the French in limiting royal power. The great political contrasts of the eighteenth century—English parliamentary monarchy and French royal absolutism—were both rooted in the Central Middle Ages.

Another lasting legacy from these centuries was the emergence in both realms of effective administrative institutions; these were critical, early steps toward the political bureaucracies that today envelop Europe and its political heirs, including the United States and Canada. During the century and a half following William the Conqueror's victory in 1066, the English government became the most effective in northern Europe. Tax collecting was managed by the exchequer, a sophisticated accounting department; written royal commands emanated from the royal chancery in ever increasing numbers; and royal justice was administered by a growing number of judges, by an accelerating flood of professional lawyers, and by an abundance of royal courts. France, although changing at a pace about a half-century behind England, followed a similar path toward administrative monarchy until, by the end of the thirteenth century, it was also governed by a complex network of political and legal institutions. The evolution from sacred monarchy—based on a ruler's holy charisma—to bureaucratic monarchy—based on a systematic royal administration—was one of the most fundamental medieval contributions to modern civilization.

TIMELINE 11.1   England, 1000–1300

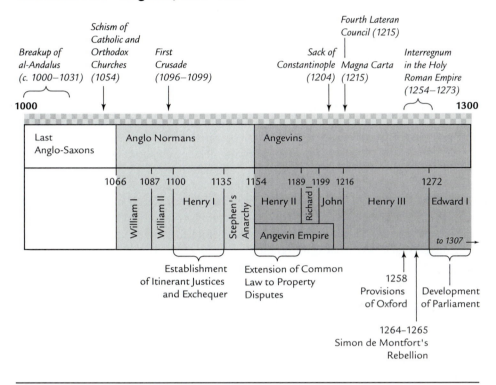

❈ England: King and Parliament

The Anglo-Saxon Heritage

The England that William the Conqueror won at Hastings in 1066 was already relatively centralized and well governed (see Timeline 11.1). Although the Anglo-Saxon court was constantly on the move, traveling around the countryside from one royal manor to another, it remained in close touch with the king's regional and local officials. Critical in this regard were the chief officers in the royal household who were, in effect, the chief administrators of the realm. They issued written notices of the king's commands and decisions, administered the royal finances, and sat as judges on royal tribunals.

England in 1066 had also long been divided into shires (or counties), each with its own shire court, staffed by important local landholders, and with its own royal agent—the "shire reeve," or **sheriff.** This official was usually a local figure whose sympathies were divided between his native shire and the king. It was his responsibility to collect royal taxes and the revenues of royal estates, to assemble the shire's military contingent when needed, and to preside over the shire court. The sheriff was, in short, the crucial link between king and countryside.

The Anglo-Norman State

William the Conqueror came to England in 1066 as a legitimate claimant to the throne, related (distantly) to King Edward the Confessor (r. 1042–1066), who had died childless earlier that year. William promised to preserve English laws and customs, some of which, in fact, were exceedingly beneficial to his monarchy, especially a smoothly functioning system of taxation and a configuration of shire courts unmatched elsewhere. But William added important new customs, many from his native Normandy, which made his government stronger than that of his Anglo-Saxon predecessors.

In the years immediately following the Conquest, William dispossessed virtually all major Anglo-Saxon landholders and replaced them with his own friends and vassals. This brutal shift was somewhat eased by marriage, for some newly enriched Norman knights married women from the newly impoverished Anglo-Saxon aristocracy. Such marriages help to encourage the development of a distinctive *Anglo-Norman* aristocratic culture, French-speaking and accustomed to continental techniques of mounted combat. William established an aristocratic regime in England more or less on the Norman pattern, but the Anglo-Norman aristocracy was more systematically organized and subordinated to his royal will. Most English estates, both lay and ecclesiastical, were transformed into fiefs, held by William's vassals in return for a specified number of mounted knights and various other obligations. The greatest of the new magnates tended to acquire these estates piecemeal as the realm passed progressively under William's control, with the result that their lands were scattered across various shires rather than consolidated into territorial blocs. For example, as we saw in Chapter 6's biography of Hugh, earl of Chester, that magnate's holdings were scattered over twenty counties. This dispersion shaped England's political future, encouraging the aristocracy to take a realm-wide perspective at a time when French and German aristocrats–who often enjoyed control over compact regional princedoms—remained politically provincial. William was also careful to reserve for his own royal demesne about one-sixth of the lands of England (similarly scattered), so that he and his successors would not be mere nominal monarchs like the early Capetian kings of France and the later Hohenstaufen emperors. His political power was buttressed by extensive landed wealth.

The king and his nobility secured their conquest by erecting dozens of castles across the land. Because castles could not be built except by royal license and because private wars between vassals were banned, this flurry of castle building both pacified the countryside and strengthened royal power. Most early castles were simply square wooden towers built on earthen mounds and encircled by wooden palisades; only later did they become elaborate works of stone. But even the earliest of them were difficult to take by siege (see Figure 11.1).

William's authority was strengthened by his loyal magnates, an extensive royal demesne, and numerous castles, but it also owed much to Anglo-Saxon traditions of strong monarchy. The new Norman barons established private courts, as had been their custom in Normandy, but the particularism of these baronial courts was muted by the endurance of shire courts. Similarly, baronial independence was restrained by an Anglo-Saxon custom of general allegiance to the crown, which enabled William and his successors to claim the primary loyalty of every vassal and sub-vassal in England. In Norman England, a knight's allegiance to his immediate lord or lady was always secondary to his allegiance to the king. In brief, the post-Conquest system of fiefs and vassals was molded into a tightly centralized regime by two forces: a powerful Anglo-Saxon tradition of royal supremacy and William's careful control of his vassals.

On the Conqueror's death, his realm passed in turn to two of his sons, William II (r. 1087–1100) and Henry I (r. 1100–1135). Both were strong leaders, but Henry I was

Figure 11.1 *Castle Acre, England*   This castle was begun soon after 1066 and completed during Stephen's Anarchy. The castle itself stood on the mound (or "motte") to the right. The larger area or "bailey" would have housed stables, storage sheds, and other unfortified buildings. As this view shows, earthworks and a commanding view of the countryside could be as important in castle building as strong walls.

the abler of the two. A skillful diplomat and administrator, Henry I rid England of rebellion, exiled troublemakers, used his royal patronage to win friends, and, through these means and others, created a docile and strongly royalist aristocracy. Indeed, at no time in its past had the English realm been as placid as under Henry I. In the words of one eyewitness, he gave his dominions "a peace such as no age remembers, such as his father himself was never able to achieve."

The reigns of William the Conqueror and his sons witnessed a significant growth in royal administration. A unique survey of landholdings known as *Domesday Book,* the product of William the Conqueror's realm-wide census of 1086, bears witness to the administrative vigor of the new regime. Within a decade or so, this regime also had its sheriffs systematically collecting and delivering royal revenues to its accounting department, the exchequer (so named because accounts were tracked by moving counters on a checkered cloth). Moreover, by Henry I's death in 1135, royal judges were extending the king's legal jurisdiction far and wide by traveling all across England to hear cases in the shire courts. Baronial courts and ecclesiastical courts continued to function, as did the ancient shire courts, but the scope of the king's **itinerant judges** (that is, traveling judges) was ever widening. Royal justice was literally on the march. In thus expanding the administrative and legal machinery of government, the Norman kings sought profit as well as power. The more closely the king's men supervised county sheriffs, the less likely it was that royal taxes would stick to sheriffs' fingers; and the more cases royal judges handled, the more fines went into the royal treasure. The Norman kings understood that strong government was good business.

William II and Henry I, each in turn, quarreled about lay investiture with their archbishop of Canterbury, the great theologian St. Anselm (1033–1109). Like their royal counterparts in the Holy Roman Empire, William and Henry were unwilling to lose their long-accepted royal authority over bishops, abbots, and abbesses. But the English dispute never raged as heatedly as in the Empire, and in 1107 a compromise, similar to the later Concordat of Worms (1122), was reached. Henry I relinquished the ceremony of lay investiture but retained considerable control over church appointments. Indeed, he even was a reformer of sorts, supporting decrees against simony and enforcing priestly celibacy. But as the father of no less than twenty-two bastards, Henry's credentials as a moral reformer were somewhat questionable. He died in 1135 of indigestion after violating his doctors' orders by eating lampreys, an eel-like delicacy that readers of this book are urged to avoid.

Ironically, Henry left only one surviving legitimate child, a daughter named Matilda (c. 1102–1167). She had been married, at age eleven, to the Holy Roman Emperor Henry V (r. 1106–1125), and after his death in 1125, she always styled herself "Empress." In 1127, however, she was married again to Count Geoffrey Plantagenet of Anjou (she was twenty-five; he was fifteen; their marriage joined two great counties in northern France). At the time of her father's death, Matilda had two advantages: first, oaths sworn by Henry I's vassals in 1127 to accept her as heir, and second, a son who could continue the male line of his grandfather. But she had disadvantages too: when her father died in 1135, she was in rebellion against him (trying to extract from him some castles he had promised as her dowry); her son Henry was only two years old; and, of course, she was a woman among warriors accustomed to male rule.

Matilda also had a serious rival in her cousin Stephen of Blois (1097–1154), a favorite of Henry I and a great landowner. At Henry's death, Stephen seized the crown; Matilda fought back; and for nineteen troubled years their struggle raged, while the barons, some supporting one side and some the other, built unlicensed castles and fought for their own interests. England suffered vast economic devastation in the course of this civil war. As one contemporary writer lamented, "Christ and his saints slept" during the tormented era commonly known as "Stephen's Anarchy."

Henry II (r. 1154–1189) and the Angevin Empire

Stephen's Anarchy ended in compromise, with Henry Plantagenet, son of Empress Matilda and Geoffrey of Anjou, named as Stephen's heir in 1153. When Stephen died the following year, Henry peacefully assumed the throne as King Henry II of England. He was, by then, also duke of Normandy, count of Anjou, and husband of Eleanor, duchess of Aquitaine (see the 1154 box on Map 11.1). His immense and diverse holdings on both sides of the Channel created an Angevin empire ("Angevin" reflecting Henry's descent from the counts of Anjou). Because Henry governed his constellation of territories separately—for example, acting differently as count of Anjou than he did as king of England—his "empire" was built on territory not political unity, and in this respect, it was very different from the Holy Roman Empire, with its sanctified emperor. But Henry's holdings were vast nonetheless, and they dwarfed the modest territory controlled by the king of France, as well as those held by other dukes and counts. In just a few years, Henry had reshaped the political landscape of France.

Henry was an energetic, brilliant, exuberant man—short, burly, and redheaded. He was a literate monarch who consorted with scholars, encouraged the growth of towns, and presided over an economic boom. He is also perhaps the only medieval English monarch known to law students today, for under his rule, significant steps were taken toward the development of English **common law,** a uniform law administered by royal courts that superseded the varied and complex jurisdictions of local and baronial courts. His first steps involved the all-important subject of feudal land tenure; all such disputes between the king's tenants-in-chief or their subtenants passed squarely under royal jurisdiction in Henry II's reign. The political unification of the Anglo-Saxon kings, begun in the late ninth century, was now paralleled by a nascent legal unification.

Henry II also sought to expand royal justice at the expense of the ecclesiastical courts, but here he ran into trouble for, as we saw in the previous chapter, canon law and papal administration were growing just as vigorously in the twelfth century as were the royal courts and bureaucracies of England. The two began to clash in the 1160s when Henry found himself locked in a bitter struggle with his former friend and new enemy, Thomas Becket (c. 1118–1170). In 1162 Henry had sought to bring the English Church under his closer control by appointing as archbishop of Canterbury his chancellor, Becket. But in raising Becket to this post, Henry had misjudged his friend. As chancellor Becket had been a devoted royal servant, but as archbishop of Canterbury he became a devoted servant of the Church—and hence, an implacable enemy of his old friend, the king. Henry and Becket clashed heatedly over two issues: an old debate about royal control of the English Church and a new debate about the jurisdiction of royal and ecclesiastical courts. Their arguments followed a predictable pattern for a while—hot exchanges, exile, excommunication—but in 1170, Becket was murdered, while standing at the altar of Canterbury Cathedral, by four of Henry's barons. This was an unspeakably horrible and sacrilegious crime.

Becket was immediately regarded as a martyr; miracles were said to have occurred at his tomb; and he was quickly canonized. Canterbury became a major pilgrimage site (the destination of Chaucer's pilgrims, among others), and the cult of St. Thomas enjoyed immense popularity. Henry, who had not ordered the killing but whose anger had prompted it, did penance by walking barefoot through the streets of Canterbury and submitting to a ceremonial flogging. But in the wake of this humiliation, Henry got most of what he had wanted. He gained effective control of appointments to high Church offices in his realm, and by the end of his reign, his royal justice had made significant inroads on the jurisdiction of Church courts. Here as elsewhere, Henry steered England toward administrative and legal centralization.

Throughout his reign, Henry divided his time between England and the French provinces of his Angevin empire, while the French monarchy did what it could to break up these dominions—encouraging rebellions on the part of Henry's sons and his estranged wife, Eleanor of Aquitaine (c. 1122–1204). Henry put down the rebellions one by one, relegated Eleanor to captivity in a royal castle, and sought to placate his sons. It did him little good. The rebellions persisted, and as Henry neared death in 1189, his two surviving sons, Richard and John, were both in arms against him. In the end he was

MEDIEVAL MYTHS

Robin Hood

What could be more medieval than Robin Hood and his band of merry men? With Friar Tuck, Little John, Will Scarlet, and Maid Marion, Robin Hood lived as an outlaw in Sherwood Forest, dressed in "Lincoln green," shot the longbow with deadly accuracy, and, most of all, stole from the rich to give to the poor. Robin Hood's primary enemy was the wicked and rich Sheriff of Nottingham; his ultimate loyalty lay with King Richard, a good king whose realm had been badly governed while he was away on crusade. Tales of Robin Hood are genuinely medieval, although the medieval Robin Hood was different from the Robin Hood of modern movies and novels. In the first tales that survive in manuscripts from the fourteenth century, Robin Hood was a heroic outlaw who fought a wicked sheriff, but he was a much rougher character—no hints that he was a noble fallen on hard times, no romance with Maid Marion, no charity to the poor, no abiding loyalty to a distant king, even, sad to say, no Sherwood Forest. Tales about Robin changed with changing times, so that he picked up over the centuries a whole range of characteristics he did not originally have. A humble yeoman with only a few buddies in late medieval stories, he was aristocratic in Elizabethan England, romantic in the Victorian era, and a rebel with a cause in the mid-twentieth century. Historians have long tried to locate a real Robin Hood in contemporary documents. Because both Robin (a nickname for Robert) and Hood were common names, several Robin Hoods have been found, most notably an outlaw in 1226 and a king's servant in 1324. Neither can be firmly fixed to the legend. In the end, what matters more than any authentic, documented Robin Hood is the *meaning* of his legend in each age that has embraced him. Medieval people seem to have enjoyed an "average Joe" sort of Robin Hood who argued with his friends, lost a lot of fights, and relied more on trickery than bravery or skill. His stories probably helped them imagine a better world than their own, one that was closer to nature, free of meaningless distinctions of status, and full of opportunity for quick-witted men who worked together for a common good. You can read about all this and more in Stephen Knight's new book, *Robin Hood, A Mythic Biography* (2003).

outmaneuvered and defeated. His dying words are said to have been, "Shame, shame on a conquered king."

The Loss of the Angevin Empire

Despite Henry's deathbed despair, his Angevin dominions passed intact into the hands of his eldest surviving son, Richard I, the Lion-Hearted (r. 1189–1199), raised in Aquitaine and a loyal son—of his mother. After liberating Queen Eleanor from captivity, Richard devoted himself chiefly to defending his French possessions and crusading against the Muslims. As we saw in the biographical sketch in Chapter 9, Richard was a skillful soldier who won renown on the Third Crusade and in his many French campaigns. But he spent little time in England and taxed it relentlessly. The royal bureaucracy stood this test well, governing England efficiently for ten kingless and expensive years until the crusader-king died, prematurely, in 1199.

His brother John (r. 1199–1216) was a master of administrative detail, but he was a suspicious, unscrupulous, and untrustworthy man. His crisis-prone reign was sabotaged repeatedly by the half-heartedness with which his overtaxed vassals supported him and the energy with which some of them opposed him. He was not at all helped by the fact that he faced two shrewd and unremitting antagonists: Philip II Augustus of France (r. 1180–1223) and Pope Innocent III (r. 1098–1216).

Philip Augustus sought to take John's French holdings for his own—and he did just that. Acting as overlord of John's continental possessions, Philip Augustus alleged a feudal slight and declared these French lands forfeit. On this pretext, he invaded Normandy in 1203 and soon seized all of John's French dominions except portions of distant Aquitaine (most importantly, Gascony). This was a political and military disaster for John, and for the next ten years he wove a dexterous web of alliances against Philip Augustus, all financed by the heavy taxation of his English subjects. His plans were shattered by Philip's decisive victory over John's Flemish and German allies at the battle of Bouvines in 1214. With the men who died at Bouvines died also John's last hope of recovering Normandy and Anjou.

Innocent III sought to assert his papal authority over the English—and he did just that. After a long and bitter quarrel with John over the appointment of an archbishop of Canterbury, he forced John to accept his candidate and then wrung even further concessions. John had to acknowledge Innocent's papal overlordship of England, and he also agreed to pay a substantial annual tribute.

John's military and diplomatic failures paved the way for an uprising of English barons that ended on the field of Runnymede in 1215, where they forced John to issue *Magna Carta* (the "Great Charter"). Magna Carta dealt with the immediate problems of 1215, but it has acquired an enormous historical legacy, albeit a confused one. To some historians, Magna Carta is a backward-looking document designed to favor the old aristocracy over the new powers of the king; to others, it is a forward-looking document that lays the foundation of England's later constitutional monarchy. In fact, it is both, for its assertion of traditional rights would eventually lead to the development of new ones. For example, Magna Carta sought to keep the king within the bounds of popular and feudal custom, stipulating, among other things, that taxes were to be levied only with the consent of the great barons. From this traditional stipulation that the monarch had to respect the rights of his vassals and rule according to custom would eventually emerge the constitutional principle of government under the law. In striving to make John a good feudal lord, the barons in 1215 moved uncertainly—and unknowingly—toward constitutional monarchy.

As soon as John could, he repudiated Magna Carta. A full-scale revolt followed that ended only with his death in 1216. As Figure 11.2 suggests, he was little mourned. The crown now passed, without objection, to his nine-year-old son, Henry III (r. 1216–1272), whose rule was initially supervised by a council of barons and churchmen. In the decades that followed, Magna Carta was reissued a number of times, but the great task of the new age was to create political institutions capable of uniting king, bureaucracy, and baronage in the governance of England. The ultimate solution to this problem would be found in a new institution: **parliament.**

Henry III (r. 1216–1272) and Baronial Government

Henry III was no improvement on his father. He was a petulant, erratic monarch who surrounded himself with foreign favorites, loved grandiose and impractical projects, and ignored the advice of his barons so completely that he gradually lost their confidence. He was eventually forced to govern in partnership with them.

Figure 11.2   *King John Assessed*   This drawing is in the
margins of a manuscript that reports the death of King John. The
upside-down royal shield is an insult, as is the tottering crown.

When the Angevin empire collapsed, John and his successors lost important estates and income on the continent; so too did many Anglo-Norman barons. They also lost
the "distraction" of continental holdings, so that after Bouvines, both crown and baronage were more focused on the power, lands, and wealth to be had in England. Henry III
still held Gascony and sought to reclaim other parts of the old Angevin domain, but these
increasingly struck his barons as "foreign" projects. They resented Frenchmen enriched
by Henry's favors.

They resented even more Henry's willingness to rule without consulting them.
Ever since its beginning, English kings had customarily arrived at important policy decisions through discussion in the **curia regis,** the "king's court," an amorphous group of
nobles, **prelates,** and officials. Although its role was only advisory, the curia regis was
a valued tradition of royal deliberation with England's lay and ecclesiastical lords. It
met in two different formats. Ordinary decisions were discussed in a small council of
household officers and royal favorites who were always with the king as he moved about
the countryside, staying in one castle and then another. But on great ceremonial occasions or at times when an important decision was pending, the king supplemented his
normal coterie of advisers by assembling around him all the important nobles and
churchmen of the realm.

Henry III, however, usually summoned great councils only for approval of new
taxes, not for substantive consultation. Resentful of his foreign schemes, his expensive
projects, and his lack of consultation, English barons eventually refused Henry's requests
for money. By 1258 Henry faced a financial crisis of major proportions, and to get money,
he submitted to a set of baronial limitations on his royal power known as the *Provisions
of Oxford.* The Provisions of Oxford went far beyond Magna Carta in creating a machinery to force the king to govern in accordance with good custom and in consultation with
his magnates. Great councils, now called "parliaments," were to be assembled three

times a year.[1] They were to include men selected by the magnates as well as those called by the king. In addition, a Council of Fifteen, chiefly barons, were to share with the king control over the royal administration—specifically, oversight of the exchequer and appointment of the chancellor and other high officers of state.

In the baronial factionalism that followed 1258, the Provisions of Oxford proved premature and unworkable. With their failure, Henry III returned to the arbitrary and inept governance that his barons found so distasteful. At length, discontent exploded into open rebellion, and Simon de Montfort, a great French lord who was also earl of Leicester in England, defeated the royal army in 1264 and captured King Henry himself. For the next fifteen months Simon de Montfort ruled England in the king's name, sharing his authority with other magnates and parliaments. But a number of barons remained royalists, as was usually the case in such crises, and with their backing the monarchy rallied under the leadership of Edward, Henry III's talented son. Edward defeated Simon's army in 1265, and the rebellion dissolved.

Neither the Provisions of Oxford nor Simon de Montfort's rebellion lasted long, but both efforts cast precious light on the attitudes of many mid-thirteenth-century English nobles toward their monarchy. These barons harassed their king, but they had no thought of abolishing the legal advances of the two previous centuries or of weakening the central government. Their interests were national rather than provincial and best served by exerting some control over royal administration rather than dismantling it. They sought to curb an incompetent, arbitrary, spendthrift king, not to curb kingship itself.

Edward I (r. 1272–1307) and the Evolution of Parliament

The reign of Edward I witnessed the culmination of many trends in law and administration, giving new force and coherence to royal administration, common law, and Parliament. In addition, Edward I was a great warrior, whose armies subdued Wales, devastated Scotland, and maintained his crown's hold on Gascony.

In 1265, just before his defeat by Edward's army, Simon de Montfort had summoned a great council that contained, for the first time, all the elements that would eventually constitute a parliament in later centuries. It included, in addition to great lords and royal officials, two knights from every shire and two burgesses from every town. Shire knights and burgesses had been called to earlier great councils, but only rarely, always for some specific purpose, and never jointly. Simon's chief motive for summoning both shire knights and burgesses was probably to broaden the base of his support, and his innovation did not stick, at least initially. For several generations, shire knights and burgesses were summoned only occasionally. Through the thirteenth century and beyond, parliaments consisted primarily of great lords, royal judges and administrators, and, of course, the king himself.

After he succeeded his father in 1272, Edward I summoned parliaments often and experimented endlessly in their composition. Like Simon de Montfort, he sometimes included shire knights and burgesses, particularly in the later years of his reign. But the composition and powers of parliaments remained fluid throughout Edward's long reign. In one respect, however, these assemblies did participate in an important Edwardian innovation. His government began to legislate—that is, govern by statute—on a larger

---

[1] "Parliament" is derived from the French word *parler*, "to talk," from which also comes our word "parley."

scale than ever before. This was a significant change from old ideas that law was a matter of custom and that, therefore, although a king might interpret or clarify the law, he seldom made new law. Of course, only a thin line separated the act of clarifying old law from the making of new law, and many of Edward's predecessors had been lawmakers in fact, if not in theory. But Edward's reign was marked by explicit lawmaking, by the appearance of a great many royal statutes that elaborated and systematized English government. Parliaments were part of this change, for new legislation was a solemn affair that required the approval of the "community of the realm" as expressed in Edward's parliaments.

Nevertheless, throughout Edward's reign, parliament remained primarily an instrument to serve his purposes and to assist him in the governance of the realm. Edward I, backed by his officials and usually by a sympathetic baronial majority, was the controlling figure in all such assemblies. He regarded parliamentary meetings as a tool of royal policy and used them to strengthen his monarchy rather than limit it. He would have been appalled to learn that his royal descendants would one day be figurehead monarchs and that Parliament was destined to rule England.

The four chief agencies of royal government under Edward I were the chancery, the exchequer, the council, and the household. Chancery and exchequer were by now both permanently established at Westminster, just outside London; they did not travel with the king. The *chancery* was, in effect, the royal secretarial office, and its chief officer, the chancellor, was the custodian of the great seal which authenticated royal documents. The *exchequer,* headed by the royal treasurer, was the king's accounting agency, and by 1300, it supervised a wide variety of local officials charged with collecting royal revenues. By 1300, it was also much enriched by Edward I's hard treatment of his Jewish subjects. After taxing English Jews in a variety of ways, Edward expelled them from his realm in 1290, taking for himself all their goods and properties.

Unlike the chancery and exchequer, the council and household accompanied the king on his endless travels. The *council* was a permanent royal entourage of judges, administrators, magnates, and prelates who advised the king on routine matters. In the Provisions of Oxford the barons had tried to wrest control of the council from the king, but in Edward's reign it was firmly under his royal authority. Traveling with the king, the *household* grew into a royal government in miniature. It had its own writing clerks, supervised by the keeper of the privy (private) seal, and its own financial office known as the *wardrobe.* By means of his household administration the king could govern on the move, without having to route all his business through Westminster.

The king's justice also took more permanent form under Edward's guidance. Cases of singular importance were brought before the king himself, sitting in parliament or surrounded by his council. Less important cases were handled by the king's itinerant justices or by one of several royal courts based at Westminster. These courts were staffed with trained professionals: lawyers or, in the case of the exchequer court, experienced accountants.

Edward's territorial ambitions led him to wars in Wales, Scotland, and France. On the first front he was highly successful, ending centuries of discord along the English-Welsh frontier by conquering Wales altogether. He then granted his eldest son the title "Prince of Wales," which male heirs-apparent to the English throne have held ever since. He came very near to conquering Scotland, too, foiled only by the dogged determination of the heroic King Robert I "the Bruce" (r. 1306–1329) of Scotland. He fought an expensive and inconclusive war with Philip IV (r. 1285–1314) of France but did protect his possession of Gascony. Eventually, Edward's wars emptied the royal treasury and aroused both baronial and popular opposition, but he survived by offering timely concessions, reissuing Magna Carta, and making sure that all extraordinary taxes were approved in parliaments.

At his death in 1307, Edward left behind him a realm exhausted by his wars but firmly under his control. He had completed the work of his predecessors in creating an effective and complex royal administrative system, bringing local justice under royal control, and building a comprehensive body of common law. More than that, he had solidified the concept of original legislation, nurtured the developing institution of parliament, and found that royal strength could come from consultation and discussion. He thereby set into motion forces that would have an immense impact not only on the future of England but also on all political systems that today trace some of their practices to the English past. Edward's England was still, in spirit, a feudal realm, but it was feudalism with a strong king, backed by a strong bureaucracy, at its center.

✳ FRANCE: THE MONARCHY TRIUMPHANT

When William of Normandy conquered England in 1066, the king of France—to whom William owed fealty as a vassal—exerted unsteady control over a modest territory around Paris known as the Ile de France. He was virtually powerless in the lands beyond (see Map 11.1). Although French monarchs *claimed* authority over such great princes as the dukes of Normandy and Aquitaine and the counts of Anjou, Flanders, and Champagne, only gradually did they acquire the power and prestige to make good these claims. From these modest beginnings, however, the Capetians slowly developed the foremost royal dynasty in Western Christendom, backed by a bureaucracy as efficient and complex as its English counterpart (see Timeline 11.2).

The Early Capetian Kings

The first Capetian, Hugh Capet (r. 987–996), had gained the crown through election by the magnates of West Francia. But he and his successors quickly sought to secure a hereditary claim to the monarchy. This they accomplished with an astonishing reproductive record, producing legitimate male heirs for no less than eleven consecutive generations, across 341 years. The stability of their dynasty was further secured by their practice of crowning heirs before the old king died and by the loyalty of younger sons who usually opted to support their royal brothers rather than rebel against them.

Yet in the early twelfth century the Capetians remained no stronger than several of their own princely vassals. While principalities such as Normandy and Anjou were becoming increasingly centralized, the Ile de France, a fertile grain-growing district of great potential value to the Capetian monarchy, was still ridden with insubordinate barons. If the Capetians were to realize the potential of their royal title, they had three great tasks before them: (1) to master and pacify the Ile de France, (2) to expand their political and economic base by bringing additional territories under direct royal authority, and (3) to make their royal claims over the great feudal principalities real rather than merely theoretical. Over the next 200 years the Capetians achieved these goals so completely that by 1300 they controlled most of France, either directly or

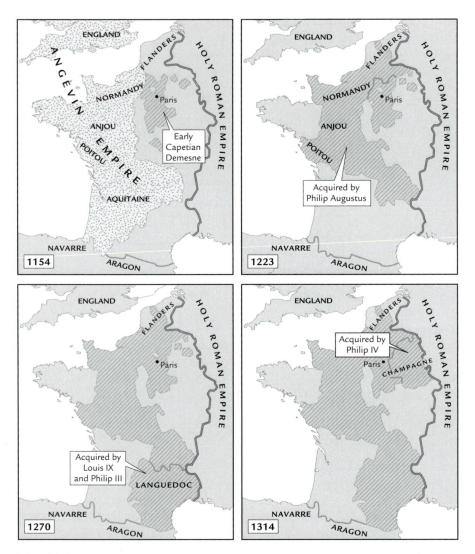

Map 11.1   *The Expansion of Royal Power in France, c. 1150–1300*   In 1154, Henry II of England controlled more of the territory we today call "France" than did the Capetian kings, who wielded power only in the region around Paris known as the Ile de France. After the Angevin Empire crumbled in the wake of the battle of Bouvines in 1214, Capetian kings slowly but surely expanded the territory under their authority.

indirectly, and they exercised that control through an efficient and sophisticated royal bureaucracy.

Aided by luck and ingenuity as well as a steady string of male heirs, the Capetians attained their objectives by exploiting their powers as kings and feudal lords, avoiding family squabbles, and maintaining comparatively good relations with the papacy. They seldom overreached themselves, preferring to extend their power gradually through favorable marriages, through reclaiming as their own the fiefs of vassals who died without

TIMELINE 11.2   France, 1000–1300

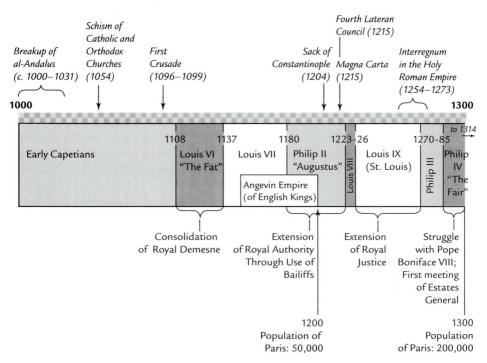

heirs, and through dispossessing vassals who violated their feudal obligations. Yet most Capetians had no grandiose desire to absorb the territories of all their vassals; rather, they sought to build a realm with a substantial royal demesne surrounded by the fiefs of loyal, obedient magnates.

The Consolidation of the Royal Demesne

Philip I (r. 1060–1108) was the first Capetian to grasp the essential fact that his dynasty had to secure its home base in the Ile de France. His policies were continued by his son, Louis VI, "the Fat" (r. 1108–1137), a gluttonous and mediocre man who was blessed with an intelligent wife, Adelaide of Murienne (d. 1154). Encouraged by Queen Adelaide, Louis the Fat battled dissident barons year after year, until he could no longer find a horse sturdy enough to carry his ever increasing weight. But no matter, for by that time he enjoyed the invaluable assistance of Abbot Suger (1098–1151) of the great royal monastery of St. Denis near Paris. This gifted statesman labored hard and effectively to extend the king's sway and systematize the royal administration. The support of his monastery of St. Denis—both the practical support of the abbey and the spiritual support of its patron saint—added much to the prestige of the Capetian house; and the king's support, in turn, enhanced the wealth and prestige of St. Denis. When Louis the Fat died in 1137, the Ile de France was orderly and prosperous, and the French monarchy was stronger than it had been since Carolingian times.

Until his own death in 1151, Abbot Suger continued to advise and support the heir, Louis VII (r. 1137–1180). Pious and gentle, Louis VII was, in the words of one contemporary observer, "a very Christian king, if somewhat simple-minded." In the 1150s, Louis VII faced a new and formidable threat: the creation of the Angevin empire of Henry Plantagenet, count of Anjou, duke of Normandy, husband (in 1152) to Eleanor, duchess of Aquitaine, and king (from 1154) of England.[2] Louis VII sought to embarrass his mighty vassal by encouraging Henry's sons to rebel, but his efforts were too half-hearted to be successful.

Still, Louis VII's reign witnessed a significant extension of royal power. On the one hand, the fertile Ile de France, now well pacified, provided more and more revenue for the Capetian treasury. On the other hand, more and more people, humble as well as great, began to turn to their genial, unassuming monarch for succor and justice. The great vassals of France, fearful of Henry II's Angevin empire and respectful of Louis VII's piety and impartiality, began for the first time to submit their disputes to his royal court. Churchmen sought his support in struggles with the nobility; so too did towns-people. In a time of growing peace, social order, and commercial growth, the Ile de France was slowly becoming the true center of France.

Philip II Augustus (r. 1180–1223) and the Extension of Royal Power

The French monarchy came of age under Louis VII's talented son, Philip II, "Augustus." A wily and clever opportunist, Philip Augustus expanded the royal demesne and tightened his lordship over the dukes and counts of France.

Philip Augustus's great achievement was the destruction of the Angevin empire, an accomplishment that both weakened the English royal house (which lost vast lands) and strengthened his own (by adding these lands to the Capetian royal demesne). For two decades Philip plotted against Henry II and Richard the Lion-Hearted, but it was not until the reign of King John that his efforts bore fruit. When Philip Augustus moved against Normandy in 1203–1204, John's unpopularity and lethargy allowed Philip to win with surprising ease the prize he had sought so long. Ten years later, with his decisive victory over John's German and Flemish allies at Bouvines in 1214, Philip extinguished John's last hope of recovering the lost territories. Settling for good the question of Normandy and Anjou, Bouvines was also a turning point in the power balance of European monarchies in the Central Middle Ages. Thereafter the Capetian monarchy overshadowed the faltering Holy Roman Empire, as well as the much-reduced territories of the kings of England. France became the great power of the thirteenth century.

Philip Augustus extended his power by administration as well as war. He used the curia regis, the high feudal court of France, as an effective instrument for the assertion of royal rights. He also relied for local governance not on local nobles but instead on salaried officials known as *baillis,* or bailiffs. These bailiffs, whose functions were at once financial, judicial, military, and administrative, owed their positions to royal favor and were devoted to the crown. Throughout the thirteenth century they worked tirelessly

---

[2] Louis VII was the first husband of Eleanor of Aquitaine, but their marriage was dissolved in 1152. The most important cause was doubtless that the union had produced no male heirs; the Capetian record of legitimate male heirs over 341 years was achieved, in part, by a ruthless readiness to unmake marriages. Since divorce was not possible in canon law, their union was declared invalid because of *consanguinity* (their close blood relationship). This was a convenient excuse, for many aristocratic marriages (and lesser ones too) involved principals who should not have married, according to the then complex and expansive rules of consanguinity. The two daughters born to the marriage were treated as legitimate. Alix became Countess of Blois; Marie became Countess of Champagne. Within two months of the dissolution, Eleanor married Henry Plantagenet, to whom she was also tied by blood relationship.

and often unscrupulously to erode the privileges of the aristocracy and extend French royal authority. Because they usually had no roots in the regions they administered, bailiffs were more loyal to the crown than their English counterparts—the sheriffs who managed the counties and shire knights who went to parliamentary assemblies. Drawn from the local gentry, English sheriffs and shire knights tended to divide their loyalties between monarchy and locality. A loyal and highly mobile bureaucracy, the bailiffs became in time a powerful instrument of royal absolutism.

Philip Augustus also transformed Paris into the true royal capital of France. Paris had long been the largest city in France, and during Philip's reign, its population doubled to some 50,000 people. It was the chief center of a royal government that, like that of England, had moved constantly from place to place. But Philip kept his government more permanently in Paris, ruling from his royal palace at the west end of an island in the Seine, the *Ile de la Cité,* which was also the site of the cathedral of Notre Dame, nearing completion at that time. Philip built great walls around the city, paved its major streets, and built a fortress, the Louvre, just outside the walls near the Seine as it flowed westward toward Normandy. (For centuries the Louvre served as a royal palace; today it is one of the world's great museums, and the walls of Philip Augustus can still be seen from an underground gallery beneath it.) Having prospered under Philip Augustus, Paris continued to flourish under his successors. By 1300, the population of Paris would have doubled and then doubled again to about 200,000 inhabitants. It was then probably Europe's largest city, even surpassing Milan, Venice, Naples, and the other great Italian city-states.

At the very end of his life, Philip Augustus made good use of another opportunity to extend his territorial sway. When Innocent III called the Albigensian Crusade against the heretics of southern France in 1208, Philip Augustus made sure that his heir Louis took an active part in it. When the son succeeded his father in 1223 as Louis VIII (r. 1223–1226), he used all the resources of his monarchy to break the power of the Cathars and extend Capetian royal authority southward to the Mediterranean.

It may seem surprising that Louis VIII, who inherited a vastly expanded royal jurisdiction and extended it still further himself, granted about one-third of these hard-won royal territories as fiefs to junior members of his family. These family fiefs, carved out of the royal domain, were known as **apanages.** As their creation shows, the growing power of the Capetian monarchy cannot be understood simply as a linear process of expanding royal demesne. The Capetians recognized the importance of keeping younger sons happy and did not hesitate to grant them counties and duchies. Indeed, given the limited facilities of communication and transportation in twelfth- and thirteenth-century France, the realm was too large to be controlled directly by any king. At least for the time being these rich cadet branches, bound to the crown by firm family ties, strengthened rather than weakened Capetian rule. So too did the bailiffs who efficiently pursued the king's interests throughout the realm.

Louis IX (r. 1226–1270) and Royal Sanctity

Louis VIII died prematurely in 1226, leaving his realm in the skillful hands of his pious widow, Blanche of Castile (1188–1252), who acted as regent for their young son Louis IX, later canonized as St. Louis. As discussed in the Biographical Sketch on pp. 284–285, Blanche put down several revolts during Louis's minority, and she continued to play a

Figure 11.3   *St. Louis*   Taken from a fifteenth-century manuscript, this image shows Louis IX, the king whose sanctity added enormous prestige to the French royal dynasty, departing on crusade.

dominant and highly capable role in his government even after he came of age in 1234. Blanche was a devout and strong-willed woman, and Louis (see Figure 11.3) inherited from her both sanctity and firmness. Determined to rule justly and to promote moral rectitude, he sought to pursue peace at home while devoting every resource to crusading against Islam.

At home, Louis oversaw great prosperity and cultural growth. In towns, where commerce flourished, newly built churches and cathedrals bore witness to urban wealth, piety, and taste for the new Gothic architectural style. Louis's own palace chapel in Paris, La Sainte Chapelle, built to house the precious relic of Jesus' crown of thorns, remains to this day a building of stunning beauty. These were also decades during which the University of Paris became, even more clearly than before, Europe's foremost intellectual center. In Paris some of the keenest minds of the age—Bonaventure (1221–1274), Albertus Magnus (c. 1200–1280), Thomas Aquinas (c. 1225–1274)—studied and taught.

On crusade, Louis was a failure, an outcome he interpreted as divine punishment for his sins. From his return in 1254 until his death in 1270 he sought to compensate for this failure abroad by creating an ideal Christian monarchy at home. He opened his royal courts to all free subjects and did everything in his power to ensure that royal justice, staffed by legal professionals, was fair and compassionate. He even sought to restrain the powers of his own royal officers, establishing a system of itinerant royal inspectors known as *enquêteurs,* who heard local complaints and corrected the abuses of other royal agents. He sponsored charitable works on an unprecedented scale. He instituted a new gold coinage of high quality, to the great benefit of French commerce. And he labored to achieve peace throughout Western Christendom, settling by treaty old disputes with Henry III of England and the king of Aragon. He came to be venerated as a peacemaker among Christians and was even selected to arbitrate between Henry III and his barons (the latter were chagrined when he decided solidly in favor of the royal authority of Henry III).

Among one group, however, Louis IX was no peacemaker. Like many other crusaders, he regarded Jews as his enemy, and he launched a major effort to persuade Jewish children to become Christians. His intolerance, born of fervent Christianity, would be followed by later royal policies, born of financial need. In 1306, his grandson Philip IV (r. 1285–1314) would arrest all the Jews in his dominions and, after seizing their property and accounts, expel them from France. As Edward I had done just a few years earlier in England, Philip IV would seek to strengthen his throne by persecuting and expelling his Jewish subjects. In this regard, the religious intolerance of Louis IX neatly matched the fiscal needs of the growing monarchies of the Central Middle Ages.

Louis died while on one final crusade, in Tunisia in 1270, with victory still eluding him. By that time, his policies at home had won him the hearts of his Christian subjects. As one contemporary put it, he exercised "kingship like a priest." His saintliness strengthened the French monarchy in ways less concrete but no less important than the territorial and administrative accomplishments of Philip Augustus. When Louis IX was canonized as St. Louis in 1297, his personal sanctity became dynastic sanctity. Henceforth, all Capetians shared in the awesome holiness of their kinsman.

Philip IV the Fair (r. 1285–1314) and an Ascendant France

St. Louis was loved and admired for keeping his ambitious officials in check, but his son Philip III (r. 1270–1285) and grandson, Philip IV "the Fair" (or "Handsome") did little to restrain the growth of the royal bureaucracy. Philip the Fair was a silent, enigmatic figure who said little and listened much. As one of his bishops observed, "He is not a man; he is not a beast; he is a statue." Yet Philip was genuinely pious, intensely so after the death of his wife in 1305, and he was by no means lacking in intelligence. He also surrounded himself with skillful and devoted ministers.

Philip and his ministers championed a lofty view of his royal authority, at the expense of the papacy, the nobility, and neighboring states. Against the papacy, as we saw in Chapter 10, Philip launched a successful campaign for the independence of the French Church, and his men even briefly arrested the proud old Pope Boniface VIII (r. 1294–1303) at Anagni. Against his nobles, Philip pursued a strongly royalist policy,

BIOGRAPHICAL SKETCH

Queen Blanche of Castile (1188–1252)

Blanche of Castile, one of medieval Europe's most gifted rulers, was born in 1188 to Alphonso VIII, King of Castile, and Eleanor, daughter of Eleanor of Aquitaine and Henry II of England. If Eleanor of Aquitaine was the most celebrated queen of the Central Middle Ages, her nearest rival was her granddaughter, Blanche of Castile.

Blanche was born in Iberia, but her destiny lay in France. At the age of twelve, she was married to the thirteen-year-old Louis, son of King Philip Augustus of France. Their marriage sealed a peace treaty between France and England, with Blanche representing the interests of her maternal uncle, King John of England. Blanche was chosen for this role by her grandmother Eleanor of Aquitaine (then almost eighty years old) who traveled to Castile, inspected her two royal granddaughters, and selected the younger. She then took Blanche to France for the wedding. The marriage might not have been immediately consummated, as Blanche did not bear her first child for five more years. That child was stillborn; three others died at birth or shortly thereafter; eight lived. Like most aristocratic and royal women, Blanche more than fulfilled her reproductive responsibilities, bearing many children to secure her husband's lineage.

When Philip Augustus died in 1223, Blanche and Louis became the queen and king of France. Louis was a gentle king who lacked his father's determination, and his regime benefited from his wife's keen intelligence and resolution. Louis devoted himself to the Albigensian Crusade (1209–1229) against the Cathars of southern France, in the process of which he established the authority of the Capetian monarchy in that region for the first time. But in 1226, at the age of thirty-nine, Louis died in the course of his campaigning, leaving his widow to rule France as regent for their twelve-year-old son, Louis IX, the future St. Louis. She was then thirty-eight, a queen for only three years, and a woman whose life to that point had been, as best we can tell, mostly devoted to motherhood and religious piety.

In the years just following Louis VIII's death, the great gains that the Capetian monarchy had achieved during the previous century were severely threatened. Rebellious coalitions of French nobles reasserted their traditional autonomy, and they were usually backed by Henry III of England, who eagerly sought to regain the French principalities that his father John had lost to Philip Augustus. The future of the Capetian monarchy hung in the balance, and it survived because of Queen Blanche's statecraft. In her young son's name, Blanche negotiated alliances, led armies, besieged castles, and in general overawed and outwitted her enemies with astute and resolute leadership.

Some French nobles, having been outmaneuvered and subdued by Blanche, attacked her with the weapon of ridicule. A proper sort of woman, they said, should not be leading armies or ruling realms; such responsibilities should be exercised by men. They accused Blanche of being too haughty, of overspending, of having an affair with a papal legate, even of having conspired to bring about her late husband's death. Men sang comic songs about Blanche in the streets of Paris, portraying her as the she-wolf, Dame Hersent, a character in the immensely popular set of fables about Renard the Fox.

As one would expect, Blanche survived these petty attacks, just as she overcame the armies and plots mounted against her young son. By the time Louis married in 1234, her policies had quelled all dissent and restored Capetian authority to its former height. During the years that followed, the young king continued to rely heavily on his mother's wise advice. He also shared her deep piety. Louis was himself frail and afflicted with poor health, yet Blanche, who had lost so many children to early death, is reported to have said that she would rather her eldest son die than that he should commit a mortal sin, for death could be a portal into paradise, whereas mortal sin, if unconfessed, doomed its perpetrator to eternal damnation.

In 1244, after nearly twenty years of close cooperation between mother and son, a sharp split arose when Louis, suffering from a nearly fatal illness, vowed to lead a crusade if he should live. Blanche was firmly opposed to such a spectacular act of militant piety, but Louis was determined to carry out his vow. He should have listened to his mother's advice, in this matter as in others. In 1248 Louis embarked on an ill-fated crusade that cost him vast treasure and, for a time, his freedom. During his absence, Blanche served as regent of France once again. Even in her sixties, with her health failing, and even in a venture that she thought foolish, Blanche supported her son. She negotiated special taxes from the Church to back his crusade; she consolidated Capetian control over the previously independent county of Toulouse; she completed construction of a vast new embarkation port at Aigues-Mortes on the Mediterranean coast (which endures to this day, behind its massive walls, as one of the most fascinating medieval sites in southern France); she carried on her son's reforms of the French royal administration; and she kept the peace.

When Blanche died, comic songs about her as Dame Hersent had not been heard in the streets of Paris for some time. Her accomplishments had stilled the vicious gossip, silenced the satirists, and brought her wide acclaim and honor. A contemporary writer paid Queen Blanche what he meant to be the greatest possible compliment when he observed that she ruled as well as any man.

demanding direct allegiance and obedience from all French subjects, regardless of what duke or count might also claim their loyalty. Against neighboring states, Philip waged an indecisive war with Edward I of England over control of Gascony, and he was also thwarted in his attempt to annex Flanders by a bloody uprising of Flemish nobles and townspeople, who routed his army at the battle of Courtrai in 1302. He was more successful to the east, with nibbling aggressions against the faltering Holy Roman Empire.

Under Philip the Fair the royal bureaucracy was a refined and supple tool of royal interest, and its middle-class officials, with their tenacious royalism, gave Philip a degree of independence from the nobility unknown to his contemporary, Edward I of England. The royal revenues were handled by a special accounting bureau, roughly parallel to the English exchequer, called the *chambre des comptes*. The king's judicial business became the responsibility of a high court known as the **Parlement** of Paris. This was a judicial court, not an advisory assembly like its homonymic counterpart the English parliament, but it was to play a significant political role in later centuries.

Still, Philip could not rule without support from his subjects, especially their financial support. He managed to fill royal coffers with his victory over the papacy on the issue of royal taxation of the clergy, with lucrative confiscations from his assault on the Knights Templars (as discussed in Chapter 9), and with similarly profitable attacks on Jews and Lombards. But soaring expenses of government and warfare forced him constantly to seek ever new sources of revenue and, as in England, to secure approval of extraordinary taxation. Instead of seeking such approval through realm-wide assemblies along the lines of the English parliaments, however, Philip usually negotiated individually with various taxpaying groups—for example, with the clergy for one tax and with townspeople for another.

Nevertheless, it was under Philip the Fair that France's first representative assembly—the Estates General—was summoned. The Estates General included members of the three great social "estates": the clergy, the nobility, and the townspeople.[3] Beginning in 1302, it was called from time to time, primarily for the purpose of giving formal support to the monarchy in moments of crisis—during the struggle with Pope Boniface VIII, for example, or in the midst of the Knights Templar controversy. But it had no real voice in royal taxation and it was, therefore, never in a position to bargain hard with Philip the Fair or his successors. Although the Estates General continued to meet occasionally over the succeeding centuries, it never became an integral organ of government as did Parliament in England.

In 1300, Philip the Fair governed the strongest realm in Western Christendom, and it was no accident that it was he—rather than the weak Holy Roman emperors or his rival, King Edward I of England—who brought Pope Boniface VIII to heel. Backed by loyal bureaucrats, armed might, and familial sanctity, he governed a large and rich realm. But his realm was too large, too segmented into cohesive principalities, and too recently brought under royal authority for its inhabitants to have acquired a strong sense of identification as a people. They were governed firmly from Paris, but their outlook remained provincial.

✳ IBERIAN AND GERMAN STATES: SOME CONSOLIDATION

In sum, over the course of the Central Middle Ages, the kings of England and France strengthened their control over extensive territories. To manage these dominions, they developed sophisticated royal administrations, with efficient offices that handled their financial, secretarial, and legal affairs. Both monarchies also tightened their control over baronial and ecclesiastical jurisdictions, although for centuries to come both would have to share their basic prerogatives—to tax, to prosecute criminals, and to adjudicate civil disputes—with others within their realms (especially nobles, bishops, and chartered towns). And in both realms, institutions developed that tempered the power of monarchy with the consultation of the governed: Parliament in England and the Estates General in France. Although these trends were especially pronounced in England and France, they were not unique to them. Other princes in Western Christendom also sought to solidify their power through administration, law, and assembly.

In Iberia, for example, the kings of Castile, Aragon, and Portugal attempted to enhance their powers by consolidating their territories through conquests, issuing laws, codes, and charters, assembling leading subjects to advise them (in a council called the **cortes**), and controlling independent aristocracies and wealthy townspeople. These monarchies faced some circumstances unique to Iberia, especially the Muslim state of Granada in the south of the peninsula, and each monarchy also faced circumstances unique to its realm. Portugal was relatively homogeneous, while Castile was a kingdom of three religions, as King Alfonso X (r. 1252–1284) liked to style it; the Aragonese

---

[3] These estates differ from the three orders advanced in medieval social theory—those who pray, fight, and work—in that peasants ("those who work") were replaced by townspeople. This was also true in English parliaments, which slowly incorporated burgesses but not peasants. This slippage from the three orders to the three estates reflects both the low status of peasants in medieval culture and the growing power of towns and townspeople. In the year 1000, when tripartite social schemas were first being advanced, there were so few townspeople that they were either included within "those who work" or entirely ignored. By the year 1300, towns and their citizens were powerful constituents of European kingdoms.

kings long continued to divide territories among sons, rather than favoring just one; and the kings of Castile dominated their cortes while the situation was roughly inverted in Aragon. Yet all three of the Christian monarchies of Iberia sought to consolidate their powers in ways not dissimilar from the administrative, legal, and territorial strategies of their English and French counterparts. They were, however, less successful, consolidating their power in some ways but remaining constrained by powerful aristocracies and towns.

Some similar strategies can also be seen in the German principalities, which, although part of a disintegrating Holy Roman Empire by the thirteenth century, were themselves becoming stronger. There, local *Landfrieden*—or peacekeeping responsibilities—provided jurisdictional powers through which local princes consolidated their powers. In 1156, for example, Frederick Barbarossa changed Austria from a march (or borderland) into a duchy, and he ordered that only the duke of Austria—and "no greater or lesser person"—should exercise justice therein. Duke Leopold VI (r. 1198–1230) soon established a distinctive regional law code for Austria, and although the duchy was later confiscated by the emperor, its regional distinctiveness, expressed in its laws, remained intact. Similar jurisdictional powers were granted to some great bishops, such as the archbishop of Salzburg, and some urban and rural communes, of which a *Landfriede* of 1291, considered today the founding act of the Swiss Confederation, is the best example. For these smaller units of the Holy Roman Empire, as for the kings of England and France, justice and law were critical elements of consolidation in the Central Middle Ages.

✵ THE STATES OF NORTHERN AND EASTERN EUROPE

In northern and eastern parts of medieval Europe, however, princes were less successful in asserting their power, whether through justice or other means. In the Scandinavian kingdoms and Poland, the centuries of the Central Middle Ages brought little royal consolidation and much political chaos. The same was true in Kiev, where the state founded by Vladimir I (r. 980–1015) had collapsed under dynastic struggle by the twelfth century; then, his many descendants held small principalities and fought incessantly among themselves. In the middle of the thirteenth century, the Mongol invasions pushed matters from bad to worse.

Led by the conqueror Genghis Khan (c. 1162–1227), Mongol horsemen from the steppes of central Asia swept outward in all directions in the early thirteenth century, terrorizing enemy armies and often slaughtering entire populations. To the east, they extended their power across Korea and northern China; to the west, they destroyed the Abbasid caliphate once and for all, took the Russian states, and even annexed Hungary and Poland. Then, in the mid-thirteenth century, the Mongols began to pull back from their western front. They departed from Hungary and Poland; they left the Middle East to the Seljuk sultans who had long been de facto rulers in Baghdad; and only over the Russians did they retain their grip. The Russian principalities became part of the *Golden Horde,* a group of conquered states that owed allegiance and tribute to the Khan. A prince of Novgorod, Alexander Nevsky (c. 1220–1263) made peace with the Mongols, paid annual tributes, and received the title of grand prince. His strength, such as it was, lay in loyal submission to the Mongols, not law, bureaucracy, or assembly. Yet even there, as we shall see in Chapter 14, a strong monarchy would emerge in the fifteenth century.

✳ CONCLUSION

By 1300, the "greater monarchies" of medieval Europe had taken three distinctive paths. The Holy Roman Empire had fallen victim to conflict with the papacy and regionalism among its princes; the English monarchy had developed a strong bureaucracy, a common law, and a tradition of cooperation with its parliaments; and the French monarchy, served by loyal bureaucrats and sanctified by the memory of St. Louis, was both powerful and unburdened by its Estates General. Of the papacy (which can reasonably be considered a fourth "greater monarchy" of the age), Boniface VIII, who called a Papal Jubilee for the year 1300, experienced both its enormous power and the dangers of that power. Of Boniface it was said, shortly after his death, that he entered the papacy like a lion, ruled like a fox, and died like a dog.

SUGGESTED READINGS

John W. Baldwin, *The Government of Philip Augustus: Foundations of French Royal Power in the Middle Ages* (1986).

Frank Barlow, *Thomas Becket* (1986). An astute, even-handed biography. For other biographical treatments, see David Bates, *William the Conqueror* (2nd edition, 2004); D. A. Carpenter, *The Minority of Henry III* (1990); Marjorie Chibnall, *The Empress Matilda: Queen Consort, Queen Mother and Lady of the English* (1991); J. R. Maddicott, *Simon de Montfort* (1994); D. D. R. Owen, *Eleanor of Aquitaine, Queen and Legend* (1993); Michael Prestwich, *Edward I* (1988); Jean Richard, *St. Louis: Crusader King of France,* trans. Jean Birrell (1992).

Marjorie Chibnall, *Anglo-Norman England* (2nd edition, 1992). The best survey. See also Michael T. Clanchy, *England and Its Rulers, 1066–1272: Foreign Lordship and National Identity* (2nd edition, 1998), and Richard Mortimer, *Angevin England, 1154–1258* (1994). For broader coverage, see especially: Nigel Saul, ed., *The Oxford Illustrated History of Medieval England* (1997); C. Warren Hollister, *The Making of England, 55 B.C. to 1399* (8th edition, 2001); and Edmund King, *Medieval England, 1066–1485* (1988).

Marjorie Chibnall, *The Debate on the Norman Conquest* (1999). A brief and accessible introduction to the historiography.

Georges Duby, *France in the Middle Ages, 987–1460,* trans. Juliet Vale (1991). A magisterial survey. See also Elizabeth M. Hallam and Judith Everard, *Capetian France, 987–1328* (1980), and Jean Dunbabin, *France in the Making, 843–1180* (2nd edition, 2000).

Leo de Hartog, *Genghis Khan: Conqueror of the World* (rev. edition, 2004). First published in Dutch in 1979, this is a well-received and readable book.

James C. Holt, *Magna Carta* (2nd edition, 1992). The definitive study.

SUGGESTED PRIMARY SOURCES

Emilie Amt, *Medieval England 1000–1500: A Reader* (2000). New and wide-ranging.

Theodore Evergates, ed., *Feudal Society in Medieval France: Documents from the County of Champagne* (1993). See also David Herlihy, ed., *The History of Feudalism* (1971).

Herbert L. Kessler and Johanna Zacharias, *Rome 1300: On the Path of the Pilgrim* (2000). This book traces the path of a pilgrim, illustrating, describing, and explaining the churches, sites, and artifacts found in Rome c. 1300.

Donald Wilkinson and John Cantrell, eds., *The Normans in Britain* (1987). Organized by debates, this short book covers the first hundred years of Norman rule.

CHAPTER 12

❦

LITERATURE, ART, AND THOUGHT, c. 1000-1300

✻ INTRODUCTION

The economic, religious, and political changes of the Central Middle Ages were matched by deeply significant cultural and intellectual developments. *Artistic images*—especially as seen in wall paintings and book illuminations—evolved from awe-inspiring idealization toward evocative realism. *Drama* shifted from the classical models used by Hroswitha (c. 935–1003) toward two quintessentially medieval forms: **mystery plays** that enacted the Christian story from Creation to Final Judgment and the musical dramas of the great twelfth-century polymath, St. Hildegard of Bingen (1098–1179). *Music* itself underwent fundamental advances with the development of the first musical notation and, in twelfth- and thirteenth-century Paris, the earliest complex polyphony (that is, music with two or more different, interrelated voice lines).

Literature saw the flourishing of warlike epic poetry, the rebirth of lyric poetry, the emergence of the **romance,** and the elaboration of richly imaginative **fabliaux** and **fables.** *Architecture* underwent similarly dramatic changes when the massive and earthbound Romanesque style slowly evolved into the soaring and delicate Gothic style. And with the advent of Gothic architecture in the mid-twelfth century came a new *sculptural style* in which Romanesque qualities of fantasy and playful distortion gave way to an idealized naturalism unmatched since classical antiquity.

These centuries also saw dramatic *intellectual* developments, especially in the new universities that were then sprouting across Europe. Law and medicine became serious intellectual disciplines, steady advances were made in natural philosophy (that is, the study of nature—the medieval equivalent of our modern "science"), and philosopher-theologians such as Thomas Aquinas (c. 1225–1274) produced vast, closely reasoned arguments that sought to reconcile human reason with religious faith.

By 1300, then, Europe had changed not only in terms of politics, economy, and society but also in terms of literature, art, and thought (see Timeline 12.1). In the process, a world that had once seemed filled with uncertainties, mysteries, and demons slowly changed into a world that seemed more knowable—built by God, structured by

TIMELINE 12.1   Cultural Change, 1000–1300

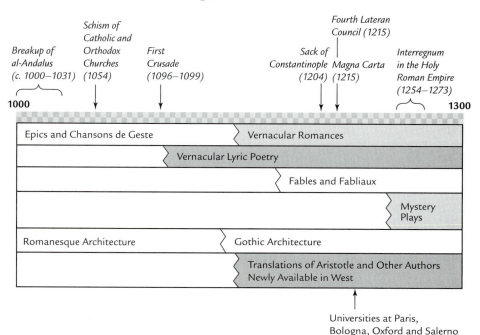

Universities at Paris,
Bologna, Oxford and Salerno

logic, and capable of human understanding. In 1107, at an early stage in this shift of worldviews, the central tower of Winchester Cathedral collapsed. To some, the explanation was obvious: the blaspheming King William II (r. 1087–1100) lay entombed beneath it. But to William of Malmesbury (c. 1096–1143), a different explanation appealed: "The structure might have fallen because of faulty construction, even if the king had never been buried there." To such a view, the future belonged.

✳ BYZANTINE AND ISLAMIC INFLUENCES

Part of that future drew on Western borrowings from Byzantium and Islam. Between 1000 and 1300, the political might of Byzantium waned, but its culture continued to flourish. As custodians of Greek culture and Roman traditions, Byzantines revered their classical heritage, nurtured art, and admired learning. Yet, although impressive and sometimes awe-inspiring, Byzantium's creative impulses were limited by devotion to ancient traditions that could be altered only slowly and cautiously, if at all. Byzantines were more preservers of ancient traditions than innovative creators: they would have liked Norman Rockwell more than Pablo Picasso. In the twelfth century, as in the sixth, Byzantine artists produced rich, abstract works that sought more to inspire reverence than to reflect reality (look again at Color Illustrations 1 and 2). When commerce, crusade, and conquest brought East and West closer during the Central Middle Ages, Byzantine art influenced the medieval West in profound and positive ways. In the words of a modern historian, "whatever else the West disliked and despised about the

East, its mosaics and enamels, its textiles and ivories, its pearl and onyx, its painting and its gold work were eagerly coveted and jealously guarded in Western treasuries." In the libraries and schools of Constantinople, Byzantine scholars in the Central Middle Ages similarly guarded their rich heritage, compiling, copying, and commenting on the great texts of the classical past. These were not small feats. Roman law and Greek authors were studied in Constantinople at a time when they were all but unknown in the West. From the twelfth century, this Byzantine learning found its way into the libraries, classrooms, and courtrooms of medieval Europe, with electrifying effect.

By the time the Abbasid empire fragmented into smaller polities in the late tenth century, Islamic learning and literature were providing a different sort of unity—a *cultural* unity—for Muslims. In the Central Middle Ages, it was through Iberia that Islamic culture most directly influenced the West. The high culture of al-Andalus was somewhat dampened by the religious fundamentalism of the two Berber regimes—first the Almoravids and later the Almohads—that dominated Muslim Iberia for most of the Central Middle Ages. But both regimes were eventually seduced by the beauty and elegance of Andalusian culture, proving, once again, the inevitable triumph of refinement over rigidity. When the West encountered the learning and literature of Iberian Islam, it was just as captivated. Muslim scholars were especially distinguished in science and philosophy, for they were able to build on the works of not only Greek and Roman scholars but also Persian and Indian astronomers and mathematicians. From these traditions, the physician Ibn Sina (980–1037), known to medieval Europeans as Avicenna, produced impressive studies of medicine, as well as a huge encyclopedia of human knowledge; his works, translated into Latin, were widely used by Western scholars in the Central Middle Ages. Also widely appreciated were the works of Ibn Rushd (1126–1198), known as Averroes in the West, who applied hardheaded logic to intractable problems of science and philosophy. His reliance on rigorous reasoning so captivated some Western scholars that a school of Latin Averrorists flourished at the University of Paris in the mid-thirteenth century. Arabic literature was graced by lyric poetry of exceptional power, and both its forms and themes—usually hunting, loving, and warring—can be traced in the romantic poetry that flourished first in southern France and then elsewhere in the Central Middle Ages.

Intellectual and cultural interchange between the medieval west, Byzantium, and Islam was not new in the Central Middle Ages, but it did intensify. In Chapter 9, we traced how the Christian kingdom of Castile conquered Muslim Toledo and its libraries in 1085, how the Norman king of Sicily, Roger the Great (r. 1130–1154), nurtured a vibrant and diverse culture in the city of Palermo, and how the Fourth Crusade's sack of Constantinople in 1204 burned many Byzantine libraries but opened others to Western eyes. In these three locations and others, Muslim, Jewish, and Christian scholars worked together to translate Greek, Arabic, and Hebrew works into Latin, and through their labors, vast quantities of texts previously unknown in the West began to be studied at Paris and other universities. For the first time, significant portions of the philosophical and scientific legacy of ancient Greece—and above all, the full Aristotelian corpus—became available to European scholars. So, too, did studies by Muslim and Jewish intellectuals. In the later twelfth and early thirteenth centuries, intellectuals in the medieval West came to grips with these new intellectual riches with, as we shall see, dramatic results.

✸ LITERATURE

The literature of the Central Middle Ages was abundant and richly varied. Poets wrote both in traditional Latin, the universal scholarly language of medieval Europe, and in the vernacular languages of ordinary speech that had long been evolving in the various regions of Western Christendom. Latin was the language of many somber and majestic hymns, such as *Jerusalem the Golden* from the twelfth century:

> The world is very evil, the times are waxing late.
> Be sober and keep vigil, the judge is at the gate. . . .
> Brief life is here our portion; brief sorrow, short lived care.
> The life that knows no ending, the tearless life, is *there*.
> Jerusalem the golden, with milk and honey blessed,
> Beneath your contemplation sink heart and voice oppressed.
> I know not, O I know not what joys await us there,
> What radiancy of glory, what light beyond compare!

But Latin was also the language for poetry of quite a different sort, composed by students and wandering scholars. Because these young men studied in Latin, they wrote their verses in Latin, too. For example, one student cast an irreverent eye on the prospect of death:

> For on this my heart is set, when the hour is near me
> Let me in the tavern die, with my ale cup by me,
> While the angels, looking down, joyously sing o'er me. . . .

For all its originality, the Latin poetry of the Central Middle Ages was outstripped in both quantity and variety of expression by vernacular poetry. We have already noted a drift toward emotionalism in medieval piety, especially as seen in the increased emphasis on Jesus' suffering at the crucifixion (look, again, at Color Illustration 7 and Figure 8.1). This same emotionalism is seen in the evolution of vernacular literature from the martial epics of the eleventh century to the sensitive romances of the twelfth and thirteenth.

The Epic

In the eleventh and early twelfth centuries, vernacular epics known as **chansons de geste** ("songs of great deeds") were enormously popular among the northern French aristocracy. Sung by minstrels in the halls of castles, these chansons were rooted in earlier heroic traditions that had produced such moody and violent masterpieces as *Beowulf* (whose lonely hero fights monsters, slays dragons, and struggles against a wild, windswept wilderness). The chansons de geste are equally heroic in mood. Like modern movies set in outer space, their stories are action-packed, their battle scenes are filled with gory realism, their protagonists fight with almost superhuman strength against fantastic odds, and their heroes (always male) tend to steer clear of sentimental entanglements with women. The heroes of the chansons are emotional, but in manly ways. They are proud men; they are loyal to their lords; they are steadfast and loving comrades; they weep at the deaths of comrades fallen in battle. In short, the chansons de geste express the warlike spirit and military brotherhood of armed knights in the earliest centuries of feudalism.

These qualities found vivid expression in the epic poetry of many languages, including the Castilian epic *The Song of My Cid,* a highly fictionalized account of the great knight Rodrigo Diaz (c. 1043–1099), who took the name El Cid. The most famous chanson de geste of all is the Old French *The Song of Roland,* which tells of a bloody battle between a Muslim army and some troops of Charlemagne (r. 768–814) who were in the rearguard of his army as it withdrew from northern Iberia. These passages describe the bravery, good vassalage, and camaraderie of two men in the midst of battle, Turpin (Archbishop of Reims) and the hero of the tale, the young Frankish count Roland:

> When Turpin of Reims feels himself struck down,
> Pierced through the body by four spears,
> He quickly jumped to his feet.
> He looks to Roland, then ran towards him
> And spoke these words: "I am not vanquished;
> A good vassal will never give up whilst still alive."
> He draws Almace, his sword of burnished steel;
> In the great throng he strikes a thousand blows and more . . . .

> Count Roland never loved a coward,
> Nor arrogant men nor those of evil character,
> Nor any knight, unless he were a good vassal.
> He called to Archbishop Turpin:
> "Lord, you are on foot and I am on horseback;
> For love of you I shall make a stand here.
> Together we shall endure both good and ill;
> I shall not abandon you because of any man."

Turpin, Roland, and all the rearguard are slain to a man, but Charlemagne returns to avenge them. He emerges victorious, after a furious battle in which he defeats the Muslim leader in single combat. Roland is avenged, not only during the battle but also during a savage assault on the retreating Muslim army.

> The pagans flee as the Lord God wishes it.
> The Franks give chase together with the emperor.
> The king said: "Lords, avenge your sorrow
> And relieve your minds and your hearts;
> For this morning I saw tears streaming from your eyes."
> The Franks reply: "Lord, this we must do."
> Each man strikes the mightiest blows he can muster;
> Of those who are there, few escaped.

The Song of Roland was sung long before it was ever written down in the 1090s, the time of the First Crusade, and this passage expresses some of the religious tension of that age, with Muslims figured as "pagans" and God depicted as unequivocally on the Christian side. But, in fact, the historical battle, fought in 778, involved Christian Basques slaughtering Christian Franks and no response—except further retreat—from Charlemagne. By and large, Charlemagne's campaign in the Iberian peninsula was a fiasco, and it was left to *The Song of Roland* to supply the happy ending.

The Lyric

During the middle and later twelfth century the martial spirit of northern French literature was gradually transformed by the influx of a new, more romantic poetry from southern France, where, particularly in Provence, Toulouse, and Aquitaine, a rich, colorful culture had flourished since the eleventh century. This culture nurtured such extraordinary figures as Eleanor of Aquitaine (c. 1122–1205) and her son Richard the Lion-Hearted (r. 1189–1199), as well as a lyric poetry of remarkable sensitivity and enduring value. The lyric poets of the south were known as *troubadours*. Many of them were court minstrels, including Bernard of Ventadour (c. 1140–1190), whose biography is featured on pp. 296–297. But some, including Duke William IX of Aquitaine (1071–1126), grandfather of Eleanor and great-grandfather of Richard, were nobles. The wit, delicacy, and romanticism of the troubadour lyrics disclose a more genteel nobility than that of the north, a nobility that preferred songs of love between women and men to songs of war, blood, and male comrades:

> I die of wounds from blissful blows,
> And love's cruel stings dry out my flesh,
> My health is lost, my vigor goes,
> And nothing can my soul refresh.
> I never knew so sad a plight,
> It should not be, it is not right.
> I'll never hold her near to me,
> My ardent joy she'll ever spurn,
> In her good grace I cannot be,
> Nor even hope, but only yearn.
> She tells me nothing, false or true,
> And neither will she ever do.

These songs of love voiced very particular—and new—ideas about male-female love. In expressing a feeling of hopeless and consuming love for a distant woman, the author of these lines, Jaufré Rudel (fl. 1148), was part of the development in lyric (and later, romance) of what is now called courtly love. Rudel and other troubadours wrote about this love as a sort of feudal relationship, as an *unrequited* love that a man felt for a woman *from afar.* The male lover was the equivalent of a humble vassal: subordinate, part of a crowd, loyal, heroic, long-suffering. The female love object was the equivalent of an empowered lord: proud, unique, distant, admired, and never acquired. In courtly love, the best love was adulterous and secretive; it was also often unrequited and unconsummated.

Courtly love drew partly on the writings of the Roman author Ovid (43 B.C.E–18 C.E.), partly on Arabic literature then flourishing in nearby Iberia, and partly on the specific circumstances of aristocratic society (with many young knights too poor to marry, and marriage more a business of property and fiefs than love). Its influence on actual aristocratic behavior was likely small, so it would be a mistake to imagine that humble knights actually prostrated themselves before imperious ladies who might occasionally have cast a smile their way, but nothing more. Poetry and stories were one thing; real life another. Yet courtly love's influence on *later* societies has been profound, for the lyric poets of southern France are the source of the tradition of romantic love as it has developed in Europe and in areas settled by Europeans. It was from the lyric poets that are derived such concepts as the idealization of women, the importance of male gallantry and courtesy, and the impulse to embroider male-female relations with emotions of eternal oneness, undying devotion, agony, and ecstasy.

In courtly love, it is generally men who love, agonize, and undertake heroic deeds to attract the attention of the women they love. Women are more passive, mere mirrors of male desire. But there were some twenty female troubadours, and their poems reverse the pattern, even twisting it a bit. This mid-twelfth-century lyric poem by Beatrice, countess of Dia (died c. 1175), expresses many of the conventional feelings of courtly love—secrecy, distance, unrequited love, adultery. But Beatrice of Dia also writes with a sexual immediacy that is less common among male poets.

> I would truly love to hold
> my knight, naked, in my arms one night,
> and that he would consider himself in ecstasy
> if only I would serve him as a pillow;
> for I am more in love with him
> than was Floris with Blanchefleur:
> I give him my heart and my love,
> my mind, my eyes and my life.
>
> Dear friend, charming and good,
> when shall I have you in my power?
> If only I might lie with you one night
> and give you a loving kiss!
> Rest assured that I would have a great desire
> to have you in place of my husband,
> provided that you would have sworn
> to do everything that I might want.

Not every lyric poet took love or life as seriously as Jaufré Rudel or Beatrice of Dia. The following verses by Duke William IX ridicule both the heroic mood of the chanson de geste and the passionate seriousness of the love lyric:

> I'll make some verses just for fun,
> Not for myself or anyone,
> Nor of great deeds that knights have done,
> Nor lovers true.
> I made them riding in the sun,
> My horse helped too.
>
> My distant love I so adore,
> Though me she has no longing for;
> We've never met, and furthermore—to my disgrace—
> I've other loves, some three or four, to fill her place.

The Romance

Midway through the twelfth century, the southern troubadour tradition began to filter into northern France, England, and the German states. It brought with it a new aristocratic ideology of courtly manners, urbane speech, and romantic idealization. Out of the convergence of vernacular epic and vernacular lyric there emerged a new poetic form known as romance.

Like the chanson de geste, the romance was a long narrative; like the southern lyric, it was sentimental and concerned with love. It was commonly based on stories

BIOGRAPHICAL SKETCH

Bernard of Ventadour (c. 1140–1190)

B ernard of Ventadour was one of the twelfth century's most celebrated and imitated troubadours. Like other troubadours, Bernard was at once a composer and a poet; he created both the music and the lyrics for his songs.

The details of Bernard's life, provided in a biography in the Old Provençal vernacular, may well be embroidered and romanticized, but very little biographical information has survived apart from this one source. It reports that Bernard's mother and father were servants at the castle of the viscount of Ventadour in southern France. At an early age Bernard showed great talent as a poet and musician, and he was singled out by the viscount of Ventadour for training as a troubadour.

The happy days ended abruptly, so the vernacular biography relates, when Bernard's patron, the viscount, found the young man in bed with the viscountess. Bernard was banished from the castle and was obliged to seek his fortune elsewhere. Undaunted, he presented himself to the greatest artistic patron in Western Europe: Eleanor, duchess of Aquitaine and queen of England.

Queen Eleanor was immediately impressed by Bernard's artistic gifts. He spent a number of years at her court, composing and performing songs for the queen and her entourage. His songs earned him fame and fortune; they were immensely popular in their time and are performed to this day. No fewer than forty-four have survived.

Bernard's songs celebrate the joys and heartaches of romantic love. His basic philosophy, like that of other troubadours of his time, is perfectly epitomized in one of his lyrics:

> Singing isn't worth a thing
> If the heart sings not the song,
> And the heart can never sing
> If it brings not love along.

Another of Bernard's songs, "The Lark," available today in several recorded versions, is an evocation of one of the most frequently encountered themes in twelfth-century romantic poetry, the agony of unrequited love:

> When I see the lark beat its wings,
> Facing the sun's rays,
> Forgetting itself, letting itself sing
> Of the sweetness that enters its
> heart—
> Ah! Such great longing enters me
> From the happiness I see,
> That only a miracle prevents my heart
> From consuming itself with desire.
> Alas! I thought I knew so much
> of love,
> And I know so little.
> For I can't help loving a lady
> Whom I cannot attain.
> She has all my heart

She has me entirely.
She has left me nothing but desire,
And a foolish heart.

His biographer reported—doubtless indulging in wishful thinking—that Bernard became Eleanor of Aquitaine's lover. Whatever the case, he accompanied the queen and her court on their travels through France, and the evidence suggests that he was in England on at least one occasion.

In later years, Bernard left Queen Eleanor's entourage to join the court of Raymond, count of Toulouse, whose name occurs in several of Bernard's songs. Like other worldly men and women—among them, Hugh, earl of Chester (1048–1101), and Eleanor of Aquitaine herself—Bernard ended his days in an abbey. He retired to the Cistercian monastery of Dalon in France and died there at the age of fifty.

from the remote past. Marie de France (died c. 1190), who wrote a dozen romances for the English court of Henry II in the late twelfth century, claimed her tales were rooted in the Breton past. Others drew stories from the Trojan War, Alexander the Great, and above all, King Arthur. A half-legendary sixth-century British king, Arthur was transformed in these romances into a twelfth-century monarch surrounded by charming ladies and chivalrous knights. His court at Camelot, as described by the late-twelfth-century French poet, Chrétien de Troyes (c. 1135–1183), was a center of romantic love and refined religious sensibilities where knights worshiped their ladies and went on daring quests in a world filled with magic and fantasy.

In the chanson de geste the great virtue had been loyalty to one's lord; in the romance it was love for one's lady. Several romances portray the old and new values in conflict. An important theme in both the Arthurian romances and the twelfth-century romance of *Tristan and Iseult* is a love affair between a vassal and his lord's wife. Romantic love and feudal loyalty stand face to face, and love wins out. Tristan loves Iseult, the wife of his lord, King Mark of Cornwall. Lancelot, trusty knight of King Arthur, loves Guinevere, Arthur's wife. In both stories the lovers are ruined by their love, yet love they must—they have no choice. Although the conduct of Tristan, Iseult, Lancelot, and Guinevere would have been regarded as nothing less than treasonable had they actually lived and loved in the twelfth century, all are presented sympathetically in the romances. Love destroys the lovers in the end, yet their destruction is romantic, even glorious. Tristan and Iseult lie dead together, side by side, and in their very death their love achieves its deepest consummation.

Alongside the theme of love in the romances is the theme of Christian purity and dedication. The rough-hewn knight of old, having been instructed to be courteous and loving, was now instructed to be holy. Lancelot was trapped in the meshes of a lawless love, but his son, Galahad, became the prototype of the Christian knight—worshipful and chaste. And Perceval, another knight of the Arthurian circle, quested not for a beloved woman but for the *Holy Grail*—that is, the cup that, in Christian tradition, held the wine at the Last Supper.

The romance flourished in twelfth- and thirteenth-century France and among the French-speaking nobility of England. It spread also into the Italian and Iberian peninsulas and became a crucial factor in the evolution of vernacular literature in the German states. The German poets, known as *Minnesingers,* were influenced by the French lyric and romance but developed these literary forms along highly original lines. The Minnesingers produced their own deeply sensitive and mystical versions of the Arthurian stories rich with exalted symbolism and deep emotion.

Yet, as the thirteenth century drew to a close, the romance was becoming a humdrum genre, drained of inspiration. The popular love story of *Aucassin et Nicolette* was actually a satire in which the hero is not fully heroic, and a battle is depicted in which the opponents cast pieces of cheese at each other. Based on earlier Byzantine material, *Aucassin et Nicolette* makes mortal love take priority over salvation itself. Indeed, Aucassin is scornful of heaven itself:

> For into Paradise go only such people as these: There go those aged priests and elderly cripples and maimed ones who day and night stoop before altars and in the crypts beneath the churches; those who go around in worn-out cloaks and shabby old clothing; who are naked and shoeless and full of sores; who are dying of hunger and thirst, of cold and misery. Such folks as these enter Paradise, and I will have nothing to do with them. I will go to hell. For to hell go the fair clerics and comely knights who are killed in tournaments and great wars, and the sturdy archer and the loyal vassal. I will go with them. There also go the fair and courteous ladies who have loving friends, two or three, together with their wedded lords. And there go the gold and silver, the ermine and all rich furs, the harpers and the minstrels, and the happy folk of the world. I will go with these, so long as I have Nicolette, my very sweet friend, at my side.

Another important product of thirteenth-century vernacular literature, the *Romance of the Rose,* was in fact not a romance in the ordinary sense but an allegory of the whole courtly love tradition in which the feelings of the lover and his lady are personified in characters such as Love, Reason, Jealousy, and Fair-Welcome. Begun by William de Lorris (died c. 1145) as an idealization of courtly love, the *Romance of the Rose* was completed after William's death by Jean de Meun (d. 1305), a man of limited talent. Jean's contribution was long-winded, encyclopedic, and contemptuous of women. The poem as a whole lacks high literary distinction, yet it appealed to contemporaries and enjoyed a great vogue.

Fabliaux, Fables, and Mystery Plays

Neither epic, lyric, nor romance had much appeal below the level of the landed aristocracy. This is scarcely surprising, given the contempt the feudal protagonists of these tales display for mere peasants and townsfolk. Ordinary people feature rarely in these genres, and if so, they are usually victims of war, objects of violence, and easy sexual prey. Andreas Capellanus (active in the 1170s and 1180s), author of a primer on courtly love, even went so far as to advise knights who desired a peasant maiden, "do not hesitate to take what you seek and embrace her by force." Scholars debate whether he was joking or serious, but the comment betrays the haughty pride and privilege with which the aristocracy viewed those who sweated on their demesne lands and paid their taxes.

There is no "peasant" literary tradition that survives for the Central Middle Ages; the stories and oral traditions of rural folk might survive in ballads, proverbs, and songs that were written down in later centuries, but such origins are difficult to trace.[1] There are, however, distinct and new "urban" traditions. As trade flourished and towns expanded, merchants and artisans started to produce a vernacular literature all their own. Their *fabliaux*, short satirical poems filled with vigor and crude humor, chiefly ridicule conventional morality. Priests and monks are portrayed as lechers; merchants' wives are depicted as easily seduced; and young men are characterized as clever upstarts who make fools of sober and stuffy merchants.

Medieval urban culture also produced the fable, an allegory in the ancient Greek tradition of *Aesop's Fables,* in which various stock characters in medieval society are thinly disguised as animals. Most of the more popular fables deal with Renard the Fox and are known collectively as the *Romance of Renard.* These tales ruthlessly parody chivalric ideals, with the clever, unscrupulous Renard persistently outwitting King Lion and his loyal but stupid vassals.

In the thirteenth century, some towns began to produce plays based on saints' lives, morality stories, and most importantly, the Bible. Because the latter were usually performed by craft guilds (also called "mysteries"), they are known as mystery plays. Each guild would enact a separate play from biblical history, usually an appropriate one (so that, for example, the carpenters might take responsibility for "The Flood," thereby building Noah's ark). The entire cycle of plays was usually offered once a year, giving urban audiences a drama that took them from Creation to the Final Judgment. Plays were sometimes mounted in rough theaters, but often the performers acted on wagons that moved throughout the town, stopping at designated spots for a performance. These plays combined coarse humor with Christian piety, both entertaining audiences and teaching them Christian history. They also expressed civic pride, as do, today, such annual events as the Tournament of Roses Parade in Pasadena and the Mummers Parade in Philadelphia. By the fourteenth and fifteenth centuries, mystery plays would be a major part of the ritual year in many Europeans towns and cities.

Dante Alighieri (1265–1321)

Vernacular poetry matured late in the Italian peninsula, but in the works of Dante Alighieri it achieved its loftiest expression. Dante wrote on a wide variety of subjects, sometimes in Latin, more often in the Tuscan vernacular. In good courtly tradition, he composed a series of lyric poems celebrating his unconsummated love for Bice di Folco Portinari (d. 1290), known as Beatrice in his poems, which were assembled, with prose commentaries, in his *La Vita Nuova (The New Life).* Dante's lyrics reflect a more mystical and idealized love than that of the troubadours:

> The power of Love borne in my lady's eyes
> imparts its grace to all she looks upon;
> men turn to gaze at her when she walks by;
> the heart of him she greets is made to quake,
> his face to whiten, forcing down his gaze;
> he sighs as all his defects flash in mind;
> all pride and indignation flee from her . . .

---

[1] See, however, the new *Medieval Folklore: An Encyclopedia of Myths, Legends, Tales, Beliefs, and Customs,* edited by Carl Lindahl et al., 2 volumes (2000).

> All sweet conception, every humblest thought
> blooms in the heart of one who hears her speak,
> and man is blessed at his first sight of her.
> The image of her when she starts to smile
> breaks out of words, the mind cannot contain it,
> a miracle too rich and strange to hold.

Firmly convinced of the literary potential of the Tuscan vernacular, Dante urged its use in his *De Vulgari Eloquentia (On Vernacular Eloquence),* which he wrote in Latin so as to appeal to scholars and writers who scorned the vulgar tongue. And he filled his own vernacular works with such grace as to convince by example those whom he could not persuade by argument. In his hands the Tuscan vernacular became the literary language of the Italian peninsula.

Dante's masterpiece, *The Divine Comedy,* was written in that Tuscan vernacular. Abounding in allegory and symbolism, it encompasses in one majestic vision the entire medieval universe. Dante tells of his own journey through hell, purgatory, and paradise to the very presence of God, a device that allows him to place all those of whom he disapproved—from local politicians to popes—in various levels of hell. The Roman poet Virgil (70–19 B.C.E.), the archetype of ancient wisdom, is Dante's guide through hell and purgatory; the lady Beatrice, a symbol of purified love, guides him through the celestial spheres of paradise; and St. Bernard of Clairvaux (1090–1153), the epitome of medieval sanctity, leads him to the threshold of God. The poem closes with Dante alone in the divine presence:

> Eternal Light, thou in thyself alone
> Abidest, and alone thine essence knows,
> And loves, and smiles, self-knowing and self-known . . .

✳ ARCHITECTURE AND SCULPTURE

During the Central Middle Ages, stone churches, abbeys, castles, hospitals, and town halls were built in prodigious numbers. More stone was quarried in central medieval France alone than by pyramid and temple builders in the 3,000 year history of ancient Egypt. The most celebrated buildings of the Central Middle Ages are great and awesome: Chartres Cathedral, Mont St. Michel Abbey, Westminster Abbey, Reims Cathedral, Notre Dame Cathedral in Paris, and many more. But throughout the European countryside are many smaller stone churches of the twelfth and thirteenth centuries, built with skill and still beautiful today. Whether large or small, these churches and cathedrals are testaments to community pride as well as faith. This was particularly the case in towns, where churches expressed the expanding wealth and solidarity of townspeople, as well as their intense piety.

Cathedrals were designed by master masons, men trained by working with stone rather than studying in universities. Only a few of them are known to us by name. Cathedral building represented an enormous investment of money and effort, and revenues were raised in a variety of ways—through episcopal taxes, fund drives, and spontaneous donations by townspeople, guilds, regional lords, great princes, and kings. One of the rose windows of Chartres displays the emblems of two of its benefactors—the Capetian fleur-de-lys of Louis IX (r. 1226–1270) in blue and gold, and the yellow castle on red background identifying the family of his mother, Blanche of Castile (1188–1252). Other windows in Chartres depict the symbols of various contributing guilds—tailors, bakers, shoemakers, and wheelwrights. Sometimes townspeople and even aristocrats would perform volunteer labor, piously pulling carts from the stone quarry to the building site or carrying food and wine to the workers. Yet at other times people objected violently to heavy episcopal taxes, and construction was sometimes delayed for a century or more for want of funds.

Two great architectural styles dominated the age: the *Romanesque style* flourished in the eleventh century, and during the middle decades of the twelfth century it gave way gradually to the *Gothic style*. From about 1150 to the early 1300s the most famous of the Gothic cathedrals were built, each an audacious architectural experiment. This change from Romanesque to Gothic mirrors the change toward greater emotional intensity and refinement that was also occurring in literature, piety, and aristocratic society. Romanesque architecture complements the solemnity of early medieval Christian piety and the rough-hewn power of the chansons de geste. Gothic architecture—dramatic, upward-reaching, aspiring—embodies the heightened sensitivity of courtly lyrics and romances.

The Romanesque Style

The key architectural ingredient in Romanesque churches was the round arch—borrowed from Greco-Roman times—which appears in the portals, windows, arcades, and stone roofs of Romanesque buildings. The chief architectural achievement of the style was to replace flat wooden ceilings with roofs made of stone vaulting; this created buildings that were less susceptible to fire, more artistically unified, acoustically resonant, and, as Figure 12.1 shows, massively built, since the immense downward and

Figure 12.1 *Romanesque Architecture: Exterior* This cathedral at Pisa was completed in the eleventh century. With its pitched roof, rounded arches, heavy stone walls, and few windows, it is a classic example of Romanesque architecture. The tower to the right is the famous Leaning Tower of Pisa.

Figure 12.2 *Romanesque Sculpture*   This lively but grotesque scene shows souls being weighed at the Last Judgment. Carved above the west door of Autun Cathedral, it was completed in the 1130s.

outward thrusts of these heavy roofs required huge pillars and thick supporting walls. The glittering mosaics and wooden roofs that had characterized the churches of late Roman, Byzantine, and Carolingian times gave way to stone as the dominant material in both Romanesque architecture and Romanesque sculpture. Indeed, the religious sculpture of the age, although highly inventive and lively, was completely fused into the structure of the church itself, with carved figures ornamenting capitals of columns, round arches over doors, and other parts of the structure of the building (see Figure 12.2).

The Romanesque style had many variations. Graceful and richly decorated in southern Europe, it tended to become more severe and austere in the north. But, in general, a church in the fully developed Romanesque style conveyed a feeling of organic unity and solidity. As Figure 12.3 shows, the shadowy interior of Romanesque churches, lit by relatively few and small windows, offered a sense of otherworldly mystery, and its

Figure 12.3   *Romanesque Architecture: Interior*   The Church of St. Sernin in Toulouse was built in the decades immediately before and after 1100. This photograph of its nave, made with the help of artificial light, illustrates how the use of stone vaulting in roofs required heavy walls and dark interiors.

sturdy arches, vaults, and walls suggested the steadfast power, amid this otherworldliness, of the universal Church.

The Gothic Style

During the first half of the twelfth century, architects began to employ new structural elements in the building of churches: first, ribs of stone crisscrossed the vaulting; next, pointed arches permitted greater height in the vaults and arcades. By the middle of the century these novel features—vault rib and pointed arch—were providing the basis for an entirely new style of architecture. They were employed with such effect c. 1140 by Abbot Suger (1098–1151) in his new abbey church of St. Denis near Paris that it has been widely regarded as the first true Gothic church. In the exciting years thereafter, each decade brought new experiments and opened new possibilities in church building.

Yet not until the 1190s was the full potential of Gothic architecture realized. By then, the vault rib, the pointed arch, and a third Gothic structural element—the **flying buttress** (that is, a roof support that stands away from the main wall)—made it possible

Figure 12.4   *Gothic Architecture: Exterior*   This view of
Reims Cathedral shows the pointed arches, flying buttresses, and
great windows that were characteristic of Gothic architecture.

to support weights and stresses in a new way. The traditional building, roof supported by
walls, was transformed into a radically new kind of structure: a skeleton, in which the
stone vault roof rested not on walls but on slender columns, aided by graceful exterior
supports (see Figure 12.4). The walls became mere screens that appeared to be struc-
turally unnecessary, and they were slowly replaced by huge windows of stained glass
that flooded the church interior with light and color. By fortunate coincidence, the
Gothic architectural revolution coincided with the development of the new art of making stained glass. The luminous windows created in the twelfth and thirteenth centuries,
with episodes from the Bible and religious legend depicted in shimmering blues and
reds, have never been equaled.

The Gothic innovations of vault rib, pointed arch, and flying buttress created the
breathtaking illusion of stone vault roofs resting on walls of glass. As Figure 12.5 illustrates, the new churches rose upward in seeming defiance of gravity, losing their earthbound quality and reaching toward the heavens. By about the mid-thirteenth century all the
structural possibilities of the Gothic skeletal design were fully realized, and in the towns of
central and northern France there then rose churches of delicate, soaring stone with walls
of lustrous glass. Never before in history had windows been so immense or buildings so
lofty, and seldom since has European architecture been at once so daring and so assured.

Gothic sculpture, like Romanesque, was intimately related to architecture, yet the
two styles differed markedly. Romanesque fantasy and exuberance gave way to a serene,
self-confident naturalism (see Figure 12.6). Human figures were no longer crowded together on the capitals of pillars; often they stood as statues—great rows of them—in
niches on the cathedral exteriors: saints, prophets, kings, angels, Christ, and the Virgin
Mary, depicted as tall, slender figures, calm yet warmly human, often young and sometimes smiling. The greatest Gothic churches of thirteenth-century France—Bourges,
Chartres, Amiens, Reims, La Sainte Chapelle—brought together many separate

Figure 12.5   *Gothic Architecture: Interior*   This view of the nave of
Beauvais Cathedral shows how Gothic architecture sought to achieve great
height and great light. Notice the relative insignificance of the walls as
compared to the windows.

arts—architecture, sculpture, stained glass, liturgical music—to the single end of providing a majestic background for the central act of medieval Christian worship, the Mass.

Cathedral Life in the Middle Ages

Stepping inside a medieval cathedral today is a bit like going to a museum: suddenly the
bustle of buses, cars, and people outside is replaced by awesome quiet and beauty. In the
Middle Ages, however, cathedrals were centers of urban life rather than refuges from it.

Figure 12.6 *Gothic Sculpture*   This naturalistic and tranquil image of the Virgin Mary was carved c. 1220 for Reims Cathedral.

Cathedral bells announced the hours of the day, called university students to their studies, and proclaimed great public events—a victory in battle, the death of a famous person, the birth of a royal heir. Cathedrals themselves were central gathering places, not only for religious services but also for civic festivals, victory celebrations, assemblies of nobles and princes, and even public meetings of town councils. On major feast days such as Christmas and Easter, cathedrals blazed with candles, and colorful processions marched noisily along their aisles and then out through their doors into narrow city streets. At other times, traveling friars addressed huge crowds from cathedral pulpits and sometimes stirred them to frenzied enthusiasm.

Cathedrals also attracted pilgrims from far and wide, many of them injured or ill and seeking a miraculous cure from the relics held by each cathedral. On any ordinary night, pilgrims might be found sleeping on the straw-covered floors of cathedrals, in company with local beggars, drunks, and prostitutes. On great feast days, most cathedrals swarmed with pilgrims and local worshipers. Abbot Suger, describing a boisterous multitude that pressed into his abbey church of St. Denis, complained of "howling men" and of women who screamed "as though they were giving birth." The crowd of visitors, shoving and struggling to see the relics of St. Denis, forced the abbey's monks "to flee through the windows, carrying the precious relics with them." All across medieval Europe cathedrals teemed with women and men from all social strata. Within these walls of glass and stone pulsed the commotion and stench, the hopes and griefs, of a turbulent cross-section of medieval Christians.

✸ INTELLECTUAL TRENDS

In the twelfth and thirteenth centuries, European cities hummed with sounds of students and their teachers. As we saw in Chapter 10, the pressure for men better trained in clerical and legal skills led to the development in the eleventh century of cathedral schools (in the north) and municipal schools (in the south). Universities—where male students were trained in the liberal arts and the specialized disciplines of medicine, law, and philosophy—soon followed.

Of these, the University of Paris was unrivaled in the twelfth and thirteenth centuries. Students flocked to Paris from all over Western Christendom. Most were about seventeen when they began their studies, and as they settled into rented rooms or boarding houses, they entered a world of extraordinary social and intellectual vibrancy. New students were hazed unmercifully and imaginatively, and unpopular professors were hissed, shouted down, or, as a last resort, pelted with stones. Philosophical disputes often developed into passionate intellectual rivalries, with some students siding with one professor and others with another. In addition to these battles of words, there were frequent tavern brawls, sometimes exploding into full-scale battles among rival student gangs or between students and townspeople.

Students at Paris began their day at five or six in the morning, when the bells of Notre Dame Cathedral summoned them to work. They streamed out of their rooms and boardinghouses into the narrow, noisy streets and on to the lecture halls, which were scattered about the university quarter of the city (hence, the "Latin Quarter"). These halls were bare and bitterly cold in the winter. Some of them had rough benches (as shown in Figure 10.1); in others students had to sit on a straw-covered floor, using their knees to support the wax tablets on which they took their lecture notes. The teacher mounted a platform at one end of the room and sat down to deliver a lecture that might run on all morning, unenlivened by audiovisual aids.

In the afternoon, students often congregated in the meadows outside the city walls to join in various sports: races, long-jump contests, lawn bowling, swimming, ball games of different sorts, and free-for-all fights pitting students from one region of Europe against those from another. In the evenings, serious students retired to their rooms for study, while fun-lovers gathered in Paris's numerous taverns and brothels. One observer complained that in one and the same house there might be classrooms above and whorehouses below.

Medieval students sought money from their parents or guardians in letters that sometimes have a curiously modern ring:

> The city is expensive and makes many demands; I have to rent lodgings, buy
> necessities, and provide for many other things that I cannot now specify.
> Wherefore I beg your paternity that by the prompting of divine pity you may assist
> me, so that I may be able to complete what I have well begun.

A father replies to his son:

> I have recently discovered that you live dissolutely, preferring play to work, and strumming a guitar while others are at their studies.

In this all-male, highly intellectual, and dynamic environment, students perfected their skills in the liberal arts. Once finished, some moved on to careers in teaching or administration, and others stayed to study at advanced levels. Only at universities could students pursue advanced study, and they could do so in only three fields: medicine, law, and philosophy.

Medicine

The University of Salerno in the southern Italian peninsula was the chief medical school of medieval Europe. Here, in a land of vigorous cultural intermingling, scholars were able to draw from the medical heritage of Islam and Byzantium. In general, medieval medicine was a bizarre medley of simple superstition, good common sense, and wise observation. In medical books, we encounter the good advice that a person should eat and drink in moderation, and we also find some remedies—such as herbs and plants recommended for birth control—that might have worked, at least a bit. But we are also instructed that onions will cure baldness, that the urine of a dog gets rid of warts, and that all a woman must do to prevent conception during intercourse is to bind her head with a red ribbon.

Yet in the midst of this good and bad advice, important progress was made. Medieval students of medicine digested the comprehensive medical writings of the Greek physician Galen (129–199 C.E.), along with the works of Arab medical scholars, particularly Ibn Sina (980–1037), or Avicenna as he was known in Western Christendom, whose works on the healing arts were especially valued. To this invaluable body of knowledge, recorded and analyzed by gifted medical scholars such as Hildegard of Bingen, Europeans began to add their own original contributions on such subjects as the curative properties of plants and the anatomy of the human body. It is probable that both animal and human dissections were performed by the scholars of twelfth-century Salerno. These doctors, rudimentary though their methods were, laid the foundations on which Western European medical science would thrive in later centuries.

Roman Law

As we saw in Chapter 10, canon law was an essential buttress of the medieval papacy. Organized by 1140 into Gratian's *Decretum,* canon law justified papal claims, expanded papal authority, and provided the papal curia with well-trained lawyers. These developments in canon law were largely stimulated by the study of Roman law, a new scholarly discipline that shaped not only canon law but also the laws of secular states throughout medieval Europe.

Roman legal principles had never entirely disappeared in the Italian peninsula, and it was in Bologna in the late eleventh century that the sixth-century *Corpus Juris Civilis* of the Emperor Justinian (r. 527–565) began to be studied after a long hiatus, and principles of Roman law began to guide legal studies. This renewed study of Roman law exposed Western Christendom to a distinctly different legal tradition from that of the custom-based law, itself derived in part from barbarian legal traditions, which had been so important throughout the Early Middle Ages. The traditions of Roman law were more coherent, more logical, and more autocratic, and they began to compete with custom-based law, rationalizing it and in some instances replacing it.

From the Italian peninsula the study of Roman law spread northward. A great school of law emerged at Montpellier, in southern France, and others flourished at Orléans, Paris, and Oxford. But Bologna remained the foremost center. There, scholars known as *glossators* wrote analytical commentaries on the *Corpus Juris,* clarifying difficult points and reconciling apparent contradictions. Later they began to produce textbooks and treatises on the *Corpus Juris* and to reorganize it into a coherent sequence of topics. Eventually such an extensive body of supplementary material existed that the glossators turned to the task of glossing the glosses—that is, clarifying the clarifications. Around the mid-thirteenth century, their efforts were synthesized into a comprehensive work—the *Glossa Ordinaria*—by the Bolognese scholar Accursius (c. 1182–1260). Thereafter, Accursius's *Glossa Ordinaria* became the authoritative supplement to the *Corpus Juris* in courts based on the principles of Roman law.

The impact of the revival of Roman law traditions was particularly strong in the Italian peninsula and southern France where elements of Roman law had survived as local custom. By the thirteenth century Roman law was beginning to make significant inroads in the north as well, for by then lawyers trained in the Roman tradition were playing dominant roles in the courts of France, Iberia, the German states, and elsewhere. Whether working in cities, duchies, or realms, these lawyers sought to organize local laws along more rational lines, molding them into systems that could emulate the coherence of the *Corpus Juris Civilis.* They also grew more confident than before about new law promulgated by statute or legislation, for Roman law allowed more room for legal innovation than had custom-based law. And many lawyers, employed in and devoted to royal service, effectively used the autocratic cast of Justinian's compilation to exalt their monarchs. Thus as the study of Roman law spread across medieval Europe, it tended to encourage legal codification, statutory legislation, and autocratic rule.

Philosophy

Medieval universities made no distinction between the study of philosophy and theology; the two projects were then one. Yet, although every important philosopher in the Central Middle Ages was a cleric of some sort, ecclesiastical authority did not stifle speculation or limit controversy. Catholic orthodoxy, which would harden noticeably at the time of the sixteenth-century Protestant Reformation, was still relatively flexible in the twelfth and thirteenth centuries, and philosophers were by no means timid apologists for official dogmas. Some philosophers tried hard to reconcile faith with reason in order to provide Christianity with a logical substructure, but there was sharp disagreement as to how this should be done and some argued against it altogether, asserting that reason cannot lead to the truth of Christian revelation. The shared faith of these philosophers did not limit the diversity of their opinions, nor did it curb their spirit of intellectual adventure.

The philosophers of the Central Middle Ages drew nourishment from six sources:

1. **Classical Greece.** Plato (c. 429–347 B.C.E.) was important; Aristotle (384–322 B.C.E.) even more so. At first these two Greek masters were known in the West only through a handful of late Roman translations and commentaries. By the thirteenth century, however, new and far more complete translations were

coming into Western Christendom from Iberia and Sicily, and Aristotelian philosophy became a matter of intense interest and controversy in Europe's universities. To many philosophers in the Central Middle Ages, Aristotle was so important that he was simply "The Philosopher."

2. **Islamic Thought.** It was from the Islamic world that many Greek scientific and philosophical works entered Europe, and they were accompanied by extensive commentaries as well as the original writings of Arab philosophers and scientists. Arab scholars came to grips with Greek learning long before Europeans did, and the rationalist arguments of the greatest of these, Ibn Rushd or Averroes (1126–1198), found many followers in European universities. In addition, Islamic advances in science and mathematics made particularly vital contributions to European philosophy.

3. **Jewish Thought.** Medieval philosophy was also enriched by the work of Jewish scholars, especially Moses Maimonides (1135–1204), whose *Guide for the Perplexed*—a penetrating reconciliation of Aristotle and the Jewish Bible—deeply influenced the work of thirteenth-century Christian philosophers and theologians.

4. **Early Christian Theologians.** Ambrose (c. 339–397), Jerome (c. 340–420), and Augustine (354–430) had been dominant intellectual forces throughout the Early Middle Ages, and their authority remained strong in the twelfth and thirteenth centuries. St. Augustine retained his singular significance and was, indeed, the chief vessel of Platonic and Neoplatonic thought in medieval universities.

5. **Early Medieval Scholars.** Gregory the Great (r. 590–604), Isidore of Seville (560–636), Bede (673–735), Alcuin (732–804), Rabanus Maurus (c. 780–856), John Scottus Eriugena (c. 810–877), and Gerbert of Aurillac (c. 945–1003) were all studied in the new universities. The original intellectual contributions of these men were less important, however, than the fact that they and their contemporaries had kept classical learning alive, thus creating the intellectual climate that made possible the reawakening of philosophical speculation in the eleventh century.

6. **Scripture.** Among medieval theologians the Vulgate Bible, the chief written source of divine revelation, was always the fundamental text and the ultimate authority.

Such were the chief elements that underlay what is today called **scholasticism,** the dominant intellectual approach to the problems of the day. As with the study of canon law and Roman law, scholastics sought to build more coherent and analytical systems. And as with these other disciplines, they sought to reconcile conflicting authorities—to create a concordance of discordant canons, to use Gratian's phrasing for canon law—in creating their systems. Their method involved careful study, respect for all past authorities, and logical thinking. In short, scholastics sought to bring together *all* knowledge—religious and worldly, past and present, classical and Christian—into one unified whole, and their method used logic to reconcile parts of knowledge that seemed to be in conflict but could, scholastics believed, be proven compatible.

The scholastics applied their method to a multitude of problems. They were concerned chiefly, however, with matters of basic significance to human existence: the nature of human beings, the purpose of human life, the existence and attributes of God, the fundamentals of human morality, and the relationship between God and humanity. It would be hard to deny that these are the most profound sorts of questions that one can ask. Many philosophers of our own day are inclined to reject them as unanswerable, but scholastic philosophers, lacking modern cynicism, were determined to make the attempt. Among the diverse investigations and conflicting opinions they produced, scholastics focused particularly on two controversies: the debate about the proper relationship between reason and revelation and the debate over **universals.**

The Relationship of Faith and Reason

All medieval scholastics believed in God, and all were also committed, to some degree, to the life of reason. But the proper balance between faith and reason was a far-reaching and perplexing problem for medieval philosophers. As we saw in Chapter 1, Tertullian (c. 150–225) had posed this question by contrasting the philosophical center of his world to its religious center, "What has Athens to do with Jerusalem?" He had answered in the negative, and in the Central Middle Ages, some philosophers agreed with him that God so transcended reason that any attempt to approach him intellectually was useless and, indeed, blasphemous. Peter Damian (1007–1072) rejected the intellectual road to God in favor of the mystical, insisting that God, whose power is limitless, cannot be bound or even approached by logic. He was followed in this view by such later mystics as Hildegard of Bingen who, to a degree, found truth in divine revelation and not scholarship, by Bernard of Clairvaux who denounced his rationalist contemporary Peter Abelard (1079–1142), and by Francis of Assisi (1182–1226) who regarded intellectual speculation as irrelevant to salvation.

The contrary view was just as old. Tertullian's counterparts in the third century, Clement of Alexandria (150–215) and his student Origen (182–251), had labored to provide Christianity with a sturdy philosophical foundation. In the next century, Ambrose, Jerome, and Augustine had wrestled with the problem of whether a Christian might properly use elements from pagan traditions in the service of the faith, and all three ended with affirmative answers. As Augustine expressed it,

> If those who are called philosophers, and especially the Platonists, have said
> anything that is true and in harmony with our faith, we must not only not shrink
> from it, but claim it for our own use.

This is the viewpoint that underlies most philosophy during the Central Middle Ages— that reason has a valuable role to play as a servant of revelation. One of its earliest proponents was Anselm (1033–1109), the archbishop of Canterbury who, as we saw in the last chapter, brought the investiture controversy to England. Anselm taught that faith must precede reason but that reason could serve to illuminate faith. He declared, following Augustine, "I believe so that I may know." He worked out several proofs of God, based on abstract reasoning rather than observation. And in his important theological treatise, *Cur Deus Homo (Why God Became Human),* he subjected the Christian doctrines of divine incarnation and atonement to rigorous logical analysis. His emphasis on reason, employed within the framework of a firm Christian conviction, set the stage for the significant philosophical developments of the following generations.

By the twelfth century, philosophers were intoxicated by the seemingly limitless possibilities of reason and logic. The most audacious of them all was Peter Abelard, the supreme logician of the twelfth century. In a famous work entitled *Sic et Non (Yes and No),* he laid the foundation for what is now known as the *scholastic method*—that is, a method that uses logic to reconcile conflicting authorities. In *Yes and No* Abelard collected opinions on a great variety of theological issues from a great variety of sources: the Bible, the Latin Fathers, the councils of the Church, and the decrees of the papacy. His collection demonstrated that these authorities disagreed on such issues as whether it is ever permissible to lie, whether anything happens by chance, and whether sin is or is not pleasing to God. Abelard argued that logic could reconcile these conflicting authorities, but he did not undertake the reconciliation himself, expecting that students should reason things out for themselves. As a result, he left himself open to attacks, especially by Bernard of Clairvaux, who was so hostile to rationalist thought that he called Abelard's theology "wild imaginations upon the Holy Scriptures." A brilliant teacher, Abelard was driven from one place to another until at length his opinions were condemned by an ecclesiastical council in 1141. Retiring to Cluny, he died there in 1142.

But Abelard's method lived. His student Peter Lombard (1100–1160) produced an important theological text, the *Book of Sentences,* which set off conflicting opinions on the pattern of the *Yes and No* but then took the further step of reconciling the contradictory authorities. Gratian's *Decretum* did the same for canon law. Both became, by the later twelfth century, the standard textbooks in their respective fields.

Most rationalists continued to agree with Anselm that reason was the servant of faith. Faith came first, but reason could perform the useful service of illuminating faith. Rationalists argued that, since truth is one, faith and reason *must* be harmonious and could not lead to contradictory conclusions. But even Thomas Aquinas, who built his intellectual system on this conviction, acknowledged that faith and reason could *appear* to disagree; in such cases, the flaw had to lie with a misuse of reason. Reason could not err, but it could be wrongly used, and logicians had always to beware of this potential misuse. As Abelard once wrote, "I do not wish to be an Aristotle if it cuts me off from Christ."

Among some medieval philosophers, however, the priorities came to be reversed. Misunderstanding Ibn Rushd's bold assertion, born of his own efforts to reconcile Aristotle with Islam, that faith and reason constitute separate paths to a single truth, a group of *Latin Averroists* emerged in the thirteenth century. They argued that reason and faith need not be compatible, and that philosophical issues (such as those raised by the writings of Aristotle) could be studied without reference to theology or faith. So, for example, Latin Averroists intellectually accepted Aristotle's eternally existing world as logically necessary, yet they nevertheless believed firmly in the Christian doctrine of the creation. Expanding on this dilemma, Latin Averroists argued that reason and revelation could produce radically different conclusions that were not merely, as rationalists such as Aquinas argued, the result of a misuse of reason. Their position came to be called the doctrine of the *twofold truth.*

The Debate over Universals

Philosophers also debated the nature of Platonic archetypes or, as they were called in the Middle Ages, "universals." Plato taught that a term such as "cat" describes not only particular cats but also a universal ideal that has reality in itself—that individual cats are imperfect reflections of a model cat, an archetypal or universal cat. Or, to take another example, Plato said that certain acts are "good" because they partake, imperfectly, of a universal good that exists in heaven. To Plato, these universals—cat, goodness, and the like—exist apart from the multitude of individual cats and good deeds in this world, and they are *more real* than their pale, individual reflections. Moreover, he taught that any-one who seeks knowledge ought to meditate on these universals rather than study the world of phenomena in which they are only imperfectly reflected.

Augustine accepted Plato's theory of universals, but he taught that the archetypes exist in the mind of God rather than in Plato's abstracted heaven. Whereas Plato thought that human knowledge of universals comes from dim memories of a prenatal past, Augustine maintained that God directly gives us knowledge of universals by a process of divine illumination. Plato and Augustine agreed, however, that the universal existed apart from the particular and, indeed, was *more real* than the particular. In the Central Middle Ages, those who followed the Platonic-Augustinian approach to universals were known as *Realists:* they believed that universals were real.

As early as the eleventh century the philosopher Roscelin (c. 1050–1125) rejected this view, declaring that universals were not real at all. "Cat" and "good" are mere words, he said, names that we have concocted for individual things that we have lumped into arbitrary categories. These categories, or universals, have no objective existence whatever. Reality is not to be found in them, but rather in the multiplicity and variety of individual objects that we can see, touch, and smell in the world around us. Those who followed Roscelin in this view were known as *Nominalists:* they argued that universals had no reality apart from their *nomina* or names. Nominalism remained in the intellec-tual background during the twelfth and thirteenth centuries, but, as we shall see, it would be revived in the fourteenth century.

Aquinas and others who studied Aristotle developed yet a third viewpoint on uni-versals: they exist, to be sure, but only through particular things or acts. In this view, the human mind draws its knowledge of the universal from observation of the particular by a process of abstraction. By studying many cats or good deeds, then, one could come to understand the universal meanings of "cat" and "goodness." Universals were real to Aquinas, but in a sense less real—or less independently real—than Plato and Augustine believed. Accordingly, philosophers who inclined toward the Aristotelian position have been called *Conceptualists:* they argued that universals existed as real and important concepts.[2]

Modern scholars sometimes accuse medieval philosophers of worrying about silly things, such as counting how many angels can dance on the head of a pin. The debate on universals might seem a good example of this high abstraction, but not so: this debate had concrete and practical implications. Realism's stress on ideas always had the poten-tial, if taken to extremes, of denigrating the natural world and the human body, thereby rejecting (as did Cathar heretics) God's creation. Nominalism was perhaps even more dangerous because its emphasis on the particular over the universal seemed to suggest that the Church was not, as medieval Christians believed, a single universal body but rather a vast accumulation of individual Christians. Conceptualism was the ideal scholastic position, for it reconciled other arguments in a synthesis that both valued par-ticular things and the abstractions to which they could lead.

---

[2] One sign of the extraordinary genius of Abelard is that he worked out a conceptualist position *before* the writings of Aristotle were available in Latin translation.

Political Theory

As scholars of the twelfth and thirteenth centuries became increasingly excited at the possibilities of logic, the remaining liberal arts began to lose out. The accomplished English scholar, John of Salisbury (c. 1115–1180), was a pupil of Abelard, a student of Greek, and a well-trained logician, but he was above all a humanist and a devotee of classical literature. He approved of logic but regretted that it was growing at the expense of other studies; he complained that the schools of his day were producing narrow logicians rather than broadly educated scholars.

In his *Policraticus* (1159), John of Salisbury made a major contribution to medieval political philosophy. Drawing on the thought of classical antiquity and the Early Middle Ages, he stressed the divine nature of kingship, but he also emphasized its responsibilities and limitations. The king drew his authority from God but was commissioned to rule for the good of his subjects rather than himself. He was bound to give his subjects peace and justice and to protect the Church. If he abused his commission and neglected his responsibilities, he lost his divine authority, ceased to be a king, and became a tyrant. As such, he forfeited his subjects' allegiance and was no longer their lawful ruler. Under extreme circumstances, and if all else failed, John of Salisbury recommended tyrannicide. In his view, a good Christian subject, although obliged to obey his *king,* might kill a *tyrant.* Apart from the highly original doctrine of tyrannicide, the views expressed in the *Policraticus* mirror the general political attitudes of the twelfth century—responsible limited monarchy and government on behalf of the governed. These theories, in turn, were idealized reflections of the actual monarchies of the day whose powers were held in check by the nobility, the Church, and ancient custom.

A century later, Thomas Aquinas would argue that the state, which most previous Christian thinkers had commonly regarded as a necessary evil—an unfortunate but indispensable consequence of the fall of Adam and Eve—was a good and natural outgrowth of human society. He echoed Aristotle's belief that politics is basic to human nature, and he regarded the justly governed state as a fitting part of the divine order. Like John of Salisbury, Aquinas insisted that kings must govern on their subjects' behalf and that a willful, unrestrained ruler who ignored God's moral imperatives was no king but a tyrant. Just as the human body could be corrupted by sin, he said, so the body politic could be corrupted by tyranny. But Aquinas argued that although good Christians must reject both sin and tyranny, they should nevertheless revere the body, the state, and indeed all physical creation as worthy products of God, inseparable from the world of spirit.

Intellectual Life outside Universities

Had the German nun Hildegard of Bingen (1098–1179) not been a woman, her intellectual power would have placed her among the greatest scholastics of her day. But cathedral schools were closed to her, so she developed her talents in other ways. She was a great composer, whose religious opera, *Ordo Virtutum (Play of the Virtues),* left songwriters such as Richard the Lion-Hearted far back in the dust. The *Ordo Virtutum* is funny, moving, and inspiring all at once, so much so that it is often performed today and is even available on compact disc. She was also a scholar of medical science, a theologian, and a political consultant whose advice was sought by popes and kings alike.

Yet the influence of Hildegard of Bingen, like that of many contemporary women, rested largely on a distinctly nonintellectual activity: mysticism. Always an element in Christian devotional life, mysticism became particularly important during the Central Middle Ages, when the most celebrated Christian visionaries were women. As the authority of male clergy increased with the development of canon law and growth of ecclesiastical bureaucracy, religious women, who were denied priestly roles and access to scholastic training in cathedral schools and universities, found an alternative and more immediate source of authority in mystical union with Christ. Hildegard of Bingen, for example, was consulted by theologians on thorny points of doctrine and by popes and emperors on questions of high politics. She answered with wisdom, eloquence, and learning acquired in her monastic schooling *and* with the power of direct revelation from God. In this way, Hildegard of Bingen (recognized for "the grace of God that is in you" by Bernard of Clairvaux) acquired an authoritative voice within an intellectual world that was turning, by her time, away from monasteries and toward the exciting dynamism of cathedral schools and nascent universities.[3]

Heloise of the Paraclete (c. 1100–1163) relied not on mysticism but her sheer brain power, and her story is more tragic. Heloise is today best known for her love affair with Peter Abelard. It began as a passionate clandestine affair; a son was born; a secret marriage was performed; and then Heloise's uncle, angry at what he perceived to be her mistreatment by Abelard, hired two thugs who broke into Abelard's rooms and castrated him. In shock, Heloise and Abelard separated, and each took monastic vows. In later years, they corresponded and worked together in the foundation of the monastery of Paraclete (where Heloise was abbess), but the sexual and physical intimacy of their earlier years was forever lost (see Color Illustration 11).

It is easy to construe Heloise as a victim. Abelard was her teacher when he deliberately (as he later confessed) set out to seduce her; she endured the difficulties of secret pregnancy and secret marriage; and much to her own expressed regret, she ended up a nun rather than a lover. Yet she was very much the intellectual equal of Abelard. She argued forcefully against their marriage (which she thought would diminish the power of their love as well as Abelard's career options); she formulated ideas about "pure love" that shaped Abelard's latter theological writings; and she enjoyed renown throughout Europe, both as a young woman and as an aged abbess, for her skilled Latinity and wisdom. As Peter the Venerable (c. 1092–1156), Abbot of Cluny, wrote to Heloise about her skill in secular learning and the liberal arts, "you have surpassed all women in carrying out your purpose, and have gone further than almost every man."

Yet, despite such praise and such talent, Heloise could never benefit from the formal education or ready employment that so aided the career and thought of a man like Peter Abelard. To put it simply, brilliant women like Hildegard of Bingen and Heloise of the Paraclete were admired during the Central Middle Ages, but they had to do their work outside the intellectual mainstream.

---

[3] For many other female mystics, however, their experiences were so ineffable that they prompted more poetic achievement than intellectual power. A century later, at the thirteenth-century abbey of Helfta in Saxony, Gertrude of Helfta (c. 1256–1302) and several other nuns of her community had visions of a Christ who was at once regal and approachable; their writings express what has aptly been called "a poised, self-confident, lyrical female mysticism."

Summations

The Latin translations of Greek, Arabic, and Hebrew texts that swept into Europe in the twelfth century answered a deep hunger on the part of Western thinkers. But they also provoked a crisis in Western Christendom because Aristotle's works in particular contained implications that seemed hostile to Christian faith. As thirteenth-century scholars sought to work through this crisis, they digested the insights of the past, cast them into comprehensive systems of thought, and produced great systematic summations.

Some philosophers, especially those drawn to the Platonic-Augustinian position that universals were real, were deeply suspicious of the newly recovered writings of Aristotle. Led in the thirteenth century by the Franciscan friar St. Bonaventure (1221–1274), they regarded Aristotle's work as pagan in viewpoint and dangerous to the faith. For them, the writings of St. Augustine sufficed, and the writings of Aristotle were an unnecessary diversion. Like Hildegard of Bingen who was at once a philosopher and a mystic, Bonaventure visualized the whole physical universe as a multitude of symbols pointing to God and glorifying him, eternally striving upward toward the Divine Presence. Human beings, he believed, stand at the fulcrum of creation, with bodies like beasts and souls like angels. We perceive the physical universe through our senses, but we know the spiritual world—the world of universals—through the grace of divine illumination. It is no accident that Bonaventure was a Franciscan as, indeed, were many philosophers who embraced Augustine and turned away from Aristotle. His entire system of thought is a kind of prayer in praise of God.

Among Dominican friars, however, a more receptive response to the new texts of Aristotle and other philosophers developed. These friars were much too devoted to the goal of reconciling faith and reason to reject the works of a man they regarded as antiquity's greatest philosopher; instead, they sought to incorporate Aristotle into Christian philosophy. Of these, the greatest were Albertus Magnus (c. 1200–1280) and his student Thomas Aquinas, both of whom were influenced by Maimonides's efforts in his *Guide for the Perplexed* to do the same for Aristotle and Judaism. Albertus Magnus, born of German parentage, was a scholar of wide-ranging interests who made important contributions to natural science, especially biology, as well as to philosophy and theology. He was a master of Aristotelian thought who sought to purge Aristotle of the heretical taint of Latin Averroism and transform his philosophy into the intellectual foundation of Christian orthodoxy. But the full achievement of this goal was left to his gifted student, Thomas Aquinas, who sought to Christianize Aristotle, much as Augustine had Christianized Plato and the Neoplatonists.

Thomas Aquinas was born of a Norman-Italian noble family in 1225. His parents hoped he would become a Benedictine monk and rise in due course to an influential abbacy. But in 1244 he shocked them by choosing a life of poverty in the new Dominican order. Shortly thereafter, he went to the University of Paris, where he spent most of his life teaching and writing. Unlike Augustine, he had no youthful follies to regret. Unlike Anselm and Bernard, he played no great role in the political affairs of his day. He persevered in his academic tasks until, in his late forties, he suddenly declared that all his books were rubbish and devoted his remaining days to mysticism. At his death, the priest who heard his last confession described it as being as innocent as that of a five-year-old.

In his copious writings—particularly his *Summa Theologica*—Aquinas explored all the great questions of philosophy, theology, political theory, and morality. He used Aristotle's logical method and categories of thought, but he arrived at conclusions that were in harmony with his Christian faith. Like Abelard, Aquinas assembled every possible argument, pro and con, on every subject that he discussed, but unlike Abelard he drew conclusions and defended them with cogent arguments. Few philosophers before or since have been so generous in presenting and exploring opinions contrary to their own, and none has been so systematic and exhaustive.

Aquinas created a vast, unified intellectual system—ranging from God to the details of the natural world—that was logically supported at every step. His theological writings have none of the passion of St. Augustine, and none of the literary elegance of Plato; rather, they have an *intellectual* elegance, an elegance of system and organization akin to that of Euclid's geometry. His *Summa Theologica* is organized into an immense series of separate sections that each deal with a particular philosophical question. Each question is subdivided into Articles, and each Article then analyzed in a predictable format: first, a list of arguments contrary to Aquinas's conclusion; then, an exposition of Aquinas's logical analysis; and finally, a refutation of the earlier objections. Aquinas then moves on to the next problem and subjects it to precisely the same process of inquiry. As in Euclidian geometry so in Thomist theology: once a problem is settled, the conclusion can be used in solving subsequent problems. Thus the system grows, problem by problem, step by step. Someone taught Thomas Aquinas how to follow an outline, and he never forgot the lesson.

Using this dense, predictable, and logical web of argumentation, Aquinas took up such matters as the nature of God, the attributes of God, the nature and destiny of humanity, human morality, law, and political theory. The result is an imposing, comprehensive edifice of thought, embracing all major theological issues. As the Gothic cathedral was the artistic embodiment of the Central Middle Ages, so the philosophy of Aquinas was its supreme intellectual expression. Both were based on clear and obvious principles of structure, and Aquinas even shared with cathedral builders the impulse to display rather than disguise the structural framework of his edifice.

Aquinas sought to encompass the totality of existence in a vast philosophical unity. At the center of his system was God, the maker of heaven and earth, who discloses portions of the truth to his followers through revelation, permits them to discover other portions through the operation of the intellect, and will lead them to all truth through salvation. Thus, for Aquinas, revelation and reason are complementary, compatible, and incapable of contradiction, if properly used. Thus also, Aquinas shared with Francis of Assisi and others the notion that the physical world, God's creation, was deeply significant in itself. In the debate over universals, he was a conceptualist, agreeing with Aristotle that universals were abstracted from the world of phenomena, but real nevertheless. Most of all, to Aquinas, heaven and earth, faith and reason worked together to one purpose: "For faith rests upon infallible truth, and therefore its contrary cannot be demonstrated." This was the essence of Aquinas's philosophical position.

Ultimately, however, Aquinas argued that God *is* truth, and he taught that it is human destiny, on reaching heaven, to stand unshielded in the divine presence—to love and to know. Thus the roads of St. Thomas, St. Bonaventure, St. Bernard, and Dante, although passing over very different terrain, arrive finally at the same destination. It is not so surprising, after all, that in the end St. Thomas rejected theology for mysticism.

Natural Philosophy: Science

As far back as the later decades of the tenth century, Gerbert of Aurillac (c. 945–1003) had visited al-Andalus, familiarized himself with Islamic thought, and made his own modest contribution to scientific knowledge. Gerbert built a simple "planetarium" of balls, rods, and bands to illustrate the motions of the stars and planets. He introduced the abacus into the West, and following the Greeks, Arabs, and earlier Western European scholars, he taught that the earth was round.

Islamic science continued thereafter to inspire Western scholars, particularly in the late eleventh and twelfth centuries. Men such as Adelard of Bath (1090–1150) retraced Gerbert's pilgrimage to Islamic libraries and returned with a new respect for scientific inquiry. Among the works that Adelard translated from Arabic into Latin were Euclid's *Elements* and important works on mathematics by al-Khwarizmi (c. 800–847) and Abu Mashar (d. 886). Through the labors of twelfth-century translators, the great scientific works of Greece and Islam were made known in the West: Aristotle's *Physics;* Ptolemy's *Almagest;* Arabic books on algebra, astrology, and medicine; and many others. And then Western scholars began to write scientific books of their own, such as Adelard of Bath's *Natural Questions.* Such works, however, were merely summaries of Greek and Arabic knowledge. This assimilative phase of Western science continued until the thirteenth century when, particularly among the Franciscans, the first serious original work began.

The mysticism of Bonaventure represents one pole of Franciscan thought; at the other stands a group of scientific thinkers who, inspired perhaps by Francis of Assisi's love of nature, applied their logical tools to the task of investigating the physical world. Oxford became Europe's chief scientific center, and it was there that Western science began to thrive in the thirteenth century. The key figure was Robert Grosseteste (c. 1170–1253), future bishop of Lincoln who, although not a Franciscan himself, was chief lecturer to the Franciscans at Oxford. Grosseteste had a comprehensive knowledge of Platonic and Neoplatonic philosophies, Aristotelian physics, and the scientific legacy of Islam. From Plato, who was thought to have once stated, "God is always doing geometry," Grosseteste derived the notion that mathematics is a basic key to understanding the physical universe. From Aristotle, Grosseteste learned the importance of abstracting knowledge from the everyday world by means of observation and experiment. By thus bridging two traditions, Grosseteste brought together the mathematical and experimental components that together underlie the rise of modern science. More than that, drawing on the suggestive work of his Islamic predecessors, he developed a far more rigorous experimental procedure than was to be found in the pages of Aristotle, a procedure of observation, hypothesis, and experimental verification that would eventually develop into the modern scientific method. The great triumphs of European science lay far in the future, but with the work of Robert Grosseteste, the basic instrument had been forged.

Grosseteste's work was carried further by his disciple, the Franciscan Roger Bacon (c. 1214–1294). The author of a fascinating body of scientific sense and nonsense, Roger Bacon dabbled in the mysteries of alchemy, and his curiosity carried him along other strange roads. He was critical of the deductive logic and metaphysical speculations that so fascinated his scholastic contemporaries. In the search for truth, he wrote succinctly and prophetically, "Reasoning does not suffice but experience does."

✳ CONCLUSION

Underlying the intellectual achievements of the Central Middle Ages was a basic change in attitude toward the natural world. To many early medieval people, the world had seemed irrelevant, disordered, chaotic, and unknowable. It was a world of happenstance and trouble, a world best avoided by contemplation of God. But in the twelfth and thirteenth centuries, some Europeans began to see the natural world in a different—and more positive—way. First, they began to see the natural world as part of God's orderly plan, a part that functioned according to consistent, divinely constituted laws and was therefore open to rational inspection. Hence, a passage from the thirteenth-century *Romance of the Rose* ridicules the notion that demons "with their hooks and cables, or their teeth and nails" cause storm damage:

> Such an explanation isn't worth
> Two turnips; those accepting it are wrong.
> For nothing but the tempest and the wind
> Are needed to explain the havoc wrought.
> These are the things that cause the injury.

Second, they began to argue that God created a natural world that was good as well as intelligible. The goodness of nature found its most eloquent expression in a text we saw in Chapter 8, Francis of Assisi's "Song of Brother Sun"; it also inspired the idealized naturalism of the Gothic sculptors, the poems of Dante in praise of Beatrice, and the philosophy of Thomas Aquinas. Some people would long continue to regard the world as threatening and unpredictable, governed by supernatural forces and possessed by the devil. Such was the traditional view, and some agree with it even today. But during the cultural awakening of the Central Middle Ages, this view began to lose ground.

SUGGESTED READINGS

John W. Baldwin, *The Language of Sex: Five Voices from Northern France around 1200* (1994). A fascinating study of the ideas of five male authors about sexuality and gender. See also Linda Paterson, *The World of the Troubadours: Medieval Occitan Society, c. 1100– c. 1300* (1995), and R. Howard Bloch, *Medieval Misogyny and the Invention of Western Romantic Love* (1991).

M. T. Clanchy, *Abelard: A Medieval Life* (1997). An outstanding new study. See also Constant J. Mews, *The Lost Love Letters of Heloise and Abelard* (1999).

Nicola Coldstream, *Medieval Architecture* (2002). A new, lavishly illustrated, and strongly written synthesis.

Marcia Colish, *Medieval Foundations of the Western Intellectual Tradition, 400–1400* (1997). An excellent new survey. See also B. B. Price, *Medieval Thought: An Introduction* (1992).

Alain Erlande-Brandenburg, *The Cathedral: The Social and Architectural Dynamics of Construction* (1994).

Edward Grant, *The Foundations of Modern Science in the Middle Ages* (1996). A new and comprehensive survey.

Jacques Le Goff, *Intellectuals in the Middle Ages* (1993). Argues cogently for the emergence of a new, intellectual class toward the beginning of the High Middle Ages. See also John W.

Baldwin, *The Scholastic Culture of the Middle Ages 1000–1300* (1971), and Anders Piltz, *The World of Medieval Learning* (1981).

Veronica Sekules, *Medieval Art* (2001). A succinct and well-illustrated introduction.

Nancy Siraisi, *Medieval and Early Renaissance Medicine: An Introduction to Knowledge and Practice* (1990). A good introduction to an exploding research field.

Colette Sirat, *A History of Jewish Philosophy in the Middle Ages* (1990). This learned and comprehensive account is the best work on the subject.

SUGGESTED PRIMARY SOURCE

Online Medieval and Classical Library (http://sunsite.berkeley.edu/OMACL/). There are many fine printed editions of literary texts, but for students who want to sample the genres, this is a good place to start.

PART III

THE LATER MIDDLE AGES
CRISIS AND CREATIVITY, 1300-1500

In the year 1300, Europeans celebrated the first-ever Papal Jubilee, proclaimed by Pope Boniface VIII (r. 1294–1303) who promised remission of sins for penitent pilgrims visiting Rome. One eyewitness reports that more than 200,000 Christians responded, flocking to the Holy City in such large numbers that a new gate had to be opened in the city's walls. For Boniface and his pilgrims, this was a bustling year of great optimism, pride, and enthusiasm. But for historians today, blessed with a hindsight that medieval popes and pilgrims could not have, the year 1300 portends more trouble than triumph.

The contrast with the year 1000 is a telling one. In 1000, Europeans had faced a bright prospect: the weather was drier and warmer than before, invaders had left or settled down, agricultural production and commerce were expanding, feudal warriors were slightly less bellicose, and monastic reform at Cluny was revitalizing the Church. In the centuries that followed, this bright prospect was fulfilled as population grew, towns grew, universities grew, and so too did the power of popes and kings. By 1300, however, the circumstances of Europe were more worrisome than bright: weather was beginning to worsen, agricultural expansion had stalled, new wars troubled the land, the papacy was less powerful and less well regarded than before, and although invasions did not threaten, devastating famine and disease did. The bright prospect offered in the year 1000 was reaching a cloudy culmination by the year 1300.

Like all turning points in history, the year 1300 is a good vantage point from which to survey developments before and after. In 1277, several of the teachings of Thomas Aquinas were condemned as heretical: a fact that suggests intellectual crisis. By 1300, the Ottoman Turks were establishing their control of Asia Minor: a new threat to the Byzantine Empire that would end with the taking of its capital in 1453. In 1309, Pope Clement V (r. 1305–1314) became the first of several popes who made their residence in Avignon rather than Rome: a sign of crisis in the papacy. In 1315, a poor harvest inaugurated the first widespread famine in centuries: an indicator of severe economic troubles. And in 1337, England and France began a war—remembered as the "Hundred Years' War"—that would bring devastation to France and aristocratic factionalism to both countries: a clear sign of political woes.

Yet the date 1300 might put the cart before the horse, because the most dramatic crisis came a half-century later with the 1347 arrival of a plague that would quickly spread throughout Western Europe. Within two years, about one of every three Europeans would die of the diseases wrought by this contagion, a horrifying event in the short term and a dramatic agent of historical change in the long term. From the perspective of the demographic collapse wrought by the Great Plague, then, 1350 is certainly a better dividing point than 1300. Yet this divider would implicitly attribute the crises of the Later Middle Ages to an external force (the happenstance arrival of a devastating disease), suggesting that the 1347–1349 plague afflicted a medieval Europe in its prime. This was clearly not so, as we can best see by approaching the Great Plague through the troubled decades that preceded it. In other words, the perspective from 1300 allows us to see the Great Plague as a fearsome disease that afflicted a Europe already troubled by various economic, political, and religious woes.

Even more than most eras of human history, then, the fourteenth and fifteenth centuries (see the accompanying timeline) were violent and unsettled. These were also violent and unsettled centuries in Byzantium. The old Byzantine Empire had been restored in 1261, after six decades of "Latin" (that is, Western) rule. But the restored Empire was a mere shadow of its former self. Its wealth had been looted; its provinces had grown into independent states; and it, too, was devastated by plague in 1347. Byzantium tottered on until the mid-fifteenth century, and its artists and scholars continued to guard the rich cultural heritage of the old Eastern Empire of Rome. But it was a small state with little authority beyond Constantinople and its region, a mere remnant of a once glorious power. When Constantinople fell to the Ottoman Turks in 1453, it was the end of a dream, not an empire.

Unsettled too were the Islamic states that came and went along the southern reaches of the Mediterranean in the fourteenth and fifteenth centuries. For the medieval West, the most momentous of these shifts occurred in 1492, when Granada, the last Muslim state in Iberia, fell to the armies of Isabella of Castile (r. 1474–1504) and Ferdinand of Aragon (r. 1479–1516). This was more than a political victory, for it signaled the Christianization of the combined kingdoms of Castile and Aragon, from which was emerging the state we today call Spain. Three months after the fall of Granada, Spanish Jews were told to convert to Christianity or emigrate; some accepted baptism, but tens of thousands emigrated to Portugal, North Africa, Constantinople, and the Low Countries. In 1504, Spanish Muslims were given the same hard choice, and many emigrated to North Africa.

These upheavals in Iberia specifically, and the southern Mediterranean more generally, were countered in the eastern Mediterranean by a new stability brought by a new Turkish dynasty, called Ottoman after its founder Osman. Like the Seljuks before them, the Ottomans had moved westward from the Asian steppes, and by the early fourteenth century, they had a firm base in western Anatolia. They then slowly but steadily supplanted the Seljuks and extended their territory even farther. In 1453, the Ottomans accomplished what the Umayyads had attempted more than seven centuries before: they took Constantinople itself. By the early sixteenth century, they controlled Anatolia, the entire Black Sea region, much of the Balkans, the Middle East, and the caliphate of Egypt. The Ottoman Empire endured until 1922.

In the West, the troubled times of the fourteenth and fifteenth centuries were also marked by a gradual ebbing of confidence in the values on which central medieval

TIMELINE FOR PART III   The Later Middle Ages, 1300–1500

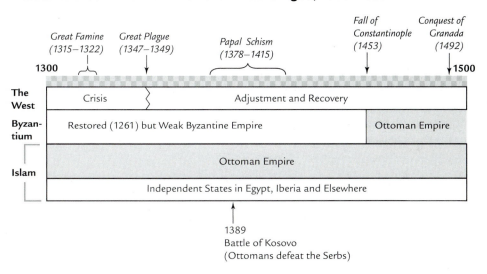

1389
Battle of Kosovo
(Ottomans defeat the Serbs)

civilization had rested. The inherent optimism of scholasticism gave way to skepticism and disillusionment; the thirteenth-century intellectual project of fusing the worlds of matter and spirit faded; some writers and artists turned from stories of love and heroism to dwell on fantasy, eccentricity, demons, and death; and everywhere pessimism and claustrophobia ruled the day. This was an age of excessive fashion, when aristocrats were happy to trip about in shoes with long upturned points and to tire their necks with absurdly high headdresses. It was also an age of excessive religiosity, with some Christians virtually starving themselves to death and others whipping themselves into frenzies of self-mutilation. And it was an age of extreme fear, with newly strengthened anxieties about God's judgment, rebellious peasants, demons, and even witches.

Yet, this violent, unsettled, and extreme age was also unusually creative, an age whose resourcefulness bridges "medieval" and "modern" Europe. In many ways, the fourteenth and fifteenth centuries built productively on the medieval past. The papacy was much battered between 1300 and 1450, but it then reestablished its supreme authority in matters of Christian faith, as would have seemed quite proper to Gregory VII (r. 1073–1085) and earlier popes. Western kingdoms were racked by civil and external wars, but by the mid-fifteenth century some monarchs were consolidating their powers in ways that built on the ideas of such earlier kings as Philip Augustus of France (r. 1180–1223) and Edward I of England (r. 1272–1307). Aristocrats had to adapt to new styles of warfare and landowning during the Later Middle Ages, but they still lived very well indeed in 1500. Towns, the quintessential new developments of the Central Middle Ages, were hard hit by the disruptions of the Great Plague, but they were growing again as the fifteenth century closed. And medieval culture—as expressed by such writers as Giovanni Boccaccio (1313–1373), Francesco Petrarch (1304–1374), Geoffrey Chaucer (c. 1340–1400), Christine de Pizan (1364–1430), and François Villon (1431–c.1463)—arguably did not just survive the crises of the Later Middle Ages but, in fact, flourished. Moreover, the products of this flourishing culture were more widely available than ever before—because more authors wrote in vernacular languages, because more people were able to read, and because, after 1450, printing presses began to produce cheaper books.

At the same time as people in these centuries built on the foundations of the medieval past, they also built toward a different sort of future. Modernity is a difficult concept to define and even more difficult to date. But many would agree that 1500 was the threshold of a *modern* Europe, a Europe distinguished from its medieval predecessor by its "renaissance" culture, its greater reliance on science, its protestant Christianities, its capitalist economy, its larger and more important cities, its geographical expansionism, its nation-states, and indeed, its witch-hunting, its revival of slavery, and its class tensions. As we shall see, all of these aspects of modernity are rooted in the fourteenth and fifteenth centuries, so that, to give just one example, the arguments of Martin Luther have intellectual precedents in the teachings of both John Wycliffe (c. 1330–1384) and Jan Hus (c. 1373–1415), as well as popular precedents in the anti-clericalism and anti-papalism of late medieval Christians. Luther's revolt produced "modern" Christian denominations, but in some critical respects, it was based on "medieval" ideas and trends. Indeed, some historians have suggested—tongue in cheek and playing on the designation of the sixteenth through eighteenth centuries as "early modern Europe"— that we should be calling the era between 1300 and 1500 "early early modern Europe."[1]

What matters more than how we label the era from 1300 to 1500, however, is its general character, and this can be best described as one of many crises *and* many creative responses. Into these centuries were poured all the strengths and weaknesses of the Central Middle Ages; to this rich inheritance were added the troubles of famine, plague, and war; and in response, Europe changed in ways that were both staggeringly awful and impressively awesome.

Suggested Readings

Thomas A. Brady, Jr. et al., *Handbook of European History 1400–1600,* 2 vols. (1994).
    Exceedingly useful essays by leading scholars that address a variety of issues in the
    social, economic, religious, and political history of the period.
Robert Fossier, ed., *The Cambridge Illustrated History of the Middle Ages, vol. 3: 1250–1520,*
    trans. Janet Sondheimer (1986). See also volumes 6 and 7 of David Abulafia et al., eds.,
    The New Cambridge Medieval History (2000 and 1998).
David Nicholas, *The Transformation of Europe, 1300–1600* (1999). A new general account. See
    also Denys Hay, *Europe in the Fourteenth and Fifteenth Centuries* (2nd edition, 1989).

---

[1] My own tongue-in-cheek response is that we might call the sixteenth through eighteenth centuries the "Very Late Middle Ages."

CHAPTER 13

❦

FAMINE, PLAGUE, AND RECOVERY, c. 1300-1500

✺ INTRODUCTION

The shift from boom to depression came gradually and unevenly to Western Europe. Even as early as the mid-thirteenth century, prosperity was starting to ebb in some regions. By the early fourteenth century, a number of related trends—shrinking population, contracting markets, devalued currencies, a lack of good land still to be claimed as arable, and a creeping mood of pessimism and retrenchment—resulted in a general economic slump.

These trends were far from universal. Economic decline was less marked in the northern Italian peninsula than elsewhere. Florence, with its large textile industry and its international bankers, prospered. So too did some enterprising individuals and families, especially those who grew wealthy from the profits of international commerce and banking. Although the great Florentine banking families of the Bardi and Peruzzi collapsed in the mid-fourteenth century, the Medici banking firm did so well that they eventually ruled Florence and married their daughters into some of the royal dynasties of Europe. Even north of the Alps, a few localities continued to expand thanks to favorable commercial situations or technological advances. The French city of Bourges flourished throughout most of the Late Middle Ages, so much so that one of its citizens, Jacques Coeur, became financier of the fifteenth-century French monarchy. The luxurious house that Coeur built in Bourges was the wonder of his day, and it still stands as an impressive monument to the prosperity of some late medieval entrepreneurs. But Coeur himself was ruined by his royal debtor, King Charles VII (r. 1422–1461), within a few months of the house's completion. So his fine home testifies to both success and collapse, the latter an all-too-common experience for merchants and bankers who undertook risky investments in the risky economy of late medieval Europe.

Even in the regions where economic decline predominated in the fourteenth and fifteenth centuries, historians disagree sharply on its magnitude and impact. No one argues that the demise of hundreds of thousands of Europeans in the Great Plague was a delightful event, but some do point out that this tragedy had positive consequences, as

TIMELINE 13.1   Economic and Social Change, 1300–1500

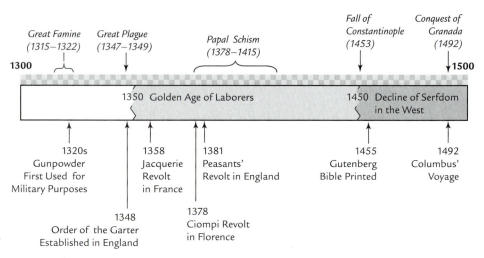

it made more land, food, and other resources available for those who survived the epidemic. Assessing the effects of other developments is often a matter of perspective. When wages rose after the Great Plague, for example, this was an excellent development for wage-laborers, who earned more money with less effort, but a terrible development for landowners, who found that hiring workers to cultivate their demesne lands was suddenly prohibitively expensive. Hence, although landowners suffered and overall economic output fell, the period after the Great Plague was, as one historian has put it, the "golden age of laborers" (see Timeline 13.1). Similarly, although the institutional Church suffered greatly in the Later Middle Ages, Christian spirituality developed in exciting new directions.

✳ ECONOMIC WOES AND DEMOGRAPHIC CRISIS (1300–1350)

By the early fourteenth century, the explosive population growth of the previous centuries had reached its limit, and Europe was overpopulated. In England, for example, there were about six million inhabitants in 1300; this was about three times as many as in 1066, and perhaps more to the point, it was more people than England would support again until the eighteenth-century industrial revolution had transformed—and expanded—the productive capacities of the English economy.

Simply put, in 1300, the number of people in Europe exceeded the productive capacities of its lands and farmers. Northern European agriculture had expanded to the limits allowed by such earlier technological innovations as the heavy plow, the three-field system, and windmills. Although peasants continued to clear new fields, these were marginal lands hitherto avoided because their soils were so poor. Indeed, land was so scarce in 1300 that some peasants tried to eke livings from poor soils that even today's farmers, aided by mechanization and chemical fertilizers, leave uncultivated.

Rising population and declining productivity were bad enough, but landowners and monarchs further aggravated the situation. Many manorial lords and ladies reacted to their own declining incomes by raising fines and rents so as to wring every last penny out of their tenants. Monarchs did much the same, for kings like Edward I of England (r. 1272–1307) and Philip IV of France (r. 1285–1314) financed their bureaucracies and wars with heavy taxes and forced requisitions. As one early fourteenth-century song-writer bitterly complained, "every fourth penny must go to the king."

For ordinary people faced with more people to feed, higher rents, new taxes, and fewer resources, all the choices were bad ones. Standards of living fell. Peasant hold-ings were subdivided into smaller and smaller plots; wages fell to very low levels; diets grew more limited and less healthy; and everyone seemed tired, ill-nourished, and demoralized.

Then, in the autumn of 1314, extraordinary rains began to fall, rains that were the prelude to several years of very cold and wet winters. The inevitable result was a series of meager harvests, and because peasants were already overworking their lands and understocking their barns, poor harvests meant famine. People prayed for better weather, mounting penitential processions of barefoot sinners and ringing bells. But famine came, and it lasted for seven hard years, from 1315 to 1322. The poorest died first, along with the very old and very young; townspeople suffered more than peasants, who had better chances to forage for food; and some died not of starvation but instead of diseases that opportunistically struck their weakened bodies. But everyone was vulnerable, and by the time it ended, the Great Famine—the *worst* famine in European history—had carried away at least 10 percent of the population.

In some regions of Europe, animals died in huge numbers as well, for these were also years of epidemic disease in herds and flocks. Some households lost half their cattle and sheep, with no meat or hides to be salvaged. People died, stock dwindled, and the land was not as productive as before. Long before the arrival of plague in the mid-fourteenth century, Europe was in trouble.

The Onset of the Great Plague

The term "Black Death" is popular today, but it is a modern term that was first introduced in 1833. Medieval people spoke about this catastrophe as the "Great Pestilence," "Great Death," or "Great Plague." It was primarily a combination of three related diseases: (1) *bubonic plague,* which is carried by rats and spread by the fleas the rats carry and in-fect; (2) *pneumonic plague,* which combines bubonic plague with respiratory infection and is therefore spread easily by coughing and sneezing; and (3) *septicemic plague,* which attacks the bloodstream and can be transmitted by fleas from one human to another. The Great Plague originated on the Asian steppes, where wild rodents still carry the disease (as they do in western parts of the United States today). Bubonic plague came first, arriving in Sicily and Sardinia from the Crimea during the winter of 1347–1348 aboard rat-infested merchant ships. It spread swiftly among a population already weakened by malnutrition, and it was quickly followed by its pneumonic and septicemic varieties. The Great Plague's swift expansion can be largely explained by the comfortable living circumstances that me-dieval castles, townhouses, and cottages offered to rats, and also by the lively European trade in grain carried by rat-infested ships. In medieval Europe, rats were everywhere.

As Map 13.1 shows, the plague advanced across Europe with terrifying speed in 1348 and 1349. The death toll cannot be determined with any precision, but about one-third of Europe's population perished. In many crowded towns the mortality rate exceeded 50 percent. Monasteries were also especially hard hit; priests, many of whom

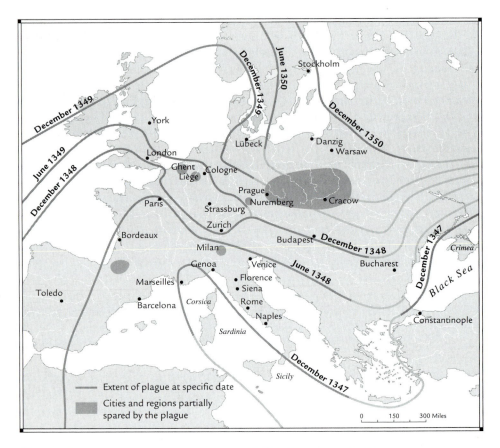

Map 13.1   *The Spread of the Great Plague, 1347–1350*   When the plague reached Europe late in 1347, it first assaulted the islands of Sicily, Sardinia, and Corsica and then the Mediterranean coast to their north. Thereafter, it moved steadily inland. By the summer of 1348, it was afflicting the people of Paris, and by the end of 1349, virtually all the medieval West was in its grip. We do not know why a few regions escaped relatively unscathed.

stayed to care for the dying, also died in large numbers. People who lived in isolated rural areas suffered comparatively less.

Europeans were stunned by the onset of the plague, especially because fourteenth-century physicians and healers were at a loss to explain the process of infection. Some attributed the plague to astrological forces; others blamed earthquakes or fogs; still others thought Jews had poisoned the wells (in Iberia, Arabs were sometimes also accused). Although some sought to control the plague through flight or quarantine, no one considered rats and rat control. Almost everyone agreed, however, on one major cause: the horrors of the plague were a sure sign of God's anger. At papal Avignon and elsewhere, clergy organized great religious processions:

> These were attended by 2,000 people from all the region round about: men and women alike, many barefoot, others wearing hairshirts or smeared with ashes. As they processed with lamentations and tears, and with loose hair, they beat themselves with cruel whips until the blood ran.

MEDIEVAL MYTHS

The Pied Piper of Hameln

Something happened—possibly—in the town of Hameln in 1284, and from it comes the story known today as the tale of the Pied Piper of Hameln. It is a simple and sad tale: Hameln, a town in north-central Germany, was infested by rats; its mayor offered a rich reward to anyone who could end the infestation; a piper played such a lovely tune that the rats followed him to a river and drowned; and, then, when the mayor refused to pay the reward, the piper played a new tune that drew all the children out of the town and to their deaths. Pied? This means that the piper wore multicolored—or pied—clothing, a notion popularized in the English-speaking world by Robert Browning's 1842 poem, "The Pied Piper of Hameln." In Germany, where the Grimm brothers studied various versions of the tale in the early nineteenth century, the piper remains less colorfully known as *der Rattenfänger* ("the Ratcatcher"). The medieval origins of the tale are mostly lost, including a stained-glass window from c. 1300 that, it is said, showed the piper leading the children away. The first surviving written evidence dates from the mid-fifteenth century. It tells of a piper and lost children, but no rats. Explaining the tale and, in particular, tracing the fate of the children has created a small historical industry: the children died of the plague, or in a landslide, or on a doomed ship, or in battle, or on crusade, or, least plausibly of all, by alien abduction in UFOs. Or, perhaps, the children did not die at all but simply left Hameln to emigrate eastward, as did so many Germans in the Central Middle Ages (if so, they must have been young adults, rather than children). To my mind, the story of the Pied Piper is best understood not as an authentic historical event but instead as a tale that reflects the troubled times and deep anxieties of the late medieval people who first created it. But try selling such skepticism to the Pied Piper who today entertains tourists in Hameln. And whether fact or fiction, it comes with a good moral: "pay the piper" or suffer the consequences. You can read various renditions of the legend at http://www.pitt.edu/~dash/hameln.html.

Other Christians attacked Jews "because they thought to please God in that way" (as one observer noted), and in those parts of Western Christendom where Jews could still live, they faced not only the dangers of plague but also frenzied mobs of frightened Christians. In February 1349, Christians murdered 2,000 Jews in Strasbourg; in July all the Jews of Frankfurt met a similar fate; in August, the Jewish communities of Mainz and Cologne were exterminated; and other smaller Jewish communities were similarly terrorized and expunged.

The horrors of the plague were further exacerbated by the swift and disgusting course of the disease. The plague offered its victims a gross death, horrible to see, to smell, and to nurse. So many people died so swiftly that proper burial was impossible (see Figure 13.1 for one mass burial). One observer spoke, for example, of ships floating aimlessly on the Mediterranean with dead crews. And, in any case, fear drove many people to abandon the sick, thereby also abandoning many basic social obligations. As one inhabitant of Siena wrote:

> Father abandoned child; wife, husband; one brother, another; for this illness
> seemed to strike through the breath and the sight. And so they died. And no one
> could be found to bury the dead for money or for friendship.... And in many

Figure 13.1 *Coffins Everywhere*   This picture shows the burial of plague victims at Tournai in 1349. The death rate in some other towns outstripped the making of coffins, requiring the disposal of corpses in mass graves.

> places in Siena huge pits were dug and piled deep with huge heaps of the dead.... And there were many corpses about the city who were so sparsely covered with earth that dogs dragged them forth and devoured their bodies.

In these first, frightening years, the Great Plague killed social ties as well as people.

✻ ADJUSTMENT AND RECOVERY (1350–1500)

The Recurring Threat of Plague

By the end of 1349, the Great Plague had run its first course, leaving its survivors traumatized and grief stricken but somewhat protected by immunities built by exposure to the disease. It is possible that unusually large numbers of marriages and births occurred in the years just after 1349, as people tried to preserve family lines and repopulate deserted lands and villages. But the plague was not done—and would not be done for a long, long time.

In 1361–1362 the plague returned to some parts of Europe, striking especially hard at young people born since the Great Plague, who lacked any immunity from prior exposure. This "children's plague" was only the first of a long series of revisitations: in 1369, 1374–1375, 1379, 1390, 1407, and in every decade throughout the fifteenth century. Plague continued, albeit less frequently, through the sixteenth and seventeenth centuries. Although none of these subsequent plagues resulted in deaths on the scale of 1347–1349, the seemingly endless recurrences kept anxieties high. Each generation saw an outbreak of the plague somewhere in Europe. And the population of Europe, having dropped drastically in the wake of the plague's first onset, stayed low for a long time. In 1500, there were still many fewer people in Europe than in 1300.

The grief brought about by the plague cannot be measured, but we can observe its more tangible effects: innumerable deserted villages whose tumbled buildings lie today beneath the grassy meadows of the European countryside, unoccupied and dilapidated districts within city walls, the temporary decline of the European wool and grain markets, and a severe shortage of labor.

Recovery in the Countryside

With grim efficiency, the Great Plague provided a sudden, radical solution to the problem of rural overpopulation. With one of every three people dead within two years, there was, by 1350, an abundance of arable land for those who survived. There was also a labor shortage, with many jobs and few workers.

Marginal lands farmed by desperate peasants in 1300 were left after 1350 to revert again to wasteland. More productive lands, available only at exorbitant rents in 1300, could be rented at better terms in the later fourteenth century. Some enterprising peasants prospered from the decline in land values, buying or leasing extra acres and hiring laborers to farm them. Their successes slowly changed peasant society, creating larger gaps between well-off and poorer peasants and laying the foundation for later classes of prosperous farmers, such as the *yeomanry* of early modern England.

Other peasants profited from labor, not land. Because the services of those laborers who survived the plague were much in demand, their wages—and hence, their standard of living—improved markedly. Employers did not pay these higher wages happily. Some attempted to hold wages down by agreeing with other employers to pay only set rates; others sought a similar end through legislation (in England, for example, the Statute of Laborers tried in 1351 to freeze wages at preplague levels). But such strategies could not hold back the economic tide, and most employers, desperate for workers, paid what the market required. This was, indeed, a golden age for workers, but it did not last long.[1] By the later fifteenth century, wages were falling again, and those who relied on wage-work were impoverished in comparison to their neighbors who had accumulated land.

For both rich and poor peasants, the post–plague economy eventually brought another benefit: the decline of serfdom. In part, this change resulted from peasant resentment and revolt. With good land and high wages widely available, some peasants simply walked away from manors that continued to demand weekly labor or other servile obligations. Others sought freedom through revolt, for in the wake of the Great Plague, rural rebellions rocked the European countryside. The first arose in 1358, when a series of protests by French peasants escalated into a widespread revolt in the region around Paris. Known as the Jacquerie (after "Jacques," the name which French nobles derisively used for any male peasant), it was crushed within a few weeks. In 1381, English

---

[1] Some historians argue that this was a golden age for women, too. In their view, because wage-workers were so much in demand, women might have been able to earn wages equal to those paid men and take jobs once reserved for men. This is an intriguing possibility, but the evidence is iffy, and quite a few wage-lists indicate that women continued to be paid about two-thirds the wages of men. See, for example, Sandy Bardsley, "Women's Work Reconsidered: Gender and Wage Differentiation in Late Medieval England," *Past and Present* 165 (1999), pp. 3–29.

peasants had their turn in a rebellion that spread through much of England and then to London, where King Richard II (r. 1377–1399) tricked and murdered its leaders. The other rebels were quickly dispersed and hunted down. Similar popular uprisings occurred—and were suppressed—in the Holy Roman Empire, Hungary, Norway, Finland, Sweden, Iberia, and the Netherlands. Only one major revolt was successful. In mid-fifteenth-century Catalonia, peasants mobilized—during a general civil war that pitted king against a coalition of nobles and townspeople—to bring an end to what even official documents called the "bad customs" (*mals usos*) that had been imposed on them some two centuries before. Their chief ally in this struggle was none other than the king.

Although most of these revolts were quickly put down, their message was not, it seems, entirely lost on the nobility. The English rebels had explicitly sought to end serfdom, and they had also questioned the social inequalities that were at the heart of aristocratic privilege. One of their leaders, John Ball, had dared to question this privilege in a dangerously memorable couplet:

> When Adam delved [dug] and Eve span,
> Who was then the gentleman?

These revolts, in other words, put the landed elite on notice, providing them with a good incentive to develop less exploitative methods of manorial management.

The economy provided a further incentive. Rising wages combined with declining grain prices to catch landowners between two blades of what has been called a "price scissors." As the expenses of farming rose and its profits declined, landowners in northwestern Europe stopped cultivating their demesne fields directly and instead rented these fields to peasants. Once the demesne was rented out, serfdom—especially the week-work that it provided for cultivation of the manorial demesne—was unnecessary, and patterns of manorial control over dependent serfs began to disintegrate. Serfs were seldom explicitly made free, but they became free in practice, as their manorial lords and ladies simply stopped requiring the work, fees, and fines of rural servitude. By 1500, serfdom had virtually disappeared from northwestern Europe, not through rebellion or manumission but simply through the withering away of its economic and ideological underpinnings.

Two other trends were less positive. First, starting in the fifteenth century, some landowners reacted to the price scissors in another way. They sought not to rent out their demesnes but instead to do just the opposite—to bring *more* or even *all* manorial land under direct management. By terminating the leases of their tenants and converting their manors into single large farms, these landowners hoped to profit through the intensive production of wool, meat, or grapes. This development is often described as *enclosure* because lands that had once been held in common by all tenants were fenced off for use by the landowner alone. In a peculiar twist, enclosure made its own contribution to the decline of serfdom, because landowners lost seigniorial authority over the tenants whose leases they refused to renew. But it had the horrible side effect of dispossessing many peasants. Some people whose families had farmed in a village for generations suddenly found themselves, in the late fifteenth century, without renewed leases, landless, and on the road.

Second, in eastern Europe, serfdom was strengthened rather than weakened. In eastern German states and Poland, landowners retained their tenants not by incentives, but instead through coercion made possible by the relative weakness of their territorial states. In other words, landowners, governed with a light hand by their princes, simply assumed new jurisdictional powers over their tenants. Thus newly empowered, they tightened the bonds of serfdom and exacted peasant labor services more rigorously than ever. By 1500 they were developing the large-scale grain-producing estates worked by serfs that would typify the Prussian and Polish agrarian economies in subsequent centuries. For the peasants of Catalonia, their king had proven a strong ally against oppressive landlords; for the peasants of Prussia and Poland, the absence of effective monarchy left uncurbed the ambitions of the landowning elite.

Recovery in Towns and Cities

The towns and cities of Western Europe lost relatively large numbers of people to the Great Plague, but they recovered relatively quickly. Although some rural villages were entirely wiped out by the plague or deserted thereafter, no towns of any importance disappeared. Also, in contrast to the countryside, with its great patches of abandoned and overgrown fields, the urban economy bounced back quickly. All told, by 1500, towns were more prominent and influential in European life than they had been before 1350.

Trade was enormously disrupted by the Great Plague. Patterns of supply and demand changed dramatically, so that, for example, the market in grain, a highly priced and profitable product before 1348, collapsed once the population was cut by one-third. Also, in the chaos of 1348 and 1349, many contracts were left unfulfilled, and in the decades that followed, merchants had to build up new alliances and contacts. And in absolute (but not per capita) terms, both production and trade declined, so that some historians speak of a late medieval urban depression.

In this climate, some urban elites did everything possible to retain their privileged position. Participation in civic government, never widely available, became even more restricted in some towns. Guilds began to enforce their trade monopolies more firmly than before, and guild masterships grew so restricted that only a lucky few were able to open shops in most trades (usually, these few were "lucky" in that they were sons of former masters or married well). Townspeople also often tried to formalize or extend control over their rural hinterlands so as to ensure a steady supply of food and also, in some cases, to assert guild control over goods produced within rural villages.

In their dealings with these hinterlands, rich merchants and guild masters sometimes antagonized local aristocrats. They also faced heated antagonism within their towns from laboring people who worried about wages and prices. After 1350, exceptionally large numbers of peasants migrated into the towns and cities of Europe. Unqualified for skilled work, many drifted into a growing mass of urban underemployed, a tenable situation only as long as wages remained high. But because high food prices, low wages, and inadequate work were always a threatening prospect, tensions between "haves" and "have-nots" were especially high. For example, Florence, ravaged by the Great Plague and burdened by years of inconclusive warfare, was briefly terrorized in 1378 by the Ciompi rebellion, an uprising of workers. It was quickly squelched, as were similar revolts in other towns, and in general, rich mercantile families retained their privileged economic status.

Yet there was creativity as well as retrenchment in urban responses to the new economic circumstances of the late fourteenth and fifteenth centuries. Some English towns developed thriving weaving industries, so that England, a great exporter of *wool* in 1300, became a great exporter of *cloth* by 1500. Some German towns began investing in mines, using new advances in mining technology to profit from the extraction of copper and iron. Others began to specialize in linen or silk production. Some Flemish towns, reacting to the improving living standards and purchasing power of late medieval consumers, switched from the production of luxury cloths to cheaper cloths that attracted a broader market. And some cities in Portugal began to make good use of improvements in ship design and navigation to establish trade links down the coast of West Africa. If some merchants responded to the challenges of the late medieval economy by seeking merely to guard the privileges they already possessed, others looked farther afield to find profit in new markets, new commodities, and new trade routes.

Three developments would be especially important for the future of Europe. First and most critical, the voyages of discovery slowly made it clear, for the first time in human history, that the oceans of the earth were linked into a single, vast body of water that could carry seaworthy ships to any coast anywhere. These voyages began not with Columbus in 1492, but almost two centuries earlier.[2] In the early fourteenth century, Venetian and Genoese ships began to venture onto the high seas of the Atlantic, making yearly expeditions through the Straits of Gibraltar to England, Flanders, and the Canary Islands. By the mid-fourteenth century, commercial links had been established with the Madeiras and Azores, and in the next century these island groups, and the Cape Verde Islands as well, passed into Spanish or Portuguese hands. By 1500, Portuguese ships had traveled down the long coast of West Africa and traversed the Indian Ocean, bringing Portugal a direct sea route to India and a vast commercial empire in the Far East. Spanish ships had traversed the Atlantic, bringing Spain an American empire and the wealth of the Incas and Aztecs. Missionary zeal, curiosity, and greed were the mixed motives of these maritime ventures, but in the long run greed—or better put, commercial profit—was the primary consideration of men who hoped to make their fortunes by risking their lives at sea. In the sixteenth century, the commercial economy of Europe would be transformed by these voyages. As new ocean routes short-circuited old trade routes, both the Ottoman Empire and the cities of the Italian peninsula fell into commercial decline. The economic future lay not in the Mediterranean Sea but in the Atlantic and Indian Oceans.

Second, some entrepreneurs began to take industrial work, especially work in cloth making, into the rural villages that surrounded their towns. These so-called *rural industries* offered entrepreneurs cheaper and less-regulated production than could be had within town walls; they offered peasants extra income, especially during the winter when agricultural demands were few. Rural industries would become a mainstay of industrial production and rural economy in early modern Europe, and, indeed, they remain important in some regions of Europe even today.

Third, technological innovation drove much of the economic expansion of the fifteenth century. In addition to improvements already mentioned in mining and shipping, water power was harnessed in better ways, mechanical clocks measured time more precisely than ever before, spinning wheels (first introduced to Europe in the late thirteenth century) continued to replace the old distaff and spindle, eyeglasses became ever more

---

[2] Of course, exploration began as early as the Viking voyages across the north Atlantic in the ninth century. But aside from Viking settlement of Greenland and Iceland, these explorations had little long-term effect.

common, and advances in the metallurgical arts gave birth to two entirely new urban industries: the production of firearms and cannon, and printing with movable type. Gunpowder, invented in eleventh-century China, was in military use—very limited military use—in Europe by the 1320s, and it became an increasingly important factor in the warfare of the later fourteenth and fifteenth centuries. Printing from movable type began with the production of the Gutenberg Bible in Mainz in 1445, and within a generation about three dozen cities in Europe—stretching from Oxford to Valencia to Krakow— boasted printing presses. Both munitions and printing gave rise to a different sort of working environment than before, slowly replacing family workshops with larger workplaces, rather like small factories, to which many employees would gather for each day's work.

New Wars and Aristocracies

By the early fourteenth century, the European aristocracy was divided into a lesser aristocracy (or *gentry*) and their greater colleagues. Both lesser and greater aristocrats shared an ethos built on military prowess, an economy based on support from manors and peasants, and an authority partly based on duties undertaken for royal masters. The gentry controlled less wealth, and their sphere of influence was the immediate locality— the parish, the county, or even the town. The greater aristocracy had a broader economic base and a broader political perspective; their world encompassed the king, the queen, and the royal court.

Both lesser and greater aristocrats suffered in the Great Plague, when many lineages ended in disease and death. In the next century and a half, other threats to their social and political power proliferated. The decline of manorialism and serfdom diluted their local power, as many became mere rentiers who wielded much less authority over their tenants than their ancestors had enjoyed as manorial lords and ladies. The importance of royal service introduced into their midst men who rose by bureaucratic expertise, not military valor; in later centuries, intense and bitter rivalries would develop between what in France were called the old *nobility of the sword* and the new *nobility of the robe*. Enterprising peasants who accumulated lands had a similar effect, introducing into the lower aristocracy persons of low birth but great wealth. In 1400, for example, Clement Paston was a simple man who "worked behind the plow both winter and summer" in the English county of Norfolk. He acquired some extra land, married wisely, and sent his son to school. By 1500 his descendants were an important gentry family, welcomed at the courts of such great men as the Duke of Norfolk and the Bishop of Norwich. And most importantly, changes in military strategy placed less emphasis on armed cavalry, thereby undermining the aristocracy's primary social role and primary source of political power.

Aristocrats reacted to these changes as had many urban elites: they sought to retain their privileges. In the face of economic troubles on their manors, they developed new ways of exploiting their land and people, sometimes leasing out the demesne and sometimes enclosing manorial lands. They also sought special economic privileges from their monarchs; by the end of the fifteenth century, for example, nobles in both France and Castile had acquired general exemptions from royal taxes. In the face of royal servants "made" into new aristocrats by grateful monarchs, they developed exclusive associations that differentiated their nobility from the lesser nobility of these newcomers.

The English Order of the Garter, founded in 1348, and the French Order of the Star, founded in 1351, are good examples. In the face of armies that relied on infantry, archers, and cannon, they developed chivalry to a point of unparalleled—some would say, excessive—refinement and splendor: shining armor, elaborate tournaments, ornate costumes, chivalric brotherhoods, and vividly colored banners and coats of arms.

All told, these strategies achieved their purpose. The late medieval aristocracy had less power over people, less control over the composition of their status group, and less military importance than before, but it remained a wealthy, well-born, and firmly entrenched elite. Aristocrats even retained much of their military importance, despite all the changes in weapons, armies, and battle strategies. The cavalry charge would continue as an important tactic in European warfare for centuries to come.

✳ LATE MEDIEVAL CHRISTIANITY

Any disease that kills one of every three people is likely to affect religious practices, and this was certainly true of the Great Plague. Although Church officers responded vigorously to the disease, organizing penitential processions and urging prayer, many religious responses to the plague—such as the hysterical attacks that Christians launched against Jews—were beyond the Church's control. And, in quite a few cases, panicked people cast angry eyes at the Church. Why had the Church not warned the faithful of God's great anger? Why were clergy dying in even greater numbers than the laity? Why were some priests deserting their parishioners, leaving them to die without last rites or hope of proper burial? Anti-clericalism, already strong in the thirteenth century, grew exceptionally strong after the Great Plague. In the fourteenth and fifteenth centuries, the Church faced serious threats to its credibility and power.

Yet late medieval Christianity was marked by vibrancy as well as crisis (see Timeline 13.2). This was a time of intense and innovative expressions of Christian piety, especially as focused on the Eucharist and particularly the Host (or consecrated bread). Eucharistic devotion was not new, for it was common among thirteenth-century beguines. But it reached new heights in late medieval celebrations of the feast of Corpus Christi (Body of Christ), a feast founded by a vision of Juliana of Liège in 1209. This feast, scheduled in the good weather days of June, grew into a major moment on the Christian calendar, a time of great processions in which the Host was carried through town streets, a time for the production of mystery plays and sports, a time for "church-ales" and other parish festivals that raised money for charity, and a time, alas, for attacks on Jews (whom slanderous rumors accused of stealing the consecrated bread in order to torture it; see Color Illustration 8). As the extraordinary popularity of this new feast illustrates, late medieval Christians developed many new forms of worship, and in so doing, they laid foundations for both spiritual reform within the Church and spiritual revolt from it.

Popes and Councils

Even during the glorious pontificate of Innocent III (r. 1198–1216), the ideal of a Christian commonwealth guided by the pope was incompletely fulfilled. By 1300, monarchs such as Philip IV of France (r. 1285–1314) and Edward I of England (r. 1272–1307) were actively eroding papal claims to supremacy. Thereafter, matters

TIMELINE 13.2   Western Christianity, 1300–1500

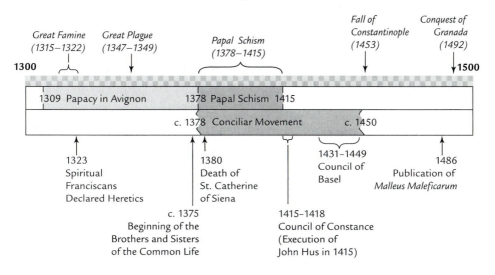

only worsened, so that by 1500 the papacy had become much weaker as an international force, and monarchs had established much more authority over their national churches. By then, papal influence in the appointment of prelates had ebbed in many European kingdoms and principalities; so too had the ability of popes to tax either clergy or laity; and even the papacy's role as the court of final appeal in canon law was under threat. More important still, the spiritual prestige of the papacy had collapsed, and a widening chasm divided many pious Christians from their Church.

Early in the fourteenth century, as we have seen, the papacy had moved to Avignon where, just outside the French realm, a series of able French popes ruled from 1309 to 1376. The Avignonese popes were subservient to the French crown only on occasion; for the most part they were capable of strong, independent action. But their very location suggested to France's enemies that the papacy was no longer an impartial international force. Moreover, the Avignonese popes were more noted for their bureaucratic skills than their sanctity, for they carried to its ultimate degree their predecessors' enthusiasm for administrative and fiscal efficiency. The smooth-working administration of the Avignonese papacy was impressive, but it failed to inspire mystics and reformers, and its taxes irritated those who regarded the papacy as a mere tool of the French crown. Thus, while the papacy was growing wealthier and more efficient, its spiritual capital was diminishing.

Several attempts were made to return the papacy to Rome, but it was not until 1376 that Pope Gregory XI (r. 1370–1378) moved back to the Holy City. He soon regretted his decision, but before he could return to Avignon, he died. Within a short time, two popes were elected to replace him. Urban VI (r. 1378–1389) was elected by the cardinals while they were intimidated by a Roman mob; he was an Italian who stayed in Rome. Clement VII (r. 1378–1394) was elected after the cardinals had retreated to Avignon and declared their first election invalid; he was a Frenchman content to keep the papacy in Avignon. For the next forty years the Church was torn by the *Great Schism.* Excommunications were hurled back and forth between Rome and Avignon, and the states of Europe chose sides according to their interests. France and its allies supported Avignon; England and the Holy Roman Empire backed Rome; and the Italian states chose one side or the other as it suited their purposes. Papal prestige plummeted.

For a while, it seemed that, in light of papal claims to supreme authority, there was no greater authority in Western Christendom that could arbitrate between the two rival papacies. But then some began to suggest that a general church council could stand above the fray. This argument was not easily made. No one was sure who, if not a pope, could summon a council. And each pope regarded councils as inferior bodies, capable of giving advice (as past councils had done) but incapable of judging *his* supreme authority. At length some cardinals from both camps called a council to meet in Pisa. There, in 1409, 500 prelates deposed both popes and elected a new one. Because neither pope recognized these conciliar depositions, however, the effect of the Council of Pisa was to transform a two-way schism into a three-way schism. The situation was not only scandalous but ludicrous. Finally the Holy Roman Emperor summoned another council to Constance (1415–1418) where, at last, the schism ended. Two popes were deposed, the third resigned, and the Church was reunited by the election of a conciliar pope, Martin V (r. 1417–1431).

The healing of the Great Schism was only the first step in what is now known as the **conciliar movement**—a movement to make Church councils, not popes, the supreme authority within the Church. Inspired by the general assemblies that were then advising secular monarchs and princes, conciliarists argued that the Church too should be so governed—that is, that popes should be firmly guided by general councils that met regularly and automatically. This was neither a new nor particularly radical argument. It had been urged by political philosophers such as Marsilius of Padua (1280–1343) and Nicholas of Cusa (1401–1464). And it was widely accepted among the prelates at Constance, who tried to reform the constitution of the Church along conciliar lines, affirming, against papal objection, that general councils should regularly meet and should exercise ultimate authority in matters of doctrine and reform.

These conciliar principles met with firm opposition from Martin V and his successors. They continued to insist on absolute papal supremacy, and although they did summon a few councils, they ensured the meetings were ineffective. The last meeting, the Council of Basel (1431–1449), petered out ingloriously, and with it died the conciliar movement. After 1449, the pope ruled the faithful of Western Christendom without any serious challenge from Church councils. But by then, papal supremacy was being slowly undermined from another direction—by the growing autonomy of national churches. In 1351 and 1353, papal control over appointments and legal cases within the English church was limited by statute; in 1438, the Pragmatic Sanction of Bourges set similar limits on papal involvement in the French (or Gallican) church; and in 1439, the Pragmatic Sanction of Mainz promised much the same for the Holy Roman Empire. In the fifteenth century, popes sometimes ignored these limits with impunity, but the principle—that national churches could manage some of their affairs without papal interference—had been asserted by national synods and conceded by the papacy.

As the international scope of the papacy slowly eroded, so too did the interests of popes. The men who sat on the papal throne between the dissolution of Basel (1449) and the beginning of the Protestant Reformation (1517) were radically different from their predecessors. Most were Italian noblemen, more interested in ruling the Papal States than ruling Western Christendom. Abandoning most of their claims over an international Church, they devoted themselves to the beguiling culture and bitter politics of the late fifteenth-century Italian states.

The fifteenth century ended with the pontificate of Alexander VI (r. 1492–1503), a caricature of all that then ailed the papacy. He was an urbane man, a great political strategist, and a generous patron of the arts. He was also, rather inappropriately, a fond lover and father. He consorted openly with his mistress Vanozza Catanei (1445–1518), who bore four of his six (or possibly eight) children, and he gave full support to the unprincipled activities of his son Cesare Borgia (c. 1475–1507) who used assassination, treachery, and cruelty to carve out a great Borgia state in the center of the Italian peninsula. By the time of Alexander VI's death, the pope had emphatically ceased to be the spiritual leader of Western Christendom. When, fourteen years later, Martin Luther (1483–1546) began to publicize his objections to some Church policies, Europeans were by no means prepared to abandon Christianity, but they were willing, in large numbers, to desert tarnished Rome.

Ordinary Christians in Search of Salvation

For ordinary Christians, the trauma of the Great Plague and its many later recurrences exacerbated anxieties about both this life and the next. These worries were further enhanced by the growing spiritual importance of *purgatory,* a place where souls were cleansed before entering heaven. Although not fully elaborated until the Council of Florence (1438–1445), teachings about purgatory had long influenced the practices of ordinary Christians. As Figure 13.2 illustrates, Christians undertook a variety of good works to free their own souls and the souls of loved ones from the purifying tortures of purgatory: pilgrimages, appeals to saints, masses for the dead, veneration of relics, charitable bequests, and the purchase of **indulgences.**[3] Increasingly, salvation seemed a goal that could be achieved through almost mechanistic means. Piety and inner spirituality mattered, of course, but so too did a myriad of pious deeds.

At the parish level, these concerns promoted a vibrant culture of communal piety. Many parish churches were built or rebuilt in these years, extended, redecorated, and beautified. Parishioners often gathered together in pious associations—called *parish guilds* or *confraternities*—that raised charitable funds, venerated specific saints, and otherwise pursued spiritual objectives. Most parish priests were better prepared for their duties than before, especially thanks to vernacular as well as Latin guidebooks that advised priests about their duties and even provided sermons for use throughout the year. At the parish level, late medieval Christians sought salvation in better churches, through more lay organizations, and with better priestly guidance than ever before.

As people worried about their salvation, they also worried about its opposite, damnation. Concerns about the devil and his demons grew more acute, old practices of magic took on new diabolic associations, and what was once seen as misguided was

---

[3] This last was the practice that so angered Martin Luther in the early sixteenth century. The medieval Church taught that even after a sin was repented and forgiven, the sinner had to submit to penitential discipline either in this life or in purgatory; an indulgence could release sinners from this punishment. Indulgences were theoretically issued only in response to repentance and good works, but to many of the faithful, it seemed they could simply be bought—that a bit of money could redeem a sin. This view was encouraged by crass salesmanship. As one Dominican friar put it to his customers, "As soon as the coin in the coffer rings, the soul from purgatory springs."

Figure 13.2 *Helping Souls out of Purgatory* This sketch shows souls being hauled out of purgatory and into heaven thanks to the good works being performed on the left: almsgiving (bottom) and masses (center). The writing just above the bucket of saved souls explains the drawing as follows, "These saules (souls) are drawne up oute of purgatory by prayer and almes dede."

increasingly seen as satanic. These worries reached their medieval culmination in a handbook for witch hunters, the *Malleus Maleficarum* (*Hammer of Witches*) written by two Dominican friars in 1486. It would be left to early modern Europeans to put this nefarious book to extensive use, for it was not well regarded in the late fifteenth century and its authors were even driven out of some towns. Yet in this respect, as in so many others, the

Later Middle Ages laid the groundwork for one quintessential aspect of modernity: the hysterical witch hunts of the sixteenth and seventeenth centuries.

Extraordinary Christians in Search of Salvation

In the meantime, other Christians were devoting their lives to spiritual practices that were individualistic, mystical, and challenging to the ecclesiastical structure. These three trends were related, since by stressing the spiritual relationship between an individual and God, mystics tended to de-emphasize the role of clergy and sacraments as channels of divine grace. Mystics were usually orthodox in their beliefs and practices, but they dwelt on the indescribable ecstasy of a mystical union with God for which no priests, no popes, and no sacraments were needed.

Desire for ineffable union with God was not new to Christians in the Later Middle Ages. Hildegard of Bingen (1098–1179) had been a "prophetess of God," and Thomas Aquinas (c. 1225–1274) had turned in his last years away from study and toward divine revelation. Mysticism's greater importance in Christian practices of the fourteenth and fifteenth centuries stemmed, in part, from the influence of late thirteenth-century beguine mystics and a Dominican friar who had worked with them, Meister Eckhart (c. 1260–1327). Eckhart linked asceticism with mysticism, teaching that mystical union with God could be achieved by purging all desire from the soul. This was the route followed by St. Catherine of Siena (1347–1380), featured in the Biographical Sketch on pp. 342–343, and many other mystics of the time who, in their search for God, denied themselves food, drink, sleep, and many basic comforts. They stressed adoration over speculation, inner spiritual purity over external good works, and direct experience of God over sacramental avenues to divine grace. They also spoke with great frankness to powerful men. Birgitta of Sweden (1302–1372) complained about abuses within the Church and urged the Avignonese popes to return to Rome (see Color Illustration 12 for a graphic depiction of the power of her mysticism); Catherine of Siena did the same, even complaining to Pope Gregory XI about the "stench" of corruption at his court; and even humble mystics, such as Lidwina of Schiedam (1400–1433), challenged the authority of their priests. Lidwina once vomited out some unconsecrated bread that her priest had attempted to pass off as the Host—and *then* claimed to receive the true Host directly from Christ himself in a miraculous vision. Most mystics remained thoroughly orthodox, but their practices included some ideas that would have great appeal to sixteenth-century Protestant reformers.

Late medieval mystics also often stood somewhat apart from the ecclesiastical structure. Catherine of Siena, for example, was not a nun, but instead a Dominican tertiary—that is, she remained a laywoman, although she adopted a life of penitential observance and good works under the direction of Dominican friars. Tertiary orders, first recognized by the Church in the late thirteenth century, provided important alternatives to late medieval Christians. So too did the *modern devotion* (*devotio moderna*) of Geert Groote (1340–1384) and his followers. Groote stressed—again, within an orthodox framework—that Christian fulfillment comes through inward piety, simplicity, religious reading, and contemplation. From his teachings grew the Brothers and Sisters of the Common Life, who, like the beguines before them, took no lifetime vows and lived in common, pooling their resources and houses. They were enormously influential in the Netherlands and other parts of northern Europe. Their schools, among Europe's finest, produced leading mystics, humanists, and reformers—among others, Desiderius Erasmus (1466–1536) and Martin Luther.

BIOGRAPHICAL SKETCH

St. Catherine of Siena (1347–1380)

The great fourteenth-century mystic St. Catherine of Siena was at once a theologian, a charismatic spiritual leader, and a significant political figure. Like other visionaries before her, such as Hildegard of Bingen (1098–1179) and Bernard of Clairvaux (1090–1153), Catherine achieved international fame and political influence through piety, intellect, and sheer force of character. Her literary output places her among the luminaries of early Italian letters. And her style of piety has led some to judge her an anorexic and others to consider her a fairly typical female mystic for her time.

Catherine was born into a prosperous urban family, the twenty-fourth of twenty-five children of a wool-dyeing couple in the bustling northern Italian city of Siena. Their home lay just down the hill from the important church of San Domenico, and from an early age Catherine fell under the spell of Dominican spirituality. As a child and young woman, she resisted her parents' pressure to live a "normal" life; in time she also defied their efforts to arrange her marriage. Instead, for several years in late adolescence, Catherine lived in virtual solitude, praying, meditating, and subsisting on a diet of bread, water, and raw vegetables. For spiritual guidance, she became a Dominican tertiary, enjoying a close affiliation with the Dominicans without having to live the narrowly cloistered life of a Dominican nun. Having thus escaped both the entanglements of a marriage and the walls of a convent, Catherine created her own self-imposed confinement, creating by force of will and spirituality a "cell within the heart."

Catherine practiced many forms of asceticism, denying herself sleep and imposing many discomforts on herself. But what Catherine called in one letter "the matter of eating" was an especially central part of her spiritual self-discipline. She consumed little food and vomited up most of what did go into her mouth. She could reliably eat only one thing—the Host. Ritual fasting was an ordinary enough piety in the Later Middle Ages, but Catherine's abstemiousness went far beyond the Christian norm. Some were impressed by Catherine's self-denial of food; some thought it was the work of the devil; and many—including the priests responsible for her spiritual guidance—urged her to try to eat more. She did try, but without success. In the end, her early death was surely hastened by her self-starvation.[4]

At the age of six or seven years, Catherine had experienced her first vision, which she later described as an image of Jesus, set against a sunset, smiling down on her. During her adolescence and young adulthood, these mystical experiences intensified. In 1370, at about the age of twenty-three, she was observed to lose consciousness and lie as though dead for some four hours, during which time, as she reported afterward, she experienced mystical union with God. Her *Dialogue,* inspired by a mystical experience in 1377, relates God's answers to questions about how individuals, the Church, and the world might be reformed and renewed. This and her other writings (including more than 400 letters) were widely influential in her own time and remain so today; she was formally honored as a "Doctor" of the Catholic Church in 1970, taking her place among such other great Catholic minds as St. Augustine (354–430) and St. Thomas Aquinas (1225–1274).

Catherine especially devoted herself to caring for the poor and ill, nursing them in their homes or in hospitals. She also devoted herself to religious study, especially with a

---

[4] For two very different interpretations of St. Catherine's food practices, see Rudolph M. Bell, *Holy Anorexia* (1985), especially pp. 22–53, and Caroline Walker Bynum, *Holy Feast and Holy Fast: The Religious Significance of Food to Medieval Women* (1987), especially pp. 165–180.

circle of like-minded women. As the depth of her spirituality grew, she began to attract a devoted group of disciples (men as well as women), and she began journeying with them from town to town in the northern Italian peninsula, urging the reform of the clergy, supporting plans to launch a new crusade, and advising repentance and renewal through total love of God.

In 1376, Catherine traveled to Avignon to urge Pope Gregory XI's return to what she and most contemporaries regarded as his rightful capital in Rome. Thanks in part to her pressure, Gregory XI did return to the Holy City, but his death in 1378 precipitated a disputed papal election and the Great Schism. Catherine devoted herself to the cause of the Roman claimant, Urban VI, staying at his papal court in Rome and urging important cardinals and princes to recognize Urban's legitimacy. At the same time—and with characteristic verve—she frequently urged Pope Urban himself to behave with greater gentleness and compassion.

In the spring of 1380, at the age of thirty-three, she suffered a stroke and died a few days later. Her final years were troubled by the tumults of the Great Schism, in the onset of which she had inadvertently played a part. Yet in her last days she felt at one with Jesus, whose life span of thirty-three years was, as she knew well from the Gospels, identical to her own.

Searching for Salvation and Achieving Heresy

Asceticism was a critical part of many forms of late medieval spirituality, but it was also carried to extremes that prompted Church condemnation. In the immediate wake of the Great Plague, men and women began repentantly flogging themselves, and groups of these *flagellants* began to travel about, making their floggings into great public displays and teaching that they were thereby cleansed of all past sins. Flagellants were condemned as heretical in October 1349, but they remained a problem well into the fifteenth century. Advocates of apostolic poverty presented a similar challenge, particularly for a Church that believed its institutional wealth was essential for its holy mission. St. Francis (1182–1226) had shown his devotion to apostolic poverty by living it rather than forcing it on others, but some of his successors, known as the Spiritual Franciscans, insisted on universal ecclesiastical poverty. By the early fourteenth century, they were virulently anti-clerical and anti-papal. Their doctrine of apostolic poverty was declared heretical in 1323, and several leaders were burned at the stake.

Many orthodox Christian mystics were strikingly individualistic in their approaches to God, but individualism was also carried to the point of heresy. John Wycliffe (c. 1330–1384), a professor at the University of Oxford, argued that the Bible was more authoritative than pronouncements of popes and councils (a position that anticipated by more than 100 years a cornerstone of Lutheranism). He also stressed the individual's inner spiritual journey toward God, questioned the real presence of Christ in the Eucharist, de-emphasized the entire sacramental system, and spoke out strongly against ecclesiastical wealth. Wycliffe was convicted of heresy but permitted to die peacefully, perhaps because professors were not deemed powerful enough to be worrisome. His followers, the Lollards, were hunted down ruthlessly, and although their threat was contained by the early fifteenth century, his doctrines spread to faraway Bohemia, where they were taken up by the Czech reformer Jan Hus (c. 1373–1415).

In the hands of Hus, heresy took a new and powerful turn, combining religious dissent with nationalism. Like Wycliffe, Hus was a professor—at the University of Prague. He was also an inspiring preacher, a religious visionary, and a Bohemian nationalist. In his hands, Wycliffe's anti-clericalism was certainly a powerful critique of the established Church, but it was also a weapon in the struggle for Bohemian (later, Czech) independence from German political and cultural influence. Lured to the Council of Constance in 1415 with the promise of a safe conduct, Hus was imprisoned, tried, and burned at the stake. His death served the interests of the Church for whom he was a dangerous heretic and the Holy Roman Emperor for whom he was a Bohemian revolutionary. But his followers survived into the Reformation era as a dissident national group. Like Joan of Arc (c. 1412–1431), a Frenchwoman burned as a heretic by the English, Jan Hus fused Christian faith with the early stirrings of nationalism in Europe. As Martin Luther would find in the early sixteenth century, this was a powerful combination.

✷ CONCLUSION

A shadow of famine and disease stretched across late medieval Europe. In the first and second decades of the fourteenth century, one in ten people died of famine; in the fifth decade, one in three died of plague; and for 150 years thereafter, plague continued to kill again and again. These terrors were matched by other troubles: rebellious peasants, disrupted trade, new sorts of warfare, popes in Avignon (and then, multiple popes). From a bird's-eye view, these terrors and troubles make late medieval Europe seem a very unwelcoming place. But viewed from the ground, the Later Middle Ages look considerably better. Many peasants had more land than before and more freedom, too. Wage-workers earned better money, and they, like peasants, lived in better houses, wore better clothing, and ate better food—especially, more meat and beer—than before. Rich townspeople began to invest in new industries, new technologies, and new explorations. And Christians—both ordinary parishioners and extraordinary visionaries—worshiped their God in new, fulfilling, and challenging ways.

SUGGESTED READINGS

Judith M. Bennett, *A Medieval Life: Cecilia Penifader of Brigstock, c. 1295–1344* (1999). An introduction to rural society, written for students. See also Duccio Balestracci, *The Renaissance in the Fields: Family Memoirs of a Fifteenth-Century Tuscan Peasant* (1999); Barbara A. Hanawalt, *The Ties That Bound: Peasant Families in Medieval England* (1986); and R. H. Hilton, *Bond Men Made Free: Medieval Peasant Movements and the English Rising of 1381* (1973).

Caroline Bynum, *Holy Feast and Holy Fast: The Religious Significance of Food to Medieval Women* (1987). A path-breaking study of female spirituality.

Carlo M. Cipolla, *Before the Industrial Revolution: European Society and Economy, 1000–1700* (3rd edition, 1993). See also Christopher Dyer, *Standards of Living in the Later Middle Ages: Social Change in England, c. 1200–1500* (rev. edition, 1998).

Michael Jones, ed., *Gentry and Lesser Nobility in Late-Medieval Europe* (1986). Innovative articles by experts.

Richard Kieckhefer, *Forbidden Rites: A Necromancer's Manual of the Fifteenth Century* (1998). An innovative study of a magician's how-to manual, accompanied by the text (in Latin).

Mavis E. Mate, *Women in Medieval English Society* (1999). A short introduction to the subject, packed with references.

David Nicholas, *The Later Medieval City, 1300–1500* (1997). A definitive new survey. See also Edwin S. Hunt and James M. Murray, *A History of Business in Medieval Europe 1200–1500* (1999).

J. R. S. Phillips, *The Medieval Expansion of Europe* (2nd edition, 1998). See also G. V. Scammell, *The First Imperial Age: European Expansion, c. 1400–1715* (1989), and Peter Russell, *Prince Henry "the Navigator": A Life* (2000).

Miri Rubin, *Corpus Christi: The Eucharist in Late Medieval Culture* (1991). An important study of a central aspect of late medieval piety. See also her *Gentile Tales: The Narrative Assault on Late Medieval Jews* (1999). For a different interpretation, see David Nirenberg, *Communities of Violence: Persecution of Minorities in the Middle Ages* (1996), and also John Christian Laursen and Cary J. Nederman, eds., *Beyond the Persecuting Society: Religious Toleration before the Enlightenment* (1997).

R. N. Swanson, *Religion and Devotion in Europe c. 1215–1515* (1995). An authoritative and wide-ranging study. See also his *Church and Society in Late Medieval England* (1989), and Eamon Duffy, *The Stripping of the Altars: Traditional Religion in England, 1400–1580* (1994).

John A. F. Thomson, *Popes and Princes 1417–1517* (1980). A good, concise history of the late medieval papacy.

Philip Ziegler, *The Black Death* (1969). The best general summary. For famine, see William C. Jordan, *The Great Famine: Northern Europe in the Early Fourteenth Century* (1996).

SUGGESTED PRIMARY SOURCES

Mark Bailey, *The English Manor, c. 1200–c. 1500* (2002). See also Edwin Brezette DeWindt, ed., *A Slice of Life: Selected Documents of Medieval English Peasant Experience* (1996), and R. B. Dobson, *The Peasant's Revolt* (2nd edition, 1983).

Rosemary Horrox, *The Black Death* (1994). A European-wide collection, but focused on England.

John Shinners, ed., *Medieval Popular Religion, 1000–1500* (1997). See also John van Engen, *Devotio Moderna: Basic Writings* (1988), and R. N. Swanson, *Catholic England: Faith, Religion and Observance before the Reformation* (1993).

CHAPTER 14

***

TOWARD THE SOVEREIGN STATE,
c. 1300-1500

✸ INTRODUCTION

In 1324, Marsilius of Padua (1280–c. 1343) wrote a far-sighted treatise on the proper relation between church and state. In *Defensor Pacis* (*Defender of the Peace*), he ruled uncompromisingly in favor of the state. The Church, Marsilius argued, should be stripped of political authority, and states should wield sovereign power over all their subjects, lay and clerical alike. Thus the Church, although united in faith, would be divided politically into numerous state churches obedient to their secular rulers, not the pope. In its glorification of the sovereign state, *Defensor Pacis* foreshadowed the evolution of late medieval and early modern politics. Sovereignty—that is, unchallenged authority over the laws, government, diplomacy, and public institutions of a state—was a critical foundation stone for the nation-states of modern Europe.

What *Defensor Pacis* foreshadowed was a long time coming. Although monarchs generally triumphed in their struggles with late medieval popes, not until the fifteenth century did the barest outlines of national churches become visible. So too with monarchical triumph over a second competing power within their realms—that is, the aristocracy. Overmighty and unruly magnates continued to undermine royal authority for much of the Later Middle Ages, and it was only after 1450 that some European monarchs began to assert their authority effectively over dukes, counts, and others who had long tried to ignore or subvert royal claims. Moreover, as we shall see in this chapter, it was only in *some* realms that the Church and aristocracy were subjected, by 1500, to new levels of royal authority; in the Holy Roman Empire in particular, imperial power remained weak and local polities strong. Yet despite changes that were partial and slow, between 1450 and 1500 monarchs in some parts of Europe began to govern in new ways—and hence, to move toward the ideal of national sovereignty.

✸ ENGLAND, FRANCE, AND THE HUNDRED YEARS' WAR

The Hundred Years' War began in 1337 and dragged on fitfully for 116 years, with periods of savage warfare alternating with long periods of truce. Arising from numerous causes, it devastated both realms, although France, where almost all the fighting took place, suffered more (see Map 14.1).

No cause for the war was sufficient in itself, but many small causes accumulated to send English armies across the Channel in 1337 to attack French forces. First, the conflict grew from continuing English claims to French lands, although these had shrunk from the days of the vast Angevin empire to only Gascony in the southwest. There, the lordship of the English king was cemented by a brisk trade in English cloth and Bordeaux wine (for which the English had developed a special thirst). Philip IV of France (r. 1285–1314) and Edward I of England (r. 1272–1307) fought an expensive but inconclusive war over Gascony from 1294 to 1303; this was a warm-up for the larger conflict that began in 1337. Second, the English and French were also competing for de facto control of Flanders. French kings claimed political lordship over the Flemish, yet English kings enjoyed a sort of economic lordship over the region, due to Flemish reliance on a profitable trade in English wool. Both wanted more authority over the rich and quasi-independent towns of Flanders.

Third, in 1328, the French royal succession was thrown into dispute, when Charles IV (r. 1322–1328) died without heirs. Edward III of England (r. 1327–1377) had the best claim to the French throne through his mother; but Philip of Valois had a plausible claim through his father. Faced with the horrific prospect of an English king on the French throne, the French nobility suddenly "invented tradition," creating a new law but enshrining it in the purported ancient customs of the Salian Franks: this law stated that the right to inherit cannot pass through a woman.[1] Edward III's claim was put aside, and Philip of Valois took the throne as Phillip VI (r. 1328–1350). Edward III initially accepted this decision, but in 1337, he used it as a pretext for war, titling himself king of France as well as England.

Chivalry itself seems to have been a fourth cause of the conflict. Edward III and Philip VI were both chivalrous, high-spirited monarchs who delighted in heroic clashes of arms. Nobles on both sides felt the same. In 1337, most welcomed war, seeing it as a chance for excitement, honor, plunder, valor, and even fun.

The French lost most of their ardor when English archers won smashing victories at Crécy (1346) and Poitiers (1356). The English lost their enthusiasm later in the century when French victories nipped away at English acquisitions and the martial Edward III was replaced by the dour Richard II (r. 1377–1399). English enthusiasm revived when Henry V (r. 1413–1422) won a momentous victory over the French at Agincourt in 1415. But he soon died, and shortly thereafter, in one of the most remarkable developments in European history, the desperate plight of France was reversed by a peasant girl, Joan of Arc (c. 1412–1431). She rallied the French troops, defeated the English,

---

[1] Some of the groundwork for this *Salic Law* had been laid just a few years earlier when, in 1316, Jeanne (1311–1349), daughter and heir of Louis X (r. 1314–1316), should have inherited the French throne. Her uncle took it instead, ruling as Philip V (r. 1316–1322) and justifying his action on the grounds that no woman could inherit the French throne (an argument that went entirely against feudal custom). As a sort of consolation gift, Jeanne received the kingdom of Navarre from her grandmother.

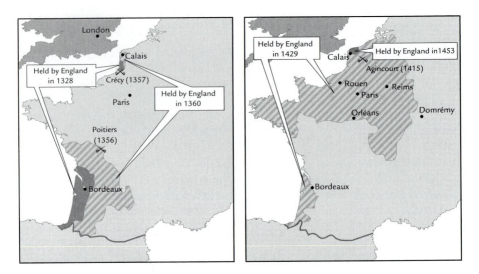

Map 14.1   *The English in France during the Hundred Years' War, 1337–1453*   When the Hundred Years' War began, the English controlled only two territories: a small outpost near the shortest crossing of the Channel and the wine-producing region around Bordeaux. By 1360, they had extended their reach in both areas, especially by capturing Calais in 1347. By 1429, the English had lost ground in the south but vastly extended their reach in the north. Then the tide turned, and within a few decades they controlled only the port of Calais.

and got the **dauphin** properly crowned as King Charles VII (r. 1422–1461) in Reims Cathedral (see Figure 14.1, as well as the Biographical Sketch on pp. 352–353).[2] By 1453, when the long struggle ended at last, the English monarchy had lost all its French lands except the port of Calais. Aside from this small outpost, the English were finally disentangled from France, and Charles VII ruled France unopposed.

Joan of Arc's role in the last phase of the Hundred Years' War is fascinating in many ways, but it is especially useful in illustrating how war was beginning to affect ordinary people in new ways. Why did a peasant girl care about this chivalric war? She cared, in part, because warfare had changed in ways that brought it directly into her home. Because infantrymen and archers were more important, peasant boys and men were trained, mustered, and marched off to war. Because armies fought for longer periods over broader areas, forced requisition of food and livestock emptied peasant larders and barns. Because armies were more expensive to feed and maintain, tax burdens grew heavier, year by year. Because military tacticians began to favor strategic devastation, armies deliberately burned fields, razed villages, and ravaged towns. And because gangs of unpaid soldiers terrorized villages and towns during intermittent truces, peace could be as dangerous as war. French peasants and townspeople suffered more than English ones, but in both countries this new sort of warfare—more infantry, more standing armies, longer campaigns, more deliberate cruelty to civilians—added

---

[2] "Dauphin" was the title given to the heir to the French throne; the title derives from the French word for "dolphin," considered in the Middle Ages to be the chief of all fish. The heraldry of dauphins often included a crowned dolphin.

Figure 14.1 *Joan of Arc* This sketch, scribbled in the margins of a document that notes the lifting of the English siege of Orléans, is the only contemporary drawing of Joan of Arc. It is more imaginative than accurate. The artist has correctly shown Joan with a sword but incorrectly shown her in women's dress.

conscriptions, taxes, requisitions, and sometimes outright terror to the burdens of working households.

Why also, we might ask, did a peasant girl care, as Joan most certainly did, about the king of *France?* In Joan's strong conviction that France should be ruled by a French king, we can see the growth of a *patriotic* or *national* consciousness among ordinary Europeans. These loyalties are hard to trace and harder to explain, but they were certainly stronger in the fifteenth century than earlier, and they would grow stronger still in later centuries. The new importance of vernacular languages—still in formation, but important nonetheless—contributed to the growth of national consciousness; so too did the importance of national universities and, eventually, national churches; and, of course, the waning influence of the most dominant international institution in Europe—the papacy with its vision of a trans-European Christendom—cannot be discounted. From these causes and others, late medieval Europeans began to feel that they shared a common history, a common interest, and a common future with *some* people (usually those with whom they also shared a monarch or a language)—and not with others. This formation of national identities would extend far beyond the confines of the Middle Ages, but by the fifteenth century in some realms, national loyalties were slowly beginning to supplement feudal loyalties as a buttress of royal power.

✳ ENGLAND: PARLIAMENT, CIVIL WAR, AND TUDOR MONARCHY

As we saw in Chapter 11, English kings strengthened their position in the Central Middle Ages through better bureaucracies, expanded legal systems, and judicious use of parliaments. In the Later Middle Ages, this process continued (see Timeline 14.1). Slowly the king's ministers came to be seen not merely as his personal servants but also as servants of the realm, answerable for their actions to the great magnates or even parliaments (from this principle derived new procedures for ministerial impeachment). Slowly too the king's justice reached more fully throughout the realm, especially with the fourteenth-century introduction of new officers called *justices of the peace* who held courts four times a year (hence, *Quarter Sessions*) in the English counties. Yet the most significant development was in the institution of Parliament, where the House of Commons took shape, not yet as an independent voice, but as a body that claimed to express the will of the English people.

In the course of the fourteenth century, the English Parliament changed from an occasional assembly into a permanent institution. It also split into two houses, *Lords* (for high-born nobility and prelates) and *Commons* (for representatives from towns and shires). Most of the shire knights and burgesses who went to parliament brought with them a wealth of local political experience. The shire knights were local gentry, skilled in county administration; the parliamentary burgesses were usually veterans of town government, skilled by past service as councilors, aldermen, and sometimes even mayors.

Faced with a monarchy hard pressed by the expenses of the Hundred Years' War, these shire knights and burgesses acted together in Commons to trade fiscal support for important political concessions, and by the end of the fourteenth century, they had gained the privilege of approving or refusing taxation not sanctioned by custom. All new taxes, in other words, had to pass through Commons. By thus gaining control of the royal purse strings, Commons also gained control over broader legislative matters. Adopting the motto 'redress before supply,' it refused to pass financial grants until the king had approved its petitions on other matters. Kings sometimes resisted, but in the end they almost always acquiesced. Slowly, it became expected not only that taxation would be approved by Commons but also that any new legislation would begin with a petition in Commons.

These were important developments, but the late medieval House of Commons remained an institution firmly subordinated to royal and aristocratic agendas. By and large, Commons was controlled by powerful nobles who rigged elections, bribed members, and sometimes simply got their way through intimidation. It is significant, to be sure, that Parliament was asked to participate in the deposition of two English kings in the fourteenth century: Edward II (r. 1307–1327) and Richard II (r. 1377–1399). But in both cases Parliament was simply ratifying aristocratic decisions already made in castles and battlefields.

These depositions illustrate a second aspect of the late medieval English state: aristocratic factionalism. Aristocratic rebellions opened and closed the fourteenth century, with one group of aristocrats rising against Edward II and another similarly attempting to control Richard II. Then, in the mid-fifteenth century, when the Hundred Years' War had been over scarcely two years, civil strife broke out between the rival

TIMELINE 14.1 England, 1300–1500

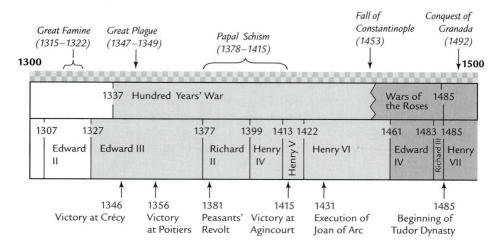

aristocratic houses of York and Lancaster, which each claimed to have the best title to the throne. The Wars of the Roses, which raged on and off between 1455 and 1485, were the last hurrah of the medieval English nobility. Long periods of peace were punctuated by wars of ferocious brutality; kings were deposed, remade, and deposed again; lives were lost and lands ravaged to very little purpose. In the midst of all this senseless brutality, one act of cruelty still especially troubles people today: the murder of the two young sons of Edward IV (r. 1461–1483) after their uncle Richard III (r. 1483–1485) had usurped the throne and lodged them in the Tower of London. William Shakespeare's ahistorical history play *Richard III* is partly responsible for the horror with which we view these murders, but so too is historical amnesia. After all, the murder of competing claimants to a throne was a venerable tradition stretching back, as we have seen, to the Carolingians, and it would continue well into Tudor times (when, for just one example, Queen Elizabeth I would execute her cousin Mary Queen of Scots in 1587). Yet the controversy about Richard III's actions and guilt still rages today; it is continued, among others, by the Richard III Society, an international group with an extensive Web site, which actively promotes new research on Richard III in order to "secure a reassessment of his reputation and of his place in history."

In any case, firm royal governance seemed the best way out of this seemingly endless civil strife, and Edward IV began to lay such a foundation. The last decade of his reign was peaceful (in part because so many rivals had perished in earlier battles), and he was the first king in more than 150 years to die solvent. After the brief and chaotic interlude of Richard III's usurpation, Edward IV's foundations were strengthened by the first Tudor king, Henry VII (r. 1485–1509). Like Edward IV, Henry VII sought peace, a full treasury, and an effective government. He was what some historians call a *new monarch,* in firm control of his nobility, his church, and his bureaucracy and strengthened by the nascent nationalism and loyalty of his subjects. Of course, none of these features was "new" in the late fifteenth century, for Henry VII drew on the work of his medieval predecessors to bring peace, stability, and strong leadership to England. The willful and determined Tudors who followed him would shape the English realm into

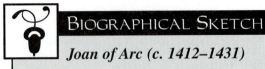

Joan of Arc (c. 1412–1431)

Joan of Arc, one of the most cherished paragons of French history, rescued the French monarchy at its lowest ebb and turned the tide of the Hundred Years' War. She was, arguably, the first French patriot. And she was just a peasant girl, who asked to be called simply, "The Maid."

Her brief but remarkable life began about 1412 in the village of Donremy in eastern France, a region afflicted by the violence and plundering of the Hundred Years' War. The child of hard-working peasants, she was lively, devout, and troubled by the savagery of a conflict that appeared to be drifting toward defeat for France. When she was twelve, Joan began hearing the voices of angels and saints who, as she reported it, told her that the English had no right to be in France and that *she* must help to drive them out. Five years later, at the age of seventeen, she persuaded the captain of a nearby garrison to give her a small military escort to the castle of Chinon, where Charles VII, the uncrowned king of France, presided falteringly over a government in exile.

The journey took eleven days, and during it, Joan dressed in male attire for the first time. The skeptical Charles kept her waiting another two days, and he then dressed in disguise in order to test her. She picked him out of the crowd immediately, urging him to believe that her voices were genuine and that she was sent by God to save the French. After spending three weeks investigating Joan's orthodoxy and chastity, Charles armed her, placed her in command of a large military force, and sent her off to relieve Orléans from its English besiegers. The fact that Charles pinned his future on a peasant maid speaks both to the utter hopelessness of his cause and to his faith in the possibility of miracles (a faith not unusual for this time).

At Orléans, Joan warned the English to lift their siege, but they were not inclined to worry much about a feisty peasant girl dressed in soldier's armor. She proved them wrong. First, she slipped through their lines with a sizable force that relieved the French troops trapped within the castle. Then, she launched a series of successful counterattacks on the English camp. Rattled and forced to lift their siege, the English retreated, leaving Joan to be forever after revered as the Maid of Orléans. The next month, she won a second major victory at the battle of Patay. By then, all French and English troops knew that a peasant maid had reversed the momentum of the war. Joan continued to campaign until she fought a path to Reims in whose cathedral Charles VII was crowned in Joan's presence in July 1429. With this coronation, the French cause was triumphant, and the author of the triumph was Joan.

Yet, having revived her king's cause, Joan's own luck turned. Charles distanced himself from her; she was wounded in an assault on Paris; she was later captured by the Burgundian allies of the English; and Charles, short of money, refused to ransom her. Sold to the English, she was put on trial for heresy and sorcery in the city of Rouen.

The trial which began in early 1431 was, of course, rigged. Joan was denied counsel and had to defend herself. Her interrogators focused especially on her cross-dressing as a male soldier, her voices, and her military successes (these were incriminating because the English believed, of course, that God was on *their* side). Joan's responses in the surviving transcript suggest that she, a young and illiterate peasant woman, answered the proud and educated men who judged her in steadfast, articulate, and clever ways. When asked whether she would submit to the authority of the Church, Joan replied, "Yes, our Sire first being served," thereby offering the necessary obedience but tempering it with the authority of her mystical revelations. When asked whether God hated the English, she replied, "Of the love or hate which God has for the English and of what He does to their souls, I know nothing; but well I know that . . . God will send victory to the French over the English." When worried that the clerk might be keeping an inaccurate record, she demanded that his notes be read aloud and then revised to reflect more truly her actual words.

Isolated, mistreated, and ill, Joan eventually gave the English court the confession they sought, and she obediently put on women's clothing. In return, she got a life sentence. But she quickly reconsidered, retracted her confession, and donned male clothing again. She was thereupon condemned. As she stood among the flames, she continued to protest her innocence, demanding that her executioner hold a cross before her eyes so that she could see it to the end. She gazed on it, crying out, "Jesus," as she died. She was not yet twenty years old.

Twenty-five years later, the pope overturned Joan's sentence and declared her innocence. It took a bit longer (until 1920) for her to achieve sainthood. She is celebrated in France today as an early patriot and a savior of France. Memorial figurines and plaques now mark the various points of her itinerary through France; a monument commemorates the place of her burning outside the great market in Rouen; and an armored statue of Joan stands proudly near the main altar of Reims Cathedral, the scene of her most dazzling triumph.

one of Europe's first nation-states, and the tools with which they worked—aristocracy, parliament, bureaucracy, and nationalism—were forged in the hot furnaces of medieval monarchy.

✳ FRANCE: CONSTITUTIONAL CRISIS, WAR, AND THE SPIDER KING

The Hundred Years' War harmed France more than England. Almost all the fighting took place on French soil, and mercenary companies continually pillaged the French countryside, even when they were not engaged in actual warfare. King John the Good (r. 1350–1364) was, in fact, a very bad king. In 1356, a decade after the French military debacle at Crécy and eight years after the first devastation of the Great Plague, he led France to another crushing defeat at Poitiers (see Timeline 14.2). Worse yet, he refused to leave the battlefield (a refusal motivated more by chivalry than wisdom), and having been taken prisoner by the English, he then had to be ransomed at great cost.

The disaster at Poitiers prompted a brief and radical political experiment. The Estates General, meeting in Paris under the leadership of Etienne Marcel, the provost (or leader) of the merchants of Paris, momentarily assumed the reins of government. In 1357 they forced the dauphin Charles to issue the *Great Ordinance,* a document that provided for a new constitutional structure. Thenceforth, France was to be governed not by its king alone, but instead by the joint rule of king and Estates General, which was to meet at regular intervals and to oversee royal finances, administration, and even foreign policy. Charles was deeply hostile to this infringement of royal authority, but he submitted for a time and then fled Paris to gather royalist support in the countryside.

TIMELINE 14.2   France, 1300–1500

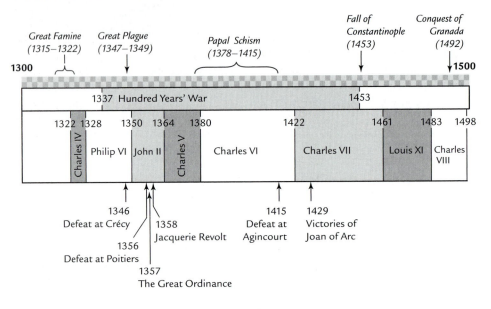

The following year, the French peasantry rose in revolt in the Jacquerie of 1358. For two weeks, angry peasants raged through northern France, until they were put down by the combined efforts of aristocrats and wealthy merchants. The terrors of this revolt were made more terrifying by exaggerated and morbid rumor. One story told, for example, of an aristocratic wife forced to eat her roasted husband; whether true or not, such tales bred more fear. And from this fear grew a conservative backlash, a longing for the law and order that, it seemed, only good kingship could bring. This surge of royalist sentiment doomed the constitutional experiment of Etienne Marcel and his followers, especially since Marcel had supported the rebels. Marcel was murdered one night as he walked along the walls of Paris, and the dauphin Charles returned to the city in triumph.

The Great Ordinance of 1357 was now a dead letter. The Estates General met less and less frequently, and its powers shriveled. Once the dauphin became King Charles V (r. 1364–1380), he instituted new tax measures that both enriched his monarchy and freed it from dependence on any representative assemblies. He and his successors also reverted to the old practice of dealing with subjects through local assemblies, rather than a realm-wide Estates General. Constitutionalism had briefly and brightly burned in Paris in 1357 and 1358, but it was then thoroughly snuffed out.

Charles V also made good headway against the English. His general Bertrand du Guesclin (c. 1320–1380), reputed to be the ugliest man in France and the best general in Europe, avoided pitched battles but so harassed the English in skirmishes that they slowly withdrew to minor outposts around Bordeaux and Calais. Charles V also reformed the French coinage, cracked down on roving bands of soldiers, assembled a royal navy, and established a royal library. When he died in 1380, Charles V—justly called "the Wise"—had turned back the disaster of Poitiers and returned glory to the French monarchy. The Estates General was subdued, the royal treasury secure, the countryside peaceful, and the English in retreat.

But he left one critical weakness: his incompetent son and heir, Charles VI "the Mad" (r. 1380–1422) who grew from a weak child into an unstable adult. In the vacuum created by his royal weakness, the old Capetian system of supporting younger brothers with independent apanages, a system that had long been a source of dynastic strength, brought bloody rivalries to the new Valois dynasty. Two cadet lineages battled for control—the houses of Orléans (headed by Charles VI's brother) and Burgundy (headed by his uncle)—and their struggle plunged France into civil strife. The Orléanist faction became identified with the cause of the Valois monarchy; the dukes of Burgundy slowly developed into a power that outrightly competed with it. Controlling most of the provinces of the Low Countries as well as their home county, the Burgundian dukes governed a powerful quasi-independent state lodged between France and the Holy Roman Empire, and they were allied, at times, with the English.

When King Henry V of England took advantage of France's weakness, triumphed at Agincourt in 1415, and won the Burgundian faction to his side, he secured a promise that *he* would succeed Charles the Mad. Briefly, it seemed the hostilities were to end where they might have never started in 1337—that is, with one English king supreme in both England and France. But Charles VI and Henry V both died in 1422. France was left with a new king, Charles VII (r. 1422–1461), who offered only halfhearted resistance as he watched the Burgundians and English divide northern France between them. Then, when the French side faced simply desperate prospects, Joan of Arc turned the tide of war against the English. As Charles VII's armies, first under her guidance and then without her, went from victory to victory, he rebuilt the royal government, established a standing army, secured tax revenues, and improved the steadily growing machinery of royal administration. But he could not subdue the great princes of France who mostly ruled as they liked within their counties and duchies, even though they recognized his royal suzerainty. The dukes of Orléans, Burgundy, Bourbon, Anjou, and others worked with Charles VII sometimes and plotted against him sometimes. So too did his son and heir, Louis.

When Louis XI (r. 1461–1483) returned from exile to take the throne in 1461, his new realm was threatened by overmighty princes but managed by an efficient bureaucracy, buttressed by a standing army, and governable without recourse to the messy demands of an Estates General. Known as "the Spider King," Louis XI's greatest accomplishment was to subdue the great aristocrats of France. He wove complicated webs to entrap some, removing them by clandestine murders, public beheadings, and various other dirty tricks. He won the loyalty of others in more traditional ways, by offering them positions in the court, the royal administration, and the army—or even marriage to his children. And he craftily turned luck to good advantage. When the duke of Burgundy died in battle in 1477, for example, Louis XI tried to force the heir, Mary duchess of Burgundy (1457–1482), to marry his son; when she refused, he seized by invasion many of her lands.[3] In all these ways, the Spider King so subdued the great nobility that by the end of his reign, only the Orléans and Bourbon dynasties remained of the great princely houses, and both were tied by marriage to the crown.

---

[3] Mary and her heirs had the last laugh. In 1477, she married Maximilian, heir to the Habsburg dynasty and the Holy Roman Empire (r. 1493–1519). Mary died in a hunting accident a few years later, but her strategic marriage brought most of the Low Countries under Habsburg influence, creating more problems for the successors of Louis XI than her duchy had ever posed.

Louis also understood, as no monarch had before him, that the economy mattered. He deliberately encouraged prosperity, establishing new fairs to attract foreign merchants, promoting industries, and reducing internal tariffs. He then taxed this expanding economy, more than doubling royal revenues. Like Henry VII of England, Louis XI was a new monarch, using old measures to produce a more stable and prosperous realm. By 1500, his successors sat securely on a well-administered and well-financed throne; French towns were flourishing once again; and the English were gone for good.

✸ THE IBERIAN STATES: CONSOLIDATION THROUGH HOMOGENIZATION

As we saw in Chapter 9, when the Christian reconquest had rolled to a stop in the second half of the thirteenth century, the Iberian Peninsula contained three strong Christian kingdoms—Castile, Aragon, and Portugal—along with the Muslim state of Granada in the south (see Map 14.2). Castile was the largest, with an economy based on sheep-raising and the production of fine merino wool. Aragon itself was rural and landlocked but because its crown controlled Catalonia, the rich port of Barcelona, and various Mediterranean islands, Aragonese merchants played an important role in Mediterranean commerce. Portugal looked out toward the Atlantic, and its sailors early began to sail westward and southward in search of trade. Granada was a small remnant of the once great Muslim caliphate of al-Andalus, but it was home to the magnificent palace of Alhambra, a wonder of architecture, art, and irrigation. Portugal and Granada were relatively homogeneous with predominantly Christian and Muslim populations, respectively; Castile and Aragon accommodated within their borders Jews and Muslims as well as Christians.

Like England and France, the three Christian kingdoms were plagued by wars—both civil conflicts and conflicts between each other—during the Later Middle Ages. King Dinas I of Portugal (r. 1279–1325) brought prosperity, security, and a navy to his realm, but his successes were undercut by later succession crises and wars with Castile. For its part, Castile was constantly torn by aristocratic uprisings, disputed royal successions, and border conflicts with Aragon and Portugal. And the Aragonese monarchy strove with only limited success to placate its nobility and merchants by granting significant concessions to regional representative assemblies, or *cortes*. A prolonged civil war in mid-fifteenth-century Catalonia—in which, as we saw in the last chapter, peasants had allied with their king against aristocrats and merchants—was put down only with the greatest difficulty.

In 1469, a single marriage began to change at least some of these problems (see Timeline 14.3). In that year, Isabella of Castile (r. 1474–1504) married Ferdinand of Aragon (r. 1479–1516), uniting their realms under one dynasty, while nevertheless preserving each realm's distinctive customs and laws. Isabella inherited her throne in 1474; Ferdinand inherited his in 1479. And thereafter—despite the continuation of regional cortes, tribunals, and customs—an efficient central administration governed the two realms and eventually transformed them into the kingdom of Spain.

Like their counterparts Henry VII in England and Louis XI in France, Isabella and Ferdinand were new monarchs, and they consolidated the power of their dynasty in three primary ways. First, they undercut aristocratic influence, filling the royal bureaucracy with middle-class lawyers rather than aristocrats, allying with towns against local

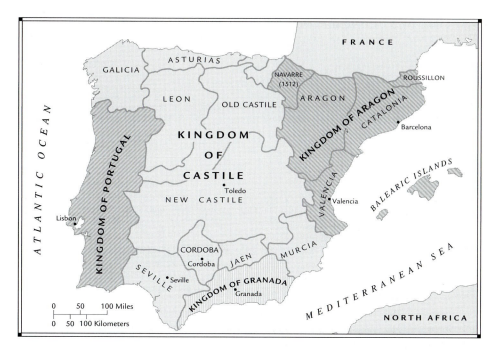

Map 14.2 *The Iberian Peninsula at the Time of Isabella and Ferdinand*   From the many small principalities of medieval Iberia, four remained powerful in the fifteenth century: predominantly Christian Portugal along the Atlantic Coast; predominantly Muslim Granada in the south; Castile in the center, born of the amalgamation of many places and peoples; and equally diverse Aragon in the northwest. When Isabella of Castile married Ferdinand of Aragon in 1469, their combined resources made them unquestioned masters of the peninsula.

landowners, and reorganizing the army to emphasize infantry over cavalry. Second, they acquired firm power over their national church, securing the pope's agreement that they, not he, could appoint most prelates within Spain. And third, they fostered national unity through religious zeal. For Isabella and Ferdinand, political obedience and national unity were tied to Christian orthodoxy.

The Jews and Muslims of Iberia had long faced worsening circumstances. The year 1391 had been particularly bad for Jews who, in the face of murderous mobs, sometimes died, sometimes emigrated, and sometimes undertook perfunctory conversion to Christianity. Muslims too had been hard pressed by their Christian rulers, slowly losing their separate law courts and even, in some cases, their knowledge of Arabic. The situation went from bad to worse in 1492 when Isabella and Ferdinand conquered Granada, finally placing all the Iberian peninsula under Christian control. In the flush of this victory, they presented their Muslim and Jewish subjects with the choice of conversion or exile. Many left, leaving the new kingdom a thoroughly Christian state but bereft of their knowledge and talents. Others converted, some genuinely and some in the hope that they could privately maintain their traditional faiths while publicly conforming as Christians.

This proved a dangerous strategy, for as public Christians, these *conversos* fell under the jurisdiction of the Inquisition. It also created dangers for Isabella and Ferdinand,

TIMELINE 14.3   European Politics, 1300–1500

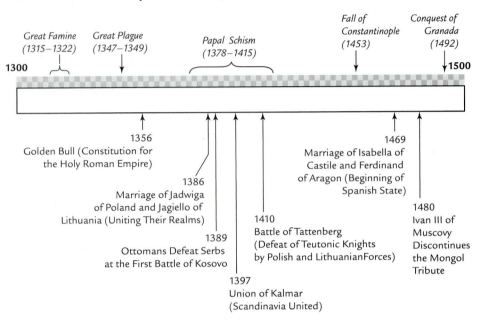

Great Famine (1315–1322)
Great Plague (1347–1349)
Papal Schism (1378–1415)
Fall of Constantinople (1453)
Conquest of Granada (1492)

1300

1500

1356
Golden Bull (Constitution for the Holy Roman Empire)

1386
Marriage of Jadwiga of Poland and Jagiello of Lithuania (Uniting Their Realms)

1389
Ottomans Defeat Serbs at the First Battle of Kosovo

1397
Union of Kalmar (Scandinavia United)

1410
Battle of Tattenberg (Defeat of Teutonic Knights by Polish and Lithuanian Forces)

1469
Marriage of Isabella of Castile and Ferdinand of Aragon (Beginning of Spanish State)

1480
Ivan III of Muscovy Discontinues the Mongol Tribute

who feared that conversos were not true Christians and, hence, not loyal subjects. The Dominican friars of the Spanish Inquisition provided a remedy, and in their search for false Christians they became important allies of a new state worried about disloyal subjects.[4] By 1500, Spain had been born from a strategic marriage, from the careful policies of Isabella and Ferdinand, and from a Christian militancy that would prove in future centuries to be both a great strength and a terrible weakness.

✷ NEW POWERS ON THE EUROPEAN PERIPHERY

The new monarchs of late fifteenth-century England, France, and Spain laid the foundations for three of the great nation-states of modern Europe. But they were not alone. To the north, Denmark, whose dominion had stretched as far as England in the eleventh century, was a more modest power in the Later Middle Ages. But it grew into a cohesive and strong force in the Baltic, and by the late fourteenth century, Queen Margaret of Denmark (1353–1412) also governed as regent over both Norway and Sweden. She consolidated her gains with the Union of Kalmar in 1397, creating a single Scandinavian state and designating her grand-nephew as nominal king of all three realms (she, in fact,

---

[4] In searching for crypto-Jews and crypto-Muslims, the Inquisition issued checklists of activities that might reveal an insincere convert to Christianity, and these checklists included considerable attention to food—what was eaten when, how it was prepared, and what was not eaten. For example, Aldonza Laínez of Almazán was reported to the Inquisition in spring 1504 for having served her workmen a turnip-and-cheese casserole. Why? Christians did not eat cheese during Lent. For a fascinating cookbook that traces the interrelations of food, crypto-Jews, and the Inquisition, see David M. Gitlitz and Linda Kay Davidson, *A Drizzle of Honey: The Lives and Recipes of Spain's Secret Jews* (1999).

governed—and very autocratically so—until her death). Sweden would break away from this confederation in the fifteenth century, but the political unity of Norway and Denmark persisted into the nineteenth century.

To the east, in the Russian states and in Asia Minor, old disunities were giving way to new and powerful states. As has been so often the case in the eastern borderlands of Europe, these developments were rooted in contact between Asia and Europe, especially the invasions of the Mongols in the thirteenth century and the rise of the Ottoman Turks in the fourteenth century.

Muscovy and the Mongols

As we saw in Chapter 4, the awesome beauty of Hagia Sophia had convinced Vladimir I (r. 980–1015) to convert to Eastern Orthodoxy, bringing all his subjects with him. His Kievan state would collapse in civil strife in the twelfth century, but his new religion survived and thrived. Thereafter, Byzantine civilization was a potent force in the development of Russian culture. So too were the Mongols, for whom the Russian principalities—made part of "The Golden Horde" in the conquests of the thirteenth century—were a source of power and income for the khan.

For the next two centuries, the Mongols allowed the Christian princes of Russia a good measure of autonomy, but they required heavy payments of tribute. As we saw in Chapter 11, Alexander Nevsky of Novgorod (c. 1220–1263) was the first to work closely with the Mongols, and they gave him the title of grand prince. This authority and power eventually passed to Moscow, whose grand princes continued to collaborate with the Mongol overlords *and* work the system to their advantage. The grand princes of Moscow became the sole collectors of the Mongol tribute, acquiring power for themselves by serving their Mongol masters well. On occasion they even helped the Mongols crush the rebellions of other Russian princes, further extending their own influence. Yet they also remained firmly loyal to the Orthodox Church, and under their guidance, Moscow became the center of Russian Orthodox Christianity, a "Third Rome."

Eventually, the servants turned on their masters when, toward the end of the fourteenth century, the Muscovite princes began to take the lead in anti-Mongol resistance. Finally, in 1480, Ivan III (r. 1462–1505), justly called "the Great," repudiated Mongol authority altogether and abolished the tribute. He annexed other Russian principalities and invaded Lithuania-Poland. He also rebuilt the Kremlin, adopted Byzantine symbols as his own, married a Byzantine princess, and began to call himself "Czar" (or Caesar) of the Russians.

Ivan III saw himself as the heir of the Byzantine Empire (which had finally fallen to the Ottomans with the capture of its capital Constantinople in 1453), and hence, also the heir of Rome. And although few in the West shared his view that Moscow was a Third Rome, Ivan III ruled in a way worthy of the most autocratic Roman or Byzantine emperors. He answered to no local or national assemblies; he had no articulate middle class to buttress his power with loyal clerks and bureaucrats; and he unhesitatingly crushed nascent opposition in such city-states as Novgorod. Not a new monarch, he was, as his chosen title suggests, more an old-fashioned emperor. But he had thrown off what he and his fellow Russians saw as the "Tartar yoke" and he had brought Muscovy, a new Russian state, into being.

Byzantium, Islam, and the Ottoman Empire

Meanwhile, to the south, a new power was replacing the attenuated empires of the Seljuks and Byzantines. By the early fourteenth century, the Ottoman Turks had replaced the Seljuks as the ruling dynasty in Asia Minor, and in 1354, they bypassed the diminutive Byzantine Empire and invaded Europe. Even today, Serbian nationalists remember with pride and bitterness the battle of Kosovo fought in 1389 and memorialized on the "Field of Blackbirds" with monuments that recall the brave but ill-fated stand of Orthodox Christian Serbians against a Muslim Ottoman army. The Ottomans won that battle and many others. By the end of the century, they had crushed Serbia and Bulgaria and extended their dominion over most of the Balkan peninsula. In 1453, the storming of Constantinople was little more than a postscript to Ottoman domination of Asia Minor and the Balkans (see Map 14.3). Yet all Europe recognized that an era had ended. It was a sign of the changing times that the Ottoman army shattered the walls of Constantinople with artillery.

Like the czars of the new Russian state, the sultans of the Ottoman Empire were autocrats. They ruled through strong centralized bureaucracy and tight military control. And they remained a threatening power to Christian Europe and its Mediterranean bases until, in 1571, a Spanish victory at the great naval battle of Lepanto definitively halted further Ottoman expansion. Yet for centuries to come, the sultans lived in Istanbul, a city built by the Roman Emperor Constantine (r. 306–337), a city sanctified as the home of Eastern Orthodox Christianity, and a city adorned by the Byzantine rulers Justinian (r. 527–565) and Theodora (500–548). They governed an Islamic empire that looked, as Constantine, Justinian, and Theodora had done before them, both east and west, both to Asia and to Europe.

✷ THE HERITAGE OF THE HOLY ROMAN EMPIRE

There is nothing inherently flawed about small states, and, as we have seen, some of the best governed states of the Central Middle Ages were of modest size. This was no accident. The princes of Europe—the bishops of tenth-century Milan, the counts of eleventh-century Champagne, the kings of twelfth-century Sicily, the dukes of thirteenth-century Austria—governed well because they governed relatively coherent areas that they could effectively protect, administer, and dominate. Modest size might also have facilitated female governance, for it seems to have been easier for a woman to claim her rightful inheritance to a duchy or county than to a realm. There were many female rulers in the Middle Ages, but like Matilda of Tuscany (1046–1115) or Jeanne of Flanders (r. 1204–1244), they usually governed relatively modest territories in which their direct personal power was able to override abstract anxieties about female governance.

In any case, small was not beautiful in the ambitions of medieval rulers, for they sought constantly to expand their borders and their authority. The dangerous dreams that

Map 14.3   *Central and Eastern Europe, c. 1490*   At the end of the fifteenth century,   ▶ there were no successful instances of "new monarchy" in central or eastern Europe. The Hapsburgs maintained only loose control over the more than one hundred quasi-independent cities, principalities, counties, and duchies of the Holy Roman Empire. The Italian peninsula was still fractured into many states. And the emerging states of eastern Europe were large but loosely governed.

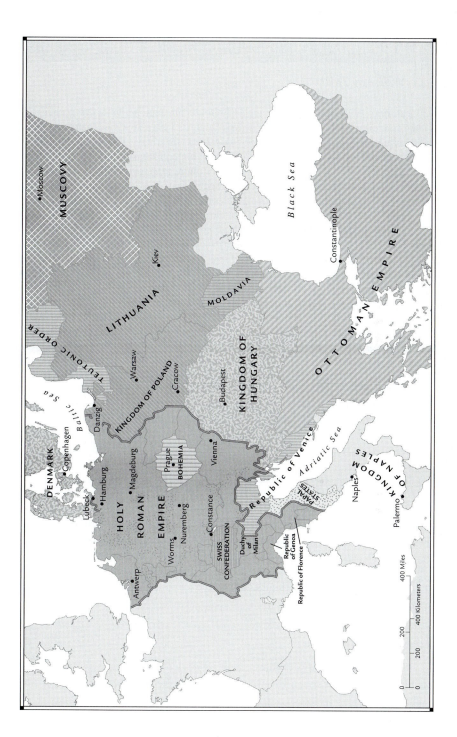

MUSCOVY

•Moscow

Black Sea

Constantinople

LITHUANIA

•Kiev

MOLDAVIA

O T T O M A N   E M P I R E

TEUTONIC ORDER

Warsaw•
Cracow•

KINGDOM OF POLAND

•Budapest

KINGDOM OF HUNGARY

Danzig•

Baltic Sea

DENMARK

Copenhagen•

Lübeck•

Hamburg•

Magdeburg•

Prague•
BOHEMIA

Vienna•

Republic of Venice

Adriatic Sea

HOLY
ROMAN
EMPIRE

Antwerp•

Worms•

Nuremberg•

Constance•

SWISS
CONFEDERATION

Duchy
of
Milan

PAPAL
STATES

Republic of Genoa
Republic of Florence

KINGDOM
OF NAPLES

Naples•

Palermo•

400 Miles

200

400 Kilometers

200

0
0

MEDIEVAL MYTHS

William Tell

The story of William Tell is set in the early fourteenth century, just a few decades after the founding pact of the Swiss Confederation in 1291. This agreement had joined three communities—Uri, Schwyz, and Unterwalden—in a defensive league against the aggrandizing interests of the Hapsburgs, the new imperial dynasty of the Holy Roman Empire. The legend of William Tell—and it is no more than legend—tells how one man from Uri took a brave stand against Hapsburg aggression. The legend has four acts. First, the scene is set: a Hapsburg official named Gessler arrives in Uri; he attempts to bring it more closely under imperial control; and as an insult to the locals, he sets his hat on a pole in the town square and orders everyone to bow before it. Second, the challenge: William Tell refuses to bow, Gessler angrily orders him to shoot an apple off his son's head, William Tell unwillingly but skillfully does the deed with his trusty cross-bow, and he then so insults Gessler that he is sentenced to life imprisonment. Third, escape: a fierce storm allows William Tell to escape from the boat transporting him to prison. Fourth, revenge: William Tell hunts Gessler down, kills him with a single arrow to the heart, and melts back into the forests of Uri. This is stirring stuff, and it especially seems to have stirred the nationalistic aspirations of those who first told the tale in the fifteenth century. By casting a personal conflict (Gessler vs. Tell) within a struggle for national sovereignty (Hapsburg empire vs. Swiss Confederation), this legend created a *national* hero: William Tell was a skilled woodsman, a trustworthy father, *and* a loyal Swiss. The national sentiments of the tale would have been lost to a twelfth-century audience, but they rang true in the fifteenth century. And they still strike a chord today; at http://www.pbs.ch/eng/ you can read about how young Swiss scouts are told about "William Tell, the National Hero of Switzerland." And if you want to hear music to stir your soul, listen to Rossini's overture to his opera *William Tell* (1829), probably best known today as the theme song for the 1950s television show *The Lone Ranger*.

fueled the history of the Holy Roman Empire and its interests in the Italian peninsula are but one example of this drive to expand. And small was not to prove competitive in modern Europe when, after 1500, small states were dwarfed and dominated by larger polities. This is true even today. The Grand Duchy of Luxembourg is a charming remnant of the small states that once dotted the medieval landscape, but it is not much of a player in the politics of the new European Union.

The German States

In the Later Middle Ages, most of these small states derived, in one way or another, from the detritus of the Holy Roman Empire, a deeply weakened institution by the time the first Habsburg sat on its throne in 1273. Its constitutional structure was set by the Golden Bull of 1356. This agreement, issued by the pope and confirmed at an imperial **diet** (or assembly), formally sanctioned imperial succession by election and designated seven great German princes as *electors:* the archbishops of Mainz, Trier, and Cologne; the count palatine of the Rhine; the duke of Saxony; the margrave of Brandenburg; and the king of Bohemia. The electoral states themselves remained relatively stable, as did some other German principalities such as the Habsburg duchy of Austria, but the Empire itself became largely powerless. In 1500, more than a hundred principalities lay within its borders—ecclesiastical city-states, free cities, counties, and duchies, all with boundaries that shifted periodically through war, marriage, and inheritance. Some were exceptionally well governed, and some, such as the Swiss Confederation and the Duchy of Austria, were precursors of modern nations. But all were relatively modest in size. And most turned inward toward local matters rather than outward toward a greater German nation, or even Europe.

Yet in the fifteenth century, the Habsburg dynasty, whose claims to the imperial title stretched back to Rudolf of Habsburg (r. 1273–1291), grew much more powerful, even though it continued to exercise only a token sway over the many states of the Holy Roman Empire. After the election of Albert II (r. 1404–1439 as Duke of Austria, r. 1438–1439 as emperor) in 1438, the Habsburgs held unchallenged control over the imperial title until 1711; it remained an elective office, but the Habsburg heir was always chosen. Albert was soon followed by his son Frederick III (r. 1440–1493), a long-lived and wily man. Although he forfeited Habsburg claims to Bohemia and Hungary, Frederick gained enormous territory by marrying his son Maximilian (r. 1493–1519) to Mary, duchess of Burgundy. Their son would eventually marry Joanna of Spain (1479–1555), heiress of the combined crowns of Aragon and Castile, creating a Habsburg dynasty that, although weak in its imperial control over the Holy Roman Empire, governed vast lands beyond the German states—especially Burgundy, the Netherlands, Spain, and large parts of the Americas. From these modest fifteenth-century foundations in the Holy Roman Empire, then, grew the most powerful dynasty of sixteenth-century Europe.

The Italian States

The Italian peninsula underwent some territorial consolidation in the Later Middle Ages, as small states were absorbed or dominated by their larger neighbors. From this process, the political crazy-quilt of the Italian peninsula in the Central Middle Ages had evolved by the fifteenth century into five dominant political units: the kingdom of Naples, the Papal States, and the three northern city-states of Florence, Milan, and Venice. Naples, formed (as we saw in Chapter 10) in the wake of the bloody War of the Sicilian Vespers (1282–1302), was ruled first by a French dynasty, and later by Aragon; in the mid-fifteenth century, it was rejoined to Sicily, briefly recreating the old extent of the Norman kingdom of Sicily. The Papal States in the center of the peninsula remained subject to the pope, but his real control of this region was compromised by the particularism of local aristocrats and the political turbulence of Rome itself. Although Milan and Florence were republics fiercely proud of their earlier struggles for independence, both fell under the rule of self-made tyrants in the Later Middle Ages. Venice remained a republic, but it was a peculiar republic, dominated by a wealthy oligarchy and exercising imperial sway over many smaller city-states in its region. There was little that was peaceful about these states or relations between them; rivalries couched in terms of Guelph and Ghibelline parties divided individual states and pitted one against another.

The internal politics of each state has a unique history, but all were marked by aristocratic factionalism, revolt, and instability. In this context, the tyrants who ruled in late medieval Milan, Florence, and other lesser city-states were welcome sources of stability. They governed more by their wits and cruelty than by tradition or custom, and because some were models for Machiavelli's *The Prince* (1513), they have often been regarded as new sorts of "renaissance" rulers. But in fact their opportunism was a quality well known to northern monarchs, and their ruthlessness would have surprised neither Charlemagne (r. 768–814) nor William the Conqueror (r. 1066–1087).

In relations with each other, these Italian states resorted often to war, usually fought with mercenary troops, or *condottieri*. Yet the fragile equilibrium of the five major Italian powers gave rise to diplomacy as well as war. Ambassadors, skilled at compliments and espionage, were exchanged on a regular basis, and complex alliances were sought to maintain a *balance of power* within the peninsula. Diplomacy as a calculated balancing act, rather than a matter of moral limitations or ecclesiastical mediation, was gaining strength throughout late medieval Europe. But it reached fruition first among the Italian states—and it would have a long history thereafter.

Poland and Lithuania

Throughout the fourteenth century, the crusading order of the Teutonic Knights continued, with brutal effectiveness, to advance German expansion to the east. In the fifteenth century they were stopped short by a new Slavic power, the combined kingdom of Poland and Lithuania, a state born of dynastic marriage and yet another case of domestic proselytization. In 1386, Jadwiga (pronounced yod-VEE-ga, r. 1384–1399), heiress to a Polish realm that had converted to Catholic Christianity around the year 1000, married the Lithuanian grand duke Jagiello (pronounced yog-YEL-low, 1377–1434), who promptly converted from paganism to Catholicism. Their union created the largest political unit in Europe, and very possibly, the least governed. Jadwiga died young, and although Jagiello did manage to defeat the Teutonic Knights at the battle of Tannenberg (1410), he ruled with little effective power and no real central administration over a nobility that would cooperate only against the hated Germans (and even then briefly and grudgingly). Stretching all the way from the Black Sea to the Baltic, incorporating many of the former lands of the Teutonic order and most of the old state of Kievan Russia, Lithuania–Poland lacked the skilled administrators and political institutions necessary to govern its vast territories.[5] Its political impotence guaranteed that, for centuries to come, no strong state would emerge between the German states and Russia.

✳ CONCLUSION

By 1500, monarchs in England, France, and Spain were, as Marsilius of Padua had argued they should be, in control of their national churches—and much more. Their administrations hummed with efficiency; their borders were securely defined and defended; and their nobles, although not tamed, had learned to think twice before rebelling. From these realms would emerge the quintessential nation-states of early modern Europe, built on medieval foundations but fortified by theories, institutions, and beliefs that took shape after 1500.

Elsewhere in Europe lay other destinies. The modern states of Germany and Italy would not form until the late nineteenth century, and historians still debate whether the

---

[5] On Map 15.3, Poland, Lithuania, and Moldavia roughly comprise the combined state of Lithuania–Poland in the early fifteenth century. Modern-day Lithuania is a tiny remnant of the great expanse of Lithuania in the Later Middle Ages.

violence of these unifications was partly rooted in nationalist sentiments that, frustrated by the political fragmentation of the Later Middle Ages, burst with dangerous fervor a half-millennium later. And on the margins of Europe loomed large and somewhat unwieldy states—Russia, the Ottoman Empire, Lithuania–Poland, and a briefly unified Scandinavia—which would each follow a different destiny to the modern day.

SUGGESTED READING

J. N. Hillgarth, *The Spanish Kingdoms, 1250–1516,* 2 vols. (1976–1978). A masterful account, with particular emphasis on Castile and Aragon.

Richard W. Kaeuper, *War, Justice, and Public Order: England and France in the Later Middle Ages* (1988). An important synthesis. See also Christopher Allmand, *The Hundred Years' War: England and France at War c. 1300–1450* (rev. edition, 2002), and Anne Curry, *The Hundred Years' War* (2nd edition, 2003).

John Larner, *Italy in the Age of Dante and Petrarch, 1216–1380* (1980). Fine coverage of social as well as political history. See also Denys Hay and John Law, *Italy in the Age of the Renaissance, 1380–1530* (1989), and Daniel Waley, *The Italian City-Republics* (3rd edition, 1988).

Joachim Leuschner, *Germany in the Late Middle Ages* (1980). See also F. R. H. Du Boulay, *Germany in the Later Middle Ages* (1983).

Janet Martin, *Medieval Russia, 940–1584* (1995). Includes extensive treatment of the Later Middle Ages. See also Robert O. Crummey, *The Formation of Muscovy, 1304–1613* (1987), and Charles J. Halperin, *Russia and the Golden Horde: The Mongol Impact on Medieval Russian History* (1985).

David Nicholas, *Medieval Flanders* (1992). Covers the entire Middle Ages, but is especially focused on the fourteenth and fifteenth centuries. See also Wim Blockmans and Walter Prevenier, *The Promised Lands: The Low Countries Under Burgundian Rule, 1369–1530,* trans. Elizabeth Fackelman (1999).

Régine Pernoud, *Joan of Arc: By Herself and Her Witnesses* (1964). A narrative built from the sources of Joan's various trials, this remains the best general introduction to Joan of Arc. For Joan's remembrance in later generations, see especially Marina Warner, *Joan of Arc: The Image of Female Heroism* (1981). For the latest research, see Bonnie Wheeler and Charles T. Wood, eds., *Fresh Verdicts on Joan of Arc* (1996).

Jean W. Sedlar, *East-Central Europe in the Middle Ages, 1000–1500* (1994). An ambitious and highly useful survey. See also John V. A. Fine, Jr., *The Late Medieval Balkans* (1987).

Alison Weir, *Lancaster and York* (1996). A lively study of the Wars of the Roses. See also John A. F. Thomson, *The Transformation of Medieval England 1370–1529* (1983).

SUGGESTED PRIMARY SOURCES

Emilie Amt, *Medieval England, 1000–1500* (2000).

Christopher Given-Wilson, *Chronicles of the Revolution, 1397–1400: The Reign of Richard II* (1993). See also A. F. Scott, *Everyone a Witness: The Plantagenet Age* (1976).

Trevor Dean, *The Towns of Italy in the Later Middle Ages* (2000).

John M. Klassen, *The Letters of the Rozmberk Sisters: Noblewomen in Fifteenth-Century Bohemia* (2001).

Thomas A. Fudge, trans., *The Crusade against Heretics in Bohemia, 1418–1437: Sources and Documents for the Hussite Crusades* (2002).

CHAPTER 15

DIVERSITY AND DYNAMISM IN LATE MEDIEVAL CULTURE, c. 1300-1500

✸ INTRODUCTION

The Great Plague affected artists and intellectuals as well as ordinary people. Some died in the plague, as did the philosopher William of Ockham (c. 1285–1349). Others lived through the Great Plague and left testimonies of the horrors they had seen. In the *Decameron,* the master storyteller Giovanni Boccaccio (1313–1373) collected stories from many sources and retold them with great narrative skill. But he prefaced his collection with an almost clinical description of the Great Plague in Florence: the blood, the boils, the swellings, the quick deaths, the mass burials. For still others, death and decay remained subjects of seemingly obsessive interest long after 1350. Some sculptors abandoned the fine effigies that traditionally graced the tombs of the dead and instead carved memorial images of the dead in decay—their rotting flesh, their skeletal remains, even their entrails being chewed by vermin. Some artists took as their special subject the *danse macabre* (or "dance of death"), drawing pictures that showed Death plucking a new victim or the dead mingling with the oblivious living. In fourteenth- and fifteenth-century Europe, death was, understandably, on everyone's mind.

Yet the contemplation of death did not lead to the death of culture—indeed, quite the opposite (see Timeline 15.1). In these centuries, ordinary people benefited more than ever before from an expansion in education and literacy, and they expressed their ideas in plays, songs, and stories of great power. Women benefited, too, for the ever growing importance of vernacular languages offered them a broader cultural forum than the Latin of the Church ever had; they responded by writing themselves and also by fostering through patronage the writings and translations of others. In literature and art, such geniuses as Giotto di Bondone (1266–1337), Geoffrey Chaucer (c. 1340–1400), and Jan van Eyck (c. 1385–1440) produced works of lasting beauty. In architecture, most of the geniuses were anonymous, but some took the Gothic style to a new, fantastic conclusion, and others began to imitate the calm serenity of old Greco-Roman styles. And in the universities and schools of Europe, philosophers chewed over old problems and turned their minds to new ones. The culture of late medieval Europe is a study in contrasts—life and

TIMELINE 15.1   Cultural Change, 1300–1500

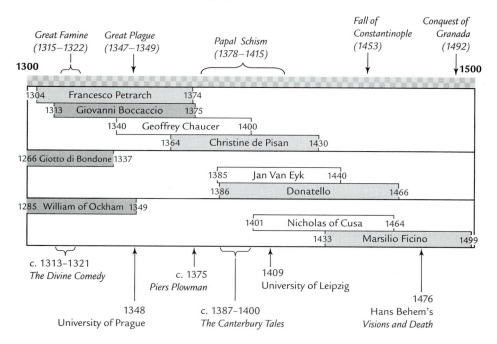

death, anti-clericalism and intense faith, old styles and new experiments—and the result was dynamic, exciting, and immensely influential for the future.

✳ LITERACY AND VERNACULAR LANGUAGES

As we saw in Chapter 10 a great expansion in education began in the eleventh century, with the proliferation of municipal schools, cathedral schools, and finally, universities. In the fourteenth and fifteenth centuries, this expansion continued, and it particularly broadened the base of literate Europeans. In other words, institutions of higher learning continued to expand in the Later Middle Ages (for example, universities were established in Prague in 1348, Vienna in 1365, Heidelberg in 1385, Cracow in 1397, Leipzig in 1409, and St. Andrews in 1412), but even more important was the proliferation of basic schools that offered young boys—and sometimes young girls—a practical education in reading, writing, and arithmetic. In Florence just before the Great Plague, about 600 boys went to *grammar schools* where they studied a traditional curriculum that prepared them for legal and ecclesiastical careers, or possibly for further study at universities. They studied in Latin, then the only language considered to have rules (or *grammar*). But twice as many boys in Florence went to schools where they learned to calculate on the abacus, to keep accounts, and to read and write in the Tuscan vernacular. These boys were preparing for careers as merchants, artisans, or clerks, not as lawyers or churchmen—and their vernacular education was growing more and more common.

Over the course of the fourteenth and fifteenth centuries, many towns in both northern and southern Europe founded *vernacular schools* for their children. Some towns boasted several. Only sons of prosperous parents could attend these schools, and few were open to girls. Peasants, of course, rarely had such schools in their villages, and they learned what they could from parents and parish priests. But the skills taught in vernacular schools percolated through society. Reliable literacy rates are impossible to come by, but by 1400, a significant minority of people could read at least a bit. The skill was especially prevalent among men, among privileged people (the gentry, nobility, and merchant class), and, it seems, among the English. Throughout Europe, more and more laypeople could keep accounts, read notarial acts, decipher court documents, and as many Italians especially started to do, write family histories and diaries. They could also pick up a vernacular book and read it for themselves—and for anyone else who wanted to listen.[1] Because many people did, in fact, want to listen, one reader meant *many* informed people. When a reader shared information—from a book, a pamphlet, a posted announcement, a court document—with an audience, he or she extended the power of the written word far beyond the literate population.

As this *culture of reading* spread throughout late medieval Europe, vernacular literature flourished: romances, epics, practical books of advice, and, of course, the vernacular writings of such authors as Dante Alighieri (1265–1321), Geoffrey Chaucer, and Christine de Pizan (1364–1430). Translations of Latin texts into vernacular languages also flourished. By 1400, the Bible could be read in French, Dutch, English, and most other European languages. So, too, could many devotional books, including saints' lives, mystical writings, and books of prayers. Wealthy women were particularly active in encouraging translations, which they sought not only for their own use but also for the guidance of their children.

A *culture of writing* also spread through late medieval Europe, as people simply wrote more down than before. As a result, we know more about the worlds of ordinary people, as seen in the texts of their mystery plays, in their diaries, in the proverbs they jotted down, in their songs, even in the doodles they drew in the margins of books. Theirs was a culture rich with ritual and festival, for throughout the year peasants and townsfolk put work aside to combine worship with play. At Christmas, Carnival (the festival that preceded the austerities of Lent), Easter, May Day, the feast of St. John the Baptist in midsummer, and a host of other more minor holidays, peasants and townspeople celebrated with song, dance, drama, bonfires, feasting, and sport. They had a disturbing fondness for cruelty (bearbaiting is the best example) and an intriguing love of inversion—electing mock bishops and mock mayors to rule over festivals and reveling in tales (such as those of Robin Hood) in which the poor triumphed over the rich.

Late medieval people also absorbed—through sermons, public readings, paintings, and conversation—a rich knowledge of Christian traditions. Margery Kempe (c. 1372–1439), a would-be mystic who dictated her autobiography (the first in English) to a scribe in the 1430s, called herself an "unlettered" woman, but she must have been a careful listener and observer, for she commanded an extensive knowledge of the Bible, mystical writings, and saints' lives. Hans Behem, an illiterate shepherd whose preaching electrified the peasants of his region for a few months in 1476 (see Biographical Sketch), similarly absorbed a great deal of what we might today consider to be "book-learning." In late medieval Europe, literacy was more widespread than ever before, but literacy was not an essential precondition for learning.

---

[1] In the Middle Ages, silent reading was rare. Even when alone, most medieval people spoke out loud the words they read, a method that, although seldom used today, helps to improve comprehension.

BIOGRAPHICAL SKETCH

Hans Behem (d. 1476)

Hans Behem was born in the 1450s near Niklashausen, a small village located just about at the center of the Holy Roman Empire (a bit to the east of Nuremberg, in Map 14.3). He was poor, and by the time he was a teenager, he worked as a shepherd, a common enough occupation for a peasant boy. He made extra money by playing his drum in taverns, a slightly unsavory sideline but nothing out of the ordinary. Then, in the spring of 1476, Behem's life took a dramatic turn. He experienced what he believed to be visits from the Virgin Mary; he began to preach about these visions and compose inspiring songs; he attracted thousands of pilgrims to Niklashausen; and within a few months, he was dead, executed by command of Rudolph von Sherenberg, Bishop of Würzburg.

In Behem's visions, the Virgin spoke to him about ordinary things, especially about why he and his neighbors were so poor and suffered so much. Some of her words echoed what Behem could have heard in a sermon in his parish church: vanity was everywhere, and people must put aside their proud possessions to stand humbly before their God (see Figure 15.1). But other lessons from Behem's visions were unlike anything he would have heard from most preachers, for, as he reported it, the Virgin spoke fervently about the sins of the clergy and the greediness of the wealthy. She also told him to prepare for a future when goods would be held in common, with no person more privileged than another. As one report put it, the Virgin told Behem, "Say to all the people that my son wishes and orders that all tolls, levies, forced labor, exactions, payments, and aids required by the prelates, princes, and nobles be abolished completely and at once. They shall oppress the poor no more." If Behem had heard such talk before, he would have heard it from other peasants, a hermit, or even a Hussite preacher. Such ideas were not the stuff of orthodox preaching. Nor was the talk that soon began about solving the problem of clerical sin by killing all the priests.

While tens of thousands of people flocked to Niklashausen, the authorities only slowly figured out what was happening. In May, the local count was pleased by the profits that came from levying tolls and selling supplies to the pilgrims, but he knew neither Behem's name nor the specifics of his teachings. Yet thousands of peasants—as many as 8,000 a day—then knew enough to leave their homes and walk to Niklashausen. How did these illiterate peasants know what nobles did not? Behem's songs might be the answer. Only two stanzas from one song have survived, but they are based on a well-known liturgical melody, and their message is powerful:

> Oh, God in heaven, on you we call
> Kyrie Eleison
> Help us seize our priests and kill them all.
> Kyrie Eleison.

Songs such as this could have spread Behem's ideas more rapidly and more powerfully than written words, preachers, or hired couriers could ever have done. No wonder they were outlawed in the very first civic ordinances issued against him.

Soon so many pilgrims were traveling to Niklashausen that all authorities—town councils, counts, and bishops—began to worry about famine and mob violence. Would there be enough food and drink for all? How could the crowds be controlled? What was this

Continued

BIOGRAPHICAL SKETCH

Hans Behem (d. 1476)   *Continued*

talk of killing priests and holding all goods in common? In early July, the Bishop of Würzburg acted. He sent spies to take incriminating notes on Behem's sermons; he ordered knights to seize Behem and bring him to his castle at Würzburg; he had Behem tried for heresy and burned at the stake. Most of the pilgrims then headed back home, but when some rose up in rebellion, the bishop's men dispersed them by firing cannons into their midst. To finish the job, the church at Niklashausen was razed, lest it become a site for future pilgrimages, and Behem's ashes were thrown into the river so that nothing remained to be revered. The bishop could not destroy the memory of Behem and his pilgrims, but he destroyed just about everything else.

Behem was poor, young, illiterate, and a threat to the established authorities. To them he was a "little fool," a "pseudo-prophet," an "ignorant half-wit," an "unlettered, common adolescent." The Bishop of Würzburg was a very different sort of person—75 years old, well-off, well educated, and powerful enough to put young boys to death. Behem played his drum to bawdy songs the bishop never heard in grimy taverns he would have never entered; the bishop read books unknown to Behem in libraries that would have made his head spin. Yet when Behem preached about vanities, he spoke about a matter that troubled his bishop too, for von Sherenberg kept an austere household and had ordered his clergy to do the same. When Behem waxed eloquent about corrupt priests, his bishop also shared this concern, for he was in the midst of a project to supply his clergy with better liturgical books and pastoral guides. When Behem spoke about miraculous visions and deeds, his bishop readily agreed that God was a powerful presence in the everyday world; at his command, agents painstakingly investigated each of the miracle stories that came out of Niklashausen. And when Behem gave his greatest sermons, he chose Christian feast days, moments of high significance to both him and the bishop he opposed. Behem and his bishop, the illiterate drummer boy and the man who ordered his death, certainly did not see the world in identical ways, but their differences—between the popular and elite cultures of late medieval Europe—were more subtle than stark. They stood at opposite ends of their world, but it was a world they shared.

✳ HUMANIST EDUCATION

At the same time that vernacular education and literature were flourishing as never before, so too did the study of Latin and classical antiquity. Francesco Petrarch (1304–1374) led the way. Deeply impressed by the writings of Cicero, Petrarch thought that the Latin of his own day suffered in comparison. He resolved to return to the "purity" of Ciceronian Latin and to build a library of manuscripts that contained this ancient Latin—what we today call *classical Latin* as opposed to *medieval Latin*. To this end, Petrarch rummaged around in monastic libraries where he found many "lost" classical texts, and adopting their style, he made his career as a poet and man of letters. He also developed a new vision of education, for he was attracted to neither the Latin (that is, *medieval* Latin) education of grammar schools and universities nor the practical education offered in vernacular schools. Instead, he argued that the study of the litera-ture of ancient Rome—its prose, its poetry, its history—was the best possible education, for it promoted clear thinking, proper morals, and satisfying life.

Petrarch was, thus, the father of **humanist** education—an education that sought through the study of classical languages and literature, history, and the arts to mold young boys into worldly men who would be both good Christians and good citizens.[2] Those who followed Petrarch trained their sons not in municipal schools, cathedral schools, or universities, but instead with tutors skilled in Ciceronian Latin or at court schools established to follow this new humanist curriculum. They were usually, there-fore, wealthy, so that at the very time that other forms of education were becoming more available to a wider spectrum of people, this new humanist program inspired rich nobles and rich merchants, but few others.

The daughters of these elite parents were sometimes educated alongside their brothers, and a few female humanists rose to positions of great fame. But, in general, the primary aim of humanist education—to produce good *public* citizens—favored men more than women. In 1528, the humanist writer Baldassare Castiglione (1478–1529) set out the difference with particular bluntness. He said that women should be well educated in classical literature and history, but only so that they might be more entertaining to men. A woman with a good humanist education was simply, it seems, a better dinner companion.

Petrarch spent most of his life in Rome and Florence, and his love of Cicero's Rome had particular resonance in the Italian peninsula. There, Italian merchants brought home great wealth from their domination of Mediterranean trade. There, the civic spirit of the northern city-states encouraged innovative forms of expression. And there, of course, the memory of the days when Cicero's Rome ruled the Mediterranean world was constantly refreshed by the Roman monuments, sculptures, and buildings that littered Italian cities. In the fourteenth century, the Italian states, battered and worn by papal-imperial wars, had little reason to be nostalgic about the immediate past, and Petrarch's humanism spoke both to the glories of ancient days and the present-day search for skilled, urbane, and moral leaders.

✸ LITERATURE

The achievements of late medieval literature reflect these changes in education, for, at one and the same time, great works were produced both in the classical Latin espoused by humanists and in the vernacular literatures that were gaining so many more readers. The first had somewhat limited reach, as the literary efforts of Petrarch and those who followed him found audiences initially only among wealthy merchants and nobles of Italian city-states. But Petrarch wrote hundreds of letters as well as vernacular poetry of great distinction, and he passed on to later generations a revised interpretation of the ide-alized lady of courtly love. Much of his poetry was inspired by Laura, a woman whom, as best we know, he once glimpsed during a church service. Just as the courtly lady of

---

[2] Eventually, "humanism" acquired many connotations in late medieval Europe, especially: *(a)* admiration for classical antiquity; *(b)* an educational curriculum that emphasized the study of literature, art, and history; and *(c)* an optimistic assessment of the potential of human beings who were, in the words of one early humanist, "confined by no bounds."

medieval romance had been an idealized and unattainable inspiration for her knightly lover, so Laura inspired Petrarch. She was ideally beautiful, ideally good, and impossibly distant—a humanist version of the courtly lady on a pedestal.

In vernacular literature, old genres such as romances continued to be popular, but the courtly tradition was slowly upstaged by authors whose gritty realism drew as much from the middling classes as from royal or ducal courts. In Italian, Boccaccio's *Decameron* relates the stories with which seven women and three men entertain themselves as they escape Florence during the Great Plague. Many of the stories dwell on fornication, adultery, and corrupt priests, and they are all told with such narrative skill that Boccaccio is today credited as the father of the short story. The popularity of his work buttressed that of Dante in establishing the Tuscan vernacular as dominant throughout the Italian peninsula.

In England, two fourteenth-century poems were wildly popular, kept in many libraries and imitated by many lesser poets. *Piers Plowman* (written c. 1375) is a long allegory that tells of one man's search for truth and salvation (see Figure 15.1). It dwells powerfully on the lives of the poor and the abuses of the wealthy, and it seems that its unknown author (conventionally identified as William Langland) was a cleric of modest means. Written a few decades later (c. 1387–1400), *The Canterbury Tales* of Geoffrey Chaucer is a livelier text that borrows its frame from Boccaccio's *Decameron:* pilgrims tell stories as they travel from London to the shrine of St. Thomas Becket at Canterbury. Chaucer was a poet of rare psychological insight and descriptive skill, and perhaps his greatest character was the Wife of Bath, a self-confident, self-supporting, and somewhat

Figure 15.1   *Pride*   Found in the margins of a manuscript of *Piers Plowman,* this drawing illustrates the vain pride that so worried its author. Note particularly the man's long sleeves, fancy belt, and elaborate headgear. Pride was one of the seven deadly sins: pride, gluttony, envy, lust, anger, greed, and sloth.

appalling wife of one husband and widow of four others. When her fifth husband persists in reading aloud to her from an anti-feminist "book of wicked wives," she takes matters into her own hands. As she tells it:

> When I saw that he would never stop
> To read this cursed book all night
> I suddenly tore three pages out
> Where he was reading, at the very place,
> And hit such a blow upon his face
> That backwards down into our fire he fell.

Literary scholars have ever since debated whether Chaucer created the Wife of Bath as a gesture of sympathy toward women or as a tool for ridiculing them.

In France, Christine de Pizan (1364–1430), a singularly gifted writer and poet, was the first woman in Europe to support herself by writing (see Figure 15.2). Educated by her father, a humanist scholar who left Venice to take up a position in the French court, Christine de Pizan wrote prose and poetry on an astonishing range of topics and in many literary forms. Besides her autobiography, she wrote lyric poems expressing her abiding love for her husband, who had left her a widow at twenty-five; a book of moral

Figure 15.2   *Christine de Pizan*   This manuscript illumination shows Christine de Pizan at work at her desk, assisted by the three inspirational muses for her defenses of women: Reason, Rectitude, and Justice.

advice for women; a companion volume for men; a verse history running from the Creation to her own time; a study of great women in history; and her deservedly celebrated treatise, *The Letter to the God of Love,* in which she effectively rebuts the antifeminist diatribes embedded in Jean de Meun's conclusion of the *Romance of the Rose.* This rebuttal marks the first clear instance in European history of a woman writing against the slanders that women had so long endured. It also gave rise to a heated debate that stretched into the sixteenth century, pitching Jean de Meun's sympathizers against Christine de Pizan's admirers—of whom there were many. None, however, could match her eloquence as she responded to age-old assumptions that women were especially wicked. As she somewhat idealistically argued, women

> do not kill people, or wound, or maim; nor do they undertake and pursue treachery;
> they do not burn out or disinherit people; they do not poison or steal gold or silver;
> they do not cheat people out of their wealth or their inheritances through false
> contracts; nor do they damage kingdoms, duchies, or empires.

Christine de Pizan could be caustic as well as idealistic. When a man once aggravated her by remarking that an educated woman is unattractive because so rare, she replied that an ignorant man is even less attractive because so common.

Both Chaucer and Pizan wrote for court audiences, but not all late medieval authors aimed so high. François Villon (1431–c.1463), a brawling Parisian vagabond, lived far from the luxuries of the French court where Christine de Pizan spent most of her life. He wrote with an anguished, sometimes brutal realism that vividly reflects the late medieval mood of insecurity and plague. To him, death was the great democrat:

> I know that rich and poor and all,
> Foolish and wise, and priest and lay,
> Mean folk and noble, great and small,
> High and low, fair and foul, and they
> That wear rich clothing on the way,
> Being of whatever stock or stem,
> And are coiffed newly every day,
> Death shall take every one of them.

❋ ART AND ARCHITECTURE

Late medieval art and architecture also headed in two directions at once: toward a revival of Greco-Roman styles that expressed in paint and stone Petrarch's love of antiquity *and* toward a further elaboration of the Gothic style. In the Italian states, architects abandoned the Gothic spire and pointed arch to create buildings reminiscent of old Rome—domes, round arches, and elegant classical facades (see Figure 15.3). Sculptors similarly turned toward their indigenous classical heritage, adopting the Greco-Roman emphasis on the contours of the perfect human body. Working in Florence, Donatello (1386–1466) studied ancient sculptures in order to replicate in his *David* and other works the idealized human forms of the classical past (see Figure 15.4); Michelangelo (1475–1564) and other later sculptors built on what he had begun. Painters had few actual classical models to follow, but they strove for lifelike figures and landscapes, and they pioneered techniques of perspective. Led by Giotto, they abandoned the more stylized forms of Byzantine and medieval art to embrace a naturalistic style that evoked

Figure 15.3   *The Revival of Classical Architecture*   This interior of St. Andrea in Mantua illustrates how architects inspired by humanist ideals sought to replicate the buildings of ancient Rome. Compare this fifteenth-century interior to the fifth-century interior of Santa Sabina in Rome (Figure 1.3).

the art of ancient Rome. As Color Illustration 13 shows, Giotto's paintings were highly realistic and detailed.

To the north, Gothic architecture became more vertical and more decorative, creating churches with sweeping vertical lines, elaborate fan vaulting, and a profusion of sculpture (see Figure 15.5). Even in the later thirteenth century, the old Gothic balance between upward aspiration and harmonious proportion—between the vertical and horizontal—had begun to shift toward an ever greater emphasis on verticality. Then, in the Later Middle Ages, all of the elements that had once introduced horizontal force—especially capitals that had punctuated the upward reach of columns and decorative lines that had balanced the soaring piers—disappeared, leaving little to disturb the dramatic upward thrust from floor to roof. Late medieval churches achieved a fluid and uncompromising verticality, a sense of heavenly aspiration that bordered on the mystical.

Also, because the basic structural potentials of the Gothic style had been fully exploited by the end of the thirteenth century, the innovations of late Gothic architecture consisted chiefly of more elaborate decoration. This created churches that today seem, according to personal taste, either rich delights of decorative exuberance or over-decorated sculptural jungles. While sculptors in the Italian city-states were emulating the work of their Roman forebears, sculptors in the north gave way to heightened emotionalism and

Figure 15.4 *Donatello's* **David**   In seeking to
sculpt a perfect male body, Donatello looked back to
Greco-Roman sculpture for both inspiration and
design. His interest in idealized representations is very
different from the realism of late Gothic sculpture
(see Figure 15.6).

an emphasis on individual peculiarities. The serenity of Gothic sculpture was replaced by
a tough realism that would have made François Villon proud: decaying corpses, images of
intense, overwhelming sorrow, and individuals shown with all their faults as well as
virtues (see Figure 15.6).

Painting north of the Alps reached a pinnacle in the precise realism of the Flemish
school. Jan van Eyck (c. 1385–1440) excelled in reproducing the natural world with a
devotion to detail that was all but photographic (see Figure 15.7). His reputation
extended throughout Europe, and even among Italian artists, focused as they were on
emulation of the classical past, van Eyck was admired for his innovative technique and
pioneering use of oil paints.

✷ Philosophy

As with the dual directions of literature, art, and architecture, so too with intellectual
trends. Philosophers moved either *(a)* toward Plato, for those inspired by Petrarch, or
(b) away from Thomas Aquinas (c. 1225–1274), for those working within the traditional
framework of medieval universities.

Figure 15.5 *Late Medieval Gothic*   Begun in the late fifteenth century, King's College Chapel in Cambridge exemplifies the verticality and decoration characteristic of late medieval Gothic architecture.

Humanist research had brought many of Plato's writings to light by the fifteenth century, generating a revival of Platonism and Neoplatonism. Marsilio Ficino (1433–1499) was skilled in Greek as well as classical Latin, and he translated all of Plato's dialogues into Latin. He also undertook to do for Plato what Aquinas had attempted for Aristotle—that is, to reconcile Platonic philosophy with Christian faith. His pupil Giovanni Pico della Mirandola (1463–1494) went still further and attempted to blend all known philosophies into one coherent framework. He began his project with an essay, *On*

Figure 15.6. *Mourners*   From the tomb of Philip the Bold,
Duke of Burgundy, these figures were sculpted by Claus Sluter
in the early fifteenth century. Their realism, typical of late
medieval Gothic sculpture, contrasts with the idealism of
Donatello's *David* (see Figure 15.4).

the Dignity of Man, that stated with exceptional eloquence his exuberance—and that of
other humanists—for the potential of the human mind and spirit. Yet neither Ficino nor
Pico della Mirandola possessed the acumen of Aquinas and other central medieval
philosophers, and neither approached the profundity of their great contemporary north of
the Alps, Nicholas of Cusa (1401–1464).

Educated by the mystical Brothers of the Common Life and at the universities of
Heidelberg and Padua, Nicholas of Cusa reached Neoplatonism by a route different
from that of the humanists Ficino and Pico della Mirandola. He came to believe that the
contradictions and diversities of the material world were reconciled and unified in an
unknowable God, a God beyond rational apprehension who could be approached only
through a mystical process he termed "learned ignorance." His concept of an unknowable God was rooted in the third-century Neoplatonism of Plotinus (205–270), whose

Figure 15.7 *Jan Van Eyck,* **Giovanni Arnolfini and His Bride** *(1434)*   The
extraordinary detail of this picture is characteristic of Van Eyck's genius. Note, for
example, the dog and the sandals in the foreground, and the chandelier above. Most
astonishingly, the mirror in the background reflects back the scene. Van Eyck's use
of oil paint facilitated his interest in a realism that seems almost photographic.

ideas had run as an undercurrent in Christian thought from St. Augustine (354–430) and
John Scottus Eriugena (c. 810–877) through the rest of the Middle Ages. Like earlier
Neoplatonists, Nicholas of Cusa conceived of the universe as a ceaseless creative un-
folding of an infinite God. But going beyond his Neoplatonic predecessors, he reasoned
that a universe emanating from an infinite deity cannot be limited by human concepts of

space and time. In short, God's created universe was *infinite*. In his synthetic vision of an ordered cosmos, Nicholas of Cusa echoed the scholastic optimism of the thirteenth century. In his emphasis on mysticism and the limitation of human reason, he was in tune with his own grittier age. And in his bold conception of an infinite universe, he anticipated modern philosophy and astronomy.

In medieval universities, the fourteenth and fifteenth centuries witnessed a widespread and largely critical reaction to Aquinas's great synthesis in the *Summa Theologica*. His hierarchical ordering and reconciliation of mind and spirit, logic and revelation had brought to a climax the central medieval search for a rational cosmic order. This climax was followed, logically enough, by critique, since Aquinas's achievement was so great that it demanded careful study and debate. So while humanists were turning back to the ideas of philosophers born nearly two millennia before, university-based philosophers were working through the implications of the extraordinary intellectual achievement of the previous century. The fourteenth-century attack on Aquinas's synthesis was founded on two related propositions: (1) that to ascribe rationality to God is to limit his omnipotence by the finite rules of human logic, and (2) that human reason can tell us nothing of God because logic and belief inhabit two separate, sealed worlds. By the first critique, the Thomist God of reason gave way to an unknowable God. By the second, knowledge of the natural world achieved a new autonomy, for it could be studied on its own terms.

The first steps toward the concept of a willful, incomprehensible God were taken by the Oxford Franciscan John Duns Scotus (c. 1266–1308), who produced a detailed critique of the Thomist theory of knowledge. Duns Scotus did not reject the possibility of elucidating faith through reason, but he was more cautious in his use of logic than Aquinas had been. Whereas Aquinas is called "The Angelic Doctor," Duns Scotus is called "The Subtle Doctor," and the extreme complexity of his thought prompted people in subsequent generations to describe anyone who bothered to follow his arguments as a "dunce." The nickname is unfair, for Duns Scotus was an important and original figure in the development of late scholasticism. Yet one is tempted to draw a parallel between the intricacies of his intellectual system and the decorative elaborations of late Gothic churches. A Christian rationalist of the most thoroughgoing kind, Duns Scotus nevertheless made the first move toward dismantling the Thomist synthesis and withdrawing reason from the realm of theology.

Another Oxford Franciscan, William of Ockham, attacked the Thomist synthesis on all fronts. Ockham argued that God and Christian doctrine were utterly undemonstrable and must be accepted on faith alone. As a consequence, human reason had to be limited to the realm of observable phenomena. In Ockham's world—an unpredictable world of an unfathomable Creator—it made sense to reason *only* about things that could be directly seen or directly experienced. His radical empiricism ruled out all metaphysical speculations, at least all couched in terms of logic and philosophy, and it gave new impetus to the logical observation of natural phenomena. By severing the bonds between revelation and reason, William of Ockham blazed two paths into the future: mysticism uninhibited by logic, and natural philosophy (that is, science) uninhibited by faith. For Ockham and many of his followers, mystical revelation and scientific empiricism coexisted, side by side. Because the two worlds never touched, they were in no way contradictory. An intelligent Christian could keep one foot in each of them.[3]

---

[3] Ockham is also famous for "Ockham's razor," the principle that the simpler explanation is always the better one.

Ockham's philosophy thus served as an appropriate foundation for both late medieval mysticism and late medieval science. Some mystics, indeed, regarded themselves as empiricists, for the empiricist is a person who accepts only those things that are directly experienced, and the mystic, abandoning the effort to *understand* God, strove to *experience* him. For those who followed Ockham's point of view on the natural world, it could now be studied on its own terms, without reference to theological underpinnings. Nicholas Oresme (1325–1382), a teacher at the University of Paris, attacked the Aristotelian theory of motion and proposed a rotating earth as a possible explanation for the apparent daily movement of the sun and stars across the sky. Oresme's theories owed more to thirteenth-century scientists such as Robert Grosseteste (1168–1253) than to Ockham, but his willingness to tinker with traditional explanations of the physical structure of God's universe was characteristic of an age in which scientific speculation was being severed from revealed truth.

Many late medieval philosophers rejected Ockham's theories and remained Thomists. But owing to the very comprehensiveness of Aquinas's achievement, his successors were reduced to detailed elaboration or minor repair work. Faced with a choice between the tedious niggling of late Thomism and the drastic limitations that Ockham's view imposed on philosophical inquiry, many of Europe's finest minds shunned philosophy altogether for the more exciting fields of science, mathematics, and classical learning. When the philosopher Jean Gerson (1364–1429), chancellor of the University of Paris, lectured against idle curiosity in matters of Christian religion, he told his students in no uncertain terms that the synthesis of faith and reason that was at the heart of the scholastic project was, quite simply, no more. It is no accident that Gerson himself was both a mystic and a natural philosopher.

✸ Political Thought

Political theory seldom neatly matches political realities, and this was as true of late medieval Europe as elsewhere. But the political changes of these centuries did prompt thoughtful commentary. Some writers continued to expound the *papalist* position that, as we have seen in Chapter 10, was so ascendant during the investiture controversy. In 1302, Pope Boniface VIII (r. 1294–1303), as a salvo in his struggle with Philip IV of France (r. 1285–1314), issued *Unam Sanctam,* a document that unequivocally stated that every Christian was subject, first and foremost, to the pope. Giles of Rome (c. 1245–1346) argued fiercely in favor of this position, and so too did other theorists, even in the fifteenth century. But as the power of the papacy waned in these centuries, so, too, did papalist theory.

A few others argued in favor of the *imperialist* perspective that an emperor should reign over Christendom, as Charlemagne (r. 768–814) had sought to do, as a benevolent ruler of both church and state. Dante argued something like this in *On Monarchy,* completed c. 1320. For Dante, the transcendent power of an emperor could bring peace, an all-important foundation for the work of the Church. But Dante was not a full-blown apologist for the imperialist position, since he never envisioned that an emperor's power would infringe in direct ways on the autonomy of his beloved Florence or any other Italian city-state. As the power of the Holy Roman emperor waned, so too did imperialist theory.

Indeed, the position that had least sway in the eleventh century—the *clericalist* position that sought to define separate jurisdictions for both church and state—proved much more compelling in the fourteenth and fifteenth centuries. Marsilius of Padua

(1280–c. 1343) fiercely attacked the claims of the Church and strongly supported the rights of secular governments, but his argument boiled down to separation of spheres: the church as a spiritual authority and the state as a temporal one. His friend William of Ockham also sought to limit the Church's power to matters of faith which, in Ockham's view, were always revealed truths, not subject to reason. Ockham's Church was one whose teachings could be obeyed but never understood; his state was a practical and rational polity.

But beyond these old arguments about the relative place of church and state, two new trends spoke directly to the political changes of the Later Middle Ages. First, Marsilius of Padua and others began to define what constituted a political community and what claims it could make. Marsilius wrote that each political community had a "ruling part" that should wield free and full authority over all within that community, including clergy. Bartolus de Sassoferrato (c. 1313–1357) put similar ideas more succinctly, stating that each Italian state was *sibi princeps*—prince to itself, a self-governing corporation with power over all within. And such ideas found expression in practice as well as theory—in, for example, the claim of English parliaments that they represented "the community of the realm." All these ideas pushed toward the clarification of the critical concept of sovereignty—that is, toward defining a sovereign state by *(a)* its autonomy in relation to external powers and *(b)* its encompassing authority over all persons within its borders. Second, a more practical bent began to emerge by the fifteenth century, with political commentators dealing less with abstract ideas and more with the nitty-gritty of how governments actually worked. Sir John Fortescue (c. 1394–1476), an English judge, wrote treatises that compared the governance of England and France and instructed rulers practically on how to govern well. His approach reflects the empiricism of the day and, in a distant way, might be seen as a precursor to Machiavelli's how-to manual for rulers, *The Prince* (1513).

❈ CONCLUSION

In the years just after 1500, the humanist movement propelled by the ideas of Francesco Petrarch would produce some of its greatest work: Desiderius Erasmus's *The Praise of Folly* in 1509, Machiavelli's *The Prince* in 1513, Thomas More's *Utopia* in 1516, Baldassare Castiglione's *Book of the Courtier* in 1528, the great works of Leonardo da Vinci (1452–1519), and much, much more. In these same years, scientific investigation would begin to gain speed, with the publication in 1543 of both *On the Revolution of the Heavenly Spheres* by Nicolaus Copernicus (1473–1543) and *The Structure of the Human Body* by Andreas Vesalius (1514–1564). The former used mathematical calculations to set forth the hypothesis of a sun-centered world system; the latter used dissection to understand the human body in more precise ways. And, of course, in 1517 Martin Luther would give impetus to a religious upheaval of huge proportions, by challenging the teachings of the Catholic Church in ways that eventually led to the creation of "protestant" denominations.

These were momentous events, but they were not sudden, and they do not represent a "renaissance" or "rebirth" from a dead medieval past. Instead, they built on firm medieval foundations, so that it would be no exaggeration to say that there would have been no Erasmus without Petrarch, no Leonardo without Giotto, no Copernicus without Ockham, and no Luther without Wycliffe and Hus. There was, to be sure, a strong sense of the new and "modern" among many creative Europeans in the early sixteenth century, but they relied on and retained many medieval ways, styles, and habits of thought.

Moreover, in 1500, the promise of the future era that we now call "early modern" (c. 1500–1800) did not depend on matters of intellect and art alone. In western Europe, many peasants were free of serfdom, better fed, and better informed than ever before. All across Europe, commerce was thriving again, cities were growing, and population was beginning to boom. More people were going to school, and they provided an eager market for the cheap editions produced by the new printing presses of Europe. Other new inventions and improvements—gunpowder, the water pump, eyeglasses, and mechanical clocks—were changing the ways people lived. The papacy that had once dreamed of ruling an international Christendom now governed a mere principality around Rome, but England, France, Spain, and Russia boasted stable, centralized governments that were well on the road toward nationhood. European ships had reached the Americas and the Indian subcontinent, and Portuguese merchants were unloading cargoes brought direct around the African coast. Medieval people had done much more than just survive famine and plague; they had built the Europe that was, by 1500, encountering the rest of the world.

SUGGESTED READINGS

Anthony Black, *Political Thought in Europe, 1250–1450* (1992). Brief and authoritative. See also J. H. Burns, *Lordship, Kingship, and Empire: The Idea of Monarchy 1400–1525* (1992).

The Geoffrey Chaucer Web site (http://icg.fas.Harvard.edu/~chaucer/). In addition to extensive information on Chaucer, this site also offers access to a wide variety of late medieval cultural materials.

Denys Hay and John Law, *Italy in the Age of the Renaissance 1380–1530* (1989). An introductory survey of social, political, and cultural history.

John Marenbon, *Later Medieval Philosophy* (1987).

Charles G. Nauert, Jr., *Humanism and the Culture of Renaissance Europe* (1995). See also Alison Brown, *The Renaissance* (2nd edition, 1999); John Hale, *The Civilization of Europe in the Renaissance* (1994); and Lisa Jardine, *Worldly Goods: A New History of the Renaissance* (1996).

Richard Wunderli, *Peasant Fires: The Drummer of Niklashausen* (1992). Written for a general audience, this is the most recent study of Hans Behem.

SUGGESTED PRIMARY SOURCES

Peter Elmer, Nick Webb, and Roberta Wood, eds., *The Renaissance in Europe: An Anthology* (2000). Each text is carefully introduced in this new collection.

Online Medieval and Classical Library (http://sunsite.berkeley.edu/OMACL). A good site for sampling the genres of medieval literature.

GLOSSARY

This is a selective list of words that might give you trouble—a list, if you will, of medieval jargon. The first time that a word from this glossary is used in the text, it has been boldfaced, so that you will know to look it up.

If you cannot find a word here, two additional resources are: *(1)* the *index,* which will lead you to many topics (and words) treated fully in the text that have not been included in this glossary, and *(2)* a good *dictionary,* which will define for you many other words not included here (for example, if you are uncertain about what is meant by the "the Balkans" or "Iberia," a dictionary will help you out).

For convenient cross-referencing, we have italicized words that are defined elsewhere in the glossary (although titles and foreign words are, of course, also italicized).

A

abbey   A monastic community, governed by an abbot or abbess. An abbey was distinct from a *priory* by its larger size, its greater autonomy, or both. See also *monastic orders.*

Albigensianism   Another word for the medieval heresy of *Catharism.*

anti-clericalism   Opposition to the influence of clergy. In the Middle Ages, anti-clericalism stressed *(a)* the greed and wickedness of the clergy, *(b)* the unnecessary role of the clergy in the *sacraments,* or *(c)* both.

apanage   A territorial holding, usually carved out of the royal demesne, that was given by the French king to a member of his own family.

apprentice   A young man (or, occasionally, young woman) training in a craft or trade. See also *journeyman/woman.*

Arians   Early Christian *heretics* who conceived of the Trinity as three unequal entities. Not to be confused with the racist concept of an Aryan race.

artisan   A skilled craftsperson, such as a goldsmith or shoemaker.

B

bailiff   In a general sense, the chief administrative officer of a manor. In a specific sense, a royal officer used by Philip II Augustus of France (r. 1180–1223) and his successors to advance royal interests in territories outside the royal demesne. See also *sheriff* and *ministerial.*

barbarian   In a general sense, a Greek term for those who spoke non-Greek languages. In a specific sense, the term used in this book to designate the frontier tribes that eventually settled within the borders of the Roman Empire—that is, Visigoths, Ostrogoths, Vandals, Franks, Saxons, Angles, Jutes, and the like. See also *Germanic.*

beguines   Women who lived in religious communities but without ecclesiastical sanction or regulation. Beguines and beguinages (as their communities were called) flourished in northwestern European cities in the thirteenth century, but they were suppressed by the Church in the early fourteenth century.

bishop   From Greek for "overseer," a bishop is the chief priest of a district (or *diocese*). Exercising authority over all the priests therein and sometimes monasteries too, the bishop is responsible for pastoral care and moral correction.

burgess (also **burgher**)   A citizen of a town. Because not all inhabitants were citizens, burgesses tended to be the wealthiest and most powerful townspeople.

C

caliph   From Arabic for "successor," the caliph succeeded, after the death of

Muhammad, to Muhammad's position as the secular and religious leader of the Islamic world. In time, however, the term came to be applied to leaders of separate polities within Islam, such as the Fatimid caliphate in Egypt or the caliphate of Cordoba.

canon   From the Greek word for "standard" or "criterion," canon has many medieval meanings, including *(a)* a Church ordinance, law, or decree (hence, *canon law*); *(b)* a cleric who works in the world but follows a quasi-monastic life, usually in association with a cathedral (women were known as "canonesses"); or *(c)* when used as an adjective, an equivalent of "authoritative," as in the seven "canonical hours," or holy services, that punctuated each monastic day.

canon law   The law of the Church.

capitulary   Laws and regulations issued by Charlemagne (r. 768–814) and his successors that were to be observed throughout his Empire.

cardinal   Created in the eleventh century, the position of cardinal entitled its holder to participate in papal elections. It was an honor that could be attached to any clerical position, so that, for example, the man who became Pope Innocent III (r. 1198–1216) spent part of his early career as a cardinal *deacon.*

Catharism   A *dualist* heresy that presented the major alternative to orthodox Christianity in the Central Middle Ages. This heresy was also known as *Albigensianism* (as in the Albigensian Crusade launched against Cathars, 1209–1229).

cathedral   The principal church of a *bishop,* located in the city that was the center of his *diocese.*

cathedral schools   Schools attached to cathedrals and therefore, unlike monastic schools, in urban settings. Cathedral schools were more common in the north; municipals schools in the south; both were part of the eleventh-century expansion of education that led in the twelfth century to the founding of the first universities.

catholic   In a general sense, "catholic" simply means "universal." In a specific sense, it designates those medieval Christians who looked to the pope in Rome for guidance (since the pope claimed authority over *all*

Christians). Eastern *Orthodox* Christians rejected the universal claims of the Roman pope, a division that hardened in 1054 when Pope Leo IX (r. 1049–1054) and Patriarch Michael Cerularius (r. 1043–1058) excommunicated each other. "Catholic" would take on new meaning when the Western Christians divided under pressure from "Protestant" reformers in the sixteenth century, but throughout the Middle Ages, "Catholic" describes the faith of all orthodox Christians in the medieval West.

chansons de geste   Literally "songs of great deeds," these epics were especially popular among the aristocracy of northern France in the eleventh and twelfth centuries.

charter   A written document that records a gift, grant, sale, or other transaction.

Christendom   Literally, a Christian realm or *imperium Christianum,* a term used to describe the lands ruled by Charlemagne (r. 768–814). In later centuries, "Christendom" had considerable ideological power for many medieval Christians, describing a territory roughly equivalent to "Europe" and expressing their vision of a unified Christian society within those lands. Historians today distinguish between Western Christendom and Eastern Christendom (the Byzantine Empire).

church   In a general sense, simply a place of worship. In a specific sense (and designated in this book by capitalization), "Church" refers to the established institution of the medieval Church, headed by the pope in Rome.

clergy (or **cleric**)   See *secular clergy* and *regular clergy.* See also *laity.*

comitatus   A barbarian war band, led by a chief to whom men owed absolute loyalty. The personal bonds of the comitatus were one precursor to *feudalism.*

common law   As developed in England from the twelfth century, common law had two critical features: *(1)* it was the king's law, available to all free people throughout the realm, and *(2)* it was based on *custom* and precedent, not statute.

communal movement   The effort of cities and towns in the Central Middle Ages to establish rights of self-governance. These movements were often led by associations of citizens who had sworn a communal oath. Also known as the charter movement, because of the *charters* of self-governance that citizens sought.

commune   A municipality that had obtained a *charter* of self-governance, as many towns did in the eleventh and twelfth centuries. In a few cases, rural villages also formed communes. See also *guild* and *communal movement.*

compurgation   Proof of innocence by oath swearing.

conciliar movement   A late medieval movement (c. 1378–1449) to make *councils,* not *popes,* the supreme authority within the *Church.*

cortes   The representative assemblies of the Christian kingdoms of the Iberian peninsula. See also *diet, Estates General,* and *parliament.*

councils   In the specific context of medieval history, this term refers to general meetings of Church officers. The earliest Church councils, such as the Council of Nicaea in 325, clarified basic matters of Christian doctrine. In the Central Middle Ages, councils were effective tools of papal monarchy, especially the Fourth Lateran Council of 1215. In the Later Middle Ages, councils briefly presented a constitutional challenge to papal authority (see *conciliar movement*). See also *synod.*

courtly love   A modern term coined to describe ideas about romantic love between women and men, as they developed in the literatures of France in the twelfth century.

crusader states   The four states established in the wake of the highly successful First Crusade: the county of Edessa, the principality of Antioch, the county of Tripoli, and the kingdom of Jerusalem (whose king was theoretically the overlord of the other three).

curia   Latin for "court," this term was especially used for the highest courts, such as the *curia regis* (the king's court) or the *papal curia.*

curia regis   The king's court or council in England. From the right of great men to advise the king in council slowly evolved

some of the advisory capacities of English *parliaments.*

custom   A practice that has legal force because of long use. Custom-based law, as opposed to statute law, took its force from the power of past practice: what had been done in the past should be done in the present. See also *common law.*

D

dauphin   The title given to the heir to the French throne.

deacon   Ranking just below a priest in the clerical hierarchy, a deacon could perform some but not all of the *sacraments.* Like priests, deacons were required to be celibate after the twelfth century. In the early Church, women served as deaconesses.

demesne   In a general sense, the land that an owner held back for direct use, as opposed to land dispersed to tenants, vassals, or others. On a *manor,* the manorial demesne consisted of the lands directly cultivated for the profit of the manorial *lord* or *lady.* In a realm, the royal demesne consisted of lands directly controlled by the monarch.

diet   From Latin for "day," an assembly in the German states. See also *cortes, Estates General,* and *parliament.*

diocese   The district supervised by a *bishop.* See also *see.*

domestic proselytization   A term coined by the historian Jane Schulenburg to describe conversions to Christianity that were accomplished by the marriages—especially royal marriages—of Christian women to pagan men.

double monastery   Monasteries that included both women and men. In the Early Middle Ages, these houses were usually ruled by abbesses. Most eventually became single-sex establishments. In the Central Middle Ages, new sorts of double monasteries were formed so that men, who were able (if ordained) to administer the *sacraments,* could assist women. Some of these eventually expelled women.

dualism   A philosophy or religion that emphasizes conflict between the two opposing forces of good and evil, such as Persian

Zoroastrianism, Manicheanism in late imperial Rome, and the *Cathar* heresy of the Central Middle Ages.

E

ecclesiastical   Related to the Church as an institutional body.

Estates General   The representative assembly of France, first called by Philip IV the Fair (r. 1285–1314). See also *cortes, diet,* and *parliament.*

Eucharist   The Christian *sacrament* that commemorates the Last Supper. By the doctrine of transubstantiation, approved by the Fourth Lateran Council in 1215, the eucharistic bread (the Host) and wine were transformed, during the Mass, into the body and blood of Christ. This miracle is celebrated in the feast of Corpus Christi ("Body of Christ"), established in the thirteenth century and celebrated about two months after Easter.

excommunication   Removal from communion with the Church. Since medieval theologians taught that the *sacraments* of the Church were essential to salvation, excommunication effectively meant damnation. See also *interdict.*

F

fable   A genre of urban literature, fables were allegories in which stock characters were presented as animals. Renard the Fox, a crafty and unscrupulous fellow who makes almost everyone he encounters into a fool, is the hero of many fables.

fabliaux   Urban tales that were filled with satire, sex, and comedy.

fallow   Unplanted land, particularly land left unplanted in order to replenish the fertility of the soil. In the *three-field system,* a field lay fallow every third year.

family   See *household.*

family church   A church (or monastery) founded by a family and treated by it as part of the family property. Such a family would endow the church and protect it, but it also expected to appoint its clerical officers and sometimes to control its resources. See also *lay investiture.*

family monastery   See *family church.*

feudalism   A modern term coined to describe the political, military, and social customs that maintained the power of the military elite ("those who fight") in the Central and Later Middle Ages. See also *manorialism.*

fief   A gift (usually an estate, but sometimes an office or annuity) given by a lord or lady to a vassal, in return for service (usually military service). Originally fiefs were for life only, but they soon became hereditary.

flying buttress   A buttress that stands apart from the roof that it supports, usually connected to the main supporting wall by arches. Flying buttresses are a critical component of the tall, window-filled walls of *Gothic* churches.

free peasant   As distinct from a *serf* or *slave,* a peasant who could move, work, marry, and otherwise make his or her own life decisions without having to seek the prior approval of a manorial lord or lady.

friar   A member of the Dominican or Franciscan orders, both founded in the early thirteenth century. Not bound to the obligation of remaining in a monastery (as were monks and nuns), friars moved about Europe, renowned as preachers, inquisitors, and professors. Known as *mendicants,* because they begged for a living, friars also include members of the Carmelite and Augustinian orders.

G

German, Germanic   In a modern sense, the people, language, and state of the contemporary Federal Republic of Germany. In medieval history, these terms are sometimes used to designate the frontier tribes that eventually settled within the borders of the Roman Empire—that is, Visigoths, Ostrogoths, Vandals, Franks, Saxons, Angles, Jutes, and the like. But Romans rarely described these tribes as "Germanic," preferring *barbarian* (the term used in this book) instead. Also, these tribes did not always share a common language that was the ancestor of modern German, and their states did not evolve into the modern Federal Republic of Germany. See also the *Holy Roman Empire.*

gloss   A comment on a text, originally written in its margins by a "glossator." This system of comments, followed by comments on comments, was a critical method of *scholasticism.*

Gothic   An architectural style that originated in twelfth-century France characterized by the use of *flying buttresses,* pointed arches, and ribbed vaults.

guild   In a general sense, a community of people engaged in a common purpose—such as the guilds of town leaders who wrested *charters* from overlords in the eleventh and twelfth centuries (these organizations were also known as *communes*); the guilds of students or faculty that comprised medieval universities; or the parish guilds that helped support local religious activities (these were also sometimes called "confraternities"). In a specific sense, however, guilds were organizations through which urban trades and crafts supervised training, quality, and sales of the products under their jurisdiction.

H

hagiography   The writing of saints' lives, a popular genre of Christian literature.

heretic   A person who diverges from established belief of his or her religion and then persists in that divergence. Note: Jews and Muslims, as non-Christians, were not heretics in the eyes of the medieval Church and therefore were outside the jurisdiction of *inquisitors.* To medieval Christians, Jews and Muslims were *infidels.*

Holy Roman Empire   Although the term was not specifically used until the twelfth century, it generally applies to the German Empire after Otto I (r. 936–973), who was crowned as emperor in 962. Otto's successors acceded to the German kingship by primogeniture or election, and their status as emperor relied on coronation by the pope. Throughout its long history, the Holy Roman Empire was usually little more than a loose net thrown over largely autonomous German states.

Host   See *Eucharist.*

household   In a general sense, a group of people who shared a common residence, as well as common work and provisioning. A household differs from our modern meaning of "family" in that it could include servants, wage–laborers, and even boarders. In medieval Latin, *familia* usually meant "household."

humanism   An intellectual movement, whose earliest beginnings are associated with Francesco Petrarch (1304–1374), that stressed: *(a)* admiration for classical antiquity, *(b)* the educational importance of literature, art, and history; and *(c)* an optimistic assessment of the potential of human beings.

I

icon   An image of a saintly or divine figure. In eighth-century Byzantium, "iconclasts" wanted to destroy these images because they feared that people wrongly attributed special power to icons. "Iconodules" wanted to retain icons because they believed icons were a useful spur to contemplation.

indulgence   Release from punishment for sin, punishment that would have otherwise been extracted either on earth or in purgatory. Theoretically, an indulgence was issued only in response to repentance and good works.

infidel   Literally, a "person without faith," this label was applied to Jews and Muslims by medieval Christians. See also *pagan.*

inquisitor   A Church official, usually a Dominican *friar,* given special powers by the pope to search out and punish *heretics.*

interdict   A form of mass *excommunication,* an interdict forbade the celebration of Christian services or *sacraments* within a specified area. Among other things, an interdict meant that no infants could be baptized, no couples wed, and no dead properly buried.

itinerant judges   As used particularly by the English crown, these judges moved about the countryside, carrying the power of the king's justice far beyond the king's immediate presence.

J

journeyman/woman   A young man or woman who had finished an apprenticeship but did not yet own a shop as an independent *master* or *mistress.* Journeymen and journeywomen were paid wages by the day (*journée* in French).

K

knight   A man trained and armed to fight on horseback. Many knights—but not all—were also *vassals.* Over the course of the Middle Ages, the training of knights—as pages and squires—became more elaborate, as did the rituals in which men were armed and "made" into knights.

L

lady   Thanks to our Victorian legacy, we associate the term "lady" with gentility and refinement. In the Middle Ages, however, a lady was a *domina,* a woman who exercised power, whether over a manor, over vassals, or even over a realm. See also *lord, vassal,* and *mistress.*

laity   In general, a person without professional knowledge or interest. As specifically used in medieval history, a term for Christians not professionally active in the Church. For Church professionals, see *regular clergy* and *secular clergy.*

lay investiture   In a strict sense, the practice of laypeople investing ecclesiastical officers with the symbols of their ecclesiastical powers. In a general sense, the control of ecclesiastical appointments by laity. See also *family church.*

legate   An ambassador of the pope who usually had the extensive powers to act on the pope's behalf.

lord   Used in many different contexts, a lord was simply a *dominus,* a man who exercised power over others—as a manorial lord, as a feudal lord, as a king, as a bishop, or otherwise. See also *lady, vassal,* and *master.*

M

magnate   A particularly wealthy or influential aristocrat, usually one with direct access to his king or prince. The greatest *nobles* of a realm were its magnates.

manorialism   The economic arrangements through which *serfs* and *free peasants* ("those who work") supported the landowning elite. A "manor" was an estate consisting of land and people who worked the land, and since each manor usually had its own court and officials, it was a jurisdictional as well as an economic unit. See also *feudalism.*

master   For the urban and peasant classes, this was the term applied to a male head of *household.* In urban guilds, it also designated a man who ran his own workshop or business (under whom might work *apprentices, journeymen,* and *journeywomen*). From this term, we get the modern title "Mr." See also *mistress* and *lord.*

mendicants   See *friars.*

military orders   Developed during the crusading movement, military orders combined the skills of soldiering with the rigors of monastic life. The greatest were the Knights Templar, the Hospitalers, the Teutonic Knights (active in the Baltic), and the Knights of Santiago de Compostela (dedicated to fighting Muslims in Iberia).

ministerial   A lowborn knight who worked for the Holy Roman Emperor, protecting his interests in the German principalities. See also *bailiff* and *sheriff.*

missi dominici   Envoys used by Charlemagne to enforce his rule throughout his wide realm. Usually the missi dominici traveled in pairs of one churchman and one layman. For later variations on the use of such officials, see *bailiff, ministerial,* and *sheriff.*

mistress   For the urban and peasant classes, this term was the equivalent of *lady,* signifying a woman who was a female head of *household* or even a woman who ran her own business. From mistress comes the modern title "Mrs." See also *master.*

monastic orders   A group of monastic houses linked by either *(a)* a common *monastic rule* or *(b)* formal structures of administration and governance (the first of these was the Cluniac order, in which Cluny is the main *abbey* and all other houses were *priories* under Cluny's governance).

monastic rules   Guides for monastic living. The most important, often known as simply *The Rule,* was written by St. Benedict of Nursia (c. 480–c. 550). Because monks and nuns follow such guidelines, they are known as *regular clergy* (rule = *regula* in Latin). See also *monastic orders.*

monastic schools   Early monasteries often included schools, but monastic schools became especially important after Charlemagne's capitulary of 789 ordered every monastery to provide some educational training. Many monastic schools trained external students as well as monks and nuns. Monastic schools were slowly superceded, for men, by *cathedral schools* and *universities,* but they remained important in female education throughout the Middle Ages.

mystery plays   Plays mounted by urban *guilds* (also known as "mysteries") that recounted stories from the Bible. An entire mystery cycle began with the Creation and ended with the Final Judgment.

mystery religions   Ancient religions and cults characterized by a promise of mystical revelation (whence "mystery") and an emphasis on individual spiritual development and salvation.

mysticism   Direct contact between humanity and divinity. Christian mystics attempted to initiate such experiences through prayer, fasting, contemplation, and other means. In medieval Islam, Sufi mystics led the way. In Judaism, cabalism was the main route to mystical union.

N

Neoplatonism   An elaboration of Plato's theory of forms especially associated with the third-century philosopher Plotinus (205–270) who taught of one infinite and unknowable God who can be approached only through mystical experience. To Neoplatonists, the human soul should seek to return, via mysticism, to the perfect oneness of God.

O

oblation   In a general sense, a gift. In a specific sense, the giving of young children to monasteries to be raised as monks or nuns (these children were known as "oblates"). This practice was discouraged by the Church, and it died out in the Central Middle Ages. The term is also applied to gifts that parishioners customarily gave to priests in return for performing marriages, funerals, and other services.

open fields   Fields surrounding villages in which many tenants held *strips* of land for growing crops. Because fences did not divide these strips, the fields were "open."

ordeal   A form of trial, derived from *barbarian* law, that relied on divine intervention to determine guilt or innocence.

orthodox   In a general sense, "orthodox" is simply a "correct opinion" as judged by a designated religious authority. See also *heresy.* In a specific sense (and indicated by capitalization), "Orthodox" signifies the Eastern Orthodox Church (which embraces self-governing branches in Greece, Russia, Serbia, and elsewhere).

P

pagan   In a general sense, an irreligious person, especially as applied by medieval Christians to Jews and Muslims. See also *infidel.* In a specific sense, a pagan is a follower of a polytheistic faith, such as the traditional deities of Rome.

papacy   The office of the *pope.*

papal bull   In a general sense, a "bull" is a document ratified by a seal (that is, a wax impression). A papal bull is an authoritative document bearing a papal seal.

papal curia   The *pope's* court and bureaucracy.

parish   The smallest geographical unit in the ecclesiastical system, a parish was the basic unit of public worship. It ideally consisted of a church and a priest who would administer to the souls of all Christians within the district.

Parlement   A judicial body, important in the administration of royal justice in France. The French representative assembly was known as the *Estates General.*

parliament   A representative assembly in England that, by the fourteenth century, was composed of great lords (both lay and ecclesiastical), and representatives from two other groups: shire knights and burgesses. See also *cortes, diets,* and *Estates General.*

patarenes   In eleventh century Milan, the patarenes (or "rag-pickers") allied with Church reformers against the great merchants of the city and the city's bishop, who was then loyal to the emperor. Since the patarenes swore a communal oath, they were precursors of the *communal movement* by which the cities of Lombardy and elsewhere sought greater rights of self-governance.

pontificate   The office of the *pope* or the period of a pope's rule.

pope   The bishop of Rome, considered by *Catholic* Christians to be the successor to St. Peter and the true head of all Christians.

prelate   A high-ranking Church officer, such as a bishop or abbot. Abbesses were sometimes included among prelates, but often not.

primogeniture   Preference in matters of inheritance to the first-born son.

prince   In a specific sense, the son of a king, but in the general sense used in this textbook, the chief ruler of a region, whether male or female.

priory   A monastic community, governed by a prior or prioress. Sometimes priories were under the authority of a superior *abbey,* but sometimes they were just relatively small communities. In some particularly large abbeys, the prior or prioress did not govern a separate community but was instead second-in-command. See also *monastic orders.*

Q

quadrivium   The study of mathematics, music, astronomy, and geometry, constituting one part of the liberal arts. The other part was the *trivium.*

R

rationalism   In general, a reliance on reason, as opposed to faith, as a critical avenue to knowledge. In the medieval debate about the proper balance between faith and reason, rationalists such as Peter Abelard (1079–1142) and Thomas Aquinas (c. 1225–1274) believed that reason was a tool which, if properly used, could illuminate the mysteries of faith.

regular clergy   From the Latin *regula* or "rule," the regular clergy are in monastic orders—that is, either monks or nuns. See *monastic rules* and *secular clergy.*

relic   An object venerated because of its association with a saint or other religious figure. Relics are often credited with miraculous powers.

ritual murder   Starting with a tale that spread through the English town of Norfolk in 1144, accusations of ritual murder became a common pretext for attacks on medieval Jews. In these stories, Jews took the role of the murderers; their victims were usually imagined as young boys; and their methods supposedly mimicked the crucifixion of Jesus. These false accusations often resulted in mass Christian assaults on Jews.

romance   A literary genre that emerged in late twelfth-century France, romances set their heroic stories in historical or legendary ages (such as the time of King Arthur). They explored the great deeds of warriors, as well as the conflicts that could arise between feudal loyalties and *courtly love.*

Romanesque   An architectural style prevalent until the twelfth century and characterized by rounded arches and stone vault roofs supported by thick walls and columns.

S

sacrament   A religious ceremony that confers God's grace upon the recipient. At the Fourth Lateran Council in 1215, the sacraments of Western Christianity were fixed at seven: baptism, confirmation, communion, penance, marriage, extreme unction, and ordination. Because ordained priests (see *secular clergy*) administer the sacraments and because the sacraments are a route to salvation, the sacramental basis of medieval Christianity was a critical part of the institutional power of its Church. See also *anti-clericalism, excommunication,* and *interdict.*

saint   In a general sense, a holy person. In a specific sense, a holy person formally recognized as such by a religious authority. As a rule, no living person is a saint; sanctity is a post-mortem recognition of holy life.

schism   A division, especially a religious division. The two greatest religious schisms of the Middle Ages are traditionally dated as occurring in 1054 (between the Catholic Church and Eastern Orthodox Church) and 1378 (between two—and later three—rival claimants to the papacy).

scholasticism   A philosophical system that reached its apogee with the work of Thomas Aquinas (c. 1225–1274). Scholastics used reason to reconcile conflicting authorities and to create coherent intellectual systems out of the messy abundance of past writings and opinions. Their method entailed careful study, respect for all past authorities, and logical thinking.

scriptorium   The place in a monastery where monks and nuns copied manuscripts.

secular   Having to do with the world, as opposed to spiritual and religious matters.

secular clergy   Unlike the *regular clergy* who submit themselves to the discipline of a monastic rule, the secular clergy—that is, priests, bishops, and archbishops—work in the world, serving the pastoral needs of the laity. Most are ordained—that is, empowered to celebrate the mass and other *sacraments* of the Church.

see   From Latin for "seat," a see is the *diocese* of a bishop, the area under his jurisdiction.

serf   Serfs could not leave their manors; they had to render labor-rent; and they had to pay various fines and fees to their manors. Serfs were distinct from both *slaves* and *free peasants.*

sheriff   An English officer who served as a link between the county where he worked and the royal administration to which he reported. Unlike French *bailiffs* whose loyalty to the crown was absolute, English sheriffs were usually local men who balanced their local interests with their royal responsibilities. See also *ministerial.*

simony   The sale and purchase of Church offices, one of the practices opposed by the Gregorian Reform of the eleventh century.

slave   Slaves were wholly at the disposal of their owners. Slavery was less common in the Middle Ages than it was in either the ancient world or early modern Europe. See also *serf* and *free peasant.*

sovereignty   Governmental authority, especially authority that is not limited by competing jurisdictions, such as those that might be posed by international bodies (for example, the Church) or internal bodies (for example, self-governing cities or autonomous principalities).

steward   A manorial officer. Sometimes, a steward was the equivalent of a *bailiff,* the

chief officer of a manor. But sometimes a steward oversaw an estate of several manors, and in such cases, he supervised the bailiffs of each manor.

strip   A long and narrow area of land within an *open field,* demarcated by stones or other markers but not fences. Each household might hold one or more strips in each of the open fields of a village.

synod   A meeting of Church officers, distinct from Church *councils* in that synods usually convened officers from only one region or realm.

T

tertiary orders   Orders of laymen and laywomen that were attached to the Dominicans or Franciscans. Formally recognized by the church in 1289, tertiaries were guided by *friars* in their prayers and rituals, but they remained active in family life and worldly affairs.

three-field system   Farming in which peasants rotated crops between three fields: the first grew a winter crop, the second a spring crop, the third lay *fallow.*

tithe   The obligation of Christians to offer one-tenth of all produce and income to the Church. From the Central Middle Ages, this was collected as a de facto tax, usually in support of the parish church and priest.

toll   A charge to use a road, cross a bridge, or even simply to trade goods. Townspeople objected to tolls, and *urban charters* usually granted them freedom from tolls.

trivium   The study of grammar, rhetoric and logic, which together with the subjects of the *quadrivium,* constituted the liberal arts studied in medieval schools and universities.

U

universals   Platonic archetypes or ideal forms. Medieval debates about the reality of these ideal forms evolved into three positions. "Realists" argued that universals were real; "nominalists" argued that they were mere names with no inherent reality; and "conceptualists" argued that universals existed as real and important concepts.

urban charter   A document that granted a town or city extensive rights of self-government. See also *commune.*

usury   Loaning money at interest, a practice condemned by the medieval Church.

V

vassal   A knight who owes loyalty and service to a feudal *lord* or *lady,* often in return for a *fief.*

vernacular language   The native spoken language—or mother tongue—of a region. In the Middle Ages, Latin long dominated all literacy and study, but vernacular literatures began to gain ground from the Central Middle Ages.

Vulgate Bible   A Latin translation of the Bible produced by St. Jerome (c. 340–420), the Vulgate remained the standard text throughout the Middle Ages.

W

wergild   Compensation paid for offenses either to the victim or the victim's family. This form of dispute resolution was common among the *barbarian* tribes.

CITATIONS

Keyed to significant phrases, citations are listed in order within each chapter, with quotes from that chapter's inserts (biographical sketch and medieval myth) at the end. Most citations will lead you to translations of medieval sources; a few others provide references to modern authors. Although most cite a specific modern edition, references of works available in multiple editions (such as those of St. Augustine) are generic so that you can use any modern version. In some cases, the authors of this textbook have translated the medieval text slightly differently from the translation given in the citation, so please remember that translators can reasonably differ on how to render medieval languages into modern English. A word might differ here or there, but each citation leads you to a modern English translation where you can examine the fuller context of the quotation.

Preface

"What I have well performed," freely translated from Henry Huntington, *Historia Anglorum,* see ed. and trans. by Diane Greenway (1996), p. 7.

Introduction

"Medieval voting machines," *New York Times,* November 11, 2000, p. A26.

"Lay dreaming," Jacob Burckhardt, *The Civilization of the Renaissance in Italy* (1860; 3rd edition, 1995), p. 87.

"A Monstrous fog," Jules Michelet, *La Sorcière* (1862), as translated in *Satanism and Witchcraft: A Study in Medieval Superstition,* trans. A. R. Allinson (1939), p. 16.

"When Adam delved," Thomas Walsingham, *Historia Angliana,* see translation in A. R. Myers, ed., *English Historical Documents, 1327–1485* (1969), p. 141.

Chapter 1

"Iron and rust," Dio Cassius, *Roman History,* Book 72.

"What has Athens," Tertullian, *The Prescription against Heretics,* Chapter 7.

"The more you cut us down," Tertullian, *Apologeticus,* Chapter 50.

"You have the will to lie," Saint Jerome, *Apology against Rufinus,* III.5

"You are a Ciceronian," Saint Jerome, *Letter to Eustochium,* 22:30.

"Charming delivery" and all quotations in the sketch, Augustine, *Confessions,* Book 5, Chapter 12 and Book 8, Chapters 5–12.

Chapter 2

"Producing in perfection," Strabo, *Geography,* 2.5.26–28.

"Happy the nose," freely translated from a poem by Sidonius Apollinaris, *Carmina,* 12 (to Catullinus).

"My tongue sticks to the roof of my mouth," Saint Jerome, *Letter to Principia,* 127:12.

"Old man of harmless simplicity," anonymous account available at http//www.fordham. edu/halsall/source/attila2.html.

"Preach to the people with the hand," Cassiodorus, *An Introduction to Divine and Human Readings,* Chapter 30.

"Oh, woe, for I travel among strangers," Gregory of Tours, *The History of the Franks,* II, 42.

"Walked before God with an upright heart," Gregory of Tours, *The History of the Franks,* II, 40.

"Whatever my Lord God orders, I will do," Bernard S. Bachrach, ed., *Liber Historiae Francorum* (1973), p. 37.

"Jesus Christ, you who Clotilda," Gregory of Tours, *The History of the Franks,* II, 30.

Chapter 3

"As a corpse to be dragged," G. W. Bowersock et al., eds., *Late Antiquity: A Guide to the Postclassical World* (1999), p. ix.

"Hazy zeal," Isidore of Seville as quoted in Kenneth R. Stow, *Alienated Minority: The Jews of Medieval Latin Europe* (1992), p. 50.

"Both sexes are seen to live together," Ludwig Bieler, ed., *The Patrician Texts in the Book of Armagh* (1979), p. 187.

"Murmuring," *The Rule of St. Benedict,* Chapter 5.

"Make a salve," *Bald's Leechbook,* see Karen Louise Jolly, ed., *Popular Religion in Late Saxon England* (1996), p. 159.

"To cut everything," letter of Gregory to Abbot Mellitus, in Bede, *Ecclesiastical History of the English People,* Book I, Chapter 30.

"The Cynocephali," Isidore of Seville, *Etymologies,* Book XI, Chapter 3.

"Wasted away with afflictions," as quoted in F. Homes Dudden, *Gregory the Great: His Place in History and Thought* (1905: reprint, 1967), v. 2, p. 19.

"Now I've copied," Falconer Madan, *Books in Manuscript* (2nd edition, 1968), p. 54.

"Taught the observance" and other quotes in this sketch, Bede, *Ecclesiastical History of the English People,* Book IV, Chapter 23.

Chapter 4

"Glory to God," as quoted in Rowland J. Mainstone, *Hagia Sophia* (1988), p. 10.

"Knew not whether," Samuel H. Cross and Olgerd P. Sherbowitz-Wetzor, eds., *The Russian Primary Chronicle* (1953), p. 111.

"The prince, a speaker of Arabic," Maria Rosa Menocal, *The Arabic Role in Medieval Literary History* (1987), p. 2.

"Sons of concubines have become so numerous," as quoted in Philip K. Hitti, *History of the Arabs* (10th edition, 2002), p. 333.

"In the name of Allah," as quoted in Hitti, *History of the Arabs,* p. 300.

"Ornament bright," Katharina M. Wilson, ed., *Hrotsvit of Gandersheim: A Florilegium of her Works* (1998), p. 29.

"Their bodies are large," the geographer Masudi, as quoted in Bernard Lewis, *The Muslim Discovery of Europe* (1982), p. 139.

"Not like any other women" and other quotes from the sketch, *Quran* 33: 32, 33, and 53.

Chapter 5

"Take pity on an old man," Thomas F. X. Noble, ed., *The Letters of Saint Boniface* (2000), p. 42.

"I will show in all things," Noble, ed., *Letters of Saint Boniface,* p. 19.

"He was moderate," Einhard, *Life of Charlemagne,* III, 24.

"He thought that his children," Einhard, *Life of Charlemagne,* III, 19.

"Pretend there was nothing," Einhard, *Life of Charlemagne,* III, 19.

"He would not have set," Einhard, *Life of Charlemagne,* III, 28.

"Let schools be established," Charlemagne, *Admonitio Generalis* of 789; see translation in Eleanor Shipley Duckett, *Alcuin, Friend of Charlemagne* (1951), p. 122.

"God is learned about through books," Dhouda, *Liber Manualis,* i, 7, as quoted in Janet L. Nelson, *The Frankish World, 750–900* (1996), p. 13.

"There is nothing better for us," Alcuin, the Latin text can be found as Letter 23 *in Epistolae Karolini Aevi,* IV (MGH, 1895), p. 61.

"Soldiers of the Church," quoted in John J. Contreni, "The Carolingian Renaissance: Education and Literary Culture," in Rosamund McKitterick, ed., *The New Cambridge Medieval History II: c. 700–900* (1995), p. 709.

"Just a table," William of Malmesbury, *The Deeds of the Bishops of England,* trans. David Preest (2002), p. 267.

"To kill, blind, or mutilate," quoted in Janet L. Nelson, "Kingship and Royal Government," in Rosamund McKitterick, ed., *The New Cambridge Medieval History II: c. 700–900* (1995), p. 399.

"As a mouse" and other quotes in sketch, Eleanor Shipley Duckett, *Carolingian Portraits* (1962), pp. 121–160.

Chapter 6

"Cattle die, kinsfolk die," Patricia Terry, ed., *Poems of the Elder Edda* (1990), p. 21.

"Heroics of virginity," see Jane Schulenburg, "The Heroics of Virginity: Brides of Christ and Sacrificial Mutilation," in *Women in the Middle Ages and the Renaissance*, ed. Mary Beth Rose (1986), pp. 26–72.

"I Ealdorman Alfred," Dorothy Whitelock, ed., *English Historical Documents, vol. 1, c. 500–1042* (1955), p. 497.

"Before everything was ravaged," Henry Sweet, ed., *The Anglo-Saxon Version of Gregory's* Pastoral Care (1871), p. 4.

"Merry sang the monks," C. E. Wright, *The Cultivation of Saga in Anglo-Saxon England* (1939), p. 37.

"He was a great lover," Marjorie Chibnall, ed., *The Ecclesiastical History of Orderic Vitalis,* vol. 3 (1972), p. 217 and vol. 2 (1990), p. 263.

Introduction to Part II

"Satan will soon be unleashed" and also "sure sign of some mysterious," Raoul Glaber, *The Five Books of the Histories,* ed. and trans. John France (1989), p. 93 and p. 111.

"For the first time in history," Robert S. Lopez, *The Commercial Revolution of the Middle Ages, 950–1350* (1971), p. vii.

Chapter 7

"Work for much less money," *Husbandry,* in Dorothea Oschinsky, ed., *Walter of Henley and other Treatises on Estate Management and Accounting* (1971), p. 427.

"They start to march," from *Chansons des Lorrains,* see version in John Gillingham, *Richard the Lion-Heart* (2nd edition, 1989), p. 118.

"London is happy" and all subsequent quotes, William fitz Stephen, "Description of the City of London," in David C. Douglas and George W. Greenaway, eds., *English Historical Documents, 1042–1189* (1953), pp. 956–962.

"When you reach England," John Appleby, ed., *The Chronicle of Richard of Devizes of the Time of King Richard the First* (1963), pp. 65–67.

"I tell you," adapted from William D. Paden et al., eds., *The Poems of the Troubadour Bertran de Born* (1986), p. 342.

"In war she rode," Marjorie Chibnall, ed., *The Ecclesiastical History of Orderic Vitalis,* vol. 4 (1973), p. 213.

"To all intents and purposes," Robert Fawtier, *The Capetian Kings of France: Monarchy and Nation* (1960), p. 29.

"Robert de Venuiz," in *Magnum Rotuli Scaccarii,* ed. Joseph Hunter (1833), pp. 37 and 110.

"And so we lost our little ones," Gregory of Tours, *The History of the Franks,* V, 34.

"Your children you dance," from "A Lamentation of the Virgin," in Margot Adamson, ed., *A Treasury of Middle English Verse* (1973), p. 152.

"Loosed her hair," Roger of Wendover's account as quoted in Katherine L. French, "The Legend of Lady Godiva and the Image of the Female Body," *Journal of Medieval History* 18 (1992), pp. 3–19.

Chapter 8

"Duties of the limbs," Bahya ibn Pakuda, *The Duties of the Heart,* as quoted in Marcia L. Colish, *Medieval Foundations of the Western Intellectual Tradition 400–1400* (1997), p. 151.

"Remember, first of all," Bernard of Clairvaux, see translation in John D. Anderson and Elizabeth T. Kennan, *Five Books on Consideration: Advice to a Pope* (1976), p. 137.

"We have besought you," see translation in James Cotter Morison, *The Life and Times of Saint Bernard* (1877), p. 174.

"Recognizing that the wickedness of women," Marchthal expulsion (1273), see translation in Penny Schine Gold, *The Lady and the Virgin: Image, Attitude, and Experience in Twelfth-Century France* (1985), p. 88.

"The archbishopric of Reims," as reported by Guibert of Nogent, see translation in Paul J. Archambault, trans., *A Monk's Confession: The Memoirs of Guibert of Nogent* (1996), p. 30.

"The man is a menace," Liemar of Bremen, as quoted in H. E. J. Cowdrey, *Pope Gregory VII* (1998), p. 105.

"Holy Satan," Peter Damian, as quoted in Uta-Renate Blumenthal, *The Investiture Controversy: Church and Monarchy from the Ninth to the Twelfth Century* (1988), p. 116.

"False monk," and later, "Hildebrand, not pope," Henry IV's letter of 1076. See translation in Ernest F. Henderson, ed., *Select Historical Documents of the Middle Ages* (1965), pp. 372–373.

"I order you to hold a free election," Writ of Henry II, 1171, as quoted in C. Warren Hollister, *The Making of England to 1399* (8th edition, 2001), p. 162.

"I have loved justice," Gregory VII, as quoted in J. W. Bowden, *The Life and Pontificate of Gregory the Seventh* (1840), II, p. 271.

"Seems altogether to have been," G. K. Chesterton, *St. Francis of Assisi* (1923), p. 45.

"Praise be to you, my Lord," St. Francis, *The Canticle of Brother Sun.* See translation in *St. Francis of Assisi: Writings and Early Biographies,* ed. Marion A. Habig (1973), pp. 130–131.

"Lord, I return to you this family," St. Francis as quoted in Paul Sabatier, *The Road to Assisi: The Essential Biography of St. Francis* (1894: new edition, 2003), p. 111.

"God has taken our wives," St. Francis as quoted in Shulamith Shahar, *The Fourth Estate: A History of Women in the Middle Ages* (1983), p. 36.

"A persecuting society," R. I. Moore, *The Formation of a Persecuting Society: Power and Deviance in Western Europe, 950–1250* (1987).

"Had not the apple," Thomas G. Duncan, ed., *Medieval English Lyrics 1200–1400* (1995), item 108.

"Curled up against her breast," Guerric of Igny, as quoted in Caroline Walker Bynum, *Jesus as Mother: Studies in the Spirituality of the High Middle Ages* (1982), p. 137.

Chapter 9

"Europeanization of Europe," the title of Chapter 11 in Robert Bartlett, *The Making of Europe: Conquest, Colonization and Cultural Change, 950–1350* (1993).

"Decapitated intellectually," Bernard F. Reilly, *The Medieval Spains* (1993), p. 197.

"The Normans are a cunning and revengeful people," Geoffery Malaterra. See version in Edward Gibbon, *The History of the Decline and Fall of the Roman Empire, vols. 5–6,* ed. David Womersley (1994), pp. 481–482.

"Ready to submit to nobody," Anna Comnena, *The Alexiad.* See translation by E. R. A. Sewter (1969), p. 54.

"When dressed in full armor," *The Alexiad,* p. 66 in Sewter translation.

"How far will you flee?" *The Alexiad,* p. 147 in Sewter translation.

"Here lies Guiscard," William of Malmesbury, *Chronicle of the Kings of England.* See translation by J. A. Giles (1847), p. 296.

"Set out on this journey," Robert the Monk, as translated in Alfred J. Andrea, *The Medieval Record: Sources of Medieval History* (1997), p. 348.

"If you had been there," Fulcher of Chartres, *Chronicle of the First Crusade,* trans. Martha Evelyn McGinty (1941), pp. 69, 70.

"I weep and am deeply grieved," as quoted in *Chronicles of the Crusades,* ed. Elizabeth Hallam (2000), p. 180.

"An abyss so deep," Bernard of Clairvaux. See translation in James A. Brundage, *The Crusades: A Documentary Survey* (1962), pp. 122–123.

"Great blessings," Innocent III, letter to Count Baldwin, November 1204.

"Against spiritual weakness," Peter the Venerable, as quoted in *The Templars,* ed. Malcolm Barber and Keith Bate (2001), p. 228.

"Rose in a spirit of cruelty," Albert of Aix, as quoted in *The First Crusade: Accounts of Eye-Witnesses and Participants,* ed. August Krey (1958), p. 54.

"About the first watch of the night," Walter Map, *De Nugis Curialium/Courtiers' Trifles,* ed. M. R. James, rev. C. N. L. Brooke and R. A. B. Mynors (1983), p. 119.

"I say with pride," Hubert Walter, as quoted in John Gillingham, *Richard the Lion-Heart* (2nd ed., 1989), p. 284.

"Richard's courage," Ibn al-Athir, as quoted in Gillingham, *Richard,* p. 288.

"Like a robber permanently on the prowl," Gerald of Wales, as quoted in Gillingham, *Richard,* p. 133.

Chapter 10

"From memory to written record," Michael Clanchy, *From Memory to Written Record, England, 1066–1307* (1979).

"Scarcely any teachers could be found," Guibert of Nogent, see translation in Paul J. Archambault, trans., *A Monk's Confession: The Memoirs of Guibert of Nogent* (1996), p. 14.

"Either to the church or to the Empire," Bartolo of Sassoferrato, as quoted in Giovanni Tabacco, *The Struggle for Power in Medieval Italy* (1989), pp. 256–257.

"Not human but rather divine" and "We declare, announce," Boniface VIII, *Unam Sanctam.*

"Praiseworthy zeal," Clement V as quoted in Brian Tierney, *The Crisis of Church and State, 1050–1300* (1964), p. 192.

"Placed between God and humans," Innocent III's "Sermon on the Consecration of a Pope." See translation in Brian Tierney, ed., *The Crisis of Church and State, 1050–1300* (1964), p. 131.

Chapter 11

"A peace such as no age remembers," William of Malmesbury, *Chronicle of the Kings of England,* p. 434 in Giles translation.

"Christ and his saints slept," *The Peterborough Chronicle,* trans. Harry A. Rositzke (1951), p. 160.

"Shame, shame on a conquered king," Gerald of Wales, *De Principis Instructione,* in Douglas and Greenaway, eds., *English Historical Documents, 1042–1189,* p. 384.

"A very Christian king," as quoted in Yves Sassier, *Louis VII* (1991), p. 9.

"Kingship like a priest," as quoted in George Duby, *France in the Middle Ages, 987–1460* (1991), p. 258.

"He is not a man," the Bishop of Pamiers, as quoted in Robert Fawtier, *The Capetian Kings of France: Monarchy and Nation* (1960), p. 39.

"No greater or lesser person," as quoted in Benjamin Arnold, *Medieval Germany, 500–1300* (1997), p. 189.

Chapter 12

"The structure might have fallen," William of Malmesbury, *Chronicle of the Kings of England,* p. 346 in Giles translation.

"Whatever else the West disliked," Romilly Jenkins, *Byzantium, The Imperial Centuries* A.D. *610–1071* (1966), p. 385.

"The world is very evil," Bernard de Morlaix, as translated in *Collected Hymns, Sequences, and Carols of John Mason Neale* (1914), pp. 203–213.

"For on this my heart is set," see version in *Selections from the Carmina Burana,* David Parlett, trans. (1986), p. 154.

"When Turpin of Reims," *The Song of Roland,* laisse 155, as translated by Glyn Burgess (1990).

"Count Roland," *The Song of Roland,* laisse 159, taken from Burgess translation.

"The pagans flee," *The Song of Roland,* laisse 269, taken from Burgess translation.

"I die of wounds," Jaufre Rudel, see translation in *The Poetry of Cercamon and Jaufre Rudel,* trans. George Wolf and Roy Rosenstein (1983), p. 135.

"I would truly love," as translated in *Troubadour Lyrics: A Bilingual Anthology,* ed. Frede Jensen (1998), p. 273.

"I'll make some verses," Duke William IX. See translation in Gerald A. Bond, ed., *The Poetry of William VII, Count of Poitiers, IX Duke of Aquitaine* (1982), pp. 14–17.

"For into Paradise," *Aucassin et Nicolette.* See translation by Eugene Mason (reprinted 1973), p. 6.

"Do not hesitate to take," Andreas Capellanus, *The Art of Courtly Love,* ed. Frederick W. Locke (1957), p. 24.

"The power of Love," Dante, *La Vita Nuova,* trans. Mark Musa (1962), p. 41.

"Eternal Light," Dante, *The Divine Comedy,* Canto 33.

"Howling men," Abbot Suger, see translation in Erwin Panofsky, *Abbot Suger on the Abbey Church of St.-Denis and its Art Treasures* (1946), pp. 87–89.

"The city is expensive," and "I have recently discovered" in Charles Homer Haskins, *Studies in Medieval Culture* (1929: reprint, 1965), p. 10 and p. 15.

"If those who are called," Augustine, *On Christian Doctrine,* c. 40.

"I believe so that," Anselm, *Proslogion.* See translation by Thomas Williams (1996), p. 99.

"Wild imaginations," Bernard of Clairvaux, as translated in Samuel J. Eales, *Life and Works of Saint Bernard* (1889), p. 565.

"I do not wish," Abelard, as translated by Betty Radice, *The Letters of Abelard and Heloise* (1974), p. 270.

"The grace of God," Bernard of Clairvaux, as translated in *The Letters and St. Bernard of Clairvaux,* trans. Bruno Scott James (1998), p. 460.

"You have surpassed all women," Peter the Venerable, as translated in Radice, *The Letters of Abelard and Heloise,* pp. 277–278.

"A poised, self-confident," Bynum, *Jesus as Mother,* p. 185.

"For faith rests on infallible truth," Thomas Aquinas, *Summa Theologiae,* question 1, article 8.

"God is always," see *Plutarch's Moralia,* trans. Edwin L. Minar et al. (1961), vol. 9, p. 119.

"Reasoning does not suffice," Roger Bacon, *Opus Majus,* as translated by Robert Belle Burke (1962), II, p. 583.

"With their hooks and cables," *Romance of the Rose,* lines 17898–17904, as translated by Harry W. Robbins (1962), p. 381.

"Singing isn't worth a thing," and "When I see the lark," Bernard of Ventadour, see translations by Stephen G. Nichols, et al. eds., *The Songs of Bernart de Ventadorn* (1962), pp. 80–82 and pp. 167–168.

Chapter 13

"Golden age of laborers," a loose rendering of James E. Thorold Rogers, *A History of Agriculture and Prices in England,* vol. 4 (1882), p. 490.

"Every fourth penny," from "Song of the Husbandman," in *Thomas Wright's Political Songs of the Fourteenth Century,* ed. Peter Coss (1996), p. 149.

"These were attended," anonymous letter translated in *The Black Death,* ed. Rosemary Horrox (1994), p. 44.

"Because they thought," quoted in Norman Cohn, *The Pursuit of the Millennium* (1957), p. 139.

"Father abandoned child," Agnolo di Tura, quoted in Philip Ziegler, *The Black Death* (1969), p. 58.

"When Adam delved," Thomas Walsingham, *Historia Angliana,* see translation in A. R. Myers, ed., *English Historical Documents, 1327–1485* (1969), p. 141.

"Worked behind the plow," quoted in Richard Barber, ed., *The Pastons: A Family in the Wars of the Roses* (1981, reprinted 1985), p. 11.

"As soon as the coin," Johann Tetzel, according to Friedrich Myconius, in *The Reformation in its Own Words,* ed. Hans J. Hillerbrand (1964), p. 43.

"Stench," *The Letters of Catherine of Siena,* vol. II, trans. Suzanne Noffke (2001), p. 345.

"Cell within the heart,' adapted from Raymond of Capua, *The Life of Catherine of Siena,* trans. Conleth Kearns (1980), pp. 46–47.

"The matter of eating," *The Letters of Catherine of Siena,* vol. I, trans. Noffke (2000), p. 161.

Chapter 14

"Secure a reassessment," see statement at http://www.richardiii.net.

"Yes, our Sire," and other quotes in the sketch from Régine Pernoud, *Joan of Arc: By Herself and Her Witnesses,* trans. Edward Hyams (1982), pp. 195, 174–175.

Chapter 15

"Unlettered," *The Book of Margery Kempe,* ed. Sanford Brown Meech (1940), p. 128.

"Confined by no bounds," Pico della Mirandola, *On the Dignity of Man,* trans. Charles Glenn Wallis (1998), p. 5.

"When I saw that he," Chaucer, "The Wife of Bath's Prologue." Middle English text found in *The Riverside Chaucer,* ed. F. N. Robinson (3rd edition, 1987), p. 115.

"Do not kill people," Christine de Pizan, "The God of Love's Letter," as translated in *The Selected Writings of Christine de Pizan,* ed. Renate Blumenfeld-Kosinski and Kevin Brownlee (1997), p. 26.

"I know that rich and poor," François Villon, in *The Testaments of François Villon,* trans. John Heron Lepper (1924), p. 312.

"Learned ignorance," Nicholas of Cusa, *De Docta Ignoranta.*

"Ruling part," as quoted in Denys Hay, *Europe in the Fourteenth and Fifteenth Centuries* (1965), p. 89.

"Say to all the people," and other quotes in the sketch from Richard Wunderli, *Peasant Fires: The Drummer of Niklashausen* (1992), pp. 70, 90, 68, 49, and 107.

SOME POPES AND MONARCHS OF MEDIEVAL EUROPE

A. Popes

A full listing of medieval popes and antipopes can be found in the *Dictionary of the Middle Ages* and in many books on the history of the medieval papacy. The popes listed here are among the most important of medieval popes (and include all those mentioned in the text).

Leo I, the Great, 440–461
Gregory I, 590–604
Zacharias, 741–752
Stephen II, 752–757
Leo III, 795–816
Sylvester II, 999–1003
Benedict IX, 1032–1048
Leo IX, 1049–1054
Gregory VII, 1073–1085
Urban II, 1088–1099
Calixtus II, 1119–1124
Hadrian IV, 1154–1159
Alexander III, 1159–1181

Celestine III, 1191–1198
Innocent III, 1198–1216
Gregory IX, 1227–1241
Innocent IV, 1243–1254
Boniface VIII, 1294–1303
Clement V, 1305–1314
Gregory XI, 1370–1378
Urban VI, 1378–1389 (at Avignon)
Clement VII, 1378–1394 (at Rome)
Martin V, 1417–1431
Sixtus IV, 1471–1484
Alexander VI, 1492–1503

B. The Early Carolingians

Pepin of Heristal, 680–714
Charles Martel, 714–741
Pepin the Short, 741–768 (king, 751–768)

Charlemagne, 768–814
Louis the Pious, 814–840

C. Kings of West Francia and France

Carolingians
Charles the Bald, 840–877; emperor, 875–877
Louis the Stammerer, 877–879
Louis III, 879–882
Carloman, 879–884
Charles the Fat, emperor, 884–887
Odo, 888–898*

Charles the Simple, 898–922
Robert I, 922–923*
Ralph, 923–936*
Louis IV, 936–954
Lothar, 954–986
Louis V, 986–987

---

* Odo, Robert I, and Ralph were not Carolingians, but were instead related by blood or marriage to the family later known as the Capetians.

Capetians
Hugh Capet, 987–996
Robert II, the Pious, 996–1031
Henry I, 1031–1060
Philip I, 1060–1108
Louis VI the Fat, 1108–1137
Louis VII, 1137–1180
Philip II, Augustus, 1180–1223
Louis VIII, 1223–1226
Louis IX, 1226–1270
Philip III, 1270–1285
Philip IV, the Fair, 1285–1314

Louis X, 1314–1316
Philip V, 1316–1322
Charles IV, 1322–1328

Valois
Philip VI, 1328–1350
John II, the Good, 1350–1364
Charles V, 1364–1380
Charles VI, 1380–1422
Charles VII, 1422–1461
Louis XI, 1461–1483
Charles VIII, 1483–1498

D. Kings of East Francia and Emperors of the German States

Carolingians
Louis the German, 840–876
Charles the Fat, 876–887 (emperor, 884–887)
Arnulf, 887–899
Louis the Child, 899–911

Franconians and Saxons
Conrad of Franconia, 911–919
Henry the Fowler, Duke of Saxony, 919–936
Otto I, the Great, 936–973 (emperor, 962–973)
Otto II, 973–983
Otto III, 983–1002
Henry II, 1002–1024

Salians
Conrad II, 1024–1039
Henry III, 1039–1056

Henry IV, 1056–1106
Henry V, 1106–1125

Welfs
Lothar, 1125–1137

Hohenstaufens
Conrad III, 1138–1152
Frederick I, Barbarossa, 1152–1190
Henry VI, 1190–1197
Frederick II, 1215–1250
Conrad IV, 1250–1254

Habsburgs (Selected)
Rudolf of Habsburg, 1273–1291
Albert II, 1438–1439
Frederick III, 1440–1493
Maximilian, 1493–1519

E. Kings of England

Some Anglo-Saxon Kings
Alfred, 871–899
Edward the Elder, 899–924
Ethelred the Unready, 978–1016
Canute, 1016–1035
Edward the Confessor, 1042–1066

Anglo-Normans
William I, the Conqueror, 1066–1087
William II, Rufus, 1087–1100
Henry I, 1100–1135
[Stephen's Anarchy, 1135–1154]

Angevins (Plantagenets)
Henry II, 1154–1189
Richard I, the Lion-Hearted, 1189–1199
John, 1199–1216

Henry III, 1216–1272
Edward I, 1272–1307
Edward II, 1307–1327
Edward III, 1327–1377
Richard II, 1377–1399

Lancastrians and Yorkists
Henry IV, 1399–1413
Henry V, 1413–1422
Henry VI, 1422–1461
Edward IV, 1461–1483
[Edward V, 1483]
Richard III, 1483–1485

The First Tudor
Henry VII, 1485–1509

PHOTO CREDITS

Chapter 1
p. 15: © Timothy McCarthy/Art Resource, NY; **pp. 18, 20:** © Scala/Art Resource, NY

Chapter 2
pp. 34, 36: © Giraudon/Art Resource, NY; **p. 41:** Photofest

Chapter 3
p. 56: © Foto Marburg/Art Resource, NY; **p. 66:** © The Trustees of Bede's World, Jarrow

Chapter 4
p. 74: © Archivo Iconografico, S.A./Corbis; **p. 75:** © Cameraphoto Arte, Venice/Art Resource, NY; **p. 90:** © Bettmann/Corbis; **p. 92:** © Paul Almasy/Corbis

Chapter 5
p. 105: © Giraudon/Art Resource, NY; **p. 109:** © Foto Marburg/Art Resource, NY; **p. 114:** From Thompson, *An Introduction to Greek & Latin Paleography*, 1912

Chapter 6
p. 125: © Werner Foreman/Art Resource, NY; **p. 142:** Bayerische Staatsbibliothek Munchen, Germany/(c) Bridgeman Art Library

Chapter 7
p. 162: © Archivo Iconografico, S.A./Corbis; **p. 172:** © Bibliotheque Nationale de France, Paris; **p. 181:** Leiden Universiteitsbibliotheek (MS. B.P.L. 20, fol. 60R)

Chapter 8
p. 189: © Alinari/Art Resource, NY; **p. 210:** © Scala/Art Resource, NY; **p. 213:** British Library, London, UK/Bridgeman Art Library

Chapter 9
p. 223: © Alinari/Art Resource, NY; **p. 230:** British Library, London, UK/© Bridgeman Art Library

Chapter 10
p. 249: © Bildarchiv Preussischer Kulturbesitz, Berlin; **p. 255:** © Scala/Art Resource, NY

Chapter 11
p. 269: © Aerofilms, Ltd.; **p. 274:** Corpus Christi College, Cambridge, MS 16 fol. 48v; **p. 282:** © Giraudon/Art Resource, NY

Chapter 12
p. 301: © Larry Lee/Corbis; **p. 302:** © Foto Marburg/Art Resource, NY; **p. 303:** © Scala/Art Resource, NY; **pp. 304, 305:** © Foto Marburg/Art Resource, NY; **p. 306:** © Sandro Vannini/Corbis

Chapter 13
p. 330: © Snark/Art Resource, NY; **p. 340:** By permission of The British Library (ADD. 37049, fol. 22v)

Chapter 14
p. 349: © Réunion des Musées Nationaux/Art Resource, NY

Chapter 15
p. 372: © The Bodleian Library, University of Oxford (MS. Douce, fol. 24r); **p. 373:** © Bibliotheque Nationale de France, Paris; **p. 375:** © Alinari/Art Resource, NY; **p. 376:** © Scala/Art Resource, NY; **pp. 377, 378, 379:** © Erich Lessing/Art Resource, NY

Color Illustrations
1: © Scala/Art Resource, NY

2: © Erich Lessing/Art Resource, NY

3: The Board of Trinity College, Dublin, Ireland/© The Bridgeman Art Library

4: Edinburgh University Library (Or. Ms. 161, f. 10v)

5: By permission of the British Library (Sloane 2435, f. 85)

6: Universitätsbibliothek, Ruprecht-Karls-Universität Heidelberg (Cod. pal. Germ. 848, fol. 52r)

7: © Erich Lessing/Art Resource, NY

8: By permission of the British Library (BL Harley 7026, fol. 13r)

9: © AKG London

10: © Sonia Halliday Photographs, Photo by Jane Taylor

11: © Giraudon/Art Resource, NY

12: © The Pierpont Morgan Library/Art Resource, NY

13: © Alinari/Art Resource, NY

INDEX

Headnote: Page references with *A* indicate appendix; *G* indicates glossary; *n* indicates note

E

F

G

J